W9-BGN-690

# Reading Advantage

## TEACHER'S EDITION
### LEVEL A

## READING LEVEL GRADES 2–3

**Laura Robb, James F. Baumann, Carol J. Fuhler, Joan Kindig**

Avon Connell-Cowell, R. Craig Roney, Jo Worthy

**GREAT SOURCE**

A Division of Houghton Mifflin Harcourt Publishing Company

## Reading Advantage Team

**Laura Robb** has more than forty years of experience in grades 4 through 8. Robb also coaches teachers of kindergarten through grade 12 in Virginia, New York, and Michigan. She speaks at conferences all over the country and conducts staff development workshops. Robb is a coauthor of these Great Source products: *Summer Success: Reading, Reader's Handbooks* grades 3, 4–5, 6–8, and *Daybooks* and *Sourcebooks* grades 2–5. In addition, she has written three books for Scholastic, *Teaching Reading in Middle School; Teaching Reading in Social Studies, Science, and Math;* and *Teaching Reading: A Complete Resource for Grades 4 and Up.*

**James F. Baumann** is a teacher and university professor. He has taught students in several school districts, and he has been a professor of reading education at three universities. His research and writing have examined how to provide students both rich, literate learning environments and effective instruction in reading skills and strategies. Baumann is also a coauthor of *Summer Success: Reading* (Great Source, 2001).

**Carol J. Fuhler** is currently an Associate Professor at Iowa State University. Dr. Fuhler is coauthor of *Teaching Reading: A Balanced Approach for Today's Classrooms* and contributed a chapter to *Young Adult Literature in the Classroom: Reading It, Teaching It, Loving It.*

**Joan Kindig** is an Associate Professor at James Madison University, where she teaches both Reading and Word Study courses. Dr. Kindig is also a frequent presenter at workshops and conferences.

**Avon Connell-Cowell** is a mentor for the New York City Department of Education. Dr. Connell-Cowell's area of interest is effective teaching practices in urban education.

**R. Craig Roney** is a Professor of Teacher Education at Wayne State University in Detroit, specializing in Children's Literature and Storytelling. He has also written numerous publications on these topics including *The Story Performance Handbook* (Lawrence Erlbaum Publishers, 2001), a research-based "how-to" text on reading aloud, mediated storytelling, and storytelling.

**Jo Worthy,** a former elementary- and middle-school teacher, teaches in the teacher preparation and graduate programs in literacy at the University of Texas at Austin. Her major research and teaching interests include reading fluency, struggling readers, and reading preferences of upper elementary- and middle-school students.

**Editorial:** Ruth Rothstein, Lea Martin, Sue Paro

**Design/Production:** Bill Smith Studio.

Printed in the United States of America

International Standard Book Number: 978-0-669-01410-5

3 4 5 6 7 8 9 10 1420 20 19 18 17 16 15 14 13
4500442619

# Contents

# Great Source Reading Advantage
# Starts with Reading

## The components in Reading Advantage were designed to help students

- develop essential reading comprehension skills, including decoding multiple-syllable words, comprehending complex syntax, and understanding context clues;
- strengthen reading fluency and gain experience reading a wide range of nonfiction genres including interviews, news articles, and photo-essays;

- build reading strategies, background knowledge, and vocabulary;
- transition from guided reading to independent reading;
- become proficient, confident readers who enjoy reading.

## For the STUDENT

### Reading, Reading, Reading

(6 copies of 4 different magazines)

**Magazines** At the heart of the program are high-interest magazines based on themes that offer original selections (primarily nonfiction) written below grade level.

**Paperback Books** (12 titles) for independent reading practice.

**eZines CD-ROMs** reinforce the skills and strategies taught in the program through additional theme-based magazine articles offering text highlighting, real voice audio, embedded strategy activities, and end-of-article comprehension quizzes and reports.

### Activities

**Student Journal** copymaster that supports students as they read each selection and provides practice in comprehension and vocabulary (also available as consumable Student Journals).

For whole classroom instruction, purchase extra copies of Theme Magazines, Paperback Books, and Student Journals separately!

# For the TEACHER

**Teacher's Edition** with point-of-use instruction wrapped around full-color theme magazine facsimiles; detailed lesson plans that follow the before, during, and after reading process; and comprehension, writing, vocabulary, and phonics/word study instruction.

**Word Study Manual** that serves as a teacher resource for expanded, in-depth word-building lessons, word sorts, and activities that target compound words, homophones, homographs, long and short vowels, multiple-syllable words, and word parts.

**Assessment** with instructions for determining students' reading level, mid- and end-of-magazine tests to track student progress, and checklists and observation notes for ongoing assessment.

**Writing Advantage** provides scaffolded instruction to support and extend students' writing.

**Also Available!** Gates-MacGinitie Reading Tests® allow teachers to assess the reading level of individual students.

**Seven levels** to help your struggling readers!

## Reading Advantage

Great Source

**Laura Robb**

James F. Baumann • Carol J. Fuhler • Joan Kindig

Each kit contains the items shown for student and teacher

# Great Source Reading Advantage
# Features the Reading Process

*Reading Advantage* is infused with the **Reading Process** to model for students that there are actions they can take **BEFORE** they read, **DURING** their reading, and **AFTER** they read to make themselves better readers.

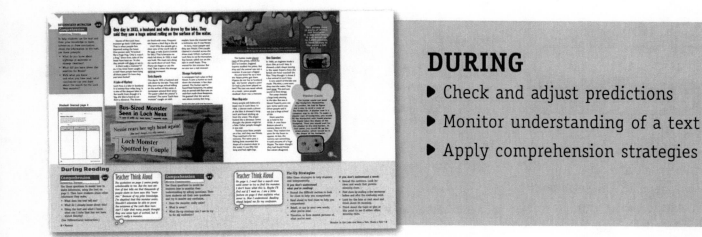

## BEFORE

▶ Activate prior knowledge

▶ Preview the selection and vocabulary

▶ Set a purpose for reading

▶ Make predictions

## DURING

▶ Check and adjust predictions

▶ Monitor understanding of a text

▶ Apply comprehension strategies

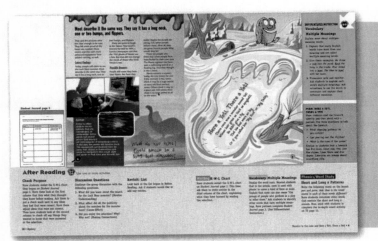

## AFTER

▶ Respond to and discuss the selection

▶ Return to the purpose

▶ Write in response to reading

▶ Learn and apply skills and strategies

# Annotated Lesson

Every lesson in *Reading Advantage* is set up to model the reading process:

**BEFORE READING**
**DURING READING**
**AFTER READING**

Each lesson is designed to last for three or four sessions when the reading period is about forty minutes long.

## Magazine Pages

The magazine pages, shown as facsimiles throughout the Teacher's Edition, were designed to look sophisticated and, therefore, appeal to students. The text, however, was constructed to be clear, provide abundant context for vocabulary, and increase gradually in difficulty across the magazines within a level.

## BEFORE READING

The first part of each lesson prepares students to read through discussion, writing, and/or graphic organizers. The selection always suggests activities for building background, previewing the selection and vocabulary, and making predictions and setting a purpose. The more support a student needs for reading, the more substantive the introduction should be. Choose the part or parts that your students need to support their reading.

LESSON **1**
## Monster in the Lake *and* Here a Yeti, There a Yeti
*Mystery*, pages 2–7

### SUMMARY
This **article** tells about the many sightings over time of the Loch Ness monster. A **poem** follows.

### COMPREHENSION STRATEGIES
Inferential Thinking
Monitor Understanding

### WRITING
K-W-L Chart

### VOCABULARY
Multiple Meanings

### PHONICS/WORD STUDY
Short and Long *a* Patterns

**Lesson Vocabulary**
claim          plaster casts
loch           sonar
sightings

### MATERIALS
*Mystery*, pp. 2–7
*Student Journal*, pp. 1–3
*Word Study Manual*, p. 34
*Writing Advantage*, pp. 30–55

For years people have claimed to see a monster in Scotland. Should we believe them?

Monster in the Lake

2

## Before Reading 🔆 *Use one or more activities.*

**Make a List** ▶
Introduce the subject of monsters. Ask: *What monsters do you know about? How would you define a monster?* Then create a list called "Why Are We Drawn to Monsters?" List students' responses. Revisit the list after students have read the selection to see if they would like to add any entries to the list.

6 • Mystery

| Why Are We Drawn to Monsters? |
| --- |
| 1. Some people like scary things. |
| 2. They're mysterious. |
| 3. |

**Vocabulary Preview**
List and say the vocabulary words. Ask students if they can make any associations with specific words. Ask: *Where have you heard the word used? Does the word remind you of anything else? Does it look like or sound like a word you know? Explain.*

Model the process of making associations with the word *loch* to help students complete the making associations activity on *Student Journal* page 1.

## Build Background
Use knowledge about students' abilities to select or adapt lesson plan suggestions or strategies as appropriate to accommodate students' needs and your instructional style.

## Graphic Organizers
Graphic organizers are used throughout the program. Black-Line Masters of most organizers are in the Appendix of this Teacher's Edition.

> "I was sitting near the lake. All at once, this black hump came out of the water. It was the size of a bus. It flipped over and made huge waves. They were three feet high. I saw it with my own eyes!"

That is how one man told of a huge beast he spotted in Scotland. It's the way others have told of it, too. Over the years, thousands of people have sworn they saw the creature known as the Loch Ness monster.

## Make Predictions/ Set Purpose

Familiarize students with a K-W-L chart. Follow these steps:

1. Read aloud and explain each column heading.
2. Explain that before reading, they will complete the first two columns, writing what they know about the topic, and questions they have.
3. Help students brainstorm ideas for the *K* column. Then help students list questions for the *W* column. Tell students to watch for answers as they read.
4. Explain that, after reading, students will complete the third column.

### Student Journal page 1

### Differentiated Instruction

Students who need deeper instruction in and/or a different approach to a strategy or skill will benefit from instruction that provides more support, or scaffolding. Use the ideas in tutorials with individual students or with a small group of students who need the support for the same skill or strategy.

### Preview the Selection

Have students look through the five pages of the article, pages 2–6 in the magazine. Use these or similar prompts as you preview the article.

- What does the title tell you?
- How has the author organized the article?
- What do the newspaper headlines tell you?

## Teacher Think Aloud

*When I first saw the title and the picture on the first two pages, I thought I was going to read a fun or scary fiction story about a monster. Then I saw the subtitle and subheads. Now I'm not so sure—maybe I'll read a nonfiction article about people who "think" they saw a monster. Let me read to find out.*

### Make Predictions/ Set Purpose

Students should use the information they gathered in previewing the selection to start a K-W-L chart on *Student Journal* page 2. If students have trouble generating a purpose for reading, suggest that they read to find answers to the questions they listed in the *W* column of their K-W-L charts. (See Differentiated Instruction.)

**Teacher Think Aloud** The Teacher Think Aloud makes the thinking of a good reader public knowledge for all students.

### English Language Learners

Students who are acquiring English as a second language will benefit from a variety of techniques and tools embedded in *Reading Advantage*. In the magazines, text provides rich context to help define unfamiliar words, illustrations and photographs provide visual support, and plays offer a natural way to practice oral fluency. In the Teacher's Edition, background concepts, oral discussion, graphic organizers, and the Differentiated Instruction feature all work together to help students build confidence in using the English language.

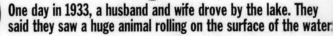

## DIFFERENTIATED INSTRUCTION

### Comprehension
INFERENTIAL THINKING

To help students use the text and their prior knowledge to make inferences or draw conclusions about the information in the text, use these prompts.

- What do you know about sightings of monsters or strange creatures?
- What did you learn about the searches for Nessie?
- With what you know and what you have read, what conclusions can you draw about the search for the Loch Ness monster?

**Student Journal page 2**

---

## One day in 1933, a husband and wife drove by the lake. They said they saw a huge animal rolling on the surface of the water.

Stories of the Loch Ness monster go back 1,500 years. That is when people first reported seeing the beast. One person said, "It looked like a huge frog. Only it wasn't a frog." Since then, tales of the beast have kept on. To this day, people still claim to see it.

Is there really a monster? If so, it has never been caught. Is it real? Have people been lying all these years? Or have they just been fooled?

### A Lake of Mystery

Loch Ness is a lake in Scotland. It is twenty-four miles long. It is one of the deepest lakes in the world. Even though it is big, the lake is hard to see from a distance. The shores are lined with trees. Frequent rain leaves a thick fog in the air.

Until 1933, few people got a close view of the north side of the loch, or lake. (*Loch* is Scottish for *lake*.) That is because no roads led there. In 1933, a road was built. The road runs along the north shore of Loch Ness. Many cars began to use the road. That is when the strange sightings increased.

### Early Reports

One day in 1933, a husband and wife drove by the lake. They said they saw a huge animal rolling on the surface of the water. A newspaper printed their story. The paper called the animal "a monster." The name "Loch Ness monster" caught on with

readers. Soon the monster ha[s] a nickname, too. It was Nessie.

In time, more people said they saw Nessie. One couple claimed it crawled across the shore road. Others rushed to Loch Ness to see for themselve[s.] Boy Scouts sailed out on the lake in small boats. They waited for the monster. But no one saw a real monster.

### Strange Footprints

A newspaper had a plan to fin[d] Nessie. It sent a hunter to trac[k] down the monster. A few day[s] passed. The hunter said he found fresh footprints. He adde[d] that an animal with four toes o[n] each foot made those footprint[s.] He guessed that the animal was about twenty feet long.

*Famous 1934 photo of the Loch Ness monst[er]*

## Bus-Sized Monster Seen in Loch Ness
"I saw it with my own eyes," reports man.

## Nessie rears her ugly head again!
(But don't forget, it is silly season.)

## Loch Monster Spotted by Couple

4

---

## During Reading

### Comprehension
INFERENTIAL THINKING

Use these questions to model how to make inferences, using the text on page 3. Then have students share other inferences they make.

- What does the text tell me?
- What do I already know about this?
- Using the text and what I know, what can I infer that has not been stated directly?

(See Differentiated Instruction.)

8 • Mystery

### Teacher Think Aloud
*The quotation on page 3 seems pretty unbelievable to me. But the next section of text tells me that thousands of people claim to have seen this "monster." Because of my prior knowledge, I'm skeptical that this monster exists. Shouldn't scientists be able to prove the existence of the Loch Ness monster? I infer that many people thought they saw some type of animal, but it wasn't really a monster.*

### Comprehension
MONITOR UNDERSTANDING

Use these questions to model for students how to monitor their understanding by asking questions. The[n] have students ask their own questions and try to resolve any confusion.

- Does the monster really exist?
- What is *sonar*?
- What fix-up strategy can I use to try to fix my confusion?

---

## DURING READING

Instruction is provided for strategies that students will learn to apply while they are reading. If students print the prompts on a bookmark or card, they will have a handy reminder for all their reading. While students are reading independently, meet with small groups or do "walk-by" conferences. In a walk-by conference, stop briefly beside a student and ask a couple of questions to assess how the student is doing. "Tell me about what you just read," "What does that word mean? How do you know?" and "Read aloud the paragraph you just finished reading" are prompts that allow you to do a quick check on a student's comprehension of text.

---

Each comprehension strategy features a **Teacher Think Aloud** that models the strategy.

There have been over 10,000 reported sightings of the Loch Ness monster. Anything could be hiding in the lake because some parts of Loch Ness are 900 feet deep.

The hunter made plaster casts of the prints, which he sent to London, England. Experts studied the prints. But they said the animal was not a monster. It was just a hippo!

No one knew for sure how the hippo prints got there. Hippos do not live in Scotland. Had the hunter played a joke? Or had a joke been played on him? The case was never solved. As a result, some people doubted there was a monster.

### More Reports

Many people still believed a beast was in Loch Ness. In 1934, a doctor took a photo at the lake. It showed a long neck and head sticking up from the water. The shape looked like a dinosaur. Some thought the photo might be a fake. Other people thought it was real.

Twenty years later, people on a bus said they saw Nessie. They watched it for ten minutes. The same year, a fishing boat recorded the shape of a creature deep in the water. It was fifty feet long and had eight legs.

### New Searches

In 1960, an engineer made a short film at Loch Ness. It showed a dark shape moving in the water. Experts from the British Air Force watched the film. They thought it showed a live animal in Loch Ness.

A new search of the lake was made. This time, a crew went deep into the water. They used sonar. This tool uses sound to find things.

The sonar showed a large body moving in the lake. But was it Nessie? Experts were not sure. Some said it was. Other people said it was just a large school of fish.

More searches were held in the 1970s. A crew from Boston placed a camera deep in the water. They waited two years for the beast to appear. At last, the camera saw something. It took pictures of a huge flipper. The team thought they had found Nessie. But others disagreed.

### Plaster Casts

The hunter could not send the footprints themselves to London. He had to figure out a way to send a copy of the footprints. A plaster cast is a common way to do this. To make a plaster cast of footprints, you would fill the footprints with liquid plaster. The liquid takes the shape of the footprint. Then you would wait for the plaster to dry and harden. At that point, you could lift up the dried plaster, which would be in the shape of the footprint.

5

---

## Teacher Think Aloud

*On page 5, I read that a search crew used sonar to try to find the monster. I don't know what this is. Maybe I'll find out if I read on. I see a little feature on page 6 that explains what sonar is. Now I understand. Reading ahead helped me fix my confusion.*

### Fix-Up Strategies

Offer these strategies to help students read independently.

**If you don't understand what you're reading:**

- Reread the difficult section to look for clues to help you comprehend.
- Read ahead to find clues to help you comprehend.
- Retell, or say in your own words, what you've read.
- Visualize, or form mental pictures of, what you've read.

**If you don't understand a word:**

- Reread the sentence. Look for ideas and words that provide meaning clues.
- Find clues by reading a few sentences before and after the confusing word.
- Look for the base or root word and think about its meaning.
- Think about the topic or plot at this point to see if either offers meaning clues.

Monster in the Lake *and* Here a Yeti, There a Yeti • **9**

**Fix-Up Strategies** Each lesson includes fix-up strategy reminders to help students become independent problem solvers.

## Most describe it the same way. They say it has a long neck, one or two humps, and flippers.

They said the pictures were not clear enough to be sure. They felt more proof of the beast was needed. More recent searches with more advanced equipment have yielded nothing, as well.

### Latest Findings
Today, people still claim to see the Loch Ness monster. Most describe it the same way. They say it has a long neck, one or two humps, and flippers.

Many are quick to laugh at the claims. How could a monster be real? In 1994, a London newspaper said that the 1934 photo of Nessie was a fake. But that did not change the minds of those who think Nessie is real.

### Possible Answers
People still swear they have seen Nessie. But have they really? Maybe the people are joking. Still, other people believe them. After all, they are good, honest people. Wh[y] would they lie?

There are people who think that other people have been fooled by their own eye[s]. The Nessie sighters may have seen a swimming animal or a floating log. And they thoug[ht] it was a beast.

Nessie remains a mystery today. No one knows for sure if the monster is real. Some think it may be a huge reptil[e] or newt left from ancient times. Others think it may be a giant seal. Still others think there is no large animal at all in the water. ◆

### Sonar
Sonar is often used to locate objects that are submerged, or underwater. Sonar sends out sound waves that bounce off solid objects. If something solid is in the way, the waves will bounce back. The equipment can measure how far away that object is. Submarines use sonar to navigate in the ocean. Bats use sonar to find their way around, too.

6

*What do you think? Could Nessie be a long lost dinosaur?*

---

**Student Journal** Reduced facsimiles are placed near the point of use to help you quickly identify which pages are used in the lesson.

Student Journal page 3

---

# After Reading  Use one or more activities.

**AFTER READING**

The After Reading section provides a variety of response ideas that include discussion, instruction, vocabulary, writing, and phonics/word study. Select the activity or activities most appropriate for your students.

### Check Purpose
Have students revisit the K-W-L chart they began on *Student Journal* page 2. Have them look at the first column that lists what they thought they knew before reading. Ask them to put a check mark next to any ideas they had that were correct. Have them adjust ideas that were not correct. Then have students look at the second column to check off any things they wanted to know that were answered in the selection.

### Discussion Questions
Continue the group discussion with the following questions.
1. What did you learn about the search for the Loch Ness monster? (Monitor Understanding)
2. What effect did all the publicity about the searches for the monster have? (Cause-Effect)
3. Did you enjoy the selection? Why? Why not? (Making Connections)

### Revisit: List
Look back at the list begun in Before Reading. Ask if students would like to add any entries.

**Discussion Questions** Strategy- and skill-based questions allow students to review their reading and teachers to check comprehension. By discussing the questions together, students learn from each other. The technique called Think-Pair-Share is sometimes recommended for discussion. In it, students think through a question, talk about it with a partner, and then share with the whole group. This technique takes the pressure off students, especially English Language Learners, because it allows them time to think and the verbal support of a partner.

## Here a Yeti, There a Yeti

There once was a monster named Yeti
Whose hair grew as thick as spaghetti.
He didn't give a fig
That his feet were so big
Or if you called him "Big Foot" or "Big Teddy."

7

DIFFERENTIATED INSTRUCTION
## Vocabulary
### Multiple Meanings

Explain more about multiple-meaning words:

1. Explain that many English words have more than one meaning and are called multiple-meaning words.

2. Give these examples: *He threw a rock into the pond. Rock the baby in the cradle. Pour cereal into a bowl. She likes to bowl with her team.*

3. Pronounce *cycle* and *monitor*. Ask students to explain each word's multiple meanings. Ask volunteers to use the words in sentences and explain their different meanings.

POEM: HERE A YETI,
THERE A YETI

Have students read the limerick silently and then aloud with a partner. Use these questions to talk about the limerick.

• What rhyming patterns do you notice?

• Can you tap out the rhythm?

• What is the tone of the poem?

Explain to students that a limerick has five lines. Lines one, two, and five rhyme. Lines three and four rhyme. Limericks are always about something silly.

## Writing K-W-L Chart

Have students revisit the K-W-L chart on *Student Journal* page 2. This time, ask them to write entries in the third column of the chart, explaining what they have learned by reading the selection.

## Vocabulary Multiple Meanings

Display the word *casts*. Remind students that in the article, *casts* is used with *plaster* to name a kind of form or mold. Explain that *casts* can also mean "the groups of people who perform in a play or other show." Ask students to identify other words that have multiple meanings. Have partners complete *Student Journal* page 3. (See Differentiated Instruction.)

## Phonics/Word Study

### Short and Long a Patterns

Write the following words on the board: *pan* and *pane*. Ask: *How is the vowel sound in each of these words different?* Have students volunteer other words that contain the short and long *a* sounds. Now, work with students to complete the in-depth vowel activity on TE page 12.

**Focus on...** Two pages at the end of every lesson provide a choice of activities:

**Phonics/Word Study** lesson (with references to *Word Study Manual*)

## Short and Long *a* Patterns

Write the following words on the board: *hat* and *name*. Tell students that these two words represent two different sounds for the letter *a*. One word has a short *a* sound, and one word has a long *a* sound. Ask students if they can identify which word has the short *a* sound and which has the long *a* sound.

▶ Ask students how they knew which was which.

▶ Using the Short and Long *a* Vowel Sort One sheet, model the sorting process for students. (See *Word Study Manual* page 34.) Write the headers *Short* a, *Long* a, and *Oddball* and the first few words in the appropriate columns.

▶ Discuss the sort, what students learned, and why the word *was* belongs in the Oddball column.

▶ Once the sort is complete, hand out copies of the Short and Long *a* Vowel Sort One sheet and ask students to cut it up and do the sort on their own or in groups.

▶ Check the final sorts.

| Short and Long *a*: Sort One | | |
|---|---|---|
| Short *a* | Long *a* | Oddball |
| lamp | flame | was |
| plant | same | |
| flat | name | |
| hat | plane | |
| trap | shade | |
| mad | frame | |
| crack | crate | |

For more information on word sorts and spelling stages, see pages 5–31 in the *Word Study Manual*.

# Focus on . . .

Use one or more activities in this section to focus on a particular area of need in your students.

## Comprehension  STRATEGY SUPPORT

To help those students who need more practice using the strategies covered in this lesson, work one-on-one or in small groups to apply the strategy prompts below. Apply the prompts to a *Reading Advantage* paperback, a classroom library book, or a new or familiar selection in the magazine. Always model your own thinking first.

### Inferential Thinking

• What are the causes or effects of this event?
• What do I learn from the character or person's thoughts, words, or actions?
• What do I know (or infer) from the text that the author hasn't stated directly?
• What conclusions can I draw?

### Monitor Understanding

• Do I understand what I'm reading? If not, what part is confusing me?
• What fix-up strategies can I use to solve the problem? (See During Reading for fix-up strategies.)
• Why did a character say (do, think, ask) that?
• What images do I visualize from the text? What parts can't I visualize?
• Why did the author include (or not include) those details?

## Writing **Point of View**

Have students use the information in the article to tell the story from Nessie's point of view. Students should first review the text to find information they want to include—the first sightings, the attempts to discover her, the newspaper publicity. Remind students to use first-person pronouns in their Nessie versions of the facts. Encourage students to gather and organize their information in a chart.

| From the text | What Nessie might say |
|---|---|
| p. 4 1933, husband and wife spot Nessie | Life was pretty peaceful until 1933. |

To help students include sensory details and strong verbs and nouns in their writing, see lessons in *Writing Advantage*, pages 30–55.

**Comprehension,** reteaching of strategies

**Writing** in response to the selection, with a reference to *Writing Advantage*

## Fluency: Pacing

Have students listen as you model how to read the poem "Here a Yeti, There a Yeti" at a smooth and even pace. Show how you pause after punctuation. Have partners first read silently to themselves to become familiar with the text, and then read aloud to each other.

As you listen to students read, use these prompts to guide them.

▶ Notice how the line breaks in the poem help you read at an even pace. They signal where to pause slightly.

▶ Keep your eyes on the text as you read so that you don't lose your place and either miss words or repeat them.

▶ Put energy into your voice as you read. It will make the poem more interesting and understandable.

When students read aloud, do they—

✓ demonstrate a smooth pace, not too fast or too slow?

✓ incorporate well-timed pauses between words and phrases?

✓ reflect an awareness and understanding of punctuation?

## English Language Learners

To support students' understanding of multiple meaning words, review the following homographs: *spotted, saw, school.*

1. Have partners choose a word. Have them divide a piece of paper into two columns and write the word at the top of each column.

2. Have each partner draw an illustration that represents one of the meanings.

## Independent Activity Options

While you work with individuals or small groups, others can work independently on one or more of the following options.

▶ Level A paperback books, see TE pages 367–372

▶ Level A *eZines*

▶ Repeat word sorts from this lesson

▶ *Student Journal* pages for this lesson

▶ *Writing Advantage* independent lessons

# Assessment

## Strategy Assessment

To help you and your students assess their use of comprehension strategies, ask the following questions. Students can complete a written response or provide verbal answers in a one-on-one reading conference.

1. **Inferential Thinking** What inferences did you make as you read this text? (Answers will vary. Students may infer that the monster must not exist, especially after reading about the many thorough searches that were done to find Nessie.)

2. **Monitor Understanding** What parts of this article were most confusing to you? What did you do to help with your understanding? (Answers will vary. Possible response: I was confused about the story of the hunter who found footprints. I tried to retell that section of the text in my own words, and that helped me understand what I was reading.)

For ongoing informal assessment, use the checklists on pages 61–64 of *Level A Assessment*.

## Word Study Assessment

Use these steps to help you and your students assess their understanding of short and long *a* patterns.

1. Create a chart like the one shown.

2. Have students read the words in the first column of the chart.

3. Then have students sort the words into the Short *a* or Long *a* column.

| Words | Short *a* | Long *a* |
|-------|-----------|----------|
| hat | hat | cape |
| blast | blast | safe |
| cape | stack | bake |
| safe | | |
| stack | | |
| bake | | |

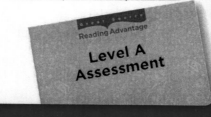

Reading Advantage

Level A Assessment

**Assessment,** ongoing assessment, helps you and your students assess what they have learned in the lesson with questions about the strategies and word study. A reference to the formal assessment appears in time for the Mid-Magazine and Magazine Tests.

**Fluency** suggestions focus on reading aloud with expression, pacing, and phrasing

**ELL** boxes target ways to accomodate English Language Learners

**Independent Activity Options** help teachers manage individuals and small groups

# Great Source Reading Advantage
# Is Supported by Research

**No Child Left Behind** has placed a national spotlight on the critical issue of reading proficiency. Educators across the nation face the challenge of helping their students read at or above grade level by the end of the third grade; however, many students continue to struggle with reading through high school. In fact, according to the National Center for Education Statistics (2003) **only 33% of eighth graders and 36% of twelfth graders are reading at or above the proficient level.**

Teachers want to help these students improve their reading and writing ability; however, the task is daunting because of a lack of appropriate instructional materials to address the specific issues with which these students struggle.

*Reading Advantage*, designed by **Laura Robb** with a team of nationally known university educators and master classroom teachers, including **James F. Baumann**, **Carol J. Fuhler**, and **Joan S. Kindig**, can help this adolescent population improve their reading and writing skills. The seven kits address the needs of at-risk adolescents who are reading between the middle of first grade and eighth grade reading level.

The program focuses on critical areas where students need the most support: comprehension, word study and phonics, vocabulary and fluency building, and assessment, and includes enough reading materials to support each student's progress.

# Great Source Reading Advantage
# Matches the Level to Your Classroom Needs!

| Program Level | Grade Level | Lexile Measure | Guided Reading Level | DRA |
|---|---|---|---|---|
| **Foundations** Motion Fun and Games Survival Arts | 1-2 | 350L–470L | J-L | 18-24 |
| **Level A** Mystery Space Odyssey Water Cities | 2-3 | 500L–630L | M-P | 28-38 |
| **Level B** Flight Underground Heroism Music | 3-4 | 630L–700L | M-Q | 28-38 |
| **Level C** Emotions Racers & Racing Boundaries Ecology | 4-5 | 730L–780L | M-Q | 28-40 |
| **Level D** Travel the World Revolution Mountains Changes | 5-6 | 820L–920L | N-R | 30-40 |
| **Level E** Communications Relationships Discoveries Money | 6-7 | 940L–990L | T-W | 44-50 |
| **Level F** Adaptation Justice Sports Disasters | 7-8 | 1030L–1100L | T-W | 44-50 |

Lexile® is a registered trademark of MetaMetrics, Inc.

Guided Reading Levels are from *Guiding Readers and Writers, Grades 3-6* by Irene Fountas and Gay Su Pinnell (Portsmouth: Heinemann, 2001).

Developmental Reading Assessment® is a registered trademark of Pearson Education, Inc. DRA is a trademark of Pearson Education, Inc.

# Great Source Reading Advantage
# Offers Differentiated Instruction

Not all students in your class need the same instruction at the same time. Therefore, using the whole-class model is not always the most effective way to teach reading. Use a pattern of whole-class, small-group, and individual instruction to address the needs of all students.

| | WHOLE CLASS | SMALL GROUP | INDEPENDENT |
|---|---|---|---|
| **Purpose** | Build community knowledge | Address students who have similar needs | Target individual needs and promote independent work |
| **Instructional Activities** | ▶ Introduce theme<br>▶ Before-reading activities<br>▶ Lesson wrap-up | ▶ During-reading strategy instruction and modeling<br>▶ Discussion questions<br>▶ After-reading skills & strategy instruction | ▶ After-reading skills & strategy instruction<br>▶ Enrichment<br>▶ Self-evaluation<br>▶ *Reading Advantage* paperback collection |

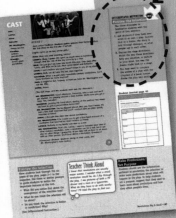

**Differentiated Instruction** Students who need deeper instruction in and/or a different approach to a strategy or skill will benefit from instruction that provides more support, or scaffolding.

**More to Read!**
Keep the *Reading Advantage* paperback books and the *eZines* CD-ROM available for students who have finished their assigned work. See the Teacher's Edition appendix for applying the reading strategies to the paperback books.

# Great Source Reading Advantage
# Is Easy to Manage

How can you address the needs of your students while still maintaining order in the classroom? Routines and schedules are key.

## Establishing Routines
Students can work independently if they know
▶ what to expect each day;
▶ how to use the material;
▶ what they can do to solve most problems on their own;
▶ how to respect their classmates.

The following charts will help your students to work productively and independently and will foster an atmosphere of respect.

Post guidelines, procedures, and schedules on a bulletin board or a wall. Have students in the independent groups take turns being the group leader to help keep the rest of the group on task.

## Behavior Guidelines During Teacher-led Group Work

▶ Come prepared.

▶ Be a good listener.

▶ Respect ideas of others.

▶ Use details from the magazine article to support your position.

▶ Participate in the discussion.

▶ Talk quietly so others can work independently.

## "I-Need-Help" Procedure Chart for Independent Work Times

If you need help, try the four steps below. (If you need to speak, use a quiet voice.)

1. Think for a moment. Try to solve the problem yourself.

2. Ask a group member for support.

3. If that person can't help, ask another student from your group.

4. If none of the steps work, put your name on the "Needs Help" clipboard. Work on something you can do until the teacher helps you.

# Is Easy to Manage continued

## Class Gathering

**Use this time to present an overview of the day's learning events.** Explain which groups you will meet with and go over the directions for the independent work other groups will do. Writing the class schedule on the board as a reference and time-management guide for you and your students lets everyone know what the plan is.

## Strategic Think Aloud or Minilesson

**Present instruction that will benefit the whole class.** Use this whole-class time to introduce a new theme, teach a new comprehension strategy, or to do the Before Reading activities. Support for all these teaching ideas is in the *Reading Advantage* Teacher's Edition.

## Read Aloud

**Why read aloud to older students?** Research shows that reading aloud to students on a daily basis develops their listening capacity, builds their background knowledge, develops their vocabulary, and enlarges their knowledge of literary language and syntax by attuning their ears to the language of different genres.

**What can you read aloud?** The *Reading Advantage* Teacher's Edition provides a theme-related read-aloud selection for each magazine in the unit opener. Use articles from the *Reading Advantage* magazines or choose short selections such as poems, short stories and folk tales, or fascinating passages from nonfiction texts.

## Small-Grouping Instruction

The following chart shows how two or three groups rotate through the major learning events related to *Reading Advantage*. Vary the rotation according to the number of groups you have (no more than 3 groups are recommended) and the length of time you have to spend on *Reading Advantage*.

**TWO GROUPS**

| | Teacher-led Group | Student Journal<br>Word Study<br>Independent Reading |
|---|---|---|
| **Time 1** | Group 1 | Group 2 |
| **Time 2** | Group 2 | Group 1 |

**THREE GROUPS**

| | Teacher-led Group | Student Journal<br>Independent Reading | Word Study<br>Independent Reading |
|---|---|---|---|
| **Time 1** | Group 1 | Group 2 | Group 3 |
| **Time 2** | Group 2 | Group 3 | Group 2 |
| **Time 3** | Group 3 | Group 1 | Group 1 |

**WRAP-UP** Bring the class back together to give any instructions, such as homework or preparation necessary for the next class.

# Establishing Schedules

Write the class schedule on the board as a reference and time-management guide. This technique enables your students to take responsibility for what they should be doing. A daily session could follow these schedules:

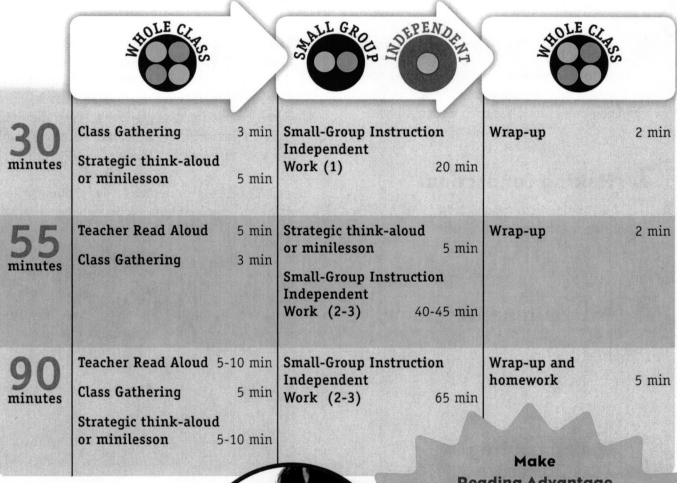

| | WHOLE CLASS | | SMALL GROUP / INDEPENDENT | | WHOLE CLASS | |
|---|---|---|---|---|---|---|
| **30 minutes** | Class Gathering | 3 min | Small-Group Instruction Independent Work (1) | 20 min | Wrap-up | 2 min |
| | Strategic think-aloud or minilesson | 5 min | | | | |
| **55 minutes** | Teacher Read Aloud | 5 min | Strategic think-aloud or minilesson | 5 min | Wrap-up | 2 min |
| | Class Gathering | 3 min | Small-Group Instruction Independent Work (2-3) | 40-45 min | | |
| **90 minutes** | Teacher Read Aloud | 5-10 min | Small-Group Instruction Independent Work (2-3) | 65 min | Wrap-up and homework | 5 min |
| | Class Gathering | 5 min | | | | |
| | Strategic think-aloud or minilesson | 5-10 min | | | | |

## Make Reading Advantage Your Own!

Use these schedules as a guide and tailor them to your schedule and teaching style.

If you use *Reading Advantage* as a supplement in your 90-minute block, for example, follow one of the shorter schedules and leave the remaining time for your other reading and language arts activities.

# Great Source Reading Advantage
# Comprehension

To become skillful readers, students must develop the reading strategies necessary to understand and learn from text. *Reading Advantage* provides for instruction in five high-utility reading strategies:

## 1 Monitor Understanding

The ability to determine whether comprehension is occurring and to take corrective (fix-up) action when comprehension becomes difficult

## 2 Making Connections

The ability to activate prior knowledge, predict, self-question, and make connections to personal experiences and other texts

## 3 Determining Importance

The ability to evaluate and determine the importance of ideas, and support one's beliefs with evidence

## 4 Understanding Text Structure

The ability to recognize and understand the organization an author uses to write a narrative or expository selection, which includes knowledge of text features and genre

## 5 Inferential Thinking

The ability to infer and synthesize ideas that are not directly stated in the text

These strategies are integrated into *Reading Advantage* lessons to provide students "point-of-use" strategy instruction and application using suitable texts. If you wish to extend these point-of-use instructional suggestions, there are references to the more robust Model Lessons that follow on pages xxiv–xxxiii.

Each Model Lesson provides a definition of the strategy, supporting research, and a three-part teaching sequence:

| | |
|---|---|
| **Explain:** | Information to help you provide students with a verbal explanation of the strategy and how to employ it |
| **Model:** | Examples for how to demonstrate to students the application of the strategy |
| **Practice:** | Guidance for how to provide students practice in the strategy to promote its independent use |

We encourage you to refer to and use the Model Lessons flexibly, drawing from them as needed when you determine that students would benefit from more extensive instruction in the strategies incorporated into *Reading Advantage*.

# REFERENCES

Alvermann, D. E., & Hagood, M. C. (2000). Critical media literacy: Research, theory, and practice in "new times." *Journal of Educational Research, 93,* 193–206.

Anderson, R. C., & Pearson, P. D. (1984). A schema-theoretic view of basic processes in reading comprehension. In P. D. Pearson (Ed.), *Handbook of reading research* (pp. 225–292). New York: Longman.

Armbruster, B. B., Anderson, T. H., & Ostertag, J. (1987). Does text structure/summarization instruction facilitate learning from expository text? *Reading Research Quarterly, 22,* 331–346.

Baker, L. (2002). Metacognition in reading comprehension. In C. C. Block and M. Pressley (Eds.), *Comprehension instruction: Research-based best practices* (pp. 77–95). New York: Guilford.

Baker, L., & Brown, A. L. (1984). Metacognitive skills and reading. In P. D. Pearson (Ed.), *Handbook of reading research* (pp. 353–394). New York: Longman.

Barron, J. B., & Sternberg, R. J. (Eds.). (1987). *Teaching thinking skills: Theory and practice.* New York: Freeman.

Brown, A. L., & Day, J. D. (1983). Macro rules for summarizing texts: The development of expertise. *Journal of Verbal Learning and Verbal Behavior, 22,* 1–14.

Commeyras, M. (1993). Promoting critical thinking through dialogical-thinking reading lessons. *The Reading Teacher, 46,* 486–494.

Duke, N. K., & Pearson, P. D. (2002). Effective practices for developing reading comprehension. In A. E. Farstrup & S. J. Samuels (Eds.), *What research has to say about reading instruction* (3rd ed., pp. 205–242). Newark, DE: International Reading Association.

Ennis, R. H. (1987). A taxonomy of critical thinking dispositions and abilities. In J. B. Baron & R. J. Sternberg (Eds.), *Teaching for thinking* (pp. 9–26). New York: Freeman.

Hahn, A. L., & Garner, R. (1984). Synthesis of research on students' ability to summarize text. *Educational Leadership, 42* (5), 52–55.

Hare, V., & Borchardt, K. M. (1984). Direct instruction of summarization skills. *Reading Research Quarterly, 20,* 62–78.

Fitzgerald, J. (1989). Research on stories: Implications for teachers. In K. D. Muth (Ed.), *Children's comprehension of text: Research into practice* (pp. 2–36). Newark, DE: International Reading Association.

Fitzgerald, J., & Spiegel, D. L. (1983). Enhancing children's reading comprehension through instruction in narrative structure. *Journal of Reading Behavior, 15,* 1–17.

Gordon, C. J. (1989). Teaching narrative text structure: A process approach to reading and writing. In K. D. Muth (Ed.). *Children's comprehension of text: Research into practice* (pp. 79–102). Newark, DE: International Reading Association.

Griffin, C. C., & Tulbert, B. L. (1995). The Effect of Graphic Organizers on students' comprehension and recall of expository text: A review of the research and implications for practice. *Reading and Writing Quarterly, 11,* 73–89.

Hansen, J., & Pearson, P. D. (1983). An instructional study: Improving the inferential comprehension of good and poor fourth-grade readers. *Journal of Educational Psychology, 75,* 821–829.

Langer, J. A. (1995). *Envisioning literature: Literary understanding and literature instruction.* New York: Teacher's College Press.

Mandler, J. M., & Johnson, N. S. (1977). Remembrance of things parsed: Story structure and recall. *Cognitive Psychology, 9,* 111–151.

McGee, L. M., & Richgels, D. J. (1988). Teaching expository text structure to elementary students. *The Reading Teacher, 38,* 739–747.

Meyer, B. J. F. (1984). Organizational aspects of text: Effects on reading comprehension and applications for the classroom. In J. Flood (Ed.), *Promoting reading comprehension* (pp. 113–138). Newark, DE: International Reading Association.

National Reading Panel. (2000). *National Reading Panel: Teaching children to read: An evidence-based assessment of the scientific research literature on reading and its implications for reading instruction: Report of the subgroups* (NIH Publication No. 00-4754). Washington, DC: National Institute of Health and National Institute of Child Health and Human Development.

Nickerson, R. S. (1988). Improving thinking through instruction. In E. Z. Rothkoph (Ed.), *Review of research in education* (pp. 3–57). Washington, DC: American Educational Research Association.

Paris, S. G., Wasik, B. A., & Turner, J. C. (1991). The development of strategic readers. In R. Barr, M. L. Kamil, P. Mosenthal, & P. D. Pearson (Eds.), *Handbook of reading research, Volume II* (pp. 609–640). White Plains, NY: Longman.

Pearson, P. D., & Camperell, K. (1981). Comprehension of text structures. In J. T. Guthrie (Ed.), *Comprehension and teaching: Research reviews* (pp. 27–55). Newark, DE: International Reading Association.

RAND Reading Study Group. (2002). *Toward an R & D program in reading comprehension.* Santa Monica, CA: RAND Corporation.

Rosenshine, B., Meister, C., & Chapman, S. (1996). Teaching students to generate questions: A review of the intervention studies. *Review of Educational Research, 66* (2), 181–221.

Tierney, R. J., Sofer, A., O'Flahavan, J. F., & McGinley, W. (1989). The effects of reading and writing upon thinking critically. *Reading Research Quarterly, 24,* 134–173.

# Monitor Understanding

**DEFINITION:** Monitoring understanding involves a reader's conscious effort to determine whether comprehension is occurring and to take corrective (fix-up) action when comprehension becomes difficult. Fix-up strategies include rereading, reading ahead, retelling, visualizing, asking questions, and using context.

## RESEARCH SUPPORT

Thoughtful reading comprehension requires that readers critically analyze why and how authors write and use ideas (Alvermann & Hagood, 2000; Ennis, 1987; Tierney, Sofer, O'Flavahan, & McGinley, 1989). Research indicates that students can be taught to understand how to read critically and analytically (Barron & Sternberg, 1987; Commeyras, 1993; Nickerson, 1988).

## MODEL LESSON

### Explain: How the Strategy Helps and When to Use It

Explain to students that monitoring understanding will help them improve comprehension and learn new information. It's especially helpful with nonfiction but can be used with any challenging text. Self-monitoring is a multi-step process that happens during reading. Here's how it works:

In Step 1, the reader reads a section of text.

In Step 2, the reader asks: *Do I understand what I just read well enough to retell it?* The reader retells the section without looking at the text.

In Step 3, the reader looks back at the section of text and evaluates the retelling. If the retelling includes the most important details from the text, the reader reads on. If the retelling includes incorrect or few details, the reader chooses a fix-up strategy to try to resolve the confusion.

### Five Fix-Up Strategies

- *Reread* a difficult section to see if that improves understanding. Rereading includes careful rereading of diagrams, captions, and photographic details. Rereading can also be done to connect newly read ideas with earlier text.

- *Read on* to see if the next section gives clues for comprehension.

- *Visualize* to form mental pictures of what's happening or of specific words and phrases.

- *Ask questions* to clarify confusing details. Then try another fix-up strategy to find the answer.

- *Use context clues* in the sentences before and after the difficult word and word-structure clues to help figure out meaning.

### Model the Strategy

**Materials** *Mystery*, "Detectives at Work," pages 39–43

**Step 1** Name the strategy and explain to students what it is and how it helps them.

**Think Aloud** Here's a good way to break down the Monitor Understanding strategy: read, pause, retell, evaluate. This process will help you confirm your understanding of a text and pinpoint areas of confusion. After reading a paragraph, section, or page of text, pause and retell in your own words what you've read. Then check the text and evaluate yourself. Ask: *Did I recall enough details to show that I understand?* If you recalled several important details, then read on. If you had trouble retelling what you read, you probably didn't understand or remember enough. Try applying a fix-up strategy to make better sense of the passage.

Now, I'll model the whole strategy. Listen as I read, pause, retell, evaluate and apply a fix-up strategy.

**Step 2** Read aloud the section called "Check for Fingerprints" on page 41.

**Think Aloud** Now I'll retell what I read, without looking at the paragraph.

*Detectives at a crime scene look for fingerprints. They dust the fingerprints with special oil. All fingerprints are different, so if a print is matched to a person, he or she will be convicted of the crime.*

When I look back at the paragraph, I see that I left out details and misunderstood others. I'll try rereading as a fix-up strategy. Here's my second retelling. Notice how I add more details and correct information from the first retelling.

*Detectives at a crime scene look for fingerprints. One way detectives save prints is by using powder. The powder sticks to the oil left by the fingerprint. A piece of foil is pressed against the print to pick up the pattern. If a person's fingerprint matches the print at the crime scene, that person will most likely be questioned.*

**Step 3** Discuss how to choose a fix-up strategy.

**Think Aloud** It can be hard to figure out which fix-up strategy to choose when you're confused about your reading. Ask yourself these questions to help you make the choice: *Do I need to slow down and reread? Do I need to connect ideas from this last section to text that came before? Am I having trouble visualizing images? What ideas are most unclear? Did a specific word confuse me?*

## Guided Practice

1. Set aside time when you can observe students as they self-monitor, evaluate, and if necessary, apply a fix-up strategy.

2. Circulate and listen to students think aloud as they monitor their understanding. Support students who have difficulty by first modeling the entire process, then sharing the process, and finally having them complete the process on their own.

## Independent Practice

1. Assign a section of text for students to monitor understanding on their own.

2. Give each student a piece of paper, have them write their retelling, evaluate it, and note the fix-up strategy they plan to apply.

## Following Up

Continue to encourage students to self-monitor their reading, especially when they need new or challenging texts.

# Comprehension continued
# Making Connections

**DEFINITION:** When readers make connections to a text, they link their life experiences and prior knowledge to the information, characters, themes, and topics in the text. Connections can be to a reader's own experience, to other texts, or to the larger world.

## RESEARCH SUPPORT

There are common patterns or structures for narrative (Fitzgerald, 1989; Mandler & Johnson, 1977) and expository texts (Duke & Pearson, 2002; Meyer, 1984; Pearson & Camperell, 1981). Research demonstrates that students can be taught to recognize and use narrative (Fitzgerald & Spiegel, 1983; Gordon, 1989) and expository (Armbruster, Anderson, & Ostertag, 1987; McGee & Richgels, 1988) text structures to enhance their comprehension, and there is evidence that the use of graphic representations of text structures can enhance students' understanding (Duke & Pearson, 2002; Griffin & Tulbert, 1995).

## MODEL LESSON

### Explain: How the Strategy Helps and When to Use It

Explain to students that when they make connections, they compare the information in a text to their own experiences, to other texts, and to issues in the larger world. The more connections they make to a text, the better they will understand and remember it. Making connections will also help students learn new information and better understand the experiences of the characters or people in a text. If a reader can't make a connection, the text will be harder to understand. In those cases, provide any necessary background and encourage students to read on and re-evaluate at the end of each section, page, or chapter. If students discover that their prior experience doesn't match what is in the text, discuss possible reasons for the mismatch.

Readers begin making connections before reading, as they preview the text to access prior knowledge. The process should then continue during and after reading. Encourage students to make connections with all texts.

### Model the Strategy

**Materials** *Space Odyssey*, "From the Diary of Sir Isaac Newton," page 46

**Step 1** Name the strategy and explain to students what it is and how it helps them.

**Think Aloud** When you make connections with a text, it strengthens your comprehension in two important ways: It makes the text more interesting, which helps you stick with it, and it helps you remember what you read. The connections you make can be to your own experience; to other texts, movies, or TV shows you know; and to issues in your community or in the world.

**Step 2** Explain that posing questions is a good way to make connections to a text. Display these questions so students can refer to them as they read:

- What do I connect to in the text?
- What makes me feel these connections?

Provide sticky notes to students and have them jot their connections on them. Students can place the sticky note next to the passage with which they connect.

**Step 3** Have students read the first diary entry on page 46. Show them how the questions help you connect to the title and diary entry.

**Think Aloud** First, I connect to the title because I keep a diary, too. I love to write about feelings and experiences. And I really like going back to reread the entries a few months later. I also connect to Newton's confusion. He wanted to understand the sun and the planets, but wasn't sure whom to believe. I can relate to his curiosity and confusion. I'm always wondering about why things happen and how things work. Thinking about my own questions and confusion helps me understand how Newton might have felt. If he became a great scientist, maybe I can, too.

**Step 4** Point out that the more specific the connections, the deeper the understanding.

**Step 5** Organize students into partners. Have partners discuss their connections to the rest of the poem, explaining why they feel them. Then have pairs share their thoughts with the class.

**Step 6** After reading, post these questions to encourage students to self-reflect.

- Which connections made the reading more meaningful?
- How did these connections help me move beyond myself to thinking about other people, other texts, and larger issues that affect the community or the world?

**Step 7** Have students share their insights with the class.

### Guided Practice

1. Provide sticky notes for students so that they can respond to the questions in Step 2 as they read.

2. Point out that you want students to begin making connections before reading, as they preview the text and begin to access what they know.

3. Have students share their connections with a partner or small group. Circulate and listen so that you can identify students who need more guidance.

4. Support students who need your expertise to make connections and reflect on them.

### Independent Practice

1. Continue to offer students opportunities to practice making connections.

2. Confer with students you supported during guided practice to make sure they can work productively on their own.

### Following Up

Periodically review this strategy and point out that making connections is a part of inferential thinking, another important comprehension strategy.

# Determining Importance

**DEFINITION:** Determining importance involves making decisions about what is important in a text. To determine the importance of ideas in a text, a reader must have a purpose for reading. Purposes can differ among readers and situations. By reflecting on important information in a text, a reader can infer big ideas and build new understandings.

## RESEARCH SUPPORT

Students are presented with large amounts of information in texts, so it is essential for them to be able to identify and remember the important ideas in selections they read. Important ideas in expository texts are the main ideas, which are supported major details. A number of studies document that students can be taught to look for and identify main ideas and major details in expository text, enabling them to comprehend and recall important information (e.g., Armbruster, Anderson, & Ostertag, 1987; Sjostrom & Hare, 1984; Taylor & Beach, 1984). Important information in narrative texts consists of central story ideas, often represented in a story map. There is considerable research demonstrating that students can be taught to identify the key ideas in stories and that this enhances their understanding and memory for narrative texts (Fitzgerald & Spiegel, 1983; Idol & Croll, 1987; Singer & Donlan, 1982).

## MODEL LESSON
### Explain: How the Strategy Helps and When to Use It

Explain to students that finding important ideas in a text is an important skill for students. When students identify what's important, they will better comprehend and remember what they read. An awareness of important ideas will also help students create and infer new understandings. Determining importance is dependent on a purpose for reading. Students can set purposes before reading a passage, a chapter, an article, or an entire book.

Point out that students should begin setting purposes and determining importance during a selection preview. Then, they should use their purposes as support for selecting important ideas both during and after reading.

### Model the Strategy
**Materials** *Water*, "The Scariest Day of My Life," pages 24–27

### Lesson 1: Determining Important Details
**Step 1** Name the strategy and explain to students what it is and how it helps them.

**Think-Aloud** Nonfiction often has a lot of information, and fiction can be complex and detailed. It can be tough to sort out what is important in both kinds of texts. A helpful way to figure out the important details is to use the purposes for reading that you set before you started reading. I will show you how I set purposes. Be on the lookout that my purposes might change as I read and gather more information.

**Step 2** Show students how you preview pages 24–27 and then set purposes for reading. Explain that to preview, you'll first read the title, the introduction on page 24, and the sidebar headings. Then, you'll study the photographs on page 27.

**Think-Aloud** After previewing, I set these purposes for reading. I would like to discover

- what happened on the scariest day of the author's life (from the title)
- if the events in this story are fiction or nonfiction (from the introduction and sidebar headings)
- if the photographs show the actual event from the author's story

**Step 3** Have students read pages 24–27 and show them how you figure out important ideas. Be sure to point out any changes in importance that occurred.

**Think-Aloud** OK, now that I've read page 24, I see that the author is writing about a tidal wave that hit Hawaii in 1960. On pages 25–26, I learn more about the details of the event. At the bottom of page 26, I see the author's note. It explains that the tsunami really did happen. And the photographs on page 27 show actual pictures of the tsunami the author wrote about.

At first, I thought the most important details were those that described how the author survived the tsunami. But as I read more, the image of the author and his family throwing sheets to save the floating people seemed important, too.

**Step 4** Have students comment on your think-aloud and add details that they believe relate to your purposes.

### Lesson 2: Finding Big Ideas
**Step 1** Explain that you will now show students how you reflect on your purposes for reading and important details to determine (or infer) a big idea.

**Think-Aloud** Now that I've read the memoir, let me think about my purposes for reading and all the important details I discovered. What big ideas grow out of everything I know? I think one big idea is that luck plays a major role in surviving a natural disaster. If the author had been home when the wave hit, he probably wouldn't have survived.

**Step 2** Organize students into partners. Have pairs discuss and suggest other big ideas.

### Guided Practice
1. Organize students into partners.
2. Have all pairs preview the same article and write their purposes for reading in a journal or notebook.
3. Have pairs discuss the selection, pinpoint important ideas, and jot them in their journals or notebooks.
4. Ask partners to share and discuss the important ideas they identified.
5. Have pairs use their purposes and important ideas to figure out a big idea. Pairs can share their big ideas with the class. Tell students that when they find big ideas, they are inferring.
6. Support pairs who need more practice with setting purposes and determining important ideas.

### Independent Practice
1. Continue to give students practice with setting purposes and determining importance.
2. Confer with individuals to determine who needs more support with finding big ideas.

### Following Up
Review this strategy throughout the year. Finding big ideas helps students comprehend, remember, and infer new meaning.

# Understanding Text Structure

**DEFINITION:** Text structure involves the organization an author uses to write a selection. There are text structures for narrative and expository texts, and readers' knowledge and recognition of various text structures can enhance their text comprehension, recall, and learning.

## RESEARCH

Students are presented with large amounts of information in texts, so it is important for them to be able to identify and remember the key ideas in selections they read. Research documents that, although creating summaries is a challenging task, preadolescents and adolescents can acquire this strategy through thoughtful instruction (e.g., Armbruster, Anderson, & Ostertag, 1987 Brown & Day, 1983; Duke & Pearson, 2002; Hahn & Garner, 1984; Hare & Borchardt, 1984; National Reading Panel, 2000).

## MODEL LESSON

### Explain: How the Strategy Helps and When to Use It

Explain to students that all selections are organized into one or more text structures. Before beginning to write, an author chooses how to organize the information. When students can identify and understand the text structures, their comprehension and recall improve. When reading fiction, students can use the **narrative structure** of **setting, characters, plot,** and **outcome** to better understand the story and remember the text. When reading nonfiction, students can identify the structures of **sequence, cause-effect, problem-solution, question-answer, compare-contrast**, and **description** to improve their understanding of the author's purpose and to identify details and big ideas. It's important to note that informational text often contains more than one structure.

Point out that skilled readers tune into text structure before reading, as they preview a text.

Being aware of the text structure before reading will help students anticipate and predict what they will read. During reading, students can use text structure to comprehend, predict, and remember. After reading, students can discuss material in terms of text structure.

### Model the Strategy

**Materials** *Space Odyssey*, "Visitors from Mars," pages 36–41; "Give Them Space," pages 14–17

**Lesson 1: Understanding Text Structure**

**Before Reading**

**Step 1** Name the strategy and explain to students what it is and how it helps them.

**Think-Aloud 1** Today, we'll preview a text to determine if it's narrative or informational. Look at pages 36–41; there are no section headings, there's dialogue between characters, and the dialogue is written in the form of a play. These are all clues that the text is narrative. To preview a narrative text, read the first two pages and look at the illustrations. We meet the Reed family. They're at home listening to the radio. The announcer says that a large flaming object has just fallen on a nearby farm. The illustrations show fire, flying saucers, and people running. This is a narrative text.

**Think-Aloud 2** Today, we'll preview to determine if this text is narrative or informational. If it's informational, we'll try to see what kind of structure the author uses. Look at pages 14-17. I know this is informational because it's about astronauts. There are photographs, headings, and sidebars, which are all features of nonfiction. Each section looks like a mini-biography of a different astronaut. Biographies are often written in chronological, or sequential, format so I'll look for clues to support that. As I scan the section on Franklin Chang-Diaz, the beginning of the text talks about his childhood. That tells me that the main text structure is sequential.

**Step 2** Organize students into pairs. Have pairs preview a text to decide whether the text is narrative or informational. Encourage students to give you the clues that led them to their conclusion.

**Step 3** Have students read the texts. Then identify and discuss the structures(s).

**Step 4** Remind students to use their knowledge of text structure as they read.

**Lesson 2: Using Text Structure After Reading**

**Step 1** Organize students into pairs. Have them read "Visitors from Mars."

**Step 2** After reading the play, have pairs complete a graphic organizer showing the structure of the play. (See TE page 390 for a plot organizer.)

**Step 3** Show students how you use the setting and plot to understand the Reeds' reactions. The Reeds' are at home listening to a breaking news report about Martians landing nearby. When Mrs. Reed wonders if the report is real, Mr. Reed says, "Of course it's happening. It's on the radio, isn't it?" This line (along with the plot and setting) helps you understand the Reeds' reactions and why people in the illustrations look frightened.

**Step 4** Ask pairs to use setting and plot to explain another reaction in the play.

**Step 5** After reading about the three astronauts, show how you use the sequential text structure to figure out a big idea. Explain that all three mini-

biographies described the years of education and training each astronaut had. This shows that becoming an astronaut probably takes many years.

**Step 6** Have pairs use the sequential structure to find another big idea.

**Guided Practice**

1. Provide guided practice before and after reading with other narrative and informational texts from the magazines.

2. Ask students to preview to figure out structure and then use structure to deepen meaning and recall.

3. Support students who need your expertise to help identify text structure to improve comprehension and recall.

**Independent Practice**

1. Provide students with opportunities to practice using text structure.

2. Confer with students you helped during guided practice to make sure that they are learning to identify and use text structure.

**Following Up**

Continue to review this strategy throughout the year. Remind students to use this strategy when they read textbooks in their other classes.

# Inferential Thinking

**DEFINITION:** Inferential thinking is the process of creating personal meaning from text. An inference is created when a reader combines prior knowledge with details from a text to create new, unstated meaning.

## RESEARCH SUPPORT

Writers rely on readers' ability to use their prior knowledge and their ability to make inferences to fill-in information that is not explicit in text. This is a challenging task for many readers (Graesser, Singer, Trabasso, 1994; RAND, 2002). Fortunately, there exist a number of studies that demonstrate that students can be taught to make inferences about the texts they read by relying on prior knowledge and by making text-based and schema-based inferences (Dewitz, Carr, & Patberg, 1987; Hansen, 1981; Hansen & Pearson, 1983; McGee & Johnson, 2003).

## MODEL LESSON

### Explain: How the Strategy Helps and When to Use It

Explain to students that writers purposely do not include all the details in a text. Writers expect readers to combine their prior knowledge with the information in the text to create new, unstated meanings. When readers infer meaning, they deepen their comprehension by becoming more involved or connected with the text and create new understandings. Students can use this strategy with fiction, poetry, biography, and informational texts. Point out that inferential thinking starts before reading, when students make logical predictions, and continues during and after reading.

### Model the Strategy

**Materials** *Cities*, "Mayor Tom Bradley," pages 38–40; "The Great Indoors," pages 21–25

**Lesson 1: Biography**

**Step 1** Name the strategy and explain to students what it is and how it helps them. Display these questions to guide students' inferring:

- What does the text tell me?
- What do I already know about the topic?
- What new meaning can I infer?

**Think-Aloud** Today, I'll show you how to make inferences with "Mayor Tom Bradley," so you can better understand his life. First, I'll notice what the text says and then I'll combine it with my prior knowledge to create an inference. I'll use the three questions to guide me.

**Step 2** Read aloud page 39 and show students how you make an inference.

**Think-Aloud** First, here's what the text tells me: Bradley worked hard at schoolwork and sports. He won a track scholarship to college. But, in 1937, times were hard, and Bradley left college to become a police officer. Now, here's my prior knowledge: I know that the Depression was happening in 1937, which meant that money was tight for most people. I also know that college costs money. Here's my inference, or new meaning: Bradley was having a hard time supporting himself and paying for college, so he had to leave school to get a job. The author does not state these details directly, but they make sense and help me better understand Bradley's situation.

**Step 3** Organize students into partners.

**Step 4** Have students read page 40 and have them infer the character traits that Bradley had that led him to his successes.

## Lesson 2: Informational Text

**Step 1** Have students read page 22 in "The Great Indoors."

**Step 2** Show students how you use the three questions to infer. (See Step 1 in Lesson 1: Biography.)

**Think-Aloud** Here are some facts from the section called "Rock Climbing." You can rock climb on a special indoor wall in a gym. The holds have different colors. Each color represents a path. Now, here's my prior knowledge about rock climbing: It's hard work, and it takes a lot of practice. Finally, here's my inference, or new meaning: You can train to become an outdoor rock climber even if you live in a city.

**Step 4** Have students find facts in one of the other sections and use the three questions to help them infer new, unstated meanings.

## Guided Practice

1. Organize students into partners.

2. Use parts of fiction and nonfiction selections from the magazines. Have pairs read or reread the same selection.

3. Have pairs use what they know to explore implied meanings. Then have partners share their findings with classmates.

4. Circulate and listen to pairs working together. Identify students who can work on their own, and those who need your support.

5. Help pairs who need extra practice and guidance until they grasp making inferences.

## Independent Practice

1. Continue to give all students practice with making inferences. Use fiction and nonfiction texts. Make sure students use the three questions to guide their inferring.

2. Confer with students in brief one-on-one meetings. Ask them to show you how they make inferences using part of an article from one of the magazines. Or have them write inferences they have made about a character, person, or information.

## Following Up

1. Keep reviewing inferential thinking with students even though they're learning another strategy.

2. Support students who need your expertise by modeling how you infer from a magazine passage. Then listen to students infer.

# Teacher Talk

# Word Study

You remember the adage: *I hear and I forget; I see and I remember; I do and I understand.* This is why active learning is so important!

## Why bother with Word Study?

Word Study promotes word knowledge and word fluency by having students take an active role in examining words and exploring patterns. Each word study activity has students engage in the following activities:

▶ **study** a group of words to find common features

▶ **sort** the words into categories

▶ **discuss** and explain the relationship between the words

## How do I do Word Study?

The *Word Study Manual* has everything you need to know about Word Study. Use it as a resource to create your own free-standing word-study program or use it as a support for the Phonics/Word Study lessons right in the *Reading Advantage* Teacher's Edition. You can do Word Study with the whole class, but you might find it more manageable to do the activities with a single small group. This will also reduce the number of card sets that you will need for sorting.

Sorting words is an important—and the most engaging—part of word study. Try these steps to familiarize yourself with word sort.

▶ First of all, read through Chapter 5, "What Is Sorting?" in the *Word Study Manual* to build background for yourself.

▶ Try a practice sort with your students.

- Prepare a set of about a dozen index cards for every two or three students by writing an animal name on each one (e.g., hippo, giraffe, deer, manatee, buffalo, whale).

- Hand out the cards to pairs or triads of students. Read aloud each animal name to be sure that everyone knows the words.

- Ask students to sort the cards into categories. Suggested categories for the animals above include these: number of syllables, double letters, land animals, water animals.

- There are no right answers, but students must have a reason for each category! Ask them to share their categories and reasons with the class. Listening to students explain how they sorted the words gives you a window into their way of thinking about words.

Here's how to go about doing a Phonics/Word Study lesson in *Reading Advantage*.

## Preparation

▶ Read through the activity.

▶ Open to the page in the *Word Study Manual* that has the words for the word sort. The page number will be in the Teacher's Edition lesson.

▶ There are three choices for sorting the words:
  - Students sort word cards.
  - Students write the words in categories on paper.
  - You and/or students work with a cut-apart transparency on an overhead projector.

If students will sort word cards, prepare a set of word cards for each pair or triad of students. Make a photocopy of the page from the *Word Study Manual* and cut apart the word cards.

If students will write the words on paper, make sure they have paper and pencil.

If you have an overhead projector, photocopy the page from the *Word Study Manual* onto a transparency and cut apart the word cards.

## Word Study

**Long e Vowel Sort from Level B**

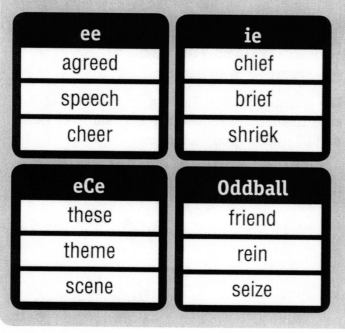

| ee | ie |
|---|---|
| agreed | chief |
| speech | brief |
| cheer | shriek |

| eCe | Oddball |
|---|---|
| these | friend |
| theme | rein |
| scene | seize |

## Sorting the Words

▶ Explain the categories for the day. For example, the activity might focus on different spellings of the Long e sound (modeled on this page), or words with prefixes or suffixes.

▶ Read each word to be sorted aloud.

▶ Model how to sort the words by placing the first few words into the appropriate columns, explaining your thinking as you work: The word *chief* has *ie*, so I will place it in the *ie* category. The word *friend* also has *ie*, but the sound is different, so I will place it in the Oddball category.

▶ Have students continue to sort the words.

▶ Help students move misplaced words to the correct category.

## Follow-up

▶ Discuss the sort and what students learned.

▶ Have students sort the words again, trying to increase their *personal* speed (this is not a competition!) and accuracy.

▶ If students keep a Word Study Notebook, they can record their sorts and add words that fit the patterns. (See *Word Study Manual*, page 13.)

# Planning a Reading Advantage Lesson

You open the *Reading Advantage* box. You lift out the Teacher's Edition and flip through the pages. Then you think, "Now what do I do?" What you want to do is to **skim through the lesson**, thinking about your students, and decide which activities will benefit them. **Then make a plan** to do those activities. (See the chart on page 30.)

## STEP 1 Skim through the lesson

Look over the lesson to get a sense of the instructional opportunities available. Think about your students' needs as you skim the activity headings: Do your students need work in comprehension? Vocabulary? Make a note of the areas on which you will concentrate.

## STEP 2 Choose how to introduce the magazine selection

Each lesson begins with a variety of activities to prepare students to read. (See Before Reading.) You know your students best and can decide whether they need a lot of support up front or just a little. Is this a topic or genre new to students? Then they might benefit from some extra pre-reading instruction. If students are comfortable with the topic and genre, then complete only Preview the Selection and Make Predictions/Set Purpose.

## STEP 3 Decide how students will read the selection

Choose any one or more of these ways to have students read the selection.

▶ Read all or part of the selection aloud.
▶ Have students read with a partner or in small groups.
▶ Have students read independently.

While students are reading in a small group, with a partner, or on their own, use the questions in During Reading to monitor students' comprehension in brief one-on-one conferences.

## STEP 4 Select after-reading activities for the whole group

The activities in After Reading, on the blue pages, are a follow-up to the reading selection. They work well in a whole-group setting.

## STEP 5 — Prepare the Phonics/Word Study activity

Check the Phonics/Word Study activity for any preparation that needs to be done before class, such as creating word cards and using resources from the *Word Study Manual*.

## STEP 6 — Select follow-up instruction

Look over the activities listed under Additional Skills/Activities. Choose one or more activities that suit your students' needs.

## STEP 7 — Assign a time frame

How long are your class periods? That will determine how much you can do in a single day. You may want to break up a lesson into two or three parts if you have short periods. To fill in around the edges, make the paperback books (see Teacher's Edition appendix) and *eZines* available to your students to use independently.

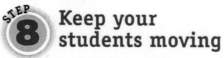

## STEP 8 — Keep your students moving

Use the Self-Reflection questions at the end of each lesson to check whether students have understood the main concepts in each lesson. Use the more formal mid-magazine and end-of-magazine tests to monitor students' progress through a level. If students do well on the mid-magazine test, consider moving them up a level or accelerating the remainder of a level by using some of the magazine selections as independent reading (without the instruction).

# Planning a **Reading Advantage** Lesson continued

## Plan Your Lesson • 3-Day Plan

Here's one way to plan a *Reading Advantage* lesson! This plan is for Lesson 3 in Level C, but it serves as a model for all *Reading Advantage* lessons.

| | Activity | Page Numbers | Time |
|---|---|---|---|
| **Before Reading** | K-W-L chart <br> Preview the Selection <br> Vocabulary <br> Make Predictions/Set Purpose | TE 20-21 <br><br> SJ 8 | Day 1 <br> 20 minutes |
| **During Reading** | Read aloud <br> Independent reading <br> Comprehension: <br> Making Connections | TE 22 | Day 1 <br> 20 minutes |
| **After Reading** | Discussion Questions <br> Revisit the KWL chart <br> Writing: Evaluate Masks | TE 24 <br><br> SJ 9 | Day 2 <br> 40 minutes |
| **Phonics/ Word Study** | Plural endings –s, -es | TE 26 <br> WSM 36 | Day 3 <br> 20 minutes |
| **Additional Instruction** | 2 groups: <br> ▶ Article: Say It with Emoticons (read on their own) <br> ▶ Comprehension: Understanding Text Structure (teacher-led group) | TE 26 | Day 3 <br> 20 minutes |
| **When students finish their work** | Paperback books <br> eZines CD-ROM | | |

TE = Teacher's Edition   SJ = Student Journal   WSM = Word Study Manual

# Great Source Reading Advantage
# Assessment

*Reading Advantage* includes assessment options to help you place students in the program, check students' progress, and plan tailored instruction:

## Place students in the right level

Use the *Reading Advantage* **Placement Test** to make sure that your students are reading text that is on their instructional level. When text is neither too hard nor too easy, students can attend to learning strategies and skills that will help them make progress in their reading ability. You have a choice of administering a Group Reading Inventory or an Individual Reading Inventory. Both have reading passages followed by multiple-choice questions and are available in each kit as well as online at http://www.greatsource.com.

## Monitor students' progress informally

Each lesson ends with an opportunity for you to check your students' understanding of the featured comprehension strategy and word study skill for the lesson.

## Assess students' progress formally

With each *Reading Advantage* kit, you will receive an Assessment book. Inside, you will find formal assessments for testing students' progress within a level. The **Mid-Magazine Tests** and **Magazine Tests** have reading passages followed by multiple-choice and extended-answer questions. The reading level and selection vocabulary in the passages match those in the magazine.

## Observe students informally

At the back of the Assessment book you will find an **Interest Survey**, a **Reading Survey,** and four **Observational Checklists.** The purpose of the surveys is to help you learn about students' interests and feelings toward reading so that you can help them choose books they will enjoy. The main purpose of the Observational Checklists is to help you monitor students' progress during the year. The information you collect will enable you to make instructional decisions based on your observations and interactions with students.

## Measure students' achievement

The *Gates-MacGinitie Reading Tests*® (GMRT®) are nationally recognized and respected for providing accurate assessment based on current research in reading. GMRT results have been directly correlated to *Reading Advantage* levels, so you can make the most of your *Reading Advantage* instruction by placing new students into the proper level, organizing instructional groups, targeting individual needs, and evaluating the effectiveness of *Reading Advantage*. GMRT is available online or in print.

# Great Source Reading Advantage

# Professional Development

Research is very clear that teacher expertise is one of the most important factors influencing student achievement. High quality professional development that is research-based, aligned with adult learning theory, and structured to promote the transfer of learning to classroom instruction is one of the most effective ways to enhance teacher expertise and student achievement.

Districts that partner with Great Source to create a sustained professional development plan for *Reading Advantage* benefit in many ways:

▶ **The professional development workshops** are based on a proven, research-based delivery model that will impact teacher instruction

▶ **Trainers are experts in the field of reading**, bringing years of experience to their work. They have used the *Reading Advantage* program and provide many suggestions for classroom use

▶ **Interactive and hands-on activities, trainer modeling, simulations, role playing, discussions, and practice teaching** prepare teachers for working with their students

▶ **The workshop** insures teachers will implement *Reading Advantage* appropriately

▶ **Well-trained teachers result in greater student achievement**

# Great Source Reading Advantage
## Scope and Sequence

The instructional lessons in Reading Advantage are set up in three parts: Before Reading, During Reading, and After Reading. Below is an outline of the skills and strategies that are taught throughout the program and where in the lesson they appear. All skills and strategies are addressed at each level.

| Leveling, Strategies, and Skills | Foundations | A | B | C | D | E | F |
|---|:-:|:-:|:-:|:-:|:-:|:-:|:-:|
| **Reading Level** | | | | | | | |
| Grade 1 Reading Level | • | | | | | | |
| Grade 2 Reading Level | • | • | | | | | |
| Grade 3 Reading Level | | • | • | | | | |
| Grade 4 Reading Level | | | • | • | | | |
| Grade 5 Reading Level | | | | • | • | | |
| Grade 6 Reading Level | | | | | • | • | |
| Grade 7 Reading Level | | | | | | • | • |
| Grade 8 Reading Level | | | | | | | • |
| **Before Reading** | | | | | | | |
| Build Background Concepts | | • | • | • | • | • | • |
| **Vocabulary** | | | | | | | |
| Context | | • | • | • | • | • | • |
| Association | | • | • | • | • | • | • |
| Categories | | • | • | • | • | • | • |
| Word Meanings | | • | • | • | • | • | • |
| **Preview/Make Predictions** | | | | | | | |
| Text Features (boldface, italics, headings, subheadings, captions, sidebars, graphics) | • | • | • | • | • | • | • |
| Text Structure (fiction, nonfiction) | | • | • | • | • | • | • |
| Genre | | • | • | • | • | • | • |
| **Set purpose** | | • | • | • | • | • | • |
| **During Reading** | | | | | | | |
| **Comprehension Strategies** | | | | | | | |
| Monitor Understanding (read on, reread, retell, visualize, ask questions, context, word structure) | | • | • | • | • | • | • |
| Making Connections (use prior knowledge, make predictions, compare to other texts) | | • | • | • | • | • | • |
| **After Reading** | | | | | | | |
| **Comprehension Strategies** | | | | | | | |
| Monitor Understanding (read on, reread, retell, visualize, ask questions, context, word structure/breaking apart long words) | | • | • | • | • | • | • |
| Making Connections (use prior knowledge, make predictions, make connections) | • | • | • | • | • | • | • |
| Determining Importance (ideas and details) | | • | • | • | • | • | • |
| Understanding Text Structure (narrative [story elements], expository [description, sequence, cause/effect, compare/contrast information, problem/solution, question/answer]; text features; genre) | | • | • | • | • | • | • |
| Inferential Thinking (make inferences, draw conclusions, identify themes) | | • | • | • | • | • | • |
| **Phonics/Word Study** | | | | | | | |
| Vowels (long, ambiguous [e.g., *oo, ew, ou*]) | | • | • | • | • | • | • |
| Consonants (digraphs, blends, doubled) | | • | • | • | • | • | • |
| Prefixes, Suffixes, Roots, Compound Words, Syllables | | • | • | • | • | • | • |
| **Vocabulary** | | | | | | | |
| Synonyms/Antonyms, Homophones, Acronyms/Initialisms, Multiple-meaning Words, Idioms, Context, Denotation/Connotation, Classification, Association, Dictionary Skills | | • | • | • | • | • | • |
| **Writing** | | • | • | • | • | • | • |
| **Ongoing Assessment** | | • | • | • | • | • | • |

# Great Source Reading Advantage

# Integration with other Great Source Products

*Great Source* offers a variety of products that enable you to group students for instruction and reach every reader in your class.

## What if my *Reading Advantage* students want more reading?

▶ The *Reading & Writing Sourcebooks* are an ideal supplement because they use a strategic approach and provide scaffolded reading and writing activities. Students in Level A of *Reading Advantage* can use Sourcebook grade 4, students in Level B can use Sourcebook grade 5, and students in Levels C and D will be comfortable using Sourcebook grade 6.

▶ Using the *Summer Success: Reading* program ensures a consistent instructional approach in summer school. Used alone, the magazines are perfect for additional independent reading.

▶ *Leveled Libraries* are ideal for independent reading and include nonfiction and fiction collections.

## How can I meet the needs of English Language Learners?

▶ *Access*, a program for ELL students, provides materials and instructional guidelines to help students learn the content information their classmates are learning.

▶ *Leveled Libraries* in English and Spanish help students practice basic reading skills.

## How can I extend reading and writing for my students?

▶ *Reader's Handbook* puts information about the reading process and reading strategies right into the students' hands.

▶ *Daybooks of Critical Reading and Writing* promote fine literature and improve students' critical reading and writing skills.

▶ *Lessons in Literacy* is a teacher resource that puts reading and writing skills and strategy lessons at your fingertips.

▶ *Science Daybooks* (Life, Earth, and Physical) help middle school students learn and review concepts in physical, life, and earth science.

▶ The *Write Source* program supports students' writing with student-friendly information on writing process, traits of effective writing, forms of writing, writing across the curriculum, and conventions.

Great Source

# Reading
# Advantage

# TEACHER'S EDITION
## LEVEL A

Great Source

**Reading Advantage**

# Mystery

In this issue: Print Mysteries, Monsters, and Mummies

Great Source

**Reading Advantage**

# Cities

In this issue: City Walls, City Sports, and City Sounds

Great Source

**Reading Advantage**

# Space
# Odyssey

In this issue: Moon Walk, Meteors, and Mars

Great Source

**Reading Advantage**

# Water

In this issue: Towering Icebergs, Underwater Life, and Underwater Sound

# Level A, Magazine 1

# Mystery

## Magazine Summary

*Mystery* magazine is a collection of nonfiction, fiction, drama, and poetry exploring unexplained events, suspenseful mystery stories, and illusions. Some mysteries are exciting, fascinating— and even a little scary!

*Content-Area Connection:* history, science
Lexile measure 500L

# *Mystery* Lesson Planner

| LESSON | BEFORE READING | DURING READING | AFTER READING |
|---|---|---|---|
| **LESSON 1**<br>**Monster in the Lake** *and* **Here a Yeti, There a Yeti**<br>(article and poem)<br>page 6 | T-Chart<br>Vocabulary Preview<br>Preview the Selection<br>Make Predictions/Set Purpose | Inferential Thinking<br>Monitor Understanding | Check Purpose<br>Discussion Questions<br>Writing K-W-L Chart<br>Vocabulary: multiple meanings<br>Phonics/Word Study: short and long *a* patterns |
| **LESSON 2**<br>**What Happened to Amelia Earhart?**<br>(biographical sketch)<br>page 14 | Character Cluster Chart<br>Vocabulary Preview<br>Preview the Selection<br>Make Predictions/Set Purpose | Understanding Text Structure | Check Purpose<br>Discussion Questions<br>Writing: timeline<br>Vocabulary: combining form *equi-*<br>Phonics/Word Study: long and short *a* patterns |
| **LESSON 3**<br>**Easter Island: Place of Many Mysteries**<br>(article)<br>page 20 | K-W-L Chart<br>Vocabulary Preview<br>Preview the Selection<br>Make Predictions/Set Purpose | Monitor Understanding | Check Purpose<br>Discussion Questions<br>Writing: summary<br>Vocabulary: homophones<br>Phonics/Word Study: long *a* patterns |
| **LESSON 4**<br>**Mysteries of the Animal World**<br>(article)<br>page 27 | Concept Web<br>Vocabulary Preview<br>Preview the Selection<br>Make Predictions/Set Purpose | Determining Importance | Check Purpose<br>Discussion Questions<br>Writing: notes for visualizing<br>Vocabulary: compound words<br>Phonics/Word Study: long *a* patterns |

# Overview

## Preview the Magazine

Give students time to thumb through the magazine to look at the selection titles, photographs, and illustrations. Explain that the magazine discusses different types of mysteries—from historical mysteries, to unexplained natural events, to fictional detective stories. Ask students to think of topics they would describe as "mysterious." Make a chart together that lists mysterious topics and why they're mysterious.

| Topic | Why is it mysterious? |
|---|---|
| Flying Saucers | Some people believe they exist and some people don't. |
|  |  |

| PHONICS/ WORD STUDY | FOCUS ON | ASSESSMENT | HIGHER-ORDER THINKING QUESTIONS |
|---|---|---|---|
| Short and Long *a* Patterns | Writing: point of view<br>Fluency: pacing<br>English Language Learners<br>Independent Activity Options | Inferential Thinking<br>Monitor Understanding<br>Short and Long *a* Patterns | Why were sightings of the Loch Ness Monster more difficult before 1933? Why did they increase after that date? Use details and information from the passage to support your answer. How has technology helped in the search for the monster? Use details and information from the passage to support your answer. |
| Long and Short *a* Patterns. | Writing: personal theory<br>Fluency: punctuation<br>English Language Learners<br>Independent Activity Options | Understanding Text Structure<br>Short and Long *a* Patterns | Why was Amelia Earhart famous? Use details and information from the passage to support your answer. How was Earhart's flight across the Atlantic different from Lindberg's? Use details and information from the passage to support your answer. |
| Long *a* Patterns | Writing: letter<br>Fluency: expression<br>English Language Learners<br>Independent Activity Options | Monitor Understanding<br>Long *a* Patterns | In what ways have the moai been altered over the years from their original state? Use details and information from the passage to support your answer. What organizational pattern did the author choose for this article? How do the text features help you understand this pattern? Use details and information from the passage to support your answer. |
| Long *a* Patterns | Writing: migration diagram<br>Fluency: pacing<br>English Language Learners<br>Independent Activity Options | Determining Importance<br>Long *a* Patterns | How are Monarch butterflies and airplanes alike? Use details and information from the passage to support your answer. How are scientists benefiting from studying bats? Use details and information from the passage to support your answer. |

# *Mystery* Lesson Planner

| LESSON | BEFORE READING | DURING READING | AFTER READING |
|---|---|---|---|
| **LESSON 5**<br>**Optical Illusions**<br>(article)<br>page 32 | Concept Web<br>Vocabulary Preview<br>Preview the Selection<br>Make Predictions/Set Purpose | Making Connections | Check Purpose<br>Discussion Questions<br>Writing: visualize<br>Vocabulary: context<br>Phonics/Word Study: long *a* patterns (*r*-controlled) |
| **LESSON 6**<br>**Three Mini Mysteries** *and* **Bermuda Triangle Mystery**<br>(poem and mystery stories)<br>page 38 | Rating Chart<br>Vocabulary Preview<br>Preview the Selection<br>Make Predictions/Set Purpose | Understanding Text Structure<br>Inferential Thinking | Check Purpose<br>Discussion Questions<br>Writing: story string<br>Vocabulary: multiple meanings<br>Phonics/Word Study: long *a* patterns review |
| **LESSON 7**<br>**The Red-Headed Club**<br>(play)<br>page 48 | Make a List<br>Vocabulary Preview<br>Preview the Selection<br>Make Predictions/Set Purpose | Understanding Text Structure<br>Determining Importance | Check Purpose<br>Discussion Questions<br>Writing: notes for visualizing<br>Vocabulary: multiple meanings<br>Phonics/Word Study: long and short *a* homophones |
| **LESSON 8**<br>**It's a Mystery** *and* **Detectives at Work**<br>(poem and article)<br>page 56 | Details Web<br>Vocabulary Preview<br>Preview the Selection<br>Make Predictions/Set Purpose | Making Connections<br>Monitor Understanding | Check Purpose<br>Discussion Questions<br>Writing: one-minute mystery<br>Vocabulary: multiple meanings<br>Phonics/Word Study: contractions |
| **LESSON 9**<br>**Frozen in Time**<br>(first-person account)<br>page 64 | Make a List<br>Vocabulary Preview<br>Preview the Selection<br>Make Predictions/Set Purpose | Monitor Understanding | Check Purpose<br>Discussion Questions<br>Writing: notes for visualizing<br>Vocabulary: related words<br>Phonics/Word Study: long and short *a* compound words |
| **LESSON 10**<br>**The Lost Colony**<br>(journal)<br>page 71 | Make a T-Chart<br>Vocabulary Preview<br>Preview the Selection<br>Make Predictions/Set Purpose | Understanding Text Structure | Check Purpose<br>Discussion Questions<br>Writing: journal entries<br>Vocabulary: multiple meanings<br>Phonics/Word Study: short and long *e* patterns |
| **LESSON 11**<br>**Code Talkers** *and* **Miscellaneous Mysteries**<br>(article and mysteries)<br>page 77 | Make a List<br>Vocabulary Preview<br>Preview the Selection<br>Make Predictions/Set Purpose | Monitor Understanding<br>Inferential Thinking | Check Purpose<br>Discussion Questions<br>Writing: summary<br>Vocabulary: context<br>Phonics/Word Study: short and long *e* patterns |
| **LESSON 12**<br>**The Silent Army** *and* **Second Glance**<br>(article and optical illusions)<br>page 86 | Make a List<br>Vocabulary Preview<br>Preview the Selection<br>Make Predictions/Set Purpose | Making Connections<br>Determining Importance | Check Purpose<br>Discussion Questions<br>Writing: notes for visualizing<br>Vocabulary: word root *terr*<br>Phonics/Word Study: short and long *e* patterns |

| PHONICS/ WORD STUDY | FOCUS ON | ASSESSMENT | HIGHER-ORDER THINKING QUESTIONS |
|---|---|---|---|
| Long *a* Patterns (*r*-controlled) | Writing: optical illusions<br>Fluency: pacing<br>English Language Learners<br>Independent Activity Options | Making Connections<br>Long *a* Patterns (*r*-controlled) | How do optical illusions fool your eyes? Use details and information from the passage to support your answer. How do the questions under the optical illusions help your brain comprehend what it is seeing? Use details and information from the passage to support your answer. |
| Long *a* Patterns | Writing: news story<br>Fluency: pacing<br>English Language Learners<br>Independent Activity Options | Understanding Text Structure<br>Inferential Thinking<br>Long *a* Patterns | What is the "mystery" of the Bermuda Triangle? Use details and information from the passage to support your answer. In the Mini Mysteries, what quality did each character that solved one of the mysteries have in common? Use details and information from the passage to support your answer. |
| Long and Short *a* Homophones | Writing: inference chart<br>Fluency: expression<br>English Language Learners<br>Independent Activity Options | Understanding Text Structure<br>Determining Importance<br>Long and Short *a* Homophones | What evidence does the author give to support the statement that Holmes is observant? Use details and information from the passage to support your answer. What inferences can you make about the character Mr. Billings? What led you to these inferences? Use details and information from the passage to support your answer. |
| Contractions | Writing: job description<br>Fluency: pacing<br>English Language Learners<br>Independent Activity Options | Making Connections<br>Monitor Understanding<br>Contractions | Why is it important for police to seal a crime scene as quickly as possible and preserve the evidence? Use details and information from the passage to support your answer. How has technology made crime solving more scientific and less guess-work? Use details and information from the passage to support your answer. |
| Long and Short *a* Compound Words | Writing: diary entry<br>Fluency: expression<br>English Language Learners<br>Independent Activity Options | Monitor Understanding<br>Long and Short *a* Compound Words | How are Egyptian mummies different from Oetzi mummies? Use details and information from the passage to support your answer. What do scientists think Oetzi's tattoos were for? Use details and information from the passage to support your answer. |
| Long and Short *e* Patterns | Writing: illustrated timeline<br>Fluency: punctuation<br>English Language Learners<br>Independent Activity Options | Understanding Text Structure<br>Short and Long *e* Patterns | Why did it take John White so long to return to the Roanoke colony? Use details and information from the passage to support your answer. Why does reading a journal entry make the events at Roanoke seem more real than a non-fiction article might? Use details and information from the passage to support your answer. |
| Long and Short *e* Patterns | Writing: codes<br>Fluency: expression<br>English Language Learners<br>Independent Activity Options | Monitor Understanding<br>Inferential Thinking<br>Short and Long *e* Patterns | How is the Navaho code different from most other codes? Why was it so successful? Use details and information from the passage to support your answer. Why would the ancient Greek method of delivering secret messages not work well in war time? Use details and information from the passage to support your answer. |
| Short and Long *e* Patterns | Writing: persuasive letter<br>Fluency: pacing<br>English Language Learners<br>Independent Activity Options | Making Connections<br>Determining Importance<br>Short and Long *e* Patterns | Why is Ying Zheng considered both a great ruler and a terrible ruler? Use details and information from the passage to support your answer. Why was the discovery of the silent army so impressive? Use details and information from the passage to support your answer. |

## LESSON 1
# Monster in the Lake *and* Here a Yeti, There a Yeti

*Mystery*, pages 2–7

### SUMMARY
This **article** tells about the many sightings over time of the Loch Ness monster. A **poem** follows.

### COMPREHENSION STRATEGIES
Inferential Thinking
Monitor Understanding

### WRITING
K-W-L Chart

### VOCABULARY
Multiple Meanings

### PHONICS/WORD STUDY
Short and Long *a* Patterns

### Lesson Vocabulary
claim      plaster casts
loch       sonar
sightings

### MATERIALS
*Mystery*, pp. 2–7
*Student Journal*, pp. 1–3
*Word Study Manual*, p. 34
*Writing Advantage*, pp. 30–55

For years people have claimed to see a monster in Scotland. Should we believe them?

Monster in the Lake

2

# Before Reading
WHOLE CLASS   Use one or more activities.

### Make a List ▶
Introduce the subject of monsters. Ask: *What monsters do you know about? How would you define a monster?* Then create a list called "Why Are We Drawn to Monsters?" List students' responses. Revisit the list after students have read the selection to see if they would like to add any entries to the list.

### Why Are We Drawn to Monsters?
1. Some people like scary things.
2. They're mysterious.
3.

### Vocabulary Preview
List and say the vocabulary words. Ask students if they can make any associations with specific words. Ask: *Where have you heard the word used? Does the word remind you of anything else? Does it look like or sound like a word you know? Explain.*

Model the process of making associations with the word *loch* to help students complete the making associations activity on *Student Journal* page 1.

"I was sitting near the lake.
All at once, this black hump
came out of the water.
It was the size of a bus.
It flipped over and made huge waves.
They were three feet high.
I saw it with my own eyes!"

That is how one man told of a huge beast he spotted in Scotland.
It's the way others have told of it, too. Over the years, thousands of people
have sworn they saw the creature known as the Loch Ness monster.

3

DIFFERENTIATED INSTRUCTION

## Make Predictions/Set Purpose

SMALL GROUP

Familiarize students with a K-W-L chart. Follow these steps:

1. Read aloud and explain each column heading.

2. Explain that before reading, they will complete the first two columns, writing what they know about the topic, and questions they have.

3. Help students brainstorm ideas for the *K* column. Then help students list questions for the *W* column. Tell students to watch for answers as they read.

4. Explain that, after reading, students will complete the third column.

### Student Journal page 1

Name _____ Date _____

**Building Vocabulary: Making Associations**
Pick two words from the vocabulary list below. Think about what you
already know about each word. Then answer the following questions.

claim          sightings          sonar
loch           plaster casts

Word _____
What do you think about when you read this word? _____

Who might use this word? _____

What do you already know about this word? _____

Word _____
What do you think about when you read this word? _____

Who might use this word? _____

What do you already know about this word? _____

Now watch for these words in the magazine selection. Were you on the right track?

Mystery • Monster in the Lake                                    1

## Preview the Selection

Have students look through the five pages of the article, pages 2–6 in the magazine. Use these or similar prompts as you preview the article.

- What does the title tell you?
- How has the author organized the article?
- What do the newspaper headlines tell you?

## Teacher Think Aloud

*When I first saw the title and the picture on the first two pages, I thought I was going to read a fun or scary fiction story about a monster. Then I saw the subtitle and subheads. Now I'm not so sure—maybe I'll read a nonfiction article about people who "think" they saw a monster. Let me read to find out.*

## Make Predictions/Set Purpose

Students should use the information they gathered in previewing the selection to start a K-W-L chart on *Student Journal* page 2. If students have trouble generating a purpose for reading, suggest that they read to find answers to the questions they listed in the *W* column of their K-W-L charts. (See Differentiated Instruction.)

## Comprehension

INFERENTIAL THINKING

To help students use the text and their prior knowledge to make inferences or draw conclusions about the information in the text, use these prompts.

- What do you know about sightings of monsters or strange creatures?
- What did you learn about the searches for Nessie?
- With what you know and what you have read, what conclusions can you draw about the search for the Loch Ness monster?

**Student Journal page 2**

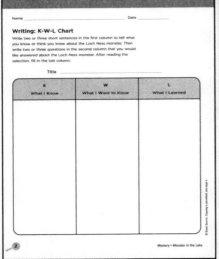

### One day in 1933, a husband and wife drove by the lake. They said they saw a huge animal rolling on the surface of the water.

Stories of the Loch Ness monster go back 1,500 years. That is when people first reported seeing the beast. One person said, "It looked like a huge frog. Only it wasn't a frog." Since then, tales of the beast have kept on. To this day, people still <u>claim</u> to see it.

Is there really a monster? If so, it has never been caught. Is it real? Have people been lying all these years? Or have they just been fooled?

#### A Lake of Mystery

Loch Ness is a lake in Scotland. It is twenty-four miles long. It is one of the deepest lakes in the world. Even though it is big, the lake is hard to see from a distance. The shores are lined with trees. Frequent rain leaves a thick fog in the air.

Until 1933, few people got a close view of the north side of the <u>loch</u>, or lake. (*Loch* is Scottish for *lake*.) That is because no roads led there. In 1933, a road was built. The road runs along the north shore of Loch Ness. Many cars began to use the road. That is when the strange <u>sightings</u> increased.

#### Early Reports

One day in 1933, a husband and wife drove by the lake. They said they saw a huge animal rolling on the surface of the water. A newspaper printed their story. The paper called the animal "a monster." The name "Loch Ness monster" caught on with readers. Soon the monster had a nickname, too. It was Nessie.

In time, more people said they saw Nessie. One couple claimed it crawled across the shore road. Others rushed to Loch Ness to see for themselves. Boy Scouts sailed out on the lake in small boats. They waited for the monster. But no one saw a real monster.

#### Strange Footprints

A newspaper had a plan to find Nessie. It sent a hunter to track down the monster. A few days passed. The hunter said he found fresh footprints. He added that an animal with four toes on each foot made those footprints. He guessed that the animal was about twenty feet long.

*Famous 1934 photo of the Loch Ness monster*

**Bus-Sized Monster Seen in Loch Ness**
"I saw it with my own eyes," reports man.

*Nessie rears her ugly head again!*
(But don't forget, it is silly season.)

**Loch Monster Spotted by Couple**

# During Reading

## Comprehension

INFERENTIAL THINKING

Use these questions to model how to make inferences, using the text on page 3. Then have students share other inferences they make.

- What does the text tell me?
- What do I already know about this?
- Using the text and what I know, what can I infer that has not been stated directly?

(See Differentiated Instruction.)

## Teacher Think Aloud

*The quotation on page 3 seems pretty unbelievable to me. But the next section of text tells me that thousands of people claim to have seen this "monster." Because of my prior knowledge, I'm skeptical that this monster exists. Shouldn't scientists be able to prove the existence of the Loch Ness monster? I infer that many people thought they saw some type of animal, but it wasn't really a monster.*

## Comprehension

MONITOR UNDERSTANDING

Use these questions to model for students how to monitor their understanding by asking questions. Then have students ask their own questions and try to resolve any confusion.

- Does the monster really exist?
- What is *sonar*?
- What fix-up strategy can I use to try to fix my confusion?

There have been over 10,000 reported sightings of the Loch Ness monster. Anything could be hiding in the lake because some parts of Loch Ness are 900 feet deep.

This animal lives in parts of Africa, not Scotland. It is big and heavy. It can weigh up to 5,800 pounds. It likes to stay in the water a lot. It is a . . .

hippopotamus

The hunter made plaster casts of the prints, which he sent to London, England. Experts studied the prints. But they said the animal was not a monster. It was just a hippo!

No one knew for sure how the hippo prints got there. Hippos do not live in Scotland. Had the hunter played a joke? Or had a joke been played on him? The case was never solved. As a result, some people doubted there was a monster.

## More Reports

Many people still believed a beast was in Loch Ness. In 1934, a doctor took a photo at the lake. It showed a long neck and head sticking up from the water. The shape looked like a dinosaur. Some thought the photo might be a fake. Other people thought it was real.

Twenty years later, people on a bus said they saw Nessie. They watched it for ten minutes. The same year, a fishing boat recorded the shape of a creature deep in the water. It was fifty feet long and had eight legs.

## New Searches

In 1960, an engineer made a short film at Loch Ness. It showed a dark shape moving in the water. Experts from the British Air Force watched the film. They thought it showed a live animal in Loch Ness.

A new search of the lake was made. This time, a crew went deep into the water. They used sonar. This tool uses sound to find things.

The sonar showed a large body moving in the lake. But was it Nessie? Experts were not sure. Some said it was. Other people said it was just a large school of fish.

More searches were held in the 1970s. A crew from Boston placed a camera deep in the water. They waited two years for the beast to appear. At last, the camera saw something. It took pictures of a huge flipper. The team thought they had found Nessie. But others disagreed.

### Plaster Casts

The hunter could not send the footprints themselves to London. He had to figure out a way to send a copy of the footprints. A plaster cast is a common way to do this. To make a plaster cast of footprints, you would fill the footprints with liquid plaster. The liquid takes the shape of the footprint. Then you would wait for the plaster to dry and harden. At that point, you could lift up the dried plaster, which would be in the shape of the footprint.

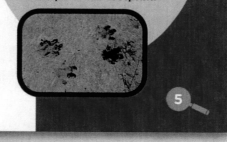

5

# Teacher Think Aloud

*On page 5, I read that a search crew used sonar to try to find the monster. I don't know what this is. Maybe I'll find out if I read on. I see a little feature on page 6 that explains what sonar is. Now I understand. Reading ahead helped me fix my confusion.*

## Fix-Up Strategies

Offer these strategies to help students read independently.

### If you don't understand what you're reading:

- Reread the difficult section to look for clues to help you comprehend.
- Read ahead to find clues to help you comprehend.
- Retell, or say in your own words, what you've read.
- Visualize, or form mental pictures of, what you've read.

### If you don't understand a word:

- Reread the sentence. Look for ideas and words that provide meaning clues.
- Find clues by reading a few sentences before and after the confusing word.
- Look for the base or root word and think about its meaning.
- Think about the topic or plot at this point to see if either offers meaning clues.

## Most describe it the same way. They say it has a long neck, one or two humps, and flippers.

They said the pictures were not clear enough to be sure. They felt more proof of the beast was needed. More recent searches with more advanced equipment have yielded nothing, as well.

### Latest Findings

Today, people still claim to see the Loch Ness monster. Most describe it the same way. They say it has a long neck, one or two humps, and flippers.

Many are quick to laugh at the claims. How could a monster be real? In 1994, a London newspaper said that the 1934 photo of Nessie was a fake. But that did not change the minds of those who think Nessie is real.

### Possible Answers

People still swear they have seen Nessie. But have they really? Maybe the people are joking. Still, other people believe them. After all, they are good, honest people. Why would they lie?

There are people who think that other people have been fooled by their own eyes. The Nessie sighters may have seen a swimming animal or a floating log. And they thought it was a beast.

Nessie remains a mystery today. No one knows for sure if the monster is real. Some think it may be a huge reptile or newt left from ancient times. Others think it may be a giant seal. Still others think there is no large animal at all in the water. ◆

### Sonar

Sonar is often used to locate objects that are submerged, or underwater. Sonar sends out sound waves that bounce off solid objects. If something solid is in the way, the waves will bounce back. The equipment can measure how far away that object is. Submarines use sonar to navigate in the ocean. Bats use sonar to find their way around, too.

6

*What do you think? Could Nessie be a long lost dinosaur?*

---

**Student Journal page 3**

---

# After Reading

**WHOLE CLASS** Use one or more activities.

## Check Purpose

Have students revisit the K-W-L chart they began on *Student Journal* page 2. Have them look at the first column that lists what they thought they knew before reading. Ask them to put a check mark next to any ideas they had that were correct. Have them adjust ideas that were not correct. Then have students look at the second column to check off any things they wanted to know that were answered in the selection.

## Discussion Questions

Continue the group discussion with the following questions.

1. What did you learn about the search for the Loch Ness monster? (Monitor Understanding)

2. What effect did all the publicity about the searches for the monster have? (Cause-Effect)

3. Did you enjoy the selection? Why? Why not? (Making Connections)

## Revisit: List

Look back at the list begun in Before Reading. Ask if students would like to add any entries.

## Here a Yeti, There a Yeti

There once was a monster named Yeti
Whose hair grew as thick as spaghetti.
He didn't give a fig
That his feet were so big
Or if you called him "Big Foot" or "Big Teddy."

7

## Vocabulary
### Multiple Meanings

Explain more about multiple-meaning words:

1. Explain that many English words have more than one meaning and are called multiple-meaning words.

2. Give these examples: *He threw a* <u>rock</u> *into the pond.* <u>Rock</u> *the baby in the cradle. Pour cereal into a* <u>bowl</u>. *She likes to* <u>bowl</u> *with her team.*

3. Pronounce *cycle* and *monitor*. Ask students to explain each word's multiple meanings. Ask volunteers to use the words in sentences and explain their different meanings.

### POEM: HERE A YETI, THERE A YETI

Have students read the limerick silently and then aloud with a partner. Use these questions to talk about the limerick.

- What rhyming patterns do you notice?
- Can you tap out the rhythm?
- What is the tone of the poem?

Explain to students that a limerick has five lines. Lines one, two, and five rhyme. Lines three and four rhyme. Limericks are always about something silly.

## Writing K-W-L Chart

Have students revisit the K-W-L chart on *Student Journal* page 2. This time, ask them to write entries in the third column of the chart, explaining what they have learned by reading the selection.

## Vocabulary Multiple Meanings

Display the word *casts*. Remind students that in the article, *casts* is used with *plaster* to name a kind of form or mold. Explain that *casts* can also mean "the groups of people who perform in a play or other show." Ask students to identify other words that have multiple meanings. Have partners complete *Student Journal* page 3. (See Differentiated Instruction.)

## Phonics/Word Study
### Short and Long *a* Patterns

Write the following words on the board: *pan* and *pane*. Ask: *How is the vowel sound in each of these words different?* Have students volunteer other words that contain the short and long *a* sounds. Now, work with students to complete the in-depth vowel activity on TE page 12.

## Short and Long *a* Patterns

Write the following words on the board: *hat* and *name*. Tell students that these two words represent two different sounds for the letter *a*. One word has a short *a* sound, and one word has a long *a* sound. Ask students if they can identify which word has the short *a* sound and which has the long *a* sound.

▶ Ask students how they knew which was which.

▶ Using the Short and Long *a* Vowel Sort One sheet, model the sorting process for students. (See *Word Study Manual* page 34.) Write the headers *Short* a, *Long* a, and *Oddball* and the first few words in the appropriate columns.

▶ Discuss the sort, what students learned, and why the word *was* belongs in the Oddball column.

▶ Once the sort is complete, hand out copies of the Short and Long *a* Vowel Sort One sheet and ask students to cut it up and do the sort on their own or in groups.

▶ Check the final sorts.

| Short and Long *a:* Sort One | | |
|---|---|---|
| Short *a* | Long *a* | Oddball |
| lamp | flame | was |
| plant | same | |
| flat | name | |
| hat | plane | |
| trap | shade | |
| mad | frame | |
| crack | crate | |

For more information on word sorts and spelling stages, see pages 5–31 in the *Word Study Manual*.

# Focus on . . .

Use one or more activities in this section to focus on a particular area of need in your students.

## Comprehension  STRATEGY SUPPORT   INDEPENDENT

To help those students who need more practice using the strategies covered in this lesson, work one-on-one or in small groups to apply the strategy prompts below. Apply the prompts to a *Reading Advantage* paperback, a classroom library book, or a new or familiar selection in the magazine. Always model your own thinking first.

### Inferential Thinking

• What are the causes or effects of this event?

• What do I learn from the character or person's thoughts, words, or actions?

• What do I know (or infer) from the text that the author hasn't stated directly?

• What conclusions can I draw?

### Monitor Understanding

• Do I understand what I'm reading? If not, what part is confusing me?

• What fix-up strategies can I use to solve the problem? (See During Reading for fix-up strategies.)

• Why did a character say (do, think, ask) that?

• What images do I visualize from the text? What parts can't I visualize?

• Why did the author include (or not include) those details?

## Writing **Point of View**   INDEPENDENT

Have students use the information in the article to tell the story from Nessie's point of view. Students should first review the text to find information they want to include—the first sightings, the attempts to discover her, the newspaper publicity. Remind students to use first-person pronouns in their Nessie versions of the facts. Encourage students to gather and organize their information in a chart.

| From the text | What Nessie might say |
|---|---|
| p. 4 1933, husband and wife spot Nessie | Life was pretty peaceful until 1933. |

To help students include sensory details and strong verbs and nouns in their writing, see lessons in *Writing Advantage*, pages 30–55.

## Fluency: Pacing

Have students listen as you model how to read the poem "Here a Yeti, There a Yeti" at a smooth and even pace. Show how you pause after punctuation. Have partners first read silently to themselves to become familiar with the text, and then read aloud to each other.

As you listen to students read, use these prompts to guide them.

▶ Notice how the line breaks in the poem help you read at an even pace. They signal where to pause slightly.

▶ Keep your eyes on the text as you read so that you don't lose your place and either miss words or repeat them.

▶ Put energy into your voice as you read. It will make the poem more interesting and understandable.

When students read aloud, do they—

✓ demonstrate a smooth pace, not too fast or too slow?

✓ incorporate well-timed pauses between words and phrases?

✓ reflect an awareness and understanding of punctuation?

## English Language Learners

To support students' understanding of multiple meaning words, review the following homographs: *spotted*, *saw*, *school*.

1. Have partners choose a word. Have them divide a piece of paper into two columns and write the word at the top of each column.

2. Have each partner draw an illustration that represents one of the meanings.

## Independent Activity Options

While you work with individuals or small groups, others can work independently on one or more of the following options.

▶ Level A paperback books, see TE pages 367–372

▶ Level A *eZines*

▶ Repeat word sorts from this lesson

▶ *Student Journal* pages for this lesson

▶ *Writing Advantage* independent lessons

# Assessment

## Strategy Assessment

To help you and your students assess their use of comprehension strategies, ask the following questions. Students can complete a written response or provide verbal answers in a one-on-one reading conference.

1. **Inferential Thinking** What inferences did you make as you read this text? (Answers will vary. Students may infer that the monster must not exist, especially after reading about the many thorough searches that were done to find Nessie.)

2. **Monitor Understanding** What parts of this article were most confusing to you? What did you do to help with your understanding? (Answers will vary. Possible response: I was confused about the story of the hunter who found footprints. I tried to retell that section of the text in my own words, and that helped me understand what I was reading.)

For ongoing informal assessment, use the checklists on pages 61–64 of *Level A Assessment*.

## Word Study Assessment

Use these steps to help you and your students assess their understanding of short and long *a* patterns.

1. Create a chart like the one shown.

2. Have students read the words in the first column of the chart.

3. Then have students sort the words into the Short *a* or Long *a* column.

| Words | Short *a* | Long *a* |
|-------|-----------|----------|
| hat | hat | cape |
| blast | blast | safe |
| cape | stack | bake |
| safe | | |
| stack | | |
| bake | | |

Great Source
Reading Advantage

Level A
Assessment

# What Happened to Amelia Earhart?

*Mystery,* pages 8–11

## SUMMARY

This **biographical sketch** tells about the life of Amelia Earhart, the famous female American aviator.

## COMPREHENSION STRATEGIES

Understanding Text Structure

## WRITING

Timeline

## VOCABULARY

Combining Form *equi*

## PHONICS/WORD STUDY

Long and Short *a* Patterns

### Lesson Vocabulary

| | |
|---|---|
| solo | equator |
| social worker | navigator |
| justify | |

## MATERIALS

*Mystery,* pp. 8–11
*Student Journal,* pp. 4–7
*Word Study Manual,* p. 35
*Writing Advantage,* pp. 152–163

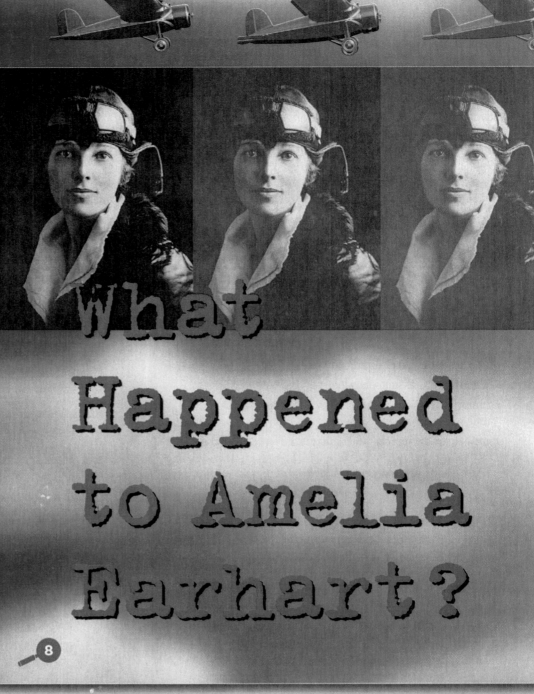

What Happened to Amelia Earhart?

8

# Before Reading

**WHOLE CLASS** Use one or more activities.

## Make a Character Cluster Chart

Tell students that they will read about Amelia Earhart, a famous pilot in the 1920s and 1930s. With students' help, create a character cluster chart. Ask students to identify character traits, skills, and talents someone would need to be a successful pilot. As each response is made, add it to the cluster. After students have finished the article, revisit the chart to add more information.

## Vocabulary Preview

With students, review the vocabulary list. Clarify pronunciations. Ask students to predict how the words will be used in the article. They can record their ideas in the second column of the chart on *Student Journal* page 4. They will finish the chart later.

## Preview the Selection

Have students look through the article. Discuss what students notice about the text and text features.

## Make Predictions/ Set Purpose

Students should use the information they gathered in previewing the selection to make some predictions about what they will learn. If students have trouble generating a purpose for reading, suggest that they read to find out more about Amelia Earhart's mysterious disappearance.

To help students understand the text structure of this selection, ask the following questions.

- If you wanted to know when Amelia Earhart became interested in flying, where in the article would you look to find out? Why?

- If you wanted to know about Amelia Earhart's final flight, where in the article would you look? Why?

Amelia Earhart is one of the most famous pilots in the world. She set flying records for women back in the 1920s and 1930s. She had planned to fly around the world, but she never made it.

Amelia Earhart was born on July 24, 1897, in Atchison, Kansas. She was an excellent student. She enjoyed reading. She also loved sports. Amelia liked to try new things.

Amelia enjoyed watching airplane stunt shows. At one show, she took a ten-minute plane ride that cost $1. She was hooked! She knew she must learn to fly.

Living in California, Amelia worked odd jobs to earn enough money to take flying lessons. Her first lesson was on January 2, 1921. Her teacher was a woman, Neta Snook Southern. After ten hours of instruction and several crashes, Amelia was ready to fly by herself, or <u>solo</u>.

Amelia continued working hard. She bought her first airplane on her twenty-fourth birthday. Flying was her hobby. But there were family problems related to money and her parents' divorce. In 1924, she sold her plane to buy a car. She drove her mother from California to her sister's house in Massachusetts. For a while she attended school in New York. But she gave that up and became a <u>social worker</u> in Boston. Amelia didn't give up on flying, though.

Amelia's flying career "took off" in 1928. She joined two other pilots on a flight from America to England. She was thrilled. She became the first woman to fly across the Atlantic.

Amelia received a great deal of attention. Still, she wasn't happy. She didn't feel she deserved it because she never actually flew the plane. She had gone only for the ride. A publisher named George Putnam covered the story. They met and fell in love. In 1931, Putnam and Earhart were married.

**9**

### Student Journal page 4

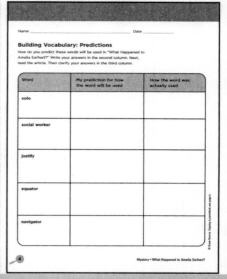

Name _____ Date _____

**Building Vocabulary: Predictions**
How do you predict these words will be used in "What Happened to Amelia Earhart?" Write your answers in the second column. Next, read the article. Then clarify your answers in the third column.

| Word | My prediction for how the word will be used | How the word was actually used |
|---|---|---|
| solo | | |
| social worker | | |
| justify | | |
| equator | | |
| navigator | | |

4      Mystery • What Happened to Amelia Earhart?

# During Reading

## Comprehension

UNDERSTANDING TEXT STRUCTURE

Use these questions to model how to identify the chronological text structure of the biographical sketch. Then have students explain how a chronological, or time sequence, text structure helps them understand the content.

- How is this selection structured?

- What clue words help me follow the structure of the text?

(See Differentiated Instruction.)

## Teacher Think Aloud

*This selection tells the story of Amelia Earhart's life. In the first sentence, I see a date: 1897. In the third paragraph, I see another date: 1921. As I continue to read, I see more dates. The dates go in time order, or chronological order. Learning the events of her life in time order helps me keep track of the information.*

## Fix-Up Strategies

Offer these strategies to help students read independently.

**If you don't understand what you're reading:**

- Reread the difficult section to look for clues to help you comprehend.

- Read ahead to find clues to help you comprehend.

- Retell, or say in your own words, what you've read.

- Visualize, or form mental pictures of, what you've read.

Earhart after her flight from Hawaii to California

Earhart tried to justify her fame by flying in contests. She also flew in stunt shows. She set and broke many speed and distance records.

In 1932, Earhart's name became a household word. She became the first woman to fly solo across the Atlantic. She was only the second person to do it. Charles Lindbergh had been the first. On May 20, 1927, Lindbergh began the 3,610-mile trip from New York to Paris, France. Earhart's flight was exactly five years after Lindbergh's. Earhart broke Lindbergh's record. She flew over the Atlantic in only 13 hours, 30 minutes. Lindbergh's trip took more than

twice that long (33½ hours). (Today, the same trip takes about 6 hours.)

Earhart was world famous. She received many awards and medals. In January 1935, Earhart set another record. She became the first person to fly solo across the Pacific Ocean. She flew from Hawaii to California. Later that year she soloed from Los Angeles to Mexico City. Then she flew back to Newark, New Jersey.

Earhart wondered what to do next. She decided to fly around the world. In July 1936, she started planning. The flight would not be the first to circle the globe. But it would be the longest. It would follow the equator and cover 29,000 miles. Fred Noonan would be Earhart's navigator. He would plan the route and keep track of where they were going. Noonan would also be her sole companion.

In June 1937, Earhart and Noonan began their journey. They departed from Miami. The pair headed east and made it to New Guinea in twenty-one days. About 22,000 miles had been completed; 7,000 miles remained. All the rest would be over the Pacific Ocean.

Earhart and Noonan left from New Guinea and headed for Howland Island. Howland Island is a tiny

Earhart after her solo flight across the Atlantic Ocean

island in the middle of the Pacific Ocean. Earhart and Noonan spoke by radio with a nearby U.S. Coast Guard ship. Many of the messages were hard to hear. Neither Earhart nor Noonan was a radio expert.

The Coast Guard received a final message on July 2 at 8:45 A.M. Earhart's tone was described as frantic.

The plane went down off the coast of Howland Island. We don't know if it sank quickly or if empty fuel tanks kept it afloat for a while. A life raft was stowed on board. No trace of it was ever found.

President Roosevelt ordered the Navy to search the area. Nine ships and sixty-six planes formed a search party. The searchers found nothing. On July 18, the search was stopped. Earhart's husband continued to seek help in the search. By October, he, too, gave up all hope.

Earhart and Noonan were never heard from again. The plane was never found. Neither were their bodies. No one knows exactly what happened. Amelia Earhart

The equator is an imaginary line around the middle of the earth. It is halfway between the North and South Poles. The equator divides the earth into two halves. The top half is known as the Northern Hemisphere. The bottom half is the Southern Hemisphere. The word *equator* comes from a word that means "equalize, or make equal."

10

**Student Journal pages 5–6**

---

# After Reading
Use one or more activities.

## Check Purpose

Have students decide if their purpose was met. Did they learn more about Amelia Earhart's disappearance?

## Discussion Questions

Continue the group discussion with the following questions.

1. Would you like to be a pilot? Why or why not? (Making Connections)

2. What effect did Amelia Earhart's plane crash have on President Roosevelt? (Cause-Effect)

3. What do you think happened to Amelia Earhart? (Inferential Thinking)

## Revisit: Character Cluster Chart

Revisit the character cluster chart started in Before Reading. Does Amelia Earhart measure up as a pilot? What new information can students add? What information would they like to amend?

## Revisit: Predictions Chart

Have students revisit the predictions chart on *Student Journal* page 4. Have students fill in the third column. How was each word actually used?

was less than a month away from her fortieth birthday.

Some people believe that Earhart and Noonan got lost. They may have simply run out of fuel. Some believe that they were captured and killed by the Japanese. (Remember, 1942 was the middle of World War II. The U.S. and Japan were fighting against each other.) Others think that President Roosevelt sent Earhart on a secret spy mission. None of these theories has ever been confirmed.

All kinds of experts have tried to solve the mystery. There are plenty of facts. Still, many questions remain unanswered. ◆

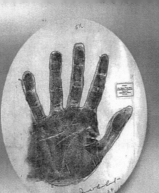

A palmist made this print of Amelia Earhart's hand. A palmist tries to tell about a person's life by looking at the lines on the palm of a hand.

Vol. IV

# Air Stunts

5¢

Air stunt shows grew out of a combination of two things. In the early 1900s, Americans were in awe of flying. They also loved to be thrilled at shows like P.T. Barnum's circuses and the Wild West shows. So by the early 1920s, pilots got the idea to do air shows.

Pilots flew planes left over from World War I. They put on shows by doing loops, rolls, and spins. They even flew upside down! The pilots then sold cheap rides and flying lessons.

People didn't always buy the airplane rides, but they loved the shows. This "barnstorming" was daring, romantic, and full of surprises.

The events became flying circuses. People paid to see more and more daring, and sometimes deadly, air stunts. There was wing-walking, air-to-air transfers, and more. This was now the world of "aerobatics."

New kinds of planes were made by the late 1920s. The new designs led to more daring stunts.

Earhart arrives in Newark, New Jersey, after flying from Los Angeles, California.

Earhart and husband George Putnam study a map before her last flight.

11

Help students understand a combining form.

1. Explain that a combining form is a word or word part only found in combination with another word or word part.

2. Use the following combining forms to make new words.

   mini (skirt)    heli (port)
   para (legal)

3. Write the word *equator* on the board. Ask students to name other words similar to it. (*equation, equality, equilibrium*) Ask: *What do you think* equi *means?* (equal)

## Student Journal page 7

Name _____ Date _____

**Building Vocabulary: Combining Form *equi-***
Write examples and meanings of words with the combining form equi in the chart. One answer is given.

equi means "equal"

| Examples | Meanings |
|---|---|
| 1. equator | imaginary circle that divides Earth from top to bottom |
| 2. | |
| 3. | |
| 4. | |
| 5. | |

Mystery • What Happened to Amelia Earhart?

## Writing Timeline

Tell students that the key, or main, events of a person's life can be shown on a timeline. Draw a quick example on the board. Have partners discuss the six most important events in Amelia Earhart's life. Then have students write on *Student Journal* page 5 a timeline of the key events in Amelia Earhart's life. Have students use the information in the timeline to write a short biographical sketch on *Student Journal* page 6.

## Vocabulary
## Combining Form *equi*

Have students work together to complete the combining form chart on *Student Journal* page 7. Have students refer to the *equi* words list to help them find words for the chart. (See Differentiated Instruction.)

## Phonics/Word Study
## Long and Short *a* Patterns

Write the following words on the board: *man, mane, main.* Ask: *How would you describe the vowel pattern in each of these words?* (short *a*, long *a* with *aCe* pattern, long *a* with *ai* pattern) Have students volunteer other words that contain these patterns, and write them on the board. Now, work with students to complete the in-depth long and short *a* patterns activity on TE page 18.

### Long and Short *a* Patterns

Write the following words on the board: *flat, flame, strain*. Tell students that they are continuing their study of short *a* and long *a* vowel patterns.

▶ Ask students to compare these new words with their last sort (*hat, name*) and identify what is different about this sort (two long *a* patterns in this one).

▶ Using the Long and Short *a*: Sort Two sheet, model the sorting process for students. (See *Word Study Manual* page 35.) Write the headings Short *a*, *aCe*, and *ai* and the first few words in the appropriate columns. Note that *aCe* and *ai* represent long *a* patterns, as in *lake* and *rain* respectively. *Cap* has a short *a* sound.

▶ Discuss the sort and what students learned.

▶ Once the model sort is complete, hand out the Long and Short *a*: Sort Two sheet and ask students to cut it up and do the sort on their own or in groups. Note that *was* is an oddball.

▶ Check the final sorts.

| Long and Short *a*: Sort Two | | |
|---|---|---|
| **Short *a*** | ***aCe*** | ***ai*** |
| flat | flame | strain |
| hat | same | sprain |
| trap | name | plain |
| mad | plane | brain |
| crack | shade | main |
| lamp | frame | vain |
| plant | crate | |

For more information on word sorts and spelling stages, see pages 5–31 in the *Word Study Manual*.

# Focus on . . .

Use one or more activities in this section to focus on a particular area of need in your students.

## Comprehension — Strategy Support — INDEPENDENT

To help those students who need more practice using the strategies covered in this lesson, work one-on-one or in small groups to apply the strategy prompts below. Apply the prompts to a *Reading Advantage* paperback, a classroom library book, or a new or familiar selection in the magazine. Always model your own thinking first.

### Understanding Text Structure

• What kind of text is this? (book, story, article, guidebook, play, manual)

• How does the author organize the text? (cause-effect, problem-solution, chronological order, description, question-answer, comparison-contrast)

• What details support my thoughts about the text structure?

• What is the cause (effect, problem, solution, order, question, answer)?

• If fiction, who are the characters? What is the setting, plot, conflict, and resolution?

## Writing Personal Theory — INDEPENDENT

Have students reread the next-to-last paragraph of the article, which gives people's theories about the circumstances of Amelia Earhart's disappearance. Ask students to write their theory of what happened to Earhart. Encourage students to organize their information in a chart similar to the one that follows.

| Known Facts | My Theory |
|---|---|
| Earhart's plane left from New Guinea. | The plane could've sunk to the bottom of the ocean, but its fuel would've risen to the ocean's surface. There was no trace of fuel. So I think the plane simply ran out of fuel. |
| The plane went down off the coast of Howland Island. | |
| Searchers found no trace of the plane. | |

To provide further instruction on taking notes, see lessons in *Writing Advantage*, pages 152–163.

## Fluency: Punctuation

After students have read the article at least once, assign a portion to partners, for practice in fluent reading. Partners should first read the portion to themselves, emphasizing the parts with the most important information. Then have partners read aloud to each other, emphasizing the important parts and using punctuation to guide their pauses.

As you listen to partners read, use these prompts to guide them.

▶ Try to make your voice sound a little stronger or livelier when you read sentences with the most important information. This will help your listeners to better follow the flow of the text.

▶ Note how information is separated by punctuation. The short or long pauses indicated by commas and periods make it easier for listeners to absorb the information.

When students read aloud, do they—

✓ demonstrate appropriate meaning and usage of punctuation marks?

✓ incorporate appropriate timing, stress, and intonation?

✓ exhibit well-timed pauses between words and phrases?

## English Language Learners

To help students make connections to the text, extend the first discussion question on TE page 16.

1. Discuss whether or not students would like to be a pilot.

2. Brainstorm a list of other occupations students are interested in.

3. Have students draw a picture that represents what they want to be when they grow up. Have each student write several sentences that describe his or her picture.

## Independent Activity Options

While you work with individuals or small groups, others can work independently on one or more of the following options.

▶ Level A paperback books, see TE pages 371–376

▶ Level A *eZines*

▶ Repeat word sorts from this lesson

▶ *Student Journal* pages for this lesson

▶ *Writing Advantage* independent lessons

# Assessment

## Strategy Assessment

To help you and your students assess their use of comprehension strategies, ask the following questions. Students can complete a written response or provide verbal answers in a one-on-one reading conference.

• **Understanding Text Structure** What clues helped you determine the time-order text structure of this article? (dates, clue words such as Amelia Earhart's age, words such as *first*)

For ongoing informal assessment, use the checklists on pages 61–64 of *Level A Assessment*.

## Word Study Assessment

Use these steps to help you and your students assess their understanding of short and long *a* patterns.

1. Display a chart like the one shown, omitting the answers.

2. Have students read the words in the first column of the chart.

3. Then have students sort the words into the correct column. The answers are shown.

4. Then have students indicate which words have long *a* patterns. (*rake, pace, jail, wait*)

| Words | Short *a* | *aCe* | *ai* |
|-------|-----------|-------|------|
| nap | nap | rake | jail |
| rake | ram | pace | wait |
| pace | | | |
| jail | | | |
| ram | | | |
| wait | | | |

Reading Advantage

Level A Assessment

## LESSON 3
# Easter Island— Place of Many Mysteries

*Mystery*, pages 12–16

### SUMMARY
This **article** tells about Easter Island, a small South Pacific island with big mysteries.

### COMPREHENSION STRATEGIES
Monitor Understanding

### WRITING
Summary

### VOCABULARY
Homophones

### PHONICS/WORD STUDY
Long *a* Patterns

### Lesson Vocabulary
| | |
|---|---|
| legends | carve |
| altars | chants |

### MATERIALS
*Mystery*, pp. 12–16
*Student Journal*, pp. 8–10
*Word Study Manual*, p. 36
*Writing Advantage*, pp. 152–163

Easter Island
Place of Many Mysteries

Easter Island has a lot of big mysteries for such a tiny place! Scientists and explorers have solved some of the mysteries. But others have not been solved. Will they ever all be solved? That's also a mystery!

12

# Before Reading
WHOLE CLASS — Use one or more activities.

## Anticipation Guide
Have students check off whether they agree or disagree with these statements:

| AGREE | DISAGREE | |
|---|---|---|
| | | 1. Easter Island is located in the Pacific Ocean. |
| | | 2. Scientists have proven that people from the Pacific Islands settled the island. |
| | | 3. There are large stone statues on Easter Island. |
| | | 4. The people of the island have always been peaceful. |

## Vocabulary Preview
With students, review the vocabulary list. Model making associations with the word *legends* to help students complete *Student Journal* page 8.

## Preview the Selection
Have students look through the five pages of the article. Discuss what students notice.

Have students write on a card or a self-stick note something they want to find out about Easter Island.

## Make Predictions/ Set Purpose
Students should use the information they gathered in previewing the selection to make some predictions about the article. If students have trouble generating a purpose for reading, suggest that they read to find out more about the solved and unsolved mysteries of Easter Island.

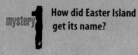

## mystery 1
**How did Easter Island get its name?**

☑ Solved ☐ Unsolved

In 1722, a Dutch sea captain landed at a tiny island. It was in the South Pacific Ocean. The island was more than 2,000 miles from other land. Since the captain landed on Easter Sunday, he named the place Easter Island. However, the natives called the island and themselves *Rapa Nui* (rah puh NOO ee).

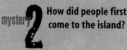

## mystery 2
**How did people first come to the island?**

☑ Solved ☐ Unsolved

Over 2,000 years ago, people paddled canoes to Easter Island. They brought food, plants, and animals. These people split into eight groups. Each group moved to a different part of the island.

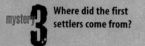

## mystery 3
**Where did the first settlers come from?**

☐ Solved ☑ Unsolved

Legends give a clue. They say that a great chief and his family came in canoes from other islands in the Pacific Ocean. Scientists think this is true. Some of the human bones on the island were tested. The tests showed that the people on Easter Island were related to people from other Pacific islands.

But there is still a mystery. The people on Easter Island had sweet potatoes. These grew only in South America. The island people built walls. These were like walls from South America. Did the islanders go to South America first? Did they take sweet potatoes back to Easter Island? Some scientists think so. Yet, there is no way to prove this.

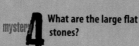

## mystery 4
**What are the large flat stones?**

☐ Solved ☑ Unsolved

The stones are called *ahu* (AH hoo). They go in a circle around the whole island. They probably had many uses. Some showed where families lived. Others were places to bury the dead. Many *ahu* were used as altars for special ceremonies and religious meetings. Some may have been calendars. We may never know the whole answer about the *ahu*.

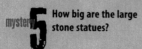

## mystery 5
**How big are the large stone statues?**

☑ Solved ☐ Unsolved

The large stone statues are the biggest mystery on the island! There are about 900 statues, called *moai* (MOH-eye). Easter Island is the only place in the world that has *moai*. Most of the statues are about twenty feet tall. They weigh up to eighty-two tons. One statue is as tall as two elephants. It weighs as much as eleven elephants.

The statues are called *moai*.

This is an *ahu* (AH hoo), one of the stone blocks that circles Easter Island.

There are about 900 *moai* on the island.

**13**

# During Reading

## Comprehension
MONITOR UNDERSTANDING

**SMALL GROUP**

Use these questions to model visualizing Mystery 9. Then have students tell about a part they visualized.

- What do I picture in my mind?
- What details help me?
- How does seeing this picture in my mind help me understand what I am reading? (See Differentiated Instruction.)

## Teacher Think Aloud
*When I read Mystery 9, I pictured a bunch of logs together, like a conveyor belt, and seventy workers pushing the statue over rolling logs. This image helps me understand just how heavy and awkward the statues must have been to move.*

## Fix-Up Strategies
Offer these strategies to help students read independently.

**If you don't understand what you're reading:**

- Reread the difficult section to look for clues to help you comprehend.
- Read ahead to find clues to help you comprehend.
- Retell, or say in your own words, what you've read.
- Visualize, or form mental pictures of, what you've read.

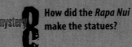

**mystery 6** Why did the *Rapa Nui* make the statues?

☐ Solved ☑ Unsolved

No one is sure why the statues were made. Legends say that the statues had special powers. They may have reminded people of their dead relatives or chiefs. They may have been a connection between the people and their gods. We also don't know why they kept making statues for hundreds of years.

**mystery 7** Why do the statues look the way they do?

☐ Solved ☑ Unsolved

You can see that the statues do not look like real people. No one knows why the statues were made this way. We may never solve this mystery.

Moai figures on Easter Island

**mystery 8** How did the *Rapa Nui* make the statues?

☑ Solved ☐ Unsolved

There is a large volcano on the island. It has a lot of ash. This ash is easy to carve. The islanders made most of the statues at this volcano. They used stone axes to carve a statue in the wall of the volcano. Then they moved it to another place. Not too long ago, a group of men started to build a *moai*. They wanted to see how long it would take to make a statue. They figured that six people could make one in about a year and a half.

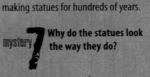

Fallen statue pieces at the volcano

**mystery 9** How did the *Rapa Nui* move the statues?

☐ Solved ☑ Unsolved

This is another mystery that may never be solved. One legend says the *moai* walked by themselves. Some people think aliens from another planet moved the *moai*. Teams of scientists have had many ideas. One woman used a computer to try out some ideas. She said the *Rapa Nui* probably put the statue on two logs. Then they rolled it along on other logs. Seventy workers could move a statue in about five days this way.

**mystery 10** How did the *Rapa Nui* get the statues up on the altars?

☑ Solved ☐ Unsolved

Think about how heavy the *moai* are. The *Rapa Nui* did not have machines. Instead, they piled rocks under the statue. The statue got straighter as the pile of rocks got bigger. Wooden poles helped keep the statue from falling over.

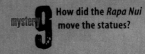

14

---

**Student Journal page 9**

Name _____ Date _____

**Writing: 5Ws and a Summary**

The 5Ws—who, what, where, when, and why—give readers the basic information about what happens in an article or a section of an article. What do the 5Ws tell you about Mystery 8, the section that tells how the islanders made their statues? Complete the chart. Use the basic information in the chart to write a summary of how the islanders made their statues. Write your summary on another sheet of paper.

| 5Ws | Information from "Easter Island" |
| --- | --- |
| **Who** made the statues? | |
| **What** did they do to make the statues? | |
| **Where** did the major events take place? | |
| **When** did the major events take place? | |
| **Why** are the events important? | |

Mystery • Easter Island: Place of Many Mysteries

9

---

# After Reading

Use one or more activities.

## Check Purpose

Have students decide if their purpose was met. Did they learn more about the solved and unsolved mysteries of Easter Island? Did they learn what they wanted to find out?

## Discussion Questions

Continue the group discussion with the following questions.

1. Which unsolved mystery would you like to learn more about? Why? (Making Connections)

2. What work is involved in building, moving, and raising a statue? (Monitor Understanding)

3. What can you infer (guess) about the lives of the islanders? (Inferential Thinking)

## Revisit: Anticipation Guide

Revisit the anticipation guide started in Before Reading. Ask students to tell which statements are true or false.

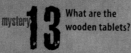

## mystery 11 How were the red tops put on some of the statues?

☐ Solved  ☑ Unsolved

Scientists still can't figure this one out.

Statues with red tops

## mystery 12 What happened to the statues?

☑ Solved  ☐ Unsolved

Over time the groups had fights. They knocked down each other's statues. Soon all of the *moai* were broken or knocked down. Many years later, scientists put up some of the fallen statues.

A tsunami in 1960 knocked down this *moai*.

## mystery 13 What are the wooden tablets?

☐ Solved  ☑ Unsolved

The tablets are called *rongorongo* (RON go ron go). They have a kind of picture writing on them. The writing may tell how to say special <u>chants</u>, rhythmic songs the islanders sang or spoke. No one knows how to read the tablets. So we may never know what they say.

Carving a *rongorongo* tablet

## mystery 14 How did the *Rapa Nui* change the island?

☑ Solved  ☐ Unsolved

At first there were many trees. Good food grew in the rich soil. The ocean was full of fish. But then things changed. The people cut down the trees. They did not plant new trees. The soil washed into the ocean. Then more crops could not grow. Without trees, the people could not make new boats. They could not sail away, or go fishing in the ocean. But they built more and more *moai*. No one knows why the *Rapa Nui* kept using up their natural resources.

## mystery 15 What happened to the people?

☑ Solved  ☐ Unsolved

The groups began to fight and many people died. Later, explorers took islanders away to other countries. Soon there were only about 750 people left on Easter Island. Then, in 1888, Easter Island became a part of the country of Chile. More people came to live on the island. More babies were born on the island. Now, about two thousand people live there. ◆

You can get to Easter Island by airplane or ship. There is one small city. Many tourists come to visit. Scientists study the stone statues. The *Rapa Nui* are once again proud of their island. Some people want Easter Island to become free from Chile. It is unclear whether the island will gain its independence.

15

## Writing Summary

Have students reread the part about how the *Rapa Nui* made the statues. Then have students complete the 5Ws chart on *Student Journal* page 9 to help them organize their thoughts for writing a summary. They can use the information in the chart to write on a separate sheet of paper a summary paragraph about how the workers made the statues.

## Vocabulary Homophones

Read aloud the sentence with the word *altars* on page 13. *Many* ahu (large, flat stones) *were used as* altars *for special ceremonies and religious meetings.* Display *altar*. Ask students what it means. (a raised place where religious services are performed)

Explain that homophones are words that sound alike but are spelled differently. Have students complete *Student Journal* page 10. (See Differentiated Instruction.)

## Phonics/Word Study

### Long *a* Patterns

List these words on the board: *shape, rake; pail, trail; ray, stay.* Then ask: *How can we categorize these long a words?* Encourage students to notice the different spelling patterns that make the long *a* sound: *aCe, ai,* and *ay.* Have students name other words with these patterns and list them on the board. Now, work with students to complete the in-depth long *a* patterns activity on TE page 25.

After a *moai* was put on the altar, the eyes were added. People believed that the eyes gave the statue its power.

PACIFIC
OCEAN

SOUTH
AMERICA

ATLANTIC
OCEAN

○ Easter
Island

# MOAI

- Most of the statues are male. Only a few are female.

- The smallest *moai* is 3.76 feet high (1.13 meters).

- The largest *moai* is 71.93 feet high (21.60 meters). It weighs about 165 tons (182 metric tons or 330,000 pounds).

- In comparison, the average African male elephant is about 11 feet tall and weighs about 6 tons. ▼

16

## Phonics/Word Study

### Long *a* Patterns

Write the following words on the board: *same, mail, day.* Tell students that they are continuing their study of long *a* patterns.

▶ Ask students to compare these new words with their last sort (*cap, lake, rain*). Have them identify what is different about this sort. (three long *a* patterns in this one)

▶ Using the Long *a*: Sort One sheet, model the sorting process for students. (See *Word Study Manual* page 36.) Write the headings *aCe, ai, ay,* and Oddball and the first few words in the appropriate columns. Note that *mail* has a long *a* sound because of its *ai* pattern.

▶ Discuss the sort and what students learned about the most common long *a* patterns. Then ask: *What do you make of* said *and* have? *They certainly fit the pattern but not the sound.*

▶ Once the model sort is complete, hand out the Long *a*: Sort One sheet and ask students to cut it up and do the sort on their own or in groups.

▶ Check the final sorts.

| Long *a*: Sort One | | | |
|---|---|---|---|
| **aCe** | **ai** | **ay** | **Oddball** |
| chase | praise | okay | said |
| quake | straight | gray | have |
| flame | sprain | pray | |
| daze | claim | payout | |
| flake | brain | sway | |
| whale | | day | |
| same | | stray | |

For more information on word sorts and spelling stages, see pages 5–31 in the *Word Study Manual.*

# Focus on . . .

Use one or more activities in this section to focus on a particular area of need in your students.

## Comprehension  STRATEGY SUPPORT  INDEPENDENT

To help those students who need more practice using the strategies covered in this lesson, work one-on-one or in small groups to apply the strategy prompts below. Apply the prompts to a *Reading Advantage* paperback, a classroom library book, or a new or familiar selection in the magazine. Always model your own thinking first.

### Monitor Understanding

• Do I understand what I'm reading? If not, what part is confusing to me?

• What fix-up strategies can I use to solve the problem? (See During Reading for fix-up strategies.)

• Why did a character say (do, think, ask) that?

• What images do I visualize from the text? What parts can't I visualize?

• Why did the author include (or not include) those details?

## Writing Letter  INDEPENDENT

Have students write a letter to a friend, from the viewpoint of either a tourist or an archaeologist, explaining why the Easter Island statues are fascinating. To help students plan for their letter, suggest that partners identify the statues' many mysteries and jot down notes about them. Students can include sketches of a statue in their letter.

Before students begin to write, explain that a friendly letter has five parts: the date, the salutation, the body, the closing, and the writer's signature.

For more instruction and practice on note-taking skills, see lessons in *Writing Advantage,* pages 152–163.

## Fluency: Expression

After students have read the article at least once, have partners choose two mysteries to read to each other. Because the article is written in a question-answer format, students may enjoy trading parts. Have one student ask the question, and the other student read the answer. Then have partners switch roles.

Point out that a question is signaled by a rising voice at the end of the sentence. If needed, model the difference between a question and a statement.

As you listen to partners read, remind them, as needed, to use a rising inflection when asking a question, and to read at an even pace.

When students read aloud, do they—

✓ reflect an understanding of the text?

✓ demonstrate appropriate timing, stress, and intonation?

✓ incorporate appropriate speed and phrasing?

## English Language Learners

To support students as they learn about homophones, provide background information for students before they complete the homophones activity in the *Student Journal*.

1. Write several homophone pairs on the board and discuss their meanings. For example: *sun/son, flew/flu*.

2. Have each pair divide a piece of paper into two columns. Have them write one word from the pair in each column.

3. Have partners draw a picture below each word that represents the meaning of each word.

## Independent Activity Options

While you work with individuals or small groups, others can work independently on one or more of the following options.

▶ Level A paperback books, see TE pages 371–376

▶ Level A *eZines*

▶ Repeat word sorts from this lesson

▶ *Student Journal* pages for this lesson

▶ *Writing Advantage* independent lessons

# Assessment

## Strategy Assessment

To help you and your students assess their use of comprehension strategies, ask the following questions. Students can complete a written response or provide verbal answers in a one-on-one reading conference.

- **Monitor Understanding** How did the pictures help you visualize the text? (Answers will vary. Possible responses may include that the pictures helped in visualizing the statues because there were not enough details in the text to create a good mental image of them.)

For ongoing informal assessment, use the checklists on pages 61–64 of *Level A Assessment*.

## Word Study Assessment

Use these steps to help you and your students assess their understanding of long *a* patterns.

1. Create a chart like the one shown, including only the words in the first column.

2. Have students read the words.

3. Then have students sort the words into the correct column. Answers are shown.

| Words | *aCe* | *ai* | *ay* |
|-------|-------|------|------|
| snail | locate | snail | delay |
| delay | grape | rain | sway |
| locate | | | |
| grape | | | |
| rain | | | |
| sway | | | |

Great Source
Reading Advantage

Level A
Assessment

# Mysteries
### of the animal world

*Bats and butterflies used to be a mystery to us. But we have learned that they are "smarter" than you may think!*

## Beautiful Butterfly

Like magic, a caterpillar turns into a beautiful butterfly. The monarch butterfly seems to have its own "magic." Only a few kinds of butterflies <u>migrate</u>. They migrate to escape the cold winter. The monarch is one of them.

Monarch butterflies travel thousands of miles each year. In midsummer, they leave their <u>breeding grounds</u>. This is where they mate and lay their eggs. Most breeding grounds are in Canada or the northern United States. By autumn, they are well on their way flying south for the winter. In spring, they fly north again. Some monarch butterflies travel as far as 4,000 miles round trip!

Few monarch butterflies that begin the journey complete the round trip. Instead, it is a relay race of several <u>generations</u> of butterflies. During the travel and the southern wintering period, some monarchs die. But others lay eggs. The eggs hatch into the new generation. Therefore, many of the butterflies that fly north are young monarchs.

*Close to 200 million monarch butterflies spend the winter in a forest near Mexico City. The trees are covered with butterflies. You can't even see the bark.*

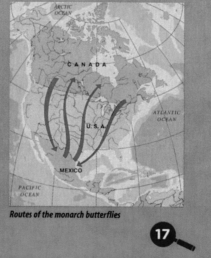

*Routes of the monarch butterflies*

**17**

## LESSON 4
# Mysteries of the Animal World
*Mystery*, pages 17–19

### SUMMARY
This **article** offers insights into the mysterious behaviors of butterflies and bats. Scientific facts debunk some of the myths and misunderstandings about the two animals.

### COMPREHENSION STRATEGIES
Determining Importance

### WRITING
Notes for Visualizing

### VOCABULARY
Compound Words

### PHONICS/WORD STUDY
Long *a* Patterns

### Lesson Vocabulary
migrate          echolocating
breeding grounds    funnels
generations    environment
nectar

### MATERIALS
*Mystery*, pp. 17–19
*Student Journal*, pp. 11–13
*Word Study Manual*, p. 37
*Writing Advantage*, pp. 113–151

# Before Reading
**WHOLE CLASS** Use one or more activities.

## Begin a K-W-L Chart
Display on the board or on chart paper the words *butterflies* and *bats*. Then begin a brief discussion of what students know about each kind of animal. Then display a K-W-L chart.

Ask students as a group to suggest entries for the *K* and *W* columns. Tell students that they will come back to the chart to list what they as a group have learned after reading the article. Remember to keep the chart for later use.

## Vocabulary Preview
List and say the vocabulary words. Ask volunteers to share what they know about the words. Have students begin the knowledge rating chart on *Student Journal* page 11. Model a response for the page. Have students complete the chart after they read the selection.

## Preview the Selection
Have students look through the three pages of the article. Discuss what students notice.

## Make Predictions/Set Purpose
Students should use the information they gathered in previewing the selection to make some predictions about the article. If students have trouble generating a purpose for reading, suggest that they read to learn about the mysterious behaviors of monarch butterflies and bats.

## DIFFERENTIATED INSTRUCTION

## Comprehension
### DETERMINING IMPORTANCE

To help students determine the importance of details in a text, use the following steps:

1. Ask students to identify a sentence from the first paragraph on page 18 that contains important details.

2. Then ask: *Why do you think that sentence is important?*

### Student Journal page 11

Name _____ Date _____

**Building Vocabulary: Knowledge Rating Chart**
Show your knowledge of each word by adding information to the other boxes in the row.

| Word | Define or Use in a Sentence | Where Have I Seen or Heard it? | How Is It Used in the Selection? | Looks Like (Words or Sketch) |
|---|---|---|---|---|
| migrate | | | | |
| breeding grounds | | | | |
| generations | | | | |
| nectar | | | | |
| echolocating | | | | |
| funnels | | | | |
| environment | | | | |

Mystery • Mysteries of the Animal World    (11)

---

Monarchs can migrate from Canada to Mexico in two months or less. They have only a four-inch wingspan. Even so, they can travel more than 1,000 miles in a few days. How do they do it? One way is by coasting and gliding to save energy. They glide on wind currents. They even ride storms and hurricanes heading south. Airplane pilots have seen monarchs flying as high as 29,000 feet! The monarchs fill up on <u>nectar</u> along the way. Some arrive south fatter than when they set out.

The return flight north is more difficult. The butterflies fly separately. They fly day and night. They rarely stop to rest or eat. Instead, they live off their stored fat.

Later generations will fly south the following year. They visit the same places that their ancestors did. Some scientists think that monarchs have a built-in compass that guides them. Other scientists believe that monarchs use the sun to guide their flight. But all scientists remain puzzled. How do these creatures find their way to a place they've never been before?

A compass is a device that shows direction. A magnetic needle inside the compass is mounted so that it will turn freely. It always points north. If you notice that the needle is pointing to your right, then north is to your right. You are facing west. The compass will not show you the direction you are facing. You have to figure that out in relationship to where north is. A pocket compass can be handy if you are hiking because it is small enough to carry. It will guide you in the direction you need to go.

(18)

---

# Going Batty

**T**he Wright brothers built the first airplane. They got their idea by watching birds. Today, scientists are going "batty." They are taking a close look at bats. They hope to learn something from these flying mammals.

Bats can see, but not very well. They find their way in the dark by <u>echolocating</u>. Bats send out high-pitched sounds. The sounds bounce off objects and return to bats' ears as echoes. Bats send out sounds through their noses! They aim their sounds through a flap of skin called a *nose leaf*. Bats have large ears. Their ears are shaped like <u>funnels</u>. This helps the bats hear even the softest echoes.

## Animal Idioms

An idiom is a phrase or sentence that doesn't mean exactly what the words say. Did you ever have "butterflies in your stomach"? People use this saying to describe how they feel when they are nervous. It doesn't mean that a person has real butterflies in his or her stomach! Something that is "for the birds" is silly and worthless. The "fly in the ointment" is something that spoils everything.

---

# During Reading

## Comprehension
### DETERMINING IMPORTANCE

Use these questions to model how to determine the importance of details in the first paragraph of the selection. Then have students determine the importance of details as they read the first paragraph on page 18.

- What do I think are the most important ideas in this paragraph?

- How can I support my beliefs?

(See Differentiated Instruction.)

## Teacher Think Aloud
*I think an important idea in the first paragraph is that some butterflies migrate to escape the cold weather. This detail is important because I think it's the beginning of the explanation for why some butterflies have a "magic" or unusual ability.*

## Fix-Up Strategies
Offer these strategies to help students read independently.

**If you don't understand what you're reading:**

- Reread the difficult section to look for clues to help you comprehend.

- Read ahead to find clues to help you comprehend.

- Retell, or say in your own words, what you've read.

- Visualize, or form mental pictures of, what you've read.

Bat sounds are too high for people to hear. Still, scientists are very interested in bats' sonar. Bats are able to pick up sound waves from a tiny beetle on a leaf. Scientists wonder about this. How do bats pick out the beetle from sound waves bouncing back from all the leaves? Scientists are amazed by the speed at which bats catch their prey. The bat's brain can tell apart different echoes in record time. The bat's sonar is better than any machine scientists have ever made.

Why do scientists want to copy bat sonar? One reason is to help the U.S. Navy. The Navy depends on man-made sonar to find distant objects. The Navy also uses the sonar of trained dolphins. Dolphins use echolocation the same way bats do. If scientists can make a sonar system like a bat's, they won't need divers or dolphins.

Scientists work with bats in bat labs. They are trying to figure out the bats' sonar system. If the bats cooperate, the scientists reward them. What's the best reward to a bat? *Mealworms*—lots of them!

Bats fly like birds. But they are mammals. (Mammals are animals that have hair or fur. In females, glands produce milk for the young.) Bats' bodies have fur. Like other mammals, mother bats make milk to feed their young. Bats are the only mammals that can fly.

Most bats eat insects, such as mosquitoes. Bats keep down harmful insect populations. By doing this, bats help protect our <u>environment</u> by controlling certain insects. ◆

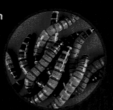

*Mealworms are the larvae, the newly hatched wormlike stage, of several kinds of beetles that get into grain and flour. Mealworms are raised for bird feed.*

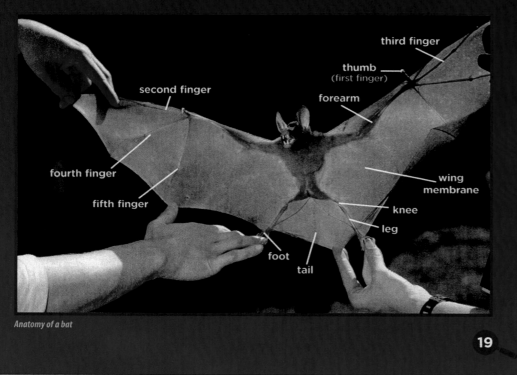

third finger

thumb
(first finger)

forearm

second finger

fourth finger

fifth finger

foot

tail

knee

leg

wing
membrane

*Anatomy of a bat*

**19**

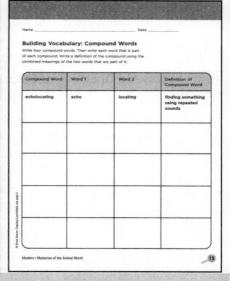

### Student Journal page 12

Name _____ Date _____

**Writing: Notes for Visualizing**
Which part of the article could you visualize best? Describe that part below. Then draw a picture to show what you "saw" in your mind.

The part I could visualize best was _____

Some details I "saw" in my mind include _____

**Now draw what you visualized.**

12                    Mystery • Mysteries of the Animal World

### Student Journal page 13

Name _____ Date _____

**Building Vocabulary: Compound Words**
Write four compound words. Then write each word that is part of each compound. Write a definition of the compound using the combined meanings of the two words that are part of it.

| Compound Word | Word 1 | Word 2 | Definition of Compound Word |
|---|---|---|---|
| echolocating | echo | locating | finding something using repeated sounds |
| | | | |
| | | | |
| | | | |

Mystery • Mysteries of the Animal World                    13

# After Reading

Use one or more activities.

## Check Purpose

Have students decide if their purpose was met. Were their predictions accurate? What facts have they learned?

## Discussion Questions

Continue the group discussion.

1. Would you prefer to study monarch butterflies or bats? Why? (Making Connections)

2. How are monarch butterflies and bats similar? (Compare-Contrast)

## Writing Notes for Visualizing

Ask students to describe the parts of the article that they could visualize best. Then have students write about them on *Student Journal* page 12.

## Vocabulary Compound Words

Display the word *echolocating*. Help students define *echo* as "a repeated sound." *Locating* means "finding." *Echolocating* means "using repeated sounds to find something." Have students complete *Student Journal* page 13.

## Phonics/Word Study

## Long *a* Patterns

Write the words *play*, *prey*, *eight*, and *break* on the board. Point out how all the words have the long *a* sound but different spelling patterns. Ask students to think of other words that contain the long *a* sound and similar spelling patterns. List them on the board. Now, work with students to complete the in-depth long *a* patterns activity on TE page 30.

## Long *a* Patterns

Write the following words on the board: *gray, prey, eight,* and *break*. Tell students that they are continuing their study of long *a* patterns.

▶ Ask students to compare these words with their last sort (*same, mail, day*). Have them identify what is different about this sort. (four long *a* patterns in this one)

▶ Using the Long *a*: Sort Two sheet, model the sorting process for students. (See *Word Study Manual* page 37.) Write the headings *ay, ey, ei, ai,* and *ea* and the first few words in the appropriate columns.

▶ Discuss the sort and what students learned. Then ask: *What do you make of prey, eight, and break? They seem to be fairly unusual, don't they?*

▶ Once the model sort is complete, hand out the Long *a*: Sort Two sheet and ask students to cut it up and do the sort on their own or in groups.

▶ Check the final sorts.

| Long *a*: Sort Two | | | |
|---|---|---|---|
| *ay* | *ey* | *ei* | *ea* |
| okay | grey | weigh | steak |
| display | they | freight | great |
| gray | prey | weight | break |
| wayside | | reign | |
| pray | | sleigh | |
| payment | | eight | |
| stray | | | |
| sway | | | |
| day | | | |

For more information on word sorts and spelling stages, see pages 5–31 in the *Word Study Manual*.

# Focus on . . .

Use one or more activities in this section to focus on a particular area of need in your students.

## Comprehension  STRATEGY SUPPORT  INDEPENDENT

To help those students who need more practice using the strategies covered in this lesson, work one-on-one or in small groups to apply the strategy prompts below. Apply the prompts to a *Reading Advantage* paperback, a classroom library book, or a new or familiar selection in the magazine. Always model your own thinking first.

### Determining Importance

• What is the most important idea in the paragraph? How can I prove it?

• Which details are unimportant? Why?

• What does the author want me to understand?

• Why is this information important (or not important) to me?

## Writing Migration Diagram  INDEPENDENT

Have students think and talk about the migration cycle of monarch butterflies. Ask volunteers to "step" what happens, beginning with the southward journey in winter. Help students record their ideas in a simple grid similar to the one shown.

### Migration Cycle Notes

| Start | Next | Then | Last |
|---|---|---|---|
| | | | |

Then have students create pictures to place in a circle diagram. Each picture should represent one step. The pictures in the circle diagram should flow clockwise. Students can review and edit their notes in the grid as labels for each picture.

If you'd like students to write sequence paragraphs based on their diagrams, see the lessons on expository writing structures in *Writing Advantage*, pages 113–151.

## Fluency: Pacing

*SMALL GROUP*

After students have read the article at least once, have them choose one paragraph from both the butterfly section and the bat section of the article. Have partners read each of their paragraphs aloud to each other. Model reading smoothly and at an even pace. You may want to have students echo each sentence you read, to experience your pacing before it is their turn to read.

As you listen to students read, use these prompts to guide them.

▶ Notice how I read smoothly, neither hesitating on some words nor repeating words.

▶ Previewing the paragraph provides an opportunity to "troubleshoot" any difficult or unfamiliar words. It also enables me to see in advance how groups of words naturally go together.

▶ Remember to read loudly enough for everyone to hear the words clearly. Put enthusiasm in your reading to make listening an enjoyable experience.

When students read aloud, do they—

✓ demonstrate a smooth pace, not too fast or too slow?

✓ incorporate well-timed pauses between words and phrases?

✓ reflect an awareness and understanding of punctuation?

## English Language Learners

*SMALL GROUP*

Provide support to students as they learn about compound words in the vocabulary activity on TE page 29.

1. Discuss what a compound word is, and write some examples on the board *(baseball, sunrise, pancake)*.

2. Have pairs copy each word and draw a line separating the two smaller words.

3. Have pairs explain how they knew where to draw the lines.

## Independent Activity Options

*INDEPENDENT*

While you work with individuals or small groups, others can work independently on one or more of the following options.

▶ Level A paperback books, see TE pages 371–376

▶ Level A *eZines*

▶ Repeat word sorts from this lesson

▶ *Student Journal* pages for this lesson

▶ *Writing Advantage* independent lessons

# Assessment

## Strategy Assessment

To help you and your students assess their use of comprehension strategies, ask the following questions. Students can complete a written response or provide verbal answers in a one-on-one reading conference.

- **Determining Importance** What were the most important details in the butterflies (or bats) section? Why were those details important? (Answers will vary. Possible response: I thought that the huge relay-race type trip of different generations of butterflies was most important. This showed me how amazing butterflies are— and it made me wonder how the baby butterflies knew where to go.)

For ongoing informal assessment, use the checklists on pages 61–64 of *Level A Assessment*.

## Word Study Assessment

Use these steps to help you and your students assess their understanding of long *a* patterns.

1. Create a chart like the one shown, omitting the answers.

2. Have students read the words.

3. Then have students sort the words into the correct column. Answers are shown.

| Words | *ay* | *ey* | *ei* | *ea* |
|---|---|---|---|---|
| steak | pay | they | neighbor | steak |
| they | way | whey | weigh | break |
| pay | | | | |
| neighbor | | | | |
| break | | | | |
| weigh | | | | |
| way | | | | |
| whey | | | | |

Great Source
Reading Advantage

Level A
Assessment

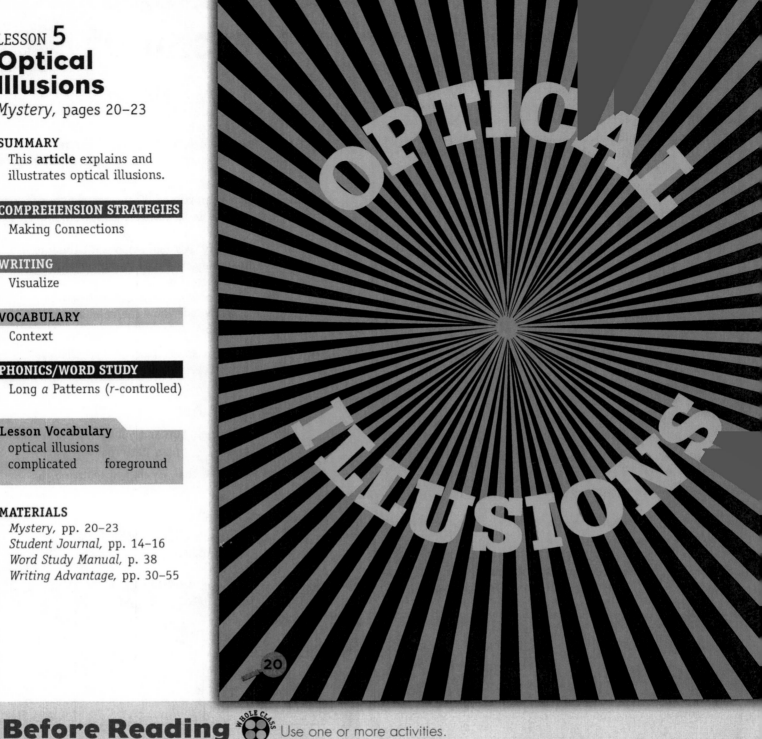

# LESSON 5
# Optical Illusions
*Mystery*, pages 20–23

### SUMMARY
This **article** explains and illustrates optical illusions.

### COMPREHENSION STRATEGIES
Making Connections

### WRITING
Visualize

### VOCABULARY
Context

### PHONICS/WORD STUDY
Long *a* Patterns (*r*-controlled)

### Lesson Vocabulary
optical illusions
complicated        foreground

### MATERIALS
*Mystery*, pp. 20–23
*Student Journal*, pp. 14–16
*Word Study Manual*, p. 38
*Writing Advantage*, pp. 30–55

OPTICAL ILLUSIONS

20

# Before Reading ⬤ Use one or more activities.

### Make a Web
Make a web with "how we see things" in the center oval. Have students identify the two organs that influence what we see when we look at things in pictures and in real life. (eyes, brain) Then talk briefly about each organ. The eye is like a camera. It "takes" a picture. The brain is like a computer. It identifies what we're looking at.

### Vocabulary Preview
Review the vocabulary list. Ask students if there are any words they know. Have them predict how the words will be used in this article in the second column on *Student Journal* page 14. They will finish the chart later.

### Preview the Selection
Have students look through the article. Discuss what they observe. Have them write questions about optical illusions to revisit later.

### Make Predictions/Set Purpose
Students should use the information they gathered in previewing the selection to make some predictions about the article. If students have trouble generating a purpose for reading, suggest that they read to see if their eyes and brains are tricked by optical illusions—and to find out how optical illusions work.

# Is seeing really believing?

**Look** at the picture above. What do you see?

Do you see a young woman? Look again, closely. Can you see the face of an old woman, too? This drawing plays a trick on your eyes. Pictures that do this are called <u>optical illusions</u>.

Optical illusions can be simple or <u>complicated</u>. To understand optical illusions, you have to understand how our eyes and brain work.

Normally, our eyes and brain work together to make sense of what we see. The eyes take a picture almost the way a camera does. The brain matches the picture with what it already knows. The brain then "decides" what we see.

What happens when we look at an optical illusion? Our eyes fool our brains. Our brains decide incorrectly about what we see.

Scientists have been studying optical illusions for many years. But they are still unsure about how they work. Look at the optical illusions on the following pages. Try to answer the questions. Then turn to page 23 for the answers.

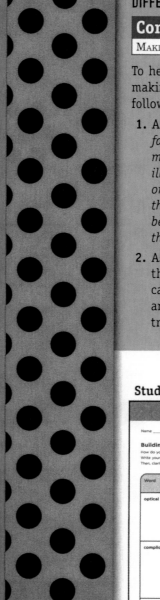

**21**

### DIFFERENTIATED INSTRUCTION

## Comprehension
MAKING CONNECTIONS

To help students practice making connections, use the following steps.

1. Ask: *What in this article seems familiar to me? I remember my brother once showed me an illusion similar to the first one on page 22. I had to measure the middle circle in both images because I didn't believe that they were both the same size!*

2. Ask volunteers to respond to the same question. Students can share experiences about any time their eyes have played tricks on them.

**SMALL GROUP**

### Student Journal page 14

Name _____ Date _____

**Building Vocabulary: Predictions**
How do you predict these words will be used in "Optical Illusions"?
Write your answers in the second column. Next, read the article.
Then, clarify your answers in the third column.

| Word | My prediction for how the word will be used | How the word was actually used |
|------|---------------------------------------------|--------------------------------|
| optical illusions | | |
| complicated | | |
| foreground | | |

14          Mystery • Optical Illusions

# During Reading

## Comprehension
MAKING CONNECTIONS

**SMALL GROUP**

Use these questions to model for students how to make connections with the text. Then have students make their own connections.

• Have I ever seen these or other optical illusions?

• Have I ever been "tricked" by an optical illusion before?

(See Differentiated Instruction.)

## Teacher Think Aloud

*I remember a salesperson once told me that vertical stripes make you look taller than horizontal stripes. I guess that's just an optical illusion. When I look at the last picture in this article, I still can't believe my eyes. Those circles just have to be a spiral! I guess the black "stripes" behind the circles make me "see" a spiral, just as vertical stripes make people seem taller.*

## Fix-Up Strategies

Offer these strategies to help students read independently.

**If you don't understand what you're reading:**

• Reread the difficult section to look for clues to help you comprehend.

• Read ahead to find clues to help you comprehend.

• Retell, or say in your own words, what you've read.

• Visualize, or form mental pictures of, what you've read.

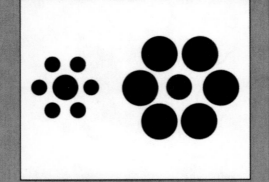

1. Which center circle is bigger? Is it the one on the left or the right?

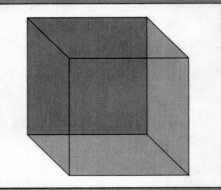

2. Look at the cube. On which side of the box is the dark panel?

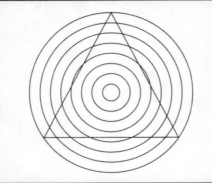

3. Are the sides of the triangle straight or curved?

4. Can you see two different pictures?

22

## Student Journal page 15

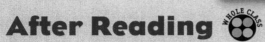

Name _____ Date _____

**Writing: Using Details to Visualize**

Look at optical illusion 5. What pictures did you see? What were some of the details?

What I saw first was _____

Some details I saw were _____

What I saw next was _____

Some details I saw were _____

**Choose one of your visualizations to illustrate.**

Mystery • Optical Illusions ⸺ 15

# After Reading  Use one or more activities.

## Check Purpose

Have students decide if their purpose was met. Did they learn more about how optical illusions work?

## Discussion Questions

Continue the group discussion with the following questions.

1. What is the effect on your brain when you look at an optical illusion? (Cause-Effect)

2. How would you answer the question: *Is seeing really believing?* Explain. (Inferential Thinking)

3. Which optical illusion did you like best? Why? (Making Connections)

## Revisit: Questions

Refer students to the questions they wrote at the outset of the lesson. Have students decide whether their questions were answered.

## Revisit: Predictions Chart

Have students complete the third column of the chart on *Student Journal* page 14.

**5.** Can you see two different pictures?

**6.** Are these circles part of a spiral or are they separate circles?

## ANSWERS

**1.** The center circles are the same size. The one on the left seems bigger. This is because we compare it to the smaller circles around it. The one on the right seems smaller because we compare it to the larger circles.

**2.** The panel that you see as dark depends on which angle your eye follows. Look at the angle formed by the line in the center and its open-Y top. Now, you "read" the angle as forming a corner of the top panel. That makes the dark panel look like it is inside the box. Look at the angle formed by the other up-and-down line and its open-Y bottom. This time, you "read" the angle as forming a corner of the front panel. Now, the dark panel looks like it is on the front of the box.

**3.** The triangle has straight sides. The sides look like they bend because of the circles. The circles pull our eyes toward the center. The sides of the triangle seem to get pulled in, too.

**4.** One picture is a musician. The other is a woman's face. Our eyes usually focus on one important object in a picture. That's the "foreground." "The rest becomes the "background." This picture is different from most. It has two possible foregrounds, the musician and the face. Our brains can stick with only one picture at a time.

**5.** This picture is similar to number four. Again, there are two possible foregrounds. If you see the light part first, you will see a candle. Otherwise, you will see two faces.

**6.** The circles are all separate from one another. However, the stripes look like they are drawn in perspective. In other words, they look like they are getting farther away. This is because they get narrow toward the center. They look like they are going down a drain! Your eyes think they are following the lines to somewhere in the distance. Therefore, the circles look like a spiral. ◆

**23**

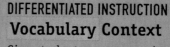

SMALL GROUP

## DIFFERENTIATED INSTRUCTION
### Vocabulary Context

Give students more experience with using context:

1. Ask: *How can you figure out the meaning of a word?*

2. Display these sentences: *Our eyes usually focus on one important object in a picture. That's the "foreground." The rest becomes the "background."*

3. Ask students how they can figure out the meaning of *foreground* by using context. (Read the next sentence.)

4. Ask students what word in the next sentence might help them. (*Background* means "the part of the picture in the back.")

### Student Journal page 16

Name _____ Date _____

**Building Vocabulary: Using Context to Understand a Word**
Select one of the words—complicated or illusion—that you defined from the context. Complete these statements and answer these questions about the word.

My Word in Context:

I think this word means _____

because _____

My word is _____

My word is not _____

Where else might I find this word? _____

What makes this an important word to know? _____

16       Mystery • Optical Illusions

## Writing Visualize

Have partners describe the picture they initially saw when they looked at Optical Illusion 5. Then have them describe the picture they saw next. Encourage them to include details in their descriptions. Then have students record their answers in the visualizing activity on *Student Journal* page 15.

## Vocabulary Context

Display these sentences: *However, the stripes look as though they are drawn in <u>perspective</u>. . . . they get narrow toward the center. Your eyes think they are following the lines to somewhere in the distance.* Point out how reading the sentences following *perspective* helps you figure out what it means. Discuss how context can help define words. Have students complete the context activity on *Student Journal* page 16. (See Differentiated Instruction.)

## Phonics/Word Study
### Long *a* Patterns (*r*-controlled)

Display the word *star*. Ask students to say it aloud. What do they notice about the vowel sound? (It looks like it should have a short *a* sound, but it doesn't.) Encourage students to notice the subtle difference in the vowel sounds in the words *star* and *cat*. The *r* changes the *a* sound. Now, work with students to complete the in-depth vowel activity on TE page 36.

## Long *a* Patterns (*r*-controlled)

▶ Write the following words on the board: *car* and *care*. Tell students that they are continuing their study of long *a* patterns. This time, however, the sort is a particularly tricky one.

▶ Point to *car*. Ask if the word *car* has a long *a* or a short *a* vowel sound.

▶ Without saying if students are right or wrong, point to *care*. Ask if *care* can help them decide which kind of vowel sound *car* has. (*Car* has a short *r*-controlled *a* sound.)

▶ Discuss the difficulty the letter *r* causes. Explain how it "robs" the vowel of its usual sound. The *a* in *cat* sounds very different from the *a* in *car*.

▶ Using the Long *a*: *r*-controlled Vowels sheet, model the sorting process for students. (See *Word Study Manual* page 38.) Write the headings *ar*, *are*, *air*, and *Oddball* and the first few words in the appropriate columns.

▶ Discuss the sort. Note that sometimes the easiest way to tell whether an *r*-controlled vowel is short or long is by saying aloud the long and short sound in the word. By doing this, it becomes clearer whether the sound is short or long. The word can then be spelled correctly.

▶ Once the model sort is complete, hand out the Long *a*: *r*-controlled Vowels sheet and ask students to cut it up and do the sort on their own or in groups.

▶ Check the final sorts.

### Long *a*: *r*-controlled Vowels

| *ar* | *are* | *air* | Oddball |
|------|-------|-------|---------|
| bar | pare | pair | wear |
| star | ware | stair | tear |
| char | bare | fair | pear |
| car | fare | air | war |
|  | stare | chair | bear |
|  | care |  | are |

For more information on word sorts and spelling stages, see pages 5–31 in the *Word Study Manual*.

# Focus on . . .

Use one or more activities in this section to focus on a particular area of need in your students.

## Comprehension  STRATEGY SUPPORT  INDEPENDENT

To help those students who need more practice using the strategies covered in this lesson, work one-on-one or in small groups to apply the strategy prompts below. Apply the prompts to a *Reading Advantage* paperback, a classroom library book, or a new or familiar selection in the magazine. Always model your own thinking first.

### Making Connections

• What does this story (article, passage) remind me of?

• What do I already know about this topic?

• Where have I heard about this topic before?

• What do I have in common with the characters, people, or situations in the text?

• What other books, stories, articles, movies, or TV shows does this text make me think about?

## Writing Optical Illusions  INDEPENDENT

Have students write about a time when they thought they knew what they were looking at but then realized they were looking at something different. For example, they mistook their own shadow for somebody following them, or they thought they were seeing a flying saucer when it was a hot-air balloon. Suggest that they first tell a partner what they experienced. Encourage partners to ask each other questions about what happened. Then have students jot down notes before they write.

Have students complete these sentences to help them organize their thoughts.

1. What I thought I saw was _____.

2. Some details I "saw" were _____ _____.

3. What I really saw was _____.

4. Some details I really saw were _____ _____.

To help students include strong verbs and specific nouns in their writing, see the lessons in *Writing Advantage*, pages 30–55.

## Fluency: Pacing

Many of the answers in "Optical Illusions" have a lot of information. Explain to students that before reading aloud, readers should silently read, and even reread, a text until they become familiar with it. Familiarity with a text helps a reader read aloud at a "just right" pace, not too fast and not too slow. After students are familiar with the information in the answers, they can practice reading aloud one question and answer at a time. Have students work in pairs and take turns reading the questions and answers.

When students read aloud, do they—

✓ demonstrate a smooth pace, not too fast or too slow?

✓ incorporate well-timed pauses between words and phrases?

✓ reflect an awareness and understanding of punctuation?

## English Language Learners

To support students as they comprehend the text "Optical Illusions," provide background knowledge.

1. Write the word *optical* on the board and underline the root *opt*.

2. Explain that the root *opt* means "having to do with the eyes," and have partners work together to think of other words that contain *opt*. (optometrist)

3. Explain that an illusion is something that deceives, or tricks, you. So, an optical illusion is something that tricks your eyes.

## Independent Activity Options

While you work with individuals or small groups, others can work independently on one or more of the following options.

▶ Level A paperback books, see TE pages 371–376

▶ Level A *eZines*

▶ Repeat word sorts from this lesson

▶ *Student Journal* pages for this lesson

▶ *Writing Advantage* independent lessons

# Assessment

## Strategy Assessment

To help you and your students assess their use of comprehension strategies, ask the following questions. Students can complete a written response or provide verbal answers in a one-on-one reading conference.

• **Making Connections** How did your prior experience with optical illusions help you understand this article? (Answers will vary. Possible responses may include that students "knew" the answers to some of the questions, even though their eyes could still trick them.)

For ongoing informal assessment, use the checklists on pages 61–64 of *Level A Assessment*.

## Word Study Assessment

Use these steps to help you and your students assess their understanding of *r*-controlled long *a* patterns.

1. Create a chart like the one shown. Include only the words in the first column.

2. Have students read the words in the first column of the chart.

3. Then have students sort the words into the correct column. Answers are shown.

| Words | *ar* | *are* | *air* |
|-------|------|-------|-------|
| care | car | care | chair |
| car | bar | dare | flair |
| chair | tart | | |
| bar | | | |
| tart | | | |
| dare | | | |
| flair | | | |

Great Source
Reading Advantage

Level A
Assessment

# Bermuda. . . *and* Three Mini Mysteries

*Mystery,* pages 24–31

## SUMMARY

Readers are invited to join the detective work in three **mini mysteries**. A **poem** precedes the mysteries.

## COMPREHENSION STRATEGIES

Understanding Text Structure
Inferential Thinking

## WRITING

Story String

## VOCABULARY

Multiple Meanings

## PHONICS/WORD STUDY

Long *a* Patterns Review

### Lesson Vocabulary

| | |
|---|---|
| theft | cooped up |
| ransom | outrageous |
| ridiculous | disgusted |
| ushered | |

## MATERIALS

*Mystery,* pp. 24–31
*Student Journal,* pp. 17–20
*Word Study Manual,* p. 39
*Writing Advantage,* pp. 56–92

## Bermuda Triangle Mystery

On the sea, under the stars,
beneath a tropical moon,
a ship sails out into the night
not to be seen again soon.

Scary tales are often told
of a place in the eastern sea.
Look at the shape on the map
as you listen closely to me.

Go west from the isle of San Juan,
to Florida's sandy shore.
Then up to sunny Bermuda,
and down to San Juan once more.

There the Triangle gets its name.
When ships and planes are lost,
they say the Triangle's to blame.
But no one knows the cause.

Some people say it's tropical storms
or the currents of the sea.
Some people say it's an unknown force
that no one can ever see.

So many ships and planes
have sunk to the ocean floor.
"Were the crews at fault?" the reader asks.
To answer we must know more.

24

# Before Reading

*WHOLE CLASS* Use one or more activities.

## Poem: Bermuda Triangle Mystery

Have students read the poem silently and then aloud with a partner. Have students discuss their interpretations.

## Make a Rating Chart

Discuss the special skills that the best detectives use to help them "crack" their cases. Display the rating chart as shown. Read through the list of skills. Then ask students to rank the skills on a scale of 1 to 5, 5 being the most important.

| Rating Chart | |
|---|---|
| **Skill** | **Rating** |
| reasoning ability | |
| logic | |
| intuition or instinct | |
| observation | |
| experience | |

## Vocabulary Preview

List and say the vocabulary words. Encourage volunteers to share their definitions of the words. Then explain that one way to think about words is to think about synonyms (words with similar meanings) and antonyms (opposites) for them. Model how to identify synonyms and antonyms for the vocabulary word *ridiculous* to help students complete the synonym and antonym chart on *Student Journal* page 17.

# Here are three Mini Mysteries for you to solve!

**25**

## DIFFERENTIATED INSTRUCTION

SMALL GROUP

### Make Predictions/ Set Purpose

Help students become "reading-purpose-setters."

1. Emphasize that having a purpose for reading gives the reader focus.

2. A reader's purpose is often based on personal interest. Suggest that students browse the text to look for headings, pictures, and special features that grab their attention. Explain that curiosity about these can help set a purpose.

3. As students browse through a selection, suggest that they talk with a partner to spark ideas and raise questions.

### Student Journal page 17

Name _____ Date _____

**Building Vocabulary: Synonym and Antonym Chart**

Read each vocabulary word. Think of three other words that are synonyms (similar in meaning) for it. Then think of three words that are antonyms (opposites) for the word. Use a thesaurus to help you.

| Vocabulary Word | Synonyms | Antonyms |
|---|---|---|
| theft | 1. robbery | 1. donation |
|  | 2. | 2. |
|  | 3. | 3. |
| outrageous | 1. | 1. |
|  | 2. | 2. |
|  | 3. | 3. |
| disgusted | 1. | 1. |
|  | 2. | 2. |
|  | 3. | 3. |

Mystery • Three Mini Mysteries

17

## Preview the Selection

Have students look through the three mini mysteries. Use these prompts to prime students for reading the stories.

• What do you think the author's purpose is?

• What do you notice about the text that gives the solutions? Why does it appear as it does?

• Do you think the three texts are fiction or nonfiction? Why?

## Teacher Think Aloud

*The text on page 25 says, "Here are three mini mysteries for you to solve!" I like mystery stories. I know it's important to notice the details in a mystery, so I'll try to remember what I read!*

## Make Predictions/ Set Purpose

Students should use the information they gathered in previewing the selection to make some predictions about the mysteries. If students have trouble generating a purpose for reading, suggest that they read to see if they can solve each of the mysteries. (See Differentiated Instruction.)

## Comprehension

UNDERSTANDING TEXT STRUCTURE

To help students understand the text structure of "Framed!" ask the following questions:

- Where does the mystery take place?
- What is the problem in the story?
- What clues does the author present when the suspects are gathered together?
- How is the mystery solved?

**Mini Mystery**

# THE BICYCLE MYSTERY

I love Sundays. That's the day I hang out with my best friend, Carla. Yesterday was a great day. It was the first weekend that it hadn't rained. The sun was shining, and the air was warm. Carla and I decided to ride our bikes on the trail in the park. It was the first time Carla was riding her brand-new ten-speed bike.

"Hey, Jenn," Carla called to me. "Let's race to the top of the hill. The loser buys the lemonade at the stand."

"You're on!" I told her. "Ready, set, go!" We took off. I got an early lead. But Carla caught up to me as we reached the top of the hill. She beat me by a foot.

"Okay," I said, catching my breath. "You win. Two cold lemonades coming up."

We put our bikes in the bike rack behind the stand. Then we walked to the front window. Carla sat at a picnic table. I ordered the lemonade—both with extra ice.

We sat in the warm sun. We sipped our drinks slowly and talked for a while. "I'm ready to ride again," Carla said.

We threw away our cups. Then we went behind the stand to get our bikes.

26

# During Reading

## Comprehension

UNDERSTANDING TEXT STRUCTURE

Using "The Bicycle Mystery" and these questions, model for students how to understand the structure of a mystery story. Then have students identify and describe the story elements in "Framed!"

- Who are the characters?
- What are the events of the mystery?
- How is the mystery solved?

(See Differentiated Instruction.)

## Teacher Think Aloud

*I read "The Bicycle Mystery" twice— once for fun, and once to look at the way the story was structured. I see that the author uses a setup to introduce the mystery: Carla and Jenn go for a bike ride, and when they stop for lemonade, Carla's bike is stolen. Jenn's search leads her to a freckle- faced boy. She questions him and gets clues. The mystery is solved when Jenn figures out that the boy is lying.*

## Comprehension

INFERENTIAL THINKING

Use these questions to model how to make inferences from "The Bicycle Mystery." Then have students reveal inferences they make as they read another mini mystery.

- What do I know about the weather?
- From my own experience, what do I know about warm days?
- Using what I know, what can I infer that the author has not stated?

Suddenly, Carla stopped short. Only one bike was in the rack. Mine.

"My new bike! It's gone!" Carla cried. "Someone stole my new bike!"

I looked around. But I didn't see anyone riding a bike.

"Now what?" Carla asked.

"Take it easy," I said. "Don't worry. Whoever took your bike must still be in the park. The road in front of the lemonade stand is the only way out. No one rode past while we were sitting there."

I told Carla to see if she could find a park ranger or police officer. Then I hopped on my bike to search the park. I checked the trail by the lake first. I rode for close to a mile without seeing anyone. Soon I arrived at the beach. A freckle-faced boy was sitting on the ground. A shiny bike lay beside him.

I pedaled toward him. At first, he didn't seem to notice me. He was putting sunblock on his nose. Then he looked up and saw me. He quickly looked down and took a big sip of lemonade.

"That's a nice bike you have," I said.

"Um, thanks," he mumbled without looking up.

"Something is strange, though," I went on. "Do you always ride a girl's bike?"

"I do when I borrow it from my sister," he answered. He quickly finished his lemonade. The ice rattled in his cup.

"My friend and I are looking for a bike that looks a lot like yours," I said. "You haven't seen anybody ride by here, have you?"

He thought hard for a moment. "Nope," he said. "I've been here for over two hours. I haven't seen a single person go by."

At that moment, I saw a beach buggy coming across the sand. Carla was sitting in the seat next to a police officer.

"You've got about ten seconds to change your story," I told the boy. "If you don't, you'll be arrested for <u>theft</u>. You stole my friend's bike."

"You think I *stole* this bike?" the boy asked.

"I don't just *think* you did. I'm *sure* you did. In fact, you just proved it yourself."

*How did Jenn know the boy was lying? What did he say that gave him away?*

*Turn the page upside down for the answer.*

The freckle-faced boy had ice rattling in his cup of lemonade. If the boy had really been at the beach for two hours, the ice in his cup would have melted in the warm sun. Clearly, he was lying about when he arrived and about the bike.

27

---

## Fix-Up Strategies

Offer these strategies to help students read independently.

**If you don't understand what you're reading:**

- Reread the difficult section to look for clues to help you comprehend.

- Read ahead to find clues to help you comprehend.

- Retell, or say in your own words, what you've read.

- Visualize, or form mental pictures of, what you've read.

**If you don't understand a word:**

- Reread the sentence. Look for ideas and words that provide meaning clues.

- Find clues by reading a few sentences before and after the confusing word.

- Look for the base or root word and think about its meaning.

- Think about the topic or plot at this point to see if either offers meaning clues.

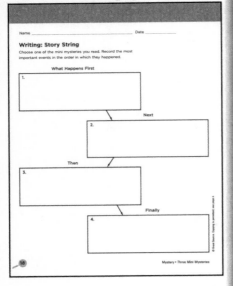

Mini Mystery

## WHO TOOK SPARKY?

Mrs. Fussbudget tiptoed upstairs to kiss her dog Sparky goodnight. "Goodness!" she exclaimed. "The door is locked! How did that happen?" She jiggled the door a few times. Then she peeked through the keyhole. Sparky looked afraid. He was watching a stranger write a note. Mrs. Fussbudget couldn't tell who the stranger was from the back.

"Oh, dear! I'm going to faint," Mrs. Fussbudget said. True to her word, she did. When she awoke, the butler was beside her.

"Oh, Hanson!" Mrs. Fussbudget gasped. "Break down the door! We must rescue Sparky!" With one swift kick, Hanson broke through the door, but it was too late. The room was empty.

"Oh, no! My baby's been dognapped!" cried Mrs. Fussbudget. "Quick! Call the police!"

In less than ten minutes, Detective Shirley Holmes was on the scene. Mrs. Fussbudget told her exactly what she had seen through

28

# After Reading
**WHOLE CLASS** Use one or more activities.

## Check Purpose

Have students decide if their purpose was met. Were they able to solve the mini mysteries?

## Discussion Questions

Continue the group discussion with the following questions.

1. Do any of the mysteries remind you of other stories you have read? In what way? (Making Connections)

2. How did the picture of what Mrs. Fussbudget saw through the keyhole help you identify the dognapper? (Inferential Thinking)

3. What caused Casey to be suspicious of Ms. Demeanor? (Cause-Effect)

## Revisit: Rating Chart

Look back at the rating chart started in Before Reading. Ask students if any of them have changed their minds about their ratings of the skills. Encourage them to explain why. Are there different skills students would like to add?

the keyhole. Then she showed the detective the ransom note from the dognapper.

"Aha," said Detective Holmes. "Whoever wrote this note knows your dog's name. The dognapper must be someone very close to you. Maybe even someone in this house."

"That's ridiculous," snapped Mrs. Fussbudget. "Everyone who lives here loves Sparky."

"No, that's not the case," said Detective Holmes. "Everyone here does *not* love Sparky. Now, please tell me who lives in this house."

"Well, there's my butler, Hanson. There's my cook, Ima Stuft. And there's my gardener, Noah Weeds."

Detective Holmes called the three suspects together. She asked each one of them to write something. Then the detective examined the handwriting samples carefully. Not one sample matched the dognapper's note.

"I knew it!" said Mrs. Fussbudget. "No one here would take Sparky."

"Not so fast, Sherlock!" the detective said with a smile. "I'm afraid you're wrong. The dognapper is in this room."

"But, what about the handwriting?" Mrs. Fussbudget asked.

"My name isn't Holmes for nothing," said the detective. "It's not the handwriting that gave the guilty person away. It's the hand that did the writing!"

**Who stole Sparky? What gave the dognapper away?**

*Turn the page upside down for the answer.*

*The dognapper is Hanson, the left-handed butler.*

29

*Turn the page upside down for the answer.*

---

## Writing Story String

**DIFFERENTIATED INSTRUCTION**
## Writing Story String

Help students complete the story string chart as a group.

1. Have students open to *Student Journal* page 18. Give them a few minutes to read the directions and preview the chart. Then call on students to explain how they would respond to the activity.

2. Choose one of the mini mysteries. Ask volunteers to identify key story events in the correct sequence.

3. Display students' responses. Review the list, asking students to agree on which events are the most important, and to finalize the correct sequence.

**Student Journal page 20**

Name _____ Date _____

**Building Vocabulary: Words with Multiple Meanings**
Write two definitions for each word below.

| Word | First Definition | Second Definition |
|------|------------------|-------------------|
| framed | made to look guilty through false evidence | put into a border |
| hang | | |
| trail | | |
| race | | |
| stand | | |

20

Mystery • Three Mini Mysteries

---

## Writing Story String

Have students select one of the mini mysteries. Then have partners retell to each other the sequence of important events in the story. Students can then write about the sequence of important events in the story string chart on *Student Journal* page 18. Then have students try writing their own mini mystery on *Student Journal* page 19. (See Differentiated Instruction.)

## Vocabulary Multiple Meanings

Write *framed* on the board. Have students recall the mini mystery "Framed!" Ask: *What does it mean to be framed?* Remind students that *framed* is used in the story to mean "made to look guilty through false evidence." Ask them to think of another meaning for *framed*. (set into a border) Have partners complete multiple meanings chart on *Student Journal* page 20.

## Phonics/Word Study

### Long *a* Patterns Review

Have students brainstorm words with the long *a* sound. (*cape, break, flake, train*) As they say the words, write them on the board. Ask: *How can we categorize these long a patterns?* Have students note the different spelling patterns of the words on the board. Work together to group the words according to their patterns. Now, work with students to complete the in-depth long *a* activity on TE page 46.

# Mini Mystery

# 3 FRAMED!

Juan and I were in the art museum looking for information for our school report. We were in a room filled with paintings. We had just finished taking our notes. Suddenly, a museum guard rushed into the room.

"Freeze!" the guard shouted. "There has been a robbery. No one can leave the museum. Everyone come with me."

The guard <u>ushered</u> everyone into the room across the hall. A police officer was already standing in the room.

"Casey, I hope this doesn't take very long," Juan whispered to me. "It's too nice outside to stay <u>cooped up</u> in a museum."

"I know what you mean," I whispered back. "Still, a robbery is kind of exciting. Maybe we can help catch the thief."

"Ladies and gentlemen," the police officer spoke up. "May I have your attention." He pointed to an empty frame on the wall. "A great work of art has been stolen. It was cut right out of this frame."

"I closed the doors the second I saw that empty frame," the museum guard said.

Juan leaned over to me. "Then, the thief is still in this room," he said softly.

30

"Come, come now. You can't think that one of us is the thief," said a male voice. "My name is Mr. Green, and I work on this block. I come here every Saturday on my lunch hour."

"You can't believe that I took it, either," said a young woman. She introduced herself as Ms. Wright. "I'm a museum member."

"Accusing one of us is <u>outrageous</u>!" said an angry woman. She pointed her umbrella at the police officer. "My name is Ms. Demeanor. I won't stand for this!"

"Tell us something about the missing art work," I said to the guard.

Juan looked <u>disgusted</u>. "This is no time for an art lesson, Casey. I want to get out of here."

"It's a city scene," the museum guard explained. "It's not too large, about two feet wide and one foot tall. Maybe the thief rolled up the painting and hid it somewhere on his or her person."

Now Ms. Demeanor pointed her umbrella at us. "I think these kids must have taken it. What are they doing in a museum, anyway?" she asked loudly.

"Duh," I said, looking at the woman. "We came to look at art, just like you did."

"And we want to get out of here as much as you do," Juan told her. "It's such a nice day."

"It is, isn't it?" I said, getting excited. "Now I know who took the painting."

I turned to the woman who was giving us a hard time. "You tried to frame us! You said we took the painting. But you're wrong. You are the real thief!"

"What are you saying?" the woman asked angrily.

"I'm saying that I know where the painting is!"

***How does Casey know? The answer is right before your eyes. Here are three clues:***

1. The painting is in the room.
2. The painting is close at *hand*.
3. It is a nice day outside.

*Turn the page upside down for the answer.* ◆

The angry woman is carrying an umbrella on a nice day. This makes it possible for her to have rolled up the painting inside the umbrella.

## Long *a* Patterns Review

► Try a review of long *a* vowel patterns. Write the following headings on the board or on a chart for students.

► Brainstorm together one word for each heading. Write the words on the board.

► Ask students what they notice about all the vowel sounds. (They're all long *a*.)

► Now have students complete the sort on *Word Study Manual* page 39. Point out that there is one oddball (*streak*).

► Check the final sorts.

### Long *a*: Review

| ai | ay | aCe | ey | ei | ea | r-controlled |
|-------|-------|-------|----|-------|-------|--------------|
| rain | bray | trace | | weigh | break | |
| trail | way | brake | | eight | steak | |
| main | hay | blame | | | | |
| plain | lay | grate | | | | |
| pain | stray | chase | | | | |
| gain | play | flake | | | | |
| train | pray | flame | | | | |
| strain | | plane | | | | |

For more information on word sorts and spelling stages, see pages 5–31 in the *Word Study Manual*.

# Focus on . . .

Use one or more activities in this section to focus on a particular area of need in your students.

## Comprehension  STRATEGY SUPPORT  INDEPENDENT

To help those students who need more practice using the strategies covered in this lesson, work one-on-one or in small groups to apply the strategy prompts below. Apply the prompts to a *Reading Advantage* paperback, a classroom library book, or a new or familiar selection in the magazine. Always model your own thinking first.

### Understanding Text Structure

• What kind of text is this? (book, story, article, guidebook, play, manual)

• How does the author organize the text? (cause-effect, problem-solution, chronological order, description, question-answer, comparison-contrast)

• What details support my thoughts about the text structure?

• What is the cause (effect, problem, solution, order, question, answer)?

• If fiction, who are the characters? What is the setting, plot, conflict, and resolution?

### Inferential Thinking

• What are the causes or effects of this event?

• What do I learn from the character or person's thoughts, words, or actions?

• What do I know (or infer) from the text that the author hasn't stated directly?

• What conclusions can I draw?

## Writing News Story  INDEPENDENT

Have students use the mini mystery "Framed!" to write a news story account about the attempted theft of the museum painting. Remind students that a good news story includes answers to the 5Ws—*who, what, where, when,* and *why*. You may want to have students use the 5Ws Chart BLM found on TE page 387. Tell students to try to think of an attention-getting headline to draw interest to their news story.

To help students edit their writing, see the editing lessons in *Writing Advantage*, pages 56–92.

## Fluency: Pacing

Have students listen as you model how to read the poem "Bermuda Triangle Mystery" at a smooth and even pace. Point out that reading too quickly or too slowly, or in a stumbling way, makes it difficult for listeners to understand the content. Then have partners take turns reading aloud to each other, following your model.

As you listen to students read, use these prompts to guide them.

▶ Notice how the line breaks and the punctuation in the poem help you read at an even pace. They signal where to pause slightly.

▶ Keep your eyes on the text as you read so you don't lose your place and either miss words or repeat them.

▶ Think about the message of the poem and its tone. Use your voice to create interest and hold attention.

When students read aloud, do they—

✓ demonstrate a smooth pace, not too fast or too slow?

✓ incorporate well-timed pauses between words and phrases?

✓ reflect an awareness and understanding of punctuation?

## English Language Learners

To support students' phonemic awareness, practice identifying rhyming words in "Bermuda Triangle Mystery" on page 24.

1. Remind students that rhyming words have the same ending sound.

2. Have students listen for rhyming words as you read the poem. Have partners identify rhyming words.

3. Say several pairs of words. Instruct students to show a thumbs-up sign if the words rhyme or a thumbs-down sign if they don't.

## Independent Activity Options

While you work with individuals or small groups, others can work independently on one or more of the following options.

▶ Level A paperback books, see TE pages 371–376

▶ Level A *eZines*

▶ Repeat word sorts from this lesson

▶ *Student Journal* pages for this lesson

▶ *Writing Advantage* independent lessons

# Assessment

## Strategy Assessment

To help you and your students assess their use of comprehension strategies, ask the following questions. Students can provide a written response or verbal answers in a one-on-one reading conference.

1. **Understanding Text Structure** How was the structure of each of the mysteries the same? (All three stories began by setting up the crime. Then, the details of the story gave clues about the suspects, through the setting and the suspects' words and actions. Finally, one of those clues gave away the guilty person, and the crime was solved.)

2. **Inferential Thinking** How did the information in the text and your prior knowledge help you figure out one of the mysteries? (Answers will vary. Possible response: In "Framed!" I wondered why Ms. Demeanor had an umbrella, and why she kept trying to blame the boys. I know that guilty people often try to blame others. I also knew that a rolled-up painting might fit in an umbrella. So I guessed that she was the person who stole the painting.)

See *Level A Assessment* page 10 for formal assessment to go with *Mystery*.

## Word Study Assessment

Use these steps to help you and your students assess their understanding of long *a* patterns.

1. Create a chart like the one shown, but don't include the answers. Display the following words: *play, scar, blame, veil, mail, vain, break weight, hey, bear.*

2. Have students read the words and sort them into the correct columns.

| ai | ay | aCe | ey | ei | ea | r-controlled |
|----|----|-----|----|----|----|--------------|
| mail | play | blame | hey | veil | break | scar |
| vain | | | | weight | | bear |

# LESSON 7
# The Red-Headed Club
*Mystery*, pages 32–37

## SUMMARY
This **play** tells about how Sherlock Holmes solves the mystery of the Red-Headed Club.

## COMPREHENSION STRATEGIES
Understanding Text Structure
Determining Importance

## WRITING
Notes for Visualizing

## VOCABULARY
Multiple Meanings

## PHONICS/WORD STUDY
Long and Short *a* Homophones

### Lesson Vocabulary
alias            elementary

## MATERIALS
*Mystery*, pp. 32–37
*Student Journal*, pp. 21–23
*Word Study Manual*, p. 40
*Writing Advantage*, pp. 56–92

*The job sounded strange. The mystery that followed was even stranger.*

# Before Reading
WHOLE CLASS  Use one or more activities.

## Make a List

Make a class list of the parts of a play. Help students identify the parts: title, characters, dialogue, scenes, stage directions, epilogue, and narrator. If necessary, explain that stage directions are instructions for directing the movements of the actors or for the arrangement of the scenery, an epilogue is a closing section added to a play, and a narrator provides background and commentary on the play for the audience.

| Parts of a Play | |
|---|---|
| title | scenes |
| characters | epilogue |
| narrator | stage directions |
| dialogue | |

## Vocabulary Preview

List and say the vocabulary words. Ask: *How have you heard these words used? What do the words make you think about?* Model making associations with the word *compliment* to help students complete the making associations activity on *Student Journal* page 21.

# The Red-Headed Club

## Based on a Sherlock Holmes story by Sir Arthur Conan Doyle

### About the Play

This play is about one of the greatest
detectives of all time—Sherlock Holmes.
He was not a real detective. He was created
by the English writer Sir Arthur Conan Doyle.
Doyle wrote many Sherlock Holmes stories.
The stories take place in England around 1890.
This play is based on one of the stories.

### Characters

**Narrator**

**Sherlock Holmes,**
*detective*

**Billings,**
*the owner of a small shop*

**Dr. Watson,**
*Holmes's friend*

**Spaulding,**
*Billings's assistant, also
known as Clay*

**Duncan Ross,**
*the manager of the
Red-Headed Club*

**Mr. Merryweather,**
*the director of the
London Bank*

**Mr. Jones,**
*an inspector from
Scotland Yard*

**33**

## DIFFERENTIATED INSTRUCTION
### Preview the Selection

To enhance the preview, use the
steps below:

1. Ask students what they know
   about Sherlock Holmes.
2. Read "About the Play" on page
   33, which lets students know
   that they are about to read a
   play about Sherlock Holmes.
3. Have students look through
   the selection and identify play
   elements. If necessary, draw
   attention to the title and list
   of characters, the numbered
   scenes, and the epilogue. Point
   out that the words in italics
   and within parentheses are the
   stage directions.

### Student Journal page 21

Name _____ Date _____

**Building Vocabulary: Making Associations**
Think about what you already know about the vocabulary words
*alias* and *elementary*. Then answer the following questions for
each word.

Word _____ **alias** _____

What do you think about when you read this word? _____

Who might use this word? _____

What do you already know about this word? _____

Word _____ **elementary** _____

What do you think about when you read this word? _____

Who might use this word? _____

What do you already know about this word? _____

Now watch for these words in the magazine selection. Were you on the right track?

Mystery • The Red-Headed Club                    21

### Preview the Selection

Have students look through the six
pages of the selection play. Ask:

• What details tell you this is a play?

• What do you know about plays?

• What do the illustrations tell you?

• What do you think it will be about?

Have students offer traits they think
make a top-notch detective. After
reading, they can see how Sherlock
Holmes measures up. (See Differentiated
Instruction.)

### Teacher Think Aloud

*I can tell right away that this
selection is going to be a play. I
see a list of characters and several
scenes. The subtitle says it's based on
a Sherlock Holmes story. I know that
Sherlock Holmes is a famous detective
character, but I don't much about
him. Maybe I'll learn something new.*

### Make Predictions/ Set Purpose

Students should use the information
they gathered in previewing the
selection to make some predictions
about the play. If students have trouble
generating a purpose for reading,
suggest that they read to learn about
the Red-Headed Club and what mystery
Sherlock Holmes will need to solve.

## Comprehension

UNDERSTANDING TEXT STRUCTURE

To help students understand the text structure of scene 2, ask the following questions:

- What is the setting of scene 2?
- Who speaks in scene 2?
- What happens in scene 2? How do you know?

*Holmes has just let in a man with bright red hair.*

### ꙮ SCENE 1 ꙮ

*(The scene takes place in Sherlock Holmes's study. There is a desk, a chair, and bookshelves. There are also two other chairs in the office. The narrator is onstage but off to the side throughout the scene.)*

**Narrator:** It is 1890. Dr. Watson is visiting his good friend, Sherlock Holmes. Holmes has just let in a man with bright red hair.

**Holmes:** Sit down, Mr. Billings. Please make yourself comfortable. *(Billings sits. He is holding a page from a newspaper.)*

**Billings:** Well, as I told you on the telephone, I have a small shop at Coburg Square. I don't make very much money. I have an assistant. His name is Spaulding. But I can pay him only a very small salary.

**Holmes:** Does he do his work well?

**Billings:** Oh, yes. There is just one problem with Spaulding. He is always going down in the cellar. He develops photographs there.

**Holmes:** I see. Go on, Mr. Billings.

**Billings:** About two months ago, Spaulding showed me this newspaper ad. *(reading aloud the ad)* "Join the Red-Headed Club. Earn four pounds a week...."

**Watson:** *(interrupting)* The Red-Headed Club— what's that?

**Billings:** That's what I wondered. Spaulding explained. He said that the club was started by a red-headed millionaire. The man left his fortune to help red-headed men.

**Narrator:** Holmes and Watson look at each other, surprised.

**Billings:** I know it sounds strange. But I needed the money. So I asked Spaulding to take me to the Red-Headed Club. *(He pauses, remembering.)*

### ꙮ SCENE 2 ꙮ

**Narrator:** The scene is the office of the Red-Headed Club. The time is two months earlier. A man with red hair is sitting at a desk. He is Duncan Ross, the manager of the club.

**Spaulding:** *(to Ross)* This is Mr. Billings. He's my boss. He wants to join the club.

 34

---

# During Reading

## Comprehension

UNDERSTANDING TEXT STRUCTURE

Use these questions to model how to understand the styles of text scene 1. Then have students identify and describe the play elements in scenes 2–4.

- What do all the different kinds of text styles mean?
- Who are the characters? What are their relationships to one another?
- How has the plot developed so far?

(See Differentiated Instruction.)

## Teacher Think Aloud

*I see different styles of type: regular, boldface, and italic. The first text is in italics. It tells me the setting of the story. I also see stage directions in italics. These help me visualize the scene as if it were on a stage. The boldface text shows me the name of the person speaking, and the regular type is what the characters say.*

## Comprehension

DETERMINING IMPORTANCE

Use these questions to model for students how to determine the importance of ideas in scene 3. Then have students determine the importance of ideas as they read scene 4.

- What are the most important details in the scene?
- How can I support my beliefs?

(See Differentiated Instruction.)

**Ross:** His red hair is perfect. *(He pulls Billings's hair.)*

**Billings:** Ouch!

**Ross:** That's good. People wearing wigs have tricked us before. You are just right for the job. When can you start?

**Billings:** What are the hours?

**Ross:** Ten in the morning until two in the afternoon. You are to copy the encyclopedia. But you must stay in this office the whole time. If you leave, you lose the job. I will pay you very well. Can you start today?

**Billings:** Certainly.

**Ross:** Congratulations! You are lucky to be a member of the Red-Headed Club.

## ❧ SCENE 3 ❧

**Narrator:** We are back in the present in Holmes's study. Billings has just finished telling Holmes and Watson his story.

**Billings:** I thought it strange that anyone would pay me so much money to copy the whole encyclopedia. But I took the job. The money was good. It was easy to pay Spaulding to mind the shop while I was away.

**Holmes:** Was Mr. Ross always there with you?

**Billings:** No. But I never left the office. He could have come in at any time.

**Watson:** How long did this go on?

**Billings:** It went on for eight weeks. This morning the office was locked. A sign on the door said, "The Red-Headed Club Is Closed." I thought something was strange about this. That's why I called you for help.

**Holmes:** Tell me more about Spaulding. What does he look like?

**Billings:** He is short and stocky. He is in his thirties. He has a scar on his forehead.

**Holmes:** I thought so! That's all I need to know for now, Mr. Billings. I'll give you an opinion soon.

**Billings:** *(shaking both men's hands)* Thank you. *(He leaves.)*

*He has a scar on his forehead.*

**35**

## DIFFERENTIATED INSTRUCTION   SMALL GROUP

### Comprehension
#### DETERMINING IMPORTANCE

To help students determine the importance of details in scene 4, ask the following questions:

- What are the most important details in the scene?

- Why do you think so? How do these details affect the story?

# Teacher Think Aloud

*I think it's strange that the office was closed today. I think that's an important detail, because it prompted Billings to talk to a detective. I also think it's important that Spaulding is short and stocky and has a scar. Holmes recognizes these traits. I don't know who Holmes thinks Spaulding is, but I have a feeling he has an important role in this mystery.*

## Fix-Up Strategies

Offer these strategies to help students read independently.

### If you don't understand what you're reading:

- Reread the difficult section to look for clues to help you comprehend.

- Read ahead to find clues to help you comprehend.

- Retell, or say in your own words, what you've read.

- Visualize, or form mental pictures of, what you've read.

### If you don't understand a word:

- Reread the sentence. Look for ideas and words that provide meaning clues.

- Find clues by reading a few sentences before and after the confusing word.

- Look for the base or root word and think about its meaning.

- Think about the topic or plot at this point to see if either offers meaning clues.

*We're here to save you a lot of money—and to catch John Clay.*

**Narrator:** Holmes and Watson go to Coburg Square. They pay a visit to Billings's shop to meet the assistant, Spaulding. When they leave, Holmes tells Watson the real reason for visiting Spaulding. That reason was to see the knees of Spaulding's pants. Holmes also tells Watson that Spaulding is an alias. His real name is John Clay. Then Holmes looks at the building next to Billings's shop. It is the London Bank. He is quiet for a moment. Then he speaks to Watson, "A serious crime is being planned. But I think we can stop it. Meet me here at ten o'clock tonight. Bring your pistol!"

### ◄◎ SCENE 4 ◎►

*(The scene is in the cellar of the London Bank. There are boxes all around.)*

**Narrator:** It is 10:00 P.M. Holmes and Watson are with two men. They are Mr. Jones of Scotland Yard and Mr. Merryweather. He is the director of the London Bank.

**Merryweather:** Why are we here?

**Holmes:** We're here to save you a lot of money—and to catch John Clay. He plans to rob the London Bank.

**Jones:** That thief! I've been after him for years.

**Holmes:** I believe you will meet him tonight.

**Jones:** Do you think Clay is planning to break into the bank?

**Merryweather:** No one could break into the bank from above or under our feet. *(He taps the floor with his cane.)* Why, it sounds hollow in this spot!

**Watson:** Why might John Clay want to get into this cellar, Mr. Merryweather?

**Merryweather:** These boxes hold 30,000 pounds of gold.

**Holmes:** And tonight, two criminals will try to steal it. We must be very careful. They are dangerous. I will stand behind these boxes. *(He points to a dark corner where there is space behind a stack of boxes.)* The rest of you, hide over there. Jones, did you do as I asked?

**Jones:** Yes. I have two officers at the front door of Billings's shop.

**Holmes:** Good. That's the only way they could escape.

---

### Student Journal page 22

---

# After Reading  ⏣ WHOLE CLASS  Use one or more activities.

## Check Purpose

Have students decide if their purpose was met. Did they discover more about the Red-Headed Club? How did Sherlock Holmes measure up to the traits they thought make a top-notch detective?

## Discussion Questions

Continue the group discussion with the following questions.

1. Would you like to be a detective? Why or why not? (Making Connections)

2. What is the problem that Sherlock Holmes must solve? (Problem-Solution)

3. What inferences can you make about Billing's character? (Inferential Thinking)

## Revisit: List

Revisit the list the class made in Before Reading. Have students identify each of the play elements in this selection.

## ✿ EPILOGUE ✿

**Narrator:** Later that night, Holmes reviewed the case with Watson. This is what Holmes concluded:

- Clay and Ross needed time to dig the tunnel from Billings's shop to the bank. So they made up the job to get Billings out of the way. Clay thought up the Red-Headed Club because Ross and Billings both had red hair.

- Billings said that Spaulding spent time in the cellar. Spaulding's pants were worn out and dirty. The London Bank was next to Billings's shop. Holmes concluded that Spaulding must have been digging a tunnel.

- Why was Holmes so sure that they would break in this night? They closed the Red-Headed Club. That meant that they didn't care about Mr. Billings anymore. So Holmes figured that they had finished the tunnel. He also knew that they had to use it soon. The tunnel might be found.

Watson complimented Holmes for solving the case. Holmes replied in his usual way. "It was elementary, my dear Watson. *Anyone* could have done it." ◆

**Narrator:** After a short while, a stone is pushed up out of the floor. Then another, and another. Two men climb up out of the hole in the floor. One is Ross. The other man is Clay—alias Spaulding.

**Clay:** *(whispering to Ross)* It's all clear.

**Narrator:** Holmes jumps out and grabs Clay. Ross jumps back down the hole.

**Jones:** Watch out! Clay has a gun!

**Narrator:** Holmes knocks the gun to the floor.

**Holmes:** Give up, John Clay. The officers at the door to the shop already have your pal.

**Clay:** You have thought of everything, Mr. Holmes. I must compliment you.

**Holmes:** And I compliment you. Your red-headed idea was very clever.

**Merryweather:** Mr. Holmes, how can the bank ever repay you?

**Holmes:** There is no need, Mr. Merryweather. This little adventure is payment enough! *(He tips his cap and shakes Merryweather's hand.)*

**Watson:** Quite, so, Holmes.
*(All exit the stage except the narrator.)*

*It was elementary, my dear Watson.*

**37**

## DIFFERENTIATED INSTRUCTION
### Vocabulary
## Multiple Meanings

Provide students with more experience identifying words with multiple meanings.

1. Draw attention to the word *inspector* on page 33.

2. Ask: *How have you heard this word used?* (a person who inspects; a high-ranking police officer)

3. Then ask: *Which meaning of* inspector *is used in "The Red-Headed Club"?* (a high-ranking police officer) *How do you know?* (The full description of the character is "an inspector from Scotland Yard." Scotland Yard is the London police.)

### Student Journal page 23

Name _____ Date _____

**Building Vocabulary: Words with Multiple Meanings**
Write two definitions for each word below.

| Word | First Definition | Second Definition |
|------|-----------------|-------------------|
| elementary | basic | a kind of school |
| place | | |
| play | | |
| pounds | | |

Mystery • The Red-Headed Club

23

## Writing Notes for Visualizing

Remind students that active readers visualize, or try to "see" what an author tells about. Have students complete the visualizing activity on *Student Journal* page 22 to describe what they "saw" best in the play. Then have students draw what they "saw" to share with others.

## Vocabulary Multiple Meanings

Have partners work together to complete *Student Journal* page 23. If needed, first brainstorm with students words with possible multiple meanings. Students can also skim the play for other words with multiple meanings. Partners can work together and check meanings in a dictionary. (See Differentiated Instruction.)

## Phonics/Word Study
### Homophones

Write the following pairs of words on the board: *packed, pact; weigh, way.* Have students read the words aloud. Ask: *What do the words in each pair have in common?* (They sound the same.) Point out that words that sound the same but have different spellings are called homophones. Ask students to list other homophone pairs. Now, work with students to complete the in-depth homophones activity on TE page 54.

### Long and Short *a* Homophones

Write the following words on the board: *plane, plain; tacks, tax; made, maid;* and *what, watt.*

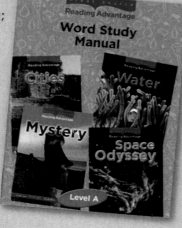

▶ Ask students if they can figure out what these pairs have in common. Students should be able to notice that the words in a pair sound the same but are spelled differently. Tell students that they've just defined a homophone.

▶ Using the list of long and short *a* homophones, play a game in which students have to turn over a homophone card worth a certain amount of points. (See *Word Study Manual* page 40.) Then they have to come up with the homophone, spell it, and define it.

▶ Have students create a section in their Word Study notebook and add any homophones that are generated.

| | | | | |
|------|-------|--------|--------|------|
| arc | ark | pear | pair | pare |
| flare | flair | chance | chants | |
| phase | faze | lamb | lam | |
| naval | navel | chased | chaste | |
| banned | band | vane | vein | |

For more information on word sorts and spelling stages, see pages 5–31 in the *Word Study Manual*.

# Focus on . . .

Use one or more activities in this section to focus on a particular area of need in your students.

## Comprehension  STRATEGY SUPPORT  *INDEPENDENT*

To help those students who need more practice using the strategies covered in this lesson, work one-on-one or in small groups to apply the strategy prompts below. Apply the prompts to a *Reading Advantage* paperback, a classroom library book, or a new or familiar selection in the magazine. Always model your own thinking first.

### Understanding Text Structure

• What kind of text is this? (book, story, article, guidebook, play, manual)

• How does the author organize the text? (cause-effect, problem-solution, chronological order, description, question-answer, comparison-contrast)

• What details support my thoughts about the text structure?

• What is the cause (effect, problem, solution, order, question, answer)?

• If fiction, who are the characters? What is the setting, plot, conflict, and resolution?

### Determining Importance

• What is the most important idea in the paragraph? How can I prove it?

• Which details are unimportant? Why?

• What does the author want me to understand?

• Why is this information important (or not) to me?

## Writing Inference Chart  *INDEPENDENT*

Brainstorm a list of clues from the play. Then have students tell the inferences that Holmes made from these clues.

**Clue:** Billings had to work from ten in the morning until two in the afternoon.

**Holmes's Inference:** Clay wanted Billings to be out of the way when he dug the tunnel.

Explain that Holmes's inferences are usually accurate, but our inferences aren't always. Use an example: *Once I found cupcakes in the kitchen. I inferred that my mom bought them for us, so I ate one. But my mom bought them for an office party. My inference was inaccurate.* Have students write about a time they made an incorrect inference. Suggest they use a format like the one above to organize their thoughts.

To help students strengthen their writing, see the lessons in *Writing Advantage*, pages 30–55.

## Fluency: Expression

After students have read the play at least once, have small groups read aloud or perform the play.

Ask students if they have ever felt like Mr. Billings—troubled about something mysterious going on—or like Sherlock Holmes—eager to help someone who's upset. *How did you sound when you were worried? How did you sound when you were helpful?* Tell students that they can use what they know about mood and voice intonation to help them speak in the role of a character. Model the difference between reading in character and out of character. Students may need to reread their lines several times before they are comfortable with them.

When students read aloud, do they—

✓ reflect an understanding of the text?

✓ demonstrate appropriate timing, stress, and intonation?

✓ incorporate appropriate speed and phrasing?

## English Language Learners

To support students as they learn about text structure, extend the text structure activity on TE page 50.

1. Have students turn to page 34 in the magazine. Have them discuss what they notice on the page with a partner.

2. Explain what a play is and what the different text styles mean.

3. Have students discuss with a partner what the setting is and who the characters are in each scene.

## Independent Activity Options

While you work with individuals or small groups, others can work independently on one or more of the following options.

▶ Level A paperback books, see TE pages 371–376

▶ Level A *eZines*

▶ Repeat word sorts from this lesson

▶ *Student Journal* pages for this lesson

▶ *Writing Advantage* independent lessons

# Assessment

## Strategy Assessment

To help you and your students assess their use of comprehension strategies, ask the following questions. Students can complete a written response or provide verbal answers in a one-on-one reading conference.

1. **Understanding Text Structure** Try retelling the plot in your own words. (Answers will vary.)

2. **Determining Importance** What details did you find most important? Why? (Answers will vary. Possible responses may include that the fake club was most important, since that was the scam that allowed the crime to be planned.)

For ongoing informal assessment, use the checklists on pages 61–64 of *Level A Assessment*.

## Word Study Assessment

Use these steps to help you and your students assess their understanding of long and short *a* homophones.

1. Create a chart like the one shown, but only include the words in the first column.

2. Have students read the words in the first column of the chart.

3. For each word, have students write a homophone and define each one. Answers are shown.

| Word | Homophone |
|------|-----------|
| stare | stair |
| main | mane |
| wrapped | rapt, rapped |
| raze | raise |
| lax | lacks |

Great Source
Reading Advantage

Level A
Assessment

## LESSON 8
# It's a Mystery and Detectives . . .
*Mystery*, pages 38–43

### SUMMARY
The **article** describes how science helps solve mysteries. It is preceded by a **riddle**.

### COMPREHENSION STRATEGIES
Making Connections
Monitor Understanding

### WRITING
One-Minute Mystery

### VOCABULARY
Multiple Meanings

### PHONICS/WORD STUDY
Contractions

**Lesson Vocabulary**

| | |
|---|---|
| forensic | splattered |
| impressions | victim |
| foil | suspect |

### MATERIALS
*Mystery*, pp. 38–43
*Student Journal*, pp. 24–26
*Word Study Manual*, p. 41
*Writing Advantage*, pp. 93–112

Little Nancy Etticoat with a White Petticoat and a Red Nose She has no feet or Hands the Longer She Stands the Shorter she Grows What is she?

Answer: a candle

38

# Before Reading
*Use one or more activities.*

## Poem: It's a Mystery
Explain that the riddle is very old. Ask a volunteer to read it. Challenge students to solve the riddle by identifying clues. If students do not arrive at the solution (candle), think aloud a few steps and invite students to participate.

## Make a Details Web
Develop a web of things someone might encounter at a crime scene—different kinds of evidence. As volunteers offer responses, add them to the web.

Important things to notice at crime scene

set of footprints

## Vocabulary Preview
Review the vocabulary list with students. Clarify pronunciations. Have students discuss how they think the vocabulary words will be used. Students should record their responses in the prediction column on *Student Journal* page 24. Students will complete the chart after they have finished the article. Model the process of predicting with the word *forensic*.

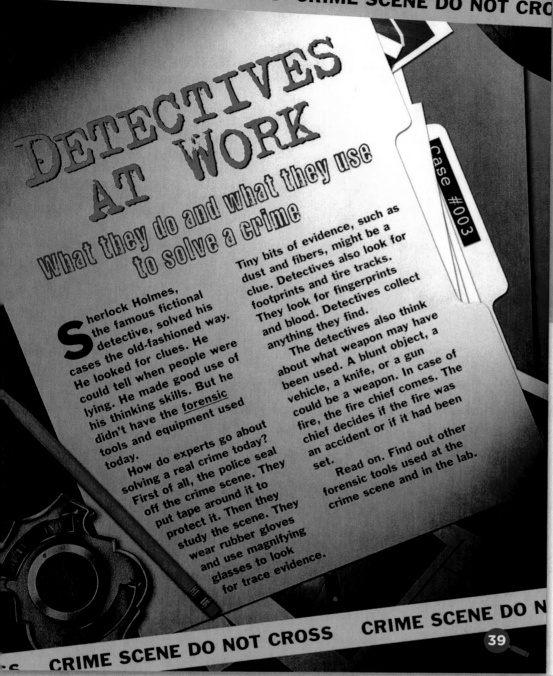

# DETECTIVES AT WORK

### What they do and what they use to solve a crime

**S**herlock Holmes, the famous fictional detective, solved his cases the old-fashioned way. He looked for clues. He could tell when people were lying. He made good use of his thinking skills. But he didn't have the <u>forensic</u> tools and equipment used today.

How do experts go about solving a real crime today? First of all, the police seal off the crime scene. They put tape around it to protect it. Then they study the scene. They wear rubber gloves and use magnifying glasses to look for trace evidence.

Tiny bits of evidence, such as dust and fibers, might be a clue. Detectives also look for footprints and tire tracks. They look for fingerprints and blood. Detectives collect anything they find.

The detectives also think about what weapon may have been used. A blunt object, a vehicle, a knife, or a gun could be a weapon. In case of fire, the fire chief comes. The chief decides if the fire was an accident or if it had been set.

Read on. Find out other forensic tools used at the crime scene and in the lab.

Case #003

CRIME SCENE DO NOT CROSS  CRIME SCENE DO NOT CRO

CRIME SCENE DO NOT CROSS  CRIME SCENE DO N

39

## DIFFERENTIATED INSTRUCTION

### Preview the Selection

**SMALL GROUP**

To enhance the preview, try the following steps:

1. Have students look at the photographs.
2. Tell students to notice what the photographs have in common.
3. Ask students what they think they will learn about in this article.
4. Make a list of students' responses.
5. Revisit the list after students finish the article to see if they learned what they thought they would.

### Student Journal page 24

Name _____  Date _____

**Building Vocabulary: Predictions**

How do you think these words will be used in "Detectives at Work"? Write your answers in the second column. Next, read the article. Then, clarify your answers in the third column.

| Word | My prediction for how the word will be used | How the word was actually used |
|------|---------------------------------------------|--------------------------------|
| forensic | | |
| impressions | | |
| foil | | |
| splattered | | |
| victim | | |
| suspect | | |

24  Mystery • Detectives at Work

## Preview the Selection

Have students look through the five pages of the article. Discuss students' reactions. Have students write a question on a self-stick note that they think will be answered in the article. As students read the article, they can check to see if their questions are answered. (See Differentiated Instruction.)

## Teacher Think Aloud

*When I look at the title page of this article, I see yellow tape. This is a familiar image to me—I've seen it on my favorite TV show about cops who solve murder cases. Looking at the photographs and subheadings, I can guess that this will be a nonfiction article about solving crimes.*

## Make Predictions/ Set Purpose

Students should use the information they gathered in previewing the selection to make some predictions about the article. If students have trouble generating a purpose for reading, suggest that they read to learn about the ways modern-day detectives solve crimes.

## Comprehension
MAKING CONNECTIONS

To help students make connections with the text, use the following prompts:

- Look at the photographs on page 40. What are these pictures of? Have you ever seen images like these in real life?

- How does your knowledge of tracks and fingerprints help you understand the way a detective gathers information about a crime?

# At the Scene of a Crime

## Make Impressions/ Take Pictures

Detectives take photos of tracks at a crime scene. Sometimes detectives make <u>impressions</u> of these tracks or footprints to study.

dog's footprint

man's boot

bicycle tread

truck tread

40

CRIME SCENE DO NOT CRO

# During Reading

## Comprehension
MAKING CONNECTIONS

Use these questions to model making connections with the text. Then have students make their own connections to the text.

- What sounds or looks familiar to me?

- Do I already know something about how detectives solve crimes?

- How does what I already know help me understand the text?

(See Differentiated Instruction.)

## Teacher Think Aloud
*On page 41, I read the section on fingerprinting. Once, my home was robbed, and the detectives who came brushed black powder all over the place. I wondered why they were doing that. Now, as I read, I see that this is a way that a detective can find fingerprints, which can identify a criminal.*

## Comprehension
MONITOR UNDERSTANDING

Use these questions to model how to monitor understanding by asking questions. Then have students ask their own questions and try to resolve any confusion.

- What is going on here?

- Why do detectives use the methods described in this article?

- What fix-up strategy can I use to fix my confusion?

## Check for Fingerprints

Just like on TV, the detectives at a crime scene dust for fingerprints. They do this because no two people have the same prints. If a person's fingerprint matches one at a crime scene, it is a good bet that that person will be questioned. Fingerprints differ. However, they do have one thing in common. They are all made up of lines that form patterns. And each type of pattern has a name.

Detectives have different ways of saving fingerprints. One way is to use powder. The powder sticks to the oil left by the print. Sometimes <u>foil</u> is pressed against the print. The print on the foil can be further studied. Highly trained scientists use other ways to save prints, too.

## Take Blood Samples

Detectives can find evidence of blood that may have been wiped off a wall or a floor. To do this, they spray a chemical called luminol on the wall or floor. They darken the room. Luminol makes blood glow a greenish-blue in the dark. Scientists guess what happened. They study how blood spilled or <u>splattered</u> onto the surface.

## Question Witnesses

Detectives on the scene question witnesses. They also question people who knew the <u>victim</u>. And every good detective asks the basic six questions: Who? What? Where? When? How? Why? Some detectives take notes in a notebook. Other detectives use a tape recorder.

Dusting for fingerprints at the scene of a crime

arch

whorl

loop

## Teacher Think Aloud

*I know that scientists use microscopes. But why would a detective use a microscope? How would a microscope help someone solve a crime? Let me reread the section on microscopes. Now I see! Evidence may be very tiny, and a microscope can help a detective identify its source. A microscope can also tell if the hairs at a crime scene belong to a human or an animal.*

## Fix-Up Strategies

Offer these strategies to help students read independently.

### If you don't understand what you're reading:

• Reread the difficult section to look for clues to help you comprehend.

• Read ahead to find clues to help you comprehend.

• Retell, or say in your own words, what you've read.

• Visualize, or form mental pictures of, what you've read.

### If you don't understand a word:

• Reread the sentence. Look for ideas and words that provide meaning clues.

• Find clues by reading a few sentences before and after the confusing word.

• Look for the base or root word and think about its meaning.

• Think about the topic or plot at this point to see if either offers meaning clues.

# In the Forensic Lab

Dog's hair

Human hair

House dust

Ceramic dust

## Study Blood Samples

Blood samples tell their own story. People have one of four blood types: A, B, AB, or O. A simple lab test can tell the blood type of the victim and/or the <u>suspect</u>. (The suspect is the person who might be guilty of the crime.)

A blood sample can also be tested to find a person's DNA. Forensic scientists use DNA to solve many crimes. DNA is a blueprint of a person's genes. Only identical twins have the same DNA. No one else does.

Forensic scientists use different tools. The tools help identify chemicals and poisons in blood.

## Use Microscopes

All evidence collected by the detectives must be studied. Scientists use microscopes to look at trace evidence. Some microscopes can magnify objects 150,000 times!

Look above. How different small things look under a microscope!

42

ME SCENE DO NOT CROSS    CRIME SCENE DO NOT CRO

## Student Journal page 25

Name _____ Date _____

**Writing: A One-Minute Mystery**
Visualize yourself as a detective. Read the questions detectives usually ask. With a partner, write answers that you can use to write a short mystery story together. Use a separate sheet of paper for the story and write the solution to your mystery on the back. Remember to title the story!

| Detectives' Questions | Answers |
|---|---|
| **Who** is the mystery about? | |
| **What** happens in the mystery? | |
| **Where** does the mystery happen? | |
| **When** does the mystery happen? | |
| **Why** does the mystery happen? | |
| **How** does the mystery get solved? | |

Mystery • Detectives at Work    25

# After Reading

WHOLE CLASS  Use one or more activities.

## Check Purpose

Have students decide if their purpose was met. Did they learn how modern-day detectives solve crime mysteries? Did they learn about new kinds of evidence?

## Discussion Questions

Continue the group discussion with the following questions.

1. What did you learn about detective work? (Details)

2. Would you like to be a detective? Why or why not? (Making Connections)

3. Why do you think this article was included in a magazine named *Mystery*? (Inferential Thinking)

## Revisit: Details Web

Revisit the web begun in Before Reading. Were students' responses correct? What new information can students add?

## Revisit: Predictions Chart

Have students complete the last column of the predictions chart on *Student Journal* page 24. Have students find the vocabulary words in the selection and read around them, using context clues to find the words' meanings.

## Work the Computers

Computers help detectives in many ways. DNA data is kept on a computer. So is a lot of other helpful information. Artists take descriptions of a suspect from a witness. Using special computer programs, an artist draws a face. The face shows what the person might look like. Detectives use computers to help find people, too.

A forensic expert uses the computer to match the remains of soldiers to military records. When she gets a match, she will know the name of a dead soldier.

## If You Want to Be a Forensic Detective

Many students today are interested in forensics. Some high schools teach classes about it. So do many colleges. If you want to work in this field, you will have to study subjects such as the following:

• chemistry

• biology

• computer science

You will also have to learn how police departments and courtrooms are run.

Who knows? Maybe you'll be a real Sherlock Holmes some day! ◆

CRIME SCENE DO NOT CROSS     CRIME SCENE DO NOT C

43

**DIFFERENTIATED INSTRUCTION**

### Writing

## One-Minute Mystery

To help students with this activity, try the following steps:

1. Help students gather ideas before they write their one-minute mystery.

2. Provide students with a three-column chart to help them develop characters, clues, and a solution to their mystery story.

| Characters | Clues | Solution |
|---|---|---|
|  |  |  |
|  |  |  |

### Student Journal page 26

Name _____ Date _____

**Building Vocabulary: Words with Multiple Meanings**

Write two definitions for each word below.

| Word | First Definition | Second Definition |
|---|---|---|
| foil | a thin metallic paper | to outwit or prevent |
| lying |  |  |
| seal |  |  |
| trace |  |  |

26    Mystery • Detectives at Work

---

## Writing One-Minute Mystery

Partners can share ideas about what kind of mystery story they want to write. Then have students complete *Student Journal* page 25. Students can then write the mystery story. Tell students to write a solution to the mystery on the back of the story. Encourage students to trade mysteries with others who can try to solve them. (See Differentiated Instruction.)

## Vocabulary Multiple Meanings

Display *foil*. Explain to students that *foil* can be a thin metallic piece of paper used for picking up fingerprints. *Foil* can also be a verb meaning "to outwit or prevent." Additionally, *foil* can refer to a narrow sword used in the sport of fencing. What other words do students know that have multiple meanings? Have partners complete *Student Journal* page 26.

## Phonics/Word Study

### Contractions

Display: *I cannot go to the store after school because I did not bring my wallet.* Ask a volunteer to read the sentence aloud. Ask: *How can the underlined words be changed to make this sentence sound more natural, or familiar?* (*can't, didn't*) Explain that these shortened words are called contractions. Now, work with students to complete the in-depth contractions activity on TE page 62.

## Contractions

Write the following words on the board: *cannot, do not, did not.*

▶ Ask students if they use the words often. If they say they do, ask them if they would say something like this: *I did not have the money with me to buy the new CD.*

▶ How else might they say *did not*?

▶ Ask students why they think people often use *can't* instead of *cannot.* Explain that the contraction is a more familiar way to say *cannot.*

▶ Write the word *didn't* under the words *did not* on the board. Ask for a volunteer to identify what changed in the original word to make it a contraction. Students should notice that the word was made shorter (contracted) and that the word *not* actually lost its *o.*

▶ With the students, generate a list of contractions. Examine whether they all follow the same pattern. For a more extensive list of contractions, see *Word Study Manual* page 41.

For more information on word sorts and spelling stages, see pages 5–31 in the *Word Study Manual.*

# Focus on . . .

Use one or more activities in this section to focus on a particular area of need in your students.

## Comprehension  STRATEGY SUPPORT  INDEPENDENT

To help those students who need more practice using the strategies covered in this lesson, work one-on-one or in small groups to apply the strategy prompts below. Apply the prompts to a *Reading Advantage* paperback, a classroom library book, or a new or familiar selection in the magazine. Always model your own thinking first.

### Making Connections

• What does this story (article, passage) remind me of?
• What do I already know about this topic?
• Where have I heard about this topic before?
• What do I have in common with the characters, people, or situations in the text?
• What other books, stories, articles, movies, or TV shows does this text make me think about?

### Monitor Understanding

• Do I understand what I'm reading? If not, what part is confusing to me?
• What fix-up strategies can I use to solve the problem? (See During Reading for fix-up strategies.)
• Why did a character say (do, think, ask) that?
• What images do I visualize from the text? What parts can't I visualize?
• Why did the author include (or not include) those details?

## Writing Job Description  INDEPENDENT

Have students use the information in the article to write a job description for a detective they need to hire. Encourage students to review "The Red-Headed Club" to identify the characteristics that detective Sherlock Holmes had. Make a class list of the characteristics they found. In the job description, make sure students include what type of forensic practices the newly hired detective should anticipate in this new job.

For related practice and instruction on writing summaries of nonfiction information, see the lessons in *Writing Advantage*, pages 93–112.

## Fluency: Pacing

SMALL GROUP

Have students read the poem "It's a Mystery" silently. Then have them read it aloud at a smooth and even pace. Remind students that reading too quickly, too slowly, or stumbling over words makes it difficult for listeners to understand the content. Have students break into pairs. Have students alternate reading lines.

As you listen to students read, use these prompts to guide them.

▶ Keep your eyes on the text as you read so you don't miss any words.

▶ Put energy in your voice at the end of the question.

▶ Although there is just one punctuation mark at the end of the poem, try to pause after each line. This will make the poem easier to understand.

When students read aloud, do they—

✓ demonstrate a smooth pace, not too fast or too slow?

✓ incorporate well-timed pauses between words and phrases?

✓ reflect an awareness and understanding of punctuation?

## English Language Learners

SMALL GROUP

To support students' understanding of multiple-meaning words, extend the vocabulary activity on page 26 of the *Student Journal*.

1. After students have completed the vocabulary activity, discuss the multiple meanings of each word.

2. Have partners create another chart similar to the one on page 26.

3. Have partners complete their chart using the following multiple-meaning words from the text: *work, cases, scene, cross.*

## Independent Activity Options

INDEPENDENT

While you work with individuals or small groups, others can work independently on one or more of the following options.

▶ Level A paperback books, see TE pages 371–376

▶ Level A *eZines*

▶ Repeat word sorts from this lesson

▶ *Student Journal* pages for this lesson

▶ *Writing Advantage* independent lessons

# Assessment

## Strategy Assessment

To help you and your students assess their use of comprehension strategies, ask the following questions. Students can complete a written response or provide verbal answers in a one-on-one reading conference.

1. **Making Connections** What part of the article did you connect to? Why? (Answers will vary.)

2. **Monitor Understanding** What parts of this article were most confusing to you? How did you fix your confusion? (Answers will vary. Possible response: I didn't understand what luminol is and how detectives use it. I reread the section and defined it in my own words to help me understand.)

For ongoing informal assessment, use the checklists on pages 61–64 of *Level A Assessment*.

## Word Study Assessment

Use these steps to help you and your students assess their understanding of contractions.

1. Create a chart like the one shown, including only the words in column A.

2. Have students read the words in column A.

3. Have students write the contraction in column B for each item. Answers are shown.

| A | B |
|---|---|
| cannot | can't |
| would not | wouldn't |
| does not | doesn't |
| did not | didn't |
| should not | shouldn't |
| will not | won't |

Great Source
Reading Advantage

Level A
Assessment

# Frozen in Time
*Mystery*, pages 44–48

### SUMMARY
This **article** describes the discovery of Oetzi, the Ice Man in the Alps mountains.

### COMPREHENSION STRATEGIES
Monitor Understanding

### WRITING
Notes for Visualizing

### VOCABULARY
Related Words

### PHONICS/WORD STUDY
Long and Short *a* Compound Words

#### Lesson Vocabulary
mummy          flints
gully

### MATERIALS
*Mystery*, pp. 44–48
*Student Journal*, pp. 27–29
*Word Study Manual*, p. 42
*Writing Advantage*, pp. 113–151

# Before Reading
WHOLE CLASS · Use one or more activities.

## Make a List
Explain that "Frozen in Time" is about a man who died and was frozen and preserved in the Alps, a mountain range in Europe. Forensic scientists have been studying the body. Have students look back at the methods used by forensic scientists in "Detectives at Work," pages 39–43 in the magazine. Make a list of the techniques. Check off any techniques students think would be used on the frozen man.

## Vocabulary Preview
Review the vocabulary list with students. Clarify pronunciations. Have students begin *Student Journal* page 27.

## Preview the Selection
Have students look through the article. Discuss their observations. Have students share a question that they think will be answered in the article. As students read the article, they can check to see if their questions are answered.

## Make Predictions/Set Purpose
Students should use the information they gathered in previewing the selection to make some predictions about the article. If students have trouble generating a purpose for reading, suggest that they read to learn about finding preserved human bodies from a long time ago.

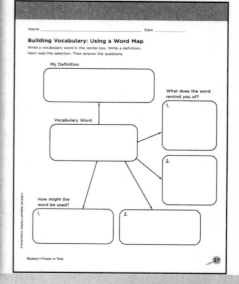

## Comprehension
MONITOR UNDERSTANDING

To help students visualize the text, use the following prompts:

- When you first pictured Oetzi in your mind, what did you picture he looked like? How did the text "show you" what he looked like?

- How do the photographs of Oetzi help you create a better picture of him in your mind?

**Student Journal page 27**

---

**Some people joke about having their bodies frozen after they die. But it's no joke. Here's a real-life story about a man who was frozen more than 5,000 years ago!**

People always come to Bolzano, Italy. They love our tall mountains, the Alps. They feel healthy here. That was before the spring of 1998. Then the Ice Man arrived. Now, people come to our city to see him.

The Ice Man doesn't sell icy sweets on our sidewalks. Instead, he is a frozen <u>mummy</u>. Actually, he is an "accidental mummy." No one prepared his body for burial to keep it in good condition. The fact that his body froze kept it in good condition.

In 1991, two people hiking in the Alps found him. They thought they were in Austria. Scientists took the mummy to a lab there. They named him Oetzi, [ET si] after the Oetz [ets] Valley where he died. Then years later, they found out that he had really died in Italy. So they shipped him here.

Oetzi is kept in a freezer in the museum. You can look at him through a window. It is the size of a TV screen. People who see the Ice Man for the first time can't get over him. "What a mystery!" they say.

The Ice Man isn't such a mystery anymore. Scientists have learned a lot about him. At first, they didn't know how old he was. They performed a "dating" test. It tells how old things are. The test told them the mummy and the things with it are 5,300 years old.

**45**

---

# During Reading

## Comprehension
MONITOR UNDERSTANDING

**SMALL GROUP**

Use these questions to model how to visualize the text. Then have students tell about a part they visualized.

- What do I picture in my mind as I read?

- Which details help me create this image in my mind?

- How does this image help me understand what I am reading?

(See Differentiated Instruction.)

## Teacher Think Aloud

*I can picture rough-looking moccasin-type shoes. The details about Oetzi's shoes, made of bear- and deerskin and bark, helped me picture this. I've seen moccasins made of animal skins, but not bark. So that's why I'm picturing crudely made shoes if they have bark on them. This helps me understand they had to rely on what they found in nature for their basic needs.*

## Fix-Up Strategies

Offer these strategies to help students read independently.

**If you don't understand what you're reading:**

- Reread the difficult section to look for clues to help you comprehend.

- Read ahead to find clues to help you comprehend.

- Retell, or say in your own words, what you've read.

- Visualize, or form mental pictures of, what you've read.

The hikers had found Oetzi in a gully. The gully probably cut into the earth by water that melted from a glacier. A glacier is a huge, slow-moving field of ice. Some glaciers are high up on mountains. The scientists wondered what Oetzi was doing there.

When they studied Oetzi, they found bits of tree pollen and plants on him. Those plants don't grow on mountains. They must have come from down in the valley. Probably Oetzi had, too.

Amazingly, the scientists found bits of what Oetzi had eaten the day he died. They studied it under a microscope. They found pieces of flat, hard wheat bread. They saw some greens and a tiny bit of meat.

Scientists know how long it takes for a person's body to digest different foods. They figured out that Oetzi had eaten about eight hours before he died.

In the lab, the scientists studied the Ice Man's clothing. He wore leggings, a jacket, a cape, and a hat. The clothing was made of layers of skins and grass. His shoes were made from bear and deer skins, and tree bark. He had a belt pouch that held flints and some other items for starting a fire. The Ice Man also had tools with him. One of the tools was a fine copper ax.

The scientists studied Oetzi for many years. They kept wondering what he was doing in that gully. They saw that some of his ribs were cracked. That wouldn't have been painful enough to make him lie down there. Finally, they saw something. It was a piece of hard rock, called flint. The flint was shaped like an arrowhead. It was sticking into his shoulder.

Some people think that the Ice Man was running away from enemies who caught up with him. They shot arrows at him. One of them struck his shoulder. Oetzi fell down in the gully. He lay there and froze to death.

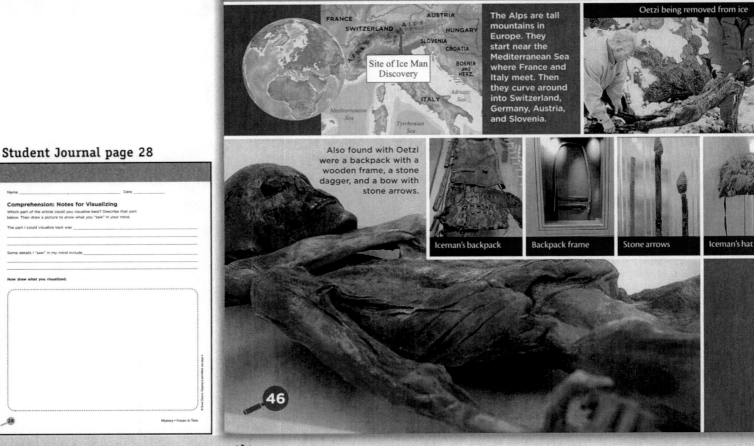

The Alps are tall mountains in Europe. They start near the Mediterranean Sea where France and Italy meet. Then they curve around into Switzerland, Germany, Austria, and Slovenia.

Site of Ice Man Discovery

Oetzi being removed from ice

Also found with Oetzi were a backpack with a wooden frame, a stone dagger, and a bow with stone arrows.

Iceman's backpack     Backpack frame     Stone arrows     Iceman's hat

46

## Student Journal page 28

Name _____ Date _____

**Comprehension: Notes for Visualizing**
Which part of the article could you visualize best? Describe that part below. Then draw a picture to show what you "saw" in your mind.

The part I could visualize best was _____

Some details I "saw" in my mind include _____

**Now draw what you visualized.**

28     Mystery • Frozen in Time

# After Reading

WHOLE CLASS  Use one or more activities.

## Check Purpose

Have students decide if their purpose was met. What did they learn about finding preserved bodies?

## Discussion Questions

Continue the group discussion with the following questions.

1. How do you think the hikers felt when they discovered Oetzi? (Inferential Thinking)

2. How is an Egyptian mummy different from the Ice Man? (Compare-Contrast)

3. What questions do you have about Oetzi? (Making Connections)

## Revisit: List

Revisit the list begun in Before Reading. Were the forensic techniques students listed mentioned in the article? What new techniques can students add?

## Revisit: Word Map

Revisit the word map begun in Before Reading and have students complete it. What does the word remind them of? Where have they seen or heard the word used?

The Ice Man had fifty-eight tattoos. They were just dots and lines. Some scientists think they were not body art. The tattoos are on or close to spots where Chinese doctors stick needles to help people who are sick or in pain.

Acupuncture (AK yoo pungck chur) is an ancient Chinese method of relieving pain and treating some kinds of disease. It involves sticking needles into parts of the body.

Acupuncture is very common in parts of Asia. It has become more popular in the United States over the last twenty years.

# MUMMIES

When you hear the word *mummy*, do you think of the Italian Alps? Probably not. Most people think of Egypt because many mummies have been dug up from burial grounds and pyramids in Egypt. The ancient Egyptians used to prepare bodies for death by embalming them. This meant that they added special ingredients to the corpses (dead bodies) to preserve them. Embalming kept the body from decaying, or rotting away. The Ice Man's body was not embalmed. Instead, it froze. Because it was frozen, it did not decay the way it would have if it had remained at a warm temperature.

This Egyptian mummy was prepared for burial. Note the linen wrapping.

47

DIFFERENTIATED INSTRUCTION   SMALL GROUP
## Vocabulary
## Related Words

To help students with this activity, use the steps below:

1. Explain that words can be related—many words can stem from just one word.

2. Write the key word *person* along with related words—*personal*, *personality*, and *personalize*—on the board or on chart paper.

3. Discuss what part of speech each word is, and ask students for the definitions, for example, *personal—adjective—having to do with or belonging to a person.*

### Student Journal page 29

Name _____ Date _____

**Building Vocabulary: Related Words**
Pick a word you are familiar with as the key word. Then write three or four words that are related to the key word. Write the part of speech and the definition of each related word.

| Related Words | Part of Speech | Definition |
|---|---|---|
| Key word: mummy | | |
| 1. mummify | verb | to make into a mummy by embalming |
| 2. mummification | | |
| 3. | | |
| 4. | | |
| Key word: | | |
| 1. | | |
| 2. | | |
| 3. | | |
| 4. | | |

Mystery • Frozen in Time   29

## Writing
### Notes for Visualizing

Ask students what part of the article they could visualize best. Write their thoughts on the board. Then have students choose a part to draw and write about in the visualizing activity on *Student Journal* page 28.

## Vocabulary Related Words

Display *mummy*. Then read the sentence on page 45 in which the word appears. Write the words *mummify* (to make into a mummy by embalming) and *mummification* (the process of becoming a mummy). Tell students that these two words stem from the word *mummy*. Then have students complete *Student Journal* page 29. (See Differentiated Instruction.)

## Phonics/Word Study
### Compound Words

Write the following "equations" on the board: *back + pack* = _____; *rain + bow* = _____. Ask students to say the answers to these equations (*backpack*, *rainbow*). Ask: *What do you notice about the words* backpack *and* rainbow? (They are made up of two smaller words.) Point out the short *a* sounds in *backpack*, and the long *a* sound in *rainbow*. Now, work with students to complete the in-depth compound words activity on TE page 69.

Who was chasing Oetzi and why? Probably we will never know.

Scientists at the museum lab continue to study Oetzi. What other secrets might he still hold? What mysteries might workers solve?

The Ice Man lived so long ago. Yet it seems right that he should be among us now. We all want to live in a safe place. We all need food, clothing, and shelter. We all hope to get where we want to go. We are not so different from Oetzi, are we?

Sometimes I like to pretend I am Oetzi. I make up a story about his last day.

The Ice Man on display in Bolzano, Italy, as he might have looked over 5,000 years ago

## Oetzi's Diary

I am running, running. I have run most of the day from my farm, my home. I am tired. I have not eaten since morning. Now it is almost dusk. I have no time to stop and think. Thoughts run through my head as I run across the land. I have lived forty years. I am no longer young. I do not know if I will live through another year. I have no time to stop and think.

It is not yet winter, but I can feel a storm coming.

The higher I climb, the more likely it will snow.

But I must climb, to lose my enemies. My ribs give me so much pain when I breathe.

I broke them running away from my chasers.

What's this? It is a huge field of ice. This will make the going harder. I must cross it quickly.

When I am standing against the white ice field, my enemies can spot me more easily.

Perhaps if I think I am a white mountain goat, it will help me escape them.

Here is a rocky ditch. Maybe I can safely rest here for the night.

With luck, my enemies will not find me. I am cold. I am seized by great hunger. I must have dozed off. What's that noise? Footsteps are crossing the ice. Can it be my enemies? I must try to remain hidden. I hear their voices. Oh! What is that pain in my shoulder?

It makes me forget the pain of my ribs. I will pretend I am dead.

Maybe they will go away and leave me alone.

My enemies are gone. I must wait until I make sure they are too far away to see me.

Then I must find the strength to get up and continue across the mountains.

I will lie here awhile and think of happier, warmer times.

What's this? It is starting to snow. This was the wrong time to be right about the weather.

I will be fine, though. I am wearing warm clothes. I will save my strength. In the morning I will go on.

48

## Long and Short *a* Compound Words

Write the following words for students: *clambake*, *racehorse*, and *bareback*.

▶ Ask students what the words have in common. They may notice that each word is actually made up of two smaller words. *Clambake* is the name of a gathering where clams are baked. *Racehorse* refers to a particular kind of horse that often runs races. *Bareback* describes a style of riding a horse without a saddle on its back.

▶ Provide students with a list of compound words they can read and take apart. (*Racehorse = race + horse*) Have partners write their "equations" together. For an extensive list of compound words, see *Word Study Manual* page 42.

For more information on word sorts and spelling stages, see pages 5–31 in the *Word Study Manual*.

# Focus on . . .

Use one or more activities in this section to focus on a particular area of need in your students.

## Comprehension  STRATEGY SUPPORT  *INDEPENDENT*

To help those students who need more practice using the strategies covered in this lesson, work one-on-one or in small groups to apply the strategy prompts below. Apply the prompts to a *Reading Advantage* paperback, a classroom library book, or a new or familiar selection in the magazine. Always model your own thinking first.

### Monitor Understanding

- Do I understand what I'm reading? If not, what part is confusing to me?
- What fix-up strategies can I use to solve the problem? (See During Reading for fix-up strategies.)
- Why did a character say (do, think, ask) that?
- What images do I visualize from the text? What parts can't I visualize?
- Why did the author include (or not include) those details?

## Writing Diary Entry  *INDEPENDENT*

Have students write an earlier diary entry that Oetzi might have written before he was wounded. The diary entry could tell about what Oetzi did in a typical day, or describe an adventure that he had.

For related instruction on writing descriptive paragraphs, see lessons in *Writing Advantage*, pages 113–151.

## Fluency: Expression

SMALL GROUP

Have students read "Oetzi's Diary" at a smooth and even pace. Have students first read the diary silently to troubleshoot for unfamiliar words and to get a sense of natural phrasing. Then have students break into groups of four. Have students divide the selection among themselves and dramatize the diary.

As you listen to students read, use these prompts to guide them.

▶ Read with expression. Put yourself in the situation of the character. How is he feeling? How would he sound?

▶ Pause at the end of every sentence. This will make it easier for listeners to understand.

When students read aloud, do they—

✓ reflect an understanding of the text?

✓ demonstrate appropriate timing, stress, and intonation?

✓ incorporate appropriate speed and phrasing?

## English Language Learners

SMALL GROUP

In response to the compare-contrast discussion question on TE page 66, help students create a Venn diagram comparing an Egyptian mummy and the Ice Man.

1. Show students how to create the Venn diagram with the appropriate headings.

2. Using facts from the text, have students complete the Venn diagram comparing an Egyptian Mummy and the Ice Man.

3. Have students use their diagrams to explain each character to a partner.

## Independent Activity Options

INDEPENDENT

While you work with individuals or small groups, others can work independently on one or more of the following options.

▶ Level A paperback books, see TE pages 371–376

▶ Level A *eZines*

▶ Repeat word sorts from this lesson

▶ *Student Journal* pages for this lesson

▶ *Writing Advantage* independent lessons

# Assessment

## Strategy Assessment

To help you and your students assess their use of comprehension strategies, ask the following questions. Students can complete a written response or provide verbal answers in a one-on-one reading conference.

• **Monitor Understanding** What part of the article did you visualize the best? Describe what you "saw." (Answers will vary. Possible answer: I could picture in my mind the Egyptian mummies. I saw a body wrapped in linen, as mentioned in the text.)

For ongoing informal assessment, use the checklists on pages 61–64 of *Level A Assessment*.

## Word Study Assessment

Use these steps to help you and your students assess their understanding of compound words.

1. Create a chart like the one shown.

2. Have students read aloud the words in each column. Have them note which words contain the long or short *a* sound.

3. Have students create compound words by combining words from column A with words in column B. (*farmland, salesman, clambake, backpack, bareback*)

| A | B |
|---|---|
| farm | bake |
| sales | land |
| clam | pack |
| back | back |
| bare | man |

Reading Advantage

Level A Assessment

# The Lost Colony

*Roanoke Island is just off the coast of present-day North Carolina. The very beginning of Roanoke is still filled with mystery.*

In March of 1584, Queen Elizabeth I gave a <u>charter</u> to the English explorer Sir Walter Raleigh. Raleigh's job was to carry out the charter to settle in the New World.

Raleigh sent 108 men to settle Roanoke Island in 1585. Life on the island was hard. So, the men left in 1586. Raleigh sent another group, 117 people, in 1587. This group included John White, an English artist; White's daughter and her husband; and other families. John White was named governor.

John White returned to England for more supplies. Three years passed before White returned to Roanoke. What if White had kept a journal? He might have written about his surprising return to Roanoke in 1590.

*Roanoke Island is surrounded by four bodies of water: the Albemarle Sound, Croatan Sound, Roanoke Sound, and the Pamlico Sound. The island is separated from the Atlantic Ocean by Bodie Island, part of a group of islands called the Outer Banks.*

49

### SUMMARY
This **article** describes the mysterious beginnings of Roanoke Island.

### COMPREHENSION STRATEGIES
Understanding Text Structure

### WRITING
Journal Entries

### VOCABULARY
Multiple Meanings

### PHONICS/WORD STUDY
Short and Long *e* Patterns

### Lesson Vocabulary
charter        colony
settlers

### MATERIALS
*Mystery,* pp. 49–52
*Student Journal,* pp. 30–32
*Word Study Manual,* p. 43
*Writing Advantage,* pp. 152–163

# Before Reading
WHOLE CLASS — Use one or more activities.

## Make a T-Chart
Tell students that they will read a selection about a group of people who moved to a new land called Roanoke Island. Encourage students to discuss the benefits and risks of moving to a new place. Write students' responses in a T-chart. Students can revisit the chart later.

| Moving to a New Land ||
|---|---|
| Benefits | Risks |
|  |  |

## Vocabulary Preview
Review the vocabulary list with students. Clarify pronunciations. Then have students complete the making associations activity on *Student Journal* page 30. Students can revisit the associations page later.

## Preview the Selection
Have students look through the four pages of the article. Discuss their observations. (See Differentiated Instruction.)

## Make Predictions/Set Purpose
Students should use the information they gathered in previewing the selection to make some predictions about what they'll learn from this selection. If students have trouble generating a purpose for reading, suggest that they read to learn about the mysteries surrounding Roanoke Island.

## Preview the Selection

Familiarize students with historical fiction.

1. Display the term *historical fiction.* Ask students to define *historical.* (actual events that occurred in the past) Then ask what *fiction* means. (something made up) Explain that *historical fiction* is a blend of historical facts and ideas created by an author.

2. Explain that authors often include journal entries (personal thoughts, memories, experiences, and feelings) in historical fiction to lend authenticity to their writing.

### Student Journal page 30

Name _____ Date _____

**Building Vocabulary: Making Associations**
Think about what you already know about each vocabulary word.
Then answer the questions for each word.

Word _____ charter _____

What do you think about when you read this word? _____

Who might use this word? _____

What do you already know about this word? _____

Word _____ colony _____

What do you think about when you read this word? _____

Who might use this word? _____

What do you already know about this word? _____

Now watch for these words in the magazine selection. Were you on the right track?

---

**June 1, 1590**

Our ship has been slowed down by terrible storms. That gives me time to think about the past. How did this all begin? Our dear Queen Elizabeth was worried about Spain. Their explorers had already been to the New World. England could not let Spain get ahead of us. So the queen sent ships to the New World.

In 1587, our group left to settle on Roanoke Island. As we came close to land, we spotted the native people. They were probably as afraid of us as we were of them.

I often lay awake thinking about those people. They were part of the Croatoan tribe. At first, they had to be sure we would not harm them. After we became friends, they taught us many things. We learned how to grow crops and catch fish.

All of us <u>settlers</u> worked hard. But hard work was not enough to keep us alive. We needed more food and supplies. That is why I had to go back to England. My plan was to bring back seeds, tools, and clothing. Little did I know how long it would take for my return.

**August 1, 1590**

So much has happened since August 1587. England was getting ready for war. Spain was planning to attack us by sea. None of our ships could leave England. When Spain did attack, we fought hard. How lucky for us that a storm destroyed many Spanish ships!

Now I am finally on my way back to Roanoke. Each day, I look for land. Oh, how I wish I had wings to fly!

50

---

# During Reading

## Comprehension

UNDERSTANDING TEXT STRUCTURE

Use these questions to model how to identify the description text structure of the selection. Then have students identify and describe the elements of a journal.

- What do I notice about the way the text is organized on the page?

- What kind of information will I find in a journal?

### Teacher Think Aloud

*I know that journals are written as a series of entries, which are usually dated. I see dates in this journal. When I read the text under each date, I know that the author is describing what happened on that day, so I can follow the events in time order. I know that a journal is a personal record of events, so it will also contain the feelings and beliefs of the writer.*

### Fix-Up Strategies

Offer these strategies to help students read independently.

**If you don't understand what you're reading:**

- Reread the difficult section to look for clues to help you comprehend.

- Read ahead to find clues to help you comprehend.

- Retell, or say in your own words, what you've read.

- Visualize, or form mental pictures of, what you've read.

## Baby Virginia

Virginia Dare was the first British child born in the New World. Virginia was the daughter of Eleanor and Ananias Dare. Eleanor was the daughter of John White, the journal's author. Thus, Virginia was John White's granddaughter.

### August 15, 1590

As we get close to the islands, my heart beats harder and harder. Surely my family will be waiting to greet me. Baby Virginia will be turning three in a few days. How well I remember the day of her birth! Eleanor and Ananias (ah nahn EYE uhs) were proud to be parents of the first child born to our colony.

### August 17, 1590

The storms have ended. The **Hopewell** is coming close to the islands. We will drop anchor tonight. Tomorrow the rowboats will carry us to Roanoke.

### August 18, 1590

Imagine how shocked we were! No one was on shore to greet us. We shouted. We sang out English tunes. But no voices shouted back. As we walked around, we came upon a tree. Its bark was pulled back. Large letters were carved into the tree. They spelled only one word: CROATOAN. What did it mean? No one knew. It's a mystery.

### August 19, 1590

Sadly, we are back on the **Hopewell**. We can hardly believe what we found. There was no sign of an attack. Yet all of the houses are gone. There is not even a nail to be found!

I ask myself many questions. Where did the settlers go? Are they with the Croatoans? Did somebody harm them? Where is Baby Virginia? I am so sad and worried. I begged the captain to take us to Croatoan Island. He says the ship is in need of repairs so that it will not sink. Food supplies are running low. He refuses to stay any longer. Oh, how sick at heart I am! Will I ever see my dear family and friends again? ◆

51

**Student Journal page 31**

Name _____  Date _____

**Writing: Journal Entries**

Write two journal entries as if you were one of the settlers on Roanoke Island. Try to incorporate answers to these questions: Where did the Roanoke settlers go? Why did they leave the island?

| June 1, 1590 | June 2, 1590 |
|---|---|
| | |

Mystery • The Lost Colony · 31

# After Reading
WHOLE CLASS  Use one or more activities.

## Check Purpose

Have students decide if their purpose was met. What mysteries surround Roanoke Island?

## Discussion Questions

Continue the group discussion with the following questions.

1. Why did it take three years for John White to get back to Roanoke Island? (Cause-Effect)

2. Why didn't John White search for his family and friends at Croatoan Island? (Making Connections)

3. What do you think happened to the settlers of Roanoke Island? Explain your thoughts. (Inferential Thinking)

## Revisit: T-Chart

Revisit the T-chart started in Before Reading. Discuss the benefits and risks of moving. Can students add more details to the chart?

## Writing Journal Entries

To help students with this activity, use the steps below:

1. Help students gather ideas before they write their journal entries.

2. Write these two questions on the board: *Where did the Roanoke settlers go? Why did they leave the island?*

3. As students discuss the questions, write their responses on the list. Encourage students to refer to the list for ideas as they write the journal entries.

**Student Journal page 32**

| Word | First Definition | Second Definition |
|------|------------------|-------------------|
| charter | a document given by a ruler, granting the right to do an activity | to hire |
| coast | | |
| ship | | |
| back | | |

Building Vocabulary: Words with Multiple Meanings
Write two definitions for each word below.

# More About the Lost Colony

Four hundred years later, people still wonder about the lost colony. These are some ideas about what might have happened to the settlers:

- They went to live with the Croatan Indians, who are now called the Lumbee.
- They packed up to move to a better place for farming.
- They were attacked by an unfriendly tribe.
- They were attacked by Spanish pirates.

The modern spelling of Croatoan is Croatan.

About one hundred years before White's journey back to Roanoke, Columbus made his voyage to the New World. Less than 50 years later, the English had settlements in Massachusetts and Virginia.

*Every summer, many people visit Roanoke Island to see a play called The Lost Colony. More than one hundred actors take the parts of settlers.*

The settlers had taken time to bury White's belongings. When he returned to Roanoke, he found three large chests buried in the sand. They were filled with books, pictures, and maps. He even found his rusted armor.

John White made paintings to show life in the colony. In one painting, he showed a small person sitting inside a hut near the fields. The person's job was to jump out, whirl around, and scare away the birds from eating the crops. The paintings are a way for us to learn about the lives of the settlers.

Roanoke Island was discovered in the late 1570s by English explorers. They thought it would be a good place for a settlement. From there, they could explore and claim new land for their country.

52

## Writing Journal Entries

Tell students that they will write two journal entries as if they were settlers on Roanoke Island. Have students complete the journal entries activity on *Student Journal* page 31. (See Differentiated Instruction.)

## Vocabulary Multiple Meanings

Display *charter*. Explain that a *charter* can be "a document given by a ruler, granting the right to do an activity," such as when Queen Elizabeth I gave a *charter* to Sir Walter Raleigh to settle Roanoke Island. Explain that *charter* can also be a verb meaning "to hire," such as to *charter* a bus for a trip. Discuss other words students know that have multiple meanings. Have partners complete *Student Journal* page 32.

## Phonics/Word Study

### Short and Long *e* Patterns

Write the following words on the board: *bet, beet.* Ask: *How is the vowel sound in each of these words different?* Have students volunteer other words that contain the short or long *e* sound. Now, work with students to complete the in-depth short and long *e* patterns activity on TE page 75.

## Introducing Short and Long *e* Patterns

Write the following words on the board: *well* and *week*. Tell students that these words represent two different sounds for the letter *e*. Both short and long sounds are represented.

▶ Ask students if they can identify which word has a short *e* sound and which word has a long *e* sound. Ask them how they knew which was which.

▶ Using the Long and Short *e:* Sort One sheet, model the sorting process for students. (See *Word Study Manual* page 43.) Write the headings Short *e*, Long *e* (*ee*), and Long *e* (*e*) and the first few words in the appropriate columns. Complete the sort as a class.

▶ Discuss the sort and what students learned. So far, there are two kinds of long *e* representations.

▶ Hand out the Long and Short *e:* Sort One sheet and ask students to cut it up and do the sort on their own or in groups.

▶ Check the final sorts.

| Long and Short *e*: Sort One | | |
|---|---|---|
| Short *e* | Long *e* (*ee*) | Long *e* (*e*) |
| crept | seem | we |
| debt | see | me |
| step | bleep | he |
| belt | peek | she |
| peck | creep | |
| well | street | |
| | meet | |
| | week | |

For more information on word sorts and spelling stages, see pages 5–31 in the *Word Study Manual*.

# Focus on . . .

Use one or more activities in this section to focus on a particular area of need in your students.

## Comprehension  STRATEGY SUPPORT  INDEPENDENT

To help those students who need more practice using the strategies covered in this lesson, work one-on-one or in small groups to apply the strategy prompts below. Apply the prompts to a *Reading Advantage* paperback, a classroom library book, or a new or familiar selection in the magazine. Always model your own thinking first.

### Understanding Text Structure

• What kind of text is this? (book, story, article, guidebook, play, manual)

• How does the author organize the text? (cause-effect, problem-solution, chronological order, description, question-answer, comparison-contrast)

• What details support my thoughts about the text structure?

• What is the cause (effect, problem, solution, order, question, answer)?

• If fiction, who are the characters? What is the setting, plot, conflict, and resolution?

## Writing Illustrated Timeline  INDEPENDENT

Explain to students that sequence of events can be shown on a timeline. Draw a timeline on the board to show an example. Then have students write and illustrate a timeline to chronicle key events surrounding Roanoke Island. Ask students to suggest the events (and the years) that might appear on the timeline. Write their ideas on the board. Students can refer to the list and the model timeline as they make their own timelines.

To give students practice in note-taking skills, see lessons in *Writing Advantage,* pages 152–163.

## Fluency: Punctuation

After students have read the journal entries at least once silently, have students pair up to read one of John White's journal entries at a smooth and even pace. Remind students that reading too quickly, too slowly, or stumbling over words makes it difficult for listeners to understand the content. Suggest that students choose a journal entry that they particularly liked to dramatize for the rest of the class.

As you listen to students read, use these prompts to guide them.

▶ Preview what you will read. Notice the different punctuation marks and what these signal to you. Pause at commas and periods. Let your voice rise at the end of sentences marked with a question mark. Put excitement in your voice when you see exclamation points.

▶ Look for groups of words that naturally go together so that you will sound natural.

▶ Try to put yourself in the situation of the character. What is his tone?

## English Language Learners

To support students as they prepare to write journal entries on *Student Journal* page 31, use a shared writing strategy to write an entry together.

1. Explain what information should be included in the journal entry.

2. Model good writing strategies and have students provide input as you write a journal entry on the board or on chart paper.

3. Have students read the journal entry aloud with you.

## Independent Activity Options

While you work with individuals or small groups, others can work independently on one or more of the following options.

▶ Level A paperback books, see TE pages 371–376

▶ Level A *eZines*

▶ Repeat word sorts from this lesson

▶ *Student Journal* pages for this lesson

▶ *Writing Advantage* independent lessons

# Assessment

## Strategy Assessment

To help you and your students assess their use of comprehension strategies, ask the following questions. Students can complete a written response or provide verbal answers in a one-on-one reading conference.

• **Understanding Text Structure** How did the dates help you understand the text? (Possible answers may include that the entry dates showed what happened in time order, making the sequence of events easier to follow.)

For ongoing informal assessment, use the checklists on pages 61–64 of *Level A Assessment*.

## Word Study Assessment

Use these steps to help you and your students assess their understanding of short and long *e* patterns.

1. Display the words *net, be, jeep, pen, me,* and *steep*, and create a chart like the one below, excluding the answers.

2. Then have students sort the words into the Short *e*, Long *e* (*ee*), or Long *e* (*e*) columns. The answers are shown.

| Short *e* | Long *e* (*ee*) | Long *e* (*e*) |
|-----------|-----------------|----------------|
| net | jeep | be |
| pen | steep | me |

Reading Advantage

Level A
Assessment

# Code Talkers

More than 25,000 Native
Americans fought in World War II.
About 3,000 of them were Navajo.
There were 540 Navajo Marines.
Of this total,
more than 400 served as
Navajo Code Talkers.

Soldiers in battle need to know where to fight. They need to know
when help is coming. Troops need to stay in touch with each other.
But they don't want the enemy to learn what they are doing. So they
send messages in code.

Some messages are sent by radio. Some are sent by telephone.
The enemy tries to listen in. When enemy soldiers hear a coded
message, they try to figure it out.

53

LESSON 11
## Code Talkers and Miscellaneous Mysteries
*Mystery*, pages 53–59

**SUMMARY**
This **article** explains how a code based on the Navajo language was used during World War II. A **short feature** follows.

**COMPREHENSION STRATEGIES**
Monitor Understanding
Inferential Thinking

**WRITING**
Summary

**VOCABULARY**
Context

**PHONICS/WORD STUDY**
Short and Long *e* Patterns

**Lesson Vocabulary**

| | |
|---|---|
| under fire | Navajo |
| unbreakable | ambush |

**MATERIALS**
*Mystery*, pp. 53–59
*Student Journal*, pp. 33–36
*Word Study Manual*, p. 44
*Writing Advantage*, pp. 93–112

---

# Before Reading 🌐 WHOLE CLASS Use one or more activities.

## Make a List

Tell students they will read a selection titled "Code Talkers" about a secret code used in World War II. Have students share their ideas about secret codes. List their responses on the board or on chart paper. You might direct the discussion by asking:

• Who uses secret codes?

• What types of codes can you think of?

## Vocabulary Preview

Read the vocabulary words aloud or write them for students to view. Have students fill in the second column on *Student Journal* page 33. They will complete the page later.

## Preview the Selection

Have students scan the article. Ask: *What do you think the article will be about? What clues help you know?*

## Make Predictions/Set Purpose

Students should use the information they gathered in previewing the selection to make some predictions about what they'll learn from the article. If students have trouble generating a purpose for reading, suggest that they read to learn about how the Navajo Marines helped the U.S. military win World War II.

## Short and Long *e* Patterns

Write the following words on the board: *best*, *mean*, and *green*. Tell students that these words have short and long *e* vowel sounds.

▶ Ask students if they can identify which words have a short *e* sound and which have a long *e* sound.

▶ Ask students how they knew which was which.

▶ Using the Long and Short *e*: Sort Two sheet, model the sorting process for students. (See *Word Study Manual* page 44.) Write the headings Short *e*, *ee*, *ea*, and Oddball and the first few words in the appropriate columns. Complete the sort as a class.

▶ Discuss the sort and what students learned. So far, there are two kinds of long *e* representations.

▶ Hand out the Long and Short *e*: Sort Two sheet and ask students to cut it up and do the sort on their own or in groups.

▶ Check the final sorts.

| Long and Short *e*: Sort Two | | | |
|---|---|---|---|
| Short *e* | *ee* | *ea* | Oddball |
| best | green | mean | been |
| web | sneer | scream | head |
| neck | peer | beach | |
| nest | bleed | stream | |
| left | queer | dear | |
| west | weed | spear | |
| | creep | reach | |
| | | dream | |
| | | steam | |

For more information on word sorts and spelling stages, see pages 5–31 in the *Word Study Manual*.

# Focus on . . .

Use one or more activities in this section to focus on a particular area of need in your students.

## Comprehension   STRATEGY SUPPORT   *INDEPENDENT*

To help those students who need more practice using the strategies covered in this lesson, work one-on-one or in small groups to apply the strategy prompts below. Apply the prompts to a *Reading Advantage* paperback, a classroom library book, or a new or familiar selection in the magazine. Always model your own thinking first.

### Monitor Understanding

• Do I understand what I'm reading? If not, what part is confusing to me?

• What fix-up strategies can I use to solve the problem? (See During Reading for fix-up strategies.)

• Why did a character say (do, think, ask) that?

• What images do I visualize from the text? What parts can't I visualize?

• Why did the author include (or not include) those details?

## Writing Codes   *INDEPENDENT*

Have partners create their own code. They should use letters, numbers, or simple symbols to create their codes. Ask students to choose a few of the titles of previous articles and translate them into their codes. Then have students try to figure out each other's codes.

For additional instruction on responding to literature, see lessons in *Writing Advantage*, pages 93–112.

## Fluency: Expression

After students have read the short feature "Miscellaneous Mysteries" at least once, they can use it to practice fluent reading. Students can work in pairs.

As you listen to students read, use these prompts to guide them.

▶ Read at an even, natural pace. Preview as needed to avoid stops and starts.

▶ Try to make your voice lively when you read. It will make your listener more interested.

▶ Let punctuation guide your pauses and the expression in your voice.

When students read aloud, do they—

✓ reflect an understanding of the text?

✓ demonstrate appropriate timing, stress, and intonation?

✓ incorporate appropriate speed and phrasing?

## English Language Learners

To support students as they examine word parts on TE page 78, review the prefix *un-*.

1. Explain that when *un-* is added to the beginning of a word, it means *not*. Give several examples.

2. Have students work with a partner to determine the meanings of the following words: *unkind*, *unhappy*, and *unable*.

3. Have partners think of other words with *un-*.

## Independent Activity Options

While you work with individuals or small groups, others can work independently on one or more of the following options.

▶ Level A paperback books, see TE pages 371–376

▶ Level A *eZines*

▶ Repeat word sorts from this lesson

▶ *Student Journal* pages for this lesson

▶ *Writing Advantage* independent lessons

# Assessment

## Strategy Assessment

To help you and your students assess their use of comprehension strategies, ask the following questions. Students can complete a written response or provide verbal answers in a one-on-one reading conference.

• **Monitor Understanding** What words were difficult for you to understand? How did you figure out their meanings? (Answers will vary. Possible response: I didn't know what the word *memorial* meant. I read the surrounding sentences and looked at the photo. This helped me see that a *memorial* is an object, such as a statue, that helps us remember people who have died.)

For ongoing informal assessment, use the checklists on pages 61–64 of *Level A Assessment*.

## Word Study Assessment

Use these steps to help you and your students assess their understanding of short and long *e* patterns.

1. Display a chart like the one below, omitting the answers.

2. Display the following words: *bean, seem, best, green, neat*, and *hem*.

3. Have students read the words and sort them into the correct columns. The answers are shown.

| Short *e* | Long *e* (*ee*) | Long *e* (*ea*) |
|-----------|-----------------|-----------------|
| best | seem | bean |
| hem | green | neat |

Great Source
Reading Advantage

Level A
Assessment

# The Silent Army *and* Second Glance

*Mystery,* pages 60–end

## SUMMARY

This **article** describes the creation of an army of clay soldiers. A **short feature** follows.

## COMPREHENSION STRATEGIES

Making Connections
Determining Importance

## WRITING

Notes for Visualizing

## VOCABULARY

Word Root *terr*

## PHONICS/WORD STUDY

Short and Long *e* Patterns

### Lesson Vocabulary

| | |
|---|---|
| ruthless | terra cotta |
| tomb | chariots |
| archaeologists | legend |

## MATERIALS

*Mystery,* pp. 60–end
*Student Journal,* pp. 37–39
*Word Study Manual,* p. 45
*Writing Advantage,* pp. 8–12

The Great Wall of China is amazing.
The emperor who had it built was amazing, too.
But the world would have to wait
2,000 years to see what else he did.

60

# Before Reading

Use one or more activities.

## Make a List

Have students discuss why rulers and states maintain large standing armies. The obvious reason is to protect a country, but students may also suggest that an army at the ready might serve as personal protection for the head of state, might fulfill civilian policing duties, might acquire new territories to extend the country, and so on. List students' responses on the board or on chart paper. Keep the list to revisit after reading.

**Why do rulers and states have armies?**
1. To protect their country
2. To develop weapons
3.

## Vocabulary Preview

List and say the vocabulary words. Have students look them over. Ask volunteers to share what they may know about a particular word or words. Encourage students to supplement each other's responses to maximize understanding of the words. Have students complete the knowledge rating chart on *Student Journal* page 37. Use the word *ruthless* to model a response to the page.

In 246 B.C., Ying Zheng (yeeng zhaing) was thirteen years old. His father, king of the Chinese state of Qin (chin), soon died. The boy became king in name only. But by the time he was twenty, things changed. He took over the reins of power. Ying Zheng had a goal. He wanted to join the warring states of China into one country.

By 221 B.C., Ying Zheng reached his goal. He gave himself the title Shi Huangdi (shee hwahng dee). It means "First Emperor." Soon, China had only one ruler. It had one written language. Next, China had one kind of money and one system of measures.

The emperor also tried to make the Chinese people think the same way. He burned books. He killed teachers. It was not surprising that such a <u>ruthless</u> ruler feared for his own life.

To keep his country safe, Shi Huangdi forced thousands of workers to build a wall. Later emperors added to it. The Great Wall of China exists today. Much of it has been rebuilt, however.

Shi Huangdi died in 210 B.C. of natural causes. Within three years, the empire he had built fell apart. Emperors from the Han state took over the throne of China. But that wasn't the last the world would hear of the First Emperor.

In A.D. 1974, some farmers were digging a well. It was near the <u>tomb</u> of Shi Huangdi. They were amazed by what they found. There were soldiers that had been buried for more than 2,000 years.

ASIA

61

**Student Journal page 37**

Name _____ Date _____

**Building Vocabulary: Knowledge Rating Chart**
Show your knowledge of each word by adding information to the other boxes in the row.

| Word | Define or Use in a Sentence | Where Have I Seen or Heard It? | How is It Used in the Selection? | Looks Like (Words or Sketch) |
|------|------|------|------|------|
| ruthless | | | | |
| tomb | | | | |
| archaeologists | | | | |
| terra cotta | | | | |
| chariots | | | | |
| legend | | | | |

Mystery • The Silent Army

37

## Preview the Selection

Have students look through the four pages of the article. Use these or similar prompts to preview the article.

- What do you think you will read about?

- Do you think the selection is fiction or nonfiction? What clues help you know?

- How did the author arrange the information in the article?

## Teacher Think Aloud

*When I look at the photographs, I'm amazed. I can't believe how many of these statues there are! I wonder who built them, and what purpose they serve. The title is "The Silent Army," so I guess these are soldiers who are meant to "protect" something. I'll read to see if I'm right.*

## Make Predictions/ Set Purpose

Students should use the information they gathered in previewing the selection to make some predictions about what they'll learn from the article. If students have trouble generating a purpose for reading, suggest that they read to learn about the life-size clay soldiers found in China.

## Comprehension
DETERMINING IMPORTANCE

To help students determine the importance of ideas on page 63, ask these questions:

- What key sentences or phrases contain important ideas?
- Why do you think so?

Archaeologists came to the tomb to dig more. They wanted to learn about the past by digging for artifacts, or old objects. These objects help archaeologists learn about how people lived long ago. In the tomb, they found three underground pits. All the pits had soldiers and horses. Some soldiers carried metal swords. In all, the diggers found more than 7,000 soldiers and horses. This was no flesh-and-blood army. It was made of a type of clay called terra cotta.

What is truly amazing about these clay figures? They are life-sized and no two are alike. People think that artists used soldiers from the First Emperor's real-life army as models. Did Shi Huangdi think he needed protection from his enemies even after death?

By the time the archaeologists stopped digging, they had dug up about five acres. That is about one one-hundredth of a square mile. Now, the archaeologists think that the whole tomb area may cover more than twenty square miles.

### The Tomb
Legend says that Shi Huangdi's tomb took 700,000 workers more than thirty-six years to build. It was completed shortly after his death only because the work had started during his lifetime.

### The Terra Cotta Army
衛 Artists made the bodies out of coils of gray clay.

衛 Then the artists covered the bodies with a layer of fine clay and sculpted the features.

衛 Next, the artists put on the arms and legs.

衛 After that, they fired the figures—put them in an oven.

衛 Finally, the artists painted the soldiers. (The bright colors have faded over the years.)

62

# During Reading

## Comprehension SMALL GROUP
MAKING CONNECTIONS

Use these questions to model making connections with the text on page 62. Then have students make their own connections.

- What does this remind me of?
- After reading this section, what do I understand now that I didn't understand before?

## Teacher Think Aloud
*I didn't know how many steps can go into making a sculpture. After reading the text under "The Terra Cotta Army," I found it interesting that artists used a fine clay to sculpt the features onto the bodies that had first been fashioned out of coils of clay. Next, the artists put them in the oven, and then painted them. Because of all these steps, I can understand just how detailed the soldiers are.*

## Comprehension SMALL GROUP
DETERMINING IMPORTANCE

Use these questions to model how to determine the importance of ideas in the first two paragraphs of the selection. Then have students determine the importance of ideas as they read page 63.

- What are the most important ideas in the section?
- How can I support my beliefs?

(See Differentiated Instruction.)

The soldiers in the third pit are different from earlier ones. Some of them ride in <u>chariots</u>. Others lead horses. Still others are kneeling, as if they are going to shoot arrows.

How many more soldiers are there to dig up? What other mysteries does the main tomb hold? There hasn't been enough money for the work to continue. It may take many years before workers unearth all the soldiers.

Digging up the tomb can be exciting. It may turn out to be like an adventure movie. One <u>legend</u> says that the tomb contains bows and arrows. If anybody enters, the arrows will shoot off. Is it true? With what we know about Shi Huangdi, it isn't hard to believe.

We may never get the full picture of Shi Huangdi's tomb. But if you visit, there is a lot to see and wonder about. There is a museum that houses many objects from around the tomb. The silent army that has guarded it is one of the most important finds of the last century. ◆

## What is truly amazing about these clay figures? They're life-sized and no two are alike.

### B.C. and A.D.

The letters B.C. and A.D. are often used to tell when an event took place or a person lived. B.C. stands for the Latin words that mean "before the Christian era." A.D. stands for the Latin words that mean "the year of our Lord," referring to Jesus Christ. We are living in the years known as A.D. The number of the year gets bigger as time goes on. In other words, A.D. 2005 comes after the year A.D. 2004. When you see years with B.C., you know that the larger the number of the year, the longer ago it was. The year 146 B.C. was before the year 145 B.C.

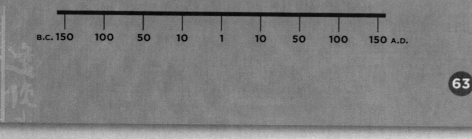

| B.C. 150 | 100 | 50 | 10 | 1 | 10 | 50 | 100 | 150 A.D. |

**63**

## Teacher Think Aloud

*When I read the first two paragraphs, I try to figure out what is most important for me to know. I learn about Ying Zheng and his main accomplishment: to unify China. I think this is the most important idea in this section because it tells me how powerful the emperor, Ying Zheng, must have been.*

## Fix-Up Strategies

Offer these strategies to help students read independently.

**If you don't understand what you're reading:**

• Reread the difficult section to look for clues to help you comprehend.

• Read ahead to find clues to help you comprehend.

• Retell, or say in your own words, what you've read.

• Visualize, or form mental pictures of, what you've read.

**If you don't understand a word:**

• Reread the sentence. Look for ideas and words that provide meaning clues.

• Find clues by reading a few sentences before and after the confusing word.

• Look for the base or root word and think about its meaning.

• Think about the topic or plot at this point to see if either offers meaning clues.

## DISCUSSION QUESTIONS

**SMALL GROUP**

For help with question 2, guide students through a compare-contrast activity.

1. Display a Venn diagram. Label the section at the left *Shi Huangdi* and the section in the middle *Both*.

2. As volunteers identify traits and accomplishments of the Chinese emperor, list them.

3. Have students name other rulers, tell what they know about them, and select one to compare with the emperor.

4. Label the diagram's third part and add students' responses. Have them identify things shared by both rulers. List those in the center of the diagram.

### Student Journal page 38

Name _____ Date _____

**Writing: Notes for Visualizing**

Which part of the article could you visualize best? Describe that part below. Then draw a picture to show what you "saw" in your mind.

The part I could visualize best was _____

Some details I "saw" in my mind include _____

Now draw what you visualized.

38    Mystery • The Silent Army

**CREDITS**

**Program Authors**
Laura Robb
James F. Baumann
Carol J. Fuhler
Joan Kindig

**Editorial Board**
Avon Cowell
Craig Roney
Jo Worthy

**Project Manager**
Ellen Sternhell

**Magazine Writers**
Della Cohen
Jeri Cipriano
Meish Goldish
Marc Gave
Steven Griffel
Judith Lechner
Barbara Linde
Liane Onish
Bernice Rappoport

**Design and Production**
Preface, Inc.

**Photography:**
Cover, © James L. Amos/Corbis; inside front cover, cl © Underwood & Underwood/Corbis; c © James L. Amos/Corbis; p. 1cl © Ed Bock/Corbis; c © Giansanti Gianni/Corbis SYGMA; cr, r Corbis; p. 4tl, 5tl © Vo Trung Dung/Corbis SYGMA; p. 5tr © Martin Harvey; Gallo Images/Corbis; b © Joe McDonald/Corbis; p. 8br © Jim Zuckerman/Corbis; b © Vo Trung Dung/Corbis SYGMA; p. 8t © Bettmann/Corbis b © Underwood & Underwood/Corbis; p. 9t © Bettmann/Corbis; b © Underwood & Underwood/Corbis; p. 10t © Corbis; b © Underwood & Underwood/Corbis; p. 11tl © Bettmann/Corbis; tr Amelia Earhart's palm print and analysis of her character prepared by Nellie Simmons Meier, June 28, 1933. *Words and Deeds in American History: Selected Documents Celebrating the Manuscript Division's First 100 years*, Library of Congress; cl © Minnesota Historical Society/Corbis; c © Bettmann/Corbis; cr © Underwood & Underwood/Corbis; b, © Corbis; p. 12, 13t © Corbis; p. 13br © Kevin Schafer/Corbis; bl © James L. Amos/Corbis; pp. 14–15b © David Forman; Eye Ubiquitous/Corbis; p. 14 © James L. Amos/Corbis; p. 15tl, tr © Wolfgang Kaehler/Corbis; tc, c © James L. Amos/Corbis; p. 16t © Richard T. Nowitz/Corbis; bl © Corbis; br © James Balog/Getty Images; p. 17l © Bob London/Corbis; r © Danny Lehman/Corbis; p. 18tl © Bob London/Corbis; tr © Joe McDonald/Corbis; b © Hans Neleman/Getty Images; p.19t © Barry Runk/Stan/Grant Heilman Photography; b © Gary Braasch/Corbis; p. 40tl © Pat O'Hara/Corbis; tr © Ralph A. Clevenger/Corbis; c © Vincenti Serge/Corbis SYGMA; bl © Ed Bock/Corbis; br © Corbis; p. 41 tr, c, br © Dave Olson/Visuals Unlimited; l © Hulton-Deutsch Collection/Corbis; p. 42tl © Dennis Kunkel/Phototake; tr © Corbis; c © Dr. Ryder/Jason Burns/Phototake; cl © Dee Breger/Photo Researchers, Inc.; b © Scimat/Photo Researchers, Inc.; p. 43 © Reuters NewMedia Inc./Corbis; p. 46t © Corbis/SYGMA; 46 c, b © Giansanti Gianni/Corbis SYGMA; p. 48 © Giansanti Gianni/Corbis SYGMA; p. 52 © Richard T. Nowitz/Corbis; p. 54t © Corbis; b © Hulton-Deutsch Collection/Corbis; p. 55t © Corbis; b © Bill Ross/Corbis; p. 56 © Rubin Steven/Corbis SYGMA; p. 57 © AP Photo/The Daily Times, Jim Snyder; p. 58t © Wolfgang Kaehler/Corbis; c © Charles & Josette Lenars/Corbis; b © Corbis; p. 59l © Asian Art & Archaeology, Inc./Corbis; r © Corbis; p. 60 © Keren Su/Corbis; p. 61 © Lowell Georgia/Corbis

**Illustration**
Inside front cover bkgd, Preface, Inc.; l, Will Terry; r, Bruce MacPherson; p. 1l, Steven Noble; pp. 2–6, Will Terry; p. 7, Jim Paillot; pp. 10–11, 16–17, 20, 23 Preface, Inc.; p. 24, Jim Paillot; p. 25, 26t, 28t, 30t Preface, Inc.; pp. 26–31, Bruce MacPherson; pp. 32–37, Steven Noble; pp. 38–39, Preface, Inc.; pp. 44–45, Tim Gabor; p. 46, Preface, Inc.; pp. 49–52, Stan Fellows; p. 49b, 50b, 51b, 53 Preface, Inc.; p. 58–59, Jim Paillot; pp. 64–65, Preface, Inc.

64

# SECOND GLANCE

Can you always believe what you see? Not with optical illusions!

Is it moving and shimmering?

---

# After Reading

**WHOLE CLASS** Use one or more activities.

## Check Purpose

Have students decide if their purpose was met. What have they learned about the army of clay soldiers discovered in China?

## Discussion Questions

Continue the group discussion with the following questions.

1. What do you think is the historical significance of the discovery of the clay army? (Inferential Thinking)

2. How is the first Chinese emperor alike and different from other rulers you know about? (Compare-Contrast)

3. Why do you think this article is important? (Making Connections)

(See Differentiated Instruction.)

## Revisit: List

Revisit the list started in Before Reading. Do students want to add or subtract ideas from the list? Now ask students to consider specifically why China's first emperor commissioned his army of clay soldiers.

## Revisit: Knowledge Rating Chart

Have students look at their responses on the knowledge rating chart on *Student Journal* page 37. Are there any changes they would like to make?

YELLOW BLUE ORANGE

BLACK RED GREEN

PURPLE YELLOW RED

ORANGE GREEN BLACK

BLUE RED PURPLE

GREEN BLUE ORANGE

Look at the chart above and say the COLOR of the word, not the word itself. Can you do it?

Are the horizontal lines parallel or do they slope?

Count the gray dots.

## Short Feature: Second Glance

## Short Feature: Second Glance

Give students a couple of minutes to preview the optical illusions. Then ask volunteers to read the text. Have students experience each illusion and then talk about their individual results. Sum up by talking briefly about why the feature is named "Second Glance."

### Student Journal page 39

Name _____ Date _____

**Building Vocabulary: Word Root *terr***
Write words you know that contain the Latin root *terr*. Write a definition for each word. Use a dictionary to help you, if you wish.

*Terr* means "earth" or "land."

| Words | Definitions |
|-------|-------------|
| terra cotta | a reddish-brown clay |
| | |
| | |
| | |
| | |

Mystery • The Silent Army

39

---

## Writing Notes for Visualizing

Remind students that active readers visualize, or try to "see" what an author tells about. Ask students which parts of the article they could visualize best. Write their ideas on the board. Have volunteers describe some of the pictures they "saw" in their minds. Then have students complete the visualizing activity on *Student Journal* page 38. Have students refer to the list on the board for help in choosing a part of the article.

## Vocabulary Word Root *terr*

Display *terra cotta*. Point out that *terra cotta* refers to both a type of clay and its reddish brown color. The term literally means "cooked earth." Have students identify the word part that means "earth." Help them brainstorm other words with *terr*. (*territory, terrestrial*) Ask volunteers to use *earth* or *land* to define each word. (*territory*: a large area of *land*; *terrestrial*: relating to *earth*) Have partners complete *Student Journal* page 39.

## Phonics/Word Study

### Short and Long *e* Patterns

List these words on the board: *head, heat*. Then ask: *How are these words different? How are they similar?* Encourage students to notice that the words have different vowel sounds (short and long *e*) but the same vowel pattern (*ea*). Have students name other words with these patterns and list them on the board. Now, work with students to complete the in-depth short and long *e* patterns activity on TE page 92.

## Phonics/Word Study

### Short and Long *e* Patterns

Write the following words on the board: *mess*, *head*, and *neat*. Tell students that the words represent two different sounds for the letter *e*. Both short and long sounds are represented.

▶ Ask students if they can identify which words have a short *e* sound and which word has a long *e* sound.

▶ Ask them how they knew which was which.

▶ Using the Long and Short *e*: Sort Three sheet, model the sorting process for students. (See *Word Study Manual* page 45.) Write the headings Short *e* (*e*), Short *e* (*ea*), and Long *e* (*ea*) and the first few words in the appropriate columns.

▶ Discuss the sort and what students learned. So far, there are two kinds of short *e* representations.

▶ Once the model sort is complete, hand out the Long and Short *e*: Sort Three sheet and ask students to cut it up and do the sort on their own or in groups. *Read* and *lead* may fall in either the second or the third column.

▶ Check the final sorts.

| Long and Short *e*: Sort Three | | |
|---|---|---|
| Short *e* (*e*) | Short *e* (*ea*) | Long *e* (*ea*) |
| mess | head | neat |
| best | read | dean |
| trek | dread | cream |
| jester | dead | clean |
| crest | bread | dream |
| text | lead | beast |
| detest | | lead |
| fret | | fear |
| | | lean |
| | | dreary |
| | | read |

For more information on word sorts and spelling stages, see pages 5–31 in the *Word Study Manual*.

# Focus on . . .

Use one or more activities in this section to focus on a particular area of need in your students.

## Comprehension  STRATEGY SUPPORT  *INDEPENDENT*

To help those students who need more practice using the strategies covered in this lesson, work one-on-one or in small groups to apply the strategy prompts below. Apply the prompts to a *Reading Advantage* paperback, a classroom library book, or a new or familiar selection in the magazine. Always model your own thinking first.

### Making Connections

• What does this story (article, passage) remind me of?

• What do I already know about this topic?

• Where have I heard about this topic before?

• What do I have in common with the characters, people, or situations in the text?

• What other books, stories, articles, movies, or TV shows does this text make me think about?

### Determining Importance

• What is the most important idea in the paragraph? How can I prove it?

• Which details are unimportant? Why?

• What does the author want me to understand?

• Why is this information important (or not important) to me?

## Writing Persuasive Letter  *INDEPENDENT*

Remind students that digging at the tomb of Shi Huangdi has stopped for the lack of money. Have students write a persuasive letter to encourage more financial supporters to help finish the job. Explain that good persuasive writing has a viewpoint, support for it, and an opposing viewpoint. Display an argument chart. Students can use the chart as a planning guide for writing their letters. Brainstorm a list of recipients of their letters.

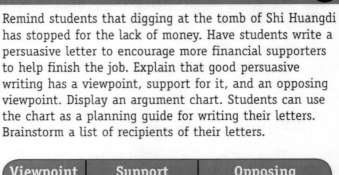

| Viewpoint | Support | Opposing Viewpoint |
|---|---|---|
| your opinion that you want to explain | facts, figures, and examples that support opinion | defending your position against arguments of the opposite side |

To give students more practice in brainstorming, see lessons in *Writing Advantage,* pages 8–12.

## Fluency: Pacing

*SMALL GROUP*

After reading the article at least once, have student pairs alternate reading aloud the paragraphs on page 62. Use the first paragraph on the page to model reading smoothly and at an even pace.

As you listen to students read, use these prompts to guide them.

▶ Read smoothly, and don't hesitate on or repeat words.

▶ Preview the paragraph to provide an opportunity to "troubleshoot" any difficult or unfamiliar words. It also enables you to see in advance how groups of words naturally go together.

▶ Use the punctuation to help you read fluently.

When students read aloud, do they—

✓ demonstrate a smooth pace, not too fast or too slow?

✓ incorporate well-timed pauses between words and phrases?

✓ reflect an awareness and understanding of punctuation?

## English Language Learners

*SMALL GROUP*

To support students as they complete the compare-contrast activity on TE page 90, use these steps to help develop their understanding of character traits.

1. Explain what character traits are, and give several examples.

2. Have students work with a partner to brainstorm a list of character traits.

3. Have students examine the Chinese emperor's actions and help them determine which character traits best describe him.

## Independent Activity Options

*INDEPENDENT*

While you work with individuals or small groups, others can work independently on one or more of the following options.

▶ Level A paperback books, see TE pages 371–376

▶ Level A *eZines*

▶ Repeat word sorts from this lesson

▶ *Student Journal* pages for this lesson

▶ *Writing Advantage* independent lessons

# Assessment

## Strategy Assessment

To help you and your students assess their use of comprehension strategies, ask the following questions. Students can complete a written response or provide verbal answers in a one-on-one reading conference.

1. **Making Connections** In what ways did you make connections with the article? Explain. (Answers will vary. Possible responses may include that students have heard of other rulers in history who have been unjustly cruel and like Ying Zheng, have killed their own people.)

2. **Determining Importance** What were the most important details about the clay soldiers? Why? (Answers will vary. Possible responses may include that they were life-size statues, and no two were the same, showing how important it was to the emperor that they were like real people.)

See *Level A Assessment* page 14 for formal assessment to go with *Mystery*.

## Word Study Assessment

Use these steps to help you and your students assess their understanding of short and long *e* patterns.

1. Create a chart like the one below, but do not include the answers.

2. Write the following words on the board: *neck, beat, instead, knead, bread, press.*

3. Have students read the words and sort them into the correct columns. The answers are provided.

| Short *e* | Short *e* (*ea*) | Long *e* (*ea*) |
|-----------|------------------|------------------|
| neck | instead | beat |
| press | bread | knead |

Great Source
Reading Advantage

Level A
Assessment

## Level A, Magazine 2

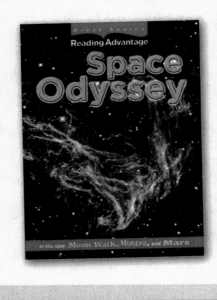

# Space Odyssey

## Magazine Summary

*Space Odyssey* magazine is a collection of nonfiction, fiction, and poetry about space. The magazine opens with a timeline of major events in space exploration that will provide some background for students who are not familiar with these events.

*Content-Area Connection:* earth and space science
Lexile measure 590L

# *Space Odyssey* Planner

| LESSON | BEFORE READING | DURING READING | AFTER READING |
|---|---|---|---|
| **LESSON 13**<br>**Great Moments in the "Space Age"**<br>(timeline)<br>page 98 | Category Chart<br>Vocabulary Preview<br>Preview the Selection<br>Make Predictions/Set Purpose | Monitor Understanding<br>Making Connections | Check Purpose<br>Discussion Questions<br>Writing: double-entry journal<br>Vocabulary: acronyms<br>Phonics/Word Study: long *e* patterns |
| **LESSON 14**<br>**Moon Walk**<br>(news stories)<br>page 108 | K-W-L Chart<br>Vocabulary Preview<br>Preview the Selection<br>Make Predictions/Set Purpose | Monitor Understanding | Check Purpose<br>Discussion Questions<br>Writing: labeled illustration<br>Vocabulary: word root *astro*<br>Phonics/Word Study: long and short *e* patterns (*r*-controlled) |
| **LESSON 15**<br>**Suited for Space**<br>(question-answer article)<br>page 114 | T-Chart<br>Vocabulary Preview<br>Preview the Selection<br>Make Predictions/Set Purpose | Understanding Text Structure | Check Purpose<br>Discussion Questions<br>Writing: explanatory paragraph<br>Vocabulary: multiple meanings<br>Phonics/Word Study: long *e* review |
| **LESSON 16**<br>**Give them Space**<br>(biographical sketches)<br>page 120 | Concept Web<br>Vocabulary Preview<br>Preview the Selection<br>Make Predictions/Set Purpose | Monitor Understanding<br>Inferential Thinking | Check Purpose<br>Discussion Questions<br>Writing: friendly letter<br>Vocabulary: word associations<br>Phonics/Word Study: long and short *e* homophones |

# Overview

## Preview the Magazine

Give students time to thumb through the magazine to look at the selection titles, photographs, and illustrations. They should look at the front and back covers for information to use to get them in a frame of mind for reading about space. Build a K-W-L chart on space, similar to the sample shown.

| Space | | |
|---|---|---|
| **What I Know** | **What I Want to Learn** | **What I Learned** |
| There are eight planets. | Is there life on other planets? | |
| No one has been to the planets, except for Earth. | What does an astronaut have to know? | |
| Earth is a planet. | | |

| PHONICS/ WORD STUDY | FOCUS ON | ASSESSMENT | HIGHER-ORDER THINKING QUESTIONS |
|---|---|---|---|
| Long *e* Patterns | Writing: personal timeline<br>Fluency: phrasing<br>English Language Learners<br>Independent Activity Options | Monitor Understanding<br>Making Connections<br>Long *e* Patterns | What did Russia and the United States send into space before they sent humans? Use details and information from the passage to support your answer. In what ways has the United States succeeded in winning the space race? In what ways has Russia succeeded in winning the space race? Use details and information from the passage to support your answer. |
| Long and Short *e* Patterns (*r*-controlled) | Writing: description<br>Fluency: pacing<br>English Language Learners<br>Independent Activity Options | Monitor Understanding<br>Long and Short *e* Patterns (*r*-controlled) | How were the Columbia and the Eagle different? How were they the same? Use details and information from the passage to support your answer. What tasks did the astronauts accomplish while in space and on the moon? Use details and information from the passage to support your answer. |
| Long *e* Review | Writing: design a mission patch<br>Fluency: expression<br>English Language Learners<br>Independent Activity Options | Understanding Text Structure<br>Long *e* Review | What is the organizational pattern the author uses for this article? Use details and information from the passage to support your answer. How have space suits evolved from early models to modern suits? Use details and information from the passage to support your answer. |
| Long and Short *e* Homophones | Writing: character traits<br>Fluency: pacing<br>English Language Learners<br>Independent Activity Options | Monitor Understanding<br>Inferential Thinking<br>Long and Short *e* Homophones | What obstacles did Chang-Diaz overcome to realize his dream of becoming an astronaut? Use details and information from the passage to support your answer. What qualities do the three astronauts have in common? Use details and information from the passage to support your answer. |

# Space Odyssey Planner

| LESSON | BEFORE READING | DURING READING | AFTER READING |
|---|---|---|---|
| **LESSON 17**<br>**Astro Quotes** *and* **Space Camp!**<br>(quotations and interview)<br>page 128 | Quotation Chart<br>Vocabulary Preview<br>Preview the Selection<br>Make Predictions/Set Purpose | Making Connections<br>Determining Importance | Check Purpose<br>Discussion Questions<br>Writing: T-chart<br>Vocabulary: suffixes *-er*, *-or*<br>Phonics/Word Study: long and short *e* compound words |
| **LESSON 18**<br>**Blaze** *and* **Solar Eclipse**<br>(story and poem)<br>page 138 | Sci-Fi Chart<br>Vocabulary Preview<br>Preview the Selection<br>Make Predictions/Set Purpose | Understanding Text Structure | Check Purpose<br>Discussion Questions<br>Writing: comparison-contrast paragraph<br>Vocabulary: word cues<br>Phonics/Word Study: sorting across vowels |
| **LESSON 19**<br>**Visitors from Mars**<br>(radio play)<br>page 144 | Concept Web<br>Vocabulary Preview<br>Preview the Selection<br>Make Predictions/Set Purpose | Inferential Thinking<br>Understanding Text Structure | Check Purpose<br>Discussion Questions<br>Writing: play summary<br>Vocabulary: word relationships<br>Phonics/Word Study: long and short *i* patterns |
| **LESSON 20**<br>**The Telescope**<br>(informational article)<br>page 152 | K-W-L Chart<br>Vocabulary Preview<br>Preview the Selection<br>Make Predictions/Set Purpose | Monitor Understanding | Check Purpose<br>Discussion Questions<br>Writing: double-entry journal<br>Vocabulary: word root *tele*<br>Phonics/Word Study: short and long *i* patterns |
| **LESSON 21**<br>**From the Diary of Sir Isaac Newton** *and* **Meteor Shower**<br>(diary entries and poem)<br>page 158 | Anticipation Guide<br>Vocabulary Preview<br>Preview the Selection<br>Make Predictions/Set Purpose | Making Connections | Check Purpose<br>Discussion Questions<br>Writing: diary entry<br>Vocabulary: multiple meanings<br>Phonics/Word Study: long *i* patterns |
| **LESSON 22**<br>**Almost Real Stars** *and* **A Very Special Visit**<br>(informational article and memoir)<br>page 164 | Concept Web<br>Vocabulary Preview<br>Preview the Selection<br>Make Predictions/Set Purpose | Inferential Thinking<br>Understanding Text Structure | Check Purpose<br>Discussion Questions<br>Writing: personal memoir<br>Vocabulary: word association<br>Phonics/Word Study: long and short *i* patterns (*r*-controlled) |
| **LESSON 23**<br>**Hercules, Star of the Skies**<br>(myth)<br>page 172 | Category Chart<br>Vocabulary Preview<br>Preview the Selection<br>Make Predictions/Set Purpose | Determining Importance | Check Purpose<br>Discussion Questions<br>Writing: description for visualizing<br>Vocabulary: homophones<br>Phonics/Word Study: long *i* review |
| **LESSON 24**<br>**Fun in Space, Meal Time,** *and* **Poems for Space Travelers**<br>(articles and poems)<br>page 178 | Activity Chart<br>Vocabulary Preview<br>Preview the Selection<br>Make Predictions/Set Purpose | Making Connections<br>Understanding Text Structure | Check Purpose<br>Discussion Questions<br>Writing: opinion paragraph<br>Vocabulary: review space terms<br>Phonics/Word Study: long and short *i* homophones |

**1961** Uri Gagarin (YOOR ee guh GAIR in) becomes the first human to orbit Earth on April 12. He is from the Soviet Union. His flight lasts one hour and forty-eight minutes.

1961

1960

1959

**1961** Ham, the U.S. chimpanzee, goes up into space. He returns safely.

**1961** Astronaut John Glenn orbits Earth. He stays in space for almost five hours.

**1961** The United States sends astronaut Alan Shepard into space on May 5. His flight takes him 116-½ miles above Earth. Shepard does not go into orbit around Earth because the United States isn't sure the capsule will make it through the drastic temperature changes of re-entry.

*The Soviet Union broke apart into separate countries in the 1990s. Now, we refer to Russia when talking about going into space.

3

## Vocabulary Preview

Tell students that using the context, the words or sentences around a word, can often help readers identify the meaning of a word. Ask students to use these steps to "read around" a word to determine its meaning.

1. Reread the sentence containing the unknown word to see if the surrounding words help define it.

2. Reread the sentences before and after the unknown word to see if they provide the needed context to define the word.

3. Look for synonyms (similar meanings), antonyms (opposite meanings), or definitions to help define the word.

### Student Journal page 40

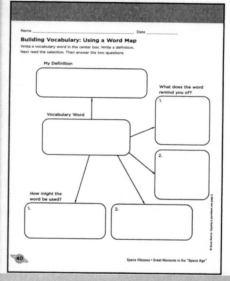

## Preview the Selection

Have students look through the article. Then ask:

- What do you notice first?
- What kind of selection is this—fiction or nonfiction? How do you know?
- What is a timeline?
- Where have you seen a timeline before?
- Why might an author write an article in the form of a timeline?

## Teacher Think Aloud

*A quick look at this selection shows it's a timeline that focuses on major events in the history of space exploration. This piece should be a good background for the content of this new magazine, Space Odyssey. It will be interesting to see how far we've come in space travel since the first date on the timeline, 1957. I also think the illustrations of the events will help me understand them better.*

## Make Predictions/ Set Purpose

Students should use the information they gathered in previewing the selection to make predictions about what they will learn. If students have trouble generating a purpose for reading, suggest that they read to answer any questions they have about the timeline.

## Comprehension

MAKING CONNECTIONS

Help students make connections with the text by asking:

- How does what you already knew about the space program connect with this article?

- Can you make a prediction based on what you knew and what you are reading?

- As you read, are you looking for the answers to questions you have?

- Can you make connections between this article and other texts you have read or other experiences you have had?

**1962** The United States sends up space probe *Mariner 2*. It spends 109 days in space and flies past the planet Venus.

**1969** Americans Neil Armstrong, Buzz Aldrin, and Michael Collins are the crew on the *Apollo 11* flight to the moon. Armstrong and Aldrin land on the moon on July 20 in the lunar module called *Eagle*. Armstrong is the first human to set foot on the moon.

197

1965

**1963** The first woman goes into space. She is from the Soviet Union. Her name is Valentina Tereshkova (val en TEE nuh tair esh KOH vuh).

4

# During Reading

## Comprehension

MONITOR UNDERSTANDING

Use these questions to model asking questions. Then have students ask their own questions and try to resolve any confusion.

- What does the word *satellite* mean?

- How do you pronounce it?

- What fix-up strategy can I use to fix my confusion?

# Teacher Think Aloud

*When I read the word* satellite, *I knew that it named something in space, but I wasn't sure what. I read ahead to see if the meaning would be explained. Two sentences later, I read: "A satellite is an object that is launched into orbit from a rocket. One purpose of a satellite is to study a heavenly body in space, often Earth." This time, reading ahead gave me the information I needed.*

## Comprehension

MAKING CONNECTIONS

Use these questions to model making connections with the text. Then have students make their own connections.

- Am I finding answers to the questions that I wrote in my double-entry journal?

- Am I coming up with new questions?

- What do I already know about the space program?

(See Differentiated Instruction.)

**1971** The Soviet Union launches the first space station, *Salyut 1*. The people on board do experiments in space.

**1973** The United States launches *Skylab*. This is the first American space station. Over the next year, three different crews live on *Skylab*. They study the universe and do medical experiments.

**1980**

**1975**

**1977** The United States launches *Voyager 2*. It is unmanned and travels for years. It flies past Jupiter, Saturn, Uranus, and Neptune between the years 1979 and 1989. Scientists learn a lot about the planets.

**1972** The United States sends *Pioneer 10* into space. It flies by Jupiter in 1973. It is unmanned, which means that there are no people on board.

5

## Teacher Think Aloud

*As I read the entry for 1958, I see that the first satellite was launched that year. Today I watch satellite weather forecasts and I know people who have satellite dishes on their houses for TV and Internet connections. So something familiar from my everyday life became possible because scientists began launching satellites 50 years ago.*

## Fix-Up Strategies

Offer these strategies to help students read independently.

**If you don't understand what you're reading:**

- Reread the difficult section to look for clues to help you comprehend.

- Read ahead to find clues to help you comprehend.

- Retell, or say in your own words, what you've read.

- Visualize, or form mental pictures of, what you've read.

**If you don't understand a word:**

- Reread the sentence. Look for ideas and words that provide meaning clues.

- Find clues by reading a few sentences before and after the confusing word.

- Look for the base or root word and think about its meaning.

- Think about the topic or plot at this point to see if either offers meaning clues.

## Writing Double-entry Journal

*SMALL GROUP*

If any students asked questions that were not answered in the selection, have them follow these steps:

1. Note in the right-hand column that the article did not answer the question. Then speculate as to where the answer might be found.

2. Add a thought or two to the right-hand column that describes some interesting thoughts you had as you read.

### Student Journal page 41

Name _____ Date _____

**Writing: Double-Entry Journal**

In the left-hand column, write five questions you think the selection might answer. Then read to see if your questions are answered. Write the answers in the right-hand column.

| Questions I Hope to Answer | Answers to My Questions |
|---|---|
| 1. | 1. |
| 2. | 2. |
| 3. | 3. |
| 4. | 4. |
| 5. | 5. |

Space Odyssey • Great Moments in the "Space Age"   41

---

**1986** The Soviet Union launches Space Station *Mir*. Cosmonauts live on *Mir*. Unlike the shuttle, *Mir* stays in space. They do experiments to learn about living in space.

**1981** The United States launches the Space Shuttle *Columbia*. It is the first space shuttle. After each mission, it comes back to Earth so that it can be flown again.

**1985**

**1986** *Challenger* explodes in January, seventy-four seconds after its launch. The whole crew is killed. The solid fuel booster rockets are redesigned to make future travel safer.

**1980**

**1983** Sally Ride becomes the first American woman to go into space. She joins the crew of the Space Shuttle *Challenger*.

6

---

# After Reading

*WHOLE CLASS* Use one or more activities.

## Check Purpose

Have students decide if their purpose was met. Were students' questions answered? What new questions do they have?

## Discussion Questions

Start a group discussion with the following questions.

1. What events from the timeline stood out to you? Why? (Details)

2. What events had you heard about before? (Making Connections)

3. Based on what you know from the article, what do you predict might happen next in the space program? What leads you to think that? (Predict, Draw Conclusions)

## Revisit: Category Chart

Revisit the category chart that was started in Before Reading. Have students recall what they read, and then add more space events to the chart.

## Revisit: Word Map

Have students complete the remaining boxes on the word map on *Student Journal* page 40. Discuss the two questions as a group: *What does the word remind you of? How might the word be used?*

**1993** Space travel began as a contest between two countries, but that changes in 1993. Russia agrees to join the United States in building an International Space Station (ISS).

**1995**

**1990**

**1988** A new space shuttle called *Discovery* replaces *Challenger*.

**1995** The American Space Shuttle *Atlantis* docks with *Mir* in June. The three Soviet cosmonauts had been on *Mir* for three months. They return to Earth with the seven U.S. astronauts aboard *Atlantis*.

7

## Answers to Student Journal page 42

| | |
|---|---|
| NASA | **N**ational **A**eronautics and **S**pace **A**dministration |
| RADAR | **R**adio **D**etecting **A**nd **R**anging |
| LASER | **L**ight **A**mplification by **S**timulated **E**mission of **R**adiation |
| SCUBA | **S**elf-**C**ontained **U**nderwater **B**reathing **A**pparatus |
| ASAP | **A**s **S**oon **A**s **P**ossible |

Name _____ Date _____

**Building Vocabulary: Acronyms**
Work with a partner to find out what these acronyms stand for. Consult a dictionary, if necessary. Then underline the letters used to form the acronym.

| Acronym | Abbreviation for |
|---|---|
| NASA | |
| RADAR | |
| LASER | |
| SCUBA | |
| ASAP | |

42     Space Odyssey • Great Moments in the "Space Age"

---

## Writing Double-entry Journal

Have students work in pairs to fill in the right-hand side of the double-entry journal on *Student Journal* page 41. They should write the questions they had and the answers to their questions (if they were found) along with any other thoughts and reactions to what they read. Have pairs share their results. (See Differentiated Instruction.)

## Vocabulary Acronyms

Point out the 1958 entry that contains the term *NASA*. Explain that the term *NASA* is an acronym. An acronym is a type of abbreviation formed from the first letter (or letters) of a phrase or a compound term. It is pronounced as a word or as letter names. *NASA* stands for National Aeronautics and Space Administration. Have students complete *Student Journal* page 42.

## Phonics/Word Study

### Long *e* Patterns

Display this sentence: *We bel_ _ve in th_s_ t_ _ ns!* Tell the students that each incomplete word has the long *e* sound. Point out that each long *e* spelling is different. Ask students to suggest the missing letters that complete each word and give it the long *e* sound. Now, work with students to complete the in-depth long *e* patterns activity on TE page 106.

**1997** The United States sends a space probe called *Pathfinder* to Mars. It takes seven months for the probe to reach Mars. When it lands, *Pathfinder's* "walls" unfold. *Sojourner* rolls out. It is a remote-controlled vehicle that scientists tell what to do through computers. It is solar-powered. Its job is to take pictures and study the weather and surface of the planet. (Since 1997, probes have been to the Sun and all the planets except Pluto.)

**1998** John Glenn at age 77 makes history again! This time Glenn is the oldest person to fly into space. Glenn flies with the *Discovery* crew. He studies how space flight affects aging. John Glenn was a United States senator from Ohio until 1999.

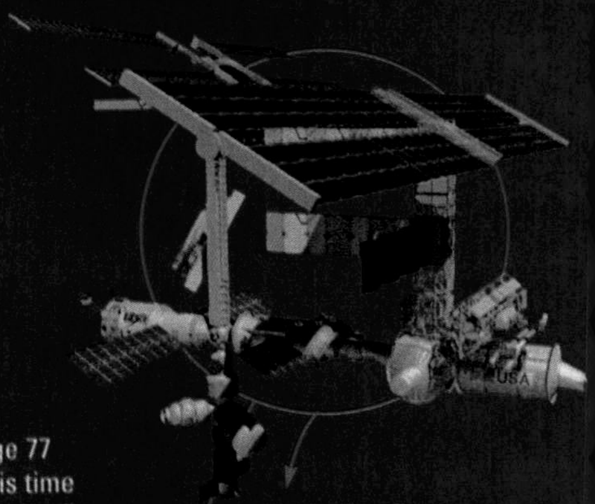

**1998** The first two parts of the ISS were launched and joined in space. One piece was launched from Russia. The other piece was launched from the United States.

1998

1996

## STAR SAILOR

The words *astronaut* and *cosmonaut* look somewhat alike. In fact, they have the same meaning. *Cosmonaut* is the Russian word for *astronaut*. *Naut* is from the Greek language. It means "sailor." *Astro* is Greek for "star." *Cosmo* is from the Greek word *kosmos,* which means "universe." The two words have similar backgrounds and meanings. They just ended up in different languages!

8

## INTERNATIONAL SPACE STATION

The International Space Station (ISS) is a place for astronauts and scientists to do experiments. The experiments have to do with many different kinds of science. People spend months at a time at the ISS. To check on the progress of the ISS, visit NASA's website at: http://spaceflight.nasa.gov. On the website, you can learn about how the space station is being built. You can hear what astronauts have to say about life aboard the U.S. Space Shuttle. You can even learn about the next mission NASA is planning.

**2001** U.S. Commander Bill Sheperd and Cosmonauts Yuri Gidzenko and Sergei Krikalev live and work together on the ISS. They have visitors in February 2001. The crew of the U.S. Space Shuttle *Atlantis* delivers the International Space Station's latest part.

**2003** The Space Shuttle *Columbia* breaks apart upon re-entry into Earth's atmosphere. The shuttle is destroyed and its crew of seven astronauts are killed.

**2002**

**2000**

**2002** The beam carries the first space railroad! The space railcar will carry the Station's robot arm. The train will carry the arm anywhere it is needed on the track.

**2002** The International Space Station is growing. The STS-110 crew adds a new forty-three-foot long beam. Astronauts work outside the Space Station. Robot arms work, too! The arms move the beam and the astronauts as they work.

## SHARING SPACE

More countries have joined the United States and Russia to learn about space. They all work to help the ISS expand. These countries include Japan, Canada, and many European countries. In the future, astronauts from all over the world will be able to stop at ISS. They will be able to rest and refuel before continuing on their journeys to the moon and beyond. ◆

9

# Phonics/Word Study

## Long *e* Patterns

▶ Write the following words on the board: *greed*, *chief*, and *these*.

▶ Ask students if these words contain short *e* or long *e*.

▶ Use the Long *e*: Sort Four sheet to model the sorting process for students. (See *Word Study Manual* page 46.) Write the headings *ee*, *ie*, *eCe* and the first few words in the appropriate columns.

▶ Students will eventually encounter words like *rein*, *friend*, and *seize*. Let them discover them on their own. Use those words to create an Oddball column.

▶ Discuss the sort, what students learned, and why *friend* belongs in the Oddball column.

▶ Once the sort is complete, hand out the Long *e*: Sort Four sheet and ask students to cut up the words and do the sort on their own or in groups.

▶ Check the final sorts.

| Long *e*: Sort Four | | | |
|---|---|---|---|
| *ee* | *ie* | *eCe* | Oddball |
| greed | chief | these | rein |
| free | brief | eve | friend |
| speech | field | scene | seize |
| creep | shriek | theme | |
| cheer | thief | | |
| tree | | | |

For more information on word sorts and spelling stages, see pages 5–31 in the *Word Study Manual*.

# Focus on . . .

Use one or more activities in this section to focus on a particular area of need in your students.

## Comprehension  STRATEGY SUPPORT  INDEPENDENT

To help those students who need more practice using the strategies covered in this lesson, work one-on-one or in small groups to apply the strategy prompts below. Apply the prompts to a *Reading Advantage* paperback, a classroom library book, or a new or familiar selection in the magazine. Always model your own thinking first.

### Monitor Understanding

• Do I understand what I'm reading? If not, what part is confusing to me?

• What fix-up strategies can I use to solve the problem? (See During Reading for fix-up strategies.)

• Why did a character say (do, think, ask) that?

• What images do I visualize from the text? What parts can't I visualize?

• Why did the author include (or not include) those details?

### Making Connections

• What does this article remind me of?

• What do I already know about this topic?

• Where have I heard about this topic before?

• What do I have in common with the characters, people, or situation in the text?

• What other books, stories, articles, movies, or TV shows does this make me think about?

## Writing Personal Timeline  INDEPENDENT

Have students label and illustrate a personal timeline of their lives. To help students organize and plan, suggest that students first list four to five events they would include on the personal timeline. Have students place the events in sequential order before adding them to the timeline.

For more sequencing practice for students, see lessons in *Writing Advantage*, pages 113–151.

## Fluency: Phrasing

SMALL GROUP

After students have read the article at least once, they can use a portion of it to practice fluent reading. Ask students to work in pairs, taking turns reading aloud every other entry. As students read, partners should listen to provide feedback that encourages even pacing. Model the difference between evenly paced reading and unevenly paced reading.

As you listen to partners reading, use these prompts to help them read at an even pace.

▶ Listen to me read. Then you read it just like I did.

▶ Reread this sentence a little bit faster (or slower) so readers can make sense of the words.

▶ Remember to use the punctuation as clues to reading evenly. Pause at the ends of sentences.

When students read aloud, do they—

✓ demonstrate quick recognition of words and phrases?

✓ exhibit an understanding of phrasal construction?

✓ incorporate appropriate timing, stress, and intonation?

## English Language Learners

SMALL GROUP

To support students as they comprehend "Great Moments in the 'Space Age,'" help students create a timeline containing the main ideas.

1. Remind students what a timeline is. Point out that the text contains one type of timeline.

2. Have partners choose dates that contain information they found interesting. Help them create their own timelines.

3. Have students explain the information on their timelines to a partner.

## Independent Activity Options

INDEPENDENT

While you work with individuals or small groups, others can work independently on one or more of the following options.

▶ Level A paperback books, see TE pages 371–376

▶ Level A *eZines*

▶ Repeat word sorts from this lesson

▶ *Student Journal* pages for this lesson

▶ *Writing Advantage* independent lessons

# Assessment

## Strategy Assessment

To help you and your students assess their use of comprehension strategies, ask the following questions. Students can complete a written response or provide verbal answers in a one-on-one reading conference.

1. **Monitor Comprehension** As you read the timeline, what did you do to monitor your own comprehension? (Answers will vary. Students may say that they read ahead to find clues to help them comprehend.)

2. **Making Connections** What connections did you make with this article? (Answers will vary. Students may say the article connected with their prior knowledge about space flights and space travel.)

For ongoing informal assessment, use the checklists on pages 61–64 of *Level A Assessment*.

## Word Study Assessment

Use these steps to help you and your students assess their understanding of long *e* spelling patterns.

1. Draw three columns on the board with the following headings: *grief, green, Chinese.*

2. Point out that each word has the long *e* sound.

3. Read the following words aloud one by one and have volunteers write each word in the column with the same spelling pattern: *these, yield, beets, Pete, shield, here, feet, pier, sweet.* The answers are shown.

| grief | green | Chinese |
| --- | --- | --- |
| yield | beets | these |
| shield | feet | Pete |
| pier | sweet | here |

Great Source
Reading Advantage

Level A
Assessment

# Moon Walk

*Space Odyssey,* pages 10–13

## SUMMARY

In July, 1969, human beings walked on the moon for the first time. The event is related here in the form of a **news story**.

## COMPREHENSION STRATEGIES

Monitor Understanding

## WRITING

Labeled Illustration

## VOCABULARY

Word Root *astro*

## PHONICS/WORD STUDY

Long and Short *e* Patterns (*r*-controlled)

### Lesson Vocabulary

| | |
|---|---|
| vehicles | dock |
| lunar module | quarantine |
| gravity | |

## MATERIALS

*Space Odyssey,* pp. 10–13
*Student Journal,* pp. 43–45
*Word Study Manual,* p. 47
*Writing Advantage,* pp. 113–151

# Moon Walk

The *Eagle* lands on the moon.

10

# Before Reading

WHOLE CLASS Use one or more activities.

## K-W-L Chart

Create a K-W-L chart like the one below. Read aloud the passage about the moon on TE page 94. Have students look for any information about the moon in "Great Moments in the 'Space Age.'" Work with students to add information to the chart.

| What We **Know** | What We **Want** to Know | What We **Learned** |
|---|---|---|
| | | |

## Vocabulary Preview

Review the vocabulary list with students. Ask each student to predict how the words might be used in the article. Then have students begin *Student Journal* page 43. Model the process for one of the words. Students will finish later.

## Preview the Selection

Have students survey the article. Point out the elements of a newspaper story: headline, subheads, date, captions. Real newspapers usually have bylines.

## Make Predictions/Set Purpose

Students should use the information they gathered in previewing the selection to make predictions about what they will learn. If students have trouble generating a purpose for reading, suggest that they read to learn what the first moonwalk was like and why it was important.

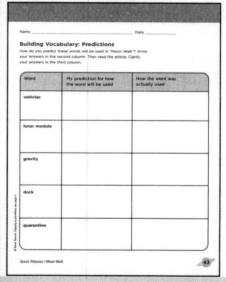

## Greenpark Times

Final Edition

July 21, 1969

# ASTRONAUTS WALK ON THE MOON!

Houston—A dream has come true! Yesterday, two American astronauts became the first people to ever walk on the moon. They landed on the moon in a small spacecraft called the *Eagle*. It had been attached to a bigger spacecraft called the *Columbia*. A third astronaut named Michael Collins stayed in the *Columbia* while the other two men landed on the moon.

### One Small Step

Neil Armstrong was the first man to step onto the moon. He climbed down a ladder from the *Eagle*. He took a step on the rocky soil. Then he spoke by radio to millions of people on Earth. "That's one small step for man, one giant leap for mankind," he said. Armstrong meant that while it was a small step for an individual, it was a huge step forward in space exploration.

Buzz Aldrin soon joined Armstrong on the moon. The astronauts set up a TV camera. People all over the world watched the two men as they moved about. The first thing they did was plant an American flag on the moon. A cloth flag was not placed on the moon because there is no air on the moon to make it wave. The flag is made of metal. It looks like it is waving, but it is not. (The metal was painted to look like it was blowing.) Then the men saluted the flag.

### The Beginning of the Moon Journey

The moon landing is the peak event in the *Apollo 11* journey. This historic trip to the moon began five days ago, at 9:32 A.M. on July 16. The place was the Kennedy Space Center in Florida. A powerful rocket sent the spacecraft *Apollo 11* into orbit around Earth. *Apollo 11* went around Earth one and one-half times. Then its rocket fired, and the spacecraft raced toward the moon.

*Apollo 11* carried the astronauts and two separate <u>vehicles</u>. One was the command module called the *Columbia*. It is the vehicle that landed on and rocketed off the moon. The other vehicle was the *Eagle*. The *Eagle* was the <u>lunar module</u>, a vehicle that could move around the moon. It was attached to the nose of the *Columbia*.

*Apollo 11* flew close to the moon on July 19. The spacecraft then fired its rockets. This sent *Columbia* and *Eagle* into orbit around the moon. Armstrong and Aldrin separated the *Eagle* from the *Columbia* twenty-four hours later. The *Eagle* traveled by itself to land on the moon with Armstrong and Aldrin aboard.

11

## Comprehension

MONITOR UNDERSTANDING

Use the photos to help students visualize any confusing text.

1. Have students look at the photo of the American flag. Ask students to read the flag's description (third paragraph). How does the photo support their understanding of it?

2. Have students look at the *Eagle* inset photo and read the fifth and sixth paragraphs. How does the photo help them visualize this text?

3. Ask how other photos support the text.

### Student Journal page 43

Name _____ Date _____

**Building Vocabulary: Predictions**
How do you predict these words will be used in "Moon Walk"? Write your answers in the second column. Then read the article. Clarify your answers in the third column.

| Word | My prediction for how the word will be used | How the word was actually used |
|------|------|------|
| vehicles | | |
| lunar module | | |
| gravity | | |
| dock | | |
| quarantine | | |

Space Odyssey • Moon Walk

43

# During Reading

## Comprehension

SMALL GROUP

MONITOR UNDERSTANDING

Use these questions to model how to visualize the text. Then have students tell about a part they visualized and what details helped them to visualize it.

- What do I picture in my mind?
- What details help me create this image in my mind?
- How does this image help me understand what I am reading?

(See Differentiated Instruction.)

## Teacher Think Aloud

*I can picture a space shuttle speeding forward, trailed by flames. The details "powerful rocket" and "its rocket fired" helped me create this picture in my mind. This image helps me understand that a lot of force is needed to launch a space shuttle into orbit around Earth and the moon.*

## Fix-Up Strategies

Offer these strategies to help students read independently.

**If you don't understand what you're reading:**

- Reread the difficult section to look for clues to help you comprehend.
- Read ahead to find clues to help you comprehend.
- Retell, or say in your own words, what you've read.
- Visualize, or form mental pictures of, what you've read.

Michael Collins pilots the *Columbia*.

Armstrong and Aldrin walk on the moon.

Astronauts left footprints on the surface of the moon.

## Exploring the Moon

Armstrong and Aldrin spent twenty-one hours on the moon. Most of the time they were inside the *Eagle*. They spent two hours and thirty-two minutes outside exploring the moon. They did experiments and collected moon rocks. They took many pictures. The two men bounced as they walked on the moon. That's because the moon's <u>gravity</u> does not pull down on the men with the same force as gravity on Earth. The men thought that they might fall down a lot, but that did not happen. They had trained well on Earth in low gravity rooms, which helped them learn what low gravity felt like.

Michael Collins had his own jobs to do in the *Columbia*. He had to orbit around the moon. He had to take some pictures, too. He also had to wait for the other astronauts to blast off from the moon.

At the end of the twenty-one hours, Armstrong and Aldrin got back into the *Eagle* and left the moon. They guided the *Eagle* to <u>dock</u>, or join together, with *Columbia*. Armstrong and Aldrin climbed back aboard the *Columbia*. Then all three men began the journey back to Earth.

## One Small—Oops!

Neil Armstrong was supposed to say, "One small step for a man, one giant leap for mankind." (When he said it, he left out the word *a*.) The meaning of the original sentence is clear. Although he was just one man taking one small step, he was taking a step on the moon! That meant that many possibilities lay ahead in space travel. The way the sentence came out is a little less clear if you stop to study it. Man and mankind sometimes mean the same thing. Still, who can blame him? Armstrong had a lot on his mind. He had no idea at the time if he would return safely to Earth. That worry plus the fear of speaking to an audience of millions of people are good reasons for making a little mistake in a speech.

12

# After Reading

WHOLE CLASS   Use one or more activities.

## Check Purpose

Have students decide if their purpose was met. What was the first moon walk like? Why was it important?

## Discussion Questions

Continue the group discussion with the following questions.

1. What was your first reaction to the article? (Making Connections)

2. What surprised you most about what you read? (Details)

3. What can you infer (guess) about the dangers involved with being an astronaut? (Inferential Thinking)

## Revisit: K-W-L Chart

Review the information in the *K* column. Have students check to see which of their questions in the *W* column were answered. Add that information to the *L* column along with other information they learned.

## Revisit: Prediction Chart

Have students complete the predictions chart on *Student Journal* page 43. How were the words actually used?

# Greenpark Times

*nal Edition*

July 24, 1969

## ASTRONAUTS HOME SAFE!

Honolulu—Astronauts Neil Armstrong, Buzz Aldrin, and Michael Collins are safely back on Earth today. The spacecraft *Columbia* splashed down into the Pacific Ocean at 12:50 P.M. It set down 812 sea miles southwest of Hawaii. A helicopter picked up the three astronauts. It took them to the USS *Hornet*. The ship will take the astronauts to Hawaii. The men will then go on to Houston, Texas.

The USS *Hornet* retrieves *Columbia* from the Pacific Ocean.

### Return Trip from the Moon

The astronauts brought moon rocks back to Earth for study.

When the three men were ready, they fired a rocket to break free from the moon's gravity. *Columbia* began falling toward Earth. *Columbia* reached a speed of 25,000 miles an hour as it entered Earth's atmosphere. The pressure of the atmosphere on the spacecraft helped to slow it down. The spacecraft had to enter the atmosphere at just the right angle, though. If the angle was wrong, the speed and pressure could have burned up the spacecraft. Lastly, two different kinds of parachutes were released to slow it down more.

Now that the astronauts are safely home, they will be placed in quarantine (KWAR un teen) for seventeen days. This is to be sure that they did not bring back any germs from the moon. ◆

13

## Writing Labeled Illustration

To help students with the accuracy of their illustrations:

1. Have students name the spaceship that carried the command module and lunar module. (*Apollo 11*) Point out that this should be the largest vehicle in students' drawings.

2. Ask students to name the command module (*Columbia*) and the lunar module (*Eagle*).

3. Have students locate the text that describes how the *Columbia* and *Eagle* are attached. (page 11) Remind students to show the connection in their illustrations.

### Student Journal page 45

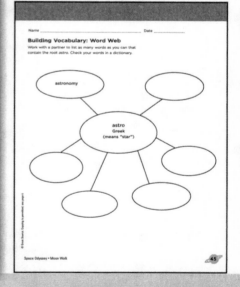

---

## Writing Labeled Illustration

Have each student draw and label his or her impression of the first vehicles that went to the moon on *Student Journal* page 44. Suggest that students reread the fifth paragraph on page 11 of the magazine to help them visualize the parts to include. Students can label *Apollo 11*, *Columbia*, and *Eagle*. (See Differentiated Instruction.)

## Vocabulary Word Root *astro*

Display *astronaut*. Ask students:

- What do you know about this word or other words that begin with *astro*?

- What might the root *astro* mean? Why?

- How could you check your guess?

Tell students that *astro* is a Greek root meaning "star." Analyze other *astro* words to see how the root gives meaning to the word. Now have partners complete *Student Journal* page 45.

## Phonics/Word Study

### Long and Short *e* Patterns

Display: *What can we* *infer* *about the* *fears* *of space* *pioneers*? Mention that each underlined word has an *r*-controlled *e*. Ask students whether this *e* has a long or a short sound, and have them suggest some other words that have the long *e* sound spelled *ear* or *eer*, or the short *e* sound spelled *er*. Now, work with students to complete the in-depth long and short *e* patterns activity on TE page 112.

## Phonics/Word Study

## Long and Short *e* Patterns (*r*-controlled)

▶ Write the following words on the board: *her, near,* and *cheer.* Tell students that they are continuing their study of the *e* patterns. The words in this sort, however, are a little tricky.

▶ Briefly review short and long *e* vowel patterns with students. Write the word *her* on the board. Ask if the *e* in *her* is long or short.

▶ Without telling students if they are right or wrong, write the word *here* on the board. Ask students if *here* helps them figure out which *e* is short and which is long.

▶ Discuss the difficulty the letter *r* causes. Explain how it "robs" the vowel of its usual sound. The *e* in *her* sounds very different from the *e* in *bet.*

▶ Use the Long and Short *e*: *r*-controlled Vowels sheet to model the sorting process for students. (See *Word Study Manual* page 47.) Write the headings Short *e* (*er*), Long *e* (*ear*), Long *e* (*eer*), and Oddball and the first few words in the appropriate columns.

▶ Discuss the sort and what students learned about *r*-controlled vowels. Note that sometimes the easiest way to tell if an *r*-controlled vowel is short or long is by saying aloud the long and short sound in the word. Doing this clarifies whether the vowel sound is short or long.

▶ Once the sort is complete, hand out the Long and Short *e*: *r*-controlled Vowels sheet and ask students to cut up the words and do the sort on their own or in groups.

▶ Check the final sorts for accuracy.

### Long and Short *e*: *r*-controlled Vowels

| Short *e* (*er*) | Long *e* (*ear*) | Long *e* (*eer*) | Oddball |
|---|---|---|---|
| her | near | cheer | heart |
| germ | clear | deer | |
| jerk | fear | queer | |
| herb | year | peer | |
| perch | spear | creep | |
| fern | beard | | |

For more information on word sorts and spelling stages, see pages 5–31 in the *Word Study Manual.*

# Focus on . . .

Use one or more activities in this section to focus on a particular area of need in your students.

## Comprehension [STRATEGY SUPPORT] INDEPENDENT

To help those students who need more practice using the strategies covered in this lesson, work one-on-one or in small groups to apply the strategy prompts below. Apply the prompts to a *Reading Advantage* paperback, a classroom library book, or a new or familiar selection in the magazine. Always model your own thinking first.

### Monitor Understanding

• Do I understand what I'm reading? If not, what part is confusing to me?

• What fix-up strategies can I use to solve the problem? (See During Reading for fix-up strategies.)

• Why did a character say (do, think, ask) that?

• What images do I visualize from the text? What parts can't I visualize?

• Why did the author include (or not include) those details?

## Writing Description INDEPENDENT

Have each student choose an object from the article that interested him or her. Then have the student draw the object and write a description of it. Suggest that students first create graphic organizers to help them include as many details as they can in their drawings and descriptions.

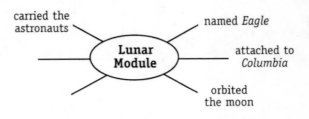

carried the astronauts — **Lunar Module** — named *Eagle*
attached to *Columbia*
orbited the moon

To provide more practice writing descriptive paragraphs, see lessons in *Writing Advantage* pages 113–151.

## Fluency: Pacing

After students have read the article at least once, they can use a small portion of it to practice reading with fluency and even pacing. Because the article is written as a news story, some students may decide to read aloud their portion as news reporters on a newscast.

Students should practice reading aloud to a partner. Point out to students that if they read too fast, too slow, or in a stopping-starting manner, their listeners will not be able to make sense of the words. Model the difference between evenly paced reading and unevenly paced reading.

As you listen to partners practice reading, use these prompts to guide them to read with an even pace:

▶ Listen to me read. Then you read it just as I did.

▶ Reread this sentence a little bit faster (or more slowly).

When students read aloud, do they—

✓ demonstrate a smooth pace, not too fast or too slow?

✓ incorporate well-timed pauses between words and phrases?

✓ reflect an awareness and understanding of punctuation?

## English Language Learners

To help students develop their understanding of text structure, extend the comprehension activity on TE page 109.

1. Remind students that photos help them understand what they are reading.

2. Explain that captions are words next to photos that provide information about what is in the photos.

3. Have students look at the photos throughout the text. Have them read and discuss the captions with a partner.

## Independent Activity Options

While you work with individuals or small groups, others can work independently on one or more of the following options.

▶ Level A paperback books, see TE pages 371–376

▶ Level A *eZines*

▶ Repeat word sorts from this lesson

▶ *Student Journal* pages for this lesson

▶ *Writing Advantage* independent lessons

# Assessment

## Strategy Assessment

To help you and your students assess their use of comprehension strategies, ask the following questions. Students can complete a written response or provide verbal answers in a one-on-one reading conference.

- **Monitor Understanding** As you read the article, how did visualizing help you monitor your understanding of the text? (Answers will vary. Students may say that they were able to use the photographs to help them visualize text descriptions that may have been confusing to them. They may say that when they tried to "see" in their minds the events and objects described, it helped them get a better understanding of what it would be like to walk on the moon.)

For ongoing informal assessment, use the checklists on pages 61–64 of *Level A Assessment*.

## Word Study Assessment

Use these steps to help you and your students assess their understanding of long and short *e* patterns (*r*-controlled).

1. Draw three columns on the board with the following headings: *fear, pioneer, infer*.

2. Point to the *e* in each word and ask whether it has a long or short *e* sound.

3. Read the following words aloud one by one and have volunteers write each word in the column with the same spelling pattern and sound: *prefer, appear, ear, confer, per, refer, shear, steer, year, deer, career*. The answers are shown.

| fear | pioneer | infer |
|------|---------|-------|
| appear | steer | prefer |
| ear | deer | confer |
| shear | career | per |
| year | | refer |

Great Source
Reading Advantage

Level A
Assessment

## LESSON 15
# Suited for Space

*Space Odyssey*, pages 14–17

### SUMMARY
This **nonfiction article**, organized in a question-answer format, is filled with facts about space suits.

### COMPREHENSION STRATEGIES
Understanding Text Structure

### WRITING
Explanatory Paragraph

### VOCABULARY
Multiple Meanings

### PHONICS/WORD STUDY
Long *e* Review

### Lesson Vocabulary
| | |
|---|---|
| air pressure | ignite |
| fabrics | mission |
| resist | |

### MATERIALS
*Space Odyssey*, pp. 14–17
*Student Journal*, pp. 46–49
*Word Study Manual*, p. 48
*Writing Advantage*, pp. 8–12

# Suited for Space

Space suits keep astronauts safe when they travel and work in space. So what are they like? How do they keep astronauts safe? Here are some questions and answers about them.

### Early Space Suits

The first space suit was made around 1935. A jet pilot wore it.

The first astronauts wore these. That was back in 1959.

14

**Q** Why do astronauts need space suits?

**A** There is no oxygen in space. It is a vacuum. You can't breathe. It gets very cold or hot. The air pressure, the weight of air pressing down, is low. Blood can boil! In space, there is much less air pressure than on Earth. Without a space suit, the gases in your blood would boil out like the bubbles in a glass of soda. The escaping gas would expand your blood vessels and cause them to burst. A space suit keeps the air pressure around your body at Earth level, so that these gases do not escape from your blood.

**Q** What are space suits made of?

**A** They are made of many different kind of fabrics, or cloths. These are in layers, like a sandwich. Gore-Tex® and Dacron® keep the wearer cool or warm. (You may have a jacket made of these fabrics.) Another fabric layer is Kevlar®. It protects the spacesuit from space dust or tears. Mylar® covers a space suit to reflect the sunlight. (Shiny silver balloons are also made of Mylar®.) The helmet is clear plastic.

# Before Reading
WHOLE CLASS Use one or more activities.

## Make a T-Chart
Ask students what they know about space suits. Encourage students to offer an explanation for the parts they mention or the facts they name. Make a T-chart to record students' responses.

| What you know about space suits | Possible use or explanation |
|---|---|
| made out of special materials | materials protect astronauts in space |
| oxygen tank or air supply | no air in space; need air supply |

## Vocabulary Preview
Display the vocabulary and read the words aloud. Help students make associations with the words. Ask: *What do you think about when you hear this word? Who might use this word?* Then have students complete *Student Journal* page 46. Model the process for one of the words.

## Preview the Selection
Have students look through the article. Discuss students' observations.

## Make Predictions/Set Purpose
Students should use the information they gathered in previewing the selection to make predictions about what they will learn. If students have trouble generating a purpose for reading, suggest that they read to build a mental image of a space suit.

**Q** What size is a space suit?

**A** Space suits are made to fit each astronaut, so they come in all sizes.

**Q** How much does a space suit weigh?

**A** Most space suits weigh around 100 pounds. The space suits that astronauts wore when they walked on the moon weighed 180 pounds on Earth. But the suits weighed only thirty pounds on the moon! That's because the moon's gravity is one-sixth that of Earth's gravity.

**Q** How much does a space suit cost?

**A** Each one costs twelve million dollars.

**Q** How long does a space suit last?

**A** It lasts about eight years.

**Q** What do astronauts on the space shuttle wear for lift-off and landing?

**A** Astronauts wear boots and orange-colored pressure suits. These will protect them if the air pressure on the shuttle fails. A back support pad goes on over the suit. Astronauts put on a helmet and gloves after they are in their seats. A parachute is put on the back of each suit to use in an emergency bailout.

**Q** What do astronauts wear while they are in orbit?

**A** They wear underwear, shirts, long pants or shorts, and slippers or socks. They have jackets to wear if they get cold. The clothes have many pockets. These all have zippers or flaps. All of the clothes are made to <u>resist</u> fire so that a spark will not <u>ignite</u> the suit.

**Q** How often do astronauts change their clothes?

**A** They change their underwear, shirts, and socks every two days. Pants and shorts are changed about once a week.

This is from the late 1960s and 1970s. It was worn for moon flights. Extra parts were added for moon walks.

This is the space suit worn for lift-off and landing.

15

## Comprehension
UNDERSTANDING TEXT STRUCTURE

Help students understand the text structure by asking these questions:

- What does each blue *Q* signal in this text? What does each red *A* signal?
- What else do you notice about the type that helps you identify the questions and answers?
- Why is the diagram on page 16 a good way to present information about space suits?

### Student Journal page 46

Name _____ Date _____

**Building Vocabulary: Making Associations**
Choose two vocabulary words. Think about what you already know about each word. Then answer the questions for each word.

| air pressure | resist | mission |
| fabrics | ignite | |

Word _____

What do you think about when you read this word? _____

Who might use this word? _____

What do you already know about this word? _____

Word _____

What do you think about when you read this word? _____

Who might use this word? _____

What do you already know about this word? _____

Now watch for these words in the magazine selection. Were you on the right track?

46     Space Odyssey • Suited for Space

# During Reading

## Comprehension
SMALL GROUP
UNDERSTANDING TEXT STRUCTURE

Use these questions to model how to identify the question-answer text structure of the selection. Then have students tell how this text structure helps them understand the information.

- What do I notice about how the information is structured?
- How does the text structure help me understand the information?

(See Differentiated Instruction.)

## Teacher Think Aloud
*The author wrote this article in a question-answer format. This format is helpful because I can focus on one piece of information at a time. I also suspect these are frequently asked questions, the types of questions you and I would be likely to ask about space suits. That's good because frequently asked questions explore the most important information on a topic.*

## Fix-Up Strategies
Offer these strategies to help students read independently.

**If you don't understand what you're reading:**

- Reread the difficult section to look for clues to help you comprehend.
- Read ahead to find clues to help you comprehend.
- Retell, or say in your own words, what you've read.
- Visualize, or form mental pictures of, what you've read.

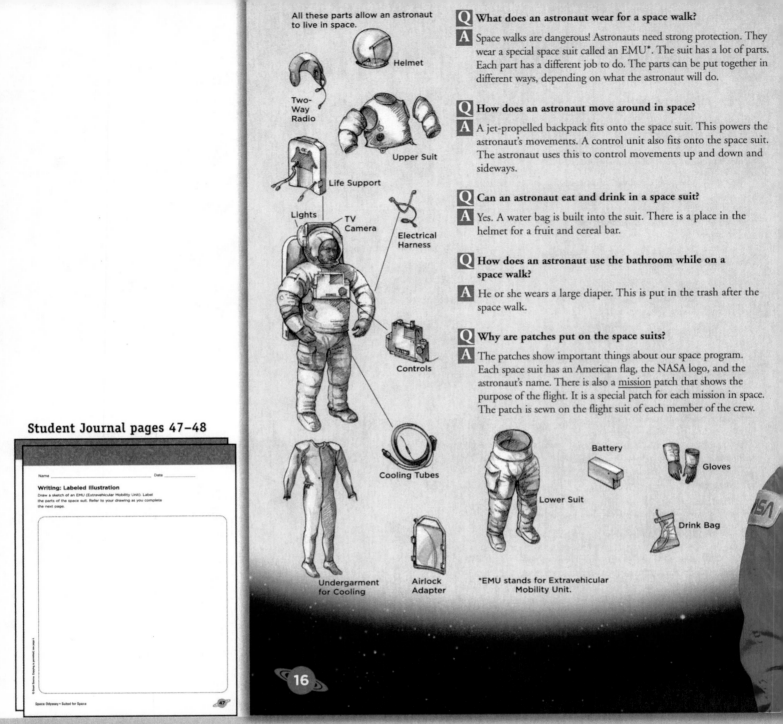

All these parts allow an astronaut to live in space.

- Helmet
- Two-Way Radio
- Upper Suit
- Life Support
- Lights
- TV Camera
- Electrical Harness
- Controls
- Cooling Tubes
- Undergarment for Cooling
- Airlock Adapter
- Lower Suit
- Battery
- Gloves
- Drink Bag

*EMU stands for Extravehicular Mobility Unit.

**Q** What does an astronaut wear for a space walk?

**A** Space walks are dangerous! Astronauts need strong protection. They wear a special space suit called an EMU*. The suit has a lot of parts. Each part has a different job to do. The parts can be put together in different ways, depending on what the astronaut will do.

**Q** How does an astronaut move around in space?

**A** A jet-propelled backpack fits onto the space suit. This powers the astronaut's movements. A control unit also fits onto the space suit. The astronaut uses this to control movements up and down and sideways.

**Q** Can an astronaut eat and drink in a space suit?

**A** Yes. A water bag is built into the suit. There is a place in the helmet for a fruit and cereal bar.

**Q** How does an astronaut use the bathroom while on a space walk?

**A** He or she wears a large diaper. This is put in the trash after the space walk.

**Q** Why are patches put on the space suits?

**A** The patches show important things about our space program. Each space suit has an American flag, the NASA logo, and the astronaut's name. There is also a mission patch that shows the purpose of the flight. It is a special patch for each mission in space. The patch is sewn on the flight suit of each member of the crew.

16

## Student Journal pages 47–48

Name _____ Date _____

**Writing: Labeled Illustration**

Draw a sketch of an EMU (Extravehicular Mobility Unit). Label the parts of the space suit. Refer to your drawing as you complete the next page.

Space Odyssey • Suited for Space          47

# After Reading

WHOLE CLASS  Use one or more activities.

## Check Purpose

Have students think about the mental models of space suits they built as they read. Were students able to visualize what a space suit looks like? Were they able to understand the different parts and purposes of the space suits?

## Discussion Questions

Start a group discussion with the following questions.

1. Describe the suit that astronauts wear for lift-off and landing and the suit they wear for space walks. (Details)

2. Do you think the question-answer format was an effective way to convey information about space suits? Why or why not? (Evaluate)

## Revisit: T-Chart

Briefly revisit the T-chart students began in Before Reading. Ask if students would like to change any of the information they listed on the chart. Then ask if students have additional information they would like to add.

**Q** Why is the mission patch important?

**A** The patch gives the name of the mission. The patch also has one or more pictures that show something about the mission.

**Q** How is a mission patch created?

**A** The crew brainstorms their ideas. An artist makes computer or hand drawings of the ideas. The astronauts look at the drawings. Other people who work on the mission from the ground also look at the drawings. When they all agree, the artist designs the final patch. Mission patches show part of the history of our space program. ◆

## Mission Patches

You can look at many of the mission patches online. Go to this address: http://www.hq.nasa.gov/office/pao/History/mission_patches.html.

first piece of International Space Station

crew names

Big Dipper shows the way for travelers

rising sun = a new program, the ISS

Space Shuttle

Space Shuttle Mission STS-88
December 4–15, 1998

Gemini 9

Mercury 9

STS-81

Skylab 2 & 3

Apollo 11

The position of the patches on the space suit remains the same for each mission. The mission patch is placed on the right side of the chest. The astronaut's name and NASA logo is placed on the left side of the chest. The U.S. flag is placed on the left shoulder.

17

DIFFERENTIATED INSTRUCTION SMALL GROUP

## Vocabulary
### Multiple Meanings

To help students with this activity, explain that a word with multiple meanings is a word that can have more than one meaning. For example, you write with a *pen*. A pig lives in a *pen*. Other examples include *hand*, *note*, *staple*, *book*, and *class*.

### Student Journal page 49

Name _____ Date _____

**Building Vocabulary: Words with Multiple Meanings**
Write two definitions for each word listed below.

| Word | First Definition | Second Definition |
|------|-----------------|-------------------|
| vacuum | an appliance used for cleaning | emptiness of space |
| suit | | |
| space | | |
| patch | | |
| mission | | |

Space Odyssey • Suited for Space

49

## Writing
### Explanatory Paragraph

To prepare for writing an explanatory paragraph, have students draw and label the various parts of an EMU on *Student Journal* page 47. Then explain that the paragraph should describe two parts of the EMU. After students choose two parts, look at *Student Journal* page 48 together. Brainstorm some details they might add for each feature. Then have students complete *Student Journal* page 48.

## Vocabulary
### Multiple Meanings

Point out the word *vacuum* in the first answer on page 14. Ask:

- What does *vacuum* mean here?
- What's a more common usage?
- How can you connect the two?
- What other words do you know that have multiple meanings?

Have students complete *Student Journal* page 49. (See Differentiated Instruction.)

## Phonics/Word Study
### Long *e* Review

Display: *This w _ _ k, w_ will r _ _ d th_s_ br _ _f selections about the car_ _ rs of l _ _ ders in space.* Explain that each incomplete word has the long *e* sound and that the spellings of these long *e* sounds differ. Ask students to suggest the missing letter or letters that complete each word. Now, work with students to complete the in-depth long *e* review activity on TE page 118.

### Long *e* Review

This is a good time to review long *e* vowel patterns. Write the following headings on the board: *ee, e, ea, ie, eCe, r*-controlled.

▶ Brainstorm together one word for each heading. Write them on the board.

▶ Ask students what they notice about all the vowel sounds. (They're all long *e*.)

▶ Now have students complete the Long *e*: Review sort on *Word Study Manual* page 48. *Seize* is the only Oddball.

▶ Check final sorts.

| Long *e* Review | | | | | |
|---|---|---|---|---|---|
| *ee* | *e* | *ea* | *ie* | *eCe* | *r*-controlled |
| sheet | she | bleak | relief | these | cheer |
| fleet | he | plead | shriek | theme | fear |
| creep | we | clean | field | eve | |

For more information on word sorts and spelling stages, see pages 5–31 in the *Word Study Manual*.

# Focus on . . .

Use one or more activities in this section to focus on a particular area of need in your students.

## Comprehension  STRATEGY SUPPORT  INDEPENDENT

To help those students who need more practice using the strategies covered in this lesson, work one-on-one or in small groups to apply the strategy prompts below. Apply the prompts to a *Reading Advantage* paperback, a classroom library book, or a new or familiar selection in the magazine. Always model your own thinking first.

### Understanding Text Structure

- What kind of text is this? (book, story, article, guidebook, play, manual)
- How does the author organize the text? (cause-effect, problem-solution, chronological order, description, question-answer, comparison-contrast)
- What details support my thoughts about the text structure?
- What is the cause (effect, problem, solution, order, question, answer)?
- If fiction, who are the characters? What is the setting, plot, conflict, and resolution?

## Writing **Design a Mission Patch**  INDEPENDENT

Have students work with partners to design original mission patches for themselves, imagining they are going on a mission to the moon. Have students brainstorm and list ideas before they begin. Students might create mission patches that incorporate a school logo or use words and signs that provide information about their personal interests. After students design their patches, have them write short explanations telling what the mission patch includes and why.

For additional brainstorming practice, see lessons in *Writing Advantage*, pages 8–12.

## Fluency: Expression

SMALL GROUP

After students have read the article at least once, have them read aloud with partners to practice fluent reading. Suggest that one student read the questions and the other read the answers. Then have partners switch roles.

As students read, caution them against reading too fast, too slow, or in a halting manner—actions that make it difficult for listeners to make sense of the words. Model the difference between evenly paced reading and unevenly paced reading. Then circulate among pairs as they read aloud, encouraging students to provide their partners with feedback on reading expressively and evenly.

As you listen to partners reading, use these prompts to help them read at an even pace.

▶ Listen to me read. Then read it just as I did.

▶ Reread this sentence a little bit faster, or more slowly.

▶ Try to make your voice sound a little stronger, or livelier, when you read. Your listeners will hear you better.

When students read aloud, do they—

✓ reflect an understanding of the text?

✓ demonstrate appropriate timing, stress, and intonation?

✓ incorporate appropriate speed and phrasing?

## English Language Learners

SMALL GROUP

To support students' comprehension of the text "Suited for Space," help them develop questions about their reading.

1. Remind students that the text is organized in a question-answer format.

2. Explain that good readers continually ask questions.

3. Have partners generate a list of questions about the topic. Provide resources to help answer them.

## Independent Activity Options

INDEPENDENT

While you work with individuals or small groups, others can work independently on one or more of the following options.

▶ Level A paperback books, see TE pages 371–376

▶ Level A *eZines*

▶ Repeat word sorts from this lesson

▶ *Student Journal* pages for this lesson

▶ *Writing Advantage* independent lessons

# Assessment

## Strategy Assessment

To help you and your students assess their use of comprehension strategy, ask the following questions. Students can complete a written response or provide verbal answers in a one-on-one reading conference.

- **Understanding Text Structure** In addition to the question-answer format, how else is the information in this article organized? (Answers will vary, but students might note a classification kind of organization. Specific information about mission patches is called out with a header in the sidebar on page 17.)

For ongoing informal assessment, use the checklists on pages 61–64 of *Level A Assessment*.

## Word Study Assessment

Use these steps to help you and your students assess their understanding of long *e* spelling patterns.

1. Draw six columns on the board with the following headings: *feet, we, meat, belief, Japanese, deer*.

2. Point out that each word has the long *e* sound.

3. Read the following words aloud one by one and have volunteers write each word in the column with the same spelling pattern: *jeer, she, seek, bean, chief, beef, Maltese, thief*. The answers are shown.

| feet | we | meat | belief | Japanese | deer |
|------|-----|------|--------|----------|------|
| seek | she | bean | chief | Maltese | jeer |
| beef |     |      | thief  |          |      |

Great Source
Reading Advantage

Level A
Assessment

## Give Them Space

*Space Odyssey*, pages 18–23

### SUMMARY

In **biographical sketches**, three astronauts describe how they realized their dreams.

### COMPREHENSION STRATEGIES

Monitor Understanding
Inferential Thinking

### WRITING

Friendly Letter

### VOCABULARY

Word Associations

### PHONICS/WORD STUDY

Long and Short *e* Homophones

### Lesson Vocabulary

| | |
|---|---|
| customs | optical system |
| engineering | monitors |
| simulator | prevented |
| weightless | video- |
| technology | conference call |

### MATERIALS

*Space Odyssey*, pp. 18–23
*Student Journal*, pp. 50–52
*Word Study Manual*, p. 49
*Writing Advantage*, pp. 113–151

## Give Them SPACE

Going into space takes training, courage, and a great love of adventure.

18

# Before Reading

WHOLE CLASS Use one or more activities.

## Make a Concept Web

Work with students to create a concept web about astronauts. Help students organize everything they know by grouping information into different categories. If students don't suggest "character traits" as a possible category, start a branch of the web dealing with character traits yourself, and guide the discussion to include the traits astronauts might need to do their jobs. (See Differentiated Instruction.)

```
          Everything We Know
           About Astronauts
   ┌──────────────┼──────────────┐
 What          Where          Their
 They          They        Character
 Do            Work          Traits
```

## Vocabulary Preview

Display the words. Have volunteers read them aloud. To preview the words, use the knowledge rating chart on *Student Journal* page 50. Model how to use context clues from the selection to define *customs* on the chart. Complete the first row of the knowledge rating chart with students. Challenge them to skim the selection to find the remaining words and to complete the chart with what they learned from using context clues.

# Franklin Chang-Diaz

The word *astronaut* comes from Greek words meaning "star sailor." Many people dream about "sailing" among the stars. This was true for Franklin Chang-Diaz. He had dreamed of becoming an astronaut since he was a child in Costa Rica, a country in Central America. His dream came true.

Chang-Diaz is the first NASA astronaut born outside the United States. His grandfather moved to Costa Rica from China. Though he lived in Costa Rica, his family kept many Chinese customs. They did a lot of Chinese cooking. They kept the Chinese New Year. Oddly, Chang-Diaz never learned to speak Chinese. He spoke Spanish instead.

Chang-Diaz came to the United States at age eighteen. He knew he wanted to be an astronaut. First, he had to learn English. Then he studied science and engineering. Engineering classes showed Chang-Diaz how to apply scientific ideas to building things and studying things. He finished school and applied to the space program. He had to go through a selection process. This lasted about a year because he had to compete with many people. He became an astronaut in 1980.

Chang-Diaz went through a lot of training. He practiced missions in a simulator, where he felt as if he was in space. Part of the practice was having things break down. Sometimes the computer would break down. Sometimes the electrical system stopped working. Chang-Diaz and other astronauts-in-training had to work to fix things. This "know-how" could save their lives in space.

As an astronaut, Chang-Diaz has flown aboard the Space Shuttle *Columbia* six times. His crew placed a large communication satellite in space.

What he enjoys most about space is being weightless. "You're away from the force of Earth's gravity, so you can float," Chang-Diaz points out. "In space, I can walk on the ceiling or the floor or the walls. After a while, you forget which wall is the ceiling. It's odd to get back to Earth and be stuck in two dimensions—down and across."

Chang-Diaz loves being an astronaut. He likes to see things that no one has seen before. He would like to take a trip beyond Earth's orbit some day. He can't wait to go on long trips to other planets and stars.

Chang-Diaz has received many honors, including six NASA Space Flight Medals (1986, 1989, 1992, 1994, 1996, 1998) and two NASA Distinguished Service Medals (1995, 1997). In addition to all of his work, he enjoys soccer, music, scuba diving, glider planes, and hiking.

19

SMALL GROUP

## DIFFERENTIATED INSTRUCTION
### CONCEPT WEB

To help students focus on the character traits aspect of the concept web, try following these steps:

1. Have students brainstorm the qualities they look for in a best friend. List them on the board.

2. Explain that these qualities are also known as character traits. They are qualities found both in real people and in fictional characters.

3. Note also that character traits can be good and bad.

### Student Journal page 50

Name _____  Date _____

**Building Vocabulary: Knowledge Rating Chart**
Show what you know about each word or phrase by completing the boxes.

| Word | Define or Use in a Sentence | Where Have I Seen or Heard It? | How Is It Used in the Selection? | Looks Like (Words or Sketch) |
|---|---|---|---|---|
| customs | | | | |
| engineering | | | | |
| simulator | | | | |
| weightless | | | | |
| technology | | | | |
| optical system | | | | |
| monitors | | | | |
| prevented | | | | |
| video conference call | | | | |

50      Space Odyssey • Give Them Space

## Preview the Selection

Have students look through the article. Use these or similar prompts to guide students to notice the important features of a piece of text:

- What do you notice about this article?

- Do you think the article is fiction or nonfiction? Why?

- How do you think the article will be organized? What makes you think that?

## Teacher Think Aloud

*When I first read the title "Give Them Space" I wondered who "them" was. As I previewed, however, I saw that the article takes a quick look at three different Shuttle astronauts. I think this article will interest me since I'm curious about the types of people who become astronauts and the skills and training they need.*

## Make Predictions/ Set Purpose

Students should use the information they gathered in previewing the selection to make predictions about what they will learn. If students have trouble generating a purpose for reading, suggest that they read to find interesting facts about the astronauts.

## Comprehension
INFERENTIAL THINKING

To help students think inferentially, ask:

- What does the text tell me about what Mae Jemison studied in college?

- What do I already know about what Franklin Chang-Diaz studied in college?

- What inference can I make about what college training astronauts often have?

# Mae C. Jemison

Mae C. Jemison knew she wanted to be a scientist when she was in kindergarten. She also knew she wanted to go into space. "The only way to get there was to become an astronaut," she explained.

## On September 12, 1992, she became the first African American woman to travel into space.

Jemison was born in Decatur, Alabama. Her family moved to Chicago, Illinois, when she was three years old.

Jemison's uncle was the person who got her interested in science. She loved all the sciences. She graduated high school in 1977 at age sixteen. She went to college and studied engineering and African studies. Then she went to medical school in New York. She graduated in 1981 and then worked as a doctor in California. She went on to practice medicine in a Cambodian refugee camp, where she treated people who had fled their government. She also worked in Africa with the Peace Corps.

Dr. Jemison is a chemical engineer, scientist, physician, teacher, astronaut, and, now, head of her own company. She shows no signs of slowing down.

20

# During Reading

## Comprehension   SMALL GROUP
MONITOR UNDERSTANDING

Use these questions to model how to monitor understanding by asking questions. Then have students ask their own questions and try to resolve any confusion.

- What am I reading about?

- Is anything confusing or unclear to me?

- What fix-up strategy can I use to resolve my confusion?

## Teacher Think Aloud
*When I first read the biography of Franklin Chang-Diaz, I noticed that he studied engineering. I wasn't sure what engineering was, though. So I read on and discovered that engineering classes taught him how to use scientific ideas to build things. That gave me the information I needed.*

## Comprehension   SMALL GROUP
INFERENTIAL THINKING

Use these questions to model how to make inferences from page 19. Then have students make inferences about another section.

- What does the text say about Chang-Diaz's education and experience?

- What do I already know about people who want to become astronauts?

- What inferences can I make?

(See Differentiated Instruction.)

It was in 1987 that Dr. Jemison left medicine to become an astronaut. She flew on the Space Shuttle *Endeavor*. The crew took off on September 12, 1992. She became the first African American woman to travel into space.

Jemison was a NASA astronaut for six years. Now she heads her own company. Her company uses science and technology, advanced machines such as computers and robots, to make everyday life better for all people around the world.

Jemison created The Earth We Share™. This is a space camp for students from around the world. She has earned many honors and awards. One of those awards includes being added to the National Women's Hall of Fame.

Other things about Mae Jemison may not be as well known. She speaks Russian, Japanese, and Swahili, as well as English. She loves jazz dancing and cats. She has even appeared on TV in *Star Trek: The Next Generation!*

Astronaut Mae Jemison on Spacelab J Flight

Dr. Jemison was Science Mission Specialist on the STS-47 Spacelab J flight. It was an American/Japanese joint mission. She conducted experiments in life sciences and was co-investigator in the Bone Cell Research experiment. She resigned from NASA in March 1993.

Men and women in the Peace Corps volunteer to help developing countries improve their living conditions. The main goals of the Peace Corps are to help the poor get their everyday needs, to promote world peace, and to help Americans and the people of other nations understand each other better. Volunteers attend special training. Then they spend about two years working in a country that has asked for help from the Peace Corps. President John F. Kennedy started the Peace Corps in 1961.

21

---

# Teacher Think Aloud

*The text tells me that Chang-Diaz studied science and engineering in college. Then he went through an astronaut selection process where he had to compete with many people. I know that many, many young people would love to become astronauts some day. From all this, I can infer that becoming an astronaut must be quite difficult.*

## Fix-Up Strategies

Offer these strategies to help students read independently.

### If you don't understand what you're reading:

- Reread the difficult section to look for clues to help you comprehend.

- Read ahead to find clues to help you comprehend.

- Retell, or say in your own words, what you've read.

- Visualize, or form mental pictures of, what you've read.

### If you don't understand a word:

- Reread the sentence. Look for ideas and words that provide meaning clues.

- Find clues by reading a few sentences before and after the confusing word.

- Look for the base or root word and think about its meaning.

- Think about the topic or plot at this point to see if either offers meaning clues.

## Writing

**SMALL GROUP**

### Friendly Letter

Before students begin writing, have them sketch out their ideas. Suggest using a graphic organizer. Tell students that they should list the steps in the order in which they should be taken. Have students list what they can accomplish now, what they can do in high school, what they can do in college, and what jobs they might do that could lead to the accomplishment of their dreams, or goals.

**Student Journal page 51**

Writing: A Friendly Letter

# Ellen Ochoa

Ellen Ochoa was the first Hispanic woman in space. She thinks of herself as a role model for all students to try their best in all they do. As a NASA astronaut, Ochoa makes time to visit schools. She encourages students to study hard and to not be afraid of success.

Ochoa comes from a family of five children. She was born in 1958 in Los Angeles, California. She earned a master's degree in 1981 and a doctorate in 1985. Both degrees were in electrical engineering.

### Ochoa's knowledge led her to develop an optical system for robots, which enables the robots to react to light and "see."

Ochoa's knowledge led her to develop an optical system for robots, which enables the robots to react to light and "see." She worked on this system from 1985 to 1988. Her system guides robots around objects. Then she began working on optical systems for exploring space. In 1990, NASA chose her to train as an astronaut. In 1993, she went on a nine-day mission aboard the Space Shuttle *Discovery*.

When Ochoa goes on a space mission, she works the robot arm that is attached to the International Space Station. That is not always easy to do. She pointed out a problem she had on one mission. She said, "I had to work with cameras and [computer] monitors because we were docked in a way that prevented me from seeing the robot arm."

Astronaut Ellen Ochoa on board the Space Shuttle *Discovery*

Astronaut Ellen Ochoa on the Space Shuttle *Atlantis*

22

# After Reading

**WHOLE CLASS** Use one or more activities.

### Check Purpose

Have students decide if their purpose was met. How are the astronauts alike and different? Are students like any of the astronauts? How?

### Discussion Questions

Continue the group discussion with the following questions.

1. What qualities or characteristics help to make a good astronaut? (Inferential Thinking)

2. What do you know now that you didn't know before reading? (Making Connections)

3. What do the three astronauts have in common? How are they different? (Compare-Contrast)

### Revisit: Concept Web

Go back over each category in the concept web. Help students identify and correct any misconceptions in the web. Then have students add any new information they learned from reading.

### Revisit: Knowledge Rating Chart

Help students review their charts. Discuss each term, and encourage students to add to or change their charts to reflect information learned while reading.

How does Ochoa keep in touch with her family when on a mission? She uses e-mail! She arranges a "visit" by having a <u>video conference call</u> from space if a mission lasts more than ten days. This way, she can keep in touch with her husband and children while she is in space.

Ellen Ochoa has earned many awards for her outstanding work in space. But winning an award is not new to her. One award goes back to the time she was in college. She won an award for playing the flute. Ochoa plays the flute on Earth *and* in space! ◆

Dr. Ellen Ochoa has been on three NASA Space Shuttle flights. She has logged over 719 hours in space. She traveled four million miles on one of the missions.

23

**Student Journal page 52**

Name _____ Date _____

**Building Vocabulary: Word Associations**
Choose two words from the vocabulary list below. Think about what you already know about each word. Then answer the following questions.

| engineering | simulator | weightless | technology |
| optical system | monitors | prevented | video conference call |

Word _____
What do you think about when you read this word? _____

Who might use this word? _____

What do you already know about this word? _____

Word _____
What do you think about when you read this word? _____

Who might use this word? _____

What do you already know about this word? _____

52                                    Space Odyssey • Give Them Space

## Writing Friendly Letter

Have each student write a letter to one of the astronauts profiled in "Give Them Space." Ask students to describe a dream that they have for the future and tell how they plan to go about achieving their dream. Suggest that students sketch out their ideas on a chart before writing their letters on *Student Journal* page 51. (See Differentiated Instruction.)

## Vocabulary Word Associations

Point out the word *optical* in the callout on page 22. Ask: *What do you think about when you read this word?* (eyes, seeing) *Who might use the word* optical? (doctor, scientist) *What do you already know about this word?* (Students may mention *optical illusion* or *optician*.) Have students complete the word association activity on *Student Journal* page 52.

## Phonics/Word Study

### Homophones

Read each sentence aloud and ask students to identify the pair of homophones in it. Then ask whether each pair has a long or short e sound. *Did I hear that you're living here? I'm feeling rather weak this week. Yesterday I read that red book.* Now, work with students to complete the in-depth long and short e homophone activity on TE page 126.

## Phonics/Word Study

### Long and Short *e* Homophones

▶ Write the following words on the board: *creek, creak; tier, tear;* and *step, steppe.*

▶ Ask students if they can figure out what these pairs have in common. They should be able to notice that the words in each pair sound the same but are spelled differently. This is the definition of a *homophone.*

▶ Using the Long and Short *e:* Homophones list on *Word Study Manual* page 49, play a game in which students turn over a homophone card worth a certain number of points. To earn the points, the student has to provide the homophone, spell it, and define it.

▶ Have each student create a homophones section in his or her Word Study notebook and add any homophones that are generated. This will become a good resource for students to use when they write.

For more information on word sorts and spelling stages, see pages 5–31 in the *Word Study Manual.*

# Focus on . . .

Use one or more activities in this section to focus on a particular area of need in your students.

## Comprehension   STRATEGY SUPPORT   INDEPENDENT

To help those students who need more practice using the strategies covered in this lesson, work one-on-one or in small groups to apply the strategy prompts below. Apply the prompts to a *Reading Advantage* paperback, a classroom library book, or a new or familiar selection in the magazine. Always model your own thinking first.

### Monitor Understanding

• Do I understand what I'm reading? If not, what part is confusing to me?

• What fix-up strategies can I use to solve the problem? (See During Reading for fix-up strategies.)

• Why did a character say (do, think, ask) that?

• What images do I visualize from the text? What parts can't I visualize?

• Why did the author include (or not include) those details?

### Inferential Thinking

• What are the causes or effects of this event?

• What do I learn from the character or person's thoughts, words, or actions?

• What do I know (or infer) from the text that the author hasn't stated directly?

• What conclusions can I draw?

## Writing Character Traits   INDEPENDENT

Have students choose one astronaut and list a character trait that they believe that astronaut has. Students should find two details in the sketch that show the character trait. Have students make a chart like the one below.

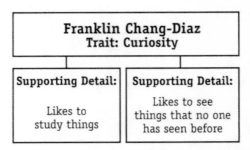

| Franklin Chang-Diaz<br>Trait: Curiosity | |
|---|---|
| **Supporting Detail:**<br><br>Likes to<br>study things | **Supporting Detail:**<br><br>Likes to see<br>things that no one<br>has seen before |

To give students more practice in writing a descriptive paragraph, see lessons in *Writing Advantage,* pages 113–151.

## Fluency: Pacing

SMALL GROUP

After students have read the biographical sketches silently at least once, they can use one to practice fluent reading. Have students choose one sketch to read aloud to a partner. Then, have them switch. Partners can provide feedback to each other. Point out that factual information needs to be read at a steady, even pace. If students read too fast, too slowly, or in a halting manner, their listeners will have difficulty making sense of the words. Model the difference between evenly paced reading and unevenly paced reading.

As you listen to partners read, use these prompts to guide them to read expressively and naturally paced.

▶ Listen to me read. Then read it just as I did.
▶ Reread this sentence more slowly (or faster).

When students read aloud, do they—

✓ demonstrate a smooth pace, not too fast or too slow?
✓ incorporate well-timed pauses between words and phrases?
✓ reflect an awareness and understanding of punctuation?

## English Language Learners

SMALL GROUP

Provide background information about the format of a friendly letter before students complete the writing activity on TE page 125.

1. Model the correct format of a friendly letter by writing a sample letter that includes the following: date, greeting, message, and closing.
2. Have students read the sample letter together.
3. Allow students to use this letter as a resource when they write their own letters.

## Independent Activity Options

INDEPENDENT

While you work with individuals or small groups, others can work independently on one or more of the following options.

▶ Level A paperback books, see TE pages 371–376
▶ Level A *eZines*
▶ Repeat word sorts from this lesson
▶ *Student Journal* pages for this lesson
▶ *Writing Advantage* independent lessons

# Assessment

## Strategy Assessment

To help you and your students assess their use of comprehension strategies, ask the following questions. Students can complete a written response or provide verbal answers in a one-on-one reading conference.

1. **Monitor Understanding** As you read these three biographies, what did you do to monitor your own comprehension? (Answers will vary. Students might say they asked themselves if they understood what they were reading, and if not, reread a passage or read on to gain more understanding.)
2. **Inferential Thinking** What inferences did you make about the astronauts based on what you read? (Answers will vary. Students might infer that many astronauts are well educated with advanced degrees and that they are trained to perform very specialized tasks.)

For ongoing informal assessment, use the checklists on pages 61–64 of *Level A Assessment*.

## Word Study Assessment

Use these steps to help you and your students assess their understanding of long and short *e* homophones.

1. Write these words on the board: *scene, creek, tents, peal, led, tense, retch, peel, wretch, lead, pedal, seen, peddle, creak*.
2. Ask students to match the pairs of homophones and tell what they know about their meanings.
3. Place a two-column chart on the board like the one shown below (the answers are shown). Ask students to write the pairs of homophones in the correct columns.

| Long *e* Homophones | Short *e* Homophones |
| --- | --- |
| scene, seen | tense, tents |
| creek, creak | led, lead |
| peal, peel | retch, wretch |
| | pedal, petal |

Great Source
Reading Advantage

Level A
Assessment

# LESSON 17
# Astro Quotes and Space Camp!

*Space Odyssey*, pages 24–31

## SUMMARY

In the main selection, two sisters are **interviewed**.

## COMPREHENSION STRATEGIES

Making Connections
Determining Importance

## WRITING

T-Chart

## VOCABULARY

Suffixes *-er, -or*

## PHONICS/WORD STUDY

Long and Short *e* Compound Words

### Lesson Vocabulary

| | |
|---|---|
| habitats | weightlessness |
| briefing | zero gravity |
| deployed | momentum |
| commander | |

## MATERIALS

*Space Odyssey*, pp. 24–31
*Student Journal*, pp. 53–55
*Word Study Manual*, p. 50
*Writing Advantage*, pp. 93–112

---

Astronauts, scientists, and inventors share their thoughts about exploring space.

# Astro Quotes

### A Space Walk

"As I was getting ready to step out [of the spacecraft], it felt for an instant like gravity was going to grab hold of me and pull me down toward Earth. I felt myself hanging onto the hand rail and saying, 'No, you're not going to fall. . . .'"

—Astronaut Dr. Bernard Harris, after a space shuttle mission in February 1995

### Space in the Future

"Within the next forty or fifty years, one of you may go to Mars. . . . Think about it. The future is coming—and it belongs to you."

—Astronaut Mike Mullane in 1995, speaking to youngsters at U.S. Space Camp in Huntsville, Alabama

### Be a Scientist

"I would encourage any young woman who thinks she wants to be a scientist or an astronomer to do it. It is enormous fun. . . . Most of the discoveries are yet to be made. We know very, very little about the universe."

—Vera Rubin, teacher, mother of four scientists, and famous astronomer, in 1994

### We Are All Part of One World

"As I looked down from orbit, I saw no lines or marks [between countries]. Before the end of our mission, all of us in the crew agreed that from space we saw only one planet, only one Earth."

—Astronaut Sultan ibn Salman al-Saud after flying on the Space Shuttle *Discovery*, 1985

24

---

# Before Reading

Use one or more activities.

## Make a Quotation Chart

Have students share thoughts about space exploration. Display comments in the form of quotations, including quotation marks and bylines. (See page 24 of *Space Odyssey* for a model.) Discuss the different quotes. Explain why you included quotation marks and bylines. Then ask: *Can you infer (guess using reasons) how each speaker might feel about space exploration?* Students can check their inferences with the speaker.

## Read Astro Quotes

Have students preview the quotations. Ask volunteers to read the quotes aloud. Discuss how the quotes look the same or different from the quotes in the group's quotation chart. Explain to students that the quotes they just read were the thoughts of a few astronomers, scientists, and inventors on the topic of space exploration. Note that they will get to read the thoughts of some fellow students in the main selection.

## Vocabulary Preview

Display the vocabulary words and read each one aloud. Assess students' prior knowledge of the words by having volunteers define words they think they know. Tell students to choose a familiar word for beginning *Student Journal* page 53. Model the process for students, using the word *commander*. Students will finish the page later. (See Differentiated Instruction.)

## Weightless

"At first just floating around is great fun, but then after a while it becomes annoying, and you want to stay in one place. . . . It's too bad you can't turn gravity off and on. . . . That would really be fun."

—Astronaut Michael Collins,
Apollo 11 flight to the Moon, July 16–24, 1969

An astronomer is a person who studies of space. Astronomy is the word study of space. As in the word astro is astronaut, the Greek word for star.

## A Dream Come True

"I'm an astronaut because I dreamed these things. I set my goals as high as I could imagine."

—Astronaut Pamela Melroy, pilot of the third space shuttle mission to the International Space Station in 2000

## Stargazing in Space

". . . as we orbit the Earth, we see a night and day every ninety-five minutes with about thirty-five minutes of darkness. What a joy it is to be able to darken the cabin and with naked eyes see the broad expanse of the Milky Way. . . ."

—Astronaut John Grunsfeld on a space shuttle mission to fix the Hubble Space Telescope in March 2002

## What Is a Galaxy?

A galaxy is a huge area of gases, dust, and hundreds of billions of stars. The Milky Way is the name of the galaxy that includes our sun, the earth, and the rest of the planets that we know about. The size of the Milky Way is hard to imagine. The distance across is about 100,000 light-years. (A light-year is the distance light can travel in one year.) This distance equals about 5.88 trillion miles!

25

### DIFFERENTIATED INSTRUCTION
## Vocabulary Preview

SMALL GROUP

If students are unfamiliar with the vocabulary, have them:

1. Choose a word that looks interesting to them or one that they would like to learn.
2. Use a dictionary to look up the word and write its definition on *Student Journal* page 53.
3. Look for the word as they read to define it in context and to learn more about it.
4. Write the details they learn on *Student Journal* page 53.

### Student Journal page 53

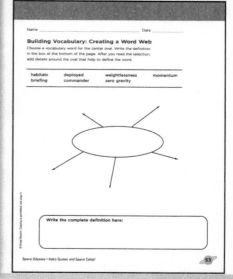

## Preview the Selection

Have students look through the six pages of the article "Space Camp!" As they preview, have students jot down on a self-stick note something from the article that looks interesting. Students can then share their thoughts with the group. Then ask students to discuss what they notice about text the structure. Discuss how interviews and quotations are similar and different.

## Teacher Think Aloud

*Previewing the article, I see it's an interview. Space Odyssey magazine is interviewing two sisters who have attended Space Camp. I like interviews because they give people a chance to express their feelings and experiences in their own words. In this interview, each sister answers each question separately. That's good because I'll get two perspectives on each question.*

## Make Predictions/ Set Purpose

Students should use the information they gathered in previewing the selection to make predictions about what they will learn. If students have trouble generating a purpose for reading, suggest that they read to find interesting information to share with the group.

## Comprehension
DETERMINING IMPORTANCE

To help students determine the importance of what they read, ask these questions:

- What does Kim mention in her first reply?
- What do you think is most important about what Kim says?
- Can you sum up the details in Kim's answer in one sentence that states her main idea?

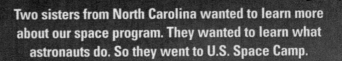

# Space Camp!

Two sisters from North Carolina wanted to learn more about our space program. They wanted to learn what astronauts do. So they went to U.S. Space Camp.

The U.S. Space and Rocket Center

26

# During Reading

## Comprehension
MAKING CONNECTIONS

Use these questions to model making connections with the text. Then have students make their own connections.

- Does anything in this interview sound familiar?
- Have I ever done anything similar to Space Camp?
- Is Space Camp something I might like to try?

## Teacher Think Aloud

*I went to a day camp one summer, where we did all kinds of things— swimming, crafts, trips, and softball. As I continued reading, however, I realized that Space Camp is a sleepaway camp with a special focus. It's probably more like the music camp that my friend went to. I can probably use what I know about summer camps to make connections with this interview.*

## Comprehension
DETERMINING IMPORTANCE

Use these questions to model determining the importance of ideas in the first two replies on page 27. Then have students determine the importance of ideas as they read subsequent answers to questions.

- What is the most important information in the first answer?
- How can I support my beliefs?

(See Differentiated Instruction.)

U.S. Space Camp is a part of the U.S. Space and Rocket Center in Huntsville, Alabama. The U.S. Space and Rocket Center is home to the Space Museum. The museum has the largest collection of rockets in the world. The museum has the rockets that carried John Glenn into space and took Alan Shepard, Jr., to the moon. The camp has programs for children and adults. The programs give people a chance to live and work like real astronauts. Chelsea and Kim were in the Space Academy program, which is for ages twelve to fourteen. They told us about the program. The letters SO below stand for *Space Odyssey* magazine.

Chelsea, Age 14

Kim, Age 13

**SO: Tell us a little about the Space Camp programs.**

Chelsea: There are programs in the fall for five days and in the summer for six days. Kim and I went during the summer. So we were there for six days.

Kim: We learned about the history of space travel. We got to go on different missions. We did science experiments. We went in simulators to feel what it is like in space.

**SO: How was your program set up?**

Chelsea: We worked on teams. Kim and I were on the same team. There were four girls and eight boys on our team. We met great kids from all across the United States.

Kim: We had counselors just like at any camp.

**SO: Where did you stay at Space Camp?**

Chelsea: We slept in <u>habitats</u>. These living spaces look like what astronauts live in when they are on the International Space Station (ISS). The girls were on the top level. The boys were on a different level. Each room had six bunk beds and lockers.

**SO: What did you do on your first day?**

Chelsea: We first got our sheets and towels. Then we put our belongings in our lockers. After that, we met our day counselors. We sat around and got to know the other team members. Then we had our first <u>briefing</u>. During the briefing, the counselors explained what we would do.

Kim: It was really interesting. We learned about the Space Shuttle. All Space Academy campers get to do a Space Shuttle mission.

27

# Teacher Think Aloud

*When the interviewer asks about space camp, Chelsea replies that the camp is held in the fall for five days and in the summer for six days. The important idea here is that Space Camp lasts for less than a week; it's a short stay. This is important because I thought Space Camp might have lasted for a month or all summer.*

## Fix-Up Strategies

Offer these strategies to help students read independently.

### If you don't understand what you're reading:

- Reread the difficult section to look for clues to help you comprehend.
- Read ahead to find clues to help you comprehend.
- Retell, or say in your own words, what you've read.
- Visualize, or form mental pictures of, what you've read.

### If you don't understand a word:

- Reread the sentence. Look for ideas and words that provide meaning clues.
- Find clues by reading a few sentences before and after the confusing word.
- Look for the base or root word and think about its meaning.
- Think about the topic or plot at this point to see if either offers meaning clues.

**SO:** We know that there are jobs on the Space Shuttle and at Mission Control on Earth. Everyone does one job in each section. What job did each of you practice first?

**Chelsea:** I was the Shuttle pilot. I <u>deployed</u> the satellite, placing it in the best position. I got to fly the Shuttle when the <u>commander</u> was doing something else.

**Kim:** I was the mission scientist on Earth. I told the people in space what experiments to do. I also had to help them solve problems with the experiments.

**SO:** Chelsea, what did you do on the second mission?

**Chelsea:** I was the weather and tracking specialist. I had to okay the landing site. I had to watch for storms. I made sure there were no weather problems on Earth for take-off and landing.

**SO:** Kim, what did you do on the second mission?

**Kim:** I was the commander. The commander heads the entire mission. He or she is responsible for the mission.

**SO:** Did you like flying the Shuttle?

**Kim:** It was a lot of fun. But it was very nerve-wracking when things went wrong—and they did! We had a major problem re-entering Earth's atmosphere. We were going twice as fast as we should have. One second we were over South America. The next second we were over Asia! It was scary to solve problems like that. Ground Control can't always help. I would not want to be the commander for real.

Chelsea and Kim have lots of photographs to help them remember their time at Space Camp.

28

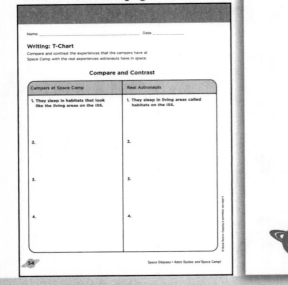

**Student Journal page 54**

Name _____ Date _____

**Writing: T-Chart**
Compare and contrast the experiences that the campers have at Space Camp with the real experiences astronauts have in space.

**Compare and Contrast**

| Campers at Space Camp | Real Astronauts |
|---|---|
| 1. They sleep in habitats that look like the living areas on the ISS. | 1. They sleep in living areas called habitats on the ISS. |
| 2. | 2. |
| 3. | 3. |
| 4. | 4. |

54                     Space Odyssey • Astro Quotes and Space Camp!

# After Reading
**WHOLE CLASS** Use one or more activities.

## Check Purpose

Have students decide if their purpose was met. Do they have a good sense of what Space Camp is like? Students should skim or reread the article, if necessary.

## Discussion Questions

Continue the group discussion with the following questions.

1. What kinds of activities did Chelsea and Kim do at Space Camp? (Details)

2. Do you think you would like to attend Space Camp? Why or why not? (Making Connections)

3. How effective was the author's use of the interview format in providing information about Space Camp? (Evaluate)

## Revisit: Quotation Chart

Refer students to the quotation chart they made in Before Reading. What quotes from the interview might they add to the chart? Why?

## Revisit: Word Web

Have students complete the word web they began on *Student Journal* page 53. Students can use the information they learned in the article to complete it.

**SO:** What else did you do at Space Academy?

Chelsea: We got to design, build, and launch our own rockets. Then there was a contest to see which rocket went highest. It was my favorite thing. We used a one-liter plastic bottle. We painted it yellow with gold stripes. Our fuel was water.

Kim: The four girls on our team built a rocket. Ours went the highest!

**SO:** You said that you went in simulators. What did you try?

Chelsea: We tried the One-sixth Gravity Chair. It's a chair that you sit in to move around as if you were on the moon. The moon has one-sixth the gravity of Earth. The chair hangs from springs on the ceiling. The springs are tightened. Then you try walking around on a rocky, moonlike surface.

Kim: It was very fun, but very hard! You take one step and you go up four feet in the air!

Chelsea and Kim pose with the rocket that the team built.

29

SMALL GROUP

**DIFFERENTIATED INSTRUCTION**

## Vocabulary

### Suffixes -er, -or

If students need additional help with suffixes, follow these steps:

1. Explain that adding the suffix -er or -or changes a verb to a noun.

2. List examples (*act/actor, write/writer*). Remind students that the suffixes mean "someone or something that does."

3. Have partners work together to complete the suffix activity on *Student Journal* page 55. Word pairs formed include: *counsel, counselor; train, trainer; command, commander; program, programmer; rescue, rescuer; design, designer.*

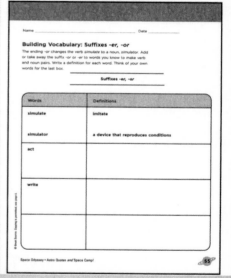

**Student Journal page 55**

Name _____ Date _____

**Building Vocabulary: Suffixes -er, -or**

The ending -or changes the verb simulate to a noun, simulator. Add or take away the suffix -or or -er to words you know to make verb and noun pairs. Write a definition for each word. Think of your own words for the last box.

Suffixes -er, -or

| Words | Definitions |
|-------|-------------|
| simulate | imitate |
| simulator | a device that reproduces conditions |
| act | |
| write | |

Space Odyssey • Astro Quotes and Space Camp!  55

---

## Writing T-Chart

Discuss the similarities and differences between the campers' experiences and an astronaut's experiences. Then have students do *Student Journal* page 54. Model the following example:

| Compare and Contrast | |
|---|---|
| Campers | Astronauts |
| Sleep in habitats like the living areas on the ISS | Sleep in living areas called habitats on the ISS |

## Vocabulary Suffixes -er, -or

Display *simulate* and *simulator*. Discuss how they are alike and different. Have students read aloud sentences in the interview that contain *simulator*. Explain that the suffixes -er and -or mean "someone or something that does." Brainstorm other words (nouns) that end with these suffixes. Have students remove the suffixes and identify the verbs that are created. Now have students complete *Student Journal* page 55. (See Differentiated Instruction.)

## Phonics/Word Study

### Compound Words

Read the following compound words aloud to the group: *redhead, beekeeper, bedspread, beanfield*. Ask students to identify the two smaller words that form each compound. Then work together to identify the short or long *e* sound in each smaller word. Now, work with students to complete the in-depth long and short *e* compound words activity on TE page 136.

**SO: Did you like that best, Chelsea?**

Chelsea: No. I liked the Multi-axis Trainer best. It lets you feel what <u>weightlessness</u> is like. The chair spins you around very fast, but your body doesn't shake. So you don't get sick to your stomach. You feel like you are floating in space with <u>zero gravity</u>. It was exciting.

Kim: I liked that best, too. I thought it was really fun.

**SO: What is the Space Shot ride?**

Chelsea: The Space Shot shoots you up to the top of a pole really fast. Coming down is like a free fall through the air. Then you bounce up again, but not as high. The bouncing slows down as the <u>momentum</u>, or motion, wears off.

Kim: We did this many times. I love Space Shot!

**SO: You have had some astronaut training. Do you think you would like to work in space for real?**

Chelsea: Working in space would be fun. But I want to be a vet and care for animals.

Kim: I always liked science. But space is too far from home for me. I think I want to be an orthodontist in Paris, France, and straighten people's teeth.

**SO: Some day we may need vets and orthodontists in space. By then, going into space might be as easy as flying . . . to Paris! You can find out more about Space Camp at www.spacecamp.com.** ◆

It looks like an amusement park ride, but it's not! The Multi-axis Trainer lets hopeful young astronauts feel what zero gravity is like.

# Chelsea's Mission Patch

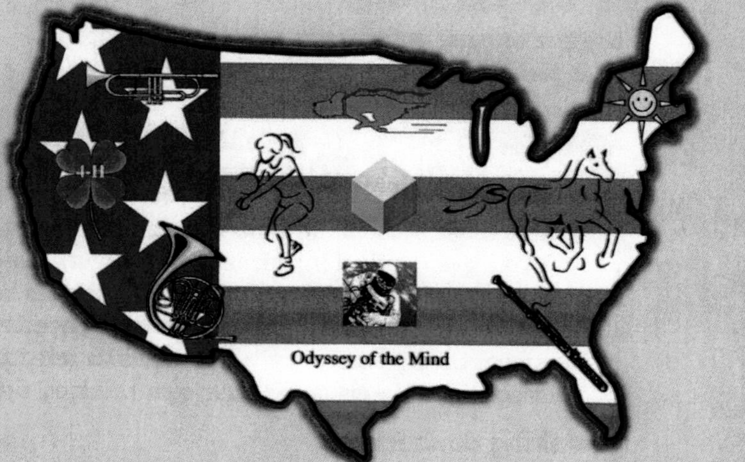

Odyssey of the Mind

Students who apply to Space Camp are asked to do a few things. One of those things is to design a patch. The patch shows their talents, awards, and things they do in their school and community. The idea of the patch comes from a patch that real astronauts create for each of their missions. Chelsea explained some of her design as follows.

"My patch is shaped like the United States and colored like the flag. I wanted to show my love for our freedom and country. . . ."

"I put in the trumpet, French horn, and bassoon because I play them. I show a four-leaf clover because I am vice president of my 4-H club. The girl with the volleyball stands for me. I play volleyball on my school team and in Junior Olympics. I show a dog because Kim and I have a dog named Sophie. We rescued her when she was ten days old. I show a horse because I love horses. I have been riding horses since I was seven years old."

## A Tasty Treat

Astronauts eat it on flights. It is dry and easy to break. It's a freeze-dried ice-cream sandwich! Chelsea said that it tastes great. Kim thought that it tasted very chalky and like powder.

OFFICIAL
Astronaut
Ice Cream Sandwich
Freeze Dried
Ready To Eat
Space Age Food

31

## Long and Short *e* Compound Words

▶ Share the following words with students: *bedroom, headband,* and *greenhouse.*

▶ Ask students what the words have in common. Someone should notice that each word is actually made up of two related words. A *bedroom* is a room with a bed for sleeping; a *headband* is a band worn around the head; and a *greenhouse* is a small house dedicated to growing green plants. Stress that compound words have a meaning connection.

▶ Provide students with a list of compound words they can read (see *Word Study Manual* page 50, Long and Short *e*: Compound Words). Have students take the words apart (*racehorse* becomes *race + horse*). Have students work in pairs to decide whether each short or long *e* word falls into a typical *e* pattern. Do not hold students responsible for the parts of words that are not in the short or long *e* family.

For more information on word sorts and spelling stages, see pages 5–31 in the *Word Study Manual.*

# Focus on . . .

Use one or more activities in this section to focus on a particular area of need in your students.

## Comprehension  STRATEGY SUPPORT   INDEPENDENT

To help those students who need more practice using the strategies covered in this lesson, work one-on-one or in small groups to apply the strategy prompts below. Apply the prompts to a *Reading Advantage* paperback, a classroom library book, or a new or familiar selection in the magazine. Always model your own thinking first.

### Making Connections

• What does this story (article, passage) remind me of?
• What do I already know about this topic?
• Where have I heard about this topic before?
• What do I have in common with the characters, people, or situations in the text?
• What other books, stories, articles, movies, or TV shows does this text make me think about?

### Determining Importance

• What is the most important idea in the paragraph? How can I prove it?
• Which details are unimportant? Why?
• What does the author want me to understand?
• Why is this information important (or not important) to me?

## Writing Double-entry Journal   INDEPENDENT

Have students complete a double-entry journal page using three of the quotes from "Astro Quotes." They should write three quotes on the left side of their paper and their responses to each one on the right side. Remind students that a double-entry journal allows readers to make connections with what they read. Students can agree or disagree with a quote, question the speaker, link the quote to their own experiences, or react to a quote in any way they wish.

To give students more practice in responding to literature, see lessons in *Writing Advantage,* pages 93–112.

## Fluency: Punctuation

SMALL GROUP

After students have read the article at least once, they can focus on reading expressively by working in groups of three to practice and then to present the interview as Readers Theater. Before students begin, discuss how an interview is conversational in nature. The dialogue should be smooth, as if students were speaking instead of reading.

Use these prompts to help students read expressively:

▶ Read your lines several times so you are comfortable with them.

▶ Read with expression. Put yourself in the role of the interviewee (camper).

▶ Use the punctuation marks for clues to reading. Raise your voice slightly at the end of a question. Read with excitement or enthusiasm when you see an exclamation mark.

▶ Put energy into your voice as you read. It will make the interview more interesting and understandable.

When students read aloud, do they—

✓ demonstrate appropriate meaning and usage of punctuation marks?

✓ incorporate appropriate timing, stress, and intonation?

✓ exhibit well-timed pauses between words and phrases?

## English Language Learners

SMALL GROUP

To support students as they learn about word parts, extend the vocabulary activity on TE page 133.

1. Remind students that the suffixes -er and -or mean "someone or something that does."

2. Have partners use this knowledge to predict the meanings of the following words: teacher, sailor, writer, creator.

## Independent Activity Options

INDEPENDENT

While you work with individuals or small groups, others can work independently on one or more of the following options.

▶ Level A paperback books, see TE pages 371–376

▶ Level A eZines

▶ Repeat word sorts from this lesson

▶ Student Journal pages for this lesson

▶ Writing Advantage independent lessons

# Assessment

## Strategy Assessment

To help you and your students assess their use of comprehension strategies, ask the following questions. Students can complete a written response or provide verbal answers in a one-on-one reading conference.

1. **Making Connections** As you read the interview, what connections did you make with it? (Answers will vary. Students may say the article connected with what they already knew about space and the space shuttle. Or, it may have provided new information and raised new questions.)

2. **Determining Importance** As you read, how did you determine the importance of what you read? (Answers will vary. Students may say that they asked themselves what was most important in each question and answer, or they might have tried to sum up various details into one main idea sentence.)

For ongoing informal assessment, use the checklists on pages 61–64 of Level A Assessment.

## Word Study Assessment

Use these steps to help you and your students assess their understanding of compound words with the long e or short e sound.

1. Write the following words on the board: downstream, sendoff, beanbag, greenhorn, infield, letterbox, meadowlark.

2. Ask students to identify the words that form each compound.

3. Place a two-column chart on the board like the one shown below (omitting the answers).

4. Reread the compound words and ask students to write each compound in the appropriate column.

5. Have students add additional compound words to each column.

| Short e | Long e |
|---|---|
| (send)(off) | (down)(stream) |
| (letter)(box) | (bean)(bag) |
| (meadow)(lark) | (green)(horn) |
| | (in)(field) |

# Blaze and Solar Eclipse
*Space Odyssey*, pages 32–35

## SUMMARY
This **short story** shows a glimpse into the life of a family living on Mars. A **poem** describing a solar eclipse follows.

## COMPREHENSION STRATEGIES
Understanding Text Structure

## WRITING
Comparison-Contrast Paragraph

## VOCABULARY
Word Cues

## PHONICS/WORD STUDY
Sorting Across Vowels

### Lesson Vocabulary

| | |
|---|---|
| harvest | pioneer |
| dome | Martian |

## MATERIALS
*Space Odyssey*, pp. 32–35
*Student Journal*, pp. 56–59
*Word Study Manual*, p. 51
*Writing Advantage*, pp. 8–12

---

# BLAZE

## The Fry family is like other families. Or is it?

It was dawn. The sun was just beginning to rise in the sky. It was spring in the year 2105. Blaze and her brother Mark rode with their dad on the tractor. Blaze was ten years old. Mark was seventeen. Blaze had been riding in the fields on weekends with her father and brother for the past two years. Their dad had been the one to invent the tractor they were riding on.

The tractor did all of the work. It broke up the deep-red soil. It planted the seeds. It gave the seeds a little water. Then it smoothed everything over.

This machine would later <u>harvest</u> the crop, too. The family would eat some of the food. Then Blaze and her family would freeze the rest.

Suddenly, the tractor went over a huge bump. This shook everyone up. Their bodies lifted off their seats and then plopped down. Mark almost fell off the tractor.

32

---

# Before Reading
WHOLE CLASS • Use one or more activities.

## Make a Sci-Fi Chart
Use what students know about science fiction to develop a chart as below.

| Genre: Science Fiction | |
|---|---|
| Characters | realistic and "alien" |
| Plot | Usually realistic with scientific "twists" |
| Setting | Generally realistic with futuristic elements |
| Theme | a problem related to a scientific advance |

## Vocabulary Preview
Review the vocabulary list with students, clarifying pronunciations as needed. Have students predict on *Student Journal* page 56 how the words might be used in the story. They will finish the page later. Model the process for one of the words.

## Preview the Selection
Have students look through the three pages of the story. Discuss their observations.

## Make Predictions/ Set Purpose
Students should use the information they gathered in previewing the selection to make predictions about what they will learn. If students have trouble generating a purpose for reading, suggest that they read to discover science-fiction elements of the story and to find out what life on Mars might be like.

"Easy does it, Dad," said Mark. "It's a good thing we're not back in New Jersey. The way you drive, you would knock down all the trees in the state!"

Dad smiled. He stopped the tractor and looked at Mark. "Hey, I'm usually the one to say, 'It's a good thing we're not in New Jersey.'"

"I know," answered Mark. "No matter where we go, you and Mom always say that. But I don't think you mean it."

"I do mean it," Dad responded. "This spot isn't perfect. We live under a dome. We are far away from our friends. But we chose to move here. It's like being a pioneer in the old days. You do remember the pioneers of the Old West?"

"Who could forget? We still learn history in school here. But we are a very different kind of pioneer, Dad," Mark replied.

"I don't feel like a pioneer," Blaze added.

Her father looked at her and smiled. "You're a little different from us," he answered. He started up the tractor again. The three of them rode in silence.

33

## DIFFERENTIATED INSTRUCTION    SMALL GROUP

### Comprehension
UNDERSTANDING TEXT STRUCTURE

Share these facts about Mars with the students.

- The temperature on Mars averages -80°F with lows of -230°.
- The Martian atmosphere is only 0.13 percent oxygen; Earth's is 21 percent.
- Mars' low gravity means a 100-pound Earthling would weigh only 32 pounds on Mars.

Ask students how these facts affect the Fry family on Mars. What has the author done to explain how the Frys can live under these conditions?

### Student Journal page 56

Name _____ Date _____

**Building Vocabulary: Predictions**
How do you predict these words will be used in "Blaze"? Write your answers in the second column. Then read the story. Clarify your answers in the third column.

| Word | My prediction for how the word will be used | How the word was actually used |
|------|------|------|
| harvest | | |
| dome | | |
| pioneer | | |
| Martian | | |

56    Space Odyssey • Blaze

# During Reading

## Comprehension    SMALL GROUP
UNDERSTANDING TEXT STRUCTURE

Use these questions to model understanding the science fiction genre. Then have students tell how their understanding of this genre helps them appreciate the story.

- What is the setting of this story?
- What futuristic developments affect the characters and plot events?
- How do I know this is science fiction?

(See Differentiated Instruction.)

## Teacher Think Aloud

*In addition to the 2105 setting on Mars, the story opens with a description of an amazing farm machine that plows, plants, waters, and finally harvests the crop. That's the sort of technological development that makes science fiction so much fun to read. By the way, it's easy to see why Blaze and Mark almost fly off the tractor when it hits a bump. On Mars, you'd weigh about one-third of what you do on Earth!*

## Fix-Up Strategies

Offer these strategies to help students read independently.

**If you don't understand what you're reading:**

- Reread the difficult section to look for clues to help you comprehend.
- Read ahead to find clues to help you comprehend.
- Retell, or say in your own words, what you've read.
- Visualize, or form mental pictures of, what you've read.

## Writing Comparison-Contrast Paragraph

If students need help, try following these steps:

1. As a class, brainstorm characteristics of life on Earth and of life on Mars according to "Blaze." Call on volunteers to circle the items that appear on both lists.

2. Have students use the items from these lists to complete their individual Venn diagrams.

3. Then work with individuals to compose opening sentences for their comparison and contrast paragraphs.

### Student Journal pages 57–58

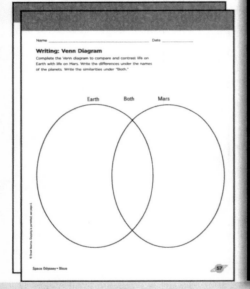

Blaze, Mark, and their father finally stopped for a drink. Blaze saw that her father was staring at a bright spot in the sky. It was always the brightest spot in the sky, except for the sun. It could even be seen in daylight.

"What do you think about when you look at that star?" Blaze asked.

"It's not a star. It's a planet," Her father replied. "You should know that."

"Well, you know what I mean," said Blaze. "What do you think about?"

"I think about New Jersey," her father said in a faraway voice. "I think about home. I think about what it would be like to feel the wind and rain on my face. It would be hard not to think about Earth when I'm watching it move across the sky."

"Why don't I feel that way?" asked Blaze.

"Maybe it's because you weren't born on Earth like Mark, your mom, and I. You were born here, Blaze." He smiled as though he had thought of something pleasant. "That's why I call you my little Martian!" Dad said. He gave her a big hug. ◆

34

# After Reading   Use one or more activities.

## Check Purpose

Have students revisit their purposes for reading and decide if they were met. What science-fiction elements did they find? What did they learn about life on Mars (according to this story)? Ask for students to share their thoughts.

## Discussion Questions

Continue the group discussion with the following questions.

1. What did you think of the story? (Making Connections)

2. How are the characters similar to and different from you? (Making Connections)

3. What could you infer from this story about the author's idea of the future? (Inferential Thinking)

## Revisit: Sci-Fi Chart

With students, go over each characteristic of science fiction listed on the chart. Have them describe how the various elements of "Blaze" fit the characteristics and make the story science fiction.

## Revisit: Predictions Chart

Have students complete the predictions chart on *Student Journal* page 56. How were the words actually used?

# SOLAR ECLIPSE

People long ago watched the sky in fear
As bit by bit the Sun would disappear.
The sky grew dark in the midst of day.
No one knew why the Sun went away.
No one knew if again the Sun would shine
Or if this would be the end of time.

Now we know the facts of this case.
The Moon can block our view of Sun in space.
Our Moon can cover the Sun so bright
Leaving just a glowing ring of light.
The sky turns black; the air turns chill.
Stars may shine, but the birds are still.

The shadow of the Moon covers the Sun.
And when the Moon has passed, the eclipse is done.
Then one dot of light, like a diamond ring,
Grows and grows until birds begin to sing.
An eclipse of the Sun makes a thrilling sight
When we know Sun's warmth will replace false "night."

The moon comes between the sun and Earth so that some or all of the sun's light is blocked out. This is called an eclipse.

35

## POEM: SOLAR ECLIPSE

Have students read the poem silently. Then have them read it aloud to a partner. Discuss the poem with questions like these:

- What does the poem tell about?
- What images could you visualize?
- Can anyone use classroom objects to model how a solar eclipse occurs? (Students can use any handy objects that represent the earth, moon, and sun.)
- How does the design, or "shape," of the poem relate to the poem's topic?

## Student Journal page 59

Name _____ Date _____

**Building Vocabulary: Noun Suffixes**

Look at the suffixes that mean "one who." Use them to make up words to name beings from the different planets. Write sentences to describe your beings.

| -an, -ian | Ohioan, Bostonian | -ese | Chinese |
|---|---|---|---|
| -ite, -ite | Akronite | -ist | tourist |
| -er, -ar, -or | Clevelander | -ling | duckling |

Mars _____

Venus _____

Earth _____

Mercury _____

Jupiter _____

Saturn _____

Uranus _____

Neptune _____

Pluto _____

Space Odyssey–Blaze      59

## Writing Comparison-Contrast Paragraph

First, have students fill in a Venn diagram that compares life on Mars to life on Earth on *Student Journal* page 57. Then have students use the information from their diagrams to write a paragraph on *Student Journal* page 58 that compares and contrasts life on Earth with life on Mars. (See Differentiated Instruction.)

## Vocabulary Word Cues

Display *Martian*. Then ask:

- What planet does a Martian come from? (Mars)
- What do you think the suffix *-ian* means? ("one who is from")
- How did the suffix change the spelling of Mars? (*s* changed to *t*)

Now, have students complete *Student Journal* page 59. Possible suffixes are included in the *Student Journal* activity.

## Phonics/Word Study

### Sorting Across Vowels

Write these spellings of the long *a* sound on the board: *ai, ay, aCe, ea*. Ask volunteers to suggest words with the long *a* sound that match each spelling pattern (*rain, tray, crate, steak*). Next, write these spellings of the long *e* sound: *ee, ie, eCe,* and *ea*. Again ask for examples of long *e* words with each spelling pattern (*sleet, piece, these, beat*). Now, work with students to complete the in-depth sorting activity on TE page 142.

## Phonics/Word Study

### Sorting Across Vowels

To review the most common patterns within the last two vowel families studied (*a* and *e*), set up a straightforward sort like the one below. While no oddballs are thrown in, students will likely falter a bit when they encounter *ea* in both vowel families. Remind students to say the word out loud and listen for the difference. For example, *ea* will show up in *break* (long *a* sound) as well as in *creak* (long *e* sound).

▶ Using the Long *a* and Long *e*: Cumulative Sort sheet on *Word Study Manual* page 51, have students look back over the two vowel patterns they have studied.

▶ As always, speed and accuracy are the goals.

| Long *a* and Long *e*: Cumultive Sort | | | | | | | |
|------|------|-------|------|-------|--------|-------|-------|
| *ai* | *ay* | *aCe* | *ea* | *ee* | *ie* | *eCe* | *ea* |
| plain | pray | shake | break | preen | shriek | these | creak |
| brain | stray | brake | | speed | piece | scene | freak |
| | | crane | | sheep | | | speak |

For more information on word sorts and spelling stages, see pages 5–31 in the *Word Study Manual*.

# Focus on . . .

Use one or more activities in this section to focus on a particular area of need in your students.

## Comprehension   STRATEGY SUPPORT   INDEPENDENT

To help those students who need more practice using the strategies covered in this lesson, work one-on-one or in small groups to apply the strategy prompts below. Apply the prompts to a *Reading Advantage* paperback, a classroom library book, or a new or familiar selection in the magazine. Always model your own thinking first.

### Understanding Text Structure

• What kind of text is this? (book, story, article, guidebook, play, manual)

• How does the author organize the text? (cause-effect, problem-solution, chronological order, description, question-answer, comparison-contrast)

• What details support my thoughts about the text structure?

• What is the cause (effect, problem, solution, order, question, answer)?

• If fiction, who are the characters? What is the setting, plot, conflict, and resolution?

## Writing Journal Entry   INDEPENDENT

Have students take on the role of Blaze and write a journal entry describing her visit to New Jersey. Brainstorm with students a list of possible issues they might cover from Blaze's point of view in the journal entries, using these questions as prompts.

• What does Blaze think of Earth?

• What surprises her?

• Which planet does she like better? Why?

• How does she feel about returning to her "home" planet?

To give students more practice in brainstorming, see lessons in *Writing Advantage*, pages 8–12.

## Fluency: Expression

*SMALL GROUP*

Have students work in groups of three, with each taking on the role of one of the story characters: Mark, Blaze, and Dad. Allow time for students to read the dialogue on pages 33–34 silently before reading it aloud together. Students can use self-stick notes to mark their places in the text. Discuss the different characters and how they might "sound" as they talk to each other. Also, remind students to use punctuation to help them read expressively.

As you listen to students read, use these or similar prompts.

▶ The story says that Dad said this sentence "in a faraway voice." What does that mean? How should you read that?

▶ This sentence ends in an exclamation point. Listen as I demonstrate how to read it with emotion. "That's why I call you my little Martian!"

When students read aloud, do they—

✓ reflect an understanding of the text?

✓ demonstrate appropriate timing, stress, and intonation?

✓ incorporate appropriate speed and phrasing?

## English Language Learners

*SMALL GROUP*

Extend the Make Predictions activity on TE page 138.

1. Remind students that active readers use the title, headings, and illustrations to make predictions.

2. Have partners look through the selection and write down one or two predictions about what might happen in the story.

3. Have students gather in small groups and share their predictions with each other.

## Independent Activity Options

*INDEPENDENT*

While you work with individuals or small groups, others can work independently on one or more of the following options.

▶ Level A paperback books, see TE pages 371–376

▶ Level A *eZines*

▶ Repeat word sorts from this lesson

▶ *Student Journal* pages for this lesson

▶ *Writing Advantage* independent lessons

# Assessment

## Strategy Assessment

To help you and your students assess their use of comprehension strategies, ask the following questions. Students can complete a written response or provide verbal answers in a one-on-one reading conference.

- **Understanding Text Structure** In addition to the 2105 setting, what details in this story help you identify it as science fiction? (Answers will vary. Students might note that the action takes place on the planet Mars where humans live under a huge dome and farm with high-tech equipment.)

See *Level A Assessment* page 22 for formal assessment to go with *Space Odyssey*.

## Word Study Assessment

Use these steps to help you and your students assess their understanding of long *a* and long *e* spelling patterns.

1. Place a four-column chart on the board with the words *pain*, *gray*, *pace*, and *great* as column headings.

2. Ask students to add words with the long *a* sound to each column that follow the spelling pattern of each heading.

3. Place a second four-column chart on the board with the words *seen*, *shriek*, *these*, and *peak* as column headings.

4. Ask students to add words with the long *e* sound to each column that follow the spelling pattern of the column heading. Sample answers are shown.

| pain | gray | pace | great |
|------|------|------|-------|
| plain | play | make | steak |

| seen | shriek | these | peak |
|------|--------|-------|------|
| sheep | piece | scene | freak |

Great Source
Reading Advantage

Level A
Assessment

# LESSON 19
## Visitors from Mars

*Space Odyssey*, pages 36–41

### SUMMARY

This **play**, based on a true story, tells about an event that happened the night before Halloween in 1938.

### COMPREHENSION STRATEGIES

Inferential Thinking
Understanding Text Structure

### WRITING

Play Summary

### VOCABULARY

Word Relationships

### PHONICS/WORD STUDY

Short and Long *i* Patterns

#### Lesson Vocabulary

meteor        jammed
shocking

### MATERIALS

*Space Odyssey*, pp. 36–41
*Student Journal*, pp. 60–63
*Word Study Manual*, p. 52
*Writing Advantage*, pp. 30–55

---

# VISITORS FROM MARS

## What is real and what is make-believe? Sometimes people aren't sure.

### CHARACTERS

**Narrators 1 and 2**
**Nancy,** the Reeds' daughter
**Mike,** the Reeds' son

**Mrs. Reed**
**Announcer,** an actor playing a news broadcaster
**Mr. Reed**

**Carl Phillips,** an actor playing a news reporter
**June Norris,** Nancy's friend and neighbor

**Narrator 1:** Before there was television, people listened to their radios. The radio was a kind of entertainment, just as television is today. The night of October 30, 1938, was a night of fear for many people in America. A radio play was aired in New York City on the night before Halloween. The idea for the play came from a book by H. G. Wells. The book was called *The War of the Worlds*. It was about invaders from Mars.

**Narrator 2:** Thousands of listeners tuned in late to the program. They did not know they were

hearing a fake radio broadcast that was part of the play. They thought that they were hearing a real news story. People believed that Martians were invading. This radio play is about that broadcast and a family who heard it.

As our play begins, the Reed family is at home. They are ready to listen to the radio. They have just tuned in to a weekly program of plays. They have missed the first few minutes of the program. Some dance music is playing.

*(sound of dance music)*

36

---

# Before Reading ⚙ WHOLE CLASS Use one or more activities.

## Make a Concept Web

Discuss students' thoughts in response to the following questions.

- How was life different before there was television?
- What do you know about the importance of radio in the early 1900s?

Create a concept web to record students' responses.

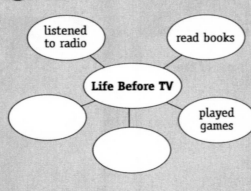

listened to radio

read books

**Life Before TV**

played games

## Vocabulary Preview

Display the vocabulary words. Call on volunteers to read the words aloud. Ask: *Have you seen this word before? How was it used? Can you use it in a sentence? Does the word look like another word or remind you of something?* Have students start *Student Journal* page 60. They will complete the page later. Model for students how to approach a word for the knowledge rating chart.

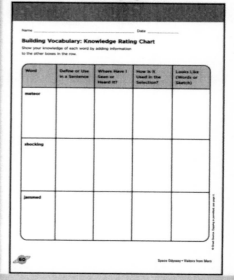
If students are having difficulty making predictions, use one or more of the following strategies.

- Read aloud the information spoken by Narrator 1. Then ask: *How do you think hearing about invaders from Mars made listeners feel?*

- Read aloud the information spoken by Narrator 2. Then ask: *What do you think the Reeds will believe? Why do you say that? What do you think the Reeds will do?*

- Call on volunteers to describe what they see in the illustrations.

**Student Journal page 60**

| Name | | | Date | |
|---|---|---|---|---|
| **Building Vocabulary: Knowledge Rating Chart** | | | | |
| Show your knowledge of each word by adding information to the other boxes in the row. | | | | |
| Word | Define or Use in a Sentence | Where Have I Seen or Heard It? | How is it Used in the Selection? | Looks Like (Words or Sketch) |
| meteor | | | | |
| shocking | | | | |
| jammed | | | | |

---

**Nancy:** Mike, turn up the radio.

**Mike:** Turn it up yourself.

**Mrs. Reed:** Quiet, kids.

*(music stops)*

**Announcer:** We break into our program to bring you a special news report. A large flaming object fell on a farm in Grovers Mill, New Jersey, at 7:40 P.M. this evening. The object is thought to be a <u>meteor</u>, matter from space that can be seen as a bright flash of light. Reporters are over at the farm now.

*(sound of police sirens off in distance)*

**Mike:** Grovers Mill is not far from here. Let's drive over, Dad.

**Mr. Reed:** Take it easy, son. Let's see what they say next.

**Narrator 1:** The report ended. The music program came on. Soon it was cut off again by another news report.

**Announcer:** I have reporter Carl Phillips on the phone. Now he can tell us more about what happened.

*(sound of sirens and people talking all at the same time, mumbling in the distance)*

---

## Preview the Selection

Have students look through the six pages of the play. Use these or similar prompts to guide students to notice the important features of a play.

- What do you notice first?

- What are the parts of a play? Point them out. (characters, lines, stage directions)

- What other plays have you read or seen?

## Teacher Think Aloud

*As I look at this selection, I can see right away that it's a play. The characters are listed at the beginning. The title—"Visitors from Mars"—also tells me it's probably science fiction. The question under the title has me thinking, though: What is real and what is make-believe? That could be a clue to the theme of the play. I think I'll keep that question in mind as I read.*

## Make Predictions/ Set Purpose

Students should use the information they gathered in previewing the selection to make predictions about what they will learn. If students have trouble generating a purpose for reading, suggest that they read to find out what happens in the play. (See Differentiated Instruction.)

## Comprehension

INFERENTIAL THINKING

To help students think inferentially, ask these questions.

- What does the introduction say about how many people reacted to the play *The War of the Worlds?* (Many people panicked.)

- What does Narrator 2 say at the very end of this radio play? ("Today we wouldn't be as easily fooled. Or would we?")

- What do I know about how people sometimes react to new or frightening situations?

- What message can I infer from Narrator 2's words at the end?

**Phillips:** This is reporter Carl Phillips in Grovers Mill, New Jersey. I can't believe my eyes! There is a big —uh— *thing* only a few feet from where I am standing. It is half buried in the ground. It looks like some kind of metal object. Lots of people are here.

**Nancy:** Oh, I wish we were there!

*(a humming and scraping noise)*

**Phillips:** Wait a minute, people! The top of this thing is starting to turn like a screw.

*(a metal clanking noise)*

**Phillips:** Now the top is off. Something that looks like a gray snake is coming out of it. Now there's another! No, these wriggling shapes are part of one body. They look like tentacles to me. Now I see two large, round, glowing circles. Could they be eyes? What else could they be? Oh, my, I see a V-shaped mouth with no lips. Ugh, goo is dripping from the mouth. This thing is as big as a bear!

*(sound of people screaming)*

38

# During Reading

## Comprehension

INFERENTIAL THINKING

Use these questions to model how to make inferences about Mr. Reed. Then have students reveal inferences they make as they read another section.

- What does the text tell me about Mr. Reed's reaction to the "invasion"?

- How have people I have known in real life reacted to emergencies?

- What can I infer about Mr. Reed?

(See Differentiated Instruction.)

## Teacher Think Aloud

*Mr. Reed decides the invasion is true because "it's on the radio." He decides to flee without a plan or trying to get more information. By contrast, most adults I know try to stay calm in emergencies. They try to get more facts from those in authority before acting. Based on this, I infer that Mr. Reed is gullible and rash; he doesn't show good judgment.*

## Comprehension

UNDERSTANDING TEXT STRUCTURE

Use these questions to model how to determine the format of a play. Then have students tell how being aware of the format of a play helps them understand the events in the play.

- What elements do I expect in a play?

- How is a radio play different from a stage play?

**Mr. Reed:** Oh, this sounds terrible.

**Phillips:** More police are here. We have to move back now.

*(sound of footsteps moving quickly)*

**Phillips:** Something is happening again!

*(hissing sound and then a humming sound that gets louder and louder)*

**Phillips:** A shape like a hump is rising from the hole. I see a small beam of light against a mirror. A flame is coming from the mirror! Oh, no! There is fire all over. This whole field is on fire. People are on fire! Now the fire is coming my way!

*(sound of a microphone crashing)*

**Mike:** What happened?

**Nancy:** I think the fire got the reporter! He must be dead.

**Mrs. Reed:** Can this really be happening?

**Mr. Reed:** Of course it's happening. It's on the radio, isn't it?

**Announcer:** I have just been handed a message. At least forty people have died in a fire. The fire was in a field near Grovers Mill. We think one of the people killed was our own reporter Carl Phillips.

**Nancy:** See, he *is* dead!

**Announcer:** There's more. I have more shocking news. There are clues that lead us to believe that strange beings have landed at Grovers Mill. They may be from Mars!

**Mrs. Reed:** Why can't the police stop them?

**Announcer:** The Martians are moving through New Jersey. They are headed for New York. Phone lines are down. People are running and screaming in the streets. Police cannot control the crowds. We have warnings of a deadly black smoke being used by the Martians.

**Mr. Reed:** Come on, everybody. Let's get ready to leave.

**Mike:** Where are we going?

**Mr. Reed:** I don't know. But we can't stay here.

**Announcer:** Oh, no, folks! We have more bad news. Our own army and air force have been wiped out. The Martians are spreading poison everywhere. This may be our last broadcast, ladies and gentlemen. But we will stay on the air until the end.

**Mrs. Reed:** Let's go! You heard him! It's the end!

*(sound of doorbell ringing)*

39

# Teacher Think Aloud

*Stage plays include stage directions that tell how the actors should move and speak. This radio play doesn't do that. Instead, it presents the sound effects. They're shown in parentheses and italic type. Sound effects are important on the radio, and I want to pay attention to them to get a feel for what this play would sound like.*

## Fix-Up Strategies

Offer these strategies to help students read independently.

**If you don't understand what you're reading:**

- Reread the difficult section to look for clues to help you comprehend.
- Read ahead to find clues to help you comprehend.
- Retell, or say in your own words, what you've read.
- Visualize, or form mental pictures of, what you've read.

**If you don't understand a word:**

- Reread the sentence. Look for ideas and words that provide meaning clues.
- Find clues by reading a few sentences before and after the confusing word.
- Look for the base or root word and think about its meaning.
- Think about the topic or plot at this point to see if either offers meaning clues.

**Nancy:** That's the doorbell. Don't answer it. It may be Martians!

**Mrs. Reed:** Don't be silly, dear. Do you really think they would ring the doorbell? I'll get it.

*(sound of door opening)*

**June:** Hello, Mrs. Reed. Happy Halloween!

**Mrs. Reed:** June, this is no time to joke.

**June:** But it is Halloween Eve. I just came over to see Nancy. Is she home?

**Mrs. Reed:** Yes, but we are on our way out. Where is the rest of your family?

**June:** Oh, they're home listening to the radio. I was, too, but—

**Mrs. Reed:** Then you must have heard. Didn't you hear about the Martians?

**June:** *(laughing)* Oh, yeah. That's a good play, isn't it?

**Nancy:** Oh, June! Come with us. I don't want you to die.

**June:** Hey, it's only a play. It's not real. No one is going to die.

**Mike:** What do you mean?

**June:** The Martian attack is part of the radio play. They said so at the beginning of the program. Didn't you hear that? Listen to the end of the program.

**Announcer:** Well, that's all folks. We hope you have enjoyed this evening's show. You have been listening to a play of *The War of the Worlds* by H. G. Wells. We hope you enjoyed it. Now we have more music for you.

**Mr. Reed:** I don't believe this! We've been fooled!

**Narrator 2:** Yes, the people were fooled. Today we wouldn't be as easily fooled. Or would we? ◆

**Student Journal pages 61–62**

# After Reading

**WHOLE CLASS** Use one or more activities.

## Check Purpose

Have students revisit their purpose for reading. Encourage students to compare their predictions to what did happen. Were any of students' predictions confirmed? What did happen in the play?

## Discussion Questions

Continue the group discussion with the following questions.

1. What did you think of the play? (Making Connections)

2. Why do you think so many people believed the radio play? (Inferential Thinking)

3. How do you think you would have reacted if you had listened to the radio play when it was first aired? (Making Connections)

## Revisit: Concept Web

Revisit the concept web that was started in Before Reading. Students may add any new information.

## Revisit: Knowledge Rating Chart

Have students finish *Student Journal* page 60. For each word, ask how they were able to define the word in context and whether their knowledge of a particular word changed.

## WAR OF THE WORLDS

- The radio show was Orson Welles's *Mercury Theater of the Air*. It was broadcast on CBS radio.
- Orson Welles was a famous actor and director. He often directed the weekly plays and starred in them.
- About six million people heard the program. It is thought that over one million people were very scared and that more than a hundred thousand people really believed the Martians had landed.

### DAILY NEWS — 1938

## FAKE RADIO 'WAR' STRIKES TERROR THROUGH U.S.

Thousands of people were fooled by *The War of the Worlds* radio show. They jammed the phone lines with calls to radio stations, newspapers, and the police. Many people fled in their cars. Some hid for weeks in the woods. The scare spread across the United States and into Canada.

41

## DIFFERENTIATED INSTRUCTION

SMALL GROUP

### Vocabulary

### Word Relationships

To help students arrange words in graduated degrees of relationships:

1. Ask students to brainstorm words that indicate temperature of varying degrees. Have them choose two words that show the greatest temperature range, for example, *hot* and *freezing*.

2. Write the words on opposite sides of the board. Help students arrange the other words in order, from *hot* to *freezing*, to show the variations in temperature and the relationship among the words. For example: **hot** warm tepid cool cold **freezing**

**Student Journal page 63**

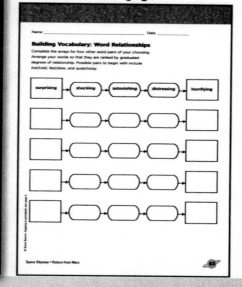

---

### Writing **Play Summary**

In preparation for writing a play summary, have partners complete *Student Journal* page 61. When pairs have completed their charts, have them decide which pieces of information should be included in a brief summary of the play. Students can circle or highlight the important details. Then they can write a summary on *Student Journal* page 62.

### Vocabulary

#### Word Relationships

List these synonyms for *shocking* on the board: *surprising, astonishing, electrifying, jarring, outrageous, stunning, horrifying, distressing, terrible.* Together rank the words from least to most upsetting. Display the array. Then have partners complete *Student Journal* page 63. Other possible array pairs include *hot, cold; fast, slow; indifferent, ecstatic;* and *quiet, noisy.* (See Differentiated Instruction.)

### Phonics/Word Study

#### Short and Long *i* Patterns

Write the word pairs *bit, bite; fin, fine;* and *kit, kite* on the board. Ask students what they notice about the sound of the vowel *i* in each word. (The first word in each pair has the short *i* sound and the second word has the long *i* sound.) Ask students to suggest other pairs of words that show this spelling pattern. Now, work with students to complete the in-depth sorting activity on TE page 150.

### Short and Long *i* Patterns

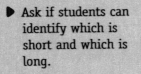

▶ Write the following words on the board: *dish* and *hike*. Tell students that these words represent both sounds the letter *i* stands for, short *i* and long *i*.

▶ Ask if students can identify which is short and which is long.

▶ Use the Long and Short *i*: Sort One sheet to model the sorting process for students. (See *Word Study Manual* page 52.)

▶ Write the headings Short *i*, Long *i*, and Oddball, and add the first few words in the appropriate columns.

▶ Introduce the word *give* and see if students note that it is a long vowel pattern with a short vowel sound. The word *give* will require a third column, the "Oddball" column. Note that *live* could have a short *i* or a long *i* sound.

▶ Discuss the sort and what students learned, pointing out the various ways each sound is spelled.

▶ Once the sort is complete, hand out the Long and Short *i*: Sort One sheet and ask students to cut up the words and do the sort on their own or in groups.

▶ Check the final sorts.

| Long and Short *i*: Sort One | | |
|---|---|---|
| Short *i* | Long *i* | Oddball |
| dish | hike | give |
| lift | smile | live |
| mitt | spy | |
| trick | fright | |
| whip | child | |
| will | swine | |
| swim | night | |
| | price | |
| | blind | |

For more information on word sorts and spelling stages, see pages 5–31 in the *Word Study Manual*.

# Focus on . . .

Use one or more activities in this section to focus on a particular area of need in your students.

## Comprehension    STRATEGY SUPPORT

INDEPENDENT

To help those students who need more practice using the strategies covered in this lesson, work one-on-one or in small groups to apply the strategy prompts below. Apply the prompts to a *Reading Advantage* paperback, a classroom library book, or a new or familiar selection in the magazine. Always model your own thinking first.

### Inferential Thinking

• What are the causes or effects of this event?

• What do I learn from the character or person's thoughts, words, or actions?

• What do I know (or infer) from the text that the author hasn't stated directly?

• What conclusions can I draw?

### Understanding Text Structure

• What kind of text is this? (book, story, article, guidebook, play, manual)

• How does the author organize the text? (cause-effect, problem-solution, chronological order, description, question-answer, comparison-contrast)

• What details support my thoughts about the text structure?

• What is the cause (effect, problem, solution, order, question, answer)?

• If fiction, who are the characters? What is the setting, plot, conflict, and resolution?

## Writing **Theme**

INDEPENDENT

Ask students to think about the message the author of "Visitors from Mars" was trying to convey. Tell students to share their ideas in small groups. Students might wish to create a concept web to record their ideas. Then have students write a brief paragraph explaining their thoughts. Students can share their paragraphs aloud.

To help students improve their writing techniques, see lessons in *Writing Advantage*, pages 30–55.

## Fluency: Expression

After students have read the play at least once, have them choose roles and work together to perform the play as Readers Theater. Have students discuss how they will read expressively to best convey the mood of the play and their characters' feelings. Discuss also how the narrators' roles differ from those of the other characters—they should speak evenly and clearly to convey information.

Use these prompts to help students read expressively.

▶ Read your lines several times so you are comfortable with them.

▶ Put yourself in the role of the characters. How would you speak if you were excited? Shocked? Frightened? Panicked? Embarrassed?

▶ Use the punctuation marks for clues to reading. Raise your voice slightly at the end of a question. Read with excitement or extra feeling when you see an exclamation mark.

When students read aloud, do they—

✓ demonstrate a smooth pace, not too fast or too slow?

✓ incorporate well-timed pauses between words and phrases?

✓ reflect an awareness and understanding of punctuation?

## English Language Learners

To support students' fluency, have them practice reading aloud sections of "Visitors from Mars."

1. Assign a role to each student.

2. Choose a selection of the text for students to read aloud, and practice reading the section in unison.

3. Have students each read their role. Provide feedback to help improve fluency and expression.

## Independent Activity Options

While you work with individuals or small groups, others can work independently on one or more of the following options.

▶ Level A paperback books, see TE pages 371–376

▶ Level A *eZines*

▶ Repeat word sorts from this lesson

▶ *Student Journal* pages for this lesson

▶ *Writing Advantage* independent lessons

# Assessment

## Strategy Assessment

To help you and your students assess their use of comprehension strategies, ask the following questions. Students can complete a written response or provide verbal answers in a one-on-one reading conference.

1. **Inferential Thinking** As you read the radio play, what inferences did you make? (Answers will vary. Students may say they made inferences about the characters, the theme, or the author's purpose for writing this play.)

2. **Understanding Text Structure** Why do you think the author chose to write a radio play about another radio play, the famous 1939 broadcast of *War of the Worlds*? (Answers will vary. Students may say that a radio play was a good way to present the impact of the original play and explore why people reacted so fearfully.)

For ongoing informal assessment, use the checklists on pages 61–64 of *Level A Assessment*.

## Word Study Assessment

Use these steps to help you and your students assess their understanding of long and short *i* sounds.

1. Write these words on the board: *pit, dine, bill, glitter, site, sin, pine, dinner, till, Nile, hilly, tide*.

2. Ask students to say each word and listen for the sound of the vowel *i*.

3. Place a two-column chart on the board like the one shown (omitting the answers). Ask students to copy the chart and write each word in the appropriate column. The answers are shown.

| Long *i* Words | Short *i* Words |
| --- | --- |
| dine | pit |
| site | bill |
| pine | glitter |
| Nile | sin |
| tide | dinner |
| | till |
| | hilly |

# The Telescope

*Space Odyssey*, pages 42–45

## SUMMARY

This **article** takes a historical look at the development of the telescope. It begins with Hans Lippershey, who is credited with the invention of the telescope in the early 1600s, and it ends with a description of the Webb telescope, set to be launched in 2010.

## COMPREHENSION STRATEGIES

Monitor Understanding

## WRITING

Double-entry Journal

## VOCABULARY

Word Root *tele*

## PHONICS/WORD STUDY

Short and Long *i* Patterns

### Lesson Vocabulary

| | |
|---|---|
| lens | atmosphere |
| craters | launched |
| magnify | |

## MATERIALS

*Space Odyssey*, pp. 42–45
*Student Journal*, pp. 64–66
*Word Study Manual*, p. 53
*Writing Advantage*, pp. 56–92

---

# THE TELESCOPE

The telescope allows us to see faraway things as though they were nearby. It opened our eyes to the skies over 400 years ago. It continues to help us discover new secrets about space.

## Who Invented the Telescope?

People who study history are not certain who really invented the telescope. They believe that it was a man who made eyeglasses! He lived in Holland, and his name was Hans Lippershey.

Glasses use lenses. A <u>lens</u> is a curved piece of glass or plastic. A convex lens makes objects appear larger. A concave lens makes objects appear smaller. A simple telescope uses both kinds of lenses.

The top drawing shows a convex lens.
The bottom drawing shows a concave lens.

Hans Lippershey of Holland may have invented the telescope in 1608. Lippershey owned an eyeglass shop. One day, two kids entered the shop. They began playing with his lenses. They held two together. They looked through them to the top of a church. It looked so close! Lippershey tried it. It was true! Lippershey had an idea. He stuck a tube in between the lenses. He had made a telescope!

Hans Lippershey invents the telescope in 1608.

42

---

# Before Reading

WHOLE CLASS — Use one or more activities.

## Make a K-W-L Chart

Write *Telescopes* as the topic of the K-W-L chart. Ask students what they know about telescopes. Add students' ideas to the *K* column. Have students scan the selection and generate questions they think will be answered. Add students' questions to the *W* column.

| What We **Know** | What We **Want** to Know | What We **Learned** |
|---|---|---|
| | | |

## Vocabulary Preview

List and pronounce the vocabulary words for students. Ask them to predict how each word might be used in the selection. They can record their answers in column two of *Student Journal* page 64. They will finish the page later. Model the process for one of the words.

## Preview the Selection

Have students look through the four pages of the article. Discuss students' reactions.

## Make Predictions/ Set Purpose

Students should use the information they gathered in previewing the selection to make predictions about what they will learn. If students have trouble generating a purpose for reading, suggest that they read to find out who invented the first telescope and how it has changed over the years.

## Galileo the Great!

Galileo Galilei was a scientist. He was from Italy. He heard about Lippershey's discovery and worked hard to improve it.

In 1609, Galileo used his telescopes to study the moon. People thought the moon was smooth. Galileo saw that it is covered with mountains. It also has valleys and craters, large bowl-shaped holes.

Galileo also looked at Jupiter. He discovered its four giant moons. He named them Io, Europa, Ganymede, and Callisto.

Galileo spent years looking through his telescopes. He made lots of notes. He told people what he saw. People used to believe that the planets and stars moved around the earth. Galileo said it wasn't true. He used the telescope to show them. Now we know the truth. Earth and the other planets move around the sun.

Galileo observed other objects. He observed the planet Venus. He studied sunspots.

Galileo did not discover the telescope. But he did make it famous. As a scientist, he was a great star!

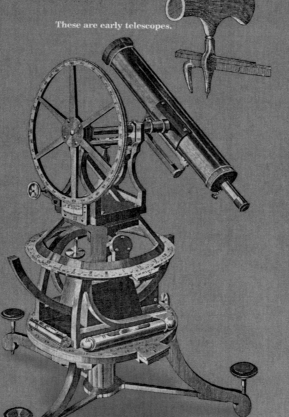

These are early telescopes.

## Naming the Planets

Most of the planets were named for characters in mythology, mostly Roman. The planet Jupiter was named for Jupiter, the king of the gods and ruler of the universe in Roman mythology. (He is like Zeus in Greek mythology.) His father was Saturn, who used to be the ruler of the universe. Two of Jupiter's brothers were Neptune and Pluto. Two of his sons were Mars and Mercury. The planet Venus was named for the Roman goddess of love and beauty. Uranus was named for the earliest supreme god in Greek mythology. Earth comes from an Old English word, *eorthe*.

Use this memory trick to remember the names and the order of the planets.

**My Very Eager Mother Just Served Us Nine Pizzas.**

(Mercury Venus Earth Mars Jupiter Saturn Uranus Neptune Pluto)

43

### Student Journal page 64

Name _____ Date _____

**Building Vocabulary: Predictions**

How do you predict these words will be used in "The Telescope"? Write your answers in the second column. Then read the article. Clarify your answers in the third column.

| Word | My prediction for how the word will be used | How the word was actually used |
|------|---------------------------------------------|--------------------------------|
| lens | | |
| craters | | |
| magnify | | |
| atmosphere | | |
| launched | | |

64 Space Odyssey • The Telescope

# During Reading

## Comprehension

MONITOR UNDERSTANDING

Use these questions to model how to visualize the text. Then have students tell about a part they visualized.

- What do I picture in my mind as I read?
- What details help me create this image in my mind?
- How does seeing this image help me understand what I am reading?

(See Differentiated Instruction.)

## Teacher Think Aloud

*When I read about what Galileo saw in his telescope, I picture a rocky surface marked with low pits and high mountains. The details about the craters and mountains help me create this picture in my mind. I can't see those surface features on an object as far away as the moon with my eyes alone, so visualizing this description helps me understand the power of a telescope.*

## Fix-Up Strategies

Offer these strategies to help students read independently.

**If you don't understand what you're reading:**

- Reread the difficult section to look for clues to help you comprehend.
- Read ahead to find clues to help you comprehend.
- Retell, or say in your own words, what you've read.
- Visualize, or form mental pictures of, what you've read.

## Bigger and Better Telescopes

Scientists began building better telescopes. These were larger and more powerful.

There are two basic kinds of telescopes that are used to look at the sky. Both magnify objects to make them look larger. Both use light. One kind uses mirrors, but the other kind uses lenses. The great scientist Sir Isaac Newton invented the mirror telescope in 1671. He used this telescope to study light. He learned that white light is made up of all colors of light.

In 1781, William Herschel used a large telescope to discover a distant planet. Today we call that planet Uranus.

In 1948, a huge telescope was built on top of a mountain in California. It uses a five-meter telescope. It is known as the Hale telescope.

Today we have the Keck II Telescope. It is the largest mirror telescope. Its main mirror is ten meters wide. That's more than thirty feet!

## Telescopes in Space

Telescopes are not always able to let us see things clearly. Lights on Earth's surface are a problem. They brighten the night sky. They make it difficult to see. Clouds are also a problem. So are dust, wind, and rain.

How can we fix these problems? Scientists finally found an answer. They decided to place a telescope above Earth's atmosphere. It would help see things more clearly.

The Hubble Space Telescope was launched into space in 1990. The Hubble gathers light from distant objects. It focuses the light with mirrors. The light is sent to scientific machines. Scientists use radio signals to control the Hubble.

The Hubble sees far into space. It can see things sharper than any telescope on Earth. It shows more details about the universe. It helps us learn how the universe works.

### Twinkling Stars

Twinkling stars are beautiful. One reason for the twinkling is pollution in Earth's atmosphere. The pollution causes the stars to look like they are shaking. Sometimes the way the star's light travels through the atmosphere makes it look to us as if the light is twinkling.

44

This is the Hale telescope at the Mt. Palomar Observatory in southern California.

# After Reading
WHOLE CLASS Use one or more activities.

## Check Purpose

Have students decide if their purpose was met. Who invented the first telescope? How has the telescope changed over the years?

## Discussion Questions

Continue the group discussion with the following questions.

1. Why were Galileo's discoveries so important? (Inferential Thinking)

2. What are the differences between the telescopes that use lenses and the telescopes that use mirrors? (Compare-Contrast)

3. What information did you like learning about most? Why? (Making Connections)

## Revisit: K-W-L Chart

Go back over the information in the *K* column and correct any misconceptions that may be there. Review the questions in the *W* column to determine which were answered. Add that information to the *L* column. Then add to the chart other facts students learned.

## Revisit: Prediction Chart

Have students complete *Student Journal* page 64. How were the words actually used?

The Hubble Space Telescope was named for Edwin Hubble (1889–1953). In the 1920s, people thought that the Milky Way galaxy was the whole universe. Hubble realized that it is just one of millions of galaxies.

Scientists are building a new kind of telescope. It will see even farther into space. The telescope will be named for James E. Webb. Webb was head of NASA during most of the 1960s. During this time, the space agency first attempted to build rockets and send people into space. Webb died in 1992.

Scientists plan to send the James E. Webb Telescope into space. It will be launched from a rocket in the year 2010. The Webb will be able to gather new information. It should tell more about stars and galaxies. We might learn how they were formed and how the universe began.

Telescopes have come a long way. Galileo used them to study the moon. Now we use them to explore the universe. That's how science works. It builds on one discovery at a time. ◆

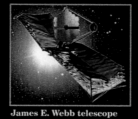
**James E. Webb telescope**

The Hubble telescope can see things ten times sharper than a ground-based telescope.

## WHAT IS IT?

Do you have any idea what this is? You might think it is a giant hamburger floating in space or a flying saucer. It really is a sunlike star nearing the end of its life. This is known as Gomez's Hamburger. The picture was taken by the Hubble Space Telescope.

45

**DIFFERENTIATED INSTRUCTION**
**SMALL GROUP**
## Writing
### Double-entry Journal
If students have trouble thinking of things to say about the quotes, try these steps.

1. Read aloud the first quote on the Double-entry Journal activity on *Student Journal* page 65.
2. Elicit responses to the quote from the whole group, and record the responses on the board.
3. Have each student choose the response that is closest to his or her own ideas and write the response as a starting point on the page.

**Student Journal page 66**

Name _____ Date _____

**Building Vocabulary: Word Part *tele***
Find six *tele* words in the puzzle by connecting letters that are next to each other. (You can move up, down, right, left, and diagonally. But you can't skip over letters!) Write the words you find on the lines below.

| x | e | m | a | r |
|---|---|---|---|---|
| i | s | i | v | g |
| o | t | e | l | e |
| n | o | h | p | g |
| e | o | t | a | r |

1. _____
2. _____
3. _____
4. _____
5. _____
6. _____

66                                    Space Odyssey • The Telescope

## Writing **Double-entry Journal**

Have students look at the double-entry journal on *Student Journal* page 65. Call on volunteers to read aloud the quotes in the left-hand column. Point out that the quotes are all from "The Telescope." Students should write what they think each entry means in the right-hand column. Ask for volunteers to share their thoughts before beginning to write. (See Differentiated Instruction.)

## Vocabulary **Word Root *tele***

Display *telescope,* and underline *tele.* Ask students to think of other words that begin with *tele.* (*television, telephone, telegram, telemarketing, telecommuting*) List their responses. Then have students tell what each word means. Ask students to think about what these word meanings all have in common. Point out, if necessary, that *tele* means "distance or distant." *Tele* is a Greek root that means "far off." Have students complete *Student Journal* page 66.

## Phonics/Word Study

### Short and Long *i* Patterns

Display: *Try not to slide on the ice. Did you slip on it?* Ask: *Which words in the first sentence have an* i *sound?* (*Try, slide, ice*) Elicit that all three words have the long *i* sound. Then ask: *Which words in the second sentence have an* i *sound?* (*did, slip, it*) Elicit that these words have the short *i* sound. Now, work with students to complete the short and long *i* patterns activity on TE page 156.

## Phonics/Word Study

### Short and Long *i* Patterns

▶ Write the following words on the board: *clip*, *mine*, and *try*. Tell students that these words represent both sounds for the letter *i*—short *i* and long *i*.

▶ Ask if students can identify which word has the short *i* sound and which words have the long *i* sound.

▶ Use the Long and Short *i*: Sort Two sheet to model the sorting process for students. (See *Word Study Manual* page 53.) Write the headings *iC*, *iCe*, *y* and Oddball and the first few words in the appropriate columns. Indicate that *iC* is a short *i* pattern and *iCe* and *y* are long *i* patterns. Introduce the word *eye* and see if students note that it is a different long vowel pattern, so it belongs in the Oddball column.

▶ Discuss the sort and what students learned, reviewing the different ways to spell the short *i* and long *i* sounds.

▶ Once the sort is complete, hand out the Long and Short *i*: Sort Two sheet and ask students to cut up the words and do the sort on their own or in groups.

▶ Check the final sorts.

| Long and Short *i*: Sort Two | | | |
|---|---|---|---|
| *iC* | *iCe* | *y* | Oddball |
| clip | mine | try | eye |
| flick | rice | fly | pink |
| nip | gripe | by | |
| strip | bride | cry | |
| | spine | | |
| | strive | | |
| | wife | | |
| | mice | | |

For more information on word sorts and spelling stages, see pages 5–31 in the *Word Study Manual*.

# Focus on . . .

Use one or more activities in this section to focus on a particular area of need in your students.

## Comprehension  SUPPORT STRATEGIES  INDEPENDENT

To help those students who need more practice using the strategies covered in this lesson, work one-on-one or in small groups to apply the strategy prompts below. Apply the prompts to a *Reading Advantage* paperback, a classroom library book, or a new or familiar selection in the magazine. Always model your own thinking first.

### Monitor Understanding

• Do I understand what I'm reading? If not, what part is confusing to me?

• What fix-up strategies can I use to solve the problem? (See During Reading for fix-up strategies.)

• Why did a character say (do, think, ask) that?

• What images do I visualize from the text? What parts can't I visualize?

• Why did the author include (or not include) those details?

## Writing Details and Main Idea  INDEPENDENT

Ask partners to list some important details from the article in a chart like the one below. (A main idea BLM can be found on page 388 of this TE.) After reading through their lists, have partners identify the main idea of the article and share. If the main ideas differ, discuss why that might be. Discuss together possible conclusions.

To extend this activity, students can use the information in the chart to write a paragraph that explains the main idea.

| Main Idea: | | |
|---|---|---|
| Detail | Detail | Detail |
| Conclusion: | | |

For instruction on editing paragraphs for main ideas, see lessons in *Writing Advantage*, pages 56–92.

## Fluency: Pacing

SMALL GROUP

After students have read "The Telescope" silently at least once, they can use portions of it to practice fluent reading. Have students work in pairs. They can first read aloud a part that they understand. Then they can read aloud a part that they don't understand. Partners can try to help each other understand the confusing parts. Remind students that factual information should be read at a smooth, even pace—one that is neither too fast nor too slow. Reading too fast or in a stop-start manner confuses listeners; they don't have time to absorb the information in one part before the reader goes on to the next part. Reading too slowly causes the listeners' attention to wander so that they lose track of the information.

As you listen to partners read, offer the following prompts to help them read at an even pace.

▶ Listen to me read. Then you read it just as I did.

▶ Reread this sentence a little faster (or more slowly).

When students read aloud, do they—

✓ demonstrate a smooth pace, not too fast or too slow?

✓ incorporate well-timed pauses between words and phrases?

✓ reflect an awareness and understanding of punctuation?

## English Language Learners

SMALL GROUP

To support students' understanding of word roots, extend the vocabulary activity on TE page 155.

1. Review the meaning of the root *tele-*. Write several examples of words that have *tele-* in them on the board.

2. Have partners create a simple picture dictionary using these words.

3. Have students share their picture dictionaries in small groups.

## Independent Activity Options

INDEPENDENT

While you work with individuals or small groups, others can work independently on one or more of the following options.

▶ Level A paperback books, see TE pages 371–376

▶ Level A *eZines*

▶ Repeat word sorts from this lesson

▶ *Student Journal* pages for this lesson

▶ *Writing Advantage* independent lessons

# Assessment

## Strategy Assessment

To help you and your students assess their use of comprehension strategies, ask the following question. Students can complete a written response or provide verbal answers in a one-on-one reading conference.

• **Monitor Understanding** As you read "The Telescope," how did visualizing help you monitor your understanding of the article? (Answers will vary. Students may mention that the measurements of the mirrors helped them visualize the telescopes to understand how big telescopes can be.)

For ongoing informal assessment, use the checklists on pages 61–64 of *Level A Assessment*.

## Word Study Assessment

Use these steps to help you and your students assess their understanding of short and long *i* sounds.

1. Place a chart like the one shown below on the board (omitting the answers) and ask students to copy it.

2. Write the following words in a list on the board and ask students to place each word in the appropriate column: *retry, spite, edit, slick, standby, slime, butterfly, crime, filth, shrimp*.

3. Have students identify which pattern denotes a short *i* sound (*iC*) and which patterns denote a long *i* sound (*iCe, y*). Answers are shown.

| iC | iCe | y |
|---|---|---|
| edit | spite | retry |
| slick | slime | standby |
| filth | crime | butterfly |
| shrimp | | |
| newsprint | | |

Reading Advantage

Level A Assessment

# From the Diary of Sir Isaac Newton *and* Meteor Shower

*Space Odyssey,* pages 46–49

## SUMMARY

In this series of **fictionalized diary entries**, Sir Isaac Newton ponders some big questions. A **poem** about meteors follows.

## COMPREHENSION STRATEGIES

Making Connections

## WRITING

Diary Entry

## VOCABULARY

Multiple Meanings

## PHONICS/WORD STUDY

Long *i* Patterns

### Lesson Vocabulary

| | |
|---|---|
| oval | credit |
| gravity | succeeded |

## MATERIALS

*Space Odyssey,* pp. 46–49
*Student Journal,* pp. 67–69
*Word Study Manual,* p. 54
*Writing Advantage,* pp. 30–55

---

## From the Diary of Sir Isaac Newton

Sir Isaac Newton (1642–1727) was an English scientist. Some have called him "the greatest scientist of all time." He gave us laws for the way things move in the universe. He gave us the laws of gravity. What if Newton had kept a diary? He might have written some of these things.

Oval    Circle

December 25, 1655

Happy birthday to me! I am thirteen years old. Grandma said I could have a party. But whom would I invite? I have no close friends. The kids in school think I'm too quiet and serious. They don't know I'm busy wondering about outer space.

I have read so many books on space. Aristotle says all planets travel around the earth. But Copernicus and Galileo say all planets travel around the sun. Who is right? I think Copernicus and Galileo are. But I want to know for sure.

Copernicus says the planets move in a perfect circle. But Kepler says they move in an <u>oval</u>, or egg-shaped, path. Who is right? I want to know the truth!

Every night I stare up at the sky. I'm filled with so many questions. What keeps the planets on their path as they travel? Why don't they ever fly off the path and fall down? How fast does something fall, anyway? Does it speed up as it falls farther?

Someday I hope to find out all the answers. I want to know the truth!

I must go now, Diary. I must finish building my toy windmill.

### The People of Newton's Diary

The people Newton writes about in the diary entry gave the world many important ideas about the universe. Those people are listed below.

- **Aristotle (384–322 B.C.),** a Greek philosopher
- **Nicolaus Copernicus (1473–1543), a Polish astronomer**
- **Galileo Galilei (1564–1642), an Italian astronomer**
- **Johann Kepler (1571–1630), a German astronomer**

46

---

# Before Reading

*WHOLE CLASS* Use one or more activities.

## Anticipation Guide

An anticipation guide is a series of statements that students respond to before reading a selection. It is not meant to quiz students, but rather to prompt discussion, build background, and create a purpose for reading. Create an anticipation guide for students. Ask students or pairs to read the statements and place a check in the AGREE or DISAGREE box before each statement. Then discuss the responses. (See Differentiated Instruction.)

## Vocabulary Preview

Display the vocabulary words. Ask for student volunteers to read the words aloud and to briefly share what they know about the words. Have students fill in the second column on *Student Journal* page 67. They will complete the page later. Model the process for students.

### Preview the Selection

Have students look through the three pages of the article. Then have them discuss their impressions.

## Make Predictions/Set Purpose

Students should use the information they gathered in previewing the selection to make predictions about what they will learn. If students have trouble generating a purpose for reading, suggest that they read to find out how Sir Isaac Newton's discoveries are important to the space program.

## The Diary

*August 10, 1665*

An amazing thing happened today! I was sitting in my garden. I was thinking about how the moon travels around Earth. Suddenly, an apple fell from a tree. It made me wonder. Why did the apple fall down? Why didn't it fall up or sideways instead?

Then, bam! The idea just came to me! There must be some force that pulled the apple down. It's a force that pulls all things down to Earth. That force is called <u>gravity</u>.

Then I wondered some more. Why doesn't gravity pull the moon down to Earth, too? I think I know the answer. The moon is too far away!

Here's how I figure: Gravity pulls on everything—the apple, the moon, everything. But the pull depends on distance. An apple falls because it's close to Earth. But the moon is too far from Earth to fall straight down. Gravity pulls on it just enough to keep it circling Earth.

I bet all the planets stay on their paths because of gravity! And I bet gravity makes things fall faster as they get closer to Earth.

I hope I can prove all this with math!

### Newton's Laws

Newton's laws of motion and gravity affect many things in our lives even today. Little things like car seatbelts and big things like space travel would not be possible without Newton's discoveries.

*47*

### Student Journal page 67

Name _____ Date _____

**Building Vocabulary: Predictions**

How do you predict these words will be used in the selection "From the Diary of Sir Isaac Newton"? Write your answers in the second column. Next, read the article. Then, clarify your answers in the third column.

| Word | My prediction for how the word will be used | How the word was actually used |
|---|---|---|
| oval | | |
| gravity | | |
| credit | | |
| succeeded | | |

Space Odyssey • From the Diary of Sir Isaac Newton | 67

# During Reading

## Comprehension SMALL GROUP

MAKING CONNECTIONS

Use these questions to model making connections with the text. Then have students make their own connections with the text.

- Have I ever heard of Sir Isaac Newton? In what context?
- Do any of Newton's ideas seem familiar?
- What do I already know about gravity?

## Teacher Think Aloud

*When I read the title of this selection, I immediately wondered if there would be a diary entry for the famous day on which Newton discovered gravity after an apple fell on him! I also know that Newton explained three important laws that tell how gravity affects our everyday lives.*

## Fix-Up Strategies

Offer these strategies to help students read independently.

**If you don't understand what you're reading:**

- Reread the difficult section to look for clues to help you comprehend.
- Read ahead to find clues to help you comprehend.
- Retell, or say in your own words, what you've read.
- Visualize, or form mental pictures of, what you've read.

## January 20, 1727

What a life I have led! People now cheer me for my ideas about gravity. They say I've solved the mysteries of space.

I know that I have done some good. Luckily, I was able to prove my ideas with math. The math book I wrote explains it all. My book shows how gravity pulls on the planets, moons, comets—even the ocean tide.

Remember all those questions I had as a child of thirteen? Well, I think I have answered most of them. I now know that planets circle the sun, not Earth. They travel in an oval, as Kepler thought. And I helped to prove it!

I'm proud of what I have done. The new telescope I invented is one of the special things I did. Now people can view Jupiter and other bodies far away in space.

I can't really take all the <u>credit</u>. I <u>succeeded</u> because I stood on the shoulders of giants. They were Copernicus, Galileo, and Kepler. These were brave men who looked for the truth even when others laughed at them.

Who knows what new truths about outer space people will learn in the future? ■

Isaac Newton received a special honor. He was knighted by the British Queen Anne in 1705. From then on, he was known as Sir Isaac Newton.

PRINCIPIA MATHEMATICA

Newton's reflecting telescope, 1671

48

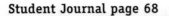
# After Reading
Use one or more activities.

## Check Purpose

Have students decide if their purpose was met. Did students learn how Sir Isaac Newton's discoveries are important to the space program?

## Discussion Questions

Continue the group discussion with the following questions.

1. In the first entry, Newton talks about astronomers who disagree with each other. Is it important for scientists always to agree? Why or why not? (Inferential Thinking)

2. What is the problem in the second diary entry? What is Newton's solution? (Problem-Solution)

3. What are three important discoveries that Newton made? (Details)

## Revisit: Anticipation Guide

Revisit the anticipation guide students completed in Before Reading. Have students changed any of their thoughts?

## Revisit: Prediction Chart

Have students complete the prediction chart on *Student Journal* page 67. They should use context clues to see how the word is being used in this selection.

## METEOR SHOWER

The midnight sky is clear.
The moon is new, not bright.
Across the black we see
A speeding streak of light.

Shooting stars, falling stars
Race across the sky.
Shooting stars, falling stars
Watch them as they fly.

A meteor shower has begun.
Across the sky they sail.
Not stars but dust on fire
From a comet's twisting tail.

Shooting stars, falling stars
Race across the sky.
Shooting stars, falling stars
Watch them as they fly.

We stare in silent wonder,
Then cheer each silver flight
Till the show is over
And darkness claims the night.

49

## Poem: Meteor Shower

First, have students read the poem silently. Then have them read it aloud with a partner. Discuss the poem with these questions.

- What is a meteor shower?
- Have you ever seen one?
- What patterns do you notice in this poem?

Have pairs perform the poem for the rest of the group. Encourage students to be creative in their performance. Pairs can alternate verses, play rhythm instruments to accompany themselves, or write music to go along with the verses. Invite students to learn more about meteors by visiting the North American Meteor Network website at http://www.namnmeteors.org.

### Student Journal page 69

| Word | First Definition | Second Definition |
|------|-----------------|-------------------|
| credit | recognition | an amount of money placed at a person's disposal by a bank |
| close | | |
| fly | | |
| down | | |
| fast | | |
| space | | |

## Writing Diary Entry

Have students brainstorm a list of scientific discoveries since Newton's time that might surprise him if he saw them today. Tell students to list on *Student Journal* page 68 the discoveries that most interest or surprise them. Then ask students to write a diary entry, using the voice of Newton, to tell what he might think of the modern world. Remind them to include in the entry some of the discoveries they listed.

## Vocabulary Multiple Meanings

Ask students to find *credit* in the fifth paragraph on page 48 of the magazine. Ask: *What does Newton mean when he says, "I can't really take all the credit"? What does* credit *mean in this context? What are some other meanings of* credit? Brainstorm a list of other words with multiple meanings. Possible words from the article include *close, space, right, fly, fall, down,* and *fast.* Have students complete *Student Journal* page 69.

## Phonics/Word Study
### Long i Patterns

Say the following sentence aloud: *The white knight was very kind.* Ask students what vowel sound they hear in the words *white, knight,* and *kind.* (long i) Write these three words on the board and ask students to identify the three different spellings of the long *i* sound that they see. (*iCe, igh,* and *iCC*) Now, work with students to complete the in-depth long *i* patterns activity on TE page 162.

### Long *i* Patterns

▶ Write the following words on the board: *kite*, *flight*, and *mind*. Tell students that these words are also examples of the vowel *i*.

▶ Ask students if the words have a short *i* or long *i* sound.

▶ Use the Long *i*: Sort Three sheet to model the sorting process for students. (See *Word Study Manual* page 54.) Write the headings *iCe*, *igh*, *iCC* and the first few words in the appropriate columns.

▶ Discuss the sort and what students learned.

▶ Once the sort is complete, hand out the Long *i*: Sort Three sheet and ask students to cut up the words and do the sort on their own or in groups.

▶ Check the final sorts.

▶ Students now have several long *i* representations. How many can they recall? Have students go back into their Word Study notebooks to refresh their memories.

| Long *i*: Sort Three | | |
|---|---|---|
| *iCe* | *igh* | *iCC* |
| kite | might | mind |
| strike | flight | blind |
| write | light | child |
| white | sigh | grind |
| spice | tight | wild |
| trite | right | kind |

For more information on word sorts and spelling stages, see pages 5–31 in the *Word Study Manual*.

# Focus on . . .

Use one or more activities in this section to focus on a particular area of need in your students.

## Comprehension  STRATEGY SUPPORT  INDEPENDENT

To help those students who need more practice using the strategies covered in this lesson, work one-on-one or in small groups to apply the strategy prompts below. Apply the prompts to a *Reading Advantage* paperback, a classroom library book, or a new or familiar selection in the magazine. Always model your own thinking first.

### Making Connections

• What does this story (article, passage) remind me of?

• What do I already know about this topic?

• Where have I heard about this topic before?

• What do I have in common with the characters, people, or situations in the text?

• What other books, stories, articles, movies or TV shows does this make me think about?

## Writing Explanatory Paragraph  INDEPENDENT

On page 48 in the magazine, Newton says that he "stood on the shoulders of giants." Explain that Newton realized that it was the accomplishments of those who came before him that paved the way for his work. Ask students who has paved the way for them. They might cite individuals from the civil rights or women's movements, or leaders in music or sports, for example. Then have students plan and write a paragraph about how one of those people paved the way for them. Students may use the following chart to plan their ideas.

| Name of Person | |
|---|---|
| Three ways the person has helped me | 1. |
| | 2. |
| | 3. |
| Conclusion | |

For additional instruction and practice writing expository paragraphs, see lessons in *Writing Advantage*, pages 114–151.

## Fluency: Expression

SMALL GROUP

After students have read the diary entries at least once, they can practice reading fluently and expressively by reading aloud one entry at a time. Have students work in pairs and take turns reading the entries.

As you listen to students read, use prompts to help them read expressively.

▶ A diary entry is written in the first person. Try to read the entry as if that person were speaking.

▶ Pay attention to punctuation marks. Pause for periods. Raise your voice slightly to signal the end of a question. Read with excitement or conviction when you see exclamation points.

▶ Read at an even pace. If you read too quickly, too slowly, or in a halting manner, listeners will have difficulty following along.

When students read aloud, do they—

✓ reflect an understanding of the text?

✓ demonstrate appropriate timing, stress, and intonation?

✓ incorporate appropriate speed and phrasing?

## English Language Learners

SMALL GROUP

To support students' understanding of a diary entry, preview the writing activity on TE page 161 by having them write a personal diary entry.

1. Explain what a diary entry is. Inform students that diary entries contain the date and thoughts about their own experiences.

2. Brainstorm several ideas students might write about.

3. Have students write their personal diary entry, then share it with a partner.

## Independent Activity Options

INDEPENDENT

While you work with individuals or small groups, others can work independently on one or more of the following options.

▶ Level A paperback books, see TE pages 371–376
▶ Level A *eZines*
▶ Repeat word sorts from this lesson
▶ *Student Journal* pages for this lesson
▶ *Writing Advantage* independent lessons

# Assessment

## Strategy Assessment

To help you and your students assess their use of comprehension strategies, ask the following question. Students can complete a written response or provide verbal answers in a one-on-one reading conference.

- **Making Connections** As you read the selection, what connections did you make? (Answers will vary. Students may mention that the article reminded them of information they already knew, provided new information, or raised questions.)

For ongoing informal assessment, use the checklists on pages 61–64 of *Level A Assessment*.

## Word Study Assessment

Use these steps to help you and your students assess their understanding of long *i* spelling patterns.

1. Place a three-column chart on the board with the headings *iCe*, *igh*, and *iCC*.

2. Read the following words aloud to students: *daylight, bind, rewrite, bite, rind, tight, satellite, unwind, fight*.

3. Ask volunteers to go to the board and write each word in the appropriate column according to its long *i* spelling pattern. The answers are shown.

| iCe | igh | iCC |
| --- | --- | --- |
| rewrite | daylight | bind |
| bite | tight | rind |
| satellite | fight | unwind |

Great Source
Reading Advantage

Level A
Assessment

# Almost Real Stars; A Very Special Visit

*Space Odyssey,* pages 50–55

## SUMMARY

An **article** and a **memoir** describe two different science museums.

## COMPREHENSION STRATEGIES

Inferential Thinking
Understanding Text Structure

## WRITING

Personal Memoir

## VOCABULARY

Word Association

## PHONICS/WORD STUDY

Long and Short *i* Patterns
(*r*-controlled)

### Lesson Vocabulary

| | |
|---|---|
| sphere | inspected |
| nebula | exhibits |
| universe | artifacts |
| cosmic | |

## MATERIALS

*Space Odyssey,* pp. 50–55
*Student Journal,* pp. 70–72
*Word Study Manual,* p. 55
*Writing Advantage,* pp. 113–151

# ALMOST REAL STARS

Look at the night sky.
Look at all those tiny lights.
A few are planets.
Most are stars, like our sun.

This is a view of the Hayden Planetarium at the Rose Center for Earth and Space. It is a part of the American Museum of Natural History in New York City. The Hayden Sphere is 87 feet in diameter and 273.3 feet in circumference. It weighs four million pounds (2,000 tons).

**50**

# Before Reading

Use one or more activities.

## Make a Concept Web

Start a concept web about science museums. Ask:

- What do you know about science museums?
- Which ones have you heard about
- What kinds of things might you find in a science museum?

Add a branch for planetariums. Revisit the web later.

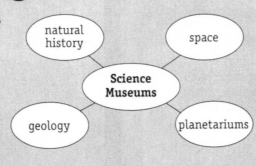

natural history

space

**Science Museums**

geology

planetariums

## Vocabulary Preview

List and pronounce the vocabulary words for students. Have them share what they know about any of the words. Remind students that they can often figure out what a word means by using clues in the text; sometimes, however, students need to look up words in a dictionary. Have students complete *Student Journal* page 70. When they're done, ask whether the context clues helped them confirm their choices. Model the process for students.

People have always relied on the stars. Sailors use them to guide their ships. Farmers use them to mark the changing seasons.

People look at the stars and wonder about them. How far away are they? How old are they? What are they made of? Where did they come from? People also wonder if we are alone. Does life exist anywhere else?

We are learning answers to these questions. Some answers are discovered at the Rose Center for Earth and Space. The Rose Center is in New York City. It is a new part of the American Museum of Natural History.

The most popular part of the Center is the Hayden Planetarium. This place is really out of this world. It offers tours of outer space. We can "visit" planets in our solar system. We can even "visit" other galaxies.

The planetarium is a <u>sphere</u>, shaped like a ball. The top half is the Space Theater. The Space Theater presents views of the night sky on a special rounded ceiling.

Powerful projectors can show **9,100** stars on the top of the sphere. They look just like tiny white twinkles!

The Space Theater uses the Digital Dome System. This is a computer system. It creates maps of our galaxy. It shows the maps on the dome. We can see every star and <u>nebula</u>, clouds of gas or dust among the stars. It looks so real that we forget we are in a theater.

The theater's sound system is amazing, too. It makes us feel like we are really moving. We feel the "lift-off" at the start of the show.

The Space Theater presents different shows. One of the most popular ones is "The Search for Life: Are We Alone?"

The "Search for Life" is a great journey. It opens our eyes to new wonders. It helps us think of life in new ways. Viewers see the depths of Earth's oceans. We take a walk on Mars. We travel to Europa, one of Jupiter's giant moons. We watch how stars are born. We see how stars die. We even visit planets outside our solar system.

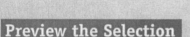

**The Zeiss Star Projector creates realistic and exciting shows.**

51

**Student Journal page 70**

Name _____  Date _____

**Building Vocabulary: Dictionary Definitions**

Read the words and the definitions below. Write the word next to its definition. Use the magazine selections for context help.

nebula       universe       inspected       artifacts
sphere       cosmic         exhibits

_____ objects made by humans, especially objects with historic or cultural interest

_____ relating to the whole universe, or cosmos

_____ displays of objects related to a topic

_____ examined carefully or officially

_____ a region or cloud of interstellar dust and gas that appears as a bright or dark patch in the sky

_____ any object similar in shape to a ball

_____ all the matter and space that exists, as a whole

Now choose two words. Tell how you used context to confirm that you matched the word with the correct definition.

_____
_____
_____
_____
_____

70       Space Odyssey • Almost Real Stars and A Very Special Visit

## Preview the Selection

Have students look through the six pages of both articles. Discuss students' impressions. Point out that both selections are nonfiction, but the first selection is an article and the second selection is a memoir. Discuss the two kinds of writing. How might each author's information be organized? Have students read and compare the first paragraph from each selection. What differences do they notice? (See Differentiated Instruction.)

## Teacher Think Aloud

*What do these selections have in common? Both tell about places to visit that tell about space. The first is a planetarium in New York. I wonder if it's like the planetarium I once visited. The other tells about the National Air and Space Museum in Washington, D.C. I wonder what space vehicles are on display there.*

## Make Predictions/ Set Purpose

Students should use the information they gathered in previewing the selection to make predictions about what they will learn. If students have trouble generating a purpose for reading, suggest that they read to find out what kind of information they can learn at a planetarium and what a trip to the National Air and Space Museum is like.

## Comprehension

INFERENTIAL THINKING

To help students think inferentially, ask these questions:

- What does the text on page 52 tell you about how the Space Theater is organized?

- What do you know about the Big Bang?

- What do you know from your own experience about chronological order as a way to organize ideas?

- What inference can you make about how information is organized along the Cosmic Pathway?

(Possible inference: Students may infer that the Cosmic Pathway takes visitors from the beginning of the universe to the present as they move from the bottom of the Space Theater up.)

The bottom half of the Space Theater is the Big Bang. Here visitors explore the beginning of time and space. They see the first moments of the universe, or cosmos. Be prepared to see, hear, and feel amazing things! The show uses a laser. It uses other kinds of light, too. It also uses special sound effects.

The journey continues. Visitors next follow the Cosmic Pathway. This walkway is 360 feet long. It explores thirteen billion years of cosmic history. We can measure how much history we cover with each step. An average step covers seventy-five million years.

There is much else to see at the Rose Center for Earth and Space. It is a great place to visit. Go there to explore the universe. You will never look at stars the same way again. ◆

**Spiral Galaxy**

Inside the Rose Center for Earth and Space

52

# During Reading

## Comprehension

INFERENTIAL THINKING

Use these questions to model making inferences from the last two paragraphs on page 51. Then have students make inferences about another section.

- What does the text tell me about the show called "The Search for Life"?

- What do I know about people's interest in life on other planets?

- What ideas can I infer?

(See Differentiated Instruction.)

## Teacher Think Aloud

*The text says that this film explores different planets and moons. It also says that it "helps us think of life in new ways." I know people are fas-cinated by aliens from space. I can infer from this that people may think they are going to see aliens when they see the film, but they may come away with a broader understanding of "life" in outer space.*

## Comprehension

UNDERSTANDING TEXT STRUCTURE

Use these questions to model for students how to identify the chronological text structure of "A Very Special Visit." Then have students tell how the text structure helps them understand the information.

- What is a memoir?

- What words in this memoir indicate the passage of time?

# A VERY SPECIAL VISIT

People sometimes write about a special event that happened at an earlier time in their lives. This writer remembers her first visit to the National Air and Space Museum.

I remember shouting, "Yippee! I'm finally in Washington, D. C. Hello, National Air and Space Museum!" Dad was happy to see how excited I was. Mom told me that the museum takes up three city blocks. The building is eighty feet high. That's as tall as a five-story building.

We walked up the steps and into the museum. There were crowds of people walking around or sitting on benches. I liked hearing people talking in many languages.

The first thing I saw was a large metal cone. I didn't know what it was until I saw the sign:

*Apollo 11* command module *Columbia*. Michael Collins had orbited the moon in this capsule! Close by, I saw a lunar module like the one that Buzz Aldrin and Neil Armstrong rode in from the *Columbia* to the moon. I looked at the models of them taking the first steps on the moon, and I imagined being there with them.

After I inspected the *Columbia*, I looked up—and almost fell over. There were real airplanes hanging from the ceiling. Part of the ceiling was glass, so it looked like the planes were in the air. What a cool sight!

## Teacher Think Aloud

*A memoir is an account of the personal experiences of the author. "The first thing," "After," and "Next" show that this piece is written in chronological order. It makes sense to describe what happened, as it happened, to show the passage of time. It would be confusing if the author wrote about the end of the day first. Time order helps me understand what the author's visit was like.*

## Fix-Up Strategies

Offer these strategies to help students read independently.

**If you don't understand what you're reading:**

- Reread the difficult section to look for clues to help you comprehend.

- Read ahead to find clues to help you comprehend.

- Retell, or say in your own words, what you've read.

- Visualize, or form mental pictures of, what you've read.

**If you don't understand a word:**

- Reread the sentence. Look for ideas and words that provide meaning clues.

- Find clues by reading a few sentences before and after the confusing word.

- Look for the base or root word and think about its meaning.

- Think about the topic or plot at this point to see if either offers meaning clues.

The command module *Columbia* from the 1969 *Apollo* mission to the moon

Strong tubes are part of the framework of the building. Cables and wires are attached to these tubes and to the aircraft that hang from the ceiling.

One plane looked very old. It had two long wings on top of each other. Between the wings was a model of a man. He was lying on his stomach. There was a small engine behind him. I knew about this from TV. Wilbur and Orville Wright built the plane and Orville flew it. This was the first plane to use an engine. I felt so lucky to see the original plane.

Dad showed us a museum map. He explained that there were <u>exhibits</u> on airplanes, pilots, the universe, aircraft carriers, and more. I really liked the moon stuff. So I asked to start at the *Apollo to the Moon* exhibit.

This exhibit is great! I saw instruments that the astronauts used. There was a broken wheel and fender from a lunar vehicle. An astronaut had taped them together but they fell apart again. Imagine using tape on the moon! Some of the other <u>artifacts</u> were spacesuits, star charts, shaving cream, and a toothbrush. Mom said it looked like I would still have to brush my teeth even if I went into space. We all laughed at that.

The best part was the collection of lunar rocks. I touched one. To this day I get a tingly feeling when I think of that.

Next, we went inside a module from a real Skylab. I carefully flipped some of the switches. I turned dials and opened drawers. The astronauts' beds were sleeping bags attached to the wall. I told my parents that I might try sleeping that way at home.

We went on to an exhibit about how things fly. There was a machine that showed how wind flows around airplane wings. The computer experiments were such fun that I did every one of them.

I was hungry by the time I finished. We ate sandwiches in the museum restaurant. For dessert, I had an astronaut ice-cream sandwich. It came in a small foil bag. It looked like a normal ice-cream sandwich, but it felt like dry chalk. I broke off a piece and put it in my mouth. Suddenly, it melted and tasted like a real ice-cream sandwich. Yummy! I bought an extra one to take home.

After lunch, we went to the planetarium. Sitting in the planetarium is like sitting under a cup that is turned upside down. We sat back and looked up at the dome. The planets whizzed by. There were stars all around us. In just twenty minutes, we zipped from one end of the universe to the other. Some of the pictures were from space satellites and telescopes. I felt like I was out there in space. That was still the best planetarium show I have ever seen.

Next, Mom and I rode in the flight simulator. We strapped ourselves into the cockpit and the top closed. It was like being in a real fighter jet.

A moon rock brought home by the *Apollo* 15 mission is on display at the museum.

54

**Student Journal page 71**

Name _____ Date _____

**Writing: A Memoir**

A memoir tells about a special event or trip from a personal point of view. Write your own memoir. Start with a topic sentence that names the event. Then list what you did in order. End with a conclusion that tells how you felt about the event.

Space Odyssey • Almost Real Stars    A Very Special Visit    71

# After Reading
Use one or more activities.

## Check Purpose

Have students decide if their purpose was met. What kind of information can they learn at a planetarium? What is a trip to the National Air and Space Museum like?

## Discussion Questions

Continue the group discussion with the following questions.

1. What similar experiences can you relate either of these articles to? (Making Connections)

2. How do "hands-on" exhibits affect a museum visit? (Cause-Effect)

3. How are "Almost Real Stars" and "A Very Special Visit" similar and different? (Compare-Contrast)

## Revisit: Concept Web

Go over the concept web about science museums that you started in Before Reading. Help students add any new information they learned about science museums from reading the two selections.

The simulator went up about twelve feet. I worked the controls and made it roll sideways and pitch up and down. Then Mom took over and we did spins and flew upside down!

Whew! I was dizzy when we got out! I teased Mom about being a hotshot pilot.

Dad looked at his watch. He told us that the museum would be closing in fifteen minutes. I begged them to come back the next day.

Mom reminded me that we had planned to go to the amusement park. I had told them I wanted to ride all the roller coasters. I quickly decided to trade the trip to the amusement park for another day at the NASM.

We all agreed to spend the whole next day at the museum. But that's another story! ◆

Planes hanging from the ceiling in the Air Transportation Gallery

## HOW MUCH DO THE HANGING PLANES WEIGH?

- The Northrop Alpha weighs 2,600 pounds.
- The Wright Brothers' Flyer weighs 605 pounds.
- The Boeing 247 weighs 17,000 pounds.
- The DC 3 weighs 25,000 pounds.

This is a model of a make-believe rocket described by Jules Verne. In the 1870s, he wrote *From the Earth to the Moon* and *Around the Moon*. These books helped people start thinking about going into space.

### MUSEUM FACTS

The National Air and Space museum is on the National Mall in Washington, D.C. It is free and is open every day except December 25.

- The museum has twenty-three exhibit rooms and many smaller displays.
- Many of the airplanes and spacecraft are original. Others are exact models.
- You can visit NASM whenever you want. Log onto the website at http://www.nasm.si.edu.

55

SMALL GROUP

### Student Journal page 72

Name _____ Date _____

**Building Vocabulary: Word Associations**
Choose two words from the vocabulary list below. Think about what you already know about each word. Then answer the following questions.

| nebula sphere | universe cosmic | inspected exhibits | artifacts |

Word _____
What do you think about when you read this word? _____
Who might use this word? _____
What do you already know about this word? _____

Word _____
What do you think about when you read this word? _____
Who might use this word? _____
What do you already know about this word? _____

72                Space Odyssey • Almost Real Stars    A Very Special Visit

## Writing Personal Memoir

Talk about how students can order events sequentially to help them write a short memoir about a school trip or a family visit to a place of interest. Then have each student write a memoir on *Student Journal* page 71. (See Differentiated Instruction.)

## Vocabulary Word Association

Display *planetarium*. Then ask:

- What do you know about this word?
- What topics do you associate with this word?
- Who might use this word?
- In what contexts have you heard this word used?

Have students complete *Student Journal* page 72.

## Phonics/Word Study
## Long and Short *i* Patterns

Display *firm, expire, dive, sir,* and *fly.* Ask: *Which are the long* i *words?* (*expire, dive, fly*) Point out the long *i* spellings—*ire, iCe, y.* Next ask: *Which are the short* i *words?* (*firm, sir*) Elicit that these short *i* words have the *ir* spelling. Now, work with students to complete the in-depth long and short *i* activity on TE page 170.

## Phonics/Word Study

### Long and Short *i* Patterns (*r*-controlled)

▶ Display *fire*. Tell students that they are continuing their study of *i* patterns. The words in this sort, however, are a little tricky.

▶ Briefly review short and long *i* vowel patterns with students. Point to the word *fire*. Ask if the *i* in *fire* is long or short.

▶ Without telling students whether they are right or wrong, write the word *fir* on the board. Ask students if *fir* helps them figure out which *i* is short and which is long.

▶ Discuss the difficulty the letter *r* causes and how it "robs" the vowel of its usual sound. The *i* in *fir* sounds very different from the *i* in *fit*.

▶ Use the Long and Short *i*: *r*-controlled Vowels sheet to model the sorting process for students. (See *Word Study Manual* page 55.) Write the headings Short *i* (*ir*), Long *i* (*ire*), Long *i* and the first few words in the appropriate columns.

▶ Discuss the sort and what students learned about *r*-controlled vowels. Note that sometimes the easiest way to tell if an *r*-controlled vowel is short or long is to say the word aloud.

▶ Once the sort is complete, hand out the Long and Short *i*: *r*-controlled Vowels sheet and ask students to cut up the words and do the sort on their own or in groups.

▶ Check the final sorts for accuracy and ask students to discuss the different spelling patterns in the Long *i* column. (*hire, strike* [iCe], *why* [y])

| Long and Short *i*: *r*-controlled Vowels | | |
|---|---|---|
| Short *i* (*ir*) | Long *i* (*ire*) | Long *i* |
| firm | fire | hive |
| whirl | dire | strike |
| quirk | wire | why |
| shirk | inspire | |
| bird | mire | |
| irk | hire | |
| girl | | |
| shirt | | |

For more information on word sorts and spelling stages, see pages 5–31 in the *Word Study Manual*.

# Focus on . . .

Use one or more activities in this section to focus on a particular area of need in your students.

## Comprehension  STRATEGY SUPPORT

To help those students who need more practice using the strategies covered in this lesson, work one-on-one or in small groups to apply the strategy prompts below. Apply the prompts to a *Reading Advantage* paperback, a classroom library book, or a new or familiar selection in the magazine. Always model your own thinking first.

### Inferential Thinking

• What are the causes or effects of this event?

• What do I learn from the character or person's thoughts, words, or actions?

• What do I know (or infer) from the text that the author hasn't stated directly?

• What conclusions can I draw?

### Understanding Text Structure

• What kind of text is this? (book, story, article, guidebook, play, manual)

• How does the author organize the text? (cause-effect, problem-solution, chronological order, description, question-answer, comparison-contrast)

• What details support my thoughts about the text structure?

• What is the cause (effect, problem, solution, order, question, answer)?

• If fiction, who are the characters? What is the setting, plot, conflict, and resolution?

## Writing  Descriptive Paragraph

Ask students to write a paragraph describing their experience with stars. Possible angles include: What do I think about when I see stars? Where have I seen the most stars? Have students use concept webs to get their thoughts on paper before they begin writing.

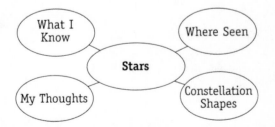

To provide additional instruction on writing paragraphs, see lessons in *Writing Advantage*, pages 113–152.

## Fluency: Punctuation

After students have read "A Very Special Visit" silently, partners can read their favorite parts aloud. First, model reading aloud the first paragraph with expression. Point out how periods let you know where to stop and exclamation points told you when to read with extra expression. Ask students to think of exciting events in their own lives so that they can put themselves in the narrator's place and read with the appropriate expression. Note that reading with good expression helps keep listeners' attention. Have students practice reading aloud to their partners, who will give feedback to encourage expressive reading.

Observe students as they read aloud. Offer prompts as needed to help students read expressively.

▶ If there's no punctuation at the end of a line, don't stop reading. Keep going until you get to the end of the sentence.

▶ That sentence ends with an exclamation point. Listen how I read it to show excitement.

When students read aloud, do they—

✓ demonstrate appropriate meaning and usage of punctuation marks?

✓ incorporate appropriate timing, stress, and intonation?

✓ exhibit well-timed pauses between words and phrases?

## English Language Learners

To support students' comprehension of "A Very Special Visit," help students make connections to the text.

1. Remind students that active readers make connections to experiences in their own lives.

2. Have them think about a time they visited a special and discuss this experience with a partner.

## Independent Activity Options

While you work with individuals or small groups, others can work independently on one or more of the following options.

▶ Level A paperback books, see TE pages 371–376

▶ Level A *eZines*

▶ Repeat word sorts from this lesson

▶ *Student Journal* pages for this lesson

▶ *Writing Advantage* independent lessons

# Assessment

## Strategy Assessment

To help you and your students assess their use of comprehension strategies, ask the following questions. Students can complete a written response or provide verbal answers in a one-on-one reading conference.

1. **Inferential Thinking** As you read the articles, what inferences did you make? (Answers will vary. Students may have made inferences about the displays at either the Rose Center or the Air and Space Museum.)

2. **Understanding Text Structure** How would you describe the text organization of the article "Almost Real Stars"? (Answers will vary. Students should note that the nonfiction article is organized by description.)

For ongoing informal assessment, use the checklists on pages 61–64 of *Level A Assessment*.

## Word Study Assessment

Use these steps to help you and your students assess their understanding of *r*-controlled long and short *i* patterns.

1. Place a three-column chart on the board with the headings Short *i* (*ir*), Long *i* (*ire*), and Long *i*. Ask students to copy it.

2. Write these words on the board: *shire*, *fir*, *miles*, *stir*, *white*, *entire*, *sir*, *reply*, *acquire*.

3. Ask students to say each word, look at its spelling, and then write it in the appropriate column on their charts. The answers are shown.

| Short *i* (*ir*) | Long *i* (*ire*) | Long *i* |
|---|---|---|
| fir | shire | miles |
| stir | entire | white |
| sir | acquire | reply |

Great Source
Reading Advantage

Level A Assessment

# Hercules: Star of the Skies

*Space Odyssey*, pages 56–59

## SUMMARY

This selection provides background information on mythology and then goes on to tell the **myth** of Hercules and why a constellation is named after him.

## COMPREHENSION STRATEGIES

Determining Importance

## WRITING

Description for Visualizing

## VOCABULARY

Homophones

## PHONICS/WORD STUDY

Long *i* Review

### Lesson Vocabulary

| | |
|---|---|
| ancient | cloak |
| constellations | boar |
| myths | Minotaur |
| resented | |

## MATERIALS

*Space Odyssey*, pp. 56–59
*Student Journal*, pp. 73–75
*Word Study Manual*, p. 56
*Writing Advantage*, pp. 13–29

# HERCULES
## STAR OF THE SKIES

Many ancient people, people who lived a very long time ago, imagined that different groups of stars formed pictures in the night sky. These groups of stars are called constellations. Ancient peoples saw a lion. They saw a bull. They saw a hunter. They saw a strong man bent down on one knee. He held a club in one hand and the neck of a many-headed monster in the other hand. The man was choking the monster to death.

Many peoples saw the star pictures. But it was the Greeks and Romans who gave us the names and stories of many of the constellations. Those stories are called myths.

What makes myths different from other kinds of stories? A myth is based on a belief of a group of people, and it usually involves gods, goddesses, and superhuman heroes. Ancient peoples didn't know many facts. So a myth was a way for people to explain something in their lives. For example, the Greeks believed that gods and goddesses with special powers ruled many areas of life. It was

what the gods and goddesses said and did that made a flood or put a star picture in the night sky.

Let's look at this star picture of the strong man. His name is Hercules. How did he get into the night sky?

According to the Greeks, Hercules' father was Zeus. Zeus was the king of all the Greek gods. He was ruler of the heavens and the earth. Hera was Zeus's wife and the goddess of marriage. However, Hera was not Hercules' mother. His mother was Alcemene. She was a human, not a goddess.

Hera was jealous of Alcemene. She sent monster snakes to kill baby Hercules in his crib. But baby Hercules was strong! He choked those snakes to death in his little hands.

Hercules grew up to be very strong—superhuman strong. He was an expert with a bow and arrow and a champion wrestler. He should have been made king, but Hera resented him. She tricked Zeus into making Hercules' cousin Eurysthesus the king. Hercules later became a sort of slave to King Eurysthesus.

56

# Before Reading

**WHOLE CLASS** Use one or more activities.

## Make a Category Chart

Ask students: *What do you know about myths?* Have students write their answers on self-stick notes or slips of paper (one thought per paper). Read the answers together and organize them into possible categories such as: mythological characters, titles of stories, qualities of superheroes. Have students explain why each note fits into each category. Write headers for each category. Stick the notes together (or to a larger piece of paper) to refer to later.

## Vocabulary Preview

Display the vocabulary words. Have students read the words aloud and discuss them. Then have students complete *Student Journal* page 73. For definition help, students can look for context clues.

## Preview the Selection

Have students look through the four pages of the selection. Discuss students' observations and the proper names they notice.

## Make Predictions/Set Purpose

Students should use the information they gathered in previewing the selection to make predictions about what they will learn. If students have trouble generating a purpose for reading, suggest that they read to discover why Hercules is a "star of the skies."

The only way Hercules could gain his freedom was to perform super-human tasks. They are known as THE TWELVE LABORS OF HERCULES.

Hercules' first labor was not easy. King Eurysthesus challenged Hercules to kill the Nemean lion. This was no ordinary lion. It had been terrorizing people in the valley of Nemea. Arrows and spears could not pierce the lion's skin. Hercules wrestled the beast in a cave. He choked the lion to death with his bare hands. To show his victory, he wore the lion's skin as a cloak, or cape, and used its giant jaws as a helmet.

Next, Hercules had to destroy an awful swamp beast known as the Hydra. The Hydra had many heads. As soon as one was chopped off, two more grew in its place. Worse, the monster had killer breath. One whiff could do it. Hercules had his nephew Iolaus help him. As soon as Hercules cut off one head, Iolaus burned the stump with a torch. This way, the Hydra could not grow more heads. One by one, Hercules chopped off the nasty heads. When the monster was dead, Hercules buried it under a large rock.

The third and fourth labors dealt with capturing other beasts. Hercules killed a swift deer with golden horns and an enormous boar, which is a male pig with large, pointed teeth. Neither task was boring!

Hercules' fifth labor was different. He had to clean out the Augean stables in a single day. Thousands of animals stayed in the stables. The animals had made a mess there for thirty years. No one had ever cleaned the stables. But Hercules managed the job. He turned the course of two rivers. He forced the waters through the stables. He did his job without even getting dirty.

57

### Comprehension
DETERMINING IMPORTANCE

Help students determine importance by asking:

- Does the text contain any vocabulary words?
- In what sentences do these key words appear?
- What are the details in those sentences and why might they be important?
- How is this information important to me?

### Student Journal page 73

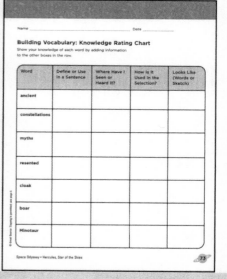

**Building Vocabulary: Knowledge Rating Chart**
Show your knowledge of each word by adding information to the other boxes in the row.

| Word | Define or Use in a Sentence | Where Have I Seen or Heard It? | How Is It Used in the Selection? | Looks Like (Words or Sketch) |
|---|---|---|---|---|
| ancient | | | | |
| constellations | | | | |
| myths | | | | |
| resented | | | | |
| cloak | | | | |
| boar | | | | |
| Minotaur | | | | |

# During Reading

## Comprehension
SMALL GROUP

DETERMINING IMPORTANCE

Use these questions to model determining the importance of ideas in the third paragraph of the selection. Then have students determine the importance of ideas in the second paragraph on page 57.

- What are the most important ideas in the paragraph?
- How can I support my beliefs?

(See Differentiated Instruction.)

## Teacher Think Aloud

*I think that an important idea is the definition of myth because the selection is about mythological figures. It's also important to know that myths provided a way for people to explain something in their lives. This is important because I can understand the idea of wanting to have an explanation of the unknown.*

## Fix-Up Strategies

Offer these strategies to help students read independently.

**If you don't understand what you're reading:**

- Reread the difficult section to look for clues to help you comprehend.
- Read ahead to find clues to help you comprehend.
- Retell, or say in your own words, what you've read.
- Visualize, or form mental pictures of, what you've read.

Hercules' sixth labor was really *fowl*. He had to get rid of a large flock of man-eating birds. First, he drove them into the air by making *very* loud noises. Then he shot them down with dozens of arrows.

The next labor required Hercules to capture the <u>Minotaur</u>. This was a half-man, half-bull monster. The fire-breathing beast lived in a maze on the island of Crete. Hercules used his great strength to overpower the beast. Go, Hercules!

Hercules' next three labors kept him very busy. First, he had to capture a wild herd of man-eating horses. Next, he had to retrieve the belt from Hippolyte. She was the Queen of the Amazons. (The Amazons were a race of great warrior women.) Then Hercules had to bring King Eurysthesus the cattle of Geryon. Geryon was a three-headed monster. Hercules took care of him with one swing of his mighty club.

Hercules' eleventh labor was a special challenge. He had to bring the golden apples to King Eurysthesus. These apples were kept in a walled garden at the edge of the world. The apples were guarded by a dragon and by the daughters of Zeus. Hercules didn't know where to find the apples, but Atlas did. Atlas was one of the first gods. He held the sky and the earth on his mighty shoulders. His job was very tiring. Atlas told Hercules he would get the apples if Hercules would do *his* job for a while. Well, a deal's a deal. Hercules got the apples!

For the final labor, Hercules had to capture the monster-dog Cerberus. This creature had three heads and a snake for a tail. It guarded the gates of Hades, the kingdom of the dead. Hercules wrestled the dog to the ground.

The labors were done. Hercules had won his freedom. ◆

HERCULES WENT ON TO OTHER ADVENTURES AND GREAT DEEDS. HE IS THOUGHT OF AS ONE OF MYTHOLOGY'S GREATEST HEROES. IT SEEMS RIGHT THAT HIS PICTURE CAN BE SEEN AMONG THE STARS.

58

## Student Journal page 74

Name _____ Date _____

**Writing: Description for Visualizing**
Which one of Hercules' labors could you visualize best? Describe that labor below. Then draw a picture to show what you "saw" in your mind.

The labor I could visualize best was _____
_____
_____

Some details I "saw" in my mind include _____
_____
_____

Now draw what you visualized.

74     Space Odyssey • Hercules, Star of the Skies

# After Reading
*WHOLE CLASS*   Use one or more activities.

## Check Purpose

Have students decide if their purpose was met. Why is Hercules the "star of the skies"? What did students discover from the story?

## Discussion Questions

Continue the group discussion with the following questions.

1. What do I know now about myths that I didn't before? (Making Connections)

2. Describe three of the twelve labors that Hercules had to perform. (Details)

3. How did Hercules manage to get the golden apples? (Problem-Solution)

## Revisit: Category Chart

Revisit the category chart that was started in Before Reading. Do students have more information about myths that they would like to add to the chart?

## Revisit: Knowledge Rating Chart

Students can revisit the chart on *Student Journal* page 73. Have their thoughts about a particular word changed or expanded? Have them revise their charts as necessary.

# GIFTS FROM THE GREEKS

Greek mythology is a source of some of the English words we use today.

## HERCULEAN

*Herculean* means "of extraordinary power or difficulty." The twelve labors that Hercules had to complete were certainly of extraordinary difficulty. Can you imagine cleaning out a stable that held thousands of animals and had never before been cleaned? Now, *that's* a herculean task.

## HYDRA

The name of the beast Hydra comes from the Greek word for water serpent. When you see an English word that contains *hydra* or *hydro*, you can be pretty sure that the word has something to do with water.

**Hydrant**—a valve with a pipe and spout that sticks out of the ground; firefighters connect hoses to it to get water to fight fires.

**Dehydrate**—to take water out of, as in food; to dry out

**Hydrate**—to combine with water, especially something that has been dehydrated, such as the food that astronauts eat in space

**Hydroplane**—a seaplane; also, to lose control (of a car) by skimming along the top of a wet road

**Hydroponics**—growing plants in a solution of water and nutrients instead of soil

## ATLAS

Atlas had to hold up the heavens and Earth on his shoulders. (Also a herculean task!) From his name comes the English word that means "a bound book of maps."

## HOW DO YOU SAY IT?

| | |
|---|---|
| Zeus (ZOOS) | Iolaus (eye OH lus) |
| Hera (HAIR uh) | Augean (aw GEE uhn) |
| Alcemene (AL seh meen) | Minotaur (MIN uh tawr) |
| Eurysthesus (yoo RIS thee sus) | Hippolyte (hip POL ih tee) |
| Nemean (Neh MEE uhn) | Geryon (GEH ree on) |
| Nemea (Neh MEE uh) | Cerberus (SIR buhr us) |
| Hydra (HI druh) | Hades (HAY deez) |

**59**

## DIFFERENTIATED INSTRUCTION

### Vocabulary

## Homophones

If students need an additional example of a homophone, try these steps:

1. Have a volunteer read aloud the first few sentences at the beginning of page 58.

2. Ask if students understand why the word *fowl* is in italics.

3. If necessary, point out the play on words that uses the homophones *fowl* (birds) and *foul* (unpleasant).

### Student Journal page 75

Name _____ Date _____

**Building Vocabulary: Homophones**
Read the homophone pairs. Write a definition for each word.

| Homophone Pair | Definition |
|---|---|
| boar | a male pig |
| bore | something that lacks interest |
| fowl | |
| foul | |

Write a homophone for each word. Then write a definition for each word.

| Homophone Pair | Definition |
|---|---|
| herd | |
| maze | |
| deer | |
| right | |
| won | |
| great | |

Space Odyssey • Hercules, Star of the Skies    75

---

## Writing

### Description for Visualizing

Remind students that active readers visualize, or try to "see," what an author tells about. Ask students which of Hercules's labors they could visualize best. Write their ideas on the board. Have volunteers describe some of the pictures they "saw" in their minds. Then have students complete *Student Journal* page 74. Have students refer to the list on the board for ideas.

## Vocabulary Homophones

Point out the paragraph on the right side of page 57 that describes the third and fourth labors, in which Hercules killed a deer and a boar. Read aloud the final sentence: *Neither task was boring!* Explain to students that *boar* and *bore* are homophones, words that sound the same but have different spellings and meanings. Have students complete *Student Journal* page 75. (See Differentiated Instruction.)

## Phonics/Word Study

### Long *i* Review

Display: __ __y ; __ i __ e ; __igh__; __ire ; ___ind. Ask students to suggest letters that complete the words and spell words that have a long *i* sound. (*why, pine, light, fire, kind*) Challenge students to think of other words for each spelling pattern. Now, work with students to complete the in-depth long *i* review on page TE 176.

## Long *i* Review

▶ Have students do the Long *i*: Review sort on *Word Study Manual* page 56.

▶ Point out that *live* and *wind* have homonyms and could be placed in more than one column depending on the pronunciation.

▶ Check the final sorts for accuracy.

| Long *i*: Review | | | | | |
|---|---|---|---|---|---|
| *iCe* | *y* | *igh* | *iCC* | *r*-controlled | Oddball |
| twine | cry | might | find | hire | live |
| strive | | thigh | wind | dire | give |
| | | flight | kind | fire | |
| | | | climb | | |

For more information on word sorts and spelling stages, see pages 5–31 in the *Word Study Manual*.

# Focus on . . .

Use one or more activities in this section to focus on a particular area of need in your students.

## Comprehension   STRATEGY SUPPORT   INDEPENDENT

To help those students who need more practice using the strategies covered in this lesson, work one-on-one or in small groups to apply the strategy prompts below. Apply the prompts to a *Reading Advantage* paperback, a classroom library book, or a new or familiar selection in the magazine. Always model your own thinking first.

### Determining Importance

• What is the most important idea in the paragraph? How can I prove it?

• Which details are unimportant? Why?

• What does the author want me to understand?

• Why is this information important (or not important) to me?

## Writing Myth   INDEPENDENT

Have students write a short original myth (or retell one they already know) about a superhero. The superhero can be known or made-up. Students should work with partners or in groups of three. Groups should share ideas about what kind of myth they want to write. Then have students fill out a chart similar to the following to help organize their ideas. Once students have written their myths, encourage them to illustrate the myth before sharing it with others.

| Characters | What It Explains | Plot Idea |
|---|---|---|
| | | |

For instruction on how to create strong images in writing, see lessons in *Writing Advantage*, pages 30–55.

## Fluency: Expression

SMALL GROUP

After students have read the selection at least once, have them work in small groups to read and dramatize the story. Students can take turns reading paragraphs while the others act out the events.

As students practice their presentations, use these prompts to guide the oral reading:

▶ Read smoothly, not hesitating on some words or repeating words. Let the punctuation be your guide.

▶ Preview the paragraph to look for words or names that might be unfamiliar or hard to pronounce. Practice reading unknown words or names aloud so you don't stumble over them as you read.

▶ Remember to read loudly enough for everyone to hear the words clearly. Put enthusiasm in what you read to make listening an enjoyable experience.

When students read aloud, do they—

✓ reflect an understanding of the text?

✓ demonstrate appropriate timing, stress, and intonation?

✓ incorporate appropriate speed and phrasing?

## English Language Learners

SMALL GROUP

To support students as they learn about the myth of "Hercules: Star of the Skies," provide background knowledge about myths.

1. Read several well-known myths to students.
2. Discuss what makes a story a myth.
3. Have students explain what a myth is to a partner and tell which of the myths they heard was their favorite.

## Independent Activity Options

INDEPENDENT

While you work with individuals or small groups, others can work independently on one or more of the following options.

▶ Level A paperback books, see TE pages 371–376
▶ Level A *eZines*
▶ Repeat word sorts from this lesson
▶ *Student Journal* pages for this lesson
▶ *Writing Advantage* independent lessons

# Assessment

## Strategy Assessment

To help you and your students assess their use of comprehension strategies, ask the following question. Students can complete a written response or provide verbal answers in a one-on-one reading conference.

- **Determining Importance** As you read the myth, how did you determine importance? (Answers will vary. Students may say that they noted information that was personally important to themselves, or that they thought the author wanted them to understand because it focused on specific vocabulary words or details related to the content of the selection.)

For ongoing informal assessment, use the checklists on pages 61–64 of *Level A Assessment*.

## Word Study Assessment

Use these steps to help you and your students assess their understanding of long *i* vowel patterns.

1. Place a five-column chart on the board with the headings *iCe, y, igh, iCC,* and *r-controlled*.

2. Say the following words aloud one by one: *bright, cry, grime, require, climb, rind, plight, rite, desire, quite*.

3. Call on students to write each word in the appropriate column of the chart. The answers are shown.

| iCe | y | igh | iCC | r-controlled |
|-----|-----|--------|-------|--------------|
| grime | cry | bright | climb | require |
| rite | | plight | rind | desire |
| quite | | | | |

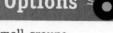

Great Source
Reading Advantage

Level A
Assessment

# Fun in Space, Meal Time, *and* Poems for Space Travelers

*Space Odyssey*, pages 60–65

## SUMMARY

Two short **informational articles** and three **poems** are included.

## COMPREHENSION STRATEGIES

Making Connections
Understanding Text Structure

## WRITING

Opinion Paragraph

## VOCABULARY

Review Space Terms

## PHONICS/WORD STUDY

Long and Short *i* Homophones

## Lesson Vocabulary

review space terms

## MATERIALS

*Space Odyssey*, pp. 60–65
*Student Journal*, pp. 76–78
*Word Study Manual*, p. 57
*Writing Advantage*, pp. 30–55

---

## Fun in

The Space Shuttle and the ISS are small places to live. But lack of room does not stop the astronauts from having fun! Here are some of the things they do.

Many astronauts say their favorite way to have fun is to look out the windows. They sure have a great view!

Jan Davis and Mark Lee were the first married couple in space.

Astronaut Jan Davis eats a cookie while in orbit.

Astronaut Ellen Ochoa looks at part of the Space Shuttle *Atlantis* from the window of the ISS.

60

---

# Before Reading

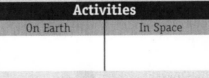 Use one or more activities.

## Make an Earth/Space Activity Chart ▶

Ask students: *What activities could you do both on Earth and in space?* Make a chart on the board or on chart paper and record students' answers. You will revisit the chart after students read the selections.

| Activities | |
|---|---|
| On Earth | In Space |
| | |

## Vocabulary Preview

Remind students that they can often figure out what a word means by using context clues, or "reading around" the word. Model the process for students. Have students use context to define other words of their choosing on *Student Journal* page 76. Students can choose a word from any selection in the magazine. (See Differentiated Instruction.)

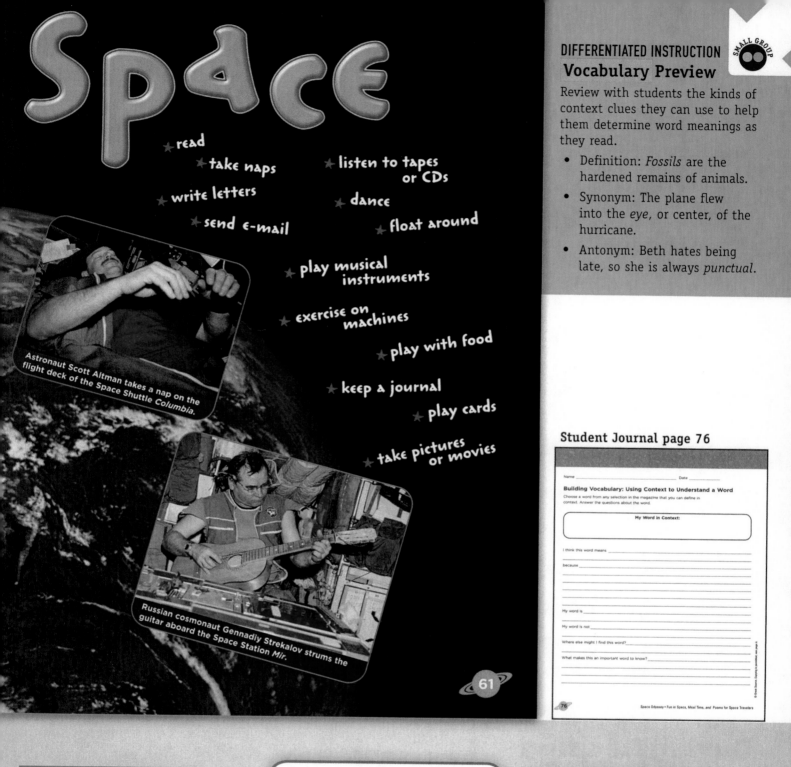

# Space

* read
* take naps
* write letters
* send e-mail
* listen to tapes or CDs
* dance
* float around
* play musical instruments
* exercise on machines
* play with food
* keep a journal
* play cards
* take pictures or movies

Astronaut Scott Altman takes a nap on the flight deck of the Space Shuttle Columbia.

Russian cosmonaut Gennadiy Strekalov strums the guitar aboard the Space Station Mir.

61

**DIFFERENTIATED INSTRUCTION**
## Vocabulary Preview

Review with students the kinds of context clues they can use to help them determine word meanings as they read.

- Definition: *Fossils* are the hardened remains of animals.
- Synonym: The plane flew into the *eye*, or center, of the hurricane.
- Antonym: Beth hates being late, so she is always *punctual*.

### Student Journal page 76

**Building Vocabulary: Using Context to Understand a Word**
Choose a word from any selection in the magazine that you can define in context. Answer the questions about the word.

**My Word in Context:**

I think this word means _____

because _____

My word is _____

My word is not _____

Where else might I find this word? _____

What makes this an important word to know? _____

76

Space Odyssey • Fun in Space, Meal Time, and Poems for Space Travelers

## Preview the Selection

Have students look through the selections. Use these or similar prompts to help students preview the short articles and poems.

- Based on the titles and illustrations, what do you think the articles will be about?
- What do you think the poems will be about? What makes you think that?

## Teacher Think Aloud

*As I look over this selection, I see right away that it's three selections in one—an article called "Fun in Space," another about mealtime in space, and finally some short poems. This, by the way, is the last selection in the Space Odyssey magazine. We've all worked hard reading about space, and we've learned a lot. Now I think it's time for us all to have a little space fun!*

## Make Predictions/ Set Purpose

Students should use the information they gathered in previewing the selection to make predictions about what they will learn. If students have trouble generating a purpose for reading, suggest that they read to check the information in the activities chart against what they read in "Fun in Space."

Help students make connections by asking:

- Now that I have read this text, what do I understand now that I didn't understand before?
- What movies or TV shows does this section make me think about?

# Meal

**Can you imagine eating upside down? Do you toss your food in the air and then float to it? Astronauts can eat like this. There is no gravity to keep them or the food on the ground.**

Astronauts eat three meals each day. They have snacks, too. All of the food is prepared on Earth. It is put into sealed packets. Then it is stored on the Space Shuttle or ISS. There is no refrigerator.

Some of the food is dried. You can put a straw in the packet and then add water. Other packages have fresh food that is sealed in. These are opened with scissors.

Everything floats, so the food packets are attached to the tray. Then the tray has to be strapped to the astronaut's leg. This is done with Velcro® straps.

Cleanup is easy. The trays are put in the trash. Knives, forks, and spoons are wiped off.

Would you like to eat this ISS meal?

62

# During Reading

Use these questions to model making connections. Then have students make their own connections.

- Do I like to do any of the same things as the astronauts?
- Would I like any of the space foods?
- What foods would I miss if I flew on a mission to space?

(See Differentiated Instruction.)

## Teacher Think Aloud
*When I saw the menu of what the astronauts eat in a typical day, I figured eating in space could be healthful—and fun! But then I looked at the food and read that the astronauts have to eat with their food trays strapped to their legs. The food didn't look very good, and eating it didn't sound like fun.*

Use these questions to model for students how to identify the classification text structure of the menu on page 63. Then have students tell about other texts that use a classification structure.

- How is the text on page 63 classified?
- How does understanding this text structure help me understand the text?

# Time

A day of meals on the Space Shuttle

## Menu

### Breakfast
Breakfast Roll
Oatmeal with Raisins
Banana
Orange Juice
Coffee

### Lunch
Macaroni and Cheese
Tuna Salad Spread
Carrot and Celery Sticks
Apple
Lemonade
Butter Cookies

### Dinner
Mushroom Soup
Sweet and Sour Chicken
Green Beans and Broccoli
Peaches
Grape Drink
Brownie

63

## Teacher Think Aloud

*I can see that the menu is classified into the foods available for breakfast, lunch, and dinner because those meals are the headings. This classification helps me understand what foods are available to astronauts at each meal of the day.*

## Fix-Up Strategies

Offer these strategies to help students read independently.

**If you don't understand what you're reading:**

- Reread the difficult section to look for clues to help you comprehend.

- Read ahead to find clues to help you comprehend.

- Retell, or say in your own words, what you've read.

- Visualize, or form mental pictures of, what you've read.

**If you don't understand a word:**

- Reread the sentence. Look for ideas and words that provide meaning clues.

- Find clues by reading a few sentences before and after the confusing word.

- Look for the base or root word and think about its meaning.

- Think about the topic or plot at this point to see if either offers meaning clues.

# DIFFERENTIATED INSTRUCTION
## Writing

### Opinion Paragraph

Help students organize their opinion paragraphs.

1. Have students cut pieces of paper into five or six strips.

2. Tell each student to write a main-idea sentence that states his or her position on space travel on one strip and to label it *1*.

3. Tell students to write, on separate strips, sentences that give their reasons for this position.

4. Students can then experiment with the order of their sentence strips to see which order is most effective. Suggest that they save their strongest reason for last.

### Student Journal page 77

Writing: Opinion Paragraph

Main Idea:

Details (reasons):

Conclusion (strongest reason):

Space Odyssey • Fun in Space, Meal Time,    Poems for Space Travelers

77

64

# After Reading
Use one or more activities.

### Check Purpose

Have students decide if their purpose was met. Ask: *What activities can astronauts do in space that we can do on Earth?* Encourage discussion of how the activities are alike and different.

### Discussion Questions

1. What do you think your favorite activity in space would be? Why? (Making Connections)

2. How do you think you would feel about space food? Why? (Details)

3. What is an example of one fact and one opinion about space food? (Fact-Opinion)

### Revisit: Chart

Review the activities chart with students. Have them add any new information they learned about activities in space.

Stars by the billions.
Universe so full we can't
visit all of them!

From the moon, they watched
the earth rise in the black sky.
A big blue marble!

Sip juice carefully!
If it spills, you must chase it
as it floats away.

## Answers to **Student Journal** page 78

**Reviewing Vocabulary: Word Search**

Find and circle 13 words you learned about space. Work with a partner to talk about what the words mean.

**Words:** artifact, commander, constellation, craters, deploy, engineering, gravity, habitat, nebula, orbit, satellite, simulator, sphere

---

## Writing **Opinion Paragraph**

Have each student write a paragraph explaining why he or she would or would not like to visit space. Students can organize their ideas on *Student Journal* page 77. Encourage students to include both facts and opinions. Review with students that a fact can be proven and an opinion is a statement of how someone thinks or feels. (See Differentiated Instruction.)

## Vocabulary

### Review Space Terms

Have students flip through the pages of *Space Odyssey*, noting all the different things they have learned about space. Ask volunteers to identify words they have learned and want to use again. Then have students find additional space terms in the word-search puzzle on *Student Journal* page 78. After students have found all the words, have them work with partners and quiz each other on the meanings of the words.

## Phonics/Word Study

### Long and Short *i* Homophones

Read the following sentences aloud and ask students to identify the homophone pairs in each and whether the *i* sound in each pair is long or short. *Which witch frightened you more? Did you get a sight of the building site? We mined her mind for information. Did you see these prints of the prince?* Now, work with students to complete the in-depth long and short *i* homophones activity on TE page 184.

## Phonics/Word Study

### Long and Short *i* Homophones

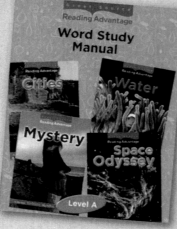

▶ Write the following words on the board: *die, dye; tied, tide;* and *wine, whine.*

▶ Ask students if they can figure out what each pair of words have in common. Students should be able to notice that the words in each pair sound the same but are spelled differently. This is the definition of a *homophone.*

▶ Using the list of long and short *i* homophones, play a game in which students turn over a homophone card worth a certain number of points. To earn the points, the student has to provide the homophone, spell it, and define it.

▶ Have each student create a section of his or her Word Study notebook and add any homophones that are generated. This will become a good resource for students to use when they write.

▶ For a more extensive list see Long and Short *i*: Homophones on *Word Study Manual* page 57.

| Long and Short *i* Homophones | | | |
|---|---|---|---|
| climb clime | bin been | knit nit | incite insight |
| liken lichen | vile vial | might mite | tick tic |
| time thyme | tied tide | die dye | vice vise |
| which witch | while wile | whine wine | knight night |
| buy by | rye wry | rite write | side sighed |

For more information on word sorts and spelling stages, see pages 5–31 in the *Word Study Manual.*

# Focus on . . .

Use one or more activities in this section to focus on a particular area of need in your students.

## Comprehension  STRATEGY SUPPORT  INDEPENDENT

To help those students who need more practice using the strategies covered in this lesson, work one-on-one or in small groups to apply the strategy prompts below. Apply the prompts to a *Reading Advantage* paperback, a classroom library book, or a new or familiar selection in the magazine. Always model your own thinking first.

### Making Connections

• What does this story (article, passage) remind me of?

• What do I already know about this topic?

• Where have I heard about this topic before?

• What do I have in common with the characters, people, or situations in the text?

• What other books, stories, articles, movies, or TV shows does this make me think about?

### Understanding Text Structure

• What kind of text is this? (book, story, article, guidebook, play, manual)

• How does the author organize the text? (cause-effect, problem-solution, chronological order, description, question-answer, comparison-contrast)

• What details support my thoughts about the text structure?

• What is the cause (effect, problem, solution, order, question, answer)?

• If fiction, who are the characters? What is the setting, plot, conflict, and resolution?

## Writing Haiku  INDEPENDENT

Have students read the haikus on page 65. Then have them write a haiku describing something they like. The pattern for a haiku is five syllables in the first line, seven syllables in the second line, and five syllables in the third line. Display a pattern such as the following.

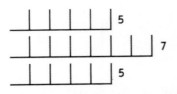

To give students more practice writing about sensory details, see lessons in *Writing Advantage,* pages 30–55.

## Fluency: Phrasing

SMALL GROUP

After students have read the three poems silently at least once, have them work in pairs to read their favorite haiku. Students should practice reading aloud to their partner, who will give feedback to encourage reading with appropriate phrasing. Tell students that there is a tendency to read poetry in a sing-song manner, stopping at the end of each line. Point out that students should stop at the end of a line only if the punctuation indicates a pause or a stop.

Monitor students as they read aloud, and prompt for correct phrasing as needed.

▶ Don't stop after *can't* in the first haiku. The phrase *can't visit* should be read together to keep the meaning clear.

▶ Listen as I read these phrases together. Then read as I did.

When students read aloud, do they—

✓ demonstrate quick recognition of words and phrases?

✓ exhibit an understanding of phrasal construction?

✓ incorporate appropriate timing, stress, and intonation?

## English Language Learners

To support students as they learn about text structure, use the following prompts to extend the lesson on TE page 180.

1. Find and read the title. What information does the title give about the selection?

2. Read the menu on page 63 and tell how it helps you understand what the astronauts eat.

3. Examine the pictures throughout the text. How do the pictures help you understand the selection?

## Independent Activity Options

While you work with individuals or small groups, others can work independently on one or more of the following options.

▶ Level A paperback books, see TE pages 371–376

▶ Level A *eZines*

▶ Repeat word sorts from this lesson

▶ *Student Journal* pages for this lesson

▶ *Writing Advantage* independent lessons

# Assessment

## Strategy Assessment

To help you and your students assess their use of comprehension strategies, ask the following questions. Students can complete a written response or provide verbal answers in a one-on-one reading conference.

1. **Making Connections** As you read the selection, what connections did you make? (Answers will vary. Students may say that the pages about fun in space and meal time remind them of information they had read in earlier *Space Odyssey* articles.)

2. **Understanding Text Structure** What details support your thoughts about the text structure of a certain section? (Answers will vary. Students may note that the stars act as bullet points separating each item in the list on page 61.)

See *Level A Assessment* page 26 for formal assessment to go with *Space Odysssey*.

## Word Study Assessment

Use these steps to help you and your students assess their understanding of long and short *i* homophones.

1. Write the following words on the board: *ring, titan, rite, whit, sink, right, tighten, sighs, wry, wring, rye, size, wit, synch*.

2. Have students identify each pair of homophones.

3. Place a two-column chart on the board with the headers Long *i* Homophones and Short *i* Homophones. Ask students to write the homophone pairs in the appropriate columns. The answers are shown.

| Long *i* Homophones | Short *i* Homophones |
|---|---|
| titan, tighten | ring, wring |
| rite, right | whit, wit |
| sighs, size | sink, synch |
| wry, rye | |

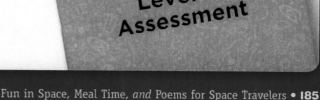

# Level A, Magazine 3

# Water

## Magazine Summary

*Water* magazine is a collection of nonfiction, fiction, drama, and poetry about different forms of water. Students will read about icebergs, life under water, and reflections about water.

*Content-Area Connection:* history, science
Lexile measure 600L

# *Water* Planner

| LESSON | BEFORE READING | DURING READING | AFTER READING |
|---|---|---|---|
| **LESSON 25**<br>**Iceberg!**<br>(informational article)<br>page 190 | K-W-L Chart<br>Vocabulary Preview<br>Preview the Selection<br>Make Predictions/Set Purpose | Making Connections<br>Monitor Understanding | Check Purpose<br>Discussion Questions<br>Writing: summary<br>Vocabulary: multiple meanings<br>Phonics/Word Study: long and short *i* compound words |
| **LESSON 26**<br>**Cool Art** *and* **Experiment with Water and Ice**<br>(informational article and experiment)<br>page 198 | Concept Web<br>Vocabulary Preview<br>Preview the Selection<br>Make Predictions/Set Purpose | Making Connections<br>Monitor Understanding | Check Purpose<br>Discussion Questions<br>Writing: feature news article<br>Vocabulary: concept ladder<br>Phonics/Word Study: sorting across vowels |
| **LESSON 27**<br>**Water Plant/Desert Plant** *and* **Seagulls and Whales**<br>(article and poem)<br>page 206 | Category Chart<br>Vocabulary Preview<br>Preview the Selection<br>Make Predictions/Set Purpose | Inferential Thinking<br>Understanding Text Structure | Check Purpose<br>Discussion Questions<br>Writing: main idea organizer<br>Vocabulary: word relationships<br>Phonics/Word Study: short and long *o* patterns |
| **LESSON 28**<br>**Yakking with a Kayaker**<br>(interview)<br>page 214 | Concept Web<br>Vocabulary Preview<br>Preview the Selection<br>Make Predictions/Set Purpose | Understanding Text Structure | Check Purpose<br>Discussion Questions<br>Writing: friendly letter<br>Vocabulary: synonyms<br>Phonics/Word Study: long *o* patterns |

# Overview

## Preview the Magazine

Give students time to thumb through the magazine to look at the selection titles, photographs, and illustrations. They should also look at the front and back covers for images of water in our world. Explain that the magazine discusses water in its liquid form, as well as in its solid form—ice. Ask students to contribute to the Venn diagram below to compare and contrast the properties of ice and water.

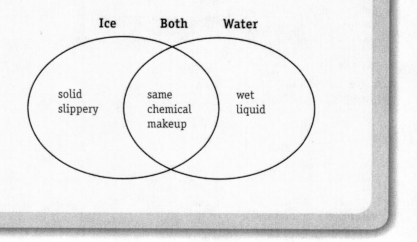

Ice · Both · Water

solid
slippery

same
chemical
makeup

wet
liquid

| PHONICS/ WORD STUDY | FOCUS ON | ASSESSMENT | HIGHER-ORDER THINKING QUESTIONS |
|---|---|---|---|
| Long and Short *i* Compound Words | Writing: poem<br>Fluency: pacing<br>English Language Learners<br>Independent Activity Options | Making Connections<br>Monitor Understanding<br>Long and Short *i* Compound Words | Where do icebergs come from? Use details and information from the passage to support your answer. Why are icebergs dangerous to ships? Use details and information from the passage to support your answer. |
| Sorting Across Vowels | Writing: experiment write-up<br>Fluency: punctuation<br>English Language Learners<br>Independent Activity Options | Making Connections<br>Monitor Understanding<br>Sorting Across Vowels | What caused people to start contests for snow sculpting around the world? Use details and information from the passage to support your answer. How is snow sculpting different from ice carving? Use details and information from the passage to support your answer. |
| Short and Long *o* Patterns | Writing: comparative paragraph<br>Fluency: phrasing<br>English Language Learners<br>Independent Activity Options | Inferential Thinking<br>Understanding Text Structure<br>Short and Long *o* Patterns | Why do plants need to adapt to the place where they live? Use details and information from the passage to support your answer. How are water plants and land plants built differently? Use details and information from the passage to support your answer. How do desert plants conserve water? Use details and information from the passage to support your answer. |
| Long *o* Patterns | Writing: interview questions<br>Fluency: expression<br>English Language Learners<br>Independent Activity Options | Understanding Text Structure<br>Long *o* Patterns | How are Kayaks and Canoes different? How are they the same? Use details and information from the passage to support your answer. What evidence does the author present to support the idea that Irma truly loves the sport of Kayaking? Use details and information from the passage to support your answer. |

# Water Planner

| LESSON | BEFORE READING | DURING READING | AFTER READING |
|---|---|---|---|
| **LESSON 29**<br>**The Scariest Day of My Life**<br>(fictional memoir)<br>page 220 | K-W-L Chart<br>Vocabulary Preview<br>Preview the Selection<br>Make Predictions/Set Purpose | Monitor Understanding | Check Purpose<br>Discussion Questions<br>Writing: notes for visualizing<br>Vocabulary: homophones<br>Phonics/Word Study: short and long *o* patterns |
| **LESSON 30**<br>**A Man for All Seas**<br>(biographical sketch)<br>page 226 | Anticipation Guide<br>Vocabulary Preview<br>Preview the Selection<br>Make Predictions/Set Purpose | Determining Importance | Check Purpose<br>Discussion Questions<br>Writing: journal entry<br>Vocabulary: multiple meanings<br>Phonics/Word Study: long and short *o* patterns (*r*-controlled) |
| **LESSON 31**<br>**Home Sweet Home, The Water Cycle,** *and* **Life of a Coral Reef**<br>(photo-essay, poem and article)<br>page 233 | T-Chart<br>Vocabulary Preview<br>Preview the Selection<br>Make Predictions/Set Purpose | Making Connections<br>Inferential Thinking | Check Purpose<br>Discussion Questions<br>Writing: notes for visualizing<br>Vocabulary: word root *auto-*<br>Phonics/Word Study: long *o* review |
| **LESSON 32**<br>**Underwater Hotel**<br>(science-fiction story)<br>page 242 | List<br>Vocabulary Preview<br>Preview the Selection<br>Make Predictions/Set Purpose | Monitor Understanding<br>Understanding Text Structure | Check Purpose<br>Discussion Questions<br>Writing: book jacket<br>Vocabulary: context<br>Phonics/Word Study: long and short *o* homophones |
| **LESSON 33**<br>**The Great Underwater Escape**<br>(radio play)<br>page 251 | Association Web<br>Vocabulary Preview<br>Preview the Selection<br>Make Predictions/Set Purpose | Making Connections<br>Monitor Understanding | Check Purpose<br>Discussion Questions<br>Writing: notes for visualizing<br>Vocabulary: multiple meanings<br>Phonics/Word Study: long and short *o* compound words |
| **LESSON 34**<br>**Oil and Water**<br>(essays)<br>page 259 | List<br>Vocabulary Preview<br>Preview the Selection<br>Make Predictions/Set Purpose | Determining Importance | Check Purpose<br>Discussion Questions<br>Writing: points of view<br>Vocabulary: multiple meanings<br>Phonics/Word Study: sorting across vowels |
| **LESSON 35**<br>**Uncle Toad Saves the World** *and* **Water, Water, Everywhere**<br>(folktale and short feature)<br>page 264 | Tally List<br>Vocabulary Preview<br>Preview the Selection<br>Make Predictions/Set Purpose | Understanding Text Structure<br>Making Connections | Check Purpose<br>Discussion Questions<br>Writing: summary<br>Vocabulary: prefixes<br>Phonics/Word Study: short and long *u* patterns |
| **LESSON 36**<br>**Like a Fish Out of Water** *and* **The Mighty Mississippi**<br>(idioms, riddles, and poems)<br>page 269 | Idiom Chart<br>Vocabulary Preview<br>Preview the Selection<br>Make Predictions/Set Purpose | Monitor Understanding | Check Purpose<br>Discussion Questions<br>Writing: notes for visualizing<br>Vocabulary: synonyms and antonyms<br>Phonics/Word Study: long *u* patterns |

| PHONICS/ WORD STUDY | FOCUS ON | ASSESSMENT | HIGHER-ORDER THINKING QUESTIONS |
|---|---|---|---|
| Short and Long *o* Patterns | Writing: short account<br>Fluency: expression<br>English Language Learners<br>Independent Activity Options | Monitor Understanding<br>Short and Long *o* Patterns | What evidence does the author give to show the power and force of a tsunami? Use details and information from the passage to support your answer. What caused the main character to suspect that something was wrong? Use details and information from the passage to support your answer. |
| Long and Short *o* Patterns (*r*-controlled) | Writing: illustrated time line<br>Fluency: pacing<br>English Language Learners<br>Independent Activity Options | Determining Importance<br>Long and Short *o* Patterns (*r*-controlled) | In what ways has Robert Ballard shared his love of the ocean with the world? Use details and information from the passage to support your answer. How did Robert Ballard become like his hero, Captain Nemo? How was he different? Use details and information from the passage to support your answer. |
| Long *o* Review | Writing: home chart<br>Fluency: phrasing<br>English Language Learners<br>Independent Activity Options | Making Connections<br>Inferential Thinking<br>Long *o* Review | What traits do all the houses in "Home Sweet Home" share? Use details and information from the passage to support your answer. Why do many of the animals in "The Water Cycle" and "Life of a Coral Reef" that make their home in the coral reef have such colorful markings? Use details and information from the passage to support your answer. |
| Long and Short *o* Homophones | Writing: story sequel<br>Fluency: expression<br>English Language Learners<br>Independent Activity Options | Monitor Understanding<br>Understanding Text Structure<br>Long and Short *o* Homophones | Which of Duane's actions let you know that he likes adventure and excitement? Use details and information from the passage to support your answer. How is the underwater hotel of the future different from a regular hotel of today? Use details and information from the passage to support your answer. |
| Long and Short *o* Compound Words | Writing: diary entry<br>Fluency: punctuation<br>English Language Learners<br>Independent Activity Options | Making Connections<br>Monitor Understanding<br>Long and Short *o* Compound Words | What can you infer about Houdini's popularity from the comments of the people in the audience? Use details and information from the passage to support your answer. What are some things Houdini did to build suspense in his water torture trick? Use details and information from the passage to support your answer. |
| Sorting Across Vowels | Writing: letter to the editor<br>Fluency: pacing<br>English Language Learners<br>Independent Activity Options | Determining Importance<br>Sorting Across Vowels | What are some of the advantages and disadvantages of drilling in the ocean for oil? Use details and information from the passage to support your answer. What was the author's purpose in writing "Oil"? What was the author's purpose in writing "Water"? Use details and information from the passage to support your answer. |
| Introducing Short and Long *u* Patterns | Writing: porquoi tale<br>Fluency: expression<br>English Language Learners<br>Independent Activity Options | Understanding Text Structure<br>Making Connections<br>Introducing Short and Long *u* Patterns | What can you infer about the Sky King's character from his actions? Use details and information from the passage to support your answer. What are the effects of having salt in most of the water on Earth? Use details and information from the passage to support your answer. |
| Long *u* Patterns | Writing: poem<br>Fluency: phrasing<br>English Language Learners<br>Independent Activity Options | Monitor Understanding<br>Long *u* Patterns | Which idioms are the closest in meaning? How are they similar? Use details and information from the passage to support your answer. What is the organizational pattern the author uses in the poem, "The Mighty Mississippi"? Use details and information from the passage to support your answer. |

## LESSON 25
# Iceberg!
*Water*, pages 2–7

### SUMMARY
This **article** describes what an iceberg is, how it is formed, and why it is beautiful *and* dangerous.

### COMPREHENSION STRATEGIES
Making Connections
Monitor Understanding

### WRITING
Summary

### VOCABULARY
Multiple Meanings

### PHONICS/WORD STUDY
Long and Short *i* Compound Words

### Lesson Vocabulary
calving
currents

### MATERIALS
*Water*, pp. 2–7
*Student Journal*, pp. 79–82
*Word Study Manual*, p. 58
*Writing Advantage*, pp. 113–151

**2**

# Before Reading  WHOLE CLASS  Use one or more activities.

### Make a K-W-L Chart ▶
Create a K-W-L chart to help students share their prior knowledge of icebergs. Then help students formulate questions about what they would like to learn about icebergs. Your chart may resemble the following example. Suggest to students that as they read the article, they try to learn the answers to their questions. They will return to the chart after reading the article, to record what they have learned.

| What We **Know** | What We **Want** to Know | What We **Learned** |
|---|---|---|
| Icebergs are floating mountains of ice. | How are icebergs formed? | |
| Icebergs are in the ocean. | Where do you find icebergs? | |
| An iceberg sank the *Titanic*. | Are all icebergs dangerous? | |

### Vocabulary Preview
Display the vocabulary. Read the words aloud or ask for volunteer readers. Help students make associations with the words. Ask students what the words remind them of. Then have students complete *Student Journal* page 79. Discuss student responses. Encourage students as they read, to use the context to help them find the meanings of the words. Students can revisit their associations later. Model the process for students.

Water in a frozen state (ice)

can cool us, but huge chunks

of ice floating freely in the

ocean are something else.

They are awesome to view.

Yet, they are also dangerous

and can be deadly.

③

DIFFERENTIATED INSTRUCTION **SMALL GROUP**

## Preview the Selection

To provide guidance for how students should preview an article, follow these steps:

1. Have students read the title and any headings or callouts.

2. Ask students to examine the photographs or graphics and to read the captions.

3. Suggest to students that they read the lead sentences of the paragraphs for a sense of what the selection is about.

### Student Journal page 79

Name _____ Date _____

**Building Vocabulary: Word Associations**
Think about what you already know about each word. Then answer the questions for each word.

**Word** _____ calving _____

What do you think about when you read this word? _____

Who might use this word? _____

What do you already know about this word? _____

**Word** _____ currents _____

What do you think about when you read this word? _____

Who might use this word? _____

What do you already know about this word? _____

Now watch for these words in the magazine selection. Were you on the right track?

Water • Iceberg! 79

## Preview the Selection

Have students look through the six pages of the article. Discuss students' observations. Have each student write on a self-stick note one or two questions that they think will be answered in the article. Students might choose from the questions on the K-W-L chart or from questions that arose during the preview of the article. (See Differentiated Instruction.)

## Teacher Think Aloud

*By reading the title and looking at the pictures, I know that this article is about icebergs. I can tell it's nonfiction because the first few paragraphs contain facts. I think the photographs are amazing, especially the one at the beginning. It shows that a lot of an iceberg is underwater. I thought they just floated on top.*

## Make Predictions/ Set Purpose

Students should use the information they gathered in previewing the selection to make predictions about what they will learn. If students have trouble generating a purpose for reading, suggest that they read to learn about the power of icebergs and to answer questions from the K-W-L chart.

## Comprehension

MAKING CONNECTIONS

To help students make connections with the text, follow these steps:

1. Ask students what they thought about in their own lives as they read the article.

2. Have students share the connections they made. Discuss how people usually make different connections with what they read, depending on their own experiences.

You've probably heard about the *Titanic*. In 1912, this great ship started to cross the Atlantic Ocean. The ship sank after it hit an iceberg. More than 1,500 people lost their lives.

Where did that iceberg come from? Why was it floating there in the water? The answer is simple: Mother Nature put it there.

An iceberg is a piece of a great sheet of ice called a *glacier*. A glacier forms on land over thousands of years. Ice forms from layers and layers of snow pressing together. A glacier "flows" or "creeps" outward because of its own weight. Finally, the glacier edges into the ocean. That is when pieces break off. Those pieces are what we call *icebergs*.

When a piece of the glacier breaks off, the process is known as <u>calving</u>. It is as if the mother glacier (cow) were giving birth to babies (calves). Calving usually happens when the motion of the water over time causes the ice to weaken and break apart. Scientists don't think that global warming causes icebergs to melt or break off.

You can find some glaciers at the tops of tall mountains. The largest glaciers cover most of the huge island of Greenland and the continent of Antarctica. There are also glaciers in Alaska.

**4**

# During Reading

## Comprehension

MAKING CONNECTIONS

Use these questions to model making connections with the topic. Then have students share their connections.

- What do I already know about icebergs?

- Where have I heard about them before?

- What books, movies, or TV shows does this make me think about?

(See Differentiated Instruction.)

## Teacher Think Aloud

*I remember seeing a movie about the Titanic. It was a huge ship that sank when it struck an iceberg, and many people lost their lives. The movie made a big impression on me. I never knew that an iceberg could be that dangerous.*

## Comprehension

MONITOR UNDERSTANDING

Use these questions to model how to monitor understanding by asking questions. Then have students ask their own questions and try to resolve any confusion.

- What is going on here?

- Why is the author being vague?

- What fix-up strategy can I use to clear up my confusion?

# Is it ever safe to see one of these amazing "ice mountains" up close?

The glacier is so heavy that it creeps downhill, toward the sea. The ice moves very slowly.

### Iceberg

The word *iceberg* was first used in the late eighteenth century. It comes from the Dutch word *ijsberg*, which is a compound word made up of *ijs*, which means "ice," and *berg*, which means "hill." An iceberg is a hill of ice.

**5**

## Teacher Think Aloud

*In the second paragraph of the article, the author says: "Where did that iceberg come from? Why was it floating there in the water? The answer is simple: Mother Nature put it there." That doesn't really answer the question. But I read on and found a more complete answer. I think the statement about Mother Nature just means that it is a natural occurrence.*

## Fix-Up Strategies

Offer these strategies to help students read independently.

**If you don't understand what you're reading:**

- Reread the difficult section to look for clues to help you comprehend.

- Read ahead to find clues to help you comprehend.

- Retell, or say in your own words, what you've read.

- Visualize, or form mental pictures of, what you've read.

**If you don't understand a word:**

- Reread the sentence. Look for ideas and words that provide meaning clues.

- Find clues by reading a few sentences before and after the confusing word.

- Look for the base or root word and think about its meaning.

- Think about the topic or plot at this point to see if either offers meaning clues.

Ice is lighter than water, so it floats. It drifts on ocean currents that are strong enough to move the ice. Only about one-eighth of an iceberg floats above the water. The rest of it, the larger part, stays hidden below. A ship's captain can be fooled into thinking that he or she can steer the ship around the iceberg. That is the reason icebergs are so dangerous to ships.

In March 2000, a huge iceberg broke away, or calved, from the Ross Ice Shelf in Antarctica. The iceberg was about 170 miles long and 25 miles wide.

It was about as long as the distance from New York City all the way to Martha's Vineyard (an island off Massachusetts). It was about as wide as Long Island, New York. Because the iceberg was so big, ships' crews could easily spot it. Therefore, it did not pose a big danger.

Is it ever safe to see one of these amazing "ice mountains" up close? In Antarctica, you can take tours to see many icebergs. Some people are trained to climb them! If you ever take a tour, you will see that icebergs are both beautiful *and* dangerous. ◆

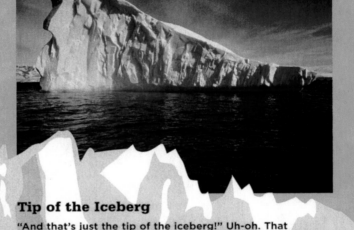

## Tip of the Iceberg

"And that's just the tip of the iceberg!" Uh-oh. That means there is trouble! When someone refers to the tip of the iceberg, they mean that the problem you see before you is quite small compared to the problem you don't know about yet. Let's say your computer screen keeps freezing. You might think that there is just a small problem that causes the frozen screen. When you call for help, though, you are told that there is a serious problem with your hard drive. The frozen screen is just the tip of the iceberg.

**6**

---

### Student Journal pages 80–81

Name _____ Date _____

**Writing: 5Ws**

Use the 5Ws chart to help you organize keys ideas for a summary of a section of "Iceberg!" Your summary might tell how icebergs are formed or might tell about the Ross Ice Shelf iceberg. You can write your summary on page 81.

| 5Ws | Details from "Iceberg!" |
|---|---|
| **Who** studies the topic? | |
| **What** happens or happened? | |
| **Where** does or did it happen? | |
| **When** does or did it happen? | |
| **Why** does or did it happen? | |

80                                      Water • Iceberg!

---

# After Reading  *Use one or more activities.*

## Check Purpose

Have students decide if their purpose was met. Were students able to answer their questions about icebergs? What did they learn about the power in icebergs?

## Discussion Questions

Continue the group discussion with the following questions.

1. Do you think icebergs are both beautiful *and* dangerous? Why or why not? (Making Connections)

2. How would you retell to a friend how icebergs are formed? (Sequence)

3. What was the most interesting thing you learned about icebergs? (Details)

## Revisit: K-W-L Chart

Revisit the K-W-L chart that students began in Before Reading. Were all students' questions about icebergs answered? What new information can they add to the chart?

## Revisit: Word Associations

Ask students to share what they wrote for the word association activity on *Student Journal* page 79. Do students need to change or adapt any word meanings?

- Icebergs are mostly white because the ice is full of tiny air bubbles. The surfaces of the air bubbles reflect white light, so the icebergs look white.
- Icebergs that do not have air bubbles look blue. The ice is blue because of the way light is scattered in the ice. The blue tint is due to the same light condition that gives the sky a blue color.
- The ice that covers Antarctica is two miles thick in places.

**Icebergs appear in many shapes and sizes.**

7

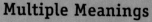

## DIFFERENTIATED INSTRUCTION
**SMALL GROUP**

## Vocabulary
### Multiple Meanings

If students need additional support, model multiple meanings with the word *current*. Write the word *current* on the board or on chart paper. Then ask these questions.

1. How is the word *current* used when talking about the way icebergs move? (An iceberg moves by floating along in an ocean *current*—a mass of liquid that is in motion.)

2. How else can the word *current* be used? (to describe a present-day event—the calving of the Ross Ice Shelf iceberg is more *current* than the sinking of the *Titanic*.)

### Student Journal page 82

Name _____ Date _____

**Building Vocabulary: Words with Multiple Meanings**
Write two definitions for each word below.

| Word | First Definition | Second Definition |
|------|-----------------|-------------------|
| calving | the process of a piece of glacier breaking off to form an iceberg | the process of a mother cow giving birth to a calf |
| view | | |
| ship | | |
| edges | | |

82                                          Water • Iceberg!

## Writing Summary

Ask students to complete the 5Ws chart on *Student Journal* page 80 to record key facts and ideas from the article. Encourage students to refer to the article and revisit the class K-W-L chart to help them complete the page. Then ask students to use the chart to write a summary of the article on *Student Journal* page 81. Remind students to include answers for the 5Ws when writing their summaries.

## Vocabulary Multiple Meanings

Display *calving*. Remind students that in the article, *calving* describes the process of a piece of glacier breaking off to form an iceberg. *Calving* is also the process of a mother cow giving birth to a calf. Ask students what other words they know that have multiple meanings. Brainstorm a list together. Other multiple-meaning words from the article include *view*, *can*, *ship*, *hit*, *sheet*, and *edges*. Have partners complete *Student Journal* page 82. (See Differentiated Instruction.)

## Phonics/Word Study

### Long and Short *i*
### Compound Words

Display the following words: *moonlight*, *bluebird*, and *timekeeper*. Ask students what the words have in common. (Each word is made up of two related words.) Ask what the relationship is between the two words that make up each compound. For example, *moonlight* refers to light that comes from the moon. Now, have students complete the in-depth word study activity on TE page 196.

## Long and Short *i* Compound Words

▶ Share the following words with students: *firehouse*, *bedtime*, and *nightlife*.

▶ Ask what the words have in common. Students should notice that each word is actually made up of two related words. A *firehouse* is a house where firefighters gather. *Bedtime* is a time for someone to go to bed. *Nightlife* refers to things people do at night. Compound words always have a meaning connection.

▶ Provide students with a list of compound words they can read and take apart (see below). (*Firehouse* becomes *fire + house*.) Have students work in pairs to decide whether each short or long *i* word within a compound falls into a typical *i* pattern. Do not hold students responsible for parts of words that are not in the short or long *i* family. For a more extensive list of long and short *i* compound words, see *Word Study Manual* page 58.

### Long and Short *i*: Compound Words

| | | |
|---|---|---|
| downsize | wildlife | lighthouse |
| housefly | highland | birthright |
| landslide | landfill | spotlight |
| footlights | headline | nighttime |
| shuteye | hairstyle | overnight |
| eyelid | footprint | hideout |

For more information on word sorts and spelling stages, see pages 5–31 in the *Word Study Manual*.

# Focus on . . .

Use one or more activities in this section to focus on a particular area of need in your students.

## Comprehension  STRATEGY SUPPORT  *INDEPENDENT*

To help those students who need more practice using the strategies covered in this lesson, work one-on-one or in small groups to apply the strategy prompts below. Apply the prompts to a *Reading Advantage* paperback, a classroom library book, or a new or familiar selection in the magazine. Always model your own thinking first.

### Making Connections

• What does this story (article, passage) remind me of?
• What do I already know about this topic?
• Where have I heard about this topic before?
• What do I have in common with the characters, people, or situations in the text?
• What other books, stories, articles, movies, or TV shows does this text make me think about?

### Monitor Understanding

• Do I understand what I'm reading? If not, what part is confusing to me?
• What fix-up strategies can I use to solve the problem? (See During Reading for fix-up strategies.)
• Why did a character say (do, think, ask) that?
• What images do I visualize from the text? What parts can't I visualize?
• Why did the author include (or not include) those details?

## Writing Poem  *INDEPENDENT*

Have students write a poem, or a paragraph, that describes icebergs. Encourage students to refer to the article and the photographs for ideas. Brainstorm with students a list of phrases related to icebergs. Write the list on the board. Students can refer to the list as they write their poems or paragraphs.

To provide additional instruction on writing a descriptive paragraph, see the lessons in *Writing Advantage*, pages 113–151.

## Fluency: Pacing

After students have read "Iceberg!" at least once, they can work with partners to take turns reading paragraphs to practice fluent reading. As needed, model the difference between evenly paced reading and unevenly paced reading. Then circulate among partners as they read.

Use these prompts to guide students to read expressively and at an even pace, and to help listeners offer positive and supportive feedback to the readers.

▶ Reread this sentence a little faster (or slower).

▶ Try reading in a louder voice so your listeners can hear you better.

▶ Let me see if I understood what you read. Listen as I retell what you read.

When students read aloud, do they—

✓ demonstrate a smooth pace, not too fast or too slow?

✓ incorporate well-timed pauses between words and phrases?

✓ reflect an awareness and understanding of punctuation?

## English Language Learners

To support students as they learn about multiple meaning words, extend the multiple meanings activity on TE page 194.

1. Remind students that many words have more than one meaning.

2. Review the meanings of the following multiple meaning words from the text: *state, tip, cross, frozen.*

3. Have students choose one word and illustrate two of its meanings. Have them share their work with a partner.

## Independent Activity Options

While you work with individuals or small groups, others can work independently on one or more of the following options.

▶ Level A paperback books, see TE pages 371–376

▶ Level A *eZines*

▶ Repeat word sorts from this lesson

▶ *Student Journal* pages for this lesson

▶ *Writing Advantage* independent lessons

# Assessment

## Strategy Assessment

To help you and your students assess their use of comprehension strategies, ask the following questions. Students can complete a written response or provide verbal answers in a one-on-one reading conference.

1. **Making Connections** Do you think you would like to go to Alaska, or even Antarctica, to see icebergs up close? Why or why not? (Answers will vary.)

2. **Monitor Understanding** What questions did you think of as you read? Were the questions answered? (Answers will vary. You might want to suggest that students do research to find answers to the questions they still have.)

For ongoing informal assessment, use the checklists on pages 61–64 of *Level A Assessment.*

## Word Study Assessment

Use these steps to help you and your students assess their understanding of long and short *i* compound words.

1. On the board or on paper to hand out, create a chart like the one shown below.

2. Ask students to match related words from both lists to create compound words. Then have them tell whether each *i* within a compound is a long or short *i*. (Answers: *spotlight*, long *i*; *babysitter*, short *i*; *lighthouse*, long *i*; *footprint*, short *i*; *landslide*, long *i*; *overnight*, long *i*.)

| List 1 | List 2 |
| --- | --- |
| spot | sitter |
| baby | night |
| light | slide |
| foot | light |
| land | print |
| over | house |

Great Source
Reading Advantage

Level A Assessment

## LESSON 26
# Cool Art *and* Experiment with Water and Ice
*Water,* pages 8–13

Genki

Yuki Matsuri Snow Festival Sculpture

8

### SUMMARY
The first **article** is about snow sculpting and ice sculpting. The **short feature** includes experiments with ice and water.

### COMPREHENSION STRATEGIES
Making Connections
Monitor Understanding

### WRITING
Feature News Article

### VOCABULARY
Concept Ladder

### PHONICS/WORD STUDY
Sorting across Vowels

### Lesson Vocabulary
| | |
|---|---|
| sculptors | chefs |
| entry | hypothesis |

### MATERIALS
*Water,* pp. 8–13
*Student Journal,* pp. 83–86
*Word Study Manual,* p. 59
*Writing Advantage,* pp. 30–55

# Before Reading
**WHOLE CLASS** Use one or more activities.

## Make a Concept Web ▶
Write *Uses for Ice* in the center oval of a concept web. Ask students to name ways in which they use ice, or ways in which they have seen ice used. Record their responses on the web. Prompt students with questions such as these:

- How does ice help us keep cool?
- How is ice used with foods?
- How is ice used for injuries?
- What sports or hobbies use ice?

to pack fish or meats

to cool beverages

to keep foods fresh

**Uses for Ice**

to reduce swelling

for ice skating

for playing ice hockey

## Vocabulary Preview
Display the vocabulary words. Ask for volunteers to read the words aloud and to briefly share what they know about the words. Have students predict how the first three words might be used in the article "Cool Art." Ask students to complete the second column of the predictions chart on *Student Journal* page 83. They will finish the chart later.

# You can use snow and ice to make totally cool art!

What can you do when your town has too much snow? That was the problem in Jackson, New Hampshire, in March 2001. Town officials had an idea, though. They invited teams of snow sculptors to come to Jackson. Instead of carving objects, animals, or people out of clay or stone, the teams would use snow.

Teams of sculptors came from all over the state. Others came from as far away as Russia and Japan. People watched in awe as blocks of snow became amazing art. The show was a big success. The town decided to hold a contest the following year. So Jackson held its first ever snow-sculpting contest in January 2002.

Each three-member team received a pillar of snow. It was eight feet high and four feet across. The teams used only hand tools to carve away at the snow. They worked all day Friday and Saturday. Some worked far into the night. Everything had to be ready for the judges on Sunday morning. The results were wonderful. The winner was Catherine Nash with her entry, "Snow Fairy."

Other places have snow-sculpting contests, too. Anchorage, Alaska, has this kind of contest. It is part of a festival called Fur Rondy. This name is short for "Fur Rendezvous" (RON day voo). It marks the time when trappers used to come to town to sell their furs. Now Fur Rondy celebrates the end of winter. The winners of the Fur Rondy contest of 2001 also won the United States Snow Sculpting Championships. This is a national contest.

## Fur Rondy

The Fur Rondy is quite a festival. It goes on for days, has several events, and raises money for community projects as well. There is a Polar Bear Party, a Grand Parade, a Fur Ball, a Dog Weight Pull, the Snow Sculpture Contest, World Championship Sled Dog Races, Snowshoe Softball, Family Nightskate, Snowboard Competition, and Junior Championship Sled Dog Races. After a cold, dark winter, people in Alaska are eager to celebrate spring!

## Rendezvous

Rendezvous is really two French words put together. Rendez-vous means "present yourselves" in French. In English, the word can be a noun or a verb. The noun means "a set time and place to meet." The verb means "to meet at a set time and place," as in, "Let's rendezvous at 4 P.M. at the food court." The word's French origins provide the reason for the way we pronounce **rendezvous**.

9

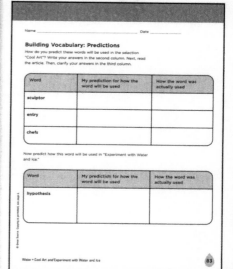
## DIFFERENTIATED INSTRUCTION
SMALL GROUP
### Preview the Selection

Offer additional support in previewing the selection by having students do these activities.

1. Examine the photographs and match up the letters on them to the legend that describes what the photographs show.

2. Read the lead sentences of paragraphs to get a sense of what the selections will be talking about.

3. Look at the structure of the experiments and relate them to other texts that use the same structure (recipes, directions, how-to instructions, science experiments).

## Preview the Selection

Have students look through pages 8–13. Use these prompts to preview the selections.

- What do you notice?
- What is different about the organization of each selection?
- What do you think each selection will be about?
- Which selection do you think will be more enjoyable to read? Why?

(See Differentiated Instruction.)

## Teacher Think Aloud

*When I looked at the photograph on the first page, I thought it was a picture of a sand sculpture. I was really surprised to discover that it was made out of snow. Now I understand that the title means both cool as in "very good" and cool as in "kind of cold."*

## Make Predictions/Set Purpose

Students should use the information they gathered in previewing the selection to make predictions about what they will learn. If students have trouble generating a purpose for reading, suggest that they read to find other ways in which ice is used.

## Comprehension
MONITOR UNDERSTANDING

Use this activity to help students understand how details help them visualize.

1. Have students give partners a detailed description of something from home. If partners need more details to help them picture the item, they should ask questions.

2. Discuss the pairs' experiences. Which details did students leave out that would have made it easier for partners to visualize the item? Which details were most helpful?

---

Sapporo, Japan, also has a snow-sculpting festival. The Sapporo Snow Festival is world-famous. It began almost by accident in the 1950s with six high school students who decided to build snow sculptures. The town loved the sculptures! The idea caught on. More and more people took part each year. A group of people from an airbase joined in, too. They built giant snow sculptures and made snow slides for children.

In 1972, Sapporo was the host for the Winter Olympics. The Snow Festival was held at the same time, and that is when it became world famous. Today it is one of the largest festivals in Japan.

Sapporo has ice carving as well as snow sculpture contests. Snow sculptors usually are allowed to use only hand tools, such as buckets or ice scrapers. Ice carvers can use power tools, like chain saws, to cut the ice. Many ice carvers are <u>chefs</u>. They learned the art of ice carving in cooking school. Chefs use ice carvings, often shaped like swans, at weddings and parties.

The top contest for ice carvers is the Olympics. Only the best in the world get to compete there. Ice carving is not a winter sports event, although ice carvers did compete for medals at the 2002 Winter Olympics in Provo, Utah. The Salt Lake Olympic Committee awarded gold, silver, and bronze medals.

Making art from ice and snow is a challenge. Although the contests are during the winter, the weather may not be cold enough. If the temperature rises too much, the snow becomes too soft to sculpt. When the temperature rises near freezing (32°F), both ice and snow melt quickly.

Carving ice or snow is hard work. Most contests have a time limit. The time limit in the Olympics is seventeen hours. Teams work straight through, with only short breaks for meals. They get cold, hungry, and tired.

The carvers have to keep the ice very cold, which keeps it clear. Carvers often use "dry ice" to help them.

(A) Ice sculptor at work    (D) Sapporo mushers

(B) Dragon    (E) Ice horse

(C) Sapporo Gothic sculpture

**10**

---

# During Reading

## Comprehension
MAKING CONNECTIONS

Use these questions to model for students how to make connections with the text. Then have students share a connection they have made.

- What does this remind me of?
- Have I experienced something similar?
- How does my experience help me understand the selection?

## Teacher Think Aloud

*In the town where I grew up, it gets very cold in the winter. On New Year's Eve, the town has a celebration called First Night. One of the events of First Night is an ice-sculpting competition. Artists use tools to carve big blocks of ice into incredible shapes, such as dragons, scenes from fairy tales, and famous buildings. Having seen these artists at work helped me understand this article.*

## Comprehension
MONITOR UNDERSTANDING

Use these questions to model visualizing the text. Then have students tell about a part they visualized.

- What do I picture in my mind as I read?
- Which details help me create this image?
- How does visualizing help me understand what I am reading?

(See Differentiated Instruction.)

The temperature of dry ice is −110°F (below zero). Carvers can't use it in the sculpture, but they can use it as a tool. They take blocks of dry ice and pack it around the sculpture. The dry ice keeps the sculpture super cold until judging time.

Then there is the question of the design: will it work? Blocks of ice weigh hundreds of pounds. The whole piece may come crashing down if the ice blocks are not put together just right.

You may think that artists feel bad when their hard work melts away. "Not at all," said one sculptor. "That's all part of the art. And you can always make another one!" ◆

| Snowy Places, USA | inches |
|---|---|
| 1. Climax, CO | 273.3 |
| 2. Mammoth Lakes, CA | 209.6 |
| 3. Truckee, CA | 207.0 |
| 4. Cooke City, MT | 204.1 |
| 5. Crested Butte, CO | 197.6 |
| 6. Tahoe City, CA | 188.5 |
| 7. Vail, CO | 187.5 |
| 8. Aspen, CO | 179.4 |
| 9. Telluride, CO | 172.5 |
| 10. Steamboat Springs, CO | 166.7 |

(average snowfall per year over a ten-year period)

## Dry Ice

Dry ice is the solid form of carbon dioxide. It is called dry ice because carbon dioxide can change from a solid to a gas without first becoming a liquid. Dry ice is used to cool food, medicine, and other materials that would be damaged by the melting of ordinary ice. Dry ice is also much colder than ordinary ice, which makes it useful in keeping ice itself cold. However, you must be careful to avoid frostbite when handling dry ice.

**(11)**

# Teacher Think Aloud

*I thought the explanation on page 13 about rising sea levels was very clear. The example of a glass of water with ice cubes in it was easy to picture. I know that I've left ice still in glasses until the ice cubes have melted. I pictured that in my mind and realized that it was true that the glass hadn't overflowed. Those details helped me understand about melting ice in the sea.*

## Fix-Up Strategies

Offer these strategies to help students read independently.

**If you don't understand what you're reading:**

- Reread the difficult section to look for clues to help you comprehend.
- Read ahead to find clues to help you comprehend.
- Retell, or say in your own words, what you've read.
- Visualize, or form mental pictures of, what you've read.

**If you don't understand a word:**

- Reread the sentence. Look for ideas and words that provide meaning clues.
- Find clues by reading a few sentences before and after the confusing word.
- Look for the base or root word and think about its meaning.
- Think about the topic or plot at this point to see if either offers meaning clues.

## Short Feature: Experiment with Water and Ice

Have students briefly look over the experiments on pages 12 and 13. Ask students to predict the meaning of the word *hypothesis* as it relates to scientific experiments. Then read aloud the introduction on page 12 and have students use the context to confirm or modify their predictions. After students read the selection, ask them to tell which experiments interest them most and why.

### Student Journal pages 84–85

# Experiment with Water and Ice

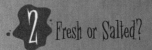

Here are some easy experiments for you to try. Each one explores water.

For each question, state your hypothesis. Then make a prediction.

Try the experiments to check on your predictions.

## 1 Melting Icebergs!

**Question:** If all the icebergs in the sea melted, would the sea level rise?

**What You Need:** glass, warm water, eight to ten ice cubes

**What You Do:**

1. Place as many ice cubes as you can fit into the glass.
2. Fill the glass to the top with warm water.
3. Watch to see what happens.

Step 1        Step 2

## 2 Fresh or Salted?

**Question:** Which is colder, iced fresh water or iced salted water?

**What You Need:** ten ice cubes, two paper cups, one tablespoon salt, two thermometers, pen

**What You Do:**

1. Label one cup "salted" and the other cup "fresh."
2. Place a thermometer in each cup.
3. Place five ice cubes around each thermometer.
4. Pour the salt in the cup you labeled "salted."
5. After 30 minutes, read the thermometers.

Fresh        Salted

The answers to the questions above are...

2. Iced salted water is colder than iced fresh water. Salted water freezes at a lower temperature. This makes the temperature colder. The thermometer in the iced fresh water will show a temperature above freezing. The thermometer in the iced salted water will show a temperature below freezing.

1. No, the sea level would not rise. The melted ice takes up the same amount of space as the part of the ice that's under the water. The main part of an iceberg is under water, just the way the ice cubes are in the glass of water.

12

---

# After Reading

**WHOLE CLASS** Use one or more activities.

## Check Purpose

Have students decide if their purpose was met. Were students able to answer their Before Reading questions? Did students find out any new uses for ice?

## Discussion Questions

Continue the group discussion with the following questions.

1. What did you learn about snow sculpting and ice sculpting? (Details)
2. Would you like to try snow sculpting or ice sculpting? Why? (Making Connections)
3. Think about the places that have snow-sculpting contests or festivals. What conclusions can you draw about winter in these places? (Draw Conclusions)

## Revisit: Concept Web

Revisit the concept web "Uses for Ice" that was started in Before Reading. What new information can students add?

## Revisit: Predictions Chart

Have students complete the predictions chart on *Student Journal* page 83. Allow students time to revisit their predictions and to then complete the page by confirming and/or correcting their definitions.

## 3 It's an Egg Trick!

**Question:** Which is denser (heavier), fresh water or salted water?

**What You Need:** two glasses, two hard-boiled eggs, ten teaspoons of salt, spoon

**What You Do:**

1. Fill each glass half-full with water.
2. Add all the salt to one glass. Stir.
3. Place a hard-boiled egg in each glass.
4. Watch what happens to the eggs.

## 4 Where's the Air?

**Question:** Can air stop water from entering a bottle?

**What You Need:** funnel; small, narrow-neck bottle; small piece of clay (molding material); small glass of water

**What You Do:**

1. Place the funnel in the bottle.
2. Roll a clay rope and press it snugly around the funnel at the bottleneck. Seal the bottleneck completely.
3. Slowly pour a small amount of water into the funnel, a little at a time. Do this until you have emptied the glass.
4. Watch what happens. ◆

### The answers to the questions above are...

3. Salted water is denser than fresh water. Salt makes the water heavier. The egg weighs less than the water it displaces (takes the place of). So the egg floats. We can float in the ocean for the same reason.

4. Yes, air can stop water from entering a bottle. Water will enter the bottle when you first begin to pour it into the funnel. But less and less water will enter the bottle as you continue to pour. Finally, no water will enter the bottle. This happens because the air in the closed bottle soon takes up all the space not taken up by water. So the air will stop any more water from entering the bottle.

### Rising Sea Levels

It seems to go against common sense that sea levels would not rise if the icebergs melted. But think of it this way. Picture a glass filled with water and ice cubes. Does the water overflow the glass when the ice cubes melt? No, it doesn't. This is because the water level already includes the mass of the frozen water. This is the same reason that scientists believe that melting icebergs will not cause worldwide ocean flooding.

However, when icebergs break apart (calve), they expose more of the ice sheet. The ice sheet is the ice that covers the polar caps, for example, Antarctica. The ice sheet is not in water, so its mass is not already included in the height of the ocean. Therefore, if the ice sheet were to melt, the ocean level would, indeed, rise.

13

## DIFFERENTIATED INSTRUCTION
### Writing Feature News Article

To provide extra support for students who might not be familiar with feature news articles, have examples ready. Choose articles that tell about upcoming events or report on events that have occurred. Use these steps to help students become familiar with this type of writing.

1. Notice with students that each article answers the questions *Who? What? Where? When? Why?*
2. Distribute the articles, one to a pair. Ask partners to read the articles and highlight or underline information that answers the 5Ws.

### Student Journal page 86

Name_____ Date_____

**Building Vocabulary: Concept Ladder**

Answer the questions to complete the concept ladder. Write words or phrases to record your responses.

- sculptor
- What other words name this person?
- What supplies might this person need?
- What tools does this person use?
- Where does this person work?
- What does this person do?

86

Water • Cool Art and Experiment with Water and Ice

## Writing Feature News Article

Invite students to write feature news articles about one of the snow-sculpting contests or festivals they read about. Preview with students *Student Journal* pages 84 and 85. Point out that a good news feature answers the 5Ws, just as a good summary does. Have partners complete *Student Journal* page 84. Students should then use their responses to write their feature news articles on *Student Journal* page 85. (See Differentiated Instruction.)

## Vocabulary Concept Ladder

Display *chef*. Ask the following questions to help students build a concept ladder for the word *chef*.

- What does this person do?
- Where does this person work?
- What tools does this person use?
- What supplies might this person need?
- What other words name this person?

Then have partners complete *Student Journal* page 86 for the word *sculptor*.

## Phonics/Word Study
### Sorting across Vowels

To remind students of the most common long *i* patterns, write these words and their vowel patterns on the board: *bike* (iCe), *fly* (y), *kind* (iCC), and *might* (igh). Point out the patterns and ask students if they can think of another word that fits each pattern, such as *like*, *by*, *mind*, and *right*. Now, work with students to complete the in-depth sorting activity on TE page 204.

## Sorting across Vowels

To review the most common long vowel patterns within the last two vowel families students have studied (*i* and *e*), set up a straightforward sort such as the one below. Note: the words *break* and *steak* are included as Oddballs.

▶ Using the Long *i* and Long *e*: Cumulative Sort sheet, have students try looking back at the vowel patterns they have studied for two vowel sounds. (See *Word Study Manual* page 59.)

▶ As always, speed and accuracy are the goals.

| Long *i* and Long *e*: Cumulative Sort | | | | | | |
|---|---|---|---|---|---|---|
| *iCe* | *y* | *iCC* | *igh* | *ee* | *ie* | *ea* |
| hike | try | mind | light | preen | shriek | creak |
| twine | cry | wild | night | screen | thief | beak |
| strike | | | fright | | | |

For more information on word sorts and spelling stages, see pages 5–31 in the *Word Study Manual*.

# Focus on . . .

Use one or more activities in this section to focus on a particular area of need in your students.

## Comprehension  STRATEGY SUPPORT  *INDEPENDENT*

To help those students who need more practice using the strategies covered in this lesson, work one-on-one or in small groups to apply the strategy prompts below. Apply the prompts to a *Reading Advantage* paperback, a classroom library book, or a new or familiar selection in the magazine. Always model your own thinking first.

### Making Connections

• What does this story (article, passage) remind me of?
• What do I already know about this topic?
• Where have I heard about this topic before?
• What do I have in common with the characters, people, or situations in the text?
• What other books, stories, articles, movies, or TV shows does this text make me think about?

### Monitor Understanding

• Do I understand what I'm reading? If not, what part is confusing to me?
• What fix-up strategies can I use to solve the problem? (See During Reading for fix-up strategies.)
• Why did a character say (do, think, ask) that?
• What images do I visualize from the text? What parts can't I visualize?
• Why did the author include (or not include) those details?

## Writing Experiment Write-Up  *INDEPENDENT*

Arrange for students to do the Melting Icebergs experiment. Have students use their knowledge about water and ice to formulate their hypotheses. Suggest that students use the Scientific Method to write up and present their findings. These are the basic steps of the Scientific Method:

**Question**—Ask a question based on observation.

**Hypothesis**—State what you think the answer will be.

**Method**—Propose an experiment to test the hypothesis.

**Result**—Conduct the experiment and record observations; repeat the experiment to confirm the results.

**Conclusion**—Write a conclusion that explains whether you proved your hypothesis.

To help students write clearly and succinctly, see the lessons on writing techniques in *Writing Advantage*, pages 30–55.

## Fluency: Punctuation

SMALL GROUP

Have each student choose one of the water and ice experiments to read aloud. Before students begin, have them discuss how they think the experiments should be read. Help students realize that experiments are similar to directions and instructions. They should be read clearly and distinctly, with slight pauses to separate the materials needed and the individual steps in the process.

Use these prompts to help students read at an even pace.

▶ Listen to me read. Then read it just as I did.

▶ Reread this sentence a little bit faster (or slower) so readers can make sense of the words.

▶ Remember to use the punctuation as clues to read evenly. Pause at the ends of sentences and between numbered items.

▶ Pay attention to the way words are grouped together (as in the list of materials) and read them as a single phrase.

When students read aloud, do they—

✓ demonstrate appropriate meaning and usage of punctuation marks?

✓ incorporate appropriate timing, stress, and intonation?

✓ exhibit well-timed pauses between words and phrases?

## English Language Learners

SMALL GROUP

To help students develop their vocabulary, extend the concept ladder activity on TE page 203.

1. Review the information on the concept ladders on page 86 of the *Student Journal*.

2. Have students draw and label a picture of a chef, including the information on the concept ladder.

3. Have students use their illustrations to explain to a partner what a chef is.

## Independent Activity Options

INDEPENDENT

While you work with individuals or small groups, others can work independently on one or more of the following options.

▶ Level A paperback books, see TE pages 371–376

▶ Level A *eZines*

▶ Repeat word sorts from this lesson

▶ *Student Journal* pages for this lesson

▶ *Writing Advantage* independent lessons

# Assessment

## Strategy Assessment

To help you and your students assess their use of comprehension strategies, ask the following questions. Students can complete a written response or provide verbal answers in a one-on-one reading conference.

1. **Making Connections** Which snow festival would you like to attend? Why? (Answers will vary. Students should use details from the article to explain why they would enjoy their chosen festival.)

2. **Monitor Understanding** Which parts of the article were the easiest to visualize? Which details helped you? (Answers will vary.)

For ongoing informal assessment, use the checklists on pages 61–64 of *Level A Assessment*.

## Word Study Assessment

Use these steps to help you and your students assess their understanding of sorting across vowels.

1. Write the following words on the board or on word cards: *sight, pry, dime, site, night, bind, sky, find*.

2. Ask students to identify the long *i* vowel pattern in each word.

| Word | Vowel Pattern |
| --- | --- |
| sight | *igh* |
| pry | *y* |
| dime | *iCe* |
| site | *iCe* |
| night | *igh* |
| bind | *iCC* |
| sky | *y* |
| find | *iCC* |

Reading Advantage

Level A Assessment

# Water Plant, Desert Plant; Seagulls and Whales

*Water,* pages 14–19

## SUMMARY

This **article** compares and contrasts water plants and desert plants. Two **poems** follow.

## COMPREHENSION STRATEGIES

Inferential Thinking
Understanding Text Structure

## WRITING

Main Idea Organizer

## VOCABULARY

Word Relationships

## PHONICS/WORD STUDY

Short and Long *o* Patterns

### Lesson Vocabulary

| | |
|---|---|
| soggy | marsh |
| adaptation | knees |
| carbon dioxide | moisture |
| limp | transpiration |

## MATERIALS

*Water,* pp. 14–19
*Student Journal,* pp. 87–89
*Word Study Manual,* p. 60
*Writing Advantage,* pp. 113–151

*You know that water is necessary for all living things. But why is it that some plants can get by with very little water, while other plants need a lot?*

Water Plant, Desert Plant

14

# Before Reading

**WHOLE CLASS** Use one or more activities.

## Make a Category Chart

Ask students the following question: *How do plants connect to your life?* Have students write their answers on self-stick notes, one thought per note. Work with students to organize the notes into possible categories. Label the categories. Have students explain their reasoning for why each note fits into a category. Possible categories for plant connections include food, shade and shelter, health, clothing. (See Differentiated Instruction.)

| Food | Shade and Shelter | Health |
|---|---|---|
| | | |

## Vocabulary Preview

Display the vocabulary. Help students share their knowledge of the words by asking: *Have you seen this word before? How was it used? Can you use it in a sentence?* Have students begin the knowledge rating chart on *Student Journal* page 87. Students will finish the chart later.

Perhaps you have taken care of a houseplant. You thought, no problem, right? You put it in good light. You watered it every day. But soon the soil in the pot was soaking wet. Then the leaves on the plant turned yellow. Finally, the plant died.

You thought the plant needed a lot of water. But could there be such a thing as too much water? The answer is *yes* for most houseplants.

Most plants that people keep in their homes like just "the right amount" of water. The "right amount" would be not too much and not too little. Most plants will die if they are watered too much and the soil in the pot becomes soggy.

But plants in nature live in all kinds of places. Plants live on land in sunny open spaces. Plants live in shady forest places with lots of rainfall. Plants live underwater. Plants live at the edges of ponds where the soil is damp most of the time. Plants live in the desert, where there is very little water. So what makes each kind of plant suited to the place in which it lives? The key word is adaptation. Plants adapt because they have special parts or special ways of growing that help them live in their environment.

The main focus here is on water plants and desert plants. First, you need to think of the basic parts of a plant. Then you can better understand how water plants and desert plants have adapted.

So how do green land plants get water, food, and other things they need? Green plants make their own food using water, oxygen, and a gas in the air called carbon dioxide. These land plants pull up water and oxygen from the soil through their **roots.** They have a system of tubes that bring the water to the **stems** and **leaves.** The leaves take in oxygen and carbon dioxide from the air. The plants use the oxygen they take in to "burn" the food for energy.

## Underwater Plants

Plants that live in water can take in water directly through all parts of the plant. They don't need tubes to carry water to the leaves. Some water plants don't even have roots.

Plants that live on land often have stiff stems or branches to hold them up. But water plants don't need stiff stems. The water holds them up. The plants would be limp, like cooked pasta, if they were removed from the water.

Some water plants may still have roots, but the roots are usually small. Others have "hold-fasts." Although these parts look like roots, they do not carry water. Their job is to hold the plant in place.

Maybe you have used water wings or an air-filled raft. Some water plants have parts that fill up with air. These parts are called "air bladders." They help the plant float on the water.

Many land plants have thick leaves with a hard, waxy coating. The coating helps keep the plant from drying out too quickly. Plants that live completely underwater don't dry out. They usually have soft, thin leaves. However, the leaves would dry out quickly if they were removed from the water.

leaves

stems

roots

15

## DIFFERENTIATED INSTRUCTION
### MAKE A CATEGORY CHART
If students have difficulty listing ways in which plants connect to their lives, prompt them with questions such as the following.

- Where do foods such as fruits and vegetables come from?
- Where does the wood used for building come from?
- What natural resources are used to make paper products?
- Wool comes from a sheep. Where does cotton come from?

### Student Journal page 87

Name _____ Date _____

**Building Vocabulary: Knowledge Rating Chart**
Show your knowledge of each word or phrase by adding information to the other boxes in the row.

| Word | Define or Use in a Sentence | Where Have I Seen or Heard It? | How Is It Used in the Selection? | Looks Like (Words or Sketch) |
|------|------|------|------|------|
| soggy | | | | |
| adaptation | | | | |
| carbon dioxide | | | | |
| limp | | | | |
| marsh | | | | |
| knees | | | | |
| moisture | | | | |
| transpiration | | | | |

Water • Water Plant, Desert Plant and Seagulls and Whales      87

## Preview the Selection
Have students look through the six pages of the article. Use these or similar prompts to orient students to the article.

- What does the title tell you about the article?
- Do you think the article is fiction or nonfiction? Why?
- What kinds of visual aids does the article provide?
- What do you think you will learn about as you read?

## Teacher Think Aloud
*The title tells me that this article is about water plants and desert plants. I predict that it will tell how these plants survive in their different environments. I'm sure the article is nonfiction. The photographs show real plants and have labels, like the ones in nonfiction books. There are also headings, diagrams, and lists of facts.*

## Make Predictions/ Set Purpose
Students should use the information they gathered in previewing the selection to make predictions about what they will learn. If students have trouble generating a purpose for reading, suggest that they read to discover why the amount of water each plant needs differs.

## Comprehension

UNDERSTANDING TEXT STRUCTURE

To help students understand text structure, follow these steps:

1. Have students study the photographs on pages 16 and 17. Ask: *What kinds of plants are in each group of pictures? Why do you think the pictures are organized in this way?*

2. Help students recognize that page 16 shows water plants, and page 17, desert plants. The pictures match what most of the text on each page is about.

Bladderwort

Mangrove

Lotus Root

Water Lilies

Reed Mace

Duckweed

*Some water plants have parts that fill up with air. These parts are called "air bladders." They help the plant float on the water.*

### Plants on the Edge

Several kinds of plants live in wetlands. These lands are on the edges of a pond or in a <u>marsh</u>. Some of the wetland plants may live with their roots in water or soggy soil, which has very little oxygen. So the plants often have hollow tubes in the stems. These tubes carry oxygen from the leaves down to the roots. The strong stems help hold the leaves in the air.

Other wetland plants, like water lilies, have large flat leaves that float on the surface of the water. The leaves often have a waxy coating on the top. This coating helps water run off the leaves.

- Plants that live in water are aquatic (uh KWAH tik) plants.
- Aquatic plants that are totally underwater have adapted to low light levels. These plants don't need direct sun.
- Aquatic plants that live totally underwater are called *hydrophytes.* (HI droh fites)

**16**

# During Reading

## Comprehension

INFERENTIAL THINKING

Use these questions with the third paragraph on page 15 to model making inferences. Then have students make inferences as they read another paragraph.

- What does the text in this paragraph tell me about plants?

- What do I already know about plants?

- What ideas can I infer that the author has not stated directly?

## Teacher Think Aloud

*In this paragraph, the author talks about how plants need "just 'the right amount' of water." In my home, we have both leafy green plants and cactus plants. The green plants need to be watered more often than the cactus plants do. I infer that "the right amount of water" varies with the kind of plant. You have to know how much water your kind of plant needs.*

## Comprehension

UNDERSTANDING TEXT STRUCTURE

Use these questions to model how to understand the classification structure of the article. Then have students identify the text structure within one of the paragraphs and explain how they know. (Most of the paragraphs fit a descriptive text structure.)

- How is the text organized?

- Which details support my thoughts?

(See Differentiated Instruction.)

Mesquite

Spring blooms

Prickly Pear Cactus

Joshua Tree

Acacia

Sedona Cactus

Ocotillo

*Most land plants lose a great deal of water through their leaves. But many desert plants have few or no leaves.*

Some trees that live in wetlands have "<u>knees</u>." Knees are part of the root system that rise above water. Wetland trees also have trunks that are wide at the base to help support the tree. The tree roots cannot support the tree the same way they would in dry soil. Can you guess why?

## Desert Plants

Plants that grow in the desert have adapted in different ways. Most land plants lose a great deal of water through their leaves. But many desert plants have few or no leaves.

Many cactus plants have short roots and thick, fleshy stems. The short roots allow the plant to quickly get a lot of water when it rains. The roots and thick stems are good for storing water. The stems have a waxy skin to seal in <u>moisture</u>, or water. The plants have spines instead of leaves. The spines collect moisture, too. The spines also protect the plants from becoming a juicy snack for animals.

Other desert plants have very long roots. This allows the plants to get moisture from deep in the ground. An example of this kind of desert plant is the mesquite (mess KEET) tree. The mesquite's roots are thought to be the longest of any desert plant. The roots can be eighty feet long!

**17**

# Teacher Think Aloud

*This article is divided into sections with headings. There is a different section for each kind of plant that is discussed. The heading above the section tells the kind of plant that that section is about. This type of text organization is called "classification," which means that the text is broken down into parts according to topic.*

## Fix-Up Strategies

Offer these strategies to help students read independently.

**If you don't understand what you're reading:**

- Reread the difficult section to look for clues to help you comprehend.

- Read ahead to find clues to help you comprehend.

- Retell, or say in your own words, what you've read.

- Visualize, or form mental pictures of, what you've read.

**If you don't understand a word:**

- Reread the sentence. Look for ideas and words that provide meaning clues.

- Find clues by reading a few sentences before and after the confusing word.

- Look for the base or root word and think about its meaning.

- Think about the topic or plot at this point to see if either offers meaning clues.

**Student Journal page 88**

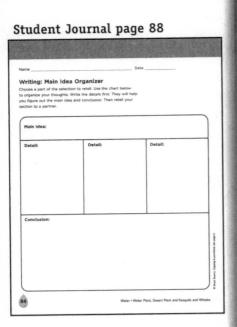

Name _____ Date _____

**Writing: Main Idea Organizer**

Choose a part of the selection to retell. Use the chart below to organize your thoughts. Write the details first. They will help you figure out the main idea and conclusion. Then retell your section to a partner.

| Main Idea: | | |
|---|---|---|
| Detail: | Detail: | Detail: |
| Conclusion: | | |

88    Water • Water Plant, Desert Plant and Seagulls and Whales

**Student Journal page 89**

Name _____ Date _____

**Building Vocabulary: Word Relationships**

Choose four other word pairs to show more word relationships. Arrange your words so that they are ranked by graduated degrees of relationship. Possible word pairs include tiny/enormous, hot/cold, and ounce/gallon.

soggy → soaked → wet → damp → dry

Water • Water Plant, Desert Plant and Seagulls and Whales    89

---

*Plants can live just about anywhere!*

The Joshua tree is another strong desert plant. It has needle-like leaves with a waxy coating. The waxy coating keeps the plant from losing water into the air through a process called transpiration.

The acacia (uh KAY shuh) tree does have leaves. But it sheds the leaves when there is very little water, which keeps the plant from losing water. The leaves grow back when it rains. Shedding leaves also helps the plant by slowing down growth. By growing slowly, desert plants use less energy, food, and water.

Many desert plants start as seeds. The seeds are able to stay alive without growing for a long time. They begin to grow when it rains. Many desert plants sprout, grow, flower, and die, all in a very short time.

It doesn't matter whether plants live in a forest, pond, marsh, or desert. Plants can be found where there is much water. Plants can be found where there is very little water. Plants can live just about anywhere! ◆

*Some desert plants live by remaining dormant (at rest) during dry periods of the year. The plants spring back to life when the rains come. The ocotillo (ock uh TEE oh) is an example. It can go through this process as many as five times a year.*

**Saguaro Cactus**

18

---

# After Reading

WHOLE CLASS  Use one or more activities.

## Check Purpose

Have students decide if their purpose was met. Were students able to answer their questions about plants? Did they learn why the amount of water each plant needs differs?

## Discussion Questions

Continue the group discussion with the following questions.

1. Do you agree with the author that plants are adapted to their environments? (Making Connections)

2. How does the way in which the author compares and contrasts plants help you understand their adaptations? (Understanding Text Structure)

3. What was the most interesting thing you learned about water plants? About desert plants? (Details)

## Revisit: Category Chart

Revisit the chart that students began in Before Reading. Are there additional categories students would like to add, or new information?

## Revisit: Knowledge Rating Chart

Ask students to complete *Student Journal* page 87. They should tell how they were able to define each word in context. Ask students what they learned.

Seagulls
gray and white
flying, soaring, swooping
garbage, beach, picnic, crumbs
landing, searching, eating
curious, useful
Cleaners

Whales
huge, mighty
swimming, diving, feeding
hunters, whaling ships, harpoons
chasing, fleeing, surviving
endangered, protected
Ocean Treasures

19

## Poems: Seagulls and Whales

Have students read the poems on page 19. Invite students to share their impressions of the poems. Discuss the poems. Tell students that the poems are *diamante poems*. Diamante poems follow a formula that gives them their diamond shape. Work with students to identify the formula:

**Line 1** noun or naming word

**Line 2** two adjectives that describe the naming word

**Line 3** three verbs or action words that end in *-ing*

**Line 4** four nouns

**Line 5** three verbs that end in *-ing*

**Line 6** two adjectives

**Line 7** noun

## Writing
### Main Idea Organizer

Ask students to choose a section of the article to retell to a partner. Have students use the main idea organizer on *Student Journal* page 88 to organize their thoughts. Then have partners take turns using their charts to retell the sections of the article they have chosen.

## Vocabulary
### Word Relationships

Ask: *Which word creates a "wetter" image*—soggy *or* moist? Moist *or* damp? *Why*? Help students arrange the words in a linear array to show the graduated relationships. Then have partners complete the activity on *Student Journal* page 89. Brainstorm other possible word pairs for students to use, such as *tiny, enormous; hot, cold.*

## Phonics/Word Study
### Short and Long *o* Patterns

Write these two words on the board: *shop* and *bone*. Pronounce each word. Point out to students that both words have the letter *o* sound. Ask students which word has a short *o* sound (*shop*) and which has a long *o* sound (*bone*). Now, work with students to complete the in-depth short and long *o* patterns activity on TE page 212.

## Phonics/Word Study

### Introducing Short and Long *o* Patterns

- Write the following words on the board: *lock* and *home*. Tell students that the words have letter *o* sounds. Both short and long *o* sounds are represented.

- Ask students to identify which word has a short *o* sound and which word has a long *o* sound. Discuss the spelling pattern of each word.

- Using the Long and Short *o*: Sort One sheet, model the sorting process for students. (See *Word Study Manual* page 60.) Write the headings Short *o*, Long *o*, and Oddball and the first few words in the appropriate columns. Introduce the word *love* and see if students recognize that the word has a long vowel pattern for a short vowel sound. The word *love* requires an Oddball column.

- Discuss the model sort and what students learned. (So far, the long *o* pattern has two different vowel sounds.)

- Once the sort is complete, hand out the Long and Short *o*: Sort One sheet. Ask students to cut up the words and do the sort on their own or in groups.

- Check the final sorts.

| Long and Short *o*: Sort One | | |
|---|---|---|
| Short *o* | Long *o* | Oddball |
| lock | home | love |
| pop | stone | gone |
| stop | ghost | |
| stock | moan | |
| prong | loan | |
| clock | groan | |
| clod | roll | |
| | drone | |
| | most | |

For more information on word sorts and spelling stages, see pages 5–31 in the *Word Study Manual*.

# Focus on . . .

Use one or more activities in this section to focus on a particular area of need in your students.

## Comprehension  STRATEGY SUPPORT

To help those students who need more practice using the strategies covered in this lesson, work one-on-one or in small groups to apply the strategy prompts below. Apply the prompts to a *Reading Advantage* paperback, a classroom library book, or a new or familiar selection in the magazine. Always model your own thinking first.

### Inferential Thinking

- What are the causes or effects of this event?
- What do I learn from the character or person's thoughts, words, or actions?
- What do I know (or infer) from the text that the author hasn't stated directly?
- What conclusions can I draw?

### Understanding Text Structure

- What kind of text is this? (book, story, article, guidebook, play, manual)
- How does the author organize the text? (cause-effect, problem-solution, chronological order, description, question-answer, comparison-contrast)
- What details support my thoughts about the text structure?
- What is the cause (effect, problem, solution, order, question, answer)?
- If fiction, who are the characters? What is the setting, plot, conflict, and resolution?

## Writing Comparative Paragraph

Have students write a comparative paragraph to compare and contrast two plants. Students can compare and contrast either plants from the article or plants with which they are familiar. Have students complete a Venn diagram to organize their thoughts. In the paragraphs, students should cite at least three ways in which the plants are alike and three ways in which they are different.

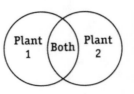

To provide additional instruction on writing a compare-contrast paragraph, see the lessons in *Writing Advantage*, pages 113–151.

## Fluency: Phrasing

SMALL GROUP

Have students silently read the poems on page 19. Discuss how reading poetry differs from reading nonfiction. (Poems are read expressively, with special attention given to phrasing, line breaks, and choice of words. Nonfiction is read deliberately, with special attention given to facts and details.) Then have students in small groups practice reading the poems aloud.

Use these prompts to guide students in reading expressively.

▶ Pay attention to the structure of the poem. Pause at the end of lines to help separate the nouns (naming words), adjectives (describing words), and verbs (action words).

▶ Listen as I read. Notice how I read the verbs in a livelier voice to give them "action."

▶ Think about the message of the poem, and its tone. Use your voice to create interest and hold attention.

When students read aloud, do they—
✓ demonstrate quick recognition of words and phrases?
✓ exhibit an understanding of phrasal construction?
✓ incorporate appropriate timing, stress, and intonation?

## English Language Learners

SMALL GROUP

To support students' comprehension of "Water Plant, Desert Plant," build students' background knowledge about deserts.

1. Read and discuss several picture books about deserts.

2. Have students make a word web. Have them write the word *desert* in the circle. Have them draw lines extending out from the circle. At the end of each line, have them write the name of a desert plant.

3. Finally, have students share their work with a partner.

## Independent Activity Options

INDEPENDENT

While you work with individuals or small groups, others can work independently on one or more of the following options.

▶ Level A paperback books, see TE pages 371–376
▶ Level A *eZines*
▶ Repeat word sorts from this lesson
▶ *Student Journal* pages for this lesson
▶ *Writing Advantage* independent lessons

# Assessment

## Strategy Assessment

To help you and your students assess their use of comprehension strategies, ask the following questions. Students can complete a written response or provide verbal answers in a one-on-one reading conference.

1. **Inferential Thinking** What is the main conclusion you draw from this article? Explain. (Answers will vary. One possible answer is that plants can live in many different kinds of places because they have adapted to their environment.)

2. **Understanding Text Structure** What are all the different ways the article conveyed information to you? (Answers will vary, but students should mention that information was conveyed in the text, captions, diagrams, and sidebars.)

For ongoing informal assessment, use the checklists on pages 61–64 of *Level A Assessment*.

## Word Study Assessment

Use these steps to help you and your students assess their understanding of short and long *o* patterns.

1. Write the following words on the board or on word cards: *dodge, jogger, chose, rocket, roast, soak, model, arrow, product, phone.*

2. Have students sort the words into two lists: one with the long *o* sound, and one with the short *o* sound. The answers are shown.

| Short *o* | Long *o* |
|-----------|----------|
| dodge | chose |
| jogger | roast |
| rocket | soak |
| model | arrow |
| product | phone |

Level A Assessment

# LESSON 28
# Yakking with a Kayaker
*Water*, pages 20–23

## SUMMARY

In this **interview**, the author describes a canoe and kayak race that takes place in upstate New York. Then she interviews Irma Sagazie, the ninety-three-year-old grandmother for whom the race was named.

## COMPREHENSION STRATEGIES

Understanding Text Structure

## WRITING

Friendly Letter

## VOCABULARY

Synonyms

## PHONICS/WORD STUDY

Long *o* Patterns

### Lesson Vocabulary
yakking
soothing

## MATERIALS

*Water*, pp. 20–23
*Student Journal*, pp. 90–92
*Word Study Manual*, p. 61
*Writing Advantage*, pp. 152–163

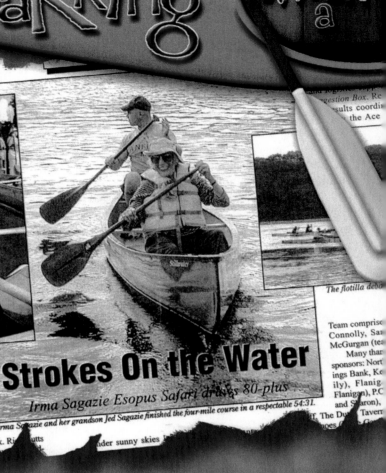

yaKKing with a

Cooper, an entrant from Rhinebeck in the "Mixed Species" class.

The flotilla debu

## Strokes On the Water

*Irma Sagazie Esopus Safari draws 80-plus*

Irma Sagazie and her grandson Jed Sagazie finished the four-mile course in a respectable 54:31.

The sun shone brightly again on Irma's Armada this past Saturday in the annual Irma Sagazie Esopus Safari.

Paddlers from all over New York braved the possibility of Hurricane Lili's remn... to Saugerties to lau... Esopus Creek. Ri... utts ... nder sunny skies

My name is Judy Lechner. October 5, 2002, was a beautiful, sunny fall day in my small town in New York State. It was the morning of a special event, the yearly Canoe and Kayak Race Day. I went down to the beach on the Esopus (eh SO puhs) Creek. The creek is very large. It flows into the Hudson River. There were about eighty people getting their canoes and kayaks ready for the race. Many people have seen a canoe. It is a long, narrow, open boat. Riders use paddles to move their canoes through the water. But fewer people know what a kayak is.

20

# Before Reading

Use one or more activities.

## Make a Concept Web

Start a concept web about boats. Ask students what they know about boats and record their responses. Revisit the web later.

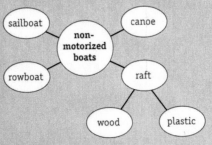

## Vocabulary Preview

List and pronounce the vocabulary words. Model how to make associations, using the word *yakking*. Tell what the word makes you think of. Then have students complete *Student Journal* page 90.

## Preview the Selection

Have students look through pages 20–23 to preview the selection. Discuss students' observations.

## Make Predictions/ Set Purpose

Students should use the information they gathered in previewing the selection to make predictions about what they will learn. If students have trouble generating a purpose for reading, suggest that they read to discover what kayaking is, and why it is a popular sport.

A kayak is a light, slim, closed boat for one or two people. The riders paddle kayaks to make them go. The boat is closed except for one or two holes called cockpits. Each of the riders sits in a cockpit.

Our canoe and kayak race is called the Irma Sagazie Esopus Race. It is named after a very special woman, Irma Sagazie. Irma is ninety-three years old. She loves kayaking and enters the race every year. No kidding! This year, she raced in a canoe with her grandson Jed. Jed is twenty-seven years old. They finished the four-mile race in about fifty-five minutes. In this interview, I talk with Irma about kayaking and canoeing. Yes, we were yakking about kayaking.

**21**

## DIFFERENTIATED INSTRUCTION
**SMALL GROUP**

### Comprehension
UNDERSTANDING TEXT STRUCTURE

To help students understand a question-answer text structure, follow these steps:

1. Ask: *What is the name of the person who is asking the questions, and the name of the person answering them? How do you know?*

2. Judy Lechner asks the questions, and Irma Sagazie answers them. Help students find where this information is provided on pages 20 and 21.

### Student Journal page 90

Name _____ Date _____

**Building Vocabulary: Making Associations**
Think about what you already know about the words listed. Then answer the following questions.

Word _____ **yakking** _____

What do you think about when you read this word? _____

Who might use this word? _____

What do you already know about this word? _____

Word _____ **soothing** _____

What do you think about when you read this word? _____

Who might use this word? _____

What do you already know about this word? _____

Now watch for these words in the magazine selection. Were you on the right track?

**90**    Water • Yakking with a Kayaker

# During Reading

### Comprehension
**SMALL GROUP**
UNDERSTANDING TEXT STRUCTURE

Use these questions to model how to identify the two text structures in this selection (first-person description and question-answer). Then have students explain how the two text structures are different.

- What do I notice about the text structure on pages 20–21? 22–23?

- Which details support my beliefs?

(See Differentiated Instruction.)

## Teacher Think Aloud
*On pages 21–22, I notice that the text is written in the first person. The author is describing what happened on a particular day. Then, on pages 22–23, I see questions and answers. Questions and answers are often clues that the text is written in the form of an interview. In this case, that's what it is.*

## Fix-Up Strategies

Offer these strategies to help students read independently.

**If you don't understand what you're reading:**

- Reread the difficult section to look for clues to help you comprehend.

- Read ahead to find clues to help you comprehend.

- Retell, or say in your own words, what you've read.

- Visualize, or form mental pictures of, what you've read.

**JL:** How did you begin kayaking?

**IS:** I started because a friend of mine had two kayaks. I told her, "Let me try that." I felt like a swan gliding over the water! Then I said to myself, "I have to have one of those!" That was in 1989.

**JL:** That was when you were eighty years old.

**IS:** Yes, and I took to kayaking like a fish to water!

**JL:** What do you like best about kayaking?

**IS:** It's the most peaceful and soothing thing that I have ever done.

**JL:** How often do you go kayaking?

**IS:** I go kayaking almost every day in the summer. I've met everyone on the creek. People who canoe and kayak are very friendly.

**JL:** How did the canoe and kayak race get started?

**IS:** A man named Ralph Childers came up with the idea of holding canoe and kayak races on the Esopus Creek. Ralph builds his own canoes. He and his wife, Erin McGurgan, put the event together. We've had the races for four years now. People come from all over New York to compete and to watch.

**JL:** So Ralph canoes while you kayak?

**IS:** Yes, he likes to use a racing canoe. It's a bit different from most canoes. It is pinched together in the middle. The shape makes it move fast in the water.

22

**JL:** I've seen those canoes. They are lighter than regular canoes. Do you think kayaking keeps you young?

**IS:** Yes, I think it does keep me young. I like to do new things and have new adventures. It's good to get out and be with people. I love people—especially kids.

**JL:** How do you stay in shape for kayaking?

**IS:** I keep in shape by walking a lot. I like to walk with my dog, Bruno. My son Pete and his wife, Cheri, live next door. They have two dogs and a cat named Peaches. We all walk together—the three dogs and the cat, too. I also do exercises on a mat on the floor. And I use a ski machine to exercise. It's just like cross-country skiing. I do that, too, in the winter.

**JL:** Well, you sure make kayaking sound like fun. You might see me in the race next year.

**IS:** I hope you try the race next year. You will enjoy it! ◆

- The Inuit (Eskimo) people were the first to use kayaks. The early kayaks were made of animal skins on a wooden frame.

- Today, kayaks are made of plastic or fiberglass. Fiberglass is a strong material made of fine threads of glass. Fiberglass does not catch fire. Fiberglass is used for skis, boats, and many other purposes.

**Student Journal page 91**

# After Reading  WHOLE CLASS  Use one or more activities.

## Check Purpose

Have students decide if their purpose was met. Were students able to answer their Before Reading questions? Did students learn what kayaking is, and why it is a popular sport?

## Discussion Questions

Continue the group discussion with the following questions.

1. What did you learn about the canoe and kayak race? (Details)

2. How is a kayak similar to and different from a canoe? (Compare-Contrast)

3. Irma Sagazie thinks that kayaking is peaceful and soothing. Would you like to try kayaking? Why or why not? (Making Connections)

## Revisit: Concept Web

Revisit the concept web started in Before Reading. What new information can students add?

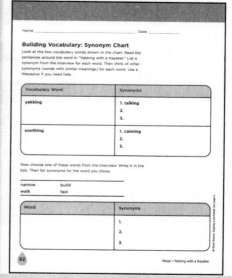

## DIFFERENTIATED INSTRUCTION
### Writing
### Friendly Letter

Talk with students about how to organize the information about kayaking, for writing their letters. Remind students that all the sentences in a paragraph should relate to the same information. Suggest that students use this model:

1. Paragraph 1: Describe kayak's parts, shape, size, and material.
2. Paragraph 2: Tell how a kayak is operated.
3. Paragraph 3: Tell whether they would like to try kayaking and why.

**Student Journal page 92**

Name _____ Date _____

**Building Vocabulary: Synonym Chart**

Look at the two vocabulary words shown in the chart. Read the sentences around the word in "Yakking with a Kayaker." List a synonym from the interview for each word. Then think of other synonyms (words with similar meanings) for each word. Use a thesaurus if you need help.

| Vocabulary Word | Synonyms |
|---|---|
| yakking | 1. talking<br>2.<br>3. |
| soothing | 1. calming<br>2.<br>3. |

Now choose one of these words from the interview. Write it in the box. Then list synonyms for the word you chose.

narrow    build
walk     fast

| Word | Synonyms |
|---|---|
|  | 1.<br>2.<br>3. |

92                                          Water • Yakking with a Kayaker

**Rules for Kayaking**

1. Always go with an adult.
2. Wear a life jacket.
3. Learn how to kayak from a teacher or other adult.
4. Wear sunscreen and a hat.
5. Pay attention to the weather.

23

## Writing Friendly Letter

Ask students to write letters in which they explain to friends what they learned about kayaks and kayaking. Also encourage students to express their opinions about the sport of boat racing. Students can write their letters on *Student Journal* page 91. (See Differentiated Instruction.)

## Vocabulary Synonyms

Write *yakking* and *talking* on the board. Ask students if they know any synonyms for the word *yakking*. List them on the board. (*chatting, gabbing, conversing*) Do the same exercise with the word *soothing* (found on page 22). Then have students work in pairs to complete the synonym chart on *Student Journal* page 92. Have students brainstorm other synonyms to complete the chart. Encourage students to use a thesaurus if they need additional help.

## Phonics/Word Study
### Long *o* Patterns

Write the following words on the board: *code, soap,* and *snow.* Ask students if the words have a long or short *o* sound. (long) Then write these vowel patterns on the board: *oa, oCe, ow.* Challenge students to match each word with one of the patterns. (*code, oCe; soap, oa; snow, ow*) Now, work with students to complete the in-depth long *o* patterns sorting activity on TE page 218.

### Long *o* Patterns

▶ Write the following words on the board: *rope*, *soap*, and *blow*.

▶ Ask students if the words have the long or short *o* sound.

▶ Using the Long *o*: Sort Two sheet, model the sorting process for students. (See *Word Study Manual* page 61.) Write the headings *oCe*, *oa*, *ow*, and Oddball and the first few words in the appropriate columns.

▶ Discuss the sort and what students learned.

▶ Once the model sort is complete, hand out the Long *o*: Sort Two sheet. Ask students to cut up the words and do the sort on their own or in groups.

▶ Check the final sorts.

| Long *o*: Sort Two | | | |
|---|---|---|---|
| *oCe* | *oa* | *ow* | Oddball |
| rope | road | blow | now |
| code | soap | snow | cow |
| stove | boat | low | |
| strode | loaf | known | |
| tone | groan | crow | |
| | | throw | |

For more information on word sorts and spelling stages, see pages 5–31 in the *Word Study Manual*.

# Focus on . . .

Use one or more activities in this section to focus on a particular area of need in your students.

## Comprehension  STRATEGY SUPPORT  INDEPENDENT

To help those students who need more practice using the strategies covered in this lesson, work one-on-one or in small groups to apply the strategy prompts below. Apply the prompts to a *Reading Advantage* paperback, a classroom library book, or a new or familiar selection in the magazine. Always model your own thinking first.

### Understanding Text Structure

• What kind of text is this? (book, story, article, guidebook, play, manual)

• How does the author organize the text? (cause-effect, problem-solution, chronological order, description, question-answer, comparison-contrast)

• What details support my thoughts about the text structure?

• What is the cause (effect, problem, solution, order, question, answer)?

• If fiction, who are the characters? What is the setting, plot, conflict, and resolution?

## Writing Interview Questions  INDEPENDENT

Have each student interview someone who is involved in an outdoor sport. Suggest that interviewers skim "Yakking with a Kayaker" to see the kinds of questions the author asked Irma Sagazie. Encourage students to prepare questions beforehand so that they elicit the information they want.

Help students brainstorm a list of possible questions, such as the following:

• What outdoor sport do you like the most?

• How did you get interested in this sport?

• Who takes part in this sport?

• Where do you practice this sport?

• When is the best time to play this sport?

• Why do you like this sport?

Students can write their questions on separate index cards and then record the answers on the same cards. Encourage students to present in either oral or written reports the results of their interviews.

For additional instruction in taking notes and compiling information, see the lessons in *Writing Advantage* pages 152–163.

## Fluency: Expression

After students have read the article silently at least once, have them work with partners. One partner should take the role of Judy Lechner, the interviewer; and the other should take the role of Irma Sagazie, the interviewee. Partners should choose a set of three questions and answers and practice reading them aloud. Remind students that the subjects are having a conversation, so students should assume a casual tone for the lines they read. Allow time for partners to present their interviews for the whole group.

As you listen to students read, use these prompts to guide them.

▶ Put yourself in the place of the interviewer or the interviewee. Think about how that person would sound.

▶ Preview what you will read, to avoid stopping and restarting unnecessarily. This will make it easier for listeners to understand what you are saying.

When students read aloud, do they—

✓ reflect an understanding of the text?

✓ demonstrate appropriate timing, stress, and intonation?

✓ incorporate appropriate speed and phrasing?

## English Language Learners

To support students' understanding of "Yakking with a Kayaker," discuss the text structure of an interview.

1. Have students discuss what they already know about interviews. Clarify what an interview is.

2. Use page 22 to point out the structure of an interview. Have students discuss how to determine who is talking.

3. Have partners brainstorm several questions they would like to ask Irma Sagazie.

## Independent Activity Options

While you work with individuals or small groups, others can work independently on one or more of the following options.

▶ Level A paperback books, see TE pages 371–376

▶ Level A *eZines*

▶ Repeat word sorts from this lesson

▶ *Student Journal* pages for this lesson

▶ *Writing Advantage* independent lessons

# Assessment

## Strategy Assessment

To help you and your students assess their use of comprehension strategies, ask the following questions. Students can complete a written response or provide verbal answers in a one-on-one reading conference.

• **Understanding Text Structure** What helped you the most in your understanding of what kayaking is like: the descriptive text, the interview, or the photographs? Explain. (Answers will vary.)

For ongoing informal assessment, use the checklists on pages 61–64 of *Level A Assessment*.

## Word Study Assessment

Use these steps to help you and your students assess their understanding of long *o* patterns.

1. Write the following words on the board or on word cards: *foam, dose, flow, coal, show, joke, soak, cone, crow, toad.*

2. Write the three different long *o* vowel patterns on the board or on a word card: *oa, oCe, ow.*

3. Ask students to identify the vowel pattern in each word. The answers are shown.

| Word | Vowel Pattern |
|------|---------------|
| foam | *oa* |
| dose | *oCe* |
| flow | *ow* |
| coal | *oa* |
| show | *ow* |
| joke | *oCe* |
| soak | *oa* |
| cone | *oCe* |
| crow | *ow* |
| toad | *oa* |

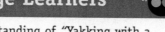

Great Source
Reading Advantage

**Level A Assessment**

**SUMMARY**

This **fictional memoir** tells about the scariest day in a boy's life—when a tsunami struck Hilo, Hawaii, in 1960.

**COMPREHENSION STRATEGIES**

Monitor Understanding

**WRITING**

Notes for Visualizing

**VOCABULARY**

Homophones

**PHONICS/WORD STUDY**

Short and Long *o* Patterns

**Lesson Vocabulary**

tsunami          swayed
swift            linen

**MATERIALS**

*Water*, pp. 24–27
*Student Journal*, pp. 93–95
*Word Study Manual*, p. 62
*Writing Advantage*, pp. 56–92

# The Scariest Day of My Life

*People remember good times and bad times in their lives. Sometimes an event happens that is painfully shocking. This kind of event can stay in one's mind for life.*

I will never forget the day when I thought the world would end. In May 1960, a huge tidal wave hit Hilo, where I lived on the big island of Hawaii. I had never seen such an ocean wave before. It was the worst thing ever. It destroyed property. It destroyed lives. It almost took my life.

The day had started like any other. It was early in the morning. I got dressed for school. Mom, Dad, and I ate breakfast. All was normal and quiet.

I left our house to walk to school. I was eleven, so I could walk by myself. The school was not very far. Most of the time I met friends along the way.

I liked to walk along the beach. There was so much to see near the ocean. On most days you saw the blue water rolling by the shore. The sun shone on the water. Fishermen were out on their boats for the day.

24

# Before Reading

WHOLE CLASS · Use one or more activities.

## Make a List

Ask students: *What do you know about tsunamis?* Make a list of what students know or have heard about tsunamis. Students will revisit the list after they finish the selection.

| TSUNAMIS |
| --- |
| 1. They have big waves. |
| 2. They can be dangerous. |

## Vocabulary Preview

Review the vocabulary list with students. Model making associations with the word *tsunami* to help students complete *Student Journal* page 93.

## Preview the Selection

Have students look through the four pages of the memoir. Discuss students' observations. (See Differentiated Instruction.)

## Make Predictions/Set Purpose

Students should use the information they gathered in previewing the selection to make predictions about what they will learn. If students have trouble generating a purpose for reading, suggest that they read to learn why the narrator felt that this was the scariest day of his life.

There were surfers, too. They rode the waves on their surfboards. It was all such a beautiful sight.

Yet, something was wrong. From the beach, I looked at the ocean. It did not look the same as always. There didn't seem to be enough water in the ocean. How strange!

I blinked my eyes and looked at the ocean again. Where did all the water go? I saw my friend Joe. "Where is all the water?" I asked.

Joe laughed. He said that maybe someone had pulled the plug out of the ocean. Maybe water was going down the drain. I tried to laugh, too. But things looked so weird to me.

Just then, a man on the beach cried, "Tidal wave!" Joe and I looked out at the ocean. I felt instant shock and fear! A tsunami (tsoo NAH mee), a huge wall of water, was rushing to shore! I think the wall was more than 100 feet high.

Joe and I ran as fast as we could. We tried to get away from the water. Then we heard a big BOOM! I thought it was a bomb. It was the wall of water crashing on land. Joe and I grabbed a rail fence. We held on as tightly as we could.

## Tsunami

The word *tsunami* comes from two Japanese words. They mean "harbor" and "wave." The word was first used around 1907.

## Tidal Wave

The term *tidal wave* means the same thing as *tsunami*. The word *tidal* refers to the flowing of the ocean in toward shore and out again. This action is caused by the gravitational pull of the moon and the sun. The result is the rise and fall of the ocean and other large bodies of water. In most coastal places, there is a high tide and a low tide at least once a day.

A tidal wave, however, is caused by an underwater earthquake or volcanic eruption. A tidal wave can have a worse effect on land if it occurs at high tide. *The Big Wave*, by Pearl S. Buck, is a story about a tidal wave.

25

## DIFFERENTIATED INSTRUCTION
## Preview the Selection

To enhance the preview, use these steps:

1. Read aloud the first paragraph. Explain that it is called a *lead*—an opening sentence or paragraph that's meant to create interest in what is to come. A good lead can "grab" the reader and "pull" the reader in.

2. Ask volunteers to tell what they thought and felt when they read the lead.

### Student Journal page 93

Name _____ Date _____

**Building Vocabulary: Making Associations**
Choose two vocabulary words. Think about what you already know about each word. Then answer the following questions for each word.

| tsunami | swayed |
| swift | linen |

Word _____

What do you think about when you read this word? _____

Who might use this word? _____

What do you already know about this word? _____

Word _____

What do you think about when you read this word? _____

Who might use this word? _____

What do you already know about this word? _____

Now watch for these words in the selection. Were you on the right track?

Water • The Scariest Day of My Life                    93

# During Reading

## Comprehension

MONITOR UNDERSTANDING

Use these questions to model visualizing the text. Then have students tell about a part they visualized, and which details helped them visualize it.

- What do I picture in my mind as I read?

- Which details help me create this image in my mind?

## Teacher Think Aloud

*On page 25, the narrator writes, "There didn't seem to be enough water in the ocean." I had trouble picturing this in my mind. Then, in the next paragraph, Joe compares the scene to water going down a drain. This helped me visualize an image. I pictured the water far from shore, as if someone had pulled a plug in the middle of the ocean, and the water was slipping away.*

## Fix-Up Strategies

Offer these strategies to help students read independently.

**If you don't understand what you're reading:**

- Reread the difficult section to look for clues to help you comprehend.

- Read ahead to find clues to help you comprehend.

- Retell, or say in your own words, what you've read.

- Visualize, or form mental pictures of, what you've read.

All at once, all kinds of things were floating in the water. Cars rode up and down on the waves. Palm trees floated into the ocean. Homes washed out, too. Some were split in two. Some crumbled like crackers. The houses that were swept away whole looked like dollhouses as they tossed about the <u>swift</u>, wild water.

It seemed like the wave of water would never stop. Joe and I kept our grip on the rail. My feet <u>swayed</u> back and forth. I thought the rail might come out of the ground and wash Joe and me into the ocean. But somehow it stayed firm in the earth.

Water splashed against my face. It stung my cheeks. I choked and turned my face away. I tried to breathe, but it was hard. Water hit my nose and mouth. I had to spit it out. As the water ran back to the sea, it actually ripped the shirt off my body.

For a long time, I just watched more and more things float into the ocean. There were chairs and tables and pots and pans. I saw telephone poles and street signs and store signs. There were clothes and toys and books. A white bathtub floated by. The whole scene looked so unreal, like in a movie. But I knew this was not a movie. It was true. It was real life. It was *my* life. At last, the wave stopped. Joe ran home to see if his house was okay. I ran home, too. But my house was not there. I knew then that it must have washed out to sea. I surely would have died if the tidal wave had come earlier in the morning.

*Water splashed against my face. It stung my cheeks. I choked and turned my face away. I tried to breathe, but it was hard.*

26

Name _____ Date _____

**Writing: Notes for Visualizing**
Which part of the selection could you visualize best? Describe that part below. Then draw a picture to show what you "saw" in your mind.

The part I could visualize best was _____

Some details I "saw" in my mind include _____

Now draw what you visualized.

94

Water • The Scariest Day of My Life

# After Reading

Use one or more activities.

## Check Purpose

Have students decide if their purpose was met. Did they learn more about why the narrator felt that this was the scariest day of his life? Was their question answered?

## Discussion Questions

Continue the group discussion with the following questions.

1. What forces of nature have you experienced? What were they like? (Making Connections)

2. What caused the tsunami that struck Hilo in 1960? (Cause-Effect)

3. What parts of the world are most likely to experience tsunamis? (Inferential Thinking)

## Revisit: List

Revisit the list started in Before Reading. Now that they've read the selection, do students want to add or revise anything?

I searched all over for Mom and Dad. At first I couldn't find them. Then I looked up high, and there they were. They were on the roof of a <u>linen</u> store that was still standing, far enough from the shore. They waved to me, and I waved back. I was so happy to see them!

Mom and Dad came down from the roof. We hugged and kissed like never before. But there was no time to lose. People were floating on the water. They held onto chairs or logs or anything they could. We quickly took sheets from the store and ripped them into long strips. We threw them to the people. They grabbed them, and we pulled them in.

Soon, many doctors and nurses arrived. People were sent to the hospital. Our family was lucky. Dad, Mom, and I were not hurt, but many other people were. A lot of people died. Lots of buildings and homes were gone.

We stayed in my aunt's home for many months afterward. She lived on the opposite side of the island in Kona. She was so grateful that we were all alive. She told me that a tidal wave wall moves 100 miles an hour as it hits the shore. I'm still not sure how my friend and I survived.

Since that day in May, I have not had to face another tsunami. I hope this will be so for the rest of my life. ◆

The photos show the aftermath of the Hilo tsunami.

**Author's note:**
The *tsunami* in the story really happened. The earthquake that triggered the tsunami occurred off the coast of South Central Chile, in South America, on May 22, 1960. The tsunami arrived at Hilo, Hawaii, around fifteen hours later. Sixty-one people were killed. More than 500 buildings were destroyed.

## Check It Out
- Scientists can predict when and where a tsunami will hit shore.
- An earlier tsunami hit several Hawaiian islands on April 1, 1946. You can read about it and stories from survivors on these websites:

pubs.usgs.gov/gip/hazards/tsunamis.html

www.nationalgeographic.com/ngkids/9610/kwave/survive.html

27

### Student Journal page 95

Name _____ Date _____

**Building Vocabulary: Homophones**
Complete each homophone pair. Then write a definition for each word in the pair.

| Homophones | Definitions |
|---|---|
| swayed | swung from side to side |
| suede | soft leather |
| seen | |
| ate | |
| way | |
| rode | |

Water • The Scariest Day of My Life

95

---

## Writing Notes for Visualizing

Remind students that active readers visualize, or try to "see" what an author tells about. Have students complete the visualizing activity on *Student Journal* page 94 to verbalize what they "saw" most clearly in the selection.

## Vocabulary Homophones

Explain that homophones are words that sound alike but are spelled differently. Point out the word *swayed* on page 26 of the selection. Ask students for the word that sounds like s-w-a-y-e-d but is spelled differently. (*suede*) Ask for a simple definition. (soft leather) Now have students complete the homophone chart on page 95 of the *Student Journal*. (See Differentiated Instruction.)

## Phonics/Word Study
### Short and Long *o* Patterns

Write these words on the board: *dock, toll, host.* Ask students which of the three words has a short *o* sound. (*dock*) Then write these vowel patterns on the board: *o*CC, *o*st. Challenge students to match each word with one of the patterns. (*dock*, *o*CC short; *toll*, *o*CC long; *host*, *o*st) Now, work with students to complete the in-depth short and long *o* patterns activity on TE page 224.

## Phonics/Word Study

### Short and Long *o* Patterns

▶ Write the following words on the board: *mock*, *roll*, and *ghost*. Tell students that the words have letter *o* sounds. Both short and long *o* sounds are represented. Note that you will be adding some oddballs to the list.

▶ Ask students if they can identify which words have a short *o* vowel sound and which have a long *o* vowel sound.

▶ Ask: *Which vowel patterns should I use as headings for the words?*

▶ Using the Long and Short *o*: Sort Three sheet, model the sorting process for students. (See *Word Study Manual* page 62.) Write the headings *oCC* (short), *oCC* (long), *ost*, and Oddball and the first few words in the appropriate columns.

▶ Introduce the word *lost* and see if students recognize that its vowel sound does not sound like the *o* in *ghost*. Note that the word *lost* requires a third column, the Oddball column. (It could also fit in the *oCC* (short) column.)

▶ Discuss the model sort and what students learned.

▶ Once the model sort is complete, hand out the Long and Short *o*: Sort Three sheet. Ask students to cut up the words and do the sort on their own or in groups.

▶ Check the final sorts.

| Long and Short *o*: Sort Three | | | |
|---|---|---|---|
| *oCC* (short) | *oCC* (long) | *ost* | Oddball |
| mock | roll | ghost | lost |
| clock | toll | host | cost |
| lock | gross | most | doll |
| shock | scold | post | botch |
| | stroll | | knob |

For more information on word sorts and spelling stages, see pages 5–31 in the *Word Study Manual*.

# Focus on . . .

Use one or more activities in this section to focus on a particular area of need in your students.

## Comprehension  STRATEGY SUPPORT  INDEPENDENT

To help those students who need more practice using the strategies covered in this lesson, work one-on-one or in small groups to apply the strategy prompts below. Apply the prompts to a *Reading Advantage* paperback, a classroom library book, or a new or familiar selection in the magazine. Always model your own thinking first.

### Monitor Understanding

- Do I understand what I'm reading? If not, what part is confusing to me?
- What fix-up strategies can I use to solve the problem? (See During Reading for fix-up strategies.)
- Why did a character say (do, think, ask) that?
- What images do I visualize from the text? What parts can't I visualize?
- Why did the author include (or not include) those details?

## Writing Short Account  INDEPENDENT

Have students write a short account of an experience they will always remember. Have them use the 5Ws to help them organize their thoughts. Have students reread and edit their drafts when finished.

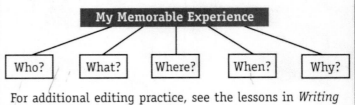

For additional editing practice, see the lessons in *Writing Advantage*, pages 56–92.

## Fluency: Expression

SMALL GROUP

After students have read the selection at least once, have partners read parts of it, first silently, then aloud.

As you listen to partners read, use these prompts.

▶ Read expressively. Think about how the narrator is feeling at different points.

▶ Look for punctuation marks to help you adjust your tone. Exclamation points signal great excitement.

▶ Reread until you can read the text expressively, without effort. With practice, you won't stumble over words or have to slow down.

When students read aloud, do they—

✓ reflect an understanding of the text?

✓ demonstrate appropriate timing, stress, and intonation?

✓ incorporate appropriate speed and phrasing?

## English Language Learners

SMALL GROUP

To support students as they make connections, extend the first discussion question on TE page 222.

1. Have students think about the forces of nature they have experienced. Also have them think about the scariest day they have ever experienced.

2. Have students write a narrative describing their scariest day.

3. Have students share their writing. Encourage them to focus on fluency and expression as they share.

## Independent Activity Options

INDEPENDENT

While you work with individuals or small groups, others can work independently on one or more of the following options.

▶ Level A paperback books, see TE pages 371–376

▶ Level A *eZines*

▶ Repeat word sorts from this lesson

▶ *Student Journal* pages for this lesson

▶ *Writing Advantage* independent lessons

# Assessment

## Strategy Assessment

To help you and your students assess their use of comprehension strategies, ask the following questions. Students can complete a written response or provide verbal answers in a one-on-one reading conference.

• **Monitor Understanding** Did the pictures in the selection help you visualize the tsunami and its aftermath? Why or why not? (Answers will vary. Students may have found the photographs on page 27 the most helpful. The illustrations may have been too abstract.)

For ongoing informal assessment, use the checklists on pages 61–64 of *Level A Assessment*.

## Word Study Assessment

Use these steps to help you and your students assess their understanding of short and long *o* patterns.

1. Write the following words on the board or on word cards: *bold, lock, colt, most, both, sock, post, rock, ghost.*

2. Write the following vowel patterns on the board or on word cards: *o*CC (long), *o*CC (short), *ost.*

3. Ask students to identify the vowel pattern in each word. The answers are shown.

| Word | Vowel Pattern |
|------|---------------|
| bold | *o*CC (long) |
| lock | *o*CC (short) |
| colt | *o*CC (long) |
| most | *ost* |
| both | *o*CC (long) |
| sock | *o*CC (short) |
| post | *ost* |
| rock | *o*CC (short) |
| ghost | *ost* |

Great Source
Reading Advantage

Level A
Assessment

# A Man for All Seas

*Water*, pages 28–32

## SUMMARY

This **biographical sketch** details the life and career of oceanographer Robert Ballard.

## COMPREHENSION STRATEGIES

Determining Importance

## WRITING

Journal Entry

## VOCABULARY

Multiple Meanings

## PHONICS/WORD STUDY

Long and Short *o* Patterns (*r*-controlled)

### Lesson Vocabulary

| | |
|---|---|
| wreck | vents |
| oceanographer | plaque |
| submersible | footage |

## MATERIALS

*Water*, pp. 28–32
*Student Journal*, pp. 96–98
*Word Study Manual*, p. 63
*Writing Advantage*, pp. 152–163

On its first voyage across the Atlantic, the *Titanic* struck an iceberg and sank. That was in 1912. For over seventy years, no one knew where the great ship lay. Finally, a team led by Robert Ballard located the ship. This was just one of many ocean successes for Robert Ballard.

# A Man for All Seas

Illustration of the sinking of the *Titanic* by Willy Stoewer

**28**

# Before Reading

WHOLE CLASS — Use one or more activities.

## Anticipation Guide

Create an anticipation guide for students. (See TE page 39.) Then discuss their responses. Students will revisit the anticipation guides later.

| AGREE | DISAGREE | |
|---|---|---|
| | | 1. The *Titanic* sank on its very first voyage. |
| | | 2. Robert Ballard built ships for a living. |
| | | 3. The *Titanic* has never been found. |

## Vocabulary Preview

Display the vocabulary words. Then ask students to predict how the words will be used. Have students complete the second column of the predictions chart on *Student Journal* page 96. Students will finish the chart later.

## Preview the Selection

Have students look through the five pages of the biographical sketch. Discuss students' observations.

## Make Predictions/ Set Purpose

Students should use the information they gathered in previewing the selection to make predictions about what they will learn. If students have trouble generating a purpose for reading, suggest that they read to discover the underwater mysteries Robert Ballard solved.

**H**e found the <u>wreck</u> of the *Titanic*. He located the wrecks of other famous ships. He discovered hot spots on the ocean floor. He started a major science program. He continues to explore the huge oceans with robots. Who is this man? He is Dr. Robert D. Ballard.

Dr. Ballard is fond of telling how he got interested in the ocean. When he was ten years old, his favorite book was *Twenty Thousand Leagues Under the Sea.* His hero was Captain Nemo from that book. Dr. Ballard decided that

*Dr. Robert D. Ballard*

he wanted to be an underwater explorer like Captain Nemo.

Ballard's parents didn't laugh at him. They encouraged him to live his dream. His parents said, "Maybe you need to become an <u>oceanographer</u> and study the oceans. Maybe you need to become a naval officer." So he did both. He believes that "all of us should try to live our dreams."

Robert Ballard began living his dreams while growing up in San Diego, California. Young Bob enjoyed scuba diving. He swam and surfed. He loved to explore tidal pools. They are pools of ocean water left in holes after the tide goes out. They are full of sea life. As a teenager, he went to a summer program at a school well known for its ocean studies.

### More on Robert Ballard

- Ballard was born June 30, 1942, in Wichita, Kansas, but grew up in San Diego, California.

- He worked at Woods Hole Oceanographic Institution for 30 years, beginning in 1966.

- He found the wreck of the *Titanic* in 1985.

- He began the JASON Project in 1989.

- He founded and heads the Mystic Aquarium Institute for Exploration in Mystic, Connecticut.

---

## DIFFERENTIATED INSTRUCTION

**SMALL GROUP**

## Comprehension
DETERMINING IMPORTANCE

Use this activity to help students recognize important ideas.

1. Have students read the feature titled "Captain Nemo" on page 30.

2. Ask what they think is the most important idea in the feature. Write their responses on the board and discuss students' reasoning.

3. Guide them to realize that details about Verne's life aren't as important as his creation of the character Captain Nemo, who inspired Ballard.

### Student Journal page 96

Name _____ Date _____

**Building Vocabulary: Predictions**

How do you predict these words will be used in "A Man for All Seas"? Write your answers in the second column. Next, read the article. Then clarify your answers in the third column.

| Word | My prediction for how the word will be used | How the word was actually used |
|---|---|---|
| wreck | | |
| oceanographer | | |
| submersible | | |
| vents | | |
| plaque | | |
| footage | | |

96         Water • A Man for All Seas

---

# During Reading

## Comprehension
DETERMINING IMPORTANCE

**SMALL GROUP**

Use these questions to model how to determine the importance of ideas in the section about Ballard finding the *Titanic*. Then have students determine the importance of ideas in the third paragraph on page 30, about the discovery of strange sea creatures.

- What are the most important ideas?

- How can I support my beliefs?

(See Differentiated Instruction.)

## Teacher Think Aloud

*I think the two most important ideas in this section are that Dr. Ballard was able to find the* Titanic *because he used a robot, and that he didn't want people to disturb the ship. The first idea explains why Ballard could find the* Titanic *when no one else could. The second idea explains his actions when he found the ship. The rest of the information contains details that support these ideas.*

## Fix-Up Strategies

Offer these strategies to help students read independently.

**If you don't understand what you're reading:**

- Reread the difficult section to look for clues to help you comprehend.

- Read ahead to find clues to help you comprehend.

- Retell, or say in your own words, what you've read.

- Visualize, or form mental pictures of, what you've read.

Like Captain Nemo, Robert Ballard traveled in a submarine. The navy sent him to Woods Hole, Massachusetts. A lot of ocean research was going on there. Ballard made dives in a small <u>submersible</u> named *Alvin*.

At Woods Hole, Ballard grew interested in an idea. The idea is that the earth's crust isn't solid. It is made up of more than a dozen pieces. The pieces float above a huge area of melted rock. In 1974, Ballard helped prove this idea. He studied mountains in the middle of the Atlantic Ocean. Sure enough, hot melted rock was oozing out of cracks in the ocean floor.

Then, in 1977, Ballard made another discovery. There were openings, or <u>vents</u>, of hot springs in the floor of the Pacific Ocean.

The submersible named *Alvin*

The *Argo* being launched

Strange sea creatures lived 9,000 feet down. They were not part of any food chain that started with the sun. For some scientists, this was the most important finding in ocean science in the last century.

If you know Robert Ballard's name at all, it is probably because you heard about him and the *Titanic*. In 1912, the *Titanic* was the largest ship in the world. On its first trip, from England to New York City, it sank

### Captain Nemo

Jules Verne (1828–1905) was a French novelist who wrote some of the first science-fiction stories. Verne had a wonderful imagination. Long before the invention of airplanes, submarines, television, and space satellites, Verne wrote about them in his novels. Published in 1870, *Twenty Thousand Leagues Under the Sea* tells about a mad sea captain who travels in a submarine. The captain's name is Captain Nemo.

**Student Journal page 97**

Name _____ Date _____

**Writing: Journal Entry**

What might Robert Ballard have written in a journal entry when he discovered the *Titanic*? Write a journal entry about it in the space below. Use what you know from the article and your own life to help you put together ideas.

September 1, 1985

_____
_____
_____
_____
_____
_____
_____
_____
_____
_____
_____
_____
_____

Water • A Man for All Seas          97

# After Reading

WHOLE CLASS  Use one or more activities.

## Check Purpose

Have students decide if their purpose was met. Ask students to discuss what they learned about the underwater discoveries of Robert Ballard.

## Discussion Questions

Continue the group discussion with the following questions.

1. What did you find interesting about Robert Ballard? (Making Connections)

2. Why was the discovery of the *Titanic* important? (Inferential Thinking)

3. What helped you keep track of all the information as you read? (Sequence)

## Revisit: Anticipation Guide

Revisit the anticipation guide that was completed in Before Reading. Have students look back at their responses. Do they agree with their original choices? Discuss with the group.

## Revisit: Predictions Chart

Have students complete the predictions chart on *Student Journal* page 96. Allow students time to confirm and/or correct their definitions.

in icy waters in the North Atlantic. It lay two miles below the surface.

No one had seen the *Titanic* for more than seventy years. Divers couldn't reach it. How could Robert Ballard ever find it? He had help from a robot named *Argo*.

### The Food Chain

A food chain follows the path of energy from one organism to the next. In most food chains, energy begins with the sun. A plant, usually, takes in energy from the sun to make its food. Then, an animal eats the plant, taking in energy from the plant. The chain continues as one creature eats another. Finally, the last creature dies and decomposes, sending nutrients back into the environment. The nutrients usually feed plants. Creatures that live in the vents on the floor of the Pacific Ocean are unusual because their food chain does not begin with the sun.

*Argo* could dive where no human could. It had a video camera and lights. It traveled along the ocean floor. It took pictures and sent them to a ship where Ballard waited and watched.

Dr. Ballard didn't tell anybody that he had found the *Titanic* in 1985. He didn't want people to take things from the ship. The next year, he sent a robot inside the ship. A camera inside the robot took more pictures. He left a <u>plaque</u> with the names of the people who went down with the *Titanic*.

About a year later, Ballard told the world. He asked people not to disturb the great ship. He thought it should lie in peace at the bottom of the sea.

Robert Ballard became famous. But he kept on working. There was so much more he wanted to do. Dr. Ballard wanted to find other wrecked ships. He wanted to solve many underwater mysteries. And he wanted to find a way to share with kids his excitement for science.

Dr. Ballard received many letters from kids. They wanted to know all about his discovery of

### Jason and Argo

In Greek mythology, Jason was a sailor. He had his own ship, the *Argo*, built for a special trip. He gathered a crew. These sailors, called *Argonauts*, went on a dangerous voyage in search of the Golden Fleece. *Argonaut* is the name Dr. Ballard gives to someone taking part in a JASON adventure.

the *Titanic*. So in 1989, he founded the JASON Project. Every year JASON goes exploring for two weeks. Dr. Ballard leads a team of scientists, teachers, and students. The JASON team has been to the deep seas. The team has traveled to rain forests, volcanoes, coral reefs, and even the icy tips of our planet.

**31**

## DIFFERENTIATED INSTRUCTION · SMALL GROUP
### Vocabulary
### Multiple Meanings

Provide further explanation of and practice with words with multiple meanings by following these steps:

1. Explain that many words in English have more than just one meaning.

2. Give some simple examples by using *ring* and *slip* in sentences: *She wore a new emerald* ring. Ring *the doorbell. Be careful not to slip on the ice. Write the address on a slip of paper.*

3. Show *plant* and *sink.* Ask students to use the words in sentences. Discuss the definition of each word.

### Student Journal page 98

Name _____ Date _____

**Building Vocabulary: Words with Multiple Meanings**
Write two definitions for each word below.

| Word | First Definition | Second Definition |
|------|------------------|-------------------|
| plaque | a flat piece of metal, wood, or stone with writing on it to honor a person or an event | a film on tooth surfaces that hardens and attracts decay-causing bacteria |
| floor | | |
| program | | |
| float | | |
| pools | | |

98 · Water • A Man for All Seas

## Writing Journal Entry

What if Robert Ballard had kept a journal? Ask students what he might have written when he discovered the *Titanic.* Have students consider these questions: *How might Ballard have felt? What might he have seen in the water the day of the discovery? What was the significance of his find to him? To the world?* Jot down students' ideas on the board. Then have students use *Student Journal* page 97 to write a journal entry in the voice of Robert Ballard.

## Vocabulary Multiple Meanings

Display the word *plaque.* Remind students that in the article, a *plaque* refers to a flat piece of metal, wood, or stone with writing on it to honor a person or an event. *Plaque* can also be a film on tooth surfaces that hardens and attracts bacteria, or it can be a material that collects on the inner walls of blood vessels. Brainstorm a list of other words with multiple meanings. Have partners complete *Student Journal* page 98. (See Differentiated Instruction.)

## Phonics/Word Study

### Long and Short *o* Patterns

Tell students that the letter *r* following a vowel changes the vowel's usual sound. Write the words *most* and *more* on the board and say them aloud. Point out how the long *o* sound in *most* is different from the long *o* sound in *more.* Have students say and listen to both words. Now, work with students to complete the in-depth long and short *o* patterns (*r*-controlled) activity on TE page 231.

Famous ships Ballard has found include *The Bismarck, a German battleship, (top left); The Britannic, twin ship of the Titanic, (top right); The Yorktown, a U.S. World War II aircraft carrier, (bottom left).*

Porthole from the *Titanic*

Silverware from the *Titanic*

More than a million other students and teachers follow the trips from classrooms and homes. Special cameras hooked up to the Internet and satellites provide live-action footage. The two-week trip becomes part of studies that can last the whole year.

What else has Robert Ballard been doing lately? He was the host of a TV show from 1989 to 1991. He has been writing books. He has published many articles. After nearly thirty years at Woods Hole, he left for a new scientific home. He founded the Mystic Aquarium Institute for Exploration. It is in Mystic, Connecticut.

Ballard has gone to study the Black Sea. This is where he has been looking for traces of the flood told about in the Bible. He has also traveled to Thunder Bay, Ontario. There he looked for sunken ships. In Pearl Harbor, Hawaii, he searched for a tiny sub that led the attack in 1941 that brought the United States into World War II.

Some people think that space is much more exciting than the ocean. But Robert Ballard doesn't think so. He has gone a long way to support his belief. And a lot of supporters have followed him to the depths of the ocean. ◆

RMS Titanic, Inc., has recovered approximately 6,000 artifacts from the *Titanic*. All the recoveries are documented. You can see photos of them at www. titanic-online.com.

## Phonics/Word Study

### Long and Short *o* Patterns (*r*-controlled)

▶ Write the following words on the board: *for*, *more*, and *door*. Tell students that they are continuing their study of *o* vowel patterns. Note that this time the sort is particularly tricky.

▶ Ask students if the word *for* has a long or short vowel sound.

▶ Discuss the problem the letter *r* causes. Explain how it "robs" the vowel of its usual sound. The *o* in *for* sounds very different from the *o* in *fog*.

▶ Using the Long and Short *o*: *r*-controlled Vowels sheet, model the sorting process for students. (See *Word Study Manual* page 63.) Write the headings *or* (short), *ore*, *oor*, and Oddball and the first few words in the appropriate columns.

▶ Discuss the sort and what students learned about *r*-controlled vowels. Note that sometimes the easiest way to tell if an *r*-controlled vowel is short or long is by saying aloud the short and long sound in the word. As is shown by the examples below, this doesn't work well with the *o* vowel sounds. The best thing to remember is that there are far fewer *or* words than there are *ore* words.

▶ Once the model sort is complete, hand out the Long and Short *o*: *r*-controlled Vowels sheet. Ask students to cut up the words and do the sort on their own or in groups.

▶ Check the final sorts for accuracy.

| Long and Short *o*: *r*-controlled Vowels | | | |
|---|---|---|---|
| *or* (short) | *ore* | *oor* | Oddball |
| for | more | door | your |
| or | shore | floor | four |
| nor | wore | poor | |
| | bore | moor | |
| | chore | | |
| | lore | | |
| | score | | |
| | adore | | |
| | gore | | |

For more information on word sorts and spelling stages, see pages 5–31 in the *Word Study Manual*.

# Focus on . . .

Use one or more activities in this section to focus on a particular area of need in your students.

## Comprehension  STRATEGY SUPPORT  *INDEPENDENT*

To help those students who need more practice using the strategies covered in this lesson, work one-on-one or in small groups to apply the strategy prompts below. Apply the prompts to a *Reading Advantage* paperback, a classroom library book, or a new or familiar selection in the magazine. Always model your own thinking first.

### Determining Importance

• What is the most important idea in the paragraph? How can I prove it?

• Which details are unimportant? Why?

• What does the author want me to understand?

• Why is this information important (or not important) to me?

## Writing Illustrated Timeline  *INDEPENDENT*

Have students use the information from the article to make an illustrated timeline of Ballard's accomplishments. Students can first talk to a partner and then take notes about Ballard's achievements and when they took place. Students can then transfer the information to a timeline and illustrate the events on separate paper. See the example below.

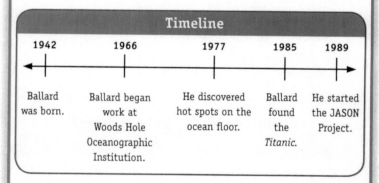

| Timeline | | | | |
|---|---|---|---|---|
| 1942 | 1966 | 1977 | 1985 | 1989 |
| Ballard was born. | Ballard began work at Woods Hole Oceanographic Institution. | He discovered hot spots on the ocean floor. | Ballard found the *Titanic*. | He started the JASON Project. |

For additional instruction and practice on taking notes, see the lessons in *Writing Advantage*, pages 152–163.

## Fluency: Pacing

**SMALL GROUP**

After students have read the entire article at least once, they can use a portion of it to practice fluent reading. Have students work with a partner to read one or two of the special features.

As you listen to students read, use these prompts to guide them.

▶ Read at an even pace. Don't read too quickly or too slowly. Let punctuation marks guide your pacing.

▶ Notice which words go together to make natural-sounding phrases.

▶ Put enthusiasm in what you read to make it sound interesting.

When students read aloud, do they—

✓ demonstrate a smooth pace, not too fast or too slow?

✓ incorporate well-timed pauses between words and phrases?

✓ reflect an awareness and understanding of punctuation?

## English Language Learners

**SMALL GROUP**

To support students in preparation for the writing activity on *Student Journal* page 97, model how to write a journal entry.

1. Explain what a journal entry is. Also discuss what Robert Ballard would have included in his journal.

2. Use chart paper to model a journal entry from the point of view of Robert Ballard.

3. Read the journal entry together. Review the components of a journal entry.

## Independent Activity Options

**INDEPENDENT**

While you work with individuals or small groups, others can work independently on one or more of the following options.

▶ Level A paperback books, see TE pages 371–376

▶ Level A *eZines*

▶ Repeat word sorts from this lesson

▶ *Student Journal* pages for this lesson

▶ *Writing Advantage* independent lessons

# Assessment

## Strategy Assessment

To help you and your students assess their use of comprehension strategies, ask the following questions. Students can complete a written response or provide verbal answers in a one-on-one reading conference.

• **Determining Importance** What do you think is the most important idea(s) the author wants readers to remember about Dr. Ballard, from reading this article? (Answers will vary. Students should consider what ideas the article as a whole covered. One possible answer might be that Dr. Ballard made many important discoveries about the ocean and has willingly shared his knowledge with others.)

See *Level A Assessment* page 34 for formal assessment to go with *Water*.

## Word Study Assessment

Use these steps to help you and your students assess their understanding of long and short *o* patterns (*r*-controlled).

1. Write the following words on the board or on word cards: *adore, indoor, snore, floor, chore, nor*.

2. Write the following vowel patterns on the board or on word cards: *ore, oor, or*.

3. Ask students to identify which vowel pattern each word has. The answers are shown.

| Word | Vowel Pattern |
| --- | --- |
| adore | *ore* |
| indoor | *oor* |
| snore | *ore* |
| floor | *oor* |
| chore | *ore* |
| nor | *or* |

Great Source
Reading Advantage

**Level A Assessment**

# Home Sweet Home

### People who live on or near water "go with the flow."

Some people live on houseboats. They can tie the houseboat to a dock and then move when they want to. But there are also people in different parts of the world who live on water in real houses! Let's visit some homes around the world that are on or near water. You may just want to "go with the flow" yourself some day!

People in Indonesia build houses in the sea. They use ladders to get into their homes. At night, they pull up the ladders.

For years, Dutch people have built dams to keep water out of the city. Now, one company is building houses on water. The houses are made of wood and aluminum. Walkways link the houses to each other. What if people want to move out of the neighborhood? No problem! They can <u>detach</u> their house from the walkway and move it by tugboat.

33

LESSON **31**

# Home Sweet Home, The Water Cycle, and Life on a Coral Reef

*Water,* pages 33–39

### SUMMARY
This **photo-essay** depicts how people around the world live on or near the water. A **poem** and a **short article** follow.

### COMPREHENSION STRATEGIES
Making Connections
Inferential Thinking

### WRITING
Notes for Visualizing

### VOCABULARY
Word Root *auto*

### PHONICS/WORD STUDY
Long *o* Review

### Lesson Vocabulary
| | |
|---|---|
| detach | automatic |
| stilts | ridges |

### MATERIALS
*Water,* pp. 33–39
*Student Journal,* pp. 99–101
*Word Study Manual,* p. 64
*Writing Advantage,* pp. 113–151

# Before Reading
*WHOLE CLASS* Use one or more activities.

## Make a T-Chart
Create a T-chart for students. See an example below. Have students share their ideas on the pros and cons of living on or near water. Record their responses on the chart. After students have finished the article, revisit the chart to see if they have changed their opinions.

| Living on or Near Water | |
|---|---|
| Pros | Cons |
| | |

## Vocabulary Preview
Read the vocabulary words aloud or write them for students to view to make sure they understand each word. Then have students complete the synonym and antonym chart on *Student Journal* page 99. (See Differentiated Instruction.)

## Preview the Selection
Have students look through the four pages of the photo-essay. Discuss students' observations.

## Make Predictions/Set Purpose
Students should use the information they gathered in previewing the selection to make predictions about what they will learn. If students have trouble generating a purpose for reading, suggest that they read to find out about the different ways in which people live near or on the water.

## DIFFERENTIATED INSTRUCTION
### Vocabulary Preview

Discuss with students the purpose and form of a thesaurus. Follow these steps:

1. Explain that a thesaurus is a special kind of word reference book. Like a dictionary, it is organized in alphabetical order.

2. A thesauraus contains synonyms for words. It also includes antonyms.

3. Share the following entry from a thesaurus. Read it together with students: "**detach**, v. separate, disconnect, unfix, loose, disjoin. *Antonyms*: see attach, connect, join."

### Student Journal page 99

Name _____ Date _____

**Building Vocabulary: Synonym and Antonym Chart**
For the word *detach*, write three words that are synonyms (similar in meaning). Then, write three words that are antonyms (opposite in meaning). Next, repeat the process for two other words you choose from the article.

| Word | Synonyms | Antonyms |
|------|----------|----------|
| detach | 1. remove | 1. attach |
| | 2. | 2. |
| | 3. | 3. |
| | 1. | 1. |
| | 2. | 2. |
| | 3. | 3. |
| | 1. | 1. |
| | 2. | 2. |
| | 3. | 3. |

*Water • Home Sweet Home, The Water Cycle, and Life on a Coral Reef*     99

People in Malaysia don't always live on the sea. Some houses are built on <u>stilts</u>. When there is a heavy rainfall, the land gets flooded. The stilts keep the houses high off the ground so that the houses stay dry.

People who live along the Mekong River in Cambodia build houses on stilts, too. During the rainy season, they use boats for transportation. The photo on the right shows how one house looks during the rainy season. The photo on the left shows a house during the dry season.

34

# During Reading

## Comprehension
### MAKING CONNECTIONS

Use these questions to model for students how to make connections with the text. Then have students share connections they have made.

- What does this article remind me of?

- How does my past experience help me understand the article?

(See Differentiated Instruction.)

## Teacher Think Aloud

*I've seen lighthouses before. In the summer, I often visit a friend who lives on an island. There's a lighthouse there, and I can hear its foghorn at night. I have always wondered what it would be like to live in a lighthouse. It might be fun for a while, but it might also get lonely. When I'm on the island, I can hear the ocean waves at night. I like that.*

## Comprehension
### INFERENTIAL THINKING

Use these questions to model how to make inferences from the bottom section on page 34. Then have students reveal inferences they make as they read another section.

- What does the text tell me?

- Using what I learn from the text and my own experience, what can I infer that the author does not state directly?

**234** • Water

Hong Kong is a very crowded place. Many people can't find living space on land. So some people live on houseboats, called *sampans*.

In Venice, Italy, the whole city is built on water. The city is built on 118 tiny islands in the Gulf of Venice. People use gondolas (GON duh luhs) to get around on the water. These boats are long and narrow. They have a flat bottom with high peaks at the ends. One person uses an oar or a pole to steer it. Today, there are powerboats as well.

35

**DIFFERENTIATED INSTRUCTION**

SMALL GROUP

## Comprehension
### MAKING CONNECTIONS

To help students make connections with the text, follow these steps:

1. On a world map or a globe, locate each of the places mentioned. Mark each one with pushpins or self-stick notes.

2. Have students speculate what the climate is like in each place. Ask: *Is this place near the equator? What do you know about the equator?*

3. Discuss how the climate affects the way the homes are constructed.

## Teacher Think Aloud

*The text tells me that people along the Mekong River live in houses on stilts and use boats in the rainy season. By looking at the photographs, I infer that people can walk everywhere during the dry season. From my own experience, I also infer that there's a time between the rainy and the dry seasons when the ground is very muddy.*

### Fix-Up Strategies

Offer these strategies to help students read independently.

**If you don't understand what you're reading:**

- Reread the difficult section to look for clues to help you comprehend.
- Read ahead to find clues to help you comprehend.
- Retell, or say in your own words, what you've read.
- Visualize, or form mental pictures of, what you've read.

**If you don't understand a word:**

- Reread the sentence. Look for ideas and words that provide meaning clues.
- Find clues by reading a few sentences before and after the confusing word.
- Look for the base or root word and think about its meaning.
- Think about the topic or plot at this point to see if either offers meaning clues.

## Vocabulary

### Word Root *auto*

Help students generate a list of words with *auto*.

1. Use prompting sentences to elicit these words: *autograph*, *autobiography*, *autocrat*.

2. Try these sentences: *He waited in line to get the star's ___. I am planning to write my ____ when I get older. The class officer tried to rule everything and everybody, so we called him an ____.* As each word is suggested, write it on the board.

3. Encourage students to look up each word in a dictionary.

### Student Journal page 100

Name _____ Date _____

**Writing: Notes for Visualizing**
Which home were you able to visualize best? Describe the home below. Use as many details as you can from the text. Then draw a picture of how you imagined it in your mind.

The part I could visualize best was _____

Some details I "saw" in my mind include _____

Now draw what you visualized.

100

Water • Home Sweet Home, The Water Cycle, *and* Life on a Coral Reef

The Rose Island Lighthouse in Newport, Rhode Island, is open for people who want a working vacation. Families are allowed to live in the tower of the lighthouse. But they must do the chores that keep the lighthouse working. For fun, they can climb to the light that has shone for more than one hundred years. The light is fully <u>automatic</u> today, running on electricity. But long ago, lighthouse keepers had to keep lanterns lit by hand. They had an important job to guide ships safely past huge rocks in the water. But life on a very small island could be lonely and difficult. ◆

Most Americans who live on houseboats do so by choice. Some people love to be near the water. Other people just like to be different. Still others find houseboats cheaper to live in than houses on land.

36

# After Reading

Use one or more activities.

## Check Purpose

Have students decide if their purpose was met. What did they find out about what it is like to live on or near the water?

## Discussion Questions

Continue the group discussion with the following questions.

1. How do you think living near the water is similar to living inland? How is it different? (Compare-Contrast)

2. Choose one of the houses you read about. How would you describe it? (Details)

3. Would you like to live near the water? Why or why not? (Making Connections)

## Revisit: T-Chart

Revisit the T-chart that was started in Before Reading, about the pros and cons of living on or near the water. What new information can students add? Have they changed their minds after reading the text?

# The Water Cycle

Welcome to Earth, our blue world
Where water moves from oceans deep
Up into the sky, then rains down again
In a moving circle that never stops.

The sun's fire heats the ocean waves.
A watery mist rises through the air.
These bits of ocean leave their salt behind.
Water vapor rises sweet and clear.

No one can see the vapor rise,
But as it cools, water drops form.
They gather into floating clouds.
The time is right for rain or snow storms.

Rain and snow fall onto our Earth
Into oceans, rivers, lakes, and streams.
Then the water cycle begins again
As the ocean feels the sun's warm beams.

37

## Poem: The Water Cycle

Have students read the poem on page 37 silently. Then have students draw a diagram to show how the water cycle works. See the example below.

Have students share their diagrams with a partner, and then discuss the diagrams as a group.

### Student Journal page 101

---

## Writing Notes for Visualizing

Ask students which home they were able to visualize best. Encourage students to picture the home in their minds, using as many details from the text as they can. Then have students write a description of that home and draw it on the visualizing activity on *Student Journal* page 100.

## Vocabulary Word Root *auto*

Write the word *automatic* on the board or on chart paper. Remind students that in the article, *automatic* refers to something that is regulated by itself and can operate without the control of a human being. Now examine the root *auto* with students. Explain that the meaning of *auto* is "self, alone." Brainstorm a list together of other words with *auto*. Have partners complete *Student Journal* page 101. (See Differentiated Instruction.)

## Phonics/Word Study

### Long *o* Review

Write the following words on the board: *knoll*, *host*, *stove*, *foal*, and *know*. Tell students that each word has one of the long *o* vowel patterns they have learned. Provide the pattern for *knoll*, *o*CC. Then ask students to identify the pattern for each of the other words. (*ost*, *o*Ce, *oa*, *ow*) Now, work with students to complete the in-depth long *o* review on TE page 240.

# LIFE ON A CORAL REEF

A coral reef is a living, underwater world all its own.

There are many beautiful and colorful places in the shallow waters of the world's warm seas. These places are coral reefs. People often describe these ridges of coral as underwater gardens. But they are so much more than that. They provide a home for as many as 2,000 sea creatures and plants.

38

### What Is a Coral Reef?

Coral reefs are formed over millions of years. They are built by millions of tiny animals called *coral polyps*. They live together in colonies, or groups.

The polyps have soft, jelly-like bodies. To protect themselves, they build cup-shaped shells by collecting a chemical that is in the seawater. The chemical is called *calcium carbonate*. This hardens to form limestone. It is white or cream colored.

The limestone shells remain after the polyps die. Then new polyps grow on the old shells. This is how the reef grows larger.

There are more than 2,500 kinds of coral. But not all corals build the reefs. The corals that build reefs are called stony corals. They are the ones that form limestone shells.

Other kinds of corals are soft. They have horn-like skeletons with tiny needles of limestone. Soft corals can bend and sway from side to side in the water.

## Coral Reef Creatures

Coral reefs are full of creatures. Only a few are shown here.

Harlequin Tuskfish

**Fish** Most coral reef fish have bright colors. The fish have unusual shapes and are decorated with spots, stripes, and other markings. The markings allow them to blend in with their surroundings. This way the fish can easily hide from their enemies.

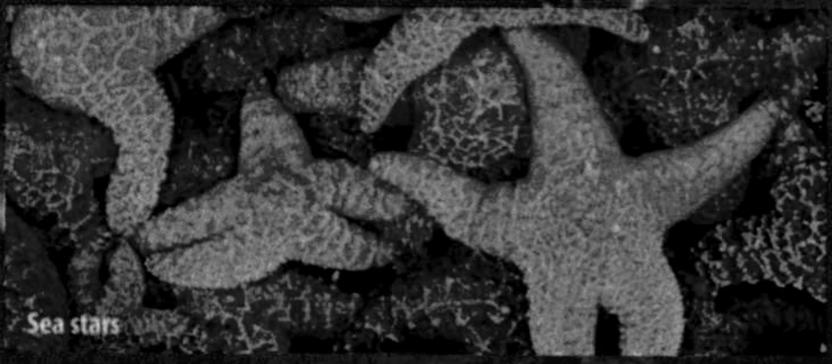

Sea stars

**Sea Star** Sea stars also have bright colors. Sea stars have five arms. A sea star has a row of suction discs under each arm. These discs help the sea star move along the coral. If a sea star loses a body part during a fight with another creature, the lost body part will grow again.

Sponges on a reef ledge

**Sponge** Sponges are animals! There are more than 5,000 different kinds. They come in all shapes and sizes. The sponges attach themselves to the hard top part of the reef. They draw water into their bodies and then strain out the tiny animals and plants that they eat.

Clown fish swimming in tentacles of sea anemone

**Sea Anemone** (un NEM uh nee) Sea anemones almost look like flowers, but they are animals. The tentacles of the sea anemone shoot poison at the slightest touch. But the poison does not bother the clown fish. It lays its eggs and raises its young within the anemone's tentacles. The clown fish leaves only to find food and bring it back. The anemone gets to eat the leftovers of the clown fish's meals. What a partnership! ◆

- Coral reefs are found in the warm seas that lie on either side of the equator. The reefs are generally within 30 degrees N and 30 degrees S latitudes.

- You can find coral reefs in or near the following places: Bermuda, the Bahamas, the Caribbean Islands, Belize, Florida, the Gulf of Mexico, the Red Sea, the Persian Gulf, the Indian and Pacific oceans, and the western coast of Panama.

39

## Phonics/Word Study

### Long *o* Review

▶ Display the following headings so that students can work on the long *o* vowel patterns: *oCC, ost, oCe, oa, ow,* r-controlled. See *Word Study Manual* page 64.

▶ Tell students that this is a review of the long *o* vowel patterns. Dictate the words shown in the chart. Have students sort each word under the correct column heading.

▶ Check the final sorts for accuracy.

| Long *o*: Review | | | | | |
|------|------|------|------|------|------|
| *oCC* | *ost* | *oCe* | *oa* | *ow* | *r-controlled* |
| roll | ghost | rope | coast | blow | shore |
| toll | most | strode | throat | know | more |
| knoll | host | stove | foal | thrown | tore |

For more information on word sorts and spelling stages, see pages 5–31 in the *Word Study Manual*.

# Focus on . . .

Use one or more activities in this section to focus on a particular area of need in your students.

## Comprehension  STRATEGY SUPPORT  INDEPENDENT

To help those students who need more practice using the strategies covered in this lesson, work one-on-one or in small groups to apply the strategy prompts below. Apply the prompts to a *Reading Advantage* paperback, a classroom library book, or a new or familiar selection in the magazine. Always model your own thinking first.

### Making Connections

• What does this story (article, passage) remind me of?

• What do I already know about this topic?

• Where have I heard about this topic before?

• What do I have in common with the characters, people, or situations in the text?

• What other books, stories, articles, movies, or TV shows does this text make me think about?

### Inferential Thinking

• What are the causes or effects of this event?

• What do I learn from the character or person's thoughts, words, or actions?

• What do I know (or infer) from the text that the author hasn't stated directly?

• What conclusions can I draw?

## Writing Home Chart  INDEPENDENT

Have students decide which house in "Home Sweet Home" they found the most interesting. Ask them to picture in their minds what living there might be like. Suggest that students think about not only the house itself but also the climate of the country, the foods they would eat, and the chores they would do. Then have students write about a typical day living in their chosen house. Encourage students to gather and organize their information in a chart similar to the one that follows.

| Home I Found Most Interesting | What I Know about It | What I Think Living There Would Be Like |
|-------------------------------|----------------------|------------------------------------------|
| 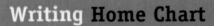 | | |

To provide additional instruction on writing descriptive paragraphs, see *Writing Advantage*, pages 113–151.

## Fluency: Phrasing

SMALL GROUP

After students have read the poem "The Water Cycle" at least once to themselves, they can use it to practice fluent reading. Model reading the poem. Emphasize pacing and natural phrasing. Then, have students work in pairs.

As you listen to pairs read, use these prompts to guide them.

▶ Read at an even, natural pace.

▶ Notice how the punctuation sometimes gives you clues for when to pause. Other times, the meaning of the words and phrases are your main clues for when to pause.

▶ Keep your eyes on the text so you don't lose your place.

▶ Think about the mood of the poem. Read expressively to convey that mood.

When students read aloud, do they—

✓ demonstrate quick recognition of words and phrases?

✓ exhibit an understanding of phrasal construction?

✓ incorporate appropriate timing, stress, and intonation?

## English Language Learners

SMALL GROUP

Provide support for students as they answer the first discussion question on TE page 236.

1. On chart paper, draw a Venn diagram with the headings "Living Near the Water" and "Living Inland."

2. Help students find similarities and differences between these two living areas.

3. Record your findings in the Venn diagram.

## Independent Activity Options

INDEPENDENT

While you work with individuals or small groups, others can work independently on one or more of the following options.

▶ Level A paperback books, see TE pages 371–376

▶ Level A eZines

▶ Repeat word sorts from this lesson

▶ Student Journal pages for this lesson

▶ Writing Advantage independent lessons

# Assessment

## Strategy Assessment

To help you and your students assess their use of comprehension strategies, ask the following questions. Students can complete a written response or provide verbal answers in a one-on-one reading conference.

1. **Making Connections** Do you think that you would like to live in a houseboat? Why or why not? (Answers will vary.)

2. **Inferential Thinking** After reading the selection, what conclusions do you draw about homes on or near the water? (Answers will vary. Students should notice that most of the homes are designed for a purpose, such as protecting people from floods, giving people who can't live on land a place to live, or—in the case of lighthouses—protecting ships at sea.)

For ongoing informal assessment, use the checklists on pages 61–64 of *Level A Assessment*.

## Word Study Assessment

Use these steps to help you and your students assess their understanding of the long *o* review.

1. Write the following words on the board or on word cards: *foam, dose, flow, both, show, toll, post, tore, most, toad.*

2. Write the following vowel patterns on the board or on word cards: *oa, oCe, ow, oCC, ost, r*-controlled.

3. Ask students to identify the vowel pattern in each word. The answers are shown.

| Word | Vowel Pattern |
|------|---------------|
| foam | *oa* |
| dose | *oCe* |
| flow | *ow* |
| both | *oCC* |
| show | *ow* |
| toll | *oCC* |
| post | *ost* |
| tore | *r*-controlled |
| most | *ost* |
| toad | *oa* |

## LESSON 32
# Underwater Hotel
*Water*, pages 40–46

### SUMMARY
In this **science-fiction story**, the Sanchez family owns and operates an underwater hotel in the year 2100. Here, the Sanchez children share an adventure with one of their guests.

### COMPREHENSION STRATEGIES
Monitor Understanding
Understanding Text Structure

### WRITING
Book Jacket

### VOCABULARY
Context

### PHONICS/WORD STUDY
Long and Short *o* Homophones

### Lesson Vocabulary
| | |
|---|---|
| scuba diving | valve |
| trio | marina |

### MATERIALS
*Water*, pp. 40–46
*Student Journal*, pp. 102–105
*Word Study Manual*, p. 65
*Writing Advantage*, pp. 30–55

# UNDERWATER Hotel

*The year is 2100. People are used to spending more time underwater. Will three teenagers have the time of their lives or the most frightening time ever?*

Hilda and Oscar Sanchez were underwater about twenty feet deep. They were in their Propel Lab. The lab was airtight with a system that provided oxygen. They pushed on the foot pedals and the Propel Lab darted through the water. They pushed one button, and the lab went up. They pushed another button, and the lab went down.

"*Mira*, Oscar. Look! There's a group of manatees!" said thirteen-year-old Hilda.

"Let's not get too close. We don't want to scare those sea cows away!" said her eighteen-year-old brother. "Years ago, many people thought that the manatees were in danger of disappearing. But people cared, and they are still around here in 2100. See how big and healthy they look!"

Hilda and Oscar watched the manatees munch on seaweed. How peaceful these huge mammals looked in the clear blue water!

"They're ready to go up for air," said Hilda. "We should head back to the hotel. There's a new group of guests who will be coming to the hotel soon. We have to help Mom and Dad."

It had taken the Sanchezes years to build their underwater hotel. It was off the Florida coast. The hotel had all the comforts of any hotel. There was always an air supply (naturally). The air came from huge oxygen tanks with 120-foot lines. People chatted with each other in the lobby. They ate good food in the dining room. They had lovely views of colorful fish from their bedroom windows.

40

---

# Before Reading
**WHOLE CLASS** Use one or more activities.

## Make a List
Discuss with students what they would expect to find if they were to stay at a hotel. List their responses on the board or on chart paper. You might direct the discussion by asking the following questions.

- What kinds of rooms does a hotel have?
- What special services might a hotel offer?

### What I'd Find in a Hotel
1. extra towels
2. coffeemaker
3.

## Vocabulary Preview
Review the vocabulary list with students, calling on volunteers to read the words aloud. Help students make associations with the words by asking: *What do you think about when you hear this word? Who might use this word? What does the word remind you of? What do you already know about the word?* Have students complete *Student Journal* page 102. Students can revisit their associations later. Model the process for students.

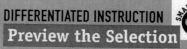

The illustration shows two children in an underwater submarine vehicle with a speech bubble: "MIRA, OSCAR. LOOK! THERE'S A GROUP OF MANATEES!" surrounded by sea creatures including manatees, fish, and a sea turtle.

**Scuba**

*Scuba* is an acronym. An acronym is a word that is formed from the first letters of the words that make up a term. The letters in scuba stand for this phrase: **S**elf-**C**ontained **U**nderwater **B**reathing **A**pparatus. Which is easier to say: "I'm off to go scuba diving" or "I'm off to go self-contained underwater breathing apparatus diving"? Now you know why people use acronyms!

41

To enhance the preview, lead students through the following steps:

1. Have students read the title and the introduction.

2. Preview the pictures, allowing students to comment on the pictures and describe what they see.

3. Help students identify the genre as science fiction—a story, either realistic or imaginary, that takes place in the future. Science fiction also uses technology or scientific knowledge that we have today, but carries it into the future.

**Student Journal page 102**

Name _____ Date _____

**Building Vocabulary: Word Associations**
Choose two vocabulary words. Think about what you already know about each word. Then answer the questions for each word.

scuba diving        valve
trio                marina

Word _____

What do you think about when you read this word? _____

Who might use this word? _____

What do you already know about this word? _____

Word _____

What do you think about when you read this word? _____

Who might use this word? _____

What do you already know about this word? _____

Now watch for these words in the magazine selection. Were you on the right track?

102                                    Water • Underwater Hotel

## Preview the Selection

Have students look through the seven pages of the story. Use these or similar prompts:

• What do you notice?

• Do you think the selection is fiction or nonfiction? Why?

• What kind of fiction do you think the story is? Why?

• What do you think the setting is? Why?

(See Differentiated Instruction.)

## Teacher Think Aloud

*When I first previewed the selection, the illustrations led me to believe that it was a story. They look like comic-book pictures. Then I noticed that the story takes place in 2100. That means the story is science fiction—a story about the future. The title is "Underwater Hotel." That is definitely something in the future! I wonder what an underwater hotel is like.*

## Make Predictions/ Set Purpose

Students should use the information they gathered in previewing the selection to make predictions about what they will learn. If students have trouble generating a purpose for reading, suggest that they read to learn what a vacation in an underwater hotel might be like.

## Comprehension
UNDERSTANDING TEXT STRUCTURE

Review the elements of fiction to help students identify them in the story they are reading.

- The *setting* is the time and place of the story. Stories that take place in the future are science fiction or fantasy.

- The *main characters* are the people or creatures the story is mostly about.

- The *plot* is the events or actions that happen in a story. Plot often tells how the characters handle a problem.

AIR TANK   FACE MASK   WET SUIT   FLIPPERS

The hotel also had a wet room where all the diving gear was kept. That was one of the main reasons people came to the hotel. They wanted to go scuba diving. They wanted to explore a coral reef that was not too far away from the Florida Keys. Mr. and Mrs. Sanchez were diving instructors. So was Oscar. Hilda knew how to scuba dive, too, but she was not old enough to be an instructor.

People got to the underwater hotel by boat. The boat stopped at a dock above the hotel. Then the people got into a watertight elevator on the dock. The elevator took them down to the hotel, where the Sanchez family always greeted their guests.

Hilda and Oscar found their mother at the front desk in the hotel. "So who are our new guests?" Oscar asked his mother.

"Mr. and Mrs. Drake and their son Duane. I think he's about Hilda's age," replied Mrs. Sanchez. "I think the boy just learned to dive. We will have to watch him carefully. He wants to see a shark!"

"I haven't seen one all summer," Hilda commented.

"Well, you never know," Oscar reminded her.

"A young couple is also due to arrive," Mrs. Sanchez added. "The Fields. They have been diving for a long time and want to takes photos at the coral reef."

"*Bueno* (BWAY noh)!" said Oscar. "Great! I love exploring the coral reef."

Just then, the elevator opened to the lobby. "Oh, here are our new guests," Mrs. Sanchez announced. The Sanchezes greeted them and introduced themselves. After Mrs. Sanchez checked them in, the guests went to unpack in their rooms.

Duane came back to the lobby first. "Hey, man," he called to Oscar. "I want to go exploring, but I don't want to go with my parents. They're going diving with your mother and the other guests. Do you want to go with me?"

42

# During Reading

## Comprehension
MONITOR UNDERSTANDING

Use these questions to model how to visualize what you read. Then have students tell about a part they visualized.

- What do I picture in my mind as I read?

- Which details help me create this image in my mind?

- How does visualizing help me understand what I am reading?

## Teacher Think Aloud
*In the first three sentences of the story, I read that Hilda and Oscar are in their Propel Lab under the water. I pictured a laboratory, like a science lab. So I was confused when the next sentence described how they pushed on foot pedals, and the Lab darted through the water. But as I read more details, I was able to visualize the Lab moving around.*

## Comprehension
UNDERSTANDING TEXT STRUCTURE

Use these questions to model how to understand the structure of science fiction. Then have students identify and describe the story elements.

- Who are the main characters in the story?

- What is the setting of the story?

- How do I know that this is science fiction?

(See Differentiated Instruction.)

"Sure," answered Oscar. "But how about taking a ride with Hilda and me in our Propel Lab? It's a special sea vehicle. It's a different way to view the sea."

"Cool," Duane replied.

The <u>trio</u> went to the area where the Propel Lab was parked. They got in. "Duane, do you want to pedal with Oscar?" asked Hilda.

"You mean pedal like a bicycle?" asked Duane.

"That's the idea," Hilda answered. "It's good exercise and it's quiet. This way we don't disturb the sea life."

"Well, this is different. No problem, easy as pie," Duane answered back. He began pedaling with Oscar.

Soon they neared the coral reef.

"Look!" said Hilda, pointing. "There's a butterfly fish. Do you see it?"

"Yeah," said Duane. "And are those angelfish?"

"You bet," said Oscar. "The coral reef is so colorful. Tiny animals and their skeletons and sea plants form this beauty. And no two reefs are alike."

"I know," said Duane. "I also know that fish come to eat the plants around the coral. Hey, do you see what I see? It's a huge turtle! Oh, man, that's so cool!"

The kids watched the turtle in silence. Then all of a sudden, the Propel Lab made a strange noise. It was a tinny, clanky noise. It sounded as if something broke. It wasn't the pedals. They were working fine.

## Teacher Think Aloud

*The main characters in this story are Hilda Sanchez and her brother, Oscar. The story takes place in their family's underwater hotel and in the water around it. I can tell the story is science fiction because it happens in the year 2100, and it has to do with technology we don't have yet, like the Propel Lab and the elevator that goes underwater.*

## Fix-Up Strategies

Offer these strategies to help students read independently.

### If you don't understand what you're reading:

- Reread the difficult section to look for clues to help you comprehend.
- Read ahead to find clues to help you comprehend.
- Retell, or say in your own words, what you've read.
- Visualize, or form mental pictures of, what you've read.

### If you don't understand a word:

- Reread the sentence. Look for ideas and words that provide meaning clues.
- Find clues by reading a few sentences before and after the confusing word.
- Look for the base or root word and think about its meaning.
- Think about the topic or plot at this point to see if either offers meaning clues.

## Marine

*Marine* comes from the Latin word *mare*, which means "sea." *Marine* means "of or relating to the sea." Other words that come from *mare* are these:

*marina*—a dock or basin with supplies for storing and repairing boats

*mariner*—sailor

*Marines*—a branch of the U.S. armed forces

They heard the noise again. Then Hilda noticed the oxygen dial. "Look, we're losing oxygen," she said. She went to check the tanks at the back of the vehicle.

"Something is wrong with the <u>valve</u> on the tanks. No matter how I turn it, it's not controlling the flow of oxygen," Hilda said when she returned. "I think we better head back to the hotel."

"Can we make it?" asked Duane. He suddenly felt uneasy.

"The hotel is only about ten minutes away. We'll be fine."

"Duane, switch seats with me," Hilda said. "I'll do the pedaling back with Oscar. We are used to working as a team."

"No problem, Hilda," answered Duane. He quickly switched seats with her. About four minutes went by. Then something unexpected happened.

A fast-moving current swept up the Propel Lab, taking it off course. Oscar and Hilda pedaled with all of their strength. But they were not going in the right direction.

Duane looked at his watch. "We only have two more minutes of air," he said.

"Okay, we're going up to the surface," Oscar stated. "Hold on. We're going to go up fast." He pushed the button that raised the Propel Lab.

Finally, they were floating on the surface. Hilda opened a window panel so they could get fresh air. But where were they? The hotel dock was nowhere in sight!

"Let's head for Sam's Marina," said Oscar. "I'll call Dad on my marine phone and tell him to meet us there. We can leave the Propel Lab at the <u>marina</u> to be fixed. No more diving in this thing for today, anyway."

Mr. Sanchez met the trio by boat at the marina. Oscar, Hilda, and Duane were quiet at first on the way back to the hotel dock. They were all thinking about how scared they were. Then all three of their stomachs started to growl.

"Man, I'm hungry now," announced Duane.

"Me, too," answered Hilda.

"Me, three," Oscar added.

They returned to the hotel dock and took the elevator down to the hotel. Mrs. Sanchez and Duane's parents had returned from their scuba diving trip. They were sitting in the lobby with the Fields. They all listened to the trio as they told about their morning experience.

"Thank goodness you're all safe," said Mrs. Sanchez. "Get washed up and we'll all have lunch. I can see that you need some food."

After lunch, Hilda had some schoolwork to do. It was Saturday, but she didn't mind doing the work. She was making a poster about a coral reef.

**44**

### Student Journal pages 103–104

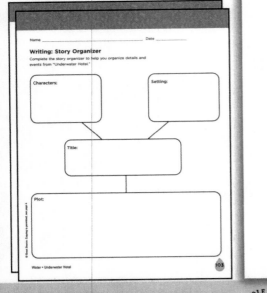

Name _____  Date _____

**Writing: Story Organizer**
Complete the story organizer to help you organize details and events from "Underwater Hotel."

Characters: | Setting:

Title:

Plot:

---

# After Reading 🌀 *WHOLE CLASS* Use one or more activities.

## Check Purpose

Have students decide if their purposes were met. Were any of students' predictions about the story correct? Are students able to tell what a vacation in an underwater hotel might be like?

## Discussion Questions

Continue the group discussion with the following questions.

1. Which details helped you visualize a place and time in the future? (Details)

2. Which futuristic aspects of the story do you think may actually happen? (Predict)

3. Which underwater activity mentioned in the story would you most like to try? Why? (Making Connections)

## Revisit: List

Review the list students began in Before Reading. Help students compare the underwater hotel in the story with an aboveground hotel.

## Revisit: Word Associations

Ask students to share what they wrote for the word associations activity on *Student Journal* page 102. Did students need to change or adapt any word meanings?

LET'S HEAD FOR SAM'S MARINA!

Oscar had some hotel work to do. Duane decided to read a magazine. An hour later, he decided that he wanted to go scuba diving. He had fully recovered from the morning event. He found Oscar in the wet room and asked him to go diving.

"Are you sure you're ready to go out?" asked Oscar.

"No problem, man. It's a piece of cake," Duane replied. "I really would like to see a shark."

Oscar looked at Duane with surprise. "You haven't had enough excitement for one day?" said Oscar.

The boys got into their gear and headed out to the coral reef. This time they saw a manta ray. It swam right up to them. And then a larger sea creature came toward them. Oscar signaled to Duane to stay very still. At first, Duane didn't know why. And then he knew. It was a shark!

"Uh-oh, this is not so cool," Duane thought.

45

**DIFFERENTIATED INSTRUCTION**

## Vocabulary Context

Tell students that using the context can often help readers identify the meaning of the unknown word. Ask students to use these steps when trying to find the meaning of a word.

1. Reread the sentence containing the unknown word to see if the words around it help define the word.

2. Reread the sentences before and after the unknown word to see if they provide the context needed to define the word.

3. Look for synonyms (similar meanings), antonyms (opposite meanings), or definitions to help define the word.

**Student Journal page 105**

Name _____ Date _____

**Building Vocabulary: Using Context to Understand a Word**
Select a vocabulary word or other word from the story that you defined from the context. Complete the statements and answer the questions about your word.

| scuba diving | valve |
| trio | marina |

My Word in Context:

I think this word means _____

because _____

My word is _____

My word is not _____

Where else might I find this word? _____

What makes this an important word to know? _____

Water • Underwater Hotel    105

## Writing Book Jacket

Ask partners to complete *Student Journal* page 103. After students record details and events from "Underwater Hotel," they can use their notes to write a synopsis of the story, as it might appear on a book jacket. The synopsis can be written on *Student Journal* page 104. Remind students that the text that appears on a book jacket tells about the story—without giving away the ending. Show some book jackets to students so that they can read some existing synopses.

## Vocabulary Context

Display these sentences, underlining the word *valve*: "*Something is wrong with the* valve *on the tanks. No matter how I turn it, it's not controlling the flow of oxygen.*" Explain that the second sentence gives context clues for the meaning of *valve*. (a device used to control the flow of gases or liquids by opening or shutting a passageway with a moving part) Now have students complete the context activity on *Student Journal* page 105. (See Differentiated Instruction.)

## Phonics/Word Study
## Homophones

Write the following word pairs on the board: *not, knot; throne, thrown;* and *forth, fourth.* Ask students what the pairs of words have in common. (The words in each pair sound alike but are spelled differently.) Remind students that words like these are called *homophones.* Now, work with students to complete the in-depth long and short *o* homophone activity on TE page 249.

It was lucky for the boys that the shark wasn't hungry. It turned and swam away.

The boys continued on their dive for a while before returning to the hotel. Duane couldn't wait to announce this latest adventure.

"We haven't seen sharks around in quite a while. Are you sure it was a shark?" asked Hilda.

"It was," Oscar answered.

"Duane, were you scared?" Hilda then asked.

"Well, a little," he admitted. "Man, I was glad that I didn't become the shark's lunch. We sure had a close shave, though!" ◆

## Close Shave

Duane seems to talk in idioms a lot! An idiom is a phrase that has a meaning different from the individual words. If Duane had a close shave, it could mean that the barber shaved his whiskers nice and close to his face. However, Duane doesn't even shave yet! More likely, he has just escaped some danger. The edge of a razor blade is very sharp. Used properly, it will cut the hairs and leave smooth skin behind. But one slip, and you end up with a nasty cut. There's not much difference between safety and danger. Narrowly escaping danger is a "close shave."

46

## Phonics/Word Study

### Long and Short *o* Homophones

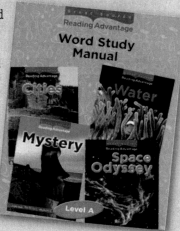

▶ Write the following word pairs on the board: *board, bored; choral, coral;* and *grown, groan.*

▶ Ask students if they can figure out what the pairs have in common. Students should recognize that the words in each pair sound the same but are spelled differently.

▶ Using the list of long and short *o* homophones below, create word cards and play a game in which students turn over a homophone card worth a certain number of points. They have to provide the homophone, spell it, and define it.

▶ Have each student create a new section of his or her Word Study notebook and add any homophones that are generated.

| Long and Short *o*: Homophones | | | |
|---|---|---|---|
| forth<br>fourth | moan<br>mown | mode<br>mowed | foreword<br>forward |
| load<br>lode | lo<br>low | locks<br>lox | doe<br>dough |
| sole<br>soul | not<br>knot | ode<br>owed | throne<br>thrown |
| yoke<br>yolk | boll<br>bowl | bough<br>bow | broach<br>brooch |

For a more extensive list of homophones, see *Word Study Manual* page 65. For more information on word sorts and spelling stages, see pages 5–31 in the *Word Study Manual.*

# Focus on . . .

Use one or more activities in this section to focus on a particular area of need in your students.

## Comprehension  STRATEGY SUPPORT

To help those students who need more practice using the strategies covered in this lesson, work one-on-one or in small groups to apply the strategy prompts below. Apply the prompts to a *Reading Advantage* paperback, a classroom library book, or a new or familiar selection in the magazine. Always model your own thinking first.

### Monitor Understanding

• Do I understand what I'm reading? If not, what part is confusing to me?

• What fix-up strategies can I use to solve the problem? (See During Reading for fix-up strategies.)

• Why did a character say (do, think, ask) that?

• What images do I visualize from the text? What parts can't I visualize?

• Why did the author include (or not include) those details?

### Understanding Text Structure

• What kind of text is this? (book, story, article, guidebook, play, manual)

• How does the author organize the text? (cause-effect, problem-solution, chronological order, description, question-answer, comparison-contrast)

• What details support my thoughts about the text structure?

• What is the cause (effect, problem, solution, order, question, answer)?

• If fiction, who are the characters? What is the setting, plot, conflict, and resolution?

## Writing **Story Sequel**

Ask partners to brainstorm other adventures or "close shaves" Hilda, Oscar, and Duane might have. Then have partners choose one of their ideas and use a Story String (see TE page 389) to outline one more adventure or "close shave" the trio might have. Students can then use their organizers to write sequels to the story. If some students want to write about a "close shave" they have encountered, encourage them to do so.

To provide instruction on writing techniques, such as using strong verbs and specific nouns, see the lessons in *Writing Advantage*, pages 30–55.

## Fluency: Expression

SMALL GROUP

After students have read the story silently at least once, discuss how reading dialogue is different from reading plain text. Help students see that when they read aloud dialogue, they should read expressively, trying to sound the same as the characters might sound.

Have students choose sections of the story to read aloud. Can students convey the feelings of the characters? Can students use their voices to show worry, confidence, relief, excitement, sadness, happiness, or gratitude?

When students read aloud, do they—

✓ reflect an understanding of the text?

✓ demonstrate appropriate timing, stress, and intonation?

✓ incorporate appropriate speed and phrasing?

## English Language Learners

SMALL GROUP

To support students as they participate in the Before Reading activity on TE page 242, help build background knowledge about hotels.

1. Have students discuss what they already know about hotels.

2. Show students pictures of hotels. Point to and name objects found in a hotel.

3. Have students work with a partner to create an illustrated list of objects found in a hotel.

## Independent Activity Options

INDEPENDENT

While you work with individuals or small groups, others can work independently on one or more of the following options.

▶ Level A paperback books, see TE pages 371–376

▶ Level A *eZines*

▶ Repeat word sorts from this lesson

▶ *Student Journal* pages for this lesson

▶ *Writing Advantage* independent lessons

# Assessment

## Strategy Assessment

To help you and your students assess their use of comprehension strategies, ask the following questions. Students can complete a written response or provide verbal answers in a one-on-one reading conference.

1. **Monitor Understanding** Which details in the text helped you visualize the underwater hotel? What in your own experience helped you? (Answers will vary. Students will probably refer to descriptions in the story, as well as their own experiences with hotels.)

2. **Understanding Text Structure** What problem arose in the story, and how was it resolved? (Students should mention the mechanical problem with the Propel Lab, and the calm manner in which Hilda and Oscar brought it safely to the marina.)

For ongoing informal assessment, use the checklists on pages 61–64 of *Level A Assessment*.

## Word Study Assessment

Use these steps to help you and your students assess their understanding of long and short *o* homophones.

1. Write the following words on the board or on word cards: *board, would, whole, flour, groan, know, fore, lone, poll, foul*.

2. Ask students to provide and spell the homophone for each word. Then have them define both words. The answers are shown.

| Homophone Pairs |
| --- |
| board, bored |
| would, wood |
| whole, hole |
| flour, flower |
| groan, grown |
| know, no |
| fore, four |
| lone, loan |
| poll, pole |
| foul, fowl |

# The Great Underwater Escape

Harry Houdini (1874–1926) was a famous magician and escape artist. He could free himself from **ANYTHING**. But what would happen when he was locked inside a tank of water?

HOUDINI'S DEATH-DEFYING MYSTERY
ESCAPE FROM A GALVANIZED IRON CAN FILLED WITH WATER AND SECURED BY MASSIVE LOCKS.

47

LESSON **33**
## The Great Underwater Escape
*Water*, pages 47–52

### SUMMARY
This **radio play** tells about Houdini's "Water Torture" escape. Special features about Houdini and his death follow the radio play.

### COMPREHENSION STRATEGIES
Making Connections
Monitor Understanding

### WRITING
Notes for Visualizing

### VOCABULARY
Multiple Meanings

### PHONICS/WORD STUDY
Long and Short *o* Compound Words

### Lesson Vocabulary
| | |
|---|---|
| daring | padlocks |
| slick | suspense |

### MATERIALS
*Water*, pp. 47–52
*Student Journal*, pp. 106–108
*Word Study Manual*, p. 66
*Writing Advantage*, pp. 30–55

# Before Reading
*WHOLE CLASS* Use one or more activities.

## Make an Association Web

Tell students they are going to read about Harry Houdini, a great magician. Then start an association web about magicians. Record students' ideas. Ask:

• What do you know about magicians?

• What kinds of tricks do magicians do?

Revisit the web after reading the play.

magician

## Vocabulary Preview

Review the vocabulary list with students. Have students begin *Student Journal* page 106. After reading, students can adjust their definitions and answer the questions.

## Preview the Selection

Have students look through the four pages of the radio play. Discuss students' observations.

## Make Predictions/ Set Purpose

Students should use the information they gathered in previewing the selection to make predictions about what they will learn. If students have trouble generating a purpose for reading, suggest that they read to learn why Houdini is still regarded as having been one of the world's greatest magicians. (See Differentiated Instruction.)

*Harry Houdini made newspaper headlines many times from about 1900 until his death in 1926. He was known worldwide as the "Handcuff King." He could pick locks and slip out of handcuffs as if they were rubber bands.*

*Houdini became famous for his courage and <u>daring</u>. No one ever figured out the secret of his tricks. Some people believed that Houdini's escapes weren't tricks. These people believed that it was the work of a superhuman person.*

*Houdini announced that he would attempt a "Water Torture" escape. This radio play is about that event.*

# Characters

| | | |
|---|---|---|
| **Narrator** | **Reporter** | **Bess (Houdini's wife)** |
| **Citizen 1** | **Manager** | **Houdini** |
| **Citizen 2** | **Announcer** | |

## Scene 1

**Narrator:** It is the early 1900s. People gather in line outside a theater. Many have been waiting for hours. They want to get good seats. A reporter is one of the crowd. The reporter wants to hear what people have to say. *(sound of voices talking softly in background, then cut)*

**Citizen 1:** We have been in this line for hours. It's a good thing that the weather is nice. I would hate to be standing in the rain.

**Citizen 2:** Rain or shine, I would be here. I wouldn't miss the chance to see the Great Houdini in person.

**Citizen 1:** He's really something. Why, he even made an elephant disappear! I saw it with my own eyes. How does he do that?

**Citizen 2:** I don't know. One time they tied him up with chains and locks. They put him in a box. Then they locked the box. He was out in no time!

**Citizen 1:** He must have a twin or a good look-alike.

**Citizen 2:** No. We know that's not true. He's <u>slick</u>, all right.

**Reporter:** Yeah, he's good. Quite skillful. I once covered a story out west. Houdini challenged the local police to handcuff him. They stripped him naked to make sure he wasn't hiding any keys! He got free.

**Citizen 2:** I think he has trained himself to do things that no other human can do. I heard that he swallows keys. Then he brings them back up. That's how he unlocks the locks to get free.

48

---

### Student Journal page 106

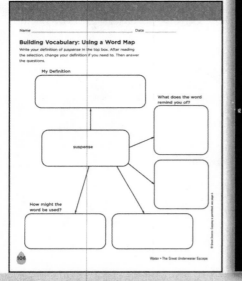

---

# During Reading

## Comprehension

SMALL GROUP

MAKING CONNECTIONS

Use these questions to model making connections with the text. Then have students share connections they have made.

- What do I already know about this topic?

- What have I read about or seen before that this reminds me of?

- How does my experience help me understand this selection?

## Teacher Think Aloud

*I have seen magicians perform on television, but I have never been to a live show. It must be really exciting to be in the audience. Today's magicians make use of lighting, music, and technology; Houdini's shows were more basic. I have read other things about him, though, and his tricks still sound amazing. He had to do everything with just his own strength and smarts.*

## Comprehension

SMALL GROUP

MONITOR UNDERSTANDING

Use these questions to model visualizing. Then have students tell about what they visualized.

- What do I picture in my mind as I read?

- Which details help me create this image in my mind?

- How does visualizing help me understand what I am reading?

(See Differentiated Instruction.)

**Citizen 1:** He must have some set of throat muscles.

**Reporter:** That's for sure.

**Narrator:** Just then, the theater manager comes out. He opens the doors wide.

**Manager:** Step right in, ladies and gentlemen! Step right in. The show will be starting in ten minutes.
*(sound of feet shuffling, people taking their seats, whispering, throat clearing, and excited chatter)*

## Scene 2

**Narrator:** The audience is seated and the show begins. It is a variety show with many different acts. There are songs, dances, and comedy skits. Then a single spotlight shines on the announcer.
*(sound of drumroll and cymbals striking)*

**Announcer:** Now we come to the moment you have all been waiting for, ladies and gentlemen. The Great Houdini will attempt his most daring escape! History will be made today if Houdini is successful.
*(sound of drumroll again)*

**Announcer:** Ladies and gentlemen, here is Houdini's lovely wife, Bess.
*(sound of cheering and clapping)*

**Bess:** Thank you, thank you. You know, Houdini is the world's greatest escape artist. But tonight he will attempt an escape that has never been done before. We are going to lock him in a big tank of water. If he can't get out quickly, he will die from lack of air.
*(sound of audience gasping)*

**Narrator:** The lights dim and the audience quiets down. Then the curtain goes up and a spotlight shines on Houdini standing there.
*(sound of cheers and applause)*

**Harry Houdini in handcuffs and shackles**

49

### DIFFERENTIATED INSTRUCTION — SMALL GROUP

## Comprehension

MONITOR UNDERSTANDING

To help students visualize the play, follow these steps:

1. Have students close their eyes as you read aloud the narrator's lines on page 50.

2. Try to capture the suspense as the narrator says things like, "Another minute passes. The audience is worried. How long can a person hold his breath underwater?"

3. Discuss the details that helped students picture what the narrator described.

## Teacher Think Aloud

*When I read what the narrator says on page 48, I can picture the scene in my mind. It's the early 1900s, so I see people in old-fashioned clothes. The people have been waiting in line for hours. I picture the people as restless but excited. I have seen reporters interviewing people, so that is easy to picture. I don't think this reporter would have had a microphone, though.*

## Fix-Up Strategies

Offer these strategies to help students read independently.

**If you don't understand what you're reading:**

• Reread the difficult section to look for clues to help you comprehend.

• Read ahead to find clues to help you comprehend.

• Retell, or say in your own words, what you've read.

• Visualize, or form mental pictures of, what you've read.

**If you don't understand a word:**

• Reread the sentence. Look for ideas and words that provide meaning clues.

• Find clues by reading a few sentences before and after the confusing word.

• Look for the base or root word and think about its meaning.

• Think about the topic or plot at this point to see if either offers meaning clues.

**Narrator:** Houdini bows to the audience. Then two men roll out a large can. The can is filled with water. Houdini climbs into the can of water. He squeezes himself into the can. Then men pour in more water. They make sure that Houdini is totally underwater. Next, they quickly close the can and lock it with six padlocks. The men put a screen in front of the can.

**Citizen 1:** My stomach is in a knot. I don't like this one bit.

**Citizen 2:** How long do you think Houdini can stay underwater without breathing? *(sound of people squirming in their seats)*

**Reporter:** I'm going to see how long I can hold my breath.

**Narrator:** The reporter holds his breath. He exhales after about twenty seconds and starts to pant.

**Reporter:** Now I'm really worried for Houdini.

**Bess:** It's been one minute, and there is no sign of Houdini. *(sound of the audience moving about in their seats)*

**Narrator:** Another minute passes. The audience is worried. How long can a person hold his breath underwater?

**Citizen 1:** Houdini must be dead by now!

**Citizen 2:** Oh, I can't take this anymore! *(sound of people crying; others are shouting "Help him!" and "Get him out!")*

**Bess:** *(shouting)* It has been three minutes! Please break him out!

**Narrator:** The crowd is screaming. Bess pulls away the screen. Houdini is standing there, safe! *(sounds of screaming and clapping)*

**50**

**Narrator:** The crowd goes crazy. They are on their feet. They are shouting and clapping. After the show, the newspaper reporter visits Houdini backstage.

**Reporter:** I have seen all your acts. But this one even scared me. I was sure you were drowned. You really are amazing!

**Houdini:** I'll tell you a secret, but it must be off the record.

**Reporter:** I promise not to reveal it.

**Houdini:** I got out of the can in thirty seconds.

**Reporter:** But you didn't come out from behind the screen. Why didn't you?

**Houdini:** I was building the suspense so that everyone would wonder whether I was alive.

**Reporter:** Wow, you really know how to put on a show!

**Student Journal page 107**

Name _____ Date _____

**Writing: Notes for Visualizing**
Which part of the play were you able to visualize best? Describe it below. Use as many details as you can from the text. Then draw a picture of how you imagined that part in your mind.

The part I could visualize best was _____

Some details I "saw" in my mind include _____

Now draw what you visualized.

Water • The Great Underwater Escape        **107**

# After Reading

Use one or more activities.

## Check Purpose

Have students decide if their purpose was met. Did they learn why Houdini is still regarded as having been one of the world's greatest magicians?

## Discussion Questions

Continue the group discussion with the following questions.

1. What did you think of the radio play? (Making Connections)

2. What effect did Houdini's being trapped in the water tank have on you? (Cause-Effect)

3. What kind of person was Houdini? What characteristics did he have? (Inferential Thinking)

## Revisit: Association Web

Revisit the association web about magicians that you started in Before Reading. What new information can students add?

## Revisit: Word Map

Have students review their word maps on *Student Journal* page 106. Students can adjust their answers to the questions, using the information they learned in the play.

## Houdini's Secret

No one knows the exact date when Houdini tried his water trick. But we know that the water trick had a secret. The secret was that the neck of the can was separate from the body. Houdini had to use great effort and pressure to lift up the neck from the inside. Then he could step out of the can. He wouldn't even have to touch the padlocks that fastened the lid down. He would simply fit the neck back on the can and be ready to greet his audience.

Still, the water trick had its dangers. The neck could become jammed at any time. Even other magicians who may have guessed the secret were unwilling to give it a try. The trick required great skill in moving and twisting the body.

## Practice Makes Perfect

Houdini worked hard onstage. But he worked even harder offstage! He practiced and practiced and practiced.

Much of Houdini's success depended on tiny picklocks. Most often, they were hidden between his teeth and worked by his tongue. Still, having a pick did not make his escapes that much easier. He had to use his muscles and his fingers and toes. No other performer has ever matched Houdini's skill and showmanship.

Harry Houdini at his desk (1925)

Harry Houdini hangs upside down from a crane after freeing himself from a straitjacket (1916).

51

**DIFFERENTIATED INSTRUCTION**

## Vocabulary

## Multiple Meanings

To help students with the vocabulary, use the steps below:

1. Explain that a word with multiple meanings is a word that can have more than one meaning. You swing a *bat*. A *bat* lives in a cave.

2. Point out the word *shine* on page 48. Discuss the two meanings of the word.

3. Now have students look through the play to find other words with multiple meanings. Make a list and have volunteers create oral sentences to convey each meaning of a listed word.

### Student Journal page 108

Name _____  Date _____

**Building Vocabulary: Words with Multiple Meanings**
Write two definitions for each word below.

| Word | First Definition | Second Definition |
|------|------------------|-------------------|
| slick | smart, clever, or tricky | smooth, glossy, or oily |
| tank | | |
| locks | | |
| bands | | |
| line | | |

108    Water • The Great Underwater Escape

## Writing Notes for Visualizing

Ask students which part of the play they were able to visualize best. Encourage students to use as many details from the text as they can to picture that part in their minds. Then have students write a description of that scene and draw it on the visualizing activity on *Student Journal* page 107.

## Vocabulary Multiple Meanings

Display the word *slick*. Mention that in the play, *slick* means "smart, clever, or tricky." Explain that *slick* also refers to something that is "smooth, glossy, or slippery." Ask students to identify other words with multiple meanings, and display them. Then have partners complete the chart on *Student Journal* page 108. (See Differentiated Instruction.)

## Phonics/Word Study

## Compound Words

Display *homeroom* and *doorknob*. Ask students what the words have in common. (Each word is made up of two related words.) Ask what the relationship is between the two words that make up each compound. For example, a *homeroom* is a room that acts as your "home" at school. Now, work with students to complete the in-depth compound word activity on TE page 257.

## Houdini's Death

In a 1957 movie about Houdini, the Houdini character died during an underwater escape. However, this was not true. Houdini died from peritonitis (pear ih tun EYE tis), which is an infection of the lining of the abdomen. A ruptured appendix caused the infection. Houdini died in Grace Hospital in Detroit, Michigan. The date was October 31, 1926.

52

### Long and Short *o* Compound Words

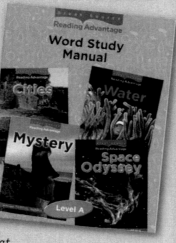

▶ Display the words *lifeboat*, *doghouse*, and *birthstone*.

▶ Ask students what the words have in common. Students should recognize that each word is actually made up of two related words. *Lifeboat* names a boat that is used for saving lives. *Doghouse* names a shelter for dogs. *Birthstone* names a precious stone associated with the month of a birth. Compound words always have a meaning connection.

▶ Provide students with a list of compound words they can read and take apart. (*Birthstone* becomes *birth + stone*.) Have students work in pairs to decide whether each short and long *o* word falls into a typical short or long vowel pattern. Do not hold students responsible for parts of words that are not in the short or long *o* family.

| Long and Short *o*: Compound Words |
| --- |
| 1. foothold |
| 2. someone |
| 3. bedrock |
| 4. homeroom |
| 5. snowplow |
| 6. undergrowth |
| 7. blacktop |
| 8. seacoast |
| 9. overflow |
| 10. workout |

For a more extensive list of compound words, see *Word Study Manual* page 66. For more information on word sorts and spelling stages, see pages 5–31 in the *Word Study Manual*.

# Focus on . . .

Use one or more activities in this section to focus on a particular area of need in your students.

## Comprehension  STRATEGY SUPPORT  INDEPENDENT

To help those students who need more practice using the strategies covered in this lesson, work one-on-one or in small groups to apply the strategy prompts below. Apply the prompts to a *Reading Advantage* paperback, a classroom library book, or a new or familiar selection in the magazine. Always model your own thinking first.

### Making Connections

• What does this story (article, passage) remind me of?

• What do I already know about this topic?

• Where have I heard about this topic before?

• What do I have in common with the characters, people, or situations in the text?

• What other books, stories, articles, movies, or TV shows does this text make me think about?

### Monitor Understanding

• Do I understand what I'm reading? If not, what part is confusing to me?

• What fix-up strategies can I use to solve the problem? (See During Reading for fix-up strategies.)

• Why did a character say (do, think, ask) that?

• What images do I visualize from the text? What parts can't I visualize?

• Why did the author include (or not include) those details?

## Writing **Diary Entry**  INDEPENDENT

Ask students to imagine what Houdini might have written in a diary entry the night before his water trick. What was he thinking? Was he afraid of anything? Was there someone in the audience he really wanted to impress? Have students use in their entries details that they learned from the radio play. Also encourage students to use specific nouns, sensory details, and strong verbs in their writing.

For additional instruction on using specific nouns, sensory details, and strong verbs, see the lessons in *Writing Advantage*, pages 30–55.

## Fluency: Punctuation

After students have read the entire play at least once, they can use a portion of it to practice fluent reading. Have them first read silently to familiarize themselves with the text. Have students work in small groups to read one of the scenes of the play.

As you listen to students, use these prompts to guide them.

▶ Read expressively. Put yourself in the place of the character. Think about how that character feels. Read to show that emotion. This is especially important in a radio play, since listeners can't see you.

▶ Pay attention to punctuation. Pause at commas and end marks. Think about how your voice should change when you see question marks and exclamation points.

When students read aloud, do they—

✓ demonstrate appropriate meaning and usage of punctuation marks?

✓ incorporate appropriate timing, stress, and intonation?

✓ exhibit well-timed pauses between words and phrases?

## English Language Learners

To support students as they develop their oral fluency, have small groups read "The Great Underwater Escape" aloud.

1. Divide students into small groups.
2. Assign each group member a different role in the play.
3. Have small groups practice reading portions of the play aloud with fluency and expression.

## Independent Activity Options

While you work with individuals or small groups, others can work independently on one or more of the following options.

▶ Level A paperback books, see TE pages 371–376
▶ Level A *eZines*
▶ Repeat word sorts from this lesson
▶ *Student Journal* pages for this lesson
▶ *Writing Advantage* independent lessons

# Assessment

## Strategy Assessment

To help you and your students assess their use of comprehension strategies, ask the following questions. Students can complete a written response or provide verbal answers in a one-on-one reading conference.

1. **Making Connections** Do you think people today would enjoy seeing a show like Houdini's? Why or why not? (Answers will vary. Some students may feel that it would be scarier because there were no special effects, just Houdini and his attempts to escape from tight places. Others might say it would be boring for the same reason.)

2. **Monitor Understanding** What phrases from the play created strong mental images for you? Skim the text to find examples. (Answers will vary.)

For ongoing informal assessment, use the checklists on pages 61–64 of *Level A Assessment*.

## Word Study Assessment

Use these steps to help you and your students assess their understanding of long and short *o* compound words.

1. On the board or on paper to hand out, create a chart like the one shown below.

2. Ask students to match related words from both lists to create compound words.

3. Then have students tell whether each *o* within a compound is a long or short *o*. (Answers: *grasshopper*, short *o*; *homemade*, long *o*; *railroad*, long *o*; *overcoat*, long *o* (two); *softball*, short *o*; *bookshelf*, short *o*.)

| List A | List B |
|--------|--------|
| grass | ball |
| home | shelf |
| rail | made |
| over | hopper |
| soft | road |
| book | coat |

Reading Advantage

**Level A Assessment**

# Oil & Water

Two Points of View

> We need water to live. We need oil to make our lives better and more comfortable. So what is the problem?

We use a lot of oil. We use it to run our cars and other machines. We use it to make paints and medicines. We use it to make plastic. And you know how many things in our world are made of plastic!

Only half the oil we use today is produced in the United States. We buy the other half from other countries. And we pay a lot for that oil.

Many people think we should drill for oil at sea. Yet others think this is a bad idea. Two essays express these different points of view.

**53**

### SUMMARY
These **essays** express two different points of view about drilling for oil in oceans.

### COMPREHENSION STRATEGIES
Determining Importance

### WRITING
Points of View

### VOCABULARY
Multiple Meanings

### PHONICS/WORD STUDY
Sorting across Vowels

### Lesson Vocabulary
platform
fumes

### MATERIALS
*Water,* pp. 53–55
*Student Journal,* pp. 109–111
*Word Study Manual,* p. 67
*Writing Advantage,* pp. 113–151

# Before Reading

**WHOLE CLASS** Use one or more activities.

## Make a List
Discuss with students how oil is an important natural resource. Begin a quick list of things that oil is used for. Point out the following facts.

- Another name for crude oil is *petroleum.*
- Petroleum can also be found in medicines, plastics, fertilizers, and explosives.

Revisit the list after the selection is read.

## Vocabulary Preview
Review the vocabulary list with students. Clarify pronunciations. Ask volunteers to tell what they know about the two words. Then have students begin the word web on *Student Journal* page 109. They will complete the web after reading the selection.

## Preview the Selection
Have students skim the essays. Discuss their observations. Ask students what they think *point of view* means.

## Make Predictions/ Set Purpose
Students should use the information they gathered in previewing the selection to make predictions about what they will learn. If students have trouble generating a purpose for reading, suggest that they read to explore two points of view about drilling for oil in the ocean.

## Comprehension
DETERMINING IMPORTANCE

Help students determine the importance of ideas in opinion pieces by applying these guidelines.

- The first paragraph states the most important, or big, ideas.
- The middle paragraphs contain details that support the big ideas.
- The conclusion, usually one or two paragraphs, restates the big ideas.

**Student Journal page 109**

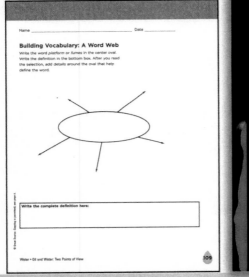

### Drilling at Sea: We Need the Oil

The United States needs more oil. We should not have to depend on buying so much oil from other countries. We need to do more offshore drilling to get the oil we need.

To drill an offshore well means drilling a <u>platform</u> into the ocean. Then the platform is attached to the seabed. These platforms are called oil rigs. Once the rigs are in place, a wide, shallow hole is drilled into the ocean floor. The hole is about 100 feet deep. This hole is filled with a casting and equipment to prevent blowouts. Then the drills are sent deeper into the ocean floor. The oil is removed through a long tube. The oil that is pumped from these rigs is shipped to many places in the United States.

Several big oil companies have oil rigs. There are some off the coast of Alaska and in the Gulf of Mexico. The rigs take oil from under the sea.

But we need many more oil rigs. These offshore rigs do not harm the environment. There have been a few oil spills over the years. But these spills were cleaned up quickly. Some fish or plants have died, but most fish and plants are doing well.

The people who work on the rigs are well trained. They know what to do in an emergency, such as a fire. The rigs themselves have special skimmers. The skimmers can collect any oil leaks or wastes before they reach the sea.

Most important of all is the cost. The more oil we take from the sea ourselves, the less we will have to buy from other countries.

Anyone can see that the benefits of offshore drilling far outweigh the risks.

**Drilling**

Blowouts are explosions from the drilling hole that throw out oil, drilling mud, pipes, and rocks into the air. Blowouts can happen when pressure builds up underground. Equipment called blowout preventers (BOPs) controls the underground well pressures and fluids during drilling.

54

# During Reading

## Comprehension
DETERMINING IMPORTANCE SMALL GROUP

Use these questions to model how to determine the most important ideas in the feature titled "Exxon Valdez," on page 55. Then have students state the most important ideas in the feature "Drilling" on page 54.

- What are the most important ideas in this feature?
- How can I support my beliefs?

(See Differentiated Instruction.)

## Teacher Think Aloud

*This feature talks mainly about the oil spilled from the tanker Exxon Valdez. I think these are the most important ideas: cleaning up the spill was very expensive, it took a long time, and many animals died. These are the facts that support my beliefs: it took two billion dollars and four months to clean up, and over 250,000 animals died.*

## Fix-Up Strategies

Offer these strategies to help students read independently.

**If you don't understand what you're reading:**

- Reread the difficult section to look for clues to help you comprehend.
- Read ahead to find clues to help you comprehend.
- Retell, or say in your own words, what you've read.
- Visualize, or form mental pictures of, what you've read.

### Drilling at Sea: Too Dangerous

The oil companies want us to believe that we need to drill for oil at sea. They want us to drill, drill, and drill for our energy. But I believe that isn't the only way to go. And I'm concerned about what it will do to our seas.

Some of these oil companies do not have enough rules in place to keep the environment safe. They also don't have enough safety measures to keep the people who work on the oil rigs safe.

There have been harmful oil spills. These spills kill plants and animals that live in the sea. If oil gets on birds' feathers, the birds cannot fly. If the birds eat the oil, they may die or become sick and cannot search for food. A mammal's fur keeps it warm. But if oil gets on its fur, the animal can get too cold and die.

You can feel the effects of an oil spill at the beach. You might find globs of oil when you wade in the water. That is neither a pleasant sight nor a pleasant smell. And it's not healthy!

Sometimes fire breaks out on an oil rig. The smoky <u>fumes</u> cause air pollution. Sometimes workers are hurt or killed on the job.

It's true we need a lot of energy to keep our machines running and to make goods. But oil should not be the only source of energy we use. Why can't we find better ways of getting energy from the sun and the wind instead of oil? Let's hope that in the future we will use other ways to get energy. Let's be sure to keep our waters clean and our sea animals and plants safe. ◆

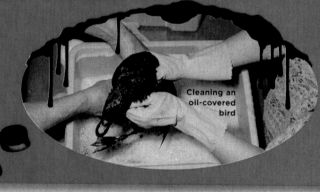

Cleaning an oil-covered bird

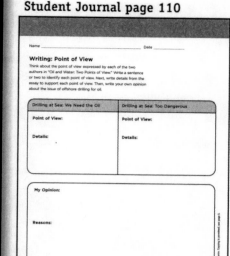

### Exxon Valdez

A big accident happened on March 24, 1989. The huge oil tanker *Exxon Valdez* was loaded with eleven tanks of oil. It ran aground off the coast of Alaska. Over ten million gallons of oil spilled into Prince Edward Sound. That's enough oil to fill 125 large swimming pools!

It took four summers to clean up the mess. The cleanup cost over two billion dollars. No one knows for sure how many animals died. The best guess is the following:

- 250,000 seabirds
- 2,800 sea otters
- 300 harbor seals
- 250 bald eagles
- 22 killer whales
- countless salmon and herring eggs

There was a huge oil spill from a tanker off the coast of Spain in 2002. The ship broke in half while at sea. The total effects of this spill have yet to be discovered. However, as a result of this accident, new regulations may require ships to be built in ways that will prevent this type of accident.

**55**

## Student Journal page 110

Name _____  Date _____

**Writing: Point of View**

Think about the point of view expressed by each of the two authors in "Oil and Water: Two Points of View." Write a sentence or two to identify each point of view. Next, write details from the essay to support each point of view. Then, write your own opinion about the issue of offshore drilling for oil.

| Drilling at Sea: We Need the Oil | Drilling at Sea: Too Dangerous |
|---|---|
| Point of View: | Point of View: |
| Details: | Details: |

| My Opinion: |
|---|
| Reasons: |

110    Water • Oil and Water: Two Points of View

## Student Journal page 111

Name _____  Date _____

**Building Vocabulary: Words with Multiple Meanings**

Write two definitions for each word below.

| Word | First Definition | Second Definition |
|---|---|---|
| fumes | irritating gases | lets off one's rage |
| platform | | |
| drill | | |
| place | | |
| rigs | | |

Water • Oil and Water: Two Points of View    111

# After Reading
*WHOLE CLASS* Use one or more activities.

## Check Purpose

Have students decide if their purpose was met.

## Discussion Questions

Continue the group discussion with the following question: *How did each author's choice of words affect how you felt about his or her opinion?* (Compare-Contrast)

## Revisit: Word Web

Have students complete the word web on *Student Journal* page 109.

## Writing Points of View

Have students briefly discuss the two viewpoints expressed by the authors. Then have students complete the activity on *Student Journal* page 110.

## Vocabulary Multiple Meanings

Display the word *fumes*. Explain that *fumes* are irritating gases that are not healthy to breathe. *Fumes* can also be a verb meaning "lets off one's rage." Have partners complete the chart on *Student Journal* page 111.

## Phonics/Word Study

### Sorting across Vowels

Write *stride* and *high* on the board. Ask students whether each word has a long or short *i*. (long i) Then challenge students to give the long vowel pattern for each word. (iCe, igh) Repeat the process with *stroll* and *float*. (oCC, oa) Now, work with students to complete the in-depth sorting across vowels activity on TE page 262.

# Phonics/Word Study

## Sorting across Vowels

To review the most common long vowel patterns within the last two vowel families that students have studied (*i* and *o*), set up a straightforward sort such as the one below. Note that no oddballs are included to confuse students. The emphasis should be that each vowel pattern is not exclusive—thinking about patterns across different vowels is helpful.

▶ Using the Long *i* and *o*: Cumulative Sort sheet, have students review the vowel patterns they have studied for the two vowel sounds. (See *Word Study Manual* page 67.)

▶ As always, speed and accuracy are the goals.

| Long *i* and *o*: Cumulative Sort | | | | | | | | |
|------|------|------|------|------|------|------|------|------|
| *iCe* | *y* | *iCC* | *igh* | *oCC* | *ost* | *oCe* | *oa* | *ow* |
| hike | try | mind | might | roll | ghost | tone | toad | blow |
| stride | fly | climb | high | stroll | most | stove | float | stow |
| tine | | | | | | | | |

For more information on word sorts and spelling stages, see pages 5–31 in the *Word Study Manual*.

# Focus on . . .

Use one or more activities in this section to focus on a particular area of need in your students.

## Comprehension  STRATEGY SUPPORT  INDEPENDENT

To help those students who need more practice using the strategies covered in this lesson, work one-on-one or in small groups to apply the strategy prompts below. Apply the prompts to a *Reading Advantage* paperback, a classroom library book, or a new or familiar selection in the magazine. Always model your own thinking first.

### Determining Importance

- What is the most important idea in the paragraph? How can I prove it?
- Which details are unimportant? Why?
- What does the author want me to understand?
- Why is this information important (or not important) to me?

## Writing Letter to the Editor  INDEPENDENT

Explain to students that people write letters expressing their views to the editor of a newspaper. If possible, show students some letters to the editor. Ask students to draft a letter on the topic of oil to the editor of their local paper. Are students for or against ocean drilling? Why or why not? Students can use the following guide to draft their letters.

| My opinion: |
|---|
| **Three reasons that support my opinion:** |
| **My opinion rephrased:** |

If students are interested, help them finalize and send their letters to the local paper.

For additional instruction on expository writing structures, see the lessons in *Writing Advantage*, pages 113–151.

## Fluency: Pacing

After they have read the article at least once, have students read aloud the *"Exxon Valdez"* feature on page 55 of the selection. Remind students that reading too quickly or too slowly, or stumbling over words makes it difficult for listeners to understand the content. Suggest that students preview the text to troubleshoot for unfamiliar words and to practice natural-sounding phrasing.

As you listen to students read, use these prompts to guide them.

▶ Read at a smooth and even pace.

▶ Pause at the end of each bulleted statistic. This will make your reading sound strong and convincing.

When students read aloud, do they—

✓ demonstrate a smooth pace, not too fast or too slow?

✓ incorporate well-timed pauses between words and phrases?

✓ reflect an awareness and understanding of punctuation?

## English Language Learners

To support students as they determine the importance of ideas in "Oil & Water," extend the comprehension activity on TE page 260.

1. Have students brainstorm a list of important ideas from the selection.

2. Have partners create a page that includes one important idea and an illustration representing the idea.

3. Compile all of the students' pages to create a class book.

## Independent Activity Options

While you work with individuals or small groups, others can work independently on one or more of the following options.

▶ Level A paperback books, see TE pages 371–376

▶ Level A *eZines*

▶ Repeat word sorts from this lesson

▶ *Student Journal* pages for this lesson

▶ *Writing Advantage* independent lessons

# Assessment

## Strategy Assessment

To help you and your students assess their use of comprehension strategies, ask the following questions. Students can complete a written response or provide verbal answers in a one-on-one reading conference.

- **Determining Importance** What are the most important ideas in each essay? (Student responses should be similar to these. Page 54: We need to depend less on buying oil from other countries. The benefits of offshore drilling outweigh the risks. Page 55: Oil spills will continue to occur, and are harmful to sea life and the environment. We should get our energy from other means.) As necessary, refer students to the guidelines in Differentiated Instruction on page 260.

For ongoing informal assessment, use the checklists on pages 61–64 of *Level A Assessment*.

## Word Study Assessment

Use these steps to help you and your students assess their understanding of sorting across vowels.

1. On the board or on paper to hand out, copy the chart shown below, mixing up the vowel patterns.

2. Ask students to match each long *i* or long *o* word to the correct vowel pattern. The answers are shown.

| Word | Vowel Pattern |
|------|---------------|
| flow | *ow* |
| sight | *igh* |
| soak | *oa* |
| like | *iCe* |
| dose | *oCe* |
| pry | *y* |
| toll | *oCC* |
| post | *ost* |
| find | *iCC* |

Great Source
**Reading Advantage**

**Level A Assessment**

# Uncle Toad Saves the World and Water, Water . . .

*Water*, pages 56–61

## SUMMARY

This **porquoi tale** tells about the call of toads. A short **question-answer feature** about oceans follows.

## COMPREHENSION STRATEGIES

Understanding Text Structure
Making Connections

## WRITING

Summary

## VOCABULARY

Prefixes

## PHONICS/WORD STUDY

Short and Long *u* Patterns

### Lesson Vocabulary

| | |
|---|---|
| lowly | vapor |
| insignificant | dissolve |
| enraged | |

## MATERIALS

*Water*, pp. 56–61
*Student Journal*, pp. 112–114
*Word Study Manual*, p. 68
*Writing Advantage*, pp. 30–55

# Uncle Toad
## Saves the World

This story is from Vietnam, a country in southeast Asia. In Vietnam, people call an important man "Uncle." It is like calling a man "Sir" in the United States.

Vietnam

56

# Before Reading ⊗ WHOLE CLASS Use one or more activities.

## Make a List

Explain that a porquoi tale explains something in the natural world. Ancient peoples used these tales to explain their environment. Now, have a short discussion about what students know about toads. Then ask students what this porquoi tale might explain about toads. Make a list of students' predictions. Revisit the list after students have finished the tale.

▶ ### What This Tale Might Explain

1. Why toads are ugly
2. Why toads cause warts
3. Why rain can be predicted by a toad's call
4.

## Vocabulary Preview

Review the vocabulary list with students. Clarify pronunciations. Have students think about any times they may have seen or heard the words. Model making associations with the word *lowly* to help students complete the making associations activity on *Student Journal* page 112.

ONCE long ago, the lowly toad was called "Uncle." Everyone used this title. The toad was called "Uncle" even by the great king of the sky. How could an insignificant toad earn the title of "Uncle"?

You see, people long ago thought that a great king ruled the sky. They believed he sent rain to the world. One year, there was no rain. Plants and animals died. People had little to eat. They were very thirsty. They needed rain badly.

One of the animals that needed rain was an ugly old toad. He lived in a garden by a pond. He stayed mostly in the pond when he was young. Now he lived on land. But the land was dry. The pond in the garden was drying out, too.

Toad was very worried. Then he had an idea. He would go to see the king of the sky and ask him to send rain. This was not an easy thing for Toad to do. You see, he was afraid of the great king. But Toad knew he must do something when he saw the dying plants and animals around him.

Toad hopped through the garden. He met some bees. They had no plants from which to get pollen. The bees agreed to go with Toad on his trip to the sky. They flew above Toad as he hopped along the road.

Soon Toad and the bees came to a farm. There they met a rooster who decided to join the trip. In the mountains, they met a tiger. This great animal also decided to come along on the trip.

Together, the animals reached the top of the highest mountain. From there, they jumped from cloud to cloud. At last, they were in the kingdom of the sky.

Toad found the king of the sky sitting on a golden throne. Toad felt very scared. He jumped too close to the king and landed on his lap! This angered the king, so he called his soldiers. He told them, "Kill the ugly toad!"

Toad cried out, "Help!" His friends the bees flew in and stung the soldiers. All the soldiers ran away.

This made the king even angrier. Toad tried to explain why he was there, but the king would not listen. The angry king ordered his drummer to make thunder.

57

### Student Journal page 112

Name _____ Date _____

**Building Vocabulary: Making Associations**
Think about what you already know about the two words listed.
Then answer the following questions for each word.

Word **insignificant**

What do you think about when you read this word? _____

Who might use this word? _____

What do you already know about this word? _____

Word **enraged**

What do you think about when you read this word? _____

Who might use this word? _____

What do you already know about this word? _____

Now watch for these words in the magazine selection. Were you on the right track?

112

Water • Uncle Toad Saves the World and Water, Water, Everywhere

## Preview the Selection

Have students look through the three pages of the article, pages 56–58 in the magazine. Use these or similar prompts to orient students to the article.

• What information does the title give you?

• Read the heading note. What does it tell you?

• Is this text fiction or nonfiction? How do you know?

(See Differentiated Instruction.)

## Teacher Think Aloud

*The title of this selection makes me think right away that it is a story, since a toad couldn't really save the world. I am guessing it's a folktale, because the pictures show different animals and a king sitting on a cloud. Kings and animals often appear in folktales.*

## Make Predictions/ Set Purpose

Students should use the information they gathered in previewing the selection to make predictions about what they will learn. If students have trouble generating a purpose for reading, suggest that they read to experience a Vietnamese porquoi tale.

## DIFFERENTIATED INSTRUCTION

SMALL GROUP

### Comprehension

UNDERSTANDING TEXT STRUCTURE

To help students understand the structure of plot in a folktale or other story, use this activity.

1. Remind students that the plot is the problem the main character has, and the solution is what he or she does to solve the problem.

2. Ask: *What is the problem that Toad has?* (Toad needs to get the king of the sky to send rain.) *How does Toad solve the problem?* (After gaining respect from the king, Toad asks for and is granted rain.)

Toad could not stand the noise. Just then, the rooster flew in and chased the drummer away.

Now the king was even angrier. <u>Enraged</u>, he called in his dog. This animal was bigger and scarier than any dog in the world. But the tiger was even tougher. He rushed in to save Toad.

The king himself became afraid when he saw the tiger. "Stop the tiger, Uncle Toad!" shouted the king. "Do not let him hurt my dog!"

Toad was very pleased to be called "Uncle" by a king. "I do not want to hurt you or your dog," Toad replied. "I just want you to send rain to the world. All the plants and animals are dying. All the people are thirsty and hungry. Please send rain to save us all."

"Ah, I understand," said the king. "Let it rain right now!" Then he turned to Toad and said. "Uncle Toad, you will never have to make this trip again. When you need rain, just make your loud call. I will hear it and send rain."

And that is why the people of Vietnam have a saying: "When the toad makes its loud call, there will soon be rain." ◆

58

### Toads

• Toads are amphibians (am FIB ee unz), which means that the young are born and live in water but spend most of their adult life on land. Toads must keep their bodies wet. They need rain to stay wet.

• Frogs and toads are related, but there are differences. Toads spend more time on land than frogs. Generally, toads are squatter and shorter than frogs.

• Frogs are better jumpers, having stronger back legs. Toads have drier, rougher skin than frogs.

# During Reading

### Comprehension

SMALL GROUP

UNDERSTANDING TEXT STRUCTURE

Use these questions to model for students how to recognize the structure of a folktale. Then have students identify and describe the story elements.

• How do I know that this is a folktale?

• What kind of folktale is it?

(See Differentiated Instruction.)

## Teacher Think Aloud

*I recognize several folktale elements in this story. One is that animals act and talk like people. Another is that things often happen in threes. In this tale, the king tries three ways in which to kill Toad, and three animals save Toad. Finally, some folktales, called porquoi tales, explain things in the natural world. This tale says that the sound a toad makes is a request for rain.*

### Comprehension

SMALL GROUP

MAKING CONNECTIONS

Use these questions to model making connections with the text. Then have students share connections they have made.

• What does this folktale make me think of?

• Does it apply to real-world issues that are a part of present-day life?

# Water, Water, Everywhere

From space, water makes Earth look like a big blue marble.

59

## Teacher Think Aloud

*This folktale is about a period when there was no rain. I know that times like that are called droughts. Today, it seems as though I often read and hear about bad droughts, in both the United States and the rest of the world. Vietnam, where the folktale comes from, has had very bad droughts in the past. It makes sense to me that people there would make up a story like this one.*

## Fix-Up Strategies

Offer these strategies to help students read independently.

**If you don't understand what you're reading:**

- Reread the difficult section to look for clues to help you comprehend.
- Read ahead to find clues to help you comprehend.
- Retell, or say in your own words, what you've read.
- Visualize, or form mental pictures of, what you've read.

**If you don't understand a word:**

- Reread the sentence. Look for ideas and words that provide meaning clues.
- Find clues by reading a few sentences before and after the confusing word.
- Look for the base or root word and think about its meaning.
- Think about the topic or plot at this point to see if either offers meaning clues.

## Short Feature:
## Water, Water, Everywhere

Have students read the short feature silently. Discuss the meanings of the words *vapor* (the gas state of a substance that is solid or liquid at other temperatures) and *dissolve* (to change from a solid to a liquid). Then read the "Water FAQs" and have volunteers read the answers. Ask:

- Which answer added information to what you already knew? How?

- Which answer amazed you the most? Why?

- What new questions do you have?

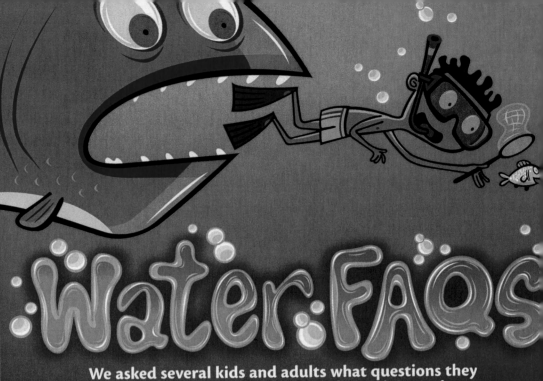

### Student Journal page 113

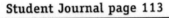

**Writing: Somebody Wanted But So**
Use this chart to help you organize your thoughts for a summary of "Uncle Toad Saves the World."

| | My Notes |
|---|---|
| **Somebody** (an important character) | |
| **Wanted** (a key problem with details) | |
| **But** (conflict for the character) | |
| **So** (an outcome) | |

Now write a summary of the tale.

113

# Water FAQs

We asked several kids and adults what questions they have about water. Here is a sampling of questions and answers. Most of the questions were about oceans.

**Q:** How wet is Earth?

Earth is a watery planet. Water covers about seventy-one percent of Earth's surface. Earth has five oceans: Atlantic, Pacific, Indian, Antarctic, and Arctic. There are also many smaller bodies of water. Because ocean water covers nearly three-quarters of Earth's surface, the planet looks blue when it is viewed from space.

*Water covers 71% of Earth's surface.*

**Q:** How much water is there to drink?

Although Earth has a lot of water on it and in it, very little of that water is fresh drinking water. Almost all the water on Earth, about ninety-seven percent, is salt water. That means that only three percent of all the water on Earth is fresh. However, about two percent of that water is frozen in icecaps and glaciers. Of all the water in the world, only one percent is available as fresh water.

*2% ice* *—1% fresh water* *97% salt water*

60

# After Reading
**WHOLE CLASS** Use one or more activities.

## Check Purpose

Have students decide if their purpose was met. What did students think of the porquoi tale?

## Discussion Questions

Continue the group discussion with the following questions.

1. What other porquoi tales have you read or heard? (Making Connections)

2. What is the problem that Toad tries to solve? (Problem-Solution)

3. What characteristics does Toad have? (Story Elements)

## Revisit: List

Revisit the list started in Before Reading. Were any of the students' ideas close to the topic of the tale? Which idea was closest?

**Q:** How deep are oceans?

**A:** The deepest ocean in the world is the Pacific Ocean. It is over 36,000 feet deep at its deepest point. That's deep enough to cover Mount Everest. But most ocean floors are about 13,000 feet deep.

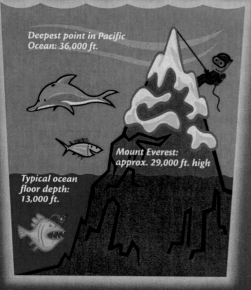

*Deepest point in Pacific Ocean: 36,000 ft.*

*Mount Everest: approx. 29,000 ft. high*

*Typical ocean floor depth: 13,000 ft.*

**Q:** How much water is in the oceans?

**A:** The world's oceans hold a huge amount of water. There is enough water to supply every person on Earth with about 100 billion gallons of water. (The water, however, would be useless for drinking because it is salt water.) This amount does not change because water leaves the ocean as <u>vapor</u>. It eventually returns as rain or snow. The process is called the water cycle.

**Q:** What causes ocean waves?

**A:** Most ocean waves are caused by wind. The stronger the wind, the larger the waves. The largest wave ever recorded was 112 feet high!

**Q:** Why is ocean water salty?

**A:** Ocean salt is a mixture of minerals that <u>dissolve</u> from rocks on land and wash into the sea. These minerals make the water taste salty. They include the salt we use to season our foods. Salt is the reason we don't drink water from the ocean.

**Q:** Is it true that no one can sink in the Dead Sea?

**A:** Yes, it is true. The Dead Sea is between Israel and Jordan. It is ten times saltier than the average ocean. The water is so salty that it is impossible for swimmers to sink. You just lie in it and float like a boat! ◆

61

## DIFFERENTIATED INSTRUCTION
### Vocabulary Prefixes

To give students more experience with identifying prefixes, try the following steps:

1. Display the word *insignificant*. Read the sentence on page 57 where the word appears.

2. Ask: *What do you think the word* insignificant *means?* (not important) *Into what parts can the word be broken?* (in and significant) *What does each part mean?* (*In-* is a prefix that means "not," and *significant* means "having importance.")

3. Then ask students what other words they know that begin with *in-* (inaccurate, invisible, inactive, indecisive, independent)

**Student Journal page 114**

Name _____  Date _____

**Building Vocabulary: Prefix en-**

Write words you know that contain the prefix *en-*. Write a definition for each word. Use a dictionary to help you, if you wish. One answer is given.

*en-* means "in," "into," "make," "make into," "make like"

| Words | Definitions |
| --- | --- |
| 1. enlarge | to make larger |
| 2. | |
| 3. | |
| 4. | |
| 5. | |

114

Water • Uncle Toad Saves the World *and* Water, Water, Everywhere

---

## Writing Summary

"Uncle Toad Saves the World" explains how the call of toads became a request for rain. But it's also a story with a problem and a solution. Have partners discuss the story's problem and solution. Then have students use the somebody-wanted-but-so chart on *Student Journal* page 113 to write a summary of the story.

## Vocabulary Prefixes

Display the word *enraged*. Ask:

- What does the word *enraged,* used on page 58, mean? (to put into a rage; to make very angry)

- What other words do you know that begin with the prefix *en-*?

- What does the prefix *en-* mean? (in or into)

Have students complete the prefix chart on *Student Journal* page 114. (See Differentiated Instruction.)

## Phonics/Word Study
### Short and Long *u* Patterns

Display the following words and read them aloud: *trust*, *rule*, and *true*. Ask students whether the vowel *u* in each word has a long or a short sound. (*trust*, short; *rule* and *true*, long) Have students identify the vowel patterns for *rule* and *true*. (uCe, ue) Now, work with students to complete the in-depth short and long *u* patterns activity on TE page 270.

## Phonics/Word Study

### Introducing Short and Long *u* Patterns

▶ Write the following words on the board: *blue*, *truth*, and *bun*. Tell students that these have sounds of the letter *u*. Both short and long sounds are represented.

▶ Ask students if they can identify which words have a short *u* sound and which have a long *u* sound. Discuss the patterns for each.

▶ Using the Long and Short *u*: Sort One sheet, model the sorting process for students. (See *Word Study Manual* page 68.) Write the headings Short *u*, *uCe*, *ue*, and *Oddball* and the first few words in the appropriate columns.

▶ Introduce the word *truth* and see if students recognize that it has a long vowel sound but a short vowel pattern. Explain how that word requires an additional column in the chart, the Oddball column.

▶ Discuss the sort and what students learned. (So far, there are three long *u* vowel patterns, although one appears to be an oddball.)

▶ Once the model sort is complete, hand out the Long and Short *u*: Sort One sheet. Ask students to cut it up and do the sort on their own or in groups.

▶ Check the final sorts.

| Long and Short *u*: Sort One | | | |
|---|---|---|---|
| Short *u* | *uCe* | Long *ue* | Oddball |
| bun | June | blue | truth |
| trust | rule | true | fuel |
| | tube | due | |
| | flute | flue | |
| | crude | clue | |
| | huge | | |

For more information on word sorts and spelling stages, see pages 5–31 in the *Word Study Manual*.

# Focus on . . .

Use one or more activities in this section to focus on a particular area of need in your students.

## Comprehension  STRATEGY SUPPORT  INDEPENDENT

To help those students who need more practice using the strategies covered in this lesson, work one-on-one or in small groups to apply the strategy prompts below. Apply the prompts to a *Reading Advantage* paperback, a classroom library book, or a new or familiar selection in the magazine. Always model your own thinking first.

### Understanding Text Structure

• What kind of text is this? (book, story, article, guidebook, play, manual)

• How does the author organize the text? (cause-effect, problem-solution, chronological order, description, question-answer, comparison-contrast)

• What details support my thoughts about the text structure?

• What is the cause (effect, problem, solution, order, question, answer)?

• If fiction, who are the characters? What is the setting, plot, conflict, and resolution?

### Making Connections

• What does this story (article, passage) remind me of?

• What do I already know about this topic?

• Where have I heard about this topic before?

• What do I have in common with the characters, people, or situations in the text?

• What other books, stories, articles, movies, or TV shows does this text make me think about?

## Writing Short Porquoi Tale  INDEPENDENT

Have students write their own short porquoi tale about a common pet. Brainstorm "why" questions about pets, for example, *Why do dogs have only one tail?* and *Why did fish get fed up with the desert?* To help students plan their tale, suggest a chart like the one shown.

| Setting | ancient land |
|---|---|
| Main Character(s) | cat |
| Problem-Solution | Why do cats have whiskers? |
| Plot | Cats used to get stuck in narrow places. One cat wove a special hat to wear to help her guess if her body would fit through a passage. |

To help students show rather than tell in their writing, see the lessons in *Writing Advantage*, pages 30–55.

## Fluency: Expression

*SMALL GROUP*

After students have read the tale at least once, have partners take turns rereading the tale to each other. Encourage students to use different voices for different characters to add drama to their retellings.

When students read aloud, do they—
- ✓ reflect an understanding of the text?
- ✓ demonstrate appropriate timing, stress, and intonation?
- ✓ incorporate appropriate speed and phrasing?

## English Language Learners

*SMALL GROUP*

To support students as they learn about text structure on TE page 266, have them make a chart.

1. Have students draw a vertical line to divide a piece of paper in half.
2. Have them label one section "Problem" and one section "Solution."
3. Have students draw and label an illustration showing the problem and solution from "Uncle Toad Saves the World."

## Independent Activity Options

*INDEPENDENT*

While you work with individuals or small groups, others can work independently on one or more of the following options.
- ▶ Level A paperback books, see TE pages 371–376
- ▶ Level A *eZines*
- ▶ Repeat word sorts from this lesson
- ▶ *Student Journal* pages for this lesson
- ▶ *Writing Advantage* independent lessons

# Assessment

## Strategy Assessment

To help you and your students assess their use of comprehension strategies, ask the following questions. Students can complete a written response or provide verbal answers in a one-on-one reading conference.

1. **Understanding Text Structure** Who is the main character in this folktale? Why do you think so? (Students should recognize that Toad is the main character. Some of the reasons are that he sets the events of the story in motion, he plays a role in each part, he resolves the problem, his name is part of the title.)

2. **Making Connections** What did reading this story make you think about? (Answers will vary.)

For ongoing informal assessment, use the checklists on pages 61–64 of *Level A Assessment*.

## Word Study Assessment

Use these steps to help you and your students assess their understanding of short and long *u* patterns.

1. Write the following words on the board or on word cards: *fun, clue, tube, must, flue, fuse, cute, crust, blue.*

2. Ask students to tell which words have a short *u* sound and which have a long *u* sound. Then have them provide the vowel patterns for the words with a long *u* sound. The answers are shown.

| Word | Vowel Pattern |
|------|---------------|
| fun | short *u* |
| clue | long *ue* |
| tube | long *uCe* |
| must | short *u* |
| flue | long *ue* |
| fuse | long *uCe* |
| cute | long *uCe* |
| crust | short *u* |
| blue | long *ue* |

Great
Reading Advantage

**Level A Assessment**

# Like a Fish Out of Water *and* The Mighty Mississippi

*Water,* pages 62–end

## SUMMARY
The main selection is about word play—**idioms** and **riddles**. A **poem** follows.

## COMPREHENSION STRATEGIES
Monitor Understanding

## WRITING
Notes for Visualizing

## VOCABULARY
Synonyms and Antonyms

## PHONICS/WORD STUDY
Long *u* Patterns

## MATERIALS
*Water,* pp. 62–end
*Student Journal,* pp. 115–117
*Word Study Manual,* p. 69
*Writing Advantage,* pp. 30–55

# Like a Fish Out of Water

*I liked my idea, but she threw cold water on it.*
When you throw water on a fire, the fire goes out. Likewise, when someone throws "cold water" on your burning hot idea, the idea fizzles like a dying fire.

*She's like a fish out of water.*
A fish belongs in the water. When a fish is out of the water, it can't breathe or swim. It doesn't know what to do. On land, a fish is definitely out of place. A person can feel out of place, too. For example, a person used to city life would feel out of place in the country and would be like a fish out of water.

**62**

What does the sea say to the sand? *Nothing, it just waves.*

What do you call a frightened skin diver? *Chicken of the sea.*

# Before Reading
**WHOLE CLASS** Use one or more activities.

## Make an Idiom Chart
Remind students that an idiom is a group of words that do not mean exactly what they say. Have students recall the two idioms from "Underwater Hotel." What other idioms do students know?

| Idiom | Meaning |
|---|---|
| It's a piece of cake! | |
| He had a very close shave. | |

## Vocabulary Riddles
In addition to reading idioms in the selection, students will be offered some riddles to solve. Have students complete the riddle-writing activity on *Student Journal* page 115 to show what they know about riddles.

## Preview the Selection
Have students look through the article, pages 62–63 in the magazine. Discuss students' observations.

## Make Predictions/ Set Purpose
Students should use the information they gathered in previewing the selection to make predictions about what they will learn. If students have trouble generating a purpose for reading, suggest that they read to learn about how idioms and riddles work.

**He was as mad as a wet hen.**
Hens don't like to get wet. When they do, they shake their feathers like crazy to get the water off. If you saw a hen shaking like this, you would think that it was in an angry rage!

**Don't be a wet blanket!**
Spread a wet blanket over a fire, and the fire might go out. It's just like throwing cold water on it! If you think something will be great fun, but your friend thinks it will be boring, your friend is a wet blanket. ◆

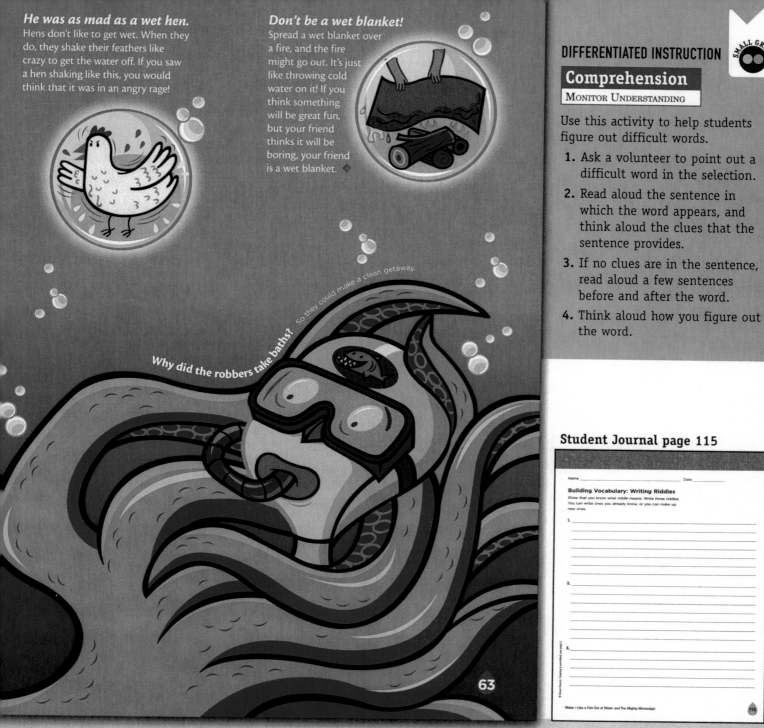

Why did the robbers take baths? So they could make a clean getaway.

63

## Comprehension
MONITOR UNDERSTANDING

Use this activity to help students figure out difficult words.

1. Ask a volunteer to point out a difficult word in the selection.
2. Read aloud the sentence in which the word appears, and think aloud the clues that the sentence provides.
3. If no clues are in the sentence, read aloud a few sentences before and after the word.
4. Think aloud how you figure out the word.

### Student Journal page 115

Name _____ Date _____

**Building Vocabulary: Writing Riddles**
Show that you know what *riddle* means. Write three riddles. You can write ones you already know, or you can make up new ones.

1. _____
2. _____
3. _____

Water • Like a Fish Out of Water and The Mighty Mississippi          115

# During Reading

## Comprehension
MONITOR UNDERSTANDING

SMALL GROUP

Use these questions to model how to figure out difficult words. Then have students identify words that they find difficult. Have students try to resolve their confusion.

- What does the word *fizzles* mean (on page 62)?
- What fix-up strategy can I use to figure it out?

(See Differentiated Instruction.)

## Teacher Think Aloud
*I don't know this word f-i-z-z-l-e-s. The first part looks like fizz. I'll try rereading the sentence to look for clues. I think the word means "slowly disappears," because the text says that "the idea fizzles like a dying fire."*

## Fix-Up Strategies
Offer these strategies to help students read independently.

**If you don't understand what you're reading:**

- Reread the difficult section to look for clues to help you comprehend.
- Read ahead to find clues to help you comprehend.
- Retell, or say in your own words, what you've read.
- Visualize, or form mental pictures of, what you've read.

## Poem:
## The Mighty Mississippi

Introduce the poem, "The Mighty Mississippi." Read aloud the poem and then ask students these questions.

- How do the ideas in the poem connect with what you already know?

- What feelings do you get from the poem?

- Which stanza best helps you visualize the Mississippi River?

### Student Journal pages 116

CREDITS

**Program Authors**
Laura Robb
James F. Baumann
Carol J. Fuhler
Joan Kindig

**Editorial Board**
Avon Cowell
Craig Roney
Jo Worthy

**Project Manager**
Ellen Sternhell

**Magazine Writers**
Janet Cassidy
Jeri Cipriano
Della Cohen
Marc Gave
Meish Goldish
Judith Lechner

**Design and Production**
Preface, Inc.

**Photography**
Cover © Brandon D. Cole/Corbis; inside front cover–1 bkgd © Christian French/Corbis; Inside front cover, l © Ralph A. Clevenger/Corbis; cl © Steve Kaufman/Corbis; c © Kevin Schafer/Corbis; cr © Bettmann/Corbis; r © Brandon D. Cole/Corbis; p. 1l © Bettmann/Corbis; r © Charles O'Rear/Corbis; pp. 2–3 © Ralph A. Clevenger/Corbis; p. 4 © Yann Arthus-Bertrand/Corbis; p. 5 © Galen Rowell/Corbis; pp. 6–7 bkgd © Peter Johnson/Corbis; p. 6l © Corbis; pp. 8–9 © Steve Kaufman/Corbis; p. 10t © Harry Walker/Index Stock; c © Richard T. Nowitz/Corbis; b © Steve Kaufman/Corbis; p. 11t © Keren Su/Corbis; b © Steve Kaufman/Corbis; p. 14t © Ralph A. Clevenger/Corbis; b © David Muench/Corbis; p. 16tl © Biophoto Associates/Photo Researchers, Inc.; tr, bl, cl © Corbis; cr © Robert Estall/Corbis; br © Joe McDonald/Corbis; p. 17tl © Lowell Georgia/Corbis; tc © Charles Krebs/Corbis; tr © Joseph Sohm, ChromoSohm Inc./Corbis; cl © Kevin Schafer/Corbis; cr © Bill Ross/Corbis; bl © Corbis; br © Corbis; p. 18 © David Muench/Corbis; p. 20 © Beth Blis; p. 21 © Bob Krist/Corbis; p. 22 © Richard Hamilton Smith/ Corbis; p. 23 © Joel W. Rogers/Corbis; pp. 27–29 © Bettmann/ Corbis; p. 30t © Ralph White/Corbis; c © AP Photo; b © Bettmann/Corbis; p. 31 © Bettmann/Corbis; p. 32tl © Historical Picture Archive/Corbis; tc © Bettmann/Corbis; tr © Ralph White/Corbis; bl © Corbis; cr © Polak Matthew Corbis SYGMA; br © Ralph White/Corbis; p. 33t © Craig Lovell/Corbis; b © Tiziana and Gianni Baldizzone/ Corbis; p. 34t © Darren Maybury; Eye Ubiquitous/Corbis; bl, br © Kevin R. Morris/Corbis; p. 35t © Buddy Mays/ Corbis; b © Dennis Degnan/Corbis; p. 36l © Morton Beebe/ Corbis; r © Rose Hartman/Corbis; p. 38 © Brandon D. Cole/ Corbis; p. 39tr, bkgd © Stephen Frink/Corbis; cl © Australian Picture Library/Corbis; cr © Japack Company/Corbis; bl © Darrell Gulin/Corbis; pp. 47, 49 © Bettmann/Corbis; p. 50 © Corbis; pp. 51–52 © Bettmann/ Corbis; p. 54 © Charles O'Rear/Corbis; p. 55t © Roy Corral/ Corbis; b © Chinch Gryniewicz, Ecoscene/Corbis; p. 58 © Kit Kittle/Corbis; pp. 64–Inside back cover © Jim Richardson/Corbis

**Illustration**
P. 1l George Toomer; c LeUyen Pham; r Jim Paillot; pp. 8–11 Preface, Inc.; pp. 12–13 John Coulter; pp. 14–15 Preface, Inc.; p. 19 Allen Garns; pp. 20–23 Preface, Inc.; pp. 24–27 John Patrick; p. 31 Preface, Inc.; pp. 33–36 Stan Fellows; p. 37 Allen Garns; pp. 40–46 George Toomer; pp. 47–48, 54–55 Preface, Inc.; pp. 56–58 LeUyen Pham; p. 58b Preface, Inc.; pp. 59–63 Jim Paillot

64

# The Mighty

The river is a winding road
From northern lake to southern shore.
From ancient days to modern ways,
The river is America's core.
*Roll on, Mighty Mississippi!*

From native tribes so long ago,
The river got its name.
Travelers, trappers, settlers, too,
Later spread its fame.
*Roll on, Mighty Mississippi!*

Pioneers came from eastern land
To farm the rich, dark shore.
The riverbank filled with people
To build new towns galore.
*Roll on, Mighty Mississippi!*

The river became a highway:
Flatboats, keelboats, steamboats, too,
Carried cotton, wheat, and rice,
Passengers, captain, and crew.
*Roll on, Mighty Mississippi!*

Now barges fill the river
Tied together like giant rafts.
A mighty tugboat pushes
These strange, but modern crafts.
*Roll on, Mighty Mississippi!*

The days of the steamboat are over,
But the river still is grand.
The mighty Mississippi keeps flowing
Through the heart of our great land.
*Roll on, Mighty Mississippi forever!*

# After Reading
WHOLE CLASS  Use one or more activities.

## Check Purpose

Have students decide if their purpose was met. What have they learned about how idioms and riddles work?

## Discussion Questions

Continue the group discussion with the following questions.

1. What is similar about all the idioms and riddles? (Draw Conclusions)

2. Which of the riddles did you solve without reading the answer? (Making Connections)

3. What other idioms do you know? (Making Connections.)

## Revisit: Idiom Chart

Revisit the idiom chart started in Before Reading. What other idioms can students add?

# Mississippi

MISSISSIPPI QUEEN

## Vocabulary

### Synonyms and Antonyms

Use these steps to provide practice with synonyms and antonyms.

1. Read each group of word pairs and ask students to identify the pair or pairs that are synonyms: *near, close; happy, glad; in, out; small, little; laugh, cry; speak, talk; first, last; walk, stroll.*

2. Have students identify the pairs in each group that are antonyms: *strong, weak; fast, quick; up, down; dark, light; near, far; tiny, huge.*

3. Turn your role over to volunteers who will create word pairs for other students to identify as synonym or antonym pairs.

### Student Journal page 117

Name _____ Date _____

**Building Vocabulary: Synonym and Antonym Chart**
Write any words you wish in the first column. Think of three other words that are synonyms (similar in meaning) for each word you write. Then think of three words that are antonyms (opposites) for each word. Use a thesaurus to help you.

| Word | Synonyms | Antonyms |
|------|----------|----------|
|      | 1.       | 1.       |
|      | 2.       | 2.       |
|      | 3.       | 3.       |
|      | 1.       | 1.       |
|      | 2.       | 2.       |
|      | 3.       | 3.       |
|      | 1.       | 1.       |
|      | 2.       | 2.       |
|      | 3.       | 3.       |

Water • Like a Fish Out of Water and The Mighty Mississippi

117

## Writing Notes for Visualizing

Remind students that active readers visualize, or try to "see," what they are reading about. Have students complete the visualizing activity on *Student Journal* page 116, so students can have an opportunity to both write and draw what they "saw" when they read one of the two riddles on page 62.

## Vocabulary

### Synonyms and Antonyms

Display these word pairs: *boring, amusing; angry, enraged; frightened, terrified.* The first word in each pair appears in the magazine selection. Ask students if each pair is an example of synonyms (similar meanings) or antonyms (opposite meanings). Have students suggest other synonym pairs and antonym pairs. Then have partners complete the chart on *Student Journal* page 117. (See Differentiated Instruction.)

## Phonics/Word Study

### Long *u* Patterns

Remind students of the long *u* patterns they learned in the last lesson. Write the words *clue* and *fuse* on the board. Have students give the pattern for each. (*ue* and *uCe*) Then introduce two additional long *u* patterns: *ui* (*suit*) and *ew* (*chew*). Ask students if they can think of other words that fit those patterns. Now, work with students to complete the in-depth long *u* patterns activity on TE page 276.

## Phonics/Word Study

### Long *u* Patterns

▶ Write the following words on the board: *rude*, *fruit*, and *new*. Tell students that these words are also examples of words with the sound of the vowel *u*.

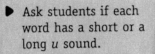

▶ Ask students if each word has a short or a long *u* sound.

▶ Using the Long *u*: Sort Two sheet, model the sorting process for students. (*See Word Study Manual* page 69.) Write the headings *uCe*, *ui*, *ew*, and Oddball and the first few words in the appropriate columns.

▶ Discuss the sort and what students learned.

▶ Once the model sort is complete, hand out the Long *u*: Sort Two sheet. Ask students to cut up the words and do the sort on their own or in groups. Within that sort, the word *fuel* may puzzle students. See if they can figure out that the word is an oddball and then tell why.

▶ Check the final sorts.

| Long *u*: Sort Two | | | |
|---|---|---|---|
| *uCe* | *ui* | *ew* | Oddball |
| flute | fruit | new | fuel |
| huge | suit | chew | |
| fume | juice | knew | |
| rule | | threw | |
| mule | | drew | |
| chute | | | |

For more information on word sorts and spelling stages, see pages 5–31 in the *Word Study Manual*.

# Focus on . . .

Use one or more activities in this section to focus on a particular area of need in your students.

## Comprehension   STRATEGY SUPPORT   INDEPENDENT

To help those students who need more practice using the strategies covered in this lesson, work one-on-one or in small groups to apply the strategy prompts below. Apply the prompts to a *Reading Advantage* paperback, a classroom library book, or a new or familiar selection in the magazine. Always model your own thinking first.

### Monitor Understanding

- Do I understand what I'm reading? If not, what part is confusing to me?
- What fix-up strategies can I use to solve the problem? (See During Reading for fix-up strategies.)
- Why did a character say (do, think, ask) that?
- What images do I visualize from the text? What parts can't I visualize?
- Why did the author include (or not include) those details?

## Writing Poem   INDEPENDENT

Have students use the poem "The Mighty Mississippi" as the inspiration for their own short poem about a body of water with which they are familiar. Ask volunteers to describe some images they might like to include. Jot down some general ideas on the board. Students can refer to the list for help. Encourage students to think about the tone of their poem before they begin to write.

For additional instruction on using sensory details in writing, see the lessons in *Writing Advantage*, pages 30–55.

## Fluency: Phrasing

After students have read "Like a Fish Out of Water" at least once, have student pairs alternate reading it. Encourage students to think about the author's tone—lighthearted and friendly. Have students use their voices to convey this tone.

As you listen to students read, use these prompts to guide them.

▶ Look for punctuation marks to help you adjust how you read certain sentences. Let your voice rise at the end of a question. Put energy and spirit into exclamations.

▶ Think about how words go together in groups, to help you sound natural as you read.

When students read aloud, do they—

✓ demonstrate quick recognition of words and phrases?

✓ exhibit an understanding of phrasal construction?

✓ incorporate appropriate timing, stress, and intonation?

## English Language Learners

To support students as they learn about idioms in "Like a Fish Out of Water," make a class book of idioms.

1. Make the idioms chart described on TE page 272.
2. Discuss the meaning of each idiom.
3. Have partners draw and label one idiom from the chart.
4. Compile all of the students' work to create a class book and read the book together.

## Independent Activity Options

While you work with individuals or small groups, others can work independently on one or more of the following options.

▶ Level A paperback books, see TE pages 371–376

▶ Level A *eZines*

▶ Repeat word sorts from this lesson

▶ *Student Journal* pages for this lesson

▶ *Writing Advantage* independent lessons

# Assessment

## Strategy Assessment

To help you and your students assess their use of comprehension strategies, ask the following questions. Students can complete a written response or provide verbal answers in a one-on-one reading conference.

• **Monitor Understanding** Reread the idioms on pages 62–63. What do they have in common? (Students should notice that they all have to do with water, which ties in with the theme of this magazine.)

See *Level A Assessment* page 38 for formal assessment to go with *Water*.

## Word Study Assessment

Use these steps to help you and your students assess their understanding of long *u* patterns.

1. Write the following words on the board or on word cards: *suit, flute, luge, crew, juice, flew, tube, fruit, grew.*

2. Ask students to identify the long *u* pattern in each word. The answers are shown.

| Word | Vowel Pattern |
|------|---------------|
| suit | *ui* |
| flute | *uCe* |
| luge | *uCe* |
| crew | *ew* |
| juice | *ui* |
| flew | *ew* |
| tube | *uCe* |
| fruit | *ui* |
| grew | *ew* |

Great Source
Reading Advantage

**Level A Assessment**

## Level A, Magazine 4

# Cities

## Magazine Summary

*Cities* magazine is a collection of nonfiction, fiction, drama, and poetry about cities. Students will read about ancient cities, aspects of current cities around the world, and even some nonhuman cities!

*Content-Area Connection:* history and social science
Lexile measure 630L

# *Cities* Planner

| LESSON | BEFORE READING | DURING READING | AFTER READING |
|---|---|---|---|
| **LESSON 37**<br>**City in the Clouds** *and* **My Days at Mesa Verde**<br>(photo-essay and diary entries)<br>page 282 | Concept Web<br>Vocabulary Preview<br>Preview the Selection<br>Make Predictions/Set Purpose | Monitor Understanding<br>Making Connections | Check Purpose<br>Discussion Questions<br>Writing: draw and write a description<br>Vocabulary: multiple meanings<br>Phonics/Word Study: long *u* patterns |
| **LESSON 38**<br>**Washington, D.C.—The Birth of a City**<br>(play)<br>page 292 | K-W-L Chart<br>Vocabulary Preview<br>Preview the Selection<br>Make Predictions/Set Purpose | Understanding Text Structure<br>Determining Importance | Check Purpose<br>Discussion Questions<br>Writing: summarize the play<br>Vocabulary: synonym-antonym chart<br>Phonics/Word Study: *r*-controlled *u* patterns |
| **LESSON 39**<br>**City Walls That Talk**<br>(article)<br>page 300 | Think-Pair-Share<br>Vocabulary Preview<br>Preview the Selection<br>Make Predictions/Set Purpose | Inferential Thinking | Check Purpose<br>Discussion Questions<br>Writing: main idea chart<br>Vocabulary: illustrated mini-dictionary<br>Phonics/Word Study: long *u* review |
| **LESSON 40**<br>**The Great Indoors**<br>(article)<br>page 306 | Concept Web<br>Vocabulary Preview<br>Preview the Selection<br>Make Predictions/Set Purpose | Making Connections<br>Monitor Understanding | Check Purpose<br>Discussion Questions<br>Writing: write about a sport<br>Vocabulary: words within a word<br>Phonics/Word Study: long and short *u* homophones |

# Overview

## Preview the Magazine

Give students time to thumb through the magazine to look at the selection titles, photographs, and illustrations. They should also look at the front and back covers for information about cities. Make a class idea web, similar to the one below, in which students can explore their own ideas about cities.

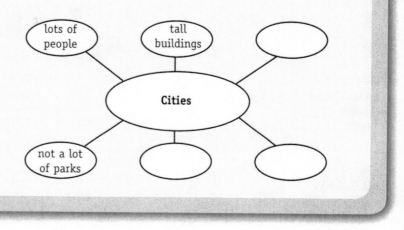

| PHONICS/ WORD STUDY | FOCUS ON | ASSESSMENT | HIGHER-ORDER THINKING QUESTIONS |
|---|---|---|---|
| Long *u* Patterns | Writing: illustrated timeline<br>Fluency: pacing<br>English Language Learners<br>Independent Activity Options | Monitor Understanding<br>Making Connections<br>Long *u* Patterns | In what ways are the Incas and the Anasazi similar? How are their two cities different? Use details and information from the passage to support your answer. In "My Days at Mesa Verde," Keesha compares the Anasazi houses to her apartment. In what ways does she think they are similar? Use details and information from the passage to support your answer. |
| *r*-controlled *u* Patterns | Writing: write a scene<br>Fluency: expression<br>English Language Learners<br>Independent Activity Options | Understanding Text Structure<br>Determining Importance<br>*r*-controlled *u* Patterns | Why did Washington end up firing L'Enfant even though he liked his designs? Use details and information from the passage to support your answer. Why was the area known as Washington, D.C. chosen for the nation's capital? Use details and information from the passage to support your answer. |
| Long *u* Patterns | Writing: descriptive paragraph<br>Fluency: phrasing<br>English Language Learners<br>Independent Activity Options | Inferential Thinking<br>Making Connections<br>Long *u* Review | What do all of the murals presented in this passage have in common? Use details and information from the passage to support your answer. What was Diego Rivera's purpose when painting his murals? Use details and information from the passage to support your answer. |
| Long and Short *u* Homophones | Writing: compare and contrast<br>Fluency: pacing<br>English Language Learners<br>Independent Activity Options | Making Connections<br>Monitor Understanding<br>Long and Short *u* Homophones | What is the difference between skateboarding on a city street and in an indoor skate park? Use details and information from the passage to support your answer. What is the author's purpose in writing this article? Use details and information from the passage to support your answer. |

# Cities Planner

| LESSON | BEFORE READING | DURING READING | AFTER READING |
|---|---|---|---|
| **LESSON 41**<br>**City Greens** *and* **Sounds of the City**<br>(essay and poem)<br>page 314 | Think-Pair-Share<br>Vocabulary Preview<br>Preview the Selection<br>Make Predictions/Set Purpose | Determining Importance<br>Making Connections | Check Purpose<br>Discussion Questions<br>Writing: fact-opinion chart<br>Vocabulary: synonym and antonym chart<br>Phonics/Word Study: long and short *u* compound words |
| **LESSON 42**<br>**Lost & Found in Chicago**<br>(realistic fiction)<br>page 322 | Think-Pair-Share<br>Vocabulary Preview<br>Preview the Selection<br>Make Predictions/Set Purpose | Understanding Text Structure<br>Making Connections | Check Purpose<br>Discussion Questions<br>Writing: personal experience<br>Vocabulary: illustrated mini-dictionary<br>Phonics/Word Study: long *o* and long *u* review |
| **LESSON 43**<br>**Mayor Tom Bradley** *and* **City Cinquains**<br>(biographical sketch)<br>page 330 | T-Chart<br>Vocabulary Preview<br>Preview the Selection<br>Make Predictions/Set Purpose | Inferential Thinking | Check Purpose<br>Discussion Questions<br>Writing: cause-effect<br>Vocabulary: context<br>Phonics/Word Study: diphthongs |
| **LESSON 44**<br>**Seattle Underground**<br>(first person account)<br>page 336 | K-W-L Chart<br>Vocabulary Preview<br>Preview the Selection<br>Make Predictions/Set Purpose | Monitor Understanding<br>Determining Importance | Check Purpose<br>Discussion Questions<br>Writing: illustrated timeline<br>Vocabulary: multiple meanings<br>Phonics/Word Study: ambiguous vowel sounds |
| **LESSON 45**<br>**Can a Sinking City Be Saved**<br>(article)<br>page 344 | Concept Web<br>Vocabulary Preview<br>Preview the Selection<br>Make Predictions/Set Purpose | Monitor Understanding | Check Purpose<br>Discussion Questions<br>Writing: 5Ws chart<br>Vocabulary: context<br>Phonics/Word Study: ambiguous vowel sounds |
| **LESSON 46**<br>**Insect Cities** *and* **Hidden Neighbors**<br>(article and poem)<br>page 349 | K-W-L Chart<br>Vocabulary Preview<br>Preview the Selection<br>Make Predictions/Set Purpose | Inferential Thinking<br>Understanding Text Structure | Check Purpose<br>Discussion Questions<br>Writing: detailed diagram<br>Vocabulary: multiple meanings<br>Phonics/Word Study: ambiguous vowel sounds |
| **LESSON 47**<br>**Atlantis & El Dorado: Fact or Fiction?**<br>(article)<br>page 356 | Concept Web<br>Vocabulary Preview<br>Preview the Selection<br>Make Predictions/Set Purpose | Making Connections<br>Determining Importance | Check Purpose<br>Discussion Questions<br>Writing: main idea chart<br>Vocabulary: multiple meanings<br>Phonics/Word Study: complex consonant clusters |
| **LESSON 48**<br>**Urban Transportation** *and* **Phone Call**<br>(articles)<br>page 364 | Concept Web<br>Vocabulary Preview<br>Preview the Selection<br>Make Predictions/Set Purpose | Making Connections | Check Purpose<br>Discussion Questions<br>Writing: compare and contrast<br>Vocabulary: words within a word<br>Phonics/Word Study: complex consonant clusters |

| PHONICS/ WORD STUDY | FOCUS ON | ASSESSMENT | HIGHER-ORDER THINKING QUESTIONS |
|---|---|---|---|
| Long and Short *u* Compound Words | Writing: write and illustrate<br><br>Fluency: expression<br><br>English Language Learners<br><br>Independent Activity Options | Determining Importance<br><br>Making Connections<br><br>Long and Short *u* Compound Words | What are some of the benefits offered by city parks? Use details and information from the passage to support your answer. What does they author mean when he uses the term "Green City?" Why is this a good thing to be "Green?" Use details and information from the passage to support your answer. |
| Long *o* and Long *u* Review | Writing: summary paragraph<br><br>Fluency: expression<br><br>English Language Learners<br><br>Independent Activity Options | Understanding Text Structure<br><br>Making Connections<br><br>Long *o* and Long *u* Review | What do Jade's and Duane's actions and reactions help you to infer about the differences in their personalities? Use details and information from the passage to support your answer. What was the main conflict in the story? Was it resolved? Use details and information from the passage to support your answer. |
| Diphthongs | Writing: persuasive paragraph<br><br>Fluency: phrasing<br><br>English Language Learners<br><br>Independent Activity Options | Inferential Thinking<br><br>Diphthongs | How did Tom Bradley's early life prepare him to face the challenges of being the mayor of Los Angeles? Use details and information from the passage to support your answer. How did Bradley improve the city during his time as mayor? Use details and information from the passage to support your answer. |
| Ambiguous Vowels | Writing: write and illustrate<br><br>Fluency: punctuation<br><br>English Language Learners<br><br>Independent Activity Options | Monitor Understanding<br><br>Determining Importance<br><br>Ambiguous Vowel Sounds | What are the reasons for rebuilding Seattle? Use details and information from the passage to support your answer. Why did they decide to build the streets so far above ground level when they rebuilt the city? What effect did it have on the buildings? Use details and information from the passage to support your answer. |
| Ambiguous Vowels | Writing: informative letter<br><br>Fluency: pacing<br><br>English Language Learners<br><br>Independent Activity Options | Monitor Understanding<br><br>Ambiguous Vowel Sounds | What are some of the problems facing Venice in the future? Use details and information from the passage to support your answer. Why do people feel that Venice should be saved? Use details and information from the passage to support your answer. |
| Ambiguous Vowels | Writing: compare and contrast<br><br>Fluency: expression<br><br>English Language Learners<br><br>Independent Activity Options | Inferential Thinking<br><br>Understanding Text Structure<br><br>Ambiguous Vowel Sounds | In what ways are ants and bees alike? In what ways are they different? Use details and information from the passage to support your answer. Why are the animals in the poem called "hidden neighbors?" Use details and information from the passage to support your answer. |
| Complex Consonant Clusters | Writing: paragraph<br><br>Fluency: punctuation<br><br>English Language Learners<br><br>Independent Activity Options | Making Connections<br><br>Determining Importance<br><br>Complex Consonant Clusters | Why do most people think Atlantis and El Dorado are nothing more than legends? Use details and information from the passage to support your answer. How did the search for El Dorado and Cibola change the native people of North America? Use details and information from the passage to support your answer. |
| Complex Consonant Clusters | Writing: time zones<br><br>Fluency: phrasing<br><br>English Language Learners<br><br>Independent Activity Options | Making Connections<br><br>Complex Consonant Clusters | How are some of the largest cities in the United States trying to cut down on people's reliance on their car? Use details and information from the passage to support your answer. Why did Jamie have to carefully plan who and when he would call during his free calling time? What was his difficulty? Use details and information from the passage to support your answer. |

# City in the Clouds *and* My Days . . .

*Cities*, pages 2–9

## SUMMARY

This **photo-essay** describes the history of a lost city. A **diary** follows.

## COMPREHENSION STRATEGIES

Monitor Understanding
Making Connections

## WRITING

Draw and Write a Description

## VOCABULARY

Multiple Meanings

## PHONICS/WORD STUDY

Long *u* Patterns

### Lesson Vocabulary

| | |
|---|---|
| dense | ancestors |
| subtropical | kivas |
| archaeologists | ceremonies |
| terraces | drought |
| thatched | pueblos |
| mesa | |

## MATERIALS

*Cities*, pp. 2–9
*Student Journal*, pp. 118–120
*Word Study Manual*, p. 70
*Writing Advantage*, pp. 152–163

---

# CITY IN THE CLOUDS

High in the mountains there is a city covered with clouds. It was lost for hundreds of years before it was found.

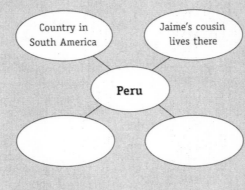

Machu Picchu (MAH choo PEEK choo) is built on a steep mountain that is covered with <u>dense</u> rain forests. An even higher peak towers over the ruins. There is a river eighteen hundred feet below. The climate is <u>subtropical</u>, as Machu Picchu is near very hot and rainy areas. There are many kinds of plants, insects, and wildlife. For example, you can find ninety kinds of orchids.

**PERU**

Lima •          ★Machu Picchu

2

---

# Before Reading

**WHOLE CLASS** Use one or more activities.

## Make a Concept Web ▶

Write "Peru" in the center oval of a concept web. Ask students what they know about Peru. Record their responses on the web. If students are unsure whether the information they contribute is correct, put a question mark next to the entry. If possible, help students locate Peru on a classroom map. Revisit the web after students have finished the article and add any new information they have learned. (See Differentiated Instruction.)

Country in South America

Jaime's cousin lives there

**Peru**

## Vocabulary Preview

Review the vocabulary list with students. Clarify pronunciations. Have students choose a word they're familiar with for *Student Journal* page 118. Then have students complete the page. They will revisit the page later to adjust definitions, if necessary. Model the process for students.

The year was 1911. The place was Peru, a country in South America. Hiram Bingham and a guide were hiking in the mountains. Bingham was a college professor, and he was looking for the remains of a lost city. They walked for hours. They walked through forests. They hiked along steep slopes.

The two men finally saw what they had been looking for. Between two mountain peaks, they saw a city unlike any other.

There were houses and staircases, fountains and temples. Everything looked old and ruined. It was also very quiet. No one lived there.

Archaeologists, people who study ancient times and people, call the place Machu Picchu. It is an ancient city. It rests on top of a mountain, about nine thousand feet above sea level.

## ABOUT MACHU PICCHU

"Machu Picchu" means "Old Peak" in the Quechua (KECH wah) language. Quechua was the language of the Incan Empire. It is still spoken in Peru, Bolivia, Ecuador, and other South American countries. The word *Inca* is from the Quechua language and means "ruler" or "man related to royalty."

Machu Picchu is in the country of Peru, which is where the Amazon River begins. The city is high in the Andes mountains, an extension of the Rocky Mountains. Compared to modern cities, the area of Machu Picchu is quite small. It is only five square miles. In contrast, the island of Manhattan is just over twenty-two square miles. The city of Chicago is 228 square miles!

## A BRIEF HISTORY

The Inca built Machu Picchu sometime before 1300. The Incan empire was great and ruled Peru for hundreds of years. The Inca ruled from about 1200 to 1532.

The Spanish invaded Incan lands in 1532. They took over Cuzco, which is a city near Machu Picchu. Luckily, the Spanish never found Machu Picchu. The city stayed a secret.

Today, Machu Picchu is a popular place. Scientists go there to study the Inca. Tourists visit, too.

3

**Student Journal page 118**

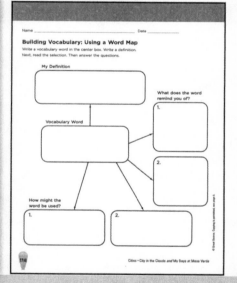

## Comprehension
MAKING CONNECTIONS

To help students make connections, ask these questions.

- Do any of these pictures look familiar to me?
- What do I already know about Peru or South America?
- What do I know about ruins of ancient cities?

Point out to students that recalling what they already know will make their reading more meaningful.

**1.** The trip to Machu Picchu is not easy. First, you have to get to Peru. Most flights land in Lima, the capital. Then, you have to take another flight to Cuzco. A train will take you near the ruins. Finally, you hike.

**2** It's not an easy hike. But the ancient city of the Inca is worth it.

**3** Farming is usually done on flat ground. But there isn't much flat ground on a steep mountain. The Inca dug "steps" into the sides of the mountain. These "steps" are called <u>terraces</u>. They are for farming—not climbing! The Inca grew different crops, including many different kinds of potatoes, in the terraces. This is one way that the Incan culture survives today.

### Hiram Bingham

Hiram Bingham taught at Yale University in Connecticut. Bingham was elected governor of Connecticut in 1925. He served for two days before he left for an opening in the United States Senate. He was a senator until 1933.

# During Reading

## Comprehension
MONITOR UNDERSTANDING

Use these questions to model how to visualize what you are reading. Then have students tell about a part they visualized.

- What do I see in my mind as I read?
- What details help me create this image in my mind?
- How does this image help me understand what I am reading?

## Teacher Think Aloud

*The second caption says, "It's not an easy hike." I'm not sure how difficult the hike is, and I can't really visualize the path one would take to the ancient city. Let's look at the photo that goes with the caption. I see the long path zigzagging up the steep mountain. Now I understand why the hike would not be easy.*

## Comprehension
MAKING CONNECTIONS

Use these questions to model making connections with the text. Then have students make their own connections.

- What sounds or looks familiar to me?
- Do I already know anything about the Inca?
- How does what I already know help me understand the text?

(See Differentiated Instruction.)

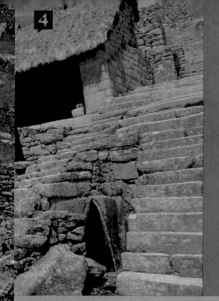

### The Incas

- ✴ Little is known about the early history of the Inca. They had no written language, so there are no written records.
- ✴ Around the year 1200, the Inca began to expand their rule.
- ✴ Around 1438, the Incan empire was formed. The empire spanned from northern Ecuador to central Chile before the Spanish conquest.
- ✴ In 1532, fighting between groups within the empire weakened the Incan empire.
- ✴ Also in 1532, the Spanish explorer Francisco Pizarro and his soldiers invaded the Incan empire. The Spaniards were able to defeat the Inca. After their victory, the Spaniards tried to wipe out every trace of the Inca.
- ✴ Today, in the mountain areas of Peru and some other countries, people still speak Quechua and use some of the farming and healing practices of the ancient Inca. ◆

**4** There have been two modern changes to the ruins. A <u>thatched</u> roof made of woven straw and leaves was added to a hut and another small building. The roofs help weak walls remain standing.

**5** Other buildings also have weak walls. Each brick in these walls has been numbered. If a wall falls down, people will be able to rebuild it.

## Teacher Think Aloud

*I remember studying about the cultures of the Aztecs, Maya, and Inca in my social studies class. One of the innovations that these cultures made was in their farming techniques. When I look at photograph 3, I remember how the Inca leveled parts of the steep mountainside for farming. This prior knowledge helps me understand the picture and the text about it.*

## Fix-Up Strategies

Offer these strategies to help students read independently.

**If you don't understand what you're reading:**

- Reread the difficult section to look for clues to help you comprehend.
- Read ahead to find clues to help you comprehend.
- Retell, or say in your own words, what you've read.
- Visualize, or form mental pictures of, what you've read.

**If you don't understand a word:**

- Reread the sentence. Look for ideas and words that provide meaning clues.
- Find clues by reading a few sentences before and after the confusing word.
- Look for the base or root word and think about its meaning.
- Think about the topic or plot at this point to see if either offers meaning clues.

## Short Feature:
## My Days At Mesa Verde

Students can read this selection independently. For background information on Mesa Verde, visit http://www.nps.gov/meve. To help students set a purpose, suggest that they read to learn who the Anasazi people were and what happened to them. After reading, brainstorm with students scenes that the Anasazi might have painted on the walls of the kivas. Students may draw one of the scenes. Or, have partners use what they learned in the article to role-play an interview with a famous archaeologist who has studied the Anasazi.

### Student Journal page 119

# My Days at MesaVer

A visit to an ancient city is special. Writing about it in a diary is a great way to remember it.

6

# After Reading
Use one or more activities.

## Check Purpose

Have students decide if their purpose was met. Why might tourists want to go to Machu Picchu?

## Discussion Questions

Continue the group discussion with the following questions.

1. Would you like to visit Machu Picchu? Why or why not? (Making Connections)

2. Why do archaeologists learn about the past? (Inferential Thinking)

3. What did you learn about the Incan civilization? (Details)

## Revisit: Concept Web

Revisit the concept web about Peru that was started in Before Reading. What new information can students add?

## Revisit: Word Map

Have students revisit the word map on *Student Journal* page 118. Students can use the information they gleaned from the selections to adjust definitions, if necessary.

Friday, 7/25

Dear Diary,

We have been on vacation in the southwestern United States. Today we went to Mesa Verde National Park in Colorado. Mesa Verde (MAY suh VER day) is Spanish for "green table." *Mesa* means "table." *Verde* means "green." The park is named for the forests that cover the <u>mesa</u>, a flat-topped mountain. The canyons are the coolest!

The Anasazi (ahn uh SAH zee) Indians lived here from about A.D. 200 to 1300. They are the <u>ancestors</u> of the Pueblo Indians. In fact, Anasazi means "the ancient ones" in the Navajo language. The Anasazi built homes in the canyon walls and rocky overhangs. The homes were built up, one on top of another. They were kind of like an apartment house. (I thought living on the fifth floor of an apartment house was modern. I found out that it's not!)

Cliff Palace is the largest cliff house. It has more than two hundred living rooms. (That's about the size of my apartment house!) About 250 to 300 Anasazi lived in Cliff Palace. (That's about how many people live in my building!) Some sections of Cliff Palace are two, three, and four stories high.

Cliff Palace also has underground rooms. These rooms are called <u>kivas</u> (KEE vahz). The Anasazi used them for all kinds of <u>ceremonies</u>. The walls of the kivas are decorated with paintings. (My building has underground rooms, too. There's a laundry room. It's next to the boiler room in the basement.) The Anasazi used ladders to go up and down. They also carved hand and foot holds in the side of the cliffs. (Lazy me. I use the elevator!)

Scientists think the Anasazi built their homes in the cliffs to protect themselves from unfriendly tribes. From the cliffs, the Anasazi could see who was coming toward them from below, and the cliffs were hard to climb.

I learned that the Anasazi were farmers and hunters. They grew beans, corn, and squash for food. They gathered wild plants and grains. The farmers also grew cotton and wove it into cloth for clothing. They grew tobacco and raised turkeys.

The Anasazi hunted deer, rabbit, and mountain sheep for food and for clothing. Rabbit fur and turkey feathers were used to make blankets and robes.

I've written enough today, Diary. I'll write more tomorrow.

Love,

Keesha

A view of Cliff Palace, the largest cliff dwelling in North America, and one of its kivas.

7

DIFFERENTIATED INSTRUCTION
SMALL GROUP
**Vocabulary**

## Multiple Meanings

If students need help with this activity, try following these steps.

1. Explain that *multiple* means "more than one." So a word with multiple meanings has more than one meaning. For example, the word *play* has two meanings. A child can *play* with toys. An actor performs in a *play*.

2. Once students understand the concept of multiple meanings, ask them to work in pairs to find the multiple meanings of these words from the article: *towers* (page 2), *ruler* (page 3), and *ruins* (page 5).

### Student Journal page 120

Name _____ Date _____

**Building Vocabulary: Words with Multiple Meanings**
Write two definitions for each word below.

| Word | First Definition | Second Definition |
|------|------------------|-------------------|
| terrace | a porch or walkway | a raised bank of earth used for planting |
| towers | | |
| ruler | | |
| ruins | | |

120  Cities • City in the Clouds *and My Days at Mesa Verde*

## Writing Draw and Write a Description

Ask students what part of Machu Picchu they could visualize best. Then have students draw that part and write a description of it on *Student Journal* page 119.

## Vocabulary Multiple Meanings

Display *terraces* on the board. Explain to students that a terrace can be a porch or walkway, a raised bank of earth used for planting (as in the article), or a strip of park in the middle of the street. What other words do students know that have multiple meanings? Have partners work together to complete the words with multiple meanings chart on *Student Journal* page 120. (See Differentiated Instruction.)

## Phonics/Word Study

### Long *u* Patterns

Tell students that sometimes, words with the long *u* sound do not contain the letter *u*. Ask students to think of some examples, and write them on the board. Point out the *ew*, *oo*, and *o* patterns (as in *knew*, *room*, and *to*). Now, work with students to complete the in-depth long *u* patterns activity on TE page 290.

## The Four Corners

There is only one place in the United States where you can stand in four states at one time! This area of the country is called the Four Corners. The corners of four states meet here: Arizona, New Mexico, Utah, and Colorado. At the Four Corners is a Navajo Tribal Park. The larger area around the actual Four Corners is mostly Navajo and Hopi reservation land. The scenery in the area is spectacular and has been featured in movies and car commercials.

## Pottery

Archaeologists use the patterns on bits of broken pottery to figure out the age of the Anasazi ruins. In fact, it is against the law to take bits of pottery that you might find on the ground. You can pick them up, hold them, and look at them. But you must put them back for others to see.

The towerlike structure behind a kiva is one of the tallest structures in Cliff Palace. The openings in the tower and other buildings let in fresh air.

The Basketmakers used **baskets** for all **kinds of things...**

Saturday, 7/26

Dear Diary,

I was really tired this morning. My older sister Janet had to drag me out of bed, but I'm glad she did. Today we went back to Mesa Verde and looked at Anasazi baskets and pottery. Wow!

Ancestors of the Anasazi made beautiful baskets. In fact, these ancestors were called the Basketmakers. The Basketmakers used baskets for all kinds of things, not just for carrying and storing stuff. Baskets were used for sifting seeds and flour and for cooking. Baskets were also used for burying the dead. The Anasazi made baskets, but pottery became their really big thing.

Janet went nuts over the Anasazi pottery. (Janet has taken one pottery class, and she thinks she's an expert!) The earliest pots we saw were made of coils of clay pinched together. These pots were used for cooking. Fancier pots had black designs on a white background.

The Anasazi later figured out how to make the background of pots in orange or red. This pottery is called redware. Redware has black and white designs on an orange or red background.

I found out more about the Anasazi. They left Mesa Verde about 1300. Scientists are not sure why. There may be one reason or many. One reason might be that there was a drought from 1276 to 1299. Since there was no rain, there was no drinking water. Without rain, the Anasazi could not grow crops. People might have died from lack of food and water. Other people might have left to find a place to live near water.

A war could have caused the Anasazi to leave. Enemy tribes might have invaded. The Anasazi might have fought each other. Whatever the reason (or reasons), the Anasazi left.

Some people moved to the Rio Grande area in New Mexico. Rio Grande means "big river" in Spanish. (*Rio* means "river." *Grande* means "big.") Others went to eastern Arizona. In Arizona, they built multi-story pueblos (PWEH blohs) that were their homes. These people are the ancestors of today's Pueblo Native Americans, the Hopi and Zuni Indians.

The Anasazi weren't the only ones to leave Mesa Verde. My family is leaving, too. Thank goodness we're not going because of a drought, famine, or war. (Janet and I did fight, but not too much.) Our vacation is over. Tomorrow we get on a plane to fly home. We'll say goodbye to the cliff dwellers and go back to being apartment house dwellers in New York City. Maybe I'll even give pottery class a try, too! ◆

Love,

Keesha

9

## Phonics/Word Study

### Long *u* Patterns

- ▶ Write the following words on the board: *groom*, *grew*, and *who*.
- ▶ Ask students if these words have the short or long *u* sound.
- ▶ Using the Long *u*: Sort Three sheet, model the sorting process for students. (See *Word Study Manual* page 70.) Write the headings *oo*, *ew*, *o*, and Oddball and the first few words in the appropriate columns.
- ▶ Once the sort is complete, discuss what students learned. Students will find one oddball: *look*.
- ▶ Hand out the Long *u*: Sort Three sheet. Ask students to cut up the words and do the sort on their own or in groups.
- ▶ Check the final sorts for accuracy.

| Long *u*: Sort Three | | | |
|---|---|---|---|
| *oo* | *ew* | *o* | Oddball |
| bloom | grew | who | look |
| doom | threw | to | |
| tooth | knew | two | |
| groom | crew | | |
| food | flew | | |
| too | blew | | |
| noon | stew | | |

For more information on word sorts and spelling stages, see pages 5–31 in the *Word Study Manual*.

# Focus on . . .

Use one or more activities in this section to focus on a particular area of need in your students.

## Comprehension  STRATEGY SUPPORT

To help those students who need more practice using the strategies covered in this lesson, work one-on-one or in small groups to apply the strategy prompts below. Apply the prompts to a *Reading Advantage* paperback, a classroom library book, or a new or familiar selection in the magazine. Always model your own thinking first.

### Monitor Understanding

- Do I understand what I'm reading? If not, what part is confusing to me?
- What fix-up strategies can I use to solve the problem? (See During Reading for fix-up strategies.)
- Why did a character say (do, think, ask) that?
- What images do I visualize from the text? What parts can't I visualize?
- Why did the author include (or not include) those details?

### Making Connections

- What does this story (article, passage) remind me of?
- What do I already know about this topic?
- Where have I heard about this topic before?
- What do I have in common with the characters, people, or situations in the text?
- What other books, stories, articles, movies, or TV shows does this text make me think about?

## Writing **Illustrated Timeline**

Have students use the information from the essay to make an illustrated timeline of the history of the Incas. Students can first take notes about the events and when they happened. Suggest that students first list six events with the dates. Then have them order the events sequentially. Students can then transfer the information to a timeline. See example below.

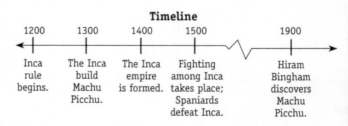

To give students more practice in taking notes, see lessons in *Writing Advantage* pages 152–163.

## Fluency: Pacing

After students have read the first selection at least once, they can use a portion of it to practice fluent reading. Because it is a photo-essay, partners can take turns reading photo captions. Students should practice reading aloud to their partner, who will provide feedback to encourage evenly paced reading. Point out to students that if they read too fast, too slow, or in a stopping-starting manner, their listeners will not be able to make sense of the words. Model the difference between evenly paced reading and unevenly paced reading.

As you listen to partners reading, use these prompts to guide them to read expressively and with an even pace.

▶ Listen to me read. Then read it just like I did.

▶ Reread this sentence a little bit faster (or slower).

▶ Try to make your voice sound a little stronger (or livelier) when you read. Your listeners will hear you better.

▶ Notice the punctuation; it will help guide your reading.

When students read aloud, do they—

✓ demonstrate a smooth pace, not too fast or too slow?

✓ incorporate well-timed pauses between words and phrases?

✓ reflect an awareness and understanding of punctuation?

## English Language Learners

To help students develop oral fluency, have them make statements about Peru using the concept webs created in the Before Reading activity on TE page 282.

1. Use a map to show students the location of Peru.

2. Read the information on the concept webs together.

3. Have students make statements about Peru using the information on the webs.

## Independent Activity Options

While you work with individuals or small groups, others can work independently on one or more of the following options.

▶ Level A paperback books, see TE pages 371–376

▶ Level A *eZines*

▶ Repeat word sorts from this lesson

▶ *Student Journal* pages for this lesson

▶ *Writing Advantage* independent lessons

# Assessment

## Strategy Assessment

To help you and your students assess their use of comprehension strategies, ask the following questions. Students can complete a written response or provide verbal answers in a one-on-one reading conference.

1. **Monitor Understanding** What parts of this article were most confusing to you? How did you figure out what the author was saying? (Answers will vary. Possible response: At first, I didn't know who Hiram Bingham was. I read on and saw a feature on him. That helped me understand more about him.)

2. **Making Connections** What connections did you make and how did they help you? (Answers will vary but should show how students can relate to the text.)

For ongoing informal assessment, use the checklists on pages 61–64 of *Level A Assessment*.

## Word Study Assessment

Use these steps to help you and your students assess their understanding of long *u* patterns.

1. Create a chart like the one shown (omitting the answers).

2. Write the following words on the board or on word cards: *bloom*, *who*, *do*, *new*, *there*, and *root*.

3. Have students read the words aloud and identify the long *u* pattern.

4. Then have students sort the words into the correct column. The answers are shown.

| *oo* | *ew* | *o* |
|------|------|-----|
| bloom | new | who |
| root | threw | do |

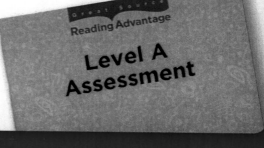

# Washington, D.C.—The Birth of a City

*Cities,* pages 10–15

## SUMMARY
In this **play**, readers learn the history of how Washington, D.C., was "born."

## COMPREHENSION STRATEGIES
Understanding Text Structure
Determining Importance

## WRITING
Summarize the Play

## VOCABULARY
Synonym-Antonym Chart

## PHONICS/WORD STUDY
*r*-controlled *u* Patterns

### Lesson Vocabulary
| | |
|---|---|
| donated | bold |
| architect | Congress |
| remodeling | precise |

## MATERIALS
*Cities,* pp. 10–15
*Student Journal,* pp. 121–123
*Word Study Manual,* p. 71
*Writing Advantage,* pp. 30–55

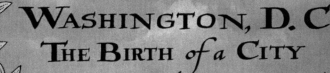

# WASHINGTON, D.C.
## THE BIRTH *of a* CITY

### Characters

NARRATOR

MARTHA WASHINGTON,
George Washington's wife
and First Lady

NELLY CUSTIS,
the Washingtons' granddaughter

GEORGE WASHINGTON,
first president of the United States

PIERRE L'ENFANT,
architect

DANIEL CARROLL,
city official

BENJAMIN BANNEKER,
surveyor

10

# Before Reading 🔆 WHOLE CLASS Use one or more activities.

## Make a K-W-L Chart ▶
Build a K-W-L chart about Washington, D.C. Ask students what they know about the city and what they want to learn about the city. Record their contributions on the chart. After students finish reading the play, they can add to the column about what they learned about the city. If possible, help students locate Washington, D.C., on a United States map. Ask for volunteers who have visited the city to share their experiences.

| What We **Know** | What We **Want** to Know | What We **Learned** |
|---|---|---|
| It's the capital of the U.S. | Is it a state? | |
| The White House is there. | How many people live there? | |

## Vocabulary Preview
Review the vocabulary list with students. Clarify pronunciations. Then have students begin working on the predictions chart on *Student Journal* page 121. Tell students that as they make and write their predictions, they shouldn't worry about whether their predictions prove to be correct. They will revisit their predictions after they read the play.

# SCENE 1

*(Time: 1792. Place: Mount Vernon, Virginia. President and Mrs. Washington sit in the parlor of their home with their granddaughter Nelly. George is seated in a chair. Martha and Nelly are on a couch. There is a round table in the room, as well as a small table next to the couch. George is reading a book. Martha is knitting. Nelly is holding a ball of yarn for her grandmother. The narrator is offstage.)*

**NARRATOR:** *(stepping out on stage)* Cities are born in different ways and grow in different ways. This play is about the great city of Washington, D.C. The building of the nation's capital began with dreams and plans. But plans do not always go smoothly. *(steps to side of stage)*

**MARTHA:** It's good that Maryland and Virginia <u>donated</u> land for our new capital city so that the nation didn't have to pay for it! We all know how much you love this part of the country, George.

**NELLY:** *(turning to her grandfather)* You often tell us about your happy childhood here, Grandfather.

**GEORGE:** *(putting the book on a table next to him)* Yes, our capital city will be only 15 miles from here. It's a fine location on the Potomac River. Martha, do you remember the Frenchman who

helped fight in the war of independence? I hired him to be the <u>architect</u> to design the new city.

**MARTHA:** *(looking up from her knitting at George)* Of course I remember Pierre L'Enfant (lon FONT). He worked on <u>remodeling</u> the Federal Hall in New York to make it a stunning building.

**GEORGE:** L'Enfant's ideas are quite <u>bold</u>. And I agree with most of his plans for the city. He wants it to have beautiful buildings and grand monuments. But I don't agree with him about one idea. He thinks the president's family should live in a palace fit for a king!

**NELLY:** I wouldn't mind that!

*(There is the sound of knocking at a door offstage.)*

11

## DIFFERENTIATED INSTRUCTION
## Preview the Selection

To enhance the preview, follow these steps:

1. Explain that *fiction* is a story the author made up. *Nonfiction* tells a true story or gives information about a topic.

2. Emphasize that in *historical fiction*, characters, places, or events can be real. However, the way the author presents the story is made up, or fictional. Make sure students understand that even though Washington, D.C., is a real city, the characters are people who truly lived, and some of the events of the story really happened, this play is a work of fiction.

### Student Journal page 121

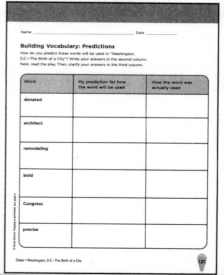

## Preview the Selection

Have students look over the six pages of the play. Point out that reading a play is very different from reading a short story or novel. In a play, the entire action is told through dialogue and stage directions. Discuss as a group what students notice from their preview. (See Differentiated Instruction.)

## Teacher Think Aloud

*I can tell right away that this selection is going to be a play. I see a list of characters and divisions into scenes. The pictures of the characters show that they are wearing clothes from a long time ago, so I think I'm going to read a play about a historical event.*

## Make Predictions/Set Purpose

Students should use the information they gathered in previewing the selection to make some predictions about the play. If students have trouble generating a purpose for reading, suggest that they read to learn how Washington, D.C., was "born."

To help students understand the problem-solution text structure of Scene 2, ask the following questions.

- What is the setting of Scene 2?
- Who speaks in Scene 2?
- What problem is solved in Scene 2?

---

**NELLY:** Excuse me. I'll see who's at the door. *(goes offstage and comes back to announce the visitor)* Pierre L'Enfant is here to see you, Grandfather.

**PIERRE:** *(entering the room, carrying a rolled-up map)* Good day, President and Mrs. Washington. I have brought my latest plans. I'm quite excited about them. *(Pierre unrolls the map on the table. Others get up and go over to the table. They look at the map as Pierre points to it.)* What do you think of these wide avenues? And notice how the streets branch out—like spokes in a wheel. I put the Congress building on a hill right in the center. This way, everyone can see the building where your laws are made.

**GEORGE:** What a fine plan! It certainly shows a lot of open spaces.

**MARTHA:** How wonderful! There will be beautiful parks. Lots of trees will keep people cool on hot summer days.

**NELLY:** *(excitedly, raising her arms and spreading them out wide)* Maybe it will feel like we're living in Paris. I read about grand palaces and gardens there.

**GEORGE:** *(looking at Pierre)* How do you plan to clear the land? There are farms and settlers all over the place.

**PIERRE:** Well, sir, clearing the land *is* a problem. There is no way to proceed without cutting trees and tearing down houses.

*(George puts his hand to his chin and looks worried. Then there is a knock at the door offstage. Nelly leaves to answer it and returns in a few seconds.)*

**NELLY:** Grandfather, there's a man who insists on seeing you now. He won't wait.

*(Daniel Carroll bursts in, angrily pointing to Pierre.)*

**DANIEL:** Excuse me, Mr. President and ladies, but I must protest this man's actions! He's gone too far with his high and mighty plans. Just who does he think he is?

12

### The Capital City

George Washington took the oath of office in New York City to become the first president of the United States. Then Philadelphia was chosen as the capital city. Ten years later, the capital was established at its present site in Washington, D.C.

Washington was named, as you might guess, for George Washington. The D.C. stands for District of Columbia, which is the land the city sits on. The land was given to the government by the state of Maryland so that the city would not be located in any state. There are no skyscrapers in Washington, D.C. A law states that no building can be taller than the Washington Monument.

George Town

---

# During Reading

### Comprehension
UNDERSTANDING TEXT STRUCTURE

Use these questions to model how to understand the text structure of a play, using page 11. Ask students to describe the problem and solution in the play.

- How is reading a play different than reading a short story?
- How do I learn about the characters?
- What are the problem and solution in this play?

(See Differentiated Instruction.)

## Teacher Think Aloud

*I first read the stage directions for Scene 1. These italicized words tell me the time and place of the play and help me picture how the characters should look on the stage. The Washington family's conversation tells about plans for building a capital city. I'll keep reading the conversation to see if any problems arise.*

### Comprehension
DETERMINING IMPORTANCE

Use these questions to model for students how to determine the importance of ideas in the first scene of the play. Then have students determine the importance of ideas as they read the second scene.

- What are the most important details in this scene?
- How can I support my beliefs?

(See Differentiated Instruction.)

MARTHA: *(looking at Daniel, puzzled)* Dear me, Mr. Carroll. What has upset you so much?

DANIEL: *(still angrily)* His workers have torn down a house that we are building! It's a brand new house! Mr. President, I demand that he be fired!

GEORGE: *(walking over to Daniel and putting his hand on the man's shoulder)* My dear Mr. Carroll, you have a right to be angry. I am sorry for any problems you have suffered. *(turning to Pierre)* Pierre, do not proceed any further. We have some important matters to discuss.

*L'Enfant's Purple Heart Medal Design*

### Pierre L'Enfant

L'Enfant lived in a castle when his father worked for the King of France.

When L'Enfant was an army major, General Washington admired his drawings.

L'Enfant designed the Purple Heart, a medal given to wounded soldiers.

PLAN of the City of WASHINGTON.

EASTERN BRANCH

13

## DIFFERENTIATED INSTRUCTION

### Comprehension
DETERMINING IMPORTANCE

To help students determine the importance of details in Scene 2, ask the following questions.

- What are the most important details in the scene?
- Why do you think so? How do those details affect building Washington, D.C.?

## Teacher Think Aloud

*I think that an important detail in the first scene is that L'Enfant tore down a house to be able to build Washington, D.C. This is important because it shows that there were problems in building the capital city. I think that this is the central problem in the play.*

### Fix-Up Strategies

Offer these strategies to help students read independently.

**If you don't understand what you're reading:**

- Reread the difficult section to look for clues to help you comprehend.
- Read ahead to find clues to help you comprehend.
- Retell, or say in your own words, what you've read.
- Visualize, or form mental pictures of, what you've read.

**If you don't understand a word:**

- Reread the sentence. Look for ideas and words that provide meaning clues.
- Find clues by reading a few sentences before and after the confusing word.
- Look for the base or root word and think about its meaning.
- Think about the topic or plot at this point to see if either offers meaning clues.

## Writing

### Summarize a Play

Try the following steps.

1. Explain that most stories or plays include a problem and solution, and that identifying them makes it easier to understand the story.

2. Explain that *but* signals a problem, and *so* signals a solution. Read this example: *I wanted to have a picnic today, but it rained. So we'll have the picnic tomorrow.* Have students create their own examples.

| My Notes | |
|---|---|
| **Somebody** (a main character) | George Washington was the president in 1792. He lived in Virginia. |
| **Wanted** (a key problem with some details) | He wanted to build a capital city called Washington, D.C. |
| **But** (conflict experienced that relates to the problem) | But his main architect wasn't following the rules George Washington proposed. |
| **So** (an outcome that relates to the problem without giving the story away; the hint of an outcome is also fine) | So Washington hired another architect who was able to do the job. |

# SCENE 2

*(Time: one week later in the same parlor. George, Martha, and Nelly are having afternoon tea. A teapot is on the table. They are seated around the table. The narrator is offstage. Then the narrator enters.)*

NARRATOR: President Washington knew it was important to keep the city officials happy. With deep regret, he decided to fire his French architect. Pierre L'Enfant was very angry. He was so angry that he took his plans with him. *(steps to the side of the stage)*

14

MARTHA: *(putting her hand on her husband's shoulder)* Dear, I know you are heartsick about this. Who will continue this great task?

NELLY: What will happen to the city of your dreams, Grandfather?

GEORGE: *(looking first at Martha and then at Nelly)* Things aren't as bad as they seem, my dears. Mr. Carroll speaks well of our surveyors. He thinks these men who measure land and draw maps can take over the job. Both Andrew Ellicott and Benjamin Banneker worked very closely with L'Enfant.

*(There is the sound of knocking at a door offstage.)*

NELLY: I hear someone at the door. I'll see who's there.

*(Nelly goes offstage and returns. Benjamin Banneker follows her into the room. He carries large rolled-up papers under his arm.)*

BENJAMIN: *(bowing with respect to George, Martha, and Nelly)* Good afternoon, Mr. President and ladies. Mr. Ellicott and I have been very busy. He asked me to come and share our plans with you. *(Martha and Nelly clear the teapot and tea cups from the table and put them on another small table. Benjamin spreads his drawings on the table. Everyone gathers around the table to look at the papers.)*

### Washington Streets

The wide avenues in Washington, D.C., are named for states. Avenues closer to the center are named after the first thirteen states. The address of the White House is 1600 Pennsylvania Avenue.

# After Reading

WHOLE CLASS

Use one or more activities.

### Check Purpose

Have students decide if their purpose was met. Do they understand how Washington, D.C., was "born"? Is anything about the play unclear to students?

### Discussion Questions

Continue the group discussion with the following questions.

1. What does this play tell you about George Washington? (Inferential Thinking)

2. Why did President Washington fire the French architect Pierre L'Enfant? (Cause-Effect)

3. What do you know now that you didn't know before reading? (Making Connections)

### Revisit: K-W-L Chart

Have students revisit the chart that was started in Before Reading. What new information can students add? What questions do they still have? How can answers be found?

### Revisit: Predictions Chart

Have students return to *Student Journal* page 121 to complete the third column of the predictions chart. How were the words actually used?

GEORGE: *(taking time to study the plans and then looking up at Benjamin)* Mr. Banneker, these look exactly like L'Enfant's plans. How were you able to get them?

BENJAMIN: Sir, I am blessed with a good memory. I worked on the first plans. So I was able to recall them. Look over these drawings. *(pointing to places on the paper)* You will see the Congress building and the president's home. And the wide avenues are still part of the plan.

GEORGE: *(excitedly)* This is remarkable, Mr. Banneker! Everything is clear. I can truly say that your <u>precise</u> memory has saved our grand city!

*(Martha and Nelly hug each other. George and Benjamin shake hands.)*

NARRATOR: *(stepping forward on stage)* George Washington died before the president's home was completed. In 1800, President John Adams and his wife, Abigail, moved in. They faced many problems. The streets were muddy, and farm animals wandered about. But the worst was yet to come. A war broke out in 1812. Most government buildings were damaged. The Capitol and the president's home were burned. However, over the years, the great efforts of many people paid off. In time, the city became the grand capital of the first president's dreams. Today, Washington, D.C., is a place that can be enjoyed by all. ◆

*(All exit the stage.)*

### The White House

★ At first, the president's home was not called the White House. Originally, it was called the President's House. Then, it was known as the Executive Mansion. In 1901, President Theodore Roosevelt declared that "White House" would be the official name.

★ Abigail Adams, wife of President John Adams, used the East Room to dry laundry. Now, guests are entertained in the East Room after formal dinners. It's the largest room in the White House.

★ In 1814, the British burned the President's House during the War of 1812.

★ The White House has 132 rooms, 35 bathrooms, 147 windows, 412 doors, 12 chimneys, 8 staircases, and 3 elevators.

*The White House*

15

**Student Journal page 122**

Name _____ Date _____
**Summarize: Somebody Wanted But So**
Use this chart to help you organize your thoughts for a summary of "Washington, D.C.—The Birth of a City." After you fill in the chart, use your notes to write a paragraph that summarizes the play.

| | My Notes |
|---|---|
| **Somebody** (an important character) | |
| **Wanted** (a key problem with details) | |
| **But** (conflict for the character) | |
| **So** (an outcome) | |

Now write your paragraph.

122    Cities • Washington, D.C.–The Birth of a City

**Student Journal page 123**

Name _____ Date _____
**Building Vocabulary: Synonym and Antonym Chart**
Think of two or three other words that are synonyms (similar in meaning) for each word in the first column. Next, think of two or three words that are antonyms (opposite in meaning) for each word in the first column. Use a thesaurus to help you.

| Vocabulary Word | Synonyms | Antonyms |
|---|---|---|
| **donated** | 1. given | 1. taken |
| | 2. | 2. |
| | 3. | 3. |
| **bold** | 1. | 1. |
| | 2. | 2. |
| | 3. | 3. |
| **precise** | 1. | 1. |
| | 2. | 2. |
| | 3. | 3. |

Cities • Washington, D.C.–The Birth of a City    123

## Writing Summarize the Play

Have students use the somebody-wanted-but-so strategy on *Student Journal* page 122 to write a paragraph summarizing the play. Model for students how to create a chart (see example on TE page 296) and take notes to organize their thoughts. Each section can be written in one or two sentences. (See Differentiated Instruction.)

## Vocabulary

### Synonym-Antonym Chart

Write the word *donate* on the board or on chart paper. Ask students:

• What do you know about this word?

• Can you think of a synonym for *donate*? (*give, contribute, present*)

• What is an antonym (opposite) for *donate*? (*take, steal*)

Now have students complete the synonym-antonym chart on *Student Journal* page 123.

## Phonics/Word Study

### *r*-controlled *u* Patterns

Write these words on the board: *purr, pure, pearl*. Ask students to say these words aloud. What do they notice about the vowel sound in *purr*? (It looks like it should have the same vowel sound as in *hut* and *rug*, but it doesn't.) The *r* changes the *u* sound. Now, work with students to complete the in-depth *r*-controlled *u* patterns activity on TE page 298.

## Phonics/Word Study

### r-controlled u Patterns

▶ Write the word *burn* on the board. Tell students that they are continuing their study of *u* patterns. Note that this time the sort is particularly tricky.

▶ Ask students if the word *burn* has a long or short vowel sound.

▶ Discuss the problem the letter *r* causes. Explain that the *r* changes the usual sound of the vowel. The *u* in *burn* sounds very different from the *u* in *bun*.

▶ Using the Long and Short *u: r*-controlled Vowels sheet, model the sorting process for students. (See *Word Study Manual* page 71.) Write the headings *ur*, *ure*, *ear* and the first few words in the appropriate columns. Complete the sort as a class.

▶ Discuss the sort and what students learned about *r*-controlled vowels. Sometimes the easiest way to tell if an *r*-controlled vowel is short or long is to try the short and long sound in the word out loud. As you can see in the examples below, this works reasonably well with *u* (*cur, cure* and *purr, pure*). The best thing to remember is that the long *u* *r*-controlled sound typically follows a standard long pattern: *uCe*, or *ure*, to be specific.

▶ After the discussion, hand out the Long and Short *u: r*-controlled Vowels sheet. Ask students to cut up the words and do the sort on their own or in groups. *Lure* is an oddball; it has a different sound than *cure* and *pure*. Also, *sure* has more than one pronunciation.

▶ Check the final sorts for accuracy.

| Long and Short *u: r*-controlled Vowels | | |
|---|---|---|
| *ur* (short) | *ure* | *ear* |
| curl | cure | learn |
| purr | pure | earth |
| burn | | pearl |
| purse | | earn |
| church | | search |
| burst | | yearn |
| hurl | | |
| turn | | |

For more information on word sorts and spelling stages, see pages 5–31 in the *Word Study Manual*.

# Focus on . . .

Use one or more activities in this section to focus on a particular area of need in your students.

## Comprehension  STRATEGY SUPPORT   INDEPENDENT

To help those students who need more practice using the strategies covered in this lesson, work one-on-one or in small groups to apply the strategy prompts below. Apply the prompts to a *Reading Advantage* paperback, a classroom library book, or a new or familiar selection in the magazine. Always model your own thinking first.

### Understanding Text Structure

• What kind of text is this? (book, story, article, guidebook, play, manual)

• How does the author organize the text? (cause-effect, problem-solution, chronological order, description, question-answer, comparison-contrast)

• What details support my thoughts about the text structure?

• What is the cause (effect, problem, solution, order, question, answer)?

• If fiction, who are the characters? What is the setting, plot, conflict, and resolution?

### Determining Importance

• What is the most important idea in the paragraph? How can I prove it?

• Which details are unimportant? Why?

• What does the author want me to understand?

• Why is this information important (or not important) to me?

## Writing Scene   INDEPENDENT

Have students write a scene of their own, using all the text elements of a play, such as setting, characters, narrator's lines, stage directions, and so forth. First, have students fill in a story string (see TE page 387) in which they plot out a brief storyline for their scene. Have them share and discuss their story strings with a partner. Then have them draft their scenes.

To give students more practice using specific nouns, see lessons in *Writing Advantage* pages 30–55.

## Fluency: Expression

SMALL GROUP

After students have read the play at least once, have groups of students do several staged readings of it. Students can change roles each time they read the play aloud.

Encourage students to read their lines in a way that shows the feelings of the character. Ask:

▶ How might the character feel in this scene?

▶ How can you show with your voice how the character might be feeling?

Provide feedback for students in regard to reading with expression, projecting their voices, and reading slowly and clearly.

When students read aloud, do they—

✓ reflect an understanding of the text?

✓ demonstrate appropriate timing, stress, and intonation?

✓ incorporate appropriate speed and phrasing?

## English Language Learners

SMALL GROUP

To support students as they develop inferential thinking skills, provide an extension activity related to the first discussion question on TE page 296.

1. Discuss the answer to the first question.

2. Have students make a concept web with George Washington's name in the center.

3. Have students write statements about George Washington at the end of each of the lines.

## Independent Activity Options

INDEPENDENT

While you work with individuals or small groups, others can work independently on one or more of the following options.

▶ Level A paperback books, see TE pages 371–376

▶ Level A *eZines*

▶ Repeat word sorts from this lesson

▶ *Student Journal* pages for this lesson

▶ *Writing Advantage* independent lessons

# Assessment

## Strategy Assessment

To help you and your students assess their use of comprehension strategies, ask the following questions. Students can complete a written response or provide verbal answers in a one-on-one reading conference.

1. **Understanding Text Structure** How did the text structure affect your understanding? (Answers should express that information in this text is in the characters' actions and words [stage directions and dialogue].)

2. **Determining Importance** What details of this play were most important to you? Why? (Answers will vary. Possible response: To me the most important detail is that Benjamin Banneker had a good memory. Without his memory, he would not have been able to recreate L'Enfant's plans for the capital city.)

For ongoing informal assessment, use the checklists on pages 61–64 of *Level A Assessment*.

## Word Study Assessment

Use these steps to help you and your students assess their understanding of *r*-controlled *u* patterns.

1. Create a chart like the one shown, omitting the answers.

2. Write the following words on the board or on word cards: *heard, pure, burn, hurt, learn,* and *secure*.

3. Have students read the words and identify the *u* sound in each one.

4. Then have students sort the words into the correct column. The answers are shown.

| ur | ure | ear |
|------|--------|-------|
| burn | pure | heard |
| hurt | secure | learn |

Great Source
Reading Advantage

**Level A Assessment**

# City Walls That Talk

*Cities*, pages 16–19

### SUMMARY

This **article** tells about the tradition of outdoor murals that brighten many city streets throughout the United States.

### COMPREHENSION STRATEGIES

Inferential Thinking

### WRITING

Main Idea Chart

### VOCABULARY

Illustrated Mini-Dictionary

### PHONICS/WORD STUDY

Long *u* Review

### Lesson Vocabulary

| | |
|---|---|
| mural | suffered |
| Aztec | customs |
| panels | |

### MATERIALS

*Cities*, pp. 16–19
*Student Journal*, pp. 124–126
*Word Study Manual*, p. 72
*Writing Advantage*, pp. 113–151

Paintings aren't just for the inside of a museum. Many cities have buildings with large paintings, called **murals**, painted right on the outside walls. Through their pictures, murals talk to us.

16

# Before Reading
WHOLE CLASS Use one or more activities.

### Think-Pair-Share

Have pairs read just the introductory paragraph on page 16. Then have them discuss their thoughts about the question: How can murals talk to us? Have pairs summarize their discussions with the group.

### Vocabulary Preview

Review the vocabulary list with students. Ask what associations students make to the words. Then have students complete the activity on *Student Journal* page 124. Model the process for a word.

### Preview the Selection

Have students survey the four pages of the article. Discuss as a group what students notice.

### Make Predictions/ Set Purpose

Students should use the information they gathered in previewing the selection to make some predictions about the article. If students have trouble generating a purpose for reading, suggest that they read to learn why artists paint outdoor murals.

The scene is a busy city street. One wall of a building is covered with a huge picture in bright, bold colors. People stop to look at it more closely. Cars slow down or pull up to the curb. What is this picture doing on the outside of a city building? It is a mural, or wall painting.

Who put this mural there? One or more artists may have planned and painted it. Often, a trained artist teaches people in a neighborhood how to help make a mural. People of all ages enjoy working on these big outdoor paintings.

Why do people paint outdoor murals? There are many answers. Some murals show people's pride in their neighborhood. The murals may tell about where people came from. They may show their different ways of life. Murals can also send a message through pictures and words. They might tell about a problem that people are facing and how they can solve it.

## Murals in Los Angeles

Los Angeles is a city with many murals. In fact, it has over 1,000 of them. John Zender Estrada is one of the mural artists. He was born and raised in East Los Angeles.

The mural on the left is by Zender. It shows an Aztec Indian warrior. He is stopping a fight between two gangs. The message is: "Don't fight among yourselves. Remember that we come from the great Aztec people. Be like them." A black eagle and a snake are on the left side of the painting. They stand for the power of the Aztec people. So does the pyramid. The Aztecs once built these great buildings.

The mural is in a place where many kids hang out. Zender hopes that a lot of kids will see it and feel proud. He hopes that the mural sends an important message: "Stop the violence. It only hurts you."

This mural is called *Hispanic Freedom.* Zender made this mural with the help of local teenagers. Some of the kids who helped Zender are now artists themselves.

### Zender Speaks

Zender believes that every person has a special "flame of fire" inside. This flame is a special talent or view of the world. Zender felt this flame himself when he was fifteen years old. He decided he wanted to be an artist. He knew he needed to get a scholarship to art school. Zender worked hard to get good grades. That helped him win a scholarship to pay for school. He went to two of the best art schools in America. Now he wants to spread the message to you. "Be what you want to be. Don't make excuses. Don't say 'I'm too poor' or 'No one is behind me.' Make your own dream come true."

17

## DIFFERENTIATED INSTRUCTION
### Comprehension
INFERENTIAL THINKING

To help students think inferentially, ask these questions.

- What does the text tell you about the topic?

- What do you already know about the topic?

- Based on your prior knowledge and the information in the text, what new information can you infer that the author does not state directly?

### Student Journal page 124

Name _____ Date _____

**Building Vocabulary: Making Associations**
Pick two words from the vocabulary list below. Think about what you already know about each word. Then answer the following questions for each word.

| mural | panels | customs |
| Aztec | suffered | |

Word _____
What do you think about when you read this word? _____
Who might use this word? _____
What do you already know about this word? _____

Word _____
What do you think about when you read this word? _____
Who might use this word? _____
What do you already know about this word? _____

Now watch for these words in the magazine selection. Were you on the right track?

124    Cities • City Walls That Talk

# During Reading

## Comprehension
INFERENTIAL THINKING

Use this question to model making inferences from the section called "Murals, Murals, Everywhere" on page 18. Then have students reveal inferences they make as they read another section.

- Using the text from this section and what I already know so far, what can I infer that the author has not stated directly?

(See Differentiated Instruction.)

## Teacher Think Aloud
*The text tells me that murals have been a part of Mexican life for over a thousand years. I see from the previous section that many famous muralists have Mexican roots. I also learned that there are murals in cities all over the United States. I can use this information to infer that Mexican culture has influenced art and culture in the United States.*

## Fix-Up Strategies

Offer these strategies to help students read independently.

**If you don't understand what you're reading:**

- Reread the difficult section to look for clues to help you comprehend.

- Read ahead to find clues to help you comprehend.

- Retell, or say in your own words, what you've read.

- Visualize, or form mental pictures of, what you've read.

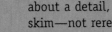

If students need help answering these questions, use the following steps:

1. If students do not know the answer to a question that asks about a detail, have them skim—not reread—the article for clues to the answer.

2. Ask students what they know about Mexican culture. What have they learned about Mexican art from this article? The answers to these questions will help them with the second discussion question.

### Student Journal page 125

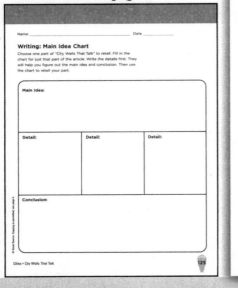

Diego Rivera's mural *Pan American Unity* is in San Francisco, California. The mural is in a theater at City College. It is made up of five panels, or sections. Thousands of students, city people, and tourists view this mural every year.

Left: **Mural by Judithe Hernandez in Los Angeles. The name of this mural is *Memories of Yesterday, Dreams of Tomorrow*. It honors the past and present of Los Angeles.**

Above: **Diego Rivera's mural *Pan American Unity* is in San Francisco, California. The mural is in a theater at City College. It is made up of five panels, or sections. Thousands of students, city people, and tourists view this mural every year.**

Judithe Hernandez is also a mural artist from Los Angeles. In 1982, the city had a special celebration. Los Angeles was two hundred years old. Hernandez made the mural above about the city and its people. The woman in the center is called the Queen of Los Angeles. The artist says she is the "spirit" that watches over the city. The mural also shows Mexican American farm workers. They helped build the city with their hard work.

## Murals, Murals, Everywhere

In every city where Mexican Americans live, you can find colorful murals. Tucson, Arizona, is certainly an example. Two mural painters from Tucson are David Tineo and Antonio Pazos. Both artists teach high school students to create murals with them.

In Chicago, young people painted several murals. Some show pictures of famous Mexican American leaders. Others show stories from Mexican and Mexican American history. Hundreds of people in San Diego painted murals under a bridge. The land around the bridge became a city park.

Murals have been a part of Mexican life for over a thousand years. Mayan Indians painted brightly colored murals on the walls of their temples. Mural painting did not stop when the Spanish conquered Mexico. Mexicans painted murals inside churches. They also painted outdoor murals on walls of shops and other buildings. The Mexican Revolution of 1911 was a time of hope for the Mexican people. Artists painted murals about their hopes for a better life for all.

18

# After Reading
WHOLE CLASS
Use one or more activities.

## Check Purpose

Have students decide whether their purpose was met. Do students understand why artists paint outdoor murals? What questions do they still have?

## Discussion Questions

Continue the group discussion with the following questions.

1. What are some of the messages that the murals in the article convey? (Details)

2. What was Diego Rivera's purpose in painting murals? (Main Idea)

3. Did you enjoy this selection? Why or why not? (Making Connections)

(See Differentiated Instruction.)

## Revisit: Word Associations

Have students revisit *Student Journal* page 124. Now that they have read the article, what new associations can students add? Were students on the right track?

## Diego Rivera

Diego Rivera (Dee AY go Ree VER uh) is perhaps the most famous mural artist. He was from Mexico. When he was young, he studied the murals of the ancient Mexicans. They inspired him. In 1921, he began to paint murals on public buildings. His purpose was to teach about Mexican history. Rivera's murals showed both the good and the bad in Mexican history. They told of how the Indians <u>suffered</u> under the rule of the Spanish. But they also praised the <u>customs</u>, art, science, and industry of his beloved country. The Mexican people are very proud of Rivera's murals.

Rivera was popular in the United States, too. In 1940, he was asked to do a special mural in San Francisco. The mural was for the World's Fair. Rivera created a mural about North and South America. He wanted to show what the many countries have in common. The mural is called *Pan American Unity*.

Rivera sends an important message in this mural. The mural tells American artists to make "real American art." To do this, they must learn from the art of the past. They must look at the art of the Native Americans and Inuits of North America.

In the mural, Rivera shows examples of native art of the past. He also shows modern machines. He wanted artists to be inspired also by the great machines of modern times. He is telling Americans to look at both their past and present. Only then can they create true American art. This was Rivera's dream. ◆

**Diego Rivera still inspires today's mural artists. He lived from 1886 to 1957.**

19

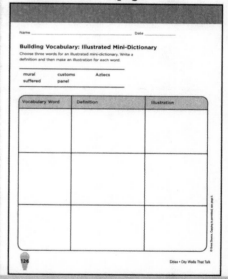

**Student Journal page 126**

---

### Writing **Main Idea Chart**

Using a main idea chart can help students retell a part of an article. Have students fill out the main idea chart on *Student Journal* page 125 for one part of the article. The text under a particular head can be considered a "part." Encourage students to fill in the details first. Both the main idea and conclusion will evolve out of the details. Then have partners use their charts to help them retell their parts of the article to each other.

### Vocabulary
### Illustrated Mini-Dictionary

Have students use the mini-dictionary activity on *Student Journal* page 126 to write, define, and illustrate three words. Students can consult the article, a dictionary, or friends for definition help.

### Phonics/Word Study
### Long *u* Patterns

Display and read aloud: *A huge blue fruit will surely cure the mule.* Ask students to point out all of the words with the long *u* sound, and to categorize them by spelling pattern (uCe: *huge, mule;* ue: *blue;* ui: *fruit;* r-controlled: *surely, cure*). Now, work with students to complete the in-depth word sort on TE page 304.

## Phonics/Word Study

### Long *u* Review

▶ Write the words *huge, glue, juice, blew, cure,* and *build* on the board. Also write the vowel patterns *uCe, ue, ui, ew, r-*controlled, and Oddball.

▶ Ask students to recall the long *u* vowel patterns they've studied and identify the long *u* vowel pattern in each word.

▶ Have partners work together to complete the Long *u*: Review sort. (See *Word Study Manual* page 72.)

▶ Check the final sort. Note that students may identify *sure* and *lure* as oddballs.

| Long *u*: Review | | | | | |
|------|-----|-----|-------|-------------|---------|
| *uCe* | *ue* | *ui* | *ew* | *r-*controlled | Oddball |
| crude | blue | fruit | threw | sure | fuel |
| huge | glue | juice | blew | cure | build |
| mule | | bruise | dew | lure | duel |
| | | | knew | | |

For more information on word sorts and spelling stages, see pages 5–31 in the *Word Study Manual*.

## Focus on . . .

Use one or more activities in this section to focus on a particular area of need in your students.

### Comprehension  STRATEGY SUPPORT

*INDEPENDENT*

To help those students who need more practice using the strategies covered in this lesson, work one-on-one or in small groups to apply the strategy prompt below. Apply the prompt to a *Reading Advantage* paperback, a classroom library book, or a new or familiar selection in the magazine. Always model your own thinking first.

#### Inferential Thinking

• What are the causes or effects of this event?

• What do I learn from the character or person's thoughts, words, or actions?

• What do I know (or infer) from the text that the author hasn't stated directly?

• What conclusions can I draw?

### Writing Descriptive Paragraph

*INDEPENDENT*

Have students study the murals in the article and choose one to write about. Students should create an idea web to jot down the symbols, images, and ideas that come to mind when observing the chosen mural. Students can write the name of their chosen mural in the center oval. Have students share their idea webs in small groups.

Students should then use their web to write a paragraph describing the message that they take away from the mural.

To give students more practice in writing descriptive paragraphs, see lessons in *Writing Advantage*, pages 113–151.

## Fluency: Phrasing

After students have read the article at least once, they can use part of it to practice fluent reading. Have partners read sections of the article into a tape recorder and then listen to and evaluate their reading. Can they understand all the words? Did they read the phrases, or words that go together, in a meaningful way? Were they reading too quickly or too slowly? Did their voices show expression? Encourage students to do the exercise again, adjusting any variables in their reading that they think should be changed.

When students read aloud, do they—

✓ demonstrate quick recognition of words and phrases?

✓ exhibit an understanding of phrasal construction?

✓ incorporate appropriate timing, stress, and intonation?

## English Language Learners

To support students' comprehension of "City Walls That Talk," build upon their background knowledge of murals.

1. Discuss what students already know about murals.

2. Show students examples of murals in books and on the Internet.

3. Have students tell a partner what they know about murals.

## Independent Activity Options

While you work with individuals or small groups, others can work independently on one or more of the following options.

▶ Level A paperback books, see TE pages 371–376

▶ Level A *eZines*

▶ Repeat word sorts from this lesson

▶ *Student Journal* pages for this lesson

▶ *Writing Advantage* independent lessons

# Assessment

## Strategy Assessment

To help you and your students assess their use of comprehension strategies, ask the following questions. Students can complete a written response or provide verbal answers in a one-on-one reading conference.

- **Inferential Thinking** What conclusions can you draw about why artists create murals? (Answers will vary. Students might answer that artists want to share their cultural heritage, or that they want to create beauty and share important messages with a lot of people.)

For ongoing informal assessment, use the checklists on pages 61–64 of *Level A Assessment*.

## Word Study Assessment

Use these steps to help you and your students assess their understanding of long *u* patterns.

1. Write these words on the board: *true, juice, loop, dew, endure, truce, bruise, smooth, glue, pure*.

2. Then create a chart with the six headings below.

3. Have students read the words and sort them into the correct column. The answers are shown.

| uCe | ue | ui | oo | ew | r-controlled |
|-----|-----|------|--------|-----|--------------|
| truce | true | juice | loop | dew | endure |
| | glue | bruise | smooth | | pure |

**Level A Assessment**

# The Great Indoors

*Cities,* pages 20–25

### SUMMARY

In this **article**, students learn about the various forms of indoor sports that are played in cities.

### COMPREHENSION STRATEGIES

Making Connections
Monitor Understanding

### WRITING

Write about a Sport

### VOCABULARY

Words within a Word

### PHONICS/WORD STUDY

Long and Short *u* Homophones

### Lesson Vocabulary

| | |
|---|---|
| ramps | maneuver |
| tournaments | sprint |

### MATERIALS

*Cities,* pp. 20–25
*Student Journal,* pp. 127–130
*Word Study Manual,* p. 73
*Writing Advantage,* pp. 113–151

Skateboarders go up and down "hills" and ride "rails" on the street course at indoor skateboard parks.

20

# Before Reading

WHOLE CLASS Use one or more activities.

## Make a Concept Web

On the board or on chart paper, make a concept web with the phrase *indoor sports* in the center oval. Have students contribute what they know about various indoor sports. Write the information on the web. Encourage students to talk about their own experiences with indoor sports. Students will return to the web after they read the article to add any new information they learned. (See Differentiated Instruction.)

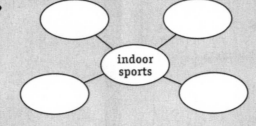

indoor sports

## Vocabulary Preview

Review the vocabulary list with students and clarify pronunciations. Have students choose a word they're familiar with for the word map on *Student Journal* page 127. Then have students write a definition for the word. They will revisit the page later.

# The Great Indoors

**Even though there is no "great outdoors" in the city, there sure is a "great indoors"— for sports, that is.**

## Skateboarding

Kids don't have many places to skateboard in a city. The streets are not safe for skateboards, and there are too many cars. The sidewalks are not good for skateboards, either. Too many people are on the sidewalks. Skateboards can also damage curbs and sidewalks. Skateboarders can be hurt because of cracks and holes in sidewalks. The best place to go is an indoor skateboard park.

An indoor skateboard park has many kinds of <u>ramps</u>. A ramp can be twelve feet high. You skate to the top. Then you flip your board and head down. The street course is like skating on a city street. Kids do the "acid drop" trick on this course. They roll along a wall. Then they jump down with the board. Another run is called a "snake run." It's a winding course. Those twists and turns will really test you!

You can learn new tricks at skateboard classes. There are contests with great prizes. So grab your board. Head for an indoor park near you!

**21**

**Student Journal page 127**

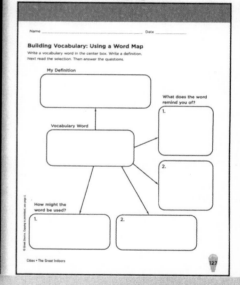

## Preview the Selection

Have students survey the six pages of the article. Ask:

- What do you notice first about the article?
- What do you think the article will be about?
- What kind of selection is this? What makes you think that?
- How does the information appear to be organized?

## Teacher Think Aloud

*When I first look at this article, I see athletes doing some pretty cool things, such as skateboarding and rock climbing. I think this will be a nonfiction article about different sports. I see headings that divide the text into different sections according to sports. I'm not sure, though, why the title is "The Great Indoors," since sports are usually played outdoors.*

## Make Predictions/ Set Purpose

Students should use the information they gathered in previewing the selection to make some predictions about the article. If students have trouble generating a purpose for reading, suggest that they read to learn how cities encourage indoor sports.

## Comprehension
### MAKING CONNECTIONS

To help students make connections, ask these questions:

- Are any of these sports familiar to me?

- Have I ever played a sport indoors? What was it like?

- How does my experience help me understand what I am reading?

## Rock Climbing

Do you need a mountain to do rock climbing? No! You can "rock climb" on a special wall. The wall can be set up in a gym. These walls have clay "holds" on them. The holds look like rocks that stick out. Your hands grab them and your feet stand on them as you climb.

On some climbing walls, the holds are different colors, such as red, yellow, and blue. Holds of the same color mark a path. You follow the path on the wall by climbing on the same-colored holds. If you are a beginner, you climb on the red holds. When you are a better climber, you can go on the blue holds.

This kind of rock climbing is called "bouldering" (BOHL duhr ing). Boulders are rocks that stick out from the ground, so "bouldering" is a good name. The climber uses just his or her hands and feet to get up or across the wall. A "spotter" watches to make sure the climber doesn't fall. A spotter helps the climber stay on the right path.

Another kind of rock climbing uses ropes. It's a kind of "buddy" climbing. One climber leads the way. He or she is the climber

22

# During Reading

## Comprehension    SMALL GROUP
### MAKING CONNECTIONS

Use these questions to model making connections with the text. Then have students make their own connections with the text.

- What sounds or looks familiar to me?

- Do I already know anything about the sports in this article?

- How does what I already know help me understand the text?

(See Differentiated Instruction.)

## Teacher Think Aloud

*I once went rock climbing in Maine. It was extremely difficult, and I was sore for a week afterward! But it was really fun and exciting. When I read the section on indoor rock climbing, I imagine that it would be just as difficult to climb fake rocks. I guess people like a physical challenge—whether it's outdoors or indoors!*

## Comprehension    SMALL GROUP
### MONITOR UNDERSTANDING

Use these questions to model for students how to monitor understanding of difficult words. Then have students identify words that they find difficult, and try to resolve any confusion.

- What does the word *holds* mean in the section on rock climbing?

- How do you pronounce it?

- What fix-up strategy can I use to figure it out?

with more experience. The other climber follows. A rope connects both climbers. The leader helps the other climber go up, down, and across on a wall.

An indoor rock-climbing park can have fifty-foot-high walls. There may be two hundred climbing paths on these walls. Some schools have rock climbing walls in their gyms. It's a great workout!

# Soccer

Think you need an outdoor field to play soccer? Think again! People have been playing soccer indoors for many years. Indoor soccer is played in indoor sports arenas and gyms.

The size of the field is usually about 80 feet by 180 feet. The playing field has a covering called *turf*. Turf is made to look and feel like grass. Nets close in the field. They keep the people watching the game from getting hit by the ball. There are no sidelines the way there are on outdoor soccer fields. Instead, players bounce the ball off the walls the way hockey players hit a puck against the boards.

Players dress in a shirt, shorts, and special shoes. The shoes help with quick starts and stops.

Indoor soccer shoes do not have cleats. For their safety, players wear shin guards.

People of all ages can play in indoor soccer tournaments. There are four to six players on a team. The games have two halves, plus a two-minute break. Each game lasts about fifty minutes.

23

# Teacher Think Aloud

*I know the word* hold. *It means "to grasp something in your hand." In this text, though, the word is used as a noun: "These walls have clay 'holds'." I'm confused. I'll read the next few sentences. I see, these are clay "rocks" that stick out from the wall. You can grab them or step on them to help you climb. I also see in the photograph what these "holds" look like.*

# Fix-Up Strategies

Offer these strategies to help students read independently.

## If you don't understand what you're reading:

- Reread the difficult section to look for clues to help you comprehend.
- Read ahead to find clues to help you comprehend.
- Retell, or say in your own words, what you've read.
- Visualize, or form mental pictures of, what you've read.

## If you don't understand a word:

- Reread the sentence. Look for ideas and words that provide meaning clues.
- Find clues by reading a few sentences before and after the confusing word.
- Look for the base or root word and think about its meaning.
- Think about the topic or plot at this point to see if either offers meaning clues.

# Wheelchair Sports

People in wheelchairs can enjoy indoor sports, too. They join teams and play in tournaments.

Wheelchair racing has become a major event at indoor track and field competitions. Racers must do a lot of strength training to prepare for races.

Wheelchair basketball uses a regular basketball. The rules are almost the same as for regular basketball. One difference is this rule: the player's wheelchair is part of the player's body. If a player's wheelchair is out of bounds, so is the player. If a player makes a move with his or her wheelchair that is not allowed, a foul is called.

Wheelchair tennis is a fast and exciting game. Tennis players in wheelchairs often play with players who are not disabled. Everyone follows the same rules. But the wheelchair player can let the ball bounce twice before he or she hits it.

Indoor wheelchair soccer is played with a ten-inch rubber ball. Players pass, catch, kick, and throw the ball to make goals.

24

**Student Journal pages 128–129**

Name _____ Date _____

**Writing: Indoor Sport Chart**
Choose one indoor sport that interested you. On the chart, record your ideas about what is involved in playing that sport and what it is like to participate in that sport.

**Indoor Sport:**

| Type of equipment needed to play the sport indoors: | Type of room needed: | What it is like to play the sport indoors: |
| --- | --- | --- |
|  |  |  |

128

Cities • The Great Indoors

# After Reading

WHOLE CLASS Use one or more activities.

## Check Purpose

Have students decide whether their purpose was met. How do cities encourage indoor sports? What questions do students still have?

## Discussion Questions

Continue the group discussion with the following questions.

1. Might it be hard for city dwellers to exercise? If so, why? How can they overcome that difficulty? (Problem-Solution)

2. Which of the sports mentioned in the article have been played outdoors and indoors for a long time? (Details)

3. Did you enjoy this selection? Why or why not? (Making Connections)

## Revisit: Concept Web

Revisit the concept web about indoor sports that was started in Before Reading. What new information can students add?

## Revisit: Word Map

Have students complete the word map on *Student Journal* page 127. Students can use the information they gleaned from the article to adjust their definitions, if necessary.

# Bike Racing

Are snowy, icy streets keeping you off your bike? Head for an indoor track. All you need is a BMX bike and a helmet. The helmet has to cover your whole face. A BMX bike is smaller than a racing bike. It has only one gear. The tires are wider. It is easier to <u>maneuver</u>, or move, into different positions.

The indoor track may be made of wood or dirt or both. A track may be 1,000 to 1,300 feet long. That is enough for a <u>sprint</u> that lasts almost a minute. The track has flat, straight parts. It also has "bumps and jumps." The bumps are made of dirt. The jumps are dirt piles to ride up on. Then you can "jump" your bike off.

BMX biking and racing moves outdoors in warm weather. BMX bikers can be as young as three years old. BMX biking is popular with families.

## Other Indoor Sports

Tennis and basketball have long been outdoor and indoor sports. This is true in cities as well as everywhere else. The court size for both sports makes it easier to do indoors.

Some tennis courts are "bubbled," or covered, for the winter months. Tennis courts have also been built inside buildings. Basketball courts most often are set up in gyms or in sports buildings.

Handball, racquetball, and squash are indoor sports. The court size is small, so clubs often have several courts. A lot of city people play these sports.

Ice-skating is done outdoors and indoors, as are both roller-skating and in-line skating. Indoor rinks—with or without ice—are available to people in many cities.

A fact of city life is that there is little open space for sports. Don't let that be an excuse! You only have to open a door to discover the "great indoors," the world of indoor sports. ◆

25

DIFFERENTIATED INSTRUCTION

## Writing
### Write about a Sport

For extra support, try the following.

1. In this activity, students are asked to draw a picture and write a brief description. Explain: *When you write to describe, you want to "paint a picture" in the reader's mind. The reader should be able to imagine the sport being played.*

2. Brainstorm a list of indoor sports not mentioned in this article.

3. Have students use the chart they filled in on *Student Journal* page 128 to help them get ideas about what to include in their pictures and writing.

### Student Journal page 130

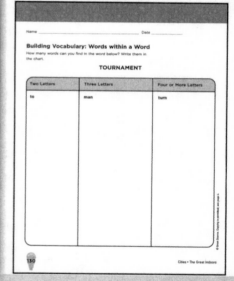

## Writing Write about a Sport

Have students choose one indoor sport and fill in the chart on *Student Journal* page 128 about what is involved in playing that sport. Then have students draw and write about that sport on *Student Journal* page 129. Students can choose a sport that was not mentioned in the article. (See Differentiated Instruction.)

## Vocabulary
### Words within a Word

Display *tournament*. Then ask:

- What do you know about this word?
- How is the word used in the article? (See page 23.)

Now ask students to look within the word *tournament* for shorter words, with or without rearranging any letters. (*to, turn, man, men, tour*) Have students list the words on *Student Journal* page 130.

## Phonics/Word Study
### Homophones

Display: *loot, lute; duct, ducked*. Have students read the words aloud. Ask: *What do the words in each pair have in common?* (They sound the same.) Explain that words that sound the same but have different spellings are called *homophones*. Ask students to list other short or long *u* homophones. Now, work with students to complete the in-depth homophones activity on TE page 312.

### Long and Short *u* Homophones

▶ Write the following words on the board: *serf, surf; due, dew;* and *brewed, brood.*

▶ Ask students if they can figure out what the pairs have in common. Students should recognize that the words in each pair sound the same but are spelled differently.

▶ Using the list of long and short *u* homophones (for a more extensive list see *Word Study Manual* page 73), create word cards with homophones on them. Each card should have one word on it. Play a game in which students turn over a homophone card worth a certain number of points. They have to provide the homophone, spell it, and define it.

▶ Have students create a new section of their Word Study notebooks and add any homophones that are generated.

| Long and Short *u*: Homophones | | | |
|---|---|---|---|
| yule you'll | blue blew | worst wurst | slew slue |
| scull skull | surf serf | surge serge | plum plumb |
| threw through | rung wrung | rumor roomer | none nun |
| rude rued | dual duel | dew due | mussel muscle |
| loot lute | chews choose | cue queue | duct ducked |
| earn urn | cruel crewel | crews cruise | but butt |
| chute shoot | brewed brood | few phew | coop coupe |

For more information on word sorts and spelling stages, see pages 5–31 in the *Word Study Manual.*

# Focus on . . .

Use one or more activities in this section to focus on a particular area of need in your students.

## Comprehension  STRATEGY SUPPORT  INDEPENDENT

To help those students who need more practice using the strategies covered in this lesson, work one-on-one or in small groups to apply the strategy prompts below. Apply the prompts to a *Reading Advantage* paperback, a classroom library book, or a new or familiar selection in the magazine. Always model your own thinking first.

### Making Connections

- What does this story (article, passage) remind me of?
- What do I already know about this topic?
- Where have I heard about this topic before?
- What do I have in common with the characters, people, or situations in the text?
- What other books, stories, articles, movies, or TV shows does this text make me think about?

### Monitor Understanding

- Do I understand what I'm reading? If not, what part is confusing to me?
- What fix-up strategies can I use to solve the problem? (See During Reading for fix-up strategies.)
- Why did a character say (do, think, ask) that?
- What images do I visualize from the text? What parts can't I visualize?
- Why did the author include (or not include) those details?

## Writing Compare and Contrast  INDEPENDENT

Have students choose two indoor sports to compare and contrast. First, have students work in pairs to discuss their ideas for comparing and contrasting. Then have students work independently to fill in a Venn diagram comparing and contrasting two indoor sports.

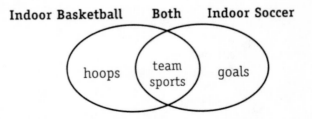

**Indoor Basketball**  **Both**  **Indoor Soccer**

hoops | team sports | goals

For instruction and practice writing compare-contrast paragraphs, see lessons in *Writing Advantage*, pages 113–151.

## Fluency: Pacing

**SMALL GROUP**

After students have read the article at least once, have them work in pairs to alternate reading the different sections aloud. Students should practice reading aloud to their partner, who will provide feedback to encourage evenly paced reading. Point out to students that if they read too fast, too slow, or in a stopping-starting manner, their listeners will not be able to make sense of the words. Model the difference between evenly paced reading and unevenly paced reading.

As you listen to partners reading, use these prompts to guide them to read expressively and with an even pace.

▶ Listen to me read. Then read it just like I did.

▶ Reread this sentence a little bit faster (or slower).

▶ Try to make your voice sound a little stronger (or livelier) when you read. Your listeners will hear you better.

▶ Notice the punctuation; it will help guide your reading.

When students read aloud, do they—

✓ demonstrate a smooth pace, not too fast or too slow?

✓ incorporate well-timed pauses between words and phrases?

✓ reflect an awareness and understanding of punctuation?

## English Language Learners

**SMALL GROUP**

To support students' understanding and use of text features in "The Great Indoors," examine the headings throughout the text.

1. Explain that headings tell the main idea of a section of text.

2. Have students identify and read the headings in "The Great Indoors."

3. Have partners tell what each section will be about.

## Independent Activity Options

**INDEPENDENT**

While you work with individuals or small groups, others can work independently on one or more of the following options.

▶ Level A paperback books, see TE pages 371–376

▶ Level A *eZines*

▶ Repeat word sorts from this lesson

▶ *Student Journal* pages for this lesson

▶ *Writing Advantage* independent lessons

# Assessment

## Strategy Assessment

To help you and your students assess their use of comprehension strategies, ask the following questions. Students can complete a written response or provide verbal answers in a one-on-one reading conference.

1. **Making Connections** What connections did you make to the text? How did those connections help with your understanding? (Answers will vary. Students may mention their own experience with a sport, or watching others participating, and should mention how that helped them relate to information in the article.)

2. **Monitor Understanding** What words in this selection were difficult to understand? How did you figure out their meanings? (Answers will vary. Possible response: I didn't know what *turf* was. I reread the sentence it was in and read on. Now I know that *turf* is "a ground covering that looks and feels like grass.")

For ongoing informal assessment, use the checklists on pages 61–64 of *Level A Assessment*.

## Word Study Assessment

Use these steps to help you and your students assess their understanding of long and short *u* homophones.

1. Create a chart like the one shown, omitting the words in the second column.

2. Have students read the words in the first column.

3. For each word, have students write a homophone in the second column. The answers are shown.

| Word | Homophone |
|-------|-----------|
| dew | due |
| billed | build |
| urn | earn |
| chute | shoot |
| none | nun |

Great Source
Reading Advantage

**Level A Assessment**

## SUMMARY
"City Greens" is an **essay** about city parks. A **poem** follows.

### COMPREHENSION STRATEGIES
Determining Importance
Making Connections

### WRITING
Fact-Opinion Chart

### VOCABULARY
Synonym and Antonym Chart

### PHONICS/WORD STUDY
Long and Short *u* Compound Words

#### Lesson Vocabulary
| | |
|---|---|
| luxury | economy |
| quality | pollution |
| urban | |

### MATERIALS
*Cities*, pp. 26–31
*Student Journal*, pp. 131–133
*Word Study Manual*, p. 74
*Writing Advantage*, pp. 113–151

# CITY GREENS

Bright flowers create a diamond design at the Golden Gate Park in San Francisco, California.

## What can a walk in the park do for you? Here is one person's opinion.

Most cities are built of concrete and steel. Grass and trees are a welcome sight. City parks aren't a <u>luxury</u>; we need them. They improve the <u>quality</u> of life. Without parks, a city can feel cold and empty. With them, a city can feel warm and relaxing.

More than two hundred million Americans live in or near a city. Where do you think they usually go to enjoy outdoor recreation? If you guessed "city parks," you're right!

Most city parks are not as famous as national parks. They are not as large. They don't have big mountains or caves or other things that national parks have. But city parks do offer a lot. You can find places to walk or to sit and talk. You can find places to play sports or play music. There are places to sit quietly and read a book. There are places to have a picnic.

Not every city park is big enough to do everything. But city parks do give us a chance to relax and have fun. And they give our eyes a feast of colors.

A park in downtown Houston, Texas, features a pond and shaded areas, making it an ideal place to escape the heat. ▼

**26**

# Before Reading
*WHOLE CLASS* Use one or more activities.

### Think-Pair-Share
Ask each student to visualize and sketch (or map) a park that he or she has visited. Then have partners share and discuss their sketches with each other. Have pairs report on the similarities and differences of their sketches.

▶

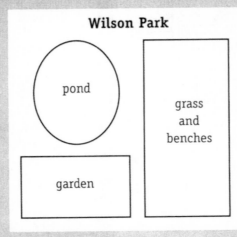

Wilson Park

pond

grass and benches

garden

### Vocabulary Preview
Review the vocabulary list with students and clarify pronunciations. Then have students begin the knowledge rating chart on *Student Journal* page 131. They will finish it later. Model the process of filling in the chart for one of the words.

Some parks have special features. There might be a place where dogs can run free. Some parks even have a zoo. There might be paths for bike riding or rinks for in-line skating. There might even be trails for horseback riding. In winter, you might sled down a snowy hill. In summer, you might nap in the sun. Parks are busy places all year round!

## Central Park

Central Park is the largest and most important park in New York City. It is 2-1/2 miles long and 1/2 mile wide. (The whole island of Manhattan, on which Central Park is located, is 12-1/2 miles long and 2-1/2 miles wide.) In Central Park, you will find a zoo, an open-air theater, and an ice-skating rink. You will also find a restaurant and a reservoir, a place to store water for the city. Even though it is in the middle of a city, Central Park is one of the best places in the United States for bird watching.

27

## DIFFERENTIATED INSTRUCTION
### Preview the Selection

Try using the following steps to enhance the preview:

1. Have students read the title, captions, and introductory paragraph. Then have them look at the photographs.

2. Ask students to share what they learned. Record their ideas in a concept web on the board or on chart paper.

3. Have students reread the introductory paragraph. Explain that this paragraph presents the main idea of the article. Ask students to use this main idea (that people who live in cities need parks) to predict what the author will say in the rest of the selection.

### Student Journal page 131

Name _____ Date _____

**Building Vocabulary: Knowledge Rating Chart**
Show your knowledge of each word by adding information to the other boxes.

| Word | Define or Use in a Sentence | Where Have I Seen or Heard It? | How Is It Used in the Selection? | Looks Like (Words or Sketch) |
|---|---|---|---|---|
| luxury | | | | |
| quality | | | | |
| urban | | | | |
| economy | | | | |
| pollution | | | | |

Cities • City Greens

131

## Preview the Selection

Have students look through the five pages of the essay, pages 26–30 in the magazine. For a previewing strategy, have students read the first sentence of each paragraph in the article to see if they can figure out some important ideas they'll learn. Discuss students' observations. (See Differentiated Instruction.)

## Teacher Think Aloud

*The title and subtitle tell me that this selection will tell about one person's opinion of parks. The pictures show me different parks. I don't see any subheadings, so I'm not sure how the text will be organized. I'll have to read to find out exactly what the opinion is and how the text is organized.*

## Make Predictions/ Set Purpose

Students should use the information they gathered in previewing the selection to make some predictions about the article. If students have trouble generating a purpose for reading, suggest that they read to learn about why city parks are important.

# DIFFERENTIATED INSTRUCTION

## Comprehension

DETERMINING IMPORTANCE

To help students determine the importance of ideas on page 28, ask these questions:

- How does the author support his or her ideas about parks?

- Which arguments do you think are most convincing? Why?

Good parks make good neighbors. Parks help people connect with one another. I like what Charles Jordan, director of Oregon Parks and Recreation, said. He said, "Parks are the most democratic spaces in the city."

Do you know what that means? It means people of any background can all enjoy the same park. It doesn't matter whether you are rich or poor. People meet there to discuss sports or politics. They talk about their lives. They discuss their neighborhoods. A park is a great place for kids and

adults. Clubs and teams can also meet there. Parks hold concerts and dances.

Urban parks also help a city's economy. Cities with quality parks are called *green cities*. Green cities offer a high quality of life, because they make city life pleasant. Businesses like to be in green cities. That's because green cities attract good workers. Green cities have a better chance of attracting and keeping businesses.

Good parks also improve property values. People want to build and buy nice homes in a city that has great parks. The homes are usually worth more money in cities with nice parks.

I'll give an example. Let's say that Mr. and Mrs. Jones have a nice home in a small city. The city is building a parking lot nearby. A parking lot is useful. But Mr. and Mrs. Jones may not want to live next to one. Suppose the city built a park near Mr. and Mrs. Jones's home. How would they feel then? I think they would be pleased. How would you feel?

Now, someone might say: "I agree. Parks are important.

▲ Indoor public gardens, or *conservatories,* are a great way for people to enjoy nature, no matter what the weather.

▶ In a housing development, all the homes look alike. There is some green space, but a nearby city park provides more room to move around.

**28**

# During Reading

## Comprehension

DETERMINING IMPORTANCE

Use these questions to model for students how to determine the importance of ideas on page 26 of the selection. Then have students determine the importance of ideas as they read page 28.

- What are the most important ideas on this page?

- How can I support my beliefs?

(See Differentiated Instruction.)

## Teacher Think Aloud

*I think the most important idea is that city parks are important. The author supports that with these ideas: city dwellers don't have a lot of green space around them, kids need a place to play sports, and parks provide a place to relax.*

## Comprehension

MAKING CONNECTIONS

Use these questions to model making connections with the text. Then have students make their own connections.

- What sounds familiar to me?

- How does what I already know help me understand the text?

A soccer team holds practice in Atlanta, Georgia's, Piedmont Park. Organized sports teams are one of the many groups that benefit from a city's planned green spaces.

They are beautiful and necessary. But they cost a lot of money. Who is going to pay for them? We have other things to pay for. We have to fix our highways. We have to build more schools. We have to repair our bridges. We don't have money to fix our parks. We can't afford to build new ones."

The answer to this problem is not simple, but volunteers can help a city save money. They can offer physical labor. People can paint benches or pick up trash. People can also donate money or other goods. There are lots of ways people can give their time or share their skills. By working together, people can help keep parks in tip-top shape.

There are other good reasons to have city parks. Did you know that parks help fight air <u>pollution</u>? Factories and cars put unhealthy gases and dirt into the air. But trees and other plants improve air quality. Leaves absorb pollutants in the air, such as ozone and sulfur dioxide. And trees give off oxygen, which is what we breathe in. You want cleaner air and water in your city? Plant some more trees!

A volunteer plants petunias in the flower beds for the summer season at her local park. Gardening requires a lot of work, but the rewards are worth the effort. Sunshine, fresh air, and exercise are just a few of the good reasons to volunteer at a park.

29

## Teacher Think Aloud

*I went to New York City last fall to visit my sister. I couldn't believe how many buildings there were. When we got to Central Park, I felt so happy to see open spaces and beautiful trees. I can see why the author feels so strongly about city parks.*

## Fix-Up Strategies

Offer these strategies to help students read independently.

### If you don't understand what you're reading:

- Reread the difficult section to look for clues to help you comprehend.
- Read ahead to find clues to help you comprehend.
- Retell, or say in your own words, what you've read.
- Visualize, or form mental pictures of, what you've read.

### If you don't understand a word:

- Reread the sentence. Look for ideas and words that provide meaning clues.
- Find clues by reading a few sentences before and after the confusing word.
- Look for the base or root word and think about its meaning.
- Think about the topic or plot at this point to see if either offers meaning clues.

## Writing

### Fact-Opinion Chart

Help students recognize a statement as fact or an opinion.

1. Say: *Central Park is the largest park in New York City.* Ask: *Is this statement a fact or an opinion? How do you know?* This statement can be proven by checking records. So it is a fact.

2. Now say: *Central Park is the most beautiful park in the United States.* Ask: *Is this a fact or an opinion?* This statement cannot be proven by checking records. So it is an opinion because it describes someone's feelings or beliefs.

### Student Journal page 132

Name _____ Date _____

**Writing: Fact and Opinion Chart**

Fill in the chart below with facts and opinions from "City Greens." An example has been done for you. Remember, a fact can be proven. An opinion is how one person thinks or feels.

| Fact | Opinion |
|------|---------|
| More than 200 million Americans live in or near a city. | Grass and trees are a welcome sight. |
| | |
| | |
| | |

132     Cities • City Greens

Cities are now paying more attention to their parks. Portland, Oregon, and Pittsburgh have new waterfront parks. Denver and Minneapolis have cleaned up polluted areas. Now they have new parks! San Francisco and Boston are turning ugly highways into parks. Philadelphia has many new community gardens. San Diego has built parks to attract tourists. Our cities are becoming greener.

There are many good reasons why we should keep parks clean and safe. They are fun places to visit. They are good for business. They help keep the air clean.

Parks are good for the soul. They make us feel better about life. Go to a park and see for yourself. ◆

This park in Laguna Beach, California, has flowers and trees typical of California.

The city of Portland, Oregon, has rebuilt its waterfront, creating attractive new public areas. The people of Portland can now enjoy beautiful surroundings as they cycle, jog, and picnic in their city's new park. The park helps to make Portland a more desirable place to live.

30

# After Reading
*Use one or more activities.*

## Check Purpose

Have students decide if their purpose was met. Why does this author believe that city parks are important?

## Discussion Questions

Continue the group discussion with the following questions.

1. What kinds of activities can people enjoy in a city park? (Details)

2. How do city parks help keep the air clean? (Cause-Effect)

3. What did this article help you understand that you didn't understand before reading it? (Making Connections)

## Revisit: Knowledge Rating Chart

After students are finished reading, have them finish their knowledge rating charts on *Student Journal* page 131.

# Sounds of the City

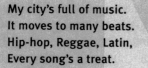

My city's full of music.
It moves to many beats.
Hip-hop, Reggae, Latin,
Every song's a treat.

Music in the subways.
Music on the street.
Singing, playing, dancing,
Drummers keep the beat.

Music sweet and soothing,
Music kind of blue.
Music with a message,
Rhythms old and new.

Jazz, Swing, and Rock,
Opera, Mozart, too.
World Beat, Afro-Pop,
Calypso, country tune.

Music keeps my city
Always on the go.
Subway stop, street corner,
Come enjoy the show.

Music in the subways.
Music on the street.
Singing, playing, dancing,
drummers keep the beat.

**31**

## Poem: Sounds of the City

Ask students to first read the poem silently. Then try reading it chorally, as a group. Discuss what students notice about the poem.

- What patterns did you notice?
- What repeated words and sounds did you hear?
- How would you describe the rhythm of the poem?
- Can you tap out the rhythm of the poem as you hear it? (Then read it with the same rhythm.)

Ask for volunteers to try writing a new verse that would fit the rhythm and rhyme scheme.

### Student Journal page 133

Name _____ Date _____

**Building Vocabulary: Synonym and Antonym Chart**

Think of three words that could be synonyms (similar in meaning) for each word. Next, think of three words that could be antonyms (opposite in meaning) for each word. Use a thesaurus to help you.

| Vocabulary Word | Synonyms | Antonyms |
|---|---|---|
| luxury | 1. fancy | 1. cheap |
| | 2. | 2. |
| | 3. | 3. |
| quality | 1. | 1. |
| | 2. | 2. |
| | 3. | 3. |
| pollution | 1. | 1. |
| | 2. | 2. |
| | 3. | 3. |

Cities • City Greens

**133**

---

## Writing Fact-Opinion Chart

Review with students the difference between a fact and an opinion. A *fact* is a piece of information that can be proven. An *opinion* is how one person thinks or feels and cannot be proven. Have students skim "City Greens" to look for examples of each. Discuss what students find. Then have pairs fill in the fact and opinion chart on *Student Journal* page 132. (See Differentiated Instruction.)

## Vocabulary
### Synonym-Antonym Chart

Display *luxury*. Read the second sentence of the article aloud. *City parks aren't a luxury; we need them.* Ask students what this sentence tells them about the word *luxury*. Students can write synonyms and antonyms (in words or phrases) for *luxury* in the chart on *Student Journal* page 133. Then they can work in pairs to complete it.

## Phonics/Word Study
### Compound Words

Write the following "equations" on the board: *butter + cup = _____; over + view = _____.* Ask students to say the answers (*buttercup, overview*). Ask: *What long and short* u *sounds do you hear in the words?* (long: *view*; short: *butter, cup*.) Now, work with students to complete the in-depth word study activity on TE page 320.

## Long and Short *u* Compound Words

▶ Share the following words with students: *haircut*, *seagull*, and *sunlight*.

▶ Ask what the words have in common. Students should notice that each word is actually made up of two related words. *Haircut* refers to hair being cut. *Seagull* is the name of a gull (a bird) that lives near the sea. *Sunlight* is light from the sun. Compound words always have a meaning connection.

▶ Provide students with a list of compound words they can read. (See *Word Study Manual* page 74.) Have them take the words apart. (*Haircut* becomes *hair + cut*.) Have students work in pairs to decide whether each short or long *u* word within a compound falls into a typical *u* pattern. Do not hold students responsible for parts of words that are not in the short or long *u* family. Typical patterns recently studied include: short *u, oo, ew, ue,* and *uCe*.

For more information on word sorts and spelling stages, see pages 5–31 in the *Word Study Manual*.

# Focus on . . .

Use one or more activities in this section to focus on a particular area of need in your students.

## Comprehension  STRATEGY SUPPORT  INDEPENDENT

To help those students who need more practice using the strategies covered in this lesson, work one-on-one or in small groups to apply the strategy prompts below. Apply the prompts to a *Reading Advantage* paperback, a classroom library book, or a new or familiar selection in the magazine. Always model your own thinking first.

### Determining Importance

• What is the most important idea in the paragraph? How can I prove it?

• Which details are unimportant? Why?

• What does the author want me to understand?

• Why is this information important (or not important) to me?

### Making Connections

• What does this story (article, passage) remind me of?

• What do I already know about this topic?

• Where have I heard about this topic before?

• What do I have in common with the characters, people, or situations in the text?

• What other books, stories, articles, movies or TV shows does this text make me think about?

## Writing Write and Illustrate  INDEPENDENT

Have students write about and illustrate an experience in a park. As a group, brainstorm some ideas together. Make a list on the board. Topics might include seeing/watching an animal, playing on equipment, talking to a friend, or attending a celebration. After students have chosen a topic, have them jot down three details they'd like to include. Then have students use their list as a guide to write about their experience.

To give students more practice in writing descriptive paragraphs, see lessons in *Writing Advantage*, pages 113–151.

## Fluency: Expression

SMALL GROUP

After students have read the poem "Sounds of the City" at least once, have them work with a partner to practice reading it aloud. Pairs can decide how they want to alternate reading different parts. Encourage pairs to do a dramatic reading for the class. Suggest that students use real (or make-shift) percussion instruments to accompany themselves.

Tell students to pay attention to expression, or the emotions they want to convey, when reading aloud.

When students read aloud, do they—

✓ reflect an understanding of the text?

✓ demonstrate appropriate timing, stress, and intonation?

✓ incorporate appropriate speed and phrasing?

## English Language Learners

SMALL GROUP

To support students as they practice making connections, provide a writing activity related to the comprehension activity on TE page 316.

1. Have students recall a time when they visited a park.

2. Have students draw a picture and write several sentences describing their experience.

3. Have students share their work with a partner.

## Independent Activity Options

INDEPENDENT

While you work with individuals or small groups, others can work independently on one or more of the following options.

▶ Level A paperback books, see TE pages 371–376

▶ Level A *eZines*

▶ Repeat word sorts from this lesson

▶ *Student Journal* pages for this lesson

▶ *Writing Advantage* independent lessons

# Assessment

## Strategy Assessment

To help you and your students assess their use of comprehension strategies, ask the following questions. Students can complete a written response or provide verbal answers in a one-on-one reading conference.

1. **Determining Importance** What details did you think were most important in this selection? Why do you think so? (Answers will vary. Possible response: Parks are good for business, which attracts workers and homeowners. I think showing the financial benefits of parks will help convince people to fund them.)

2. **Making Connections** What connections did you make to the text? How did those connections help with your understanding? (Answers will vary. An answer should report one or more relevant details from the student's own experience, and explain how it helped the student understand or relate to the text.)

For ongoing informal assessment, use the checklists on pages 61–64 of *Level A Assessment*.

## Word Study Assessment

Use these steps to help you and your students assess their understanding of compound words.

1. Create a chart like the one shown, including all the words.

2. Have students read aloud the words in column A and column B. Have them note which words contain a long or short *u* sound.

3. Have students pair words from column A and column B to create compound words. (ladybug, handcuffs, overused, haircut, butterfly)

| A | B |
|---|---|
| lady | used |
| hand | fly |
| over | cuffs |
| hair | cut |
| butter | bug |

Great Source
Reading Advantage

Level A
Assessment

# Lost & Found in Chicago
*Cities*, pages 32–37

## SUMMARY
In this **short story**, twins Jade and Duane have just moved away from their friends to a new home in Chicago. One of their first adventures takes place at the Lincoln Park Zoo.

## COMPREHENSION STRATEGIES
Understanding Text Structure
Making Connections

## WRITING
Personal Experience

## VOCABULARY
Illustrated Mini-Dictionary

## PHONICS/WORD STUDY
Long *o* and Long *u* Review

### Lesson Vocabulary
| | |
|---|---|
| long-winded | grooming |
| midway | frantic |

## MATERIALS
*Cities*, pp. 32–37
*Student Journal*, pp. 134–136
*Word Study Manual*, p. 75
*Writing Advantage*, pp. 93–112

Duane and Jade Green were not very happy. Dad accepted a new job at Northwestern University. It was near downtown Chicago. He was going to teach writing there. Mom found a job at a big clothing store. She was the new buyer of sports clothes.

So the twins, Duane and Jade, had to move away from their small farm town in Illinois to the big city of Chicago. They had to move away from their friends in middle school. And they had to give up their pet pig, Spot. He could do tricks just like a dog. He was their most treasured pet.

Mom and Dad tried their best to make Duane and Jade feel comfortable in their new city home. The family went on many trips to the downtown area. They went to the Field Museum and saw "Sue." She is the oldest and most complete fossil of a Tyrannosaurus Rex. They visited the Sears Tower, which, if you count the roof antennas, is the tallest building in the world.

## Lost & Found in Chicago

32

# Before Reading
*WHOLE CLASS* Use one or more activities.

## Think-Pair-Share
Ask students how they might feel if they had to move away and leave their friends. Have each student make a short list of positives and negatives of such an experience. Then have pairs read and discuss their lists.

| Positives | Negatives |
|---|---|
| • make new friends | • miss old friends |
| • meet new people | • feel homesick |

## Vocabulary Preview
Review the vocabulary list with students. Have students begin working on the predictions chart on *Student Journal* page 134. Model the process for students. Tell students not to worry about whether their predictions prove to be correct. They will revisit their predictions later.

They even went on a bike trip along the Lake Michigan waterfront and picnicked in Grant Park.

Duane and Jade enjoyed the family trips. Still, they missed their small farm town.

"I'll never make new friends," said Duane. "These kids are city dudes."

"I miss our old school," added Jade. "Lincoln School is so much bigger than our other school."

"I don't know what they are studying here. Suppose I don't understand the work?" Duane asked.

"I'll help you with your homework," Dad replied.

"Yeah, right," said Duane.

"I just learned something new," Mom chimed in. "I always thought that Chicago was nicknamed 'The Windy City' because it gets really windy. But it got its name from a newspaper editor in 1893. He was tired of the people in the mayor's office who kept bragging about the Chicago World's Fair of 1893. He said they were <u>long-winded</u> because they never stopped talking. From that came the term 'windy city.' Of course, the wind does blow in off Lake Michigan, too."

"Big deal," said Duane.

"Wait a minute, Duane," said Dad. "That World's Fair marked the first appearance of the Ferris wheel. George W. Ferris spent $250,000 to build the big wheel. He also paid $25,000 for the spot on the Fair's <u>midway</u>."

"Hey, that's very cool," said Jade. "Who knew?"

### Midway

The word *midway* was first used at Chicago's Columbian Exposition in 1893. It was the site of the amusement section. Now *midway* refers to the place at any fair, carnival, or amusement park where the concessions (food stands) and amusements (the rides) are located.

33

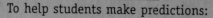

## DIFFERENTIATED INSTRUCTION
## Make Predictions/Set Purpose

To help students make predictions:

1. Explain that when you make predictions, you use the information you already know to predict what will happen next.

2. Ask a volunteer to read the first two paragraphs aloud. Then ask: *How did the twins feel about their home in a small farm town? What problems do you predict they will have living in a big city?*

3. Tell students that as they read, they should periodically stop to predict what will happen next. This will help them better focus on details, and understand what they read.

### Student Journal page 134

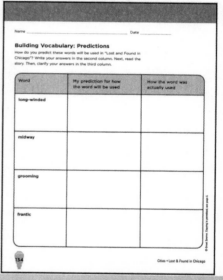

## Preview the Selection

Have students look through the six pages of the story, pages 32–37 in the magazine. Use these or similar questions to orient students to the story.

- What do the illustrations tell you about the setting of the story?

- Do you think this story is fiction or nonfiction? How can you tell?

## Teacher Think Aloud

*As I flip through the selection, I see illustrations of buildings, and kids at a zoo. I don't see any subheadings, and I see lots of dialogue, so I think I'm going to read a fiction story. I'll read to see what the story is about.*

## Make Predictions/Set Purpose

Students should use the information they gathered in previewing the selection to make some predictions about the story. If students have trouble generating a purpose for reading, suggest that they read to learn about two kids who move from a farm town to a big city. (See Differentiated Instruction.)

## Comprehension
### UNDERSTANDING TEXT STRUCTURE

To help students understand the features of realistic fiction, ask:

- Do the characters seem like real people? Do they speak and act like people you know?
- Does the story take place in a realistic place?
- Does the problem seem like a problem that can happen in real life? Is the solution realistic?

### The Chicago World's Fair

Was the Chicago World's Fair of 1893 really "fair" to all people? It was considered a major event in American history and culture.

The official name of the fair was the World's Columbian Exposition. It was named in honor of Christopher Columbus, to mark the 400th anniversary of Columbus's arrival in the New World. (The exposition was delayed by one year.)

The exhibits promoted progress in science, industry, and culture. However, few African Americans were part of the fair. Black men were not allowed to participate. Only two black women were given clerical jobs.

34

The next day was Saturday. Dad had a meeting at the university. Mom had to work at the store.

"I have an idea," said Dad. "What if I drop you guys off at the Lincoln Park Zoo? You're old enough to go around the park by yourselves. I will pick you up at four o'clock at the same spot where I drop you off. Do you want to go?"

"Yes!" yelled Jade.

"Yeah, okay," added Duane. He didn't sound excited, but he did love animals as much as his sister.

"Take the cell phone," Mom told them, "just in case you need us for any reason."

"There are plenty of park people you can go to if you have any questions," reminded Dad.

"We're not babies," said Duane. "Don't worry. We'll be fine."

The twins went to the gate as soon as they left the car. They were ready to pay to get in when they found out that the zoo was free.

# During Reading

## Comprehension
### UNDERSTANDING TEXT STRUCTURE

Use these questions to model for students how to recognize the structure of realistic fiction. Then have students identify and describe the plot and conflict.

- Who are the main characters in the story?
- What is the setting, plot, and conflict in the story?

(See Differentiated Instruction.)

## Teacher Think Aloud

*The first page of the story introduces the two main characters: Duane and Jade Green. The setting is Chicago. Duane and Jade don't seem very happy about leaving their school, friends, and pet pig to move to Chicago. My guess is this will be the problem in the story, but I'll read to find out.*

## Comprehension
### MAKING CONNECTIONS

Use these questions to model making connections with the text. Then have students make their own connections with the text.

- Does the plot of this story remind me of other stories I've read?
- Have I, or anyone I know, been in the same situation as Duane and Jade?

"Amazing!" said Duane. He shoved the money back into his pocket. "Now we'll have more money to spend on food."

"Let's take this map of the zoo," Jade told Duane. "It is a pretty big place."

"I see they have different trails for us to follow. Let's go to the Great Ape House first," Duane told Jade.

"No problem," Jade answered. "Let's get to the Green Trail. That's where they are."

The twins saw gorillas and chimpanzees. A few ran around and beat their chests. Some mothers were grooming their young ones by picking off bugs and combing their hair with their claws. After a while, the twins went to see the lions and other big cats.

"Man, I need food," Duane suddenly said. "Let's go get some eats!"

"You're always hungry," Jade replied, giving him a disgusted look. "Okay, let's go."

The twins went off to the snack bar nearby. Jade went to the restroom while Duane stood in line for food. When Jade came out of the restroom, she forgot her way. She walked toward the sea lion pool instead of the snack bar.

Duane, in the meantime, had bought food and found a place to sit. He looked for Jade, but she was nowhere in sight!

Jade thought she was walking in the right direction, but she ended up near the Children's Zoo. She stopped at a bench to think things out. Duane had both the cell phone and the map. So she wasn't sure which trail to take.

Just then, Jade saw a little boy about three years old, walking alone and crying. He was lost, too. She stopped the boy and asked who he was looking for.

He said, "Soo-lin, Soo-lin."

35

## Fix-Up Strategies

Offer these strategies to help students read independently.

### If you don't understand what you're reading:

- Reread the difficult section to look for clues to help you comprehend.
- Read ahead to find clues to help you comprehend.
- Retell, or say in your own words, what you've read.
- Visualize, or form mental pictures of, what you've read.

### If you don't understand a word:

- Reread the sentence. Look for ideas and words that provide meaning clues.
- Find clues by reading a few sentences before and after the confusing word.
- Look for the base or root word and think about its meaning.
- Think about the topic or plot at this point to see if either offers meaning clues.

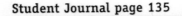

Name _____ Date _____

**Writing: Personal Experience**

As you reflect on "Lost & Found in Chicago," think about an
experience you have had in an unfamiliar setting. Describe
how you felt being in a new place. Use the lines below to
write a paragraph telling about your experience.

_____

_____

_____

_____

_____

_____

_____

_____

_____

_____

Cities • Lost & Found in Chicago                                    135

A girl came running out of the Children's Zoo. She looked <u>frantic</u>. Her breathing was fast; tears stained her cheek. Then she saw Jade with her brother. "Oh, I'm so glad you found Lee," said Soo-lin. "I turned my back to buy some food so he could feed the goats. When I turned around, he was gone! I was so scared."

"I know how you feel," said Jade. "I don't know if I should laugh or cry, because I'm a little lost, too."

"Where are you supposed to be?" asked Soo-lin.

"I'm supposed to be at the snack bar with my brother," Jade explained.

**36**

"No problem," said Soo-lin. "Follow me. I've been to this zoo many times."

Soo-lin led Jade to the snack bar. They talked all the way over.

"I go to Lincoln. It's my first year here," Jade told Soo-lin.

"You won't believe this," said Soo-lin. "I go to Lincoln, too."

Then the girls found out that they lived three blocks from each other.

Duane looked happy to see his sister. Then he got mad.

# After Reading

Use one or more activities.

## Check Purpose

Have students decide whether their purpose was met. Did they learn why moving away from friends and family can be difficult?

## Discussion Questions

Continue the group discussion with the following questions.

1. How do Duane and Jade's parents try to make the twins feel comfortable in their new home? (Details)

2. What can you tell about Jade's character from the way she responds when she finds Lee? (Inferential Thinking)

3. Does Duane remind you of anyone you know? What do you think about his attitude? (Making Connections)

## Revisit: Predictions Chart

Have students return to *Student Journal* page 134 to complete the predictions chart. How were the words actually used? Students can clarify their predictions in the right-hand column of the chart.

"Where were you? I've been waiting forever!"

Jade explained what happened and introduced Soo-lin. "You're twins, huh?" said Soo-lin. "Some twin boys live on my block. They go to Lincoln, too. I'll bring them over Monday morning, and we can all walk to school together." Soo-lin turned and waved goodbye. She walked away with Lee.

"Okay," Jade called out. Then she turned to Duane. "Maybe getting lost is just what we needed to find new friends."

"Yeah, right," answered Duane. He wasn't so sure about that. But he told Jade that he would walk with all of them to school on Monday.

When Dad picked up the twins, he saw smiling faces. Well, at least Jade was smiling. Jade told Dad what had happened.

"Well, maybe living in a big city won't be so bad after all," he said.

"Maybe not," answered Jade.

"Yeah, right," answered Duane. ◆

Navy Pier is located on Chicago's lakefront and includes an IMAX theater, a giant Ferris wheel, and a sculpture park.

37

## Writing

### Personal Experience

If students need help with this activity, try following these steps:

1. Before students write their paragraphs, have them write their topic in the center of a piece of paper. Then have them create an idea web in which they record some of the details and feelings they had about the experience of being in an unfamiliar place.

2. Have pairs of students share their webs and discuss their experiences with each other. Then have students work independently to complete the activity.

### Student Journal page 136

Name _____  Date _____

**Building Vocabulary: Illustrated Mini-Dictionary**
Write a definition and then make an illustration for each vocabulary word.

| Vocabulary Word | Definition | Illustration |
|---|---|---|
| long-winded | | |
| midway | | |
| grooming | | |
| frantic | | |

136                    Cities • Lost & Found in Chicago

## Writing Personal Experience

Have students use *Student Journal* page 135 to write a paragraph about an experience they have had in an unfamiliar setting. Brainstorm some ideas together before students begin. Encourage students to provide as many details as possible. (See Differentiated Instruction.)

## Vocabulary
### Illustrated Mini-Dictionary

Have students use *Student Journal* page 136 to write and illustrate a mini-dictionary for the four vocabulary words.

## Phonics/Word Study
### Long *o* and Long *u* Review

Display these vowel patterns: oCC, ost, oCe, oa, ow, ure, ue, ui, ew. Have students list words with the long *o* and long *u* sound, and try to match them with their vowel pattern. (Examples include: *lock, most, tone, boat, now, cure, blue, fruit, flew.*) Now, work with students to complete the in-depth vowel activity on TE page 328.

## Long *o* and Long *u* Review

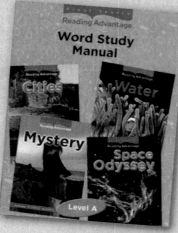

▶ To review the most common long vowel patterns within the last two vowel families students have studied (*o* and *u*), set up a straightforward sort such as the one below. Note that no oddballs are included to confuse students. The emphasis should be that each vowel pattern is not exclusive—thinking about patterns across different vowels is helpful.

▶ Using the Long *o* and *u*: Cumulative Sort sheet, have students sort across the vowel patterns they have studied for the two vowel sounds. (See *Word Study Manual* page 75.)

▶ As always, speed and accuracy are the goals.

| Long *o* and *u*: Cumulative Sort | | | | | | | | |
|---|---|---|---|---|---|---|---|---|
| *oCC* | *ost* | *oCe* | *oa* | *ow* | *ure* | *ue* | *ui* | *ew* |
| roll | ghost | tone | toast | blow | pure | true | fruit | blew |
| troll | most | gnome | boast | show | cure | blue | suit | stew |

For more information on word sorts and spelling stages, see pages 5–31 in the *Word Study Manual*.

# Focus on . . .

Use one or more activities in this section to focus on a particular area of need in your students.

## Comprehension   STRATEGY SUPPORT   INDEPENDENT

To help those students who need more practice using the strategies covered in this lesson, work one-on-one or in small groups to apply the strategy prompts below. Apply the prompts to a *Reading Advantage* paperback, a classroom library book, or a new or familiar selection in the magazine. Always model your own thinking first.

### Understanding Text Structure

- What kind of text is this? (book, story, article, guidebook, play, manual)
- How does the author organize the text? (cause-effect, problem-solution, chronological order, description, question-answer, comparison-contrast)
- What details support my thoughts about the text structure?
- What is the cause (effect, problem, solution, order, question, answer)?
- If fiction, who are the characters? What is the setting, plot, conflict, and resolution?

### Making Connections

- What does this story (article, passage) remind me of?
- What do I already know about this topic?
- Where have I heard about this topic before?
- What do I have in common with the characters, people, or situations in the text?
- What other books, stories, articles, movies, or TV shows does this text make me think about?

## Writing Summary Paragraph   INDEPENDENT

Provide a copy of the somebody-wanted-but-so chart for each student. (See TE page 386.) Help students fill in the chart with information about "Lost & Found in Chicago." Then have students write a summary paragraph story.

| | My Notes |
|---|---|
| **Somebody** | Duane and Jade took a trip to the zoo. |
| **Wanted** | They wanted to get food from the snack bar. |
| **But** | But Jade got lost. |
| **So** | So Soo-lin helped Jade. |

For additional instruction on responses to literature, see the lessons in *Writing Advantage,* pages 93–112.

## Fluency: Expression

SMALL GROUP

After students have read the story at least once, have them work in pairs to create a script for part of the story. Students can write the script in play or dialogue form. Have pairs first choose the part of the story they'd like to use. Then pairs should jot down the general idea of the action that will occur in the scripts. After the scripts are written, pairs can practice reading them to each other and then do a dramatic reading for the rest of the group. Students should focus on reading with expression, or showing the feelings of the characters.

When students read aloud, do they—

✓ reflect an understanding of the text?

✓ demonstrate appropriate timing, stress, and intonation?

✓ incorporate appropriate speed and phrasing?

## English Language Learners

SMALL GROUP

To support students' understanding of the elements of realistic fiction, extend the comprehension activity on TE page 324.

1. Discuss the answers to the comprehension questions.
2. Have students divide a piece of paper into four sections and label the sections "Setting," "Characters," "Problem," and "Solution."
3. Have students complete the story map with information from "Lost & Found in Chicago."

## Independent Activity Options

INDEPENDENT

While you work with individuals or small groups, others can work independently on one or more of the following options.

▶ Level A paperback books, see TE pages 371–376
▶ Level A *eZines*
▶ Repeat word sorts from this lesson
▶ *Student Journal* pages for this lesson
▶ *Writing Advantage* independent lessons

# Assessment

## Strategy Assessment

To help you and your students assess their use of comprehension strategies, ask the following questions. Students can complete a written response or provide verbal answers in a one-on-one reading conference.

1. **Understanding Text Structure** What is the problem in this story? How is the problem resolved? (Duane and Jade move to Chicago and are not happy about the change. They go to the zoo, and when Jade gets lost, she makes a new friend, who promises to introduce the twins to more kids.)

2. **Making Connections** What connections did you make to the story? How did those connections help with your understanding? (Answers will vary. Students might compare Duane and Jade's relationship to their own relationship with a sibling, or mention which character's attitude is most like their own. Answers should show how students can relate to the text.)

See *Level A Assessment* page 46 for formal assessment to go with *Cities*.

## Word Study Assessment

Use these steps to help you and your students assess their understanding of long *o* and long *u* patterns.

1. Create a chart like the one shown, omitting the answers.

2. Display these words: *roll, stew, suit, true, pure, show, boast, tone, ghost, troll, blew, fruit, blue, cure, blow, toast, poke,* and *most.*

3. Have students read the words aloud.

4. Then have students sort the words into the column with the correct spelling pattern. The answers are shown.

| *oCC* | *ost* | *oCe* | *oa* | *ow* | *ure* | *ue* | *ui* | *ew* |
|-------|-------|-------|------|------|-------|------|------|------|
| roll | ghost | tone | toast | blow | pure | true | fruit | blew |
| troll | most | poke | boast | show | cure | blue | suit | stew |

Reading Advantage

Level A
Assessment

# Mayor Tom Bradley *and* City Cinquains

*Cities*, pages 38–41

## SUMMARY

This **biographical sketch** looks at the significant life accomplishments of Tom Bradley, the former mayor of Los Angeles. The following **poems** are about city life.

## COMPREHENSION STRATEGIES

Inferential Thinking

## WRITING

Cause-Effect

## VOCABULARY

Context

## PHONICS/WORD STUDY

Diphthongs

### Lesson Vocabulary

| | |
|---|---|
| major | determined |
| ethnic | opportunity |
| conflicts | mourned |

## MATERIALS

*Cities*, pp. 38–41
*Student Journal*, pp. 137–140
*Word Study Manual*, p. 76
*Writing Advantage*, pp. 30–55

California
Los Angeles

# Mayor Tom Bradley

This is the story of an American dream. A poor boy from Texas becomes mayor of the great city of Los Angeles, California.

38

# Before Reading

Use one or more activities.

## Make a T-Chart

Start a discussion with students. Ask: *What is the American dream? What is your dream for your future?* Write students' responses on a T-chart. Students can revisit the chart later to add any new information. (See Diifferentiated Instruction.)

| The American Dream | My Dreams |
|---|---|
| big house | go to college |
| good job | get a scholarship |

## Vocabulary Preview

Review the vocabulary list with students. Discuss each word. Then have students complete the word association activity on *Student Journal* page 137. Model the process for one of the words.

## Preview the Selection

Have students survey the three pages of the article. Discuss what students notice.

## Make Predictions/Set Purpose

Students should use the information they gathered in previewing the selection to make some predictions about the article. If students have trouble generating a purpose for reading, suggest that they read to learn why Mayor Tom Bradley is an admirable person.

The people of Los Angeles will never forget Tom Bradley. He was their mayor for 20 years. No other mayor had ever been elected five times! But Tom Bradley made history in an even bigger way. He was the first African American to be the mayor of Los Angeles. In fact, he was the first African American to be the mayor of a <u>major</u> American city.

Bradley was first elected in 1973. At that time, the city had many more white than black voters. Bradley was popular with people of all <u>ethnic</u> backgrounds. They believed he could make Los Angeles a better place for everyone.

Being mayor of a big city is a very hard job. A mayor has to make sure that many different kinds of people work and live in peace. A big city like Los Angeles is a great challenge. A good mayor must help people solve <u>conflicts</u>. Everyone must learn to "give a little, get a little." Tom Bradley tried to create "win-win" solutions.

## From Track Star to Mayor

Solving hard problems was not new to Tom Bradley. He learned to do that when he was very young. Bradley was born in 1917 to a poor family in Texas. At the age of seven, he had to help his family pick cotton. This hard work made him <u>determined</u> to have a better life. The young boy was happy when his family moved to Los Angeles, because he thought life would be better there. But they still had little money. Bradley helped out by delivering newspapers.

Bradley worked hard at both his schoolwork and at sports. This paid off when he won a scholarship college as a track star. But in 1937, times were hard. Bradley left college to become a police officer.

### Racial Discrimination

To discriminate against someone is to make decisions based on a whole class of people, rather than on a single person's characteristics. When the decisions are made because of race, it is called racial discrimination. Tom Bradley felt that he was held back by racial discrimination in the Los Angeles Police Department (LAPD) during his career. Bradley felt that the LAPD did not look at him as an individual. He believed that the LAPD did not promote him because he was black.

39

## DIFFERENTIATED INSTRUCTION
### MAKE A T-CHART

If the students have not heard of the term "American dream," share this information with them:

- Many immigrants came to America seeking a better life. They hoped to be part of the "American dream"—opportunities to work and make money for their families.

- Some Americans grow up in poverty or in situations where they do not have a lot of opportunities. Through hard work and determination, they can gain the education and resources they need to succeed in business, politics, or any field they choose. They are living the "American dream."

### Student Journal page 137

**Building Vocabulary: Making Associations**
Pick two words from the vocabulary list below. Think about what you already know about each word. Then answer the following questions for each word.

| major | conflicts | opportunity |
|-------|-----------|-------------|
| ethnic | determined | mourned |

Word _____
What do you think about when you read this word? _____

Who might use this word? _____

What do you already know about this word? _____

Word _____
What do you think about when you read this word? _____

Who might use this word? _____

What do you already know about this word? _____

Now watch for these words in the magazine selection. Were you on the right track?

Cities • Mayor Tom Bradley                    137

# During Reading

## Comprehension
### INFERENTIAL THINKING

Use these questions to model for students how to make inferences from the section called "From Track Star to Mayor" on page 39. Then have students reveal inferences they make as they read the next section.

- What does the text tell me?

- Using what I already know from the text and my own experience, what can I infer about Tom Bradley's character?

## Teacher Think Aloud

*The text tells me that Tom Bradley grew up poor and suffered discrimination in his first job. He worked hard to overcome obstacles that stood in his way. I know that people who overcome obstacles are often brave. I can infer that Tom Bradley was a brave person.*

## Fix-Up Strategies

Offer these strategies to help students read independently.

**If you don't understand what you're reading:**

- Reread the difficult section to look for clues to help you comprehend.

- Read ahead to find clues to help you comprehend.

- Retell, or say in your own words, what you've read.

- Visualize, or form mental pictures of, what you've read.

## DIFFERENTIATED INSTRUCTION
### Writing Cause-Effect

SMALL GROUP

If students need help with this activity, offer these two cause-effect examples from the article.

**Cause:** Bradley had to work hard as a child.

**Effect:** He was determined to make a better life for himself.

**Cause:** Bradley worked hard at schoolwork and sports.

**Effect:** Bradley won a track scholarship to college.

## City Council

A city council is a group of people who govern, or run, a city. The city council works with the mayor to make decisions and set laws for the city. The people who live in the city elect the members of the city council to their positions.

Bradley stayed at this job for twenty-one years. He worked his way up to the rank of lieutenant (loo TEN ent). Finally, he realized that he could not rise higher in the police department because he was black. So he began to study law at night. After he got his law degree, he left his police job.

Bradley enjoyed being a lawyer. But his real goal was to be in politics. In 1963, he was elected to the City Council. He served three terms. Bradley knew he could make a big difference if he were mayor. In 1973, his dream came true. He was elected mayor of Los Angeles.

### A Great Mayor

At that time, Los Angeles was the third largest U.S. city. The city grew and got stronger with Bradley as its leader. The new mayor helped people start new businesses. He helped them improve their neighborhoods. He told them, "Los Angeles is the city of hope and opportunity. I am a living example of that." If Tom Bradley could become mayor, other people could succeed, too.

Bradley wanted Los Angeles to be a center of trade with Asia. To do that, he improved the airport and the seaport. He also had a subway built. But, Bradley's biggest triumph came in 1984. He brought the Olympic Games to Los Angeles. The people were proud and excited. The city hosted thousands of visitors from all over the world.

Tom Bradley died at the age of eighty in 1998. Many people in Los Angeles mourned him. They were proud of what Bradley had done for their city. Los Angeles was now the second largest city in the United States. Many people had better jobs and lives because of Tom Bradley. He never gave up trying to make life better for the people of his city. ◆

### Student Journal pages 138–139

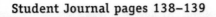

Name _____  Date _____

**Writing: Cause and Effect Chart**

Fill in the following chart with information you gathered from reading "Mayor Tom Bradley." An example has been done for you.

| Cause | Effect |
|-------|--------|
| Bradley had a hard childhood. | He was determined to have a better life. |
| | |
| | |
| | |
| | |

138

Cities • Mayor Tom Bradley

GAMES of the XXIIIrd OLYMPIA

40

# After Reading

WHOLE CLASS

Use one or more activities.

## Check Purpose

Have students decide whether their purpose was met. Did they learn what makes an outstanding mayor? What questions do they still have?

## Discussion Questions

Continue the group discussion with the following questions.

1. Did Tom Bradley's childhood experiences prepare him for the job of mayor? If so, how did they? (Inferential Thinking)

2. Why did Tom Bradley decide to go to law school at night? (Problem-Solution)

3. Based on what you have read, what do you think of Tom Bradley? (Making Connections)

## Revisit: Word Association

Have students revisit *Student Journal* page 137. Now that they have read the article, what new associations can students add?

**Skyscraper**
**Proud, powerful**
**Humming, buzzing, scurrying**
**People rush in and out.**
**Beehive.**

# city cinquains

**Park**
**Soothing, leafy**
**Strolling, skating, cycling**
**City folks glad to relax.**
**Everyone's green place.**

**Subway**
**Noisy, crowded**
**Complaining, pushing, shoving**
**Everyone wants to get home.**
**Rush hour!**

41

## Poems: City Cinquains

Have students read the three cinquains. What patterns do they see? Explain the pattern of a cinquain:

Line 1—Title (one word)

Line 2—Two words to describe the title

Line 3—Three related words that express actions (ending with -ing)

Line 4—Four words that express feelings (complete sentence)

Line 5—Another word or phrase that describes the topic

Point out the word part *cinq*. If students are familiar with French, Spanish, or Italian, they will recognize that *cinq* means "five." A cinquain has five lines.

### Student Journal page 140

Name _____ Date _____
**Building Vocabulary: Using Context**
Choose three of the following vocabulary words to include in a mini-speech that you would give if you were running for public office. Define the words. Then write and perform your speech.

| major | conflicts | opportunity |
|-------|-----------|-------------|
| ethnic | determined | mourned |

1. The word _____ means _____

2. The word _____ means _____

3. The word _____ means _____

Use the lines below to write your mini-speech. When you finish, give your speech to the group.

140                                     Cities • Mayor Tom Bradley

## Writing Cause-Effect

Review the concept of cause and effect. A *cause* is an event that makes something else happen. An *effect* is an event that happens as a result of the cause. Discuss some cause and effect relationships in "Mayor Tom Bradley." Then have students complete the chart on *Student Journal* page 138 and use their charts to write a paragraph on *Student Journal* page 139. (See Differentiated Instruction.)

## Vocabulary Context

When Tom Bradley gave campaign speeches, he probably spoke about helping people start new businesses and improving neighborhoods. What would students speak about if they were running for public office? Have students identify three vocabulary words they might use in a speech to voters. Students can use *Student Journal* page 140 to define the three words and then write a mini-speech in which the words are used.

## Phonics/Word Study

### Diphthongs

Say the word *boy* slowly, exaggerating the diphthong. Ask: *What vowel sounds do you hear in the word* boy? Elicit that the sounds *o* and *e* glide together to make a new vowel sound (*oy*). Write the word *boy* on the board. Then ask students to name other words with the *oy* sound and list them on the board. Now, work with students to complete the in-depth vowel activity on TE page 334.

## Diphthongs

*Ambiguous vowels* are unusual and confusing vowel sounds that many students find difficult. Ambiguous vowels include *dipthongs*, which are vowel sounds that start out with one vowel sound and glide into another sound (*toy, coin, noise*). These vowels have little in common with regular vowels and are often studied separately.

▶ Write the following words on the board: *toy, coin,* and *noise*. Tell students that these words include diphthongs. Explain what that means.

▶ Ask: *Do any of these words have a short or long a sound?* Have students revisit the sounds of short and long *a* and compare the *oi* sound to them. Do the same with *e, i, o,* and *u* as well. Students will notice that the *oi* sound is distinct and cannot be confused with any of those vowels.

▶ Using the Diphthongs sheet, model the sorting process. (See *Word Study Manual* page 76.) Write the headings *oy, oi, oiCe,* and the first few words in the appropriate columns. Complete the sort as a class.

▶ Discuss the sort and what students learned. There are three kinds of *oy* diphthong patterns.

▶ Hand out the Diphthongs sheet. Ask students to cut up the words and do the sort on their own or in groups.

▶ Check the final sorts for accuracy.

| Dipthongs | | |
|---|---|---|
| *oy* | *oi* | *oiCe* |
| ploy | coin | voice |
| joy | moist | noise |
| employ | hoist | poise |
| boy | broil | choice |
| enjoy | foist | |
| toy | spoil | |
| | point | |
| | joist | |

For more information on word sorts and spelling stages, see pages 5–31 in the *Word Study Manual*.

# Focus on . . .

Use one or more activities in this section to focus on a particular area of need in your students.

## Comprehension STRATEGY SUPPORT INDEPENDENT

To help those students who need more practice using the strategies covered in this lesson, work one-on-one or in small groups to apply the strategy prompts below. Apply the prompts to a *Reading Advantage* paperback, a classroom library book, or a new or familiar selection in the magazine. Always model your own thinking first.

### Inferential Thinking

- What are the causes or effects of this event?
- What do I learn from the character or person's thoughts, words, or actions?
- What do I know (or infer) from the text that the author hasn't stated directly?
- What conclusions can I draw?

## Writing Persuasive Paragraph INDEPENDENT

Tom Bradley worked to make Los Angeles a better, fairer place. Ask students how they think their city could be a better, fairer place. First, have them fill in a T-chart as follows:

| What My City Is Like Now | How It Could Be Better |
|---|---|
| There is a lot of garbage in the streets. | We should have clean-up day once a month to clean the streets and raise awareness about litter. |
| Our schools don't have music programs. | People could pay higher taxes so schools can hire music teachers to help kids learn to play instruments. |

Have students choose an issue from the chart. They should then write a paragraph persuading the reader to take the action noted in the right-hand column of their chart.

To give students more practice in writing problem-solution paragraphs, see the lessons in *Writing Advantage,* pages 113–151.

## Fluency: Phrasing

**SMALL GROUP**

After students have read "City Cinquains" at least once, they can use the poems to practice fluent reading. Have partners read the poems into a tape recorder and then listen to and evaluate their reading. Encourage students to read with expression, insert pauses where appropriate, and reread to vary their approaches. Encourage students to read meaningful groups of words (phrases) together.

When students read aloud, do they—

✓ demonstrate quick recognition of words and phrases?

✓ exhibit an understanding of phrasal construction?

✓ incorporate appropriate timing, stress, and intonation?

## English Language Learners

**SMALL GROUP**

To support students' comprehension of the concepts in "Mayor Tom Bradley," make a vocabulary word chart.

1. Make a 3-column chart. In the first column, write vocabulary words from the text: *mayor, accomplishments, lawyer.*

2. Discuss the meanings of the words.

3. Write definitions and draw an illustration in the second column.

4. Brainstorm sentences using the words. Write sentences in the third column.

## Independent Activity Options

**INDEPENDENT**

While you work with individuals or small groups, others can work independently on one or more of the following options.

▶ Level A paperback books, see TE pages 371–376

▶ Level A *eZines*

▶ Repeat word sorts from this lesson

▶ *Student Journal* pages for this lesson

▶ *Writing Advantage* independent lessons

# Assessment

## Strategy Assessment

To help you and your students assess their use of comprehension strategies, ask the following questions. Students can complete a written response or provide verbal answers in a one-on-one reading conference.

- **Inferential Thinking** What can you learn about Tom Bradley from his decision to study law? (Answers will vary. Students might answer that he did not stand for racial discrimination, or that he wanted to do whatever it took to make change.)

For ongoing informal assessment, use the checklists on pages 61–64 of *Level A Assessment*.

## Word Study Assessment

Use these steps to help you and your students assess their understanding of diphthongs.

1. Create a chart like the one shown, including only the words in the first column.

2. Have students read the words aloud.

3. Then have students sort the words into the column with the correct spelling pattern. The answers are shown.

| Words | *oy* | *oi* | *oiCe* |
|-------|------|------|--------|
| noise | joy | coin | noise |
| coin | boy | soil | voice |
| joy | | | |
| boy | | | |
| soil | | | |
| voice | | | |

Great Source
Reading Advantage

**Level A Assessment**

# Seattle Underground

*Cities*, pages 42–47

## SUMMARY

This **article** provides an account of the history of Seattle, a city whose layers reveal a subterranean city beneath the streets.

## COMPREHENSION STRATEGIES

Monitor Understanding
Determining Importance

## WRITING

Illustrated Timeline

## VOCABULARY

Multiple Meanings

## PHONICS/WORD STUDY

Ambiguous Vowel Sounds

### Lesson Vocabulary

historical district
network          professional
unique           shady
musty            stalls

## MATERIALS

*Cities*, pp. 42–47
*Student Journal*, pp. 141–143
*Word Study Manual*, p. 77
*Writing Advantage*, pp. 113–151

# Seattle Underground

When you rebuild the city streets eight to thirty feet higher than they used to be, you end up with a city under the ground.

Washington state is in the Pacific Northwest. It is the only state named for a president. The state capital is Olympia, but Washington's largest and best-known city is Seattle.

Seattle's modern history dates from 1851, shortly after gold was discovered in California. A lot of people moved west, hoping to find gold so that they would become rich. Arthur Denny led a group of pioneers west from Illinois that year. They were the first white settlers to stay in the area. Seattle grew quickly. In 1800, about three hundred people lived in Seattle. By 1900, there were 80,000 people.

This explosion of growth caused major growing pains for the city. To make room for all the new people, Seattle had to be built more than once. There was also a big problem with the city's sewers. Then, in 1889, a major fire burned down most of the city.

Today's city is a familiar sight. Most people know the Space Needle that rises in the skyline, for example. What most people don't know is that some of Seattle's history lies below their feet. The underground city was forgotten for a long time. But it has many visitors today. In fact, a great way to learn about Seattle's history is to visit this beautiful city. You can see all the modern sights. Then you can learn the history by going on the Seattle Underground Tour.

Arthur Denny

42

# Before Reading

Use one or more activities.

## Make a K-W-L Chart ▶

Make a K-W-L chart about the Pacific Northwest. Guide students to contribute information they know or would like to know. Elicit what students know about the states in the region, the weather, the history, and current facts about life in this area. Revisit the chart after students finish the article to add any new information. (See Differentiated Instruction.)

| What We **Know** | What We **Want** to Know | What We **Learned** |
|---|---|---|
| The Pacific Northwest is Washington, Oregon, and Idaho. | What does "Seattle Underground" mean? | |

## Vocabulary Preview

Review the vocabulary list with students. Have students choose a word they're familiar with for the word map on *Student Journal* page 141. Then have students fill in only the definition box before reading the article. Students can complete the word map after they finish the article. Model the process with one of the words.

The Pioneer building stands in the historic Pioneer Square District.

Inset: Historic buildings in Pioneer Square surround Doc Maynard's, the entrance to the Underground Tour.

## Pioneer Square

Pioneer Square is the oldest neighborhood in Seattle. It is in the area known as downtown Seattle. It was the site of the great fire of Seattle in 1889. The fire lasted about a day. It burned down twenty-nine city blocks. The square was restored in 1970 and made into a historical district. This was done because Pioneer Square is where Seattle's history began. The remains of old Seattle lie under your feet as you walk along the sidewalks.

The eighteen blocks that make up Pioneer Square are a mix of old and new places. There are many famous buildings. Some are more than one hundred years old. You will learn about them from your guide for the underground tour.

### Doc Maynard

David Swinson Maynard was a medical doctor who came to Seattle in 1863. He founded Seattle's first hospital. He also had a salmon salting business and a bar with rooms to rent. He made a lot of money in business. He devoted himself and his money to making Seattle a better place.

Make your way over to Pioneer Place Park to the Pioneer Building. It was built in 1892. Doc Maynard's Tavern is there. You meet at the tavern for the underground tour. The tour takes ninety minutes. The remains aren't much to look at. But the network of dimly lit walkways and rooms is unique. As you walk through them, you go back into another time.

So you are now gathered with the tour group. Your guide begins by telling you about old Seattle.

43

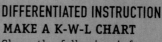

**DIFFERENTIATED INSTRUCTION**
**MAKE A K-W-L CHART**
Share the following information about the Pacific Northwest:

- The Pacific Northwest region includes Washington, Oregon, and Idaho. This area contains mountain ranges, rivers, beaches, two national volcanic monuments, and nineteen national forests.

- The Pacific Northwest generally has warm, wet winters and cool, dry summers. Seattle has about thirty-seven inches of rain a year. The moist climate helps plants and trees flourish and makes the landscape green. This is why the city has the nickname "the Emerald City."

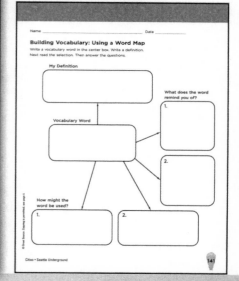

**Student Journal page 141**

### Preview the Selection

Have students survey the six pages of the article, pages 42–47 in the magazine. Use these or similar questions to guide students.

- Who might the men in the ovals be on the first three pages? Why might they be important?

- What do you think this article will be about? Why?

## Teacher Think Aloud

*When I read the title, "Seattle Underground," I'm not sure what the article will be about. The pictures show city scenes and portraits of people. I'm still not sure what the title means. Maybe the article will tell me about Seattle's subway system or some other part of the city that is underground. I'll read to find out.*

### Make Predictions/ Set Purpose

Students should use the information they gathered in previewing the selection to make some predictions about the article. If students have trouble generating a purpose for reading, suggest that they read to learn about a hidden city beneath a city's streets.

## Comprehension
MONITOR UNDERSTANDING

To help students visualize the text, use these steps.

1. Ask students if they have ever been in a cave or a damp basement. Ask: *How do you think that experience would be like taking the underground tour?*

2. Point out the descriptive language in this article. For example, read the first paragraph on page 45 aloud. Ask students to describe what they "see."

Men chopped down trees from the forests at the top of the hill. Then the trees slid down the hill to the sawmill at the bottom. The road that the trees slid down was called "Skid Road."

## The Tour

The tour guide begins:

*In 1851, Arthur A. Denny led a group of settlers from Illinois to the Northwest. They founded a town on Alki Point, a Puget Sound beach. The area today is called West Seattle. The weather was so bad there in the winter that most of the settlers moved in 1852. They went to the eastern side of Elliott Bay. Today, this is Pioneer Square and the rest of downtown Seattle.*

You hear more about Seattle as you make your way underground. Your guide will probably tease you about seeing big cockroaches and rats. But that is just a joke. However, the air feels cool and damp, and it smells <u>musty</u> as you move underground.

*Denny and other settlers had been in this new town for about a year when a man named Henry Yesler arrived from Ohio. He came to make money. He built a sawmill at the bottom of a hill, near Puget Sound. The mill was very successful. Yesler made lots of money, as did other people, because lumber became an important part of the economy. People also began making paper. The city grew.*

44

### Henry Yesler

Yesler built many things in Seattle. He built the cable line for the original trolley. He built the Seattle Hotel. The only remaining part of what was once the Seattle Hotel is the Sinking Ship Garage. The rest of the hotel was destroyed in 1962. After fire destroyed the business section of Seattle in 1889, Yesler urged people to start rebuilding.

*All kinds of shops opened near the mill. The town received a city charter in 1859. By 1870, about a thousand people lived here.*

*As times changed and Seattle grew, all sorts of people came here. They displayed both the good and bad sides of human nature. There were <u>professional</u> people who wanted to work. Sailors, loggers, and gold miners found jobs. Lots of <u>shady</u> people came to Seattle, too. They wanted to make money, but not always by working.*

*The town had been built on mud with wooden streets, shops, and homes. Even the water system was made of wooden pipes.*

# During Reading

## Comprehension  SMALL GROUP
MONITOR UNDERSTANDING

Use these questions to model visualizing. Then have students tell about a part they visualized.

• What strong images do I see in my mind?

• How do these images help me understand what I am reading?

(See Differentiated Instruction.)

## Teacher Think Aloud
*When I read the section called "The Tour," I imagine I'm actually underground and on the tour. The sensory details help me imagine and feel what it's like: "the air feels cool and damp, and it smells musty."*

## Comprehension  SMALL GROUP
DETERMINING IMPORTANCE

Use these questions to model how to determine the importance of ideas in the second paragraph of the selection. Then have students determine the importance of ideas as they read the section called "Pioneer Square."

• What are the most important ideas in this paragraph?

• How can I support my beliefs?

The Space Needle rises behind a statue of *Chief Seattle*.

Thirty minutes after the alarm sounded, firefighters battled the blaze that soon burned most of downtown Seattle (1889).

*The drainage system that was built didn't work very well. Wastes went downhill, into Puget Sound. During high tide, the wastes came back up to the street. Imagine the smells, the rats, and the disease! Some people actually built outhouses on stilts with ladders up to their toilets!*

*The engineers decided that the city was too low. It needed to be higher up. Yesler and some shopkeepers were against the idea. They wanted things to stay the same so they could keep on making money. The engineers won. But before they could do anything, part of the city burned in a fire in 1889.*

*By 1890, workers rebuilt the city. They built streets from eight to thirty feet higher than they were before. They put ladders down from the road to the stores and sidewalks below. The people used bricks and cement instead of wood. Raising the streets caused the first floor of buildings to become the basements. Sometimes even the second floor became a basement.*

### Chief Seattle

Native Americans lived in the Northwest long before white settlers arrived.

In 1884, the United States government made a treaty with the Washington Indians. It was called the *Port Elliot Treaty*.

The treaty required that the tribes move to reservations. Chief Seattle, of the Suquamish, wanted to keep things peaceful. He was the first signer of this treaty. He died eleven years later. Grateful settlers named their town in his honor.

*New sidewalks were later built above the old ones. These new sidewalks were level with the street. Glass skylights were put in on some of the sidewalks to let light down to the "ground floors" that were now below ground. After a few years, most building owners were tired of going below street level. They gave up on their old basement ground floors and moved up to street level. Sometimes the old ground floor was left empty or used for storage.*

*The underground Seattle slowly became a mess. Then it became the Forgotten City.*

45

## Teacher Think Aloud

*It seems that there are a lot of important ideas about Seattle's history in the second paragraph. I think the most important idea is that the population grew from 300 to 80,000 in just 100 years. That population explosion probably had a huge effect on the city's history.*

## Fix-Up Strategies

Offer these strategies to help students read independently.

### If you don't understand what you're reading:

- Reread the difficult section to look for clues to help you comprehend.

- Read ahead to find clues to help you comprehend.

- Retell, or say in your own words, what you've read.

- Visualize, or form mental pictures of, what you've read.

### If you don't understand a word:

- Reread the sentence. Look for ideas and words that provide meaning clues.

- Find clues by reading a few sentences before and after the confusing word.

- Look for the base or root word and think about its meaning.

- Think about the topic or plot at this point to see if either offers meaning clues.

Glass skylights can be seen in the sidewalks near Pioneer Square.

You don't have too much room to move around as you follow the walkways. But you will see up close the mess that was left. Some buildings collapsed into sections of the underground, so most of it was closed off or filled in. You see only a few sections on the tour.

During your walk, you see right in front of you the remains of some stores. You also look up and see purple glass skylights. The sun's rays turned the glass purple. Look for the purple glass "patches" on the sidewalks when you get to the street level again.

Your eyes have gotten used to the darkness. When you go up to street level, it is very bright. You need to let your eyes adjust. And you need to let your mind come back to the present.

Tourists on the Underground Tour look up at a glass skylight.

**46**

Student Journal page 142

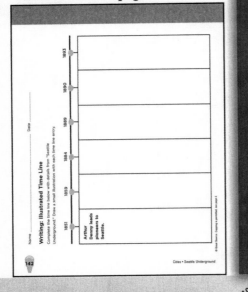

# After Reading
*WHOLE CLASS* Use one or more activities.

## Check Purpose

Have students decide whether their purpose was met. Did they learn how an underground city exists below a modern city?

## Discussion Questions

Continue the group discussion with the following questions.

1. Why does Seattle have an underground city? (Cause-Effect)

2. Why do you think the engineers won the battle to rebuild the city? (Inferential Thinking)

3. Would you like to take a tour of Seattle's underground city? Explain your answer. (Making Connections)

## Revisit: K-W-L Chart

Return to the K-W-L chart started in Before Reading and have students contribute any new information. Were questions answered? Do students have new questions?

## Revisit: Word Map

Have students complete their word maps on *Student Journal* page 141. Students can use the information they learned in the article to answer the questions.

## Back on the Street

If you've worked up an appetite after your underground tour, you might want to go to Pike Place Market. The market is on the Seattle waterfront. Colorful <u>stalls</u> sell all kinds of food, including seafood, flowers, and crafts. Your eyes will love the sights. So will your stomach! There are plenty of good restaurants as well.

Seattle is one of my favorite cities. I hope that you will visit some day and see it for yourself. ◆

Pike Place Market began in August 1907. The nine acres of shops have everything from fish to fruit, books to bagels, and tea to tattoos!

## THE GROWTH OF SEATTLE

 ← **1893** The Great Northern Railroad arrived in Seattle. The railroads brought more settlers and opened up many new markets for Seattle's natural resources, such as lumber and fish.

**1897** The Klondike and Alaska gold rush brought thousands of settlers to the Puget Sound region because it was on the route to the gold-mining fields in Canada and Alaska. →

← **1913** The ports at Seattle and Tacoma grew into centers of international shipping after the opening of the Panama Canal. Agriculture and fishing, particularly salmon fishing, also increased in importance.

✗ SEATTLE

**1916** William Boeing started the Boeing Company. The company soon became a leading aircraft maker and brought many workers and their families to the Seattle area. →

 ← **1975** Paul Allen and Bill Gates developed a software application that made PCs more useful for the general public. That led to the founding of Microsoft, which provides jobs for many people in the Seattle area.

47

## DIFFERENTIATED INSTRUCTION
### Vocabulary
## Multiple Meanings

If students need help with this activity, try following these steps:

1. Explain that *multiple* means "more than one." So a word with multiple meanings has more than one meaning. For example, the word *run* has two meanings: A person can *run* in a race. A manager can *run* a business.

2. Once students understand the concept of multiple meanings of words, ask them to work in pairs to find the multiple meanings of these words from the selection: *shady* (page 44), *stalls* (page 47).

### Student Journal page 143

Name _____ Date _____

**Building Vocabulary: Words with Multiple Meanings**
What are two meanings for each of the words below? Write them in the chart. Then choose your own word that has multiple meanings. Write the definitions in the chart.

| Word | First Definition | Second Definition |
|------|-----------------|-------------------|
| network | an interconnected system | a radio or television company |
| shady | | |
| stalls | | |
| | | |

Cities • Seattle Underground                                                143

## Writing Illustrated Timeline

Have students look at the timeline on *Student Journal* page 142. Discuss with students how they can find the appropriate information for the dates on the timeline. Help students develop a strategy such as scanning the text for the dates. Then have students work in pairs to write and illustrate the timeline.

## Vocabulary Multiple Meanings

Write the words *network*, *shady*, and *stalls* on the board or on chart paper. Discuss the meanings of each word. Point out that each word has more than one meaning. Ask for volunteers to provide the multiple meanings. Then have students complete the multiple meanings chart on *Student Journal* page 143. (See Differentiated Instruction.)

## Phonics/Word Study
### Ambiguous Vowel Sounds

Say the word *proud* slowly, exaggerating the vowel sound. Ask: *What vowel sounds do you hear?* Elicit that the vowel sound cannot be classified as short or long, since it contains more than one vowel sound. Ask students to name other words with the same *ou* sound and list them on the board. Now, work with students to complete the in-depth vowel activity on TE page 342.

## Ambiguous Vowel Sounds

▶ Write the following words on the board: *town* and *sound*. Tell the students that these words have ambiguous, or undecided, vowel sounds and explain what that means.

▶ Ask: *Do any of these words have a short or long a sound?* Have students revisit the sounds of short and long *a* and compare the *ow* sound to them. Do the same with *e, i, o,* and *u.* Students will notice that the *ow* sound is distinct and cannot be confused with any of those vowels.

▶ Using the Ambiguous Vowels: Sort One sheet, model the sorting process. (See *Word Study Manual* page 77.) Write the headings *ow, ou,* Oddball and the first few words in the appropriate columns. Complete the sort as a class.

▶ Discuss the sort and what students learned. There are three patterns that create the *ow* sound.

▶ Hand out the Ambiguous Vowels: Sort One sheet. Ask students to cut up the words and do the sort on their own or in groups.

▶ Check the final sorts for accuracy.

### Ambiguous Vowels: Sort One

| *ow* | *ou* | Oddball |
|-------|--------|---------|
| brown | ground | tough |
| crowd | sound | grown |
| drown | proud | rough |
| scowl | around | |
| wow | mouth | |
| growl | doubt | |
| plow | cloud | |
| gown | | |

For more information on word sorts and spelling stages, see pages 5–31 in the *Word Study Manual.*

# Focus on . . .

Use one or more activities in this section to focus on a particular area of need in your students.

## Comprehension    STRATEGY SUPPORT    INDEPENDENT

To help those students who need more practice using the strategies covered in this lesson, work one-on-one or in small groups to apply the strategy prompts below. Apply the prompts to a *Reading Advantage* paperback, a classroom library book, or a new or familiar selection in the magazine. Always model your own thinking first.

### Monitor Understanding

• Do I understand what I'm reading? If not, what part is confusing to me?
• What fix-up strategies can I use to solve the problem? (See During Reading for fix-up strategies.)
• Why did a character say (do, think, ask) that?
• What images do I visualize from the text? What parts can't I visualize?
• Why did the author include (or not include) those details?

### Determining Importance

• What is the most important idea in the paragraph? How can I prove it?
• Which details are unimportant? Why?
• What does the author want me to understand?
• Why is this information important (or not important) to me?

## Writing Write and Illustrate    INDEPENDENT

Have students choose one part of the article that they could visualize well. Have students share their ideas about that part with the class. Encourage them to use specific, descriptive words. Then have students "quickwrite" a list of images and ideas they have about the part of the article they chose. They should then use their list to illustrate and write about that part.

For additional instruction on writing descriptive paragraphs, see the lessons in *Writing Advantage,* pages 113–151.

## Fluency: Punctuation

SMALL GROUP

After students have read the selection at least once silently, have them take turns reading the italicized text on pages 44–45, which is the tour guide's presentation. Students should practice reading aloud to their partner, who can provide feedback. Partners should encourage each other to read with an even pace and with expression. Partners should help each other pause appropriately at commas and periods.

When students read aloud, do they—

✓ demonstrate appropriate meaning and usage of punctuation marks?

✓ incorporate appropriate timing, stress, and intonation?

✓ exhibit well-timed pauses between words and phrases?

## English Language Learners

SMALL GROUP

To support students as they practice visualizing, extend the comprehension activity on TE page 338.

1. Follow the steps outlined in the comprehension activity.

2. Have students draw a picture showing what they "saw" after reading the first paragraph on page 45 of the article.

3. Have students use their drawings to explain the scene to a partner.

## Independent Activity Options

INDEPENDENT

While you work with individuals or small groups, others can work independently on one or more of the following options.

▶ Level A paperback books, see TE pages 371–376

▶ Level A *eZines*

▶ Repeat word sorts from this lesson

▶ *Student Journal* pages for this lesson

▶ *Writing Advantage* independent lessons

# Assessment

## Strategy Assessment

To help you and your students assess their use of comprehension strategies, ask the following questions. Students can complete a written response or provide verbal answers in a one-on-one reading conference.

1. **Monitor Understanding** What part of this article did you have trouble visualizing? What did you do to help you "see" what was being described? (Answers will vary. An answer should identify a particular section or detail, and then specify the strategy the student used to better understand it, such as rereading, or reading ahead to look for clarification.)

2. **Determining Importance** What was the most important thing you learned on the "tour"? Why was that important? (Answers will vary. An answer should state a fact or concept from the article, and explain its importance.)

For ongoing informal assessment, use the checklists on pages 61–64 of *Level A Assessment*.

## Word Study Assessment

Use these steps to help you and your students assess their understanding of ambiguous vowels.

1. Create a chart like the one shown, including only the words in the first column.

2. Have students read the words.

3. Then have students sort the words into the column with the correct spelling pattern. The answers are shown.

| Words | *ou* | *ow* | Oddball |
|-------|------|------|---------|
| crown | proud | crown | cough |
| proud | foul | cow | enough |
| cow | | | |
| cough | | | |
| foul | | | |
| enough | | | |

Great Source
Reading Advantage

**Level A Assessment**

# Can a Sinking City Be Saved?

*Cities,* pages 48–50

## SUMMARY

This **article** explains why Venice is sinking and how scientists are hoping to prevent further damage to one of Europe's oldest and most beloved cities.

## COMPREHENSION STRATEGIES

Monitor Understanding

## WRITING

5Ws Chart

## VOCABULARY

Context

## PHONICS/WORD STUDY

Ambiguous Vowel Sounds

### Lesson Vocabulary

| | |
|---|---|
| canals | environmentalists |
| lagoon | cesspool |
| drastic | inflate |
| forecast | |

## MATERIALS

*Cities,* pp. 48–50
*Student Journal,* pp. 144–146
*Word Study Manual,* p. 78
*Writing Advantage,* pp. 152–163

---

**Venice, Italy,** is one of the world's most famous and unusual cities. It has one problem that most other cities do not have—it is sinking.

# CAN A SINKING CITY BE SAVED?

Venice is on the coast of the Adriatic Sea. It is a city of islands. The major streets are <u>canals</u>, and boats are used instead of cars. Bridges cross the canals to link the islands. Part of the city also lies on the mainland. A <u>lagoon</u>, or shallow lake, separates the islands from the rest of Italy.

The city is built on wooden piles driven into marshy ground. (This kind of land is low, wet, and covered with grasses.) Old information said that the city sank almost one and a half inches over a thousand years. A new study shows more <u>drastic</u> results.

## New Study Shows Drastic Results

The new study shows that Venice is sinking faster now than in the past. It notes that global warming will increase flooding. The study says that Venice sank almost ten inches in just the last hundred years. The report predicts that Venice may sink within the next hundred years. The study also says that plans to build dams to hold back the water will not work.

**ABOVE:** Gondolas (GON duh luhz) are flat-bottomed boats and were once the main way to travel around Venice.

**LEFT AND RIGHT:** Saint Mark's Square, a popular spot for tourists in Venice, often floods after a heavy rainfall.

48

---

# Before Reading

**WHOLE CLASS** Use one or more activities.

## Make a Concept Web

Start a concept web with *Venice* in the center oval. Then ask students: *What do you know about the city of Venice in Italy?* If possible, locate Italy and Venice on a world map. Return to the web after students finish reading the article. (See Differentiated Instruction.)

```
( city in Italy )        ( the streets
                           are canals )
           \              /
            ( Venice )
```

## Vocabulary Preview

Review the vocabulary list with students. Have students begin the knowledge rating chart on *Student Journal* page 144. They will revisit it later.

## Preview the Selection

Have students look through the three pages of the article, pages 48–50 in the magazine. Discuss what students notice.

## Make Predictions/ Set Purpose

Students should use the information they gathered in previewing the selection to make some predictions about the article. If students have trouble generating a purpose for reading, suggest that they read to learn why Venice is sinking.

## The Importance of Venice

Venice was once an important sea power and trading center. It was also the center of the rebirth of art and learning. Today, Venice's art treasures make it one of the world's most important art centers.

Art keeps Venice afloat in an important way. It attracts tourists who spend their money there. But other things are sinking the city. Winter storms sweep through the canals and buildings. Heavy rains flood public squares. High tides combined with south or southeast winds also cause flooding. Water weakens stone building foundations. Air and water pollution damage buildings and works of art.

## Some Disagree with Study

Most people in Venice agree that something should be done. But not everyone agrees with the new study. People say that the report does not reflect steps taken to slow the city's sinking. The city stopped pumping water from under the lagoon. The underground water supply acts as a cushion. This cushion has slowed the city's sinking. People note that the study is based on predictions for future global warming. The people of Venice have their own <u>forecast</u>.

## Dams or Floodgates?

In the 1960s, scientists began work on a project to save the city with dams. The project was named Moses. The dams would go at the mouth of the lagoon and hold back rising sea levels. The dams would control the water flow into the lagoon.

### Global Warming

**Global warming is a long-term increase in the temperature of the earth's atmosphere. If the earth's air heats up and stays warmer than usual for a long time, then polar icecaps—huge masses of ice at the poles—will begin to melt. If the icecaps melt, they will pour millions of gallons of water into the oceans. This could cause flooding in coastal areas around the world as the oceans rise.**

49

### DIFFERENTIATED INSTRUCTION  SMALL GROUP
### MAKE A CONCEPT WEB

To help students fill in the web, give some background information.

- More than a thousand years ago, people created the city of Venice on water and swampland. It was the center of trade between Europe and Asia for hundreds of years.

- All the "roads" are made of water. The only ways to get around are by walking or taking boats. To cross a street, you must walk over a bridge.

- Sometimes, high tides flood the city, and may be causing the city to sink. Guide students to look at the following website to learn more about Venice: www.pbs.org/wgbh/nova/venice.

### Student Journal page 144

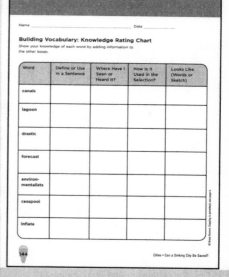

Name _____ Date _____

**Building Vocabulary: Knowledge Rating Chart**
Show your knowledge of each word by adding information to the other boxes.

| Word | Define or Use in a Sentence | Where Have I Seen or Heard It? | How Is It Used in the Selection? | Looks Like (Words or Sketch) |
|---|---|---|---|---|
| canals | | | | |
| lagoon | | | | |
| drastic | | | | |
| forecast | | | | |
| environmentalists | | | | |
| cesspool | | | | |
| inflate | | | | |

144

Cities • Can a Sinking City Be Saved?

# During Reading

## Comprehension  SMALL GROUP
MONITOR UNDERSTANDING

Use these questions to model how to monitor understanding by asking questions. Then have students ask their own questions and try to resolve any confusion.

- What ideas are confusing in this selection?

- What fix-up strategy can I use to resolve my confusion?

## Teacher Think Aloud

*When I read about the underwater floodgates, I was confused. I asked questions to help me clarify what I needed to know. What are floodgates? How do they work? Why would floodgates be preferable to a dam? I read page 50 several times until I could answer these questions in my own words.*

## Fix-Up Strategies

Offer these strategies to help students read independently.

**If you don't understand what you're reading:**

- Reread the difficult section to look for clues to help you comprehend.

- Read ahead to find clues to help you comprehend.

- Retell, or say in your own words, what you've read.

- Visualize, or form mental pictures of, what you've read.

Environmentalists cared about keeping the lagoon clean; they protested. "Closing off the lagoon will turn it into a cesspool of human waste," they claimed. The people of Venice also protested. They objected to ugly dams in their beautiful city. So a new plan was developed.

The new plan called for underwater floodgates that inflate when filled with air. The floodgates would rest on the bottom of the lagoon. They would stay out of sight until needed. During storms and very high tides, these dams would be pumped full of air. The inflated dams would lift up to block the rising tide. The cost of the eight-year project is $4 billion.

### Moses

In Italy, the dam project is called MoSE. MoSE is an acronym for the full project name. However, *Mose* is also Italian for *Moses*. Moses is a character in the Old Testament of the Bible. In one story, Moses held back the waters of the Red Sea so that he and the Israelites could escape from Egypt on foot across the dry ocean floor.

### Tides

The water in the ocean moves in and out on a regular basis. This is called the *tide*. High tide is when the water comes as far in to shore as it will come. Low tide is the opposite; the water is as far out from the shore as it will get.

A report about the new plan says that it won't work. It may be too late, anyway. Decades of climate study have changed people's forecasts. Scientists now think sea levels will rise so high that the dams will not work. The mayor of Venice disagrees. He believes that Moses will save the city. He said, ". . . Venice has a long life ahead of it. We are already working to guarantee that life." The world hopes so. ◆

**Venice has more than 118 islands, 150 canals, 400 bridges, 450 historic palaces and homes, and about 3 million tourists a year.**

Workers on an inflatable rubber dam in Venice

50

# After Reading
Use one or more activities.

## Check Purpose
Have students decide whether their purpose was met. Do they understand why Venice is sinking?

## Discussion Question
- Why do people feel strongly about saving Venice? (Draw Conclusions)

## Revisit: Concept Web
Ask students what new information they can add to the concept web.

## Writing 5Ws Chart
Have students fill in the 5Ws chart on *Student Journal* page 145. Then have them use the information in the chart to summarize the article to a partner.

## Vocabulary Context
Have students use *Student Journal* page 146 to write a brief news report about the situation in Venice. Have students use three (or more) vocabulary words in their report.

## Phonics/Word Study
### Ambiguous Vowel Sounds
Say the word *claw* very slowly, exaggerating the vowel sound. Ask: *What vowel sound do you hear in the word* claw? Elicit that the vowel sound cannot be classified as short or long. Ask students to name other words that have the *aw* sound and list them on the board. Now, work with students to complete the in-depth ambiguous vowel activity on TE page 347.

## Phonics/Word Study

### Ambiguous Vowel Sounds

▶ Write the following words on the board: *hawk*, *salt*, and *fault*. Tell students that these words have ambiguous, or undecided, vowel sounds and explain what that means.

▶ Ask: *Do any of these words have a short or long a sound?* Have the students revisit the sounds of short and long *a* and compare the *aw* sound to them. Do the same with *e, i, o,* and *u* as well. Students will notice that the *aw* sound is distinct and cannot be confused with any of those vowels.

▶ Using the Ambiguous Vowels: Sort Two sheet, model the sorting process. (See *Word Study Manual* page 78.) Write the headings *aw, au,* and Oddball and the first few words in the appropriate columns. Complete the sort as a class.

▶ Discuss the sort and what students learned. There are three kinds of ambiguous *aw* patterns.

▶ Hand out the Ambiguous Vowels: Sort Two sheet. Ask students to cut up the words and do the sort on their own or in groups.

▶ Check the final sorts for accuracy.

| Ambiguous Vowels: Sort Two | | |
|---|---|---|
| *aw* | *au* | Oddball |
| claw | fault | laugh |
| dawn | caught | ought |
| straw | launch | fought |
| brawn | pause | chalk |
| crawl | aunt | |
| drawn | haunt | |
| | Paul | |

For more information on word sorts and spelling stages, see pages 5–31 in the *Word Study Manual*.

## Focus on . . .

Use one or more activities in this section to focus on a particular area of need in your students.

### Comprehension   STRATEGY SUPPORT

INDEPENDENT

To help those students who need more practice using the strategy covered in this lesson, work one-on-one or in small groups to apply the strategy prompts below. Apply the prompts to a *Reading Advantage* paperback, a classroom library book, or a new or familiar selection in the magazine. Always model your own thinking first.

#### Monitor Understanding

• Do I understand what I'm reading? If not, what part is confusing to me?

• What fix-up strategies can I use to solve the problem? (See During Reading for fix-up strategies.)

• Why did a character say (do, think, ask) that?

• What images do I visualize from the text? What parts can't I visualize?

• Why did the author include (or not include) those details?

### Writing **Informative Letter**

INDEPENDENT

Have students write a letter from the point of view of a Venetian who is explaining the city's sinking problem to a cousin or friend in the United States. To help students prepare, brainstorm ideas together and write them on the board. Students can refer to the list and the article when they write.

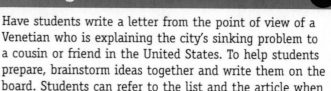

| Important Details to Include |
|---|
| where Venice is |
| people ride in boats instead of cars |
| the city is sinking |
| why the city is sinking |
| ways to fix the problem |

To provide additional instruction on extracting information from a text, see the lessons in *Writing Advantage*, pages 152–163.

## Fluency: Pacing

*SMALL GROUP*

After students have read the article at least once silently, have partners read the article as if it's a news story. Students can alternate between sections. Have partners provide feedback to each other. Point out that if students read too fast, too slowly, or in a halting manner, their listeners will have difficulty making sense of the words. Model the difference between evenly paced and unevenly paced reading.

As you listen to partners reading, use these prompts to guide them to read expressively and evenly.

▶ Listen to me read. Then read it just as I did.

▶ Reread this sentence more slowly, or faster.

▶ Try to make your voice livelier when you read.

▶ Notice the punctuation; it can help you know when to pause.

When students read aloud, do they—

✓ demonstrate a smooth pace, not too fast or too slow?

✓ incorporate well-timed pauses between words and phrases?

✓ reflect an awareness and understanding of punctuation?

## English Language Learners

*SMALL GROUP*

Provide support for students as they answer the first discussion question on TE page 345.

1. Ask students to think about ideas in the selection that may have been confusing to them.

2. Have partners write down two or three questions about the selection.

3. Pairs should work together to answer each other's questions.

## Independent Activity Options

*INDEPENDENT*

While you work with individuals or small groups, others can work independently on one or more of the following options.

▶ Level A paperback books, see TE pages 371–376

▶ Level A *eZines*

▶ Repeat word sorts from this lesson

▶ *Student Journal* pages for this lesson

▶ *Writing Advantage* independent lessons

# Assessment

## Strategy Assessment

To help you and your students assess their use of comprehension strategies, ask the following questions. Students can complete a written response or provide verbal answers in a one-on-one reading conference.

- **Monitor Understanding** What parts of this article were most confusing to you? How did you figure out what you were reading? (Answers will vary. Students should tell one or more details or concepts from the article that were confusing, and describe the strategies they used to understand the passages, such as looking at illustrations, or rereading.)

For ongoing informal assessment, use the checklists on pages 61–64 of *Level A Assessment*

## Word Study Assessment

Use these steps to help you and your students assess their understanding of ambiguous vowels.

1. Create a chart like the one shown, including only the words in the first column.

2. Have students read the words.

3. Then have students sort the words into the column with the correct spelling pattern. The answers are shown.

| Words | *aw* | *au* | Oddball |
|-------|------|------|---------|
| launch | straw | launch | bought |
| haul | paw | haul | laugh |
| straw | | | |
| bought | | | |
| paw | | | |
| laugh | | | |

Great Source
Reading Advantage

Level A
Assessment

# Insect Cities

People are not the only ones who live in cities. Some insects do, too!

## An Ant Colony

Ants are <u>social</u> insects. They like to live together, not alone. Ants live in a group called a <u>colony</u>. A small colony might have only a dozen members. But a large colony could have millions of ants.

## Classes of Ants

Every ant in a colony belongs to one of three classes, or <u>castes</u>. They are the queen, the males, and the workers. Each kind of ant has a different role. A queen's job is to lay eggs, and a male's job is to mate with the queen. A worker's job, as the name hints, is to do all the work. Workers build the home, or nest. They look for food, care for the young, and fight enemies. All workers are females.

**Inside an Anthill**

Nurseries

Queen's Chamber

Workers' Rest Chambers

Storage Chamber

51

## LESSON 46
# Insect Cities and Hidden Neighbors
*Cities*, pages 51–55

### SUMMARY
This **article** includes information about and photographs of insect cities. A **poem** about city animals that come out at night follows.

### COMPREHENSION STRATEGIES
Inferential Thinking
Understanding Text Structure

### WRITING
Detailed Diagram

### VOCABULARY
Multiple Meanings

### PHONICS/WORD STUDY
Ambiguous Vowel Sounds

### Lesson Vocabulary

| | |
|---|---|
| social | cells |
| colony | pollen |
| castes | nectar |
| chambers | nocturnal |

### MATERIALS
*Cities*, pp. 51–55
*Student Journal*, pp. 147–149
*Word Study Manual*, p. 79
*Writing Advantage*, pp. 13–39

# Before Reading
**WHOLE CLASS** Use one or more activities.

## Make a K-W-L Chart

Create a K-W-L chart. Ask students what they know about ants and bees, and what they want to learn. Record responses in columns 1 and 2. Tell students that after they read the article, they will fill in column 3.

| What We Know | What We Want to Know | What We Learned |
|---|---|---|
| Ants can sting. | Where do ants live? | |
| Bees can sting. | Can killer bees really kill you? | |

## Vocabulary Preview

Review the vocabulary list with students. Discuss how each word might relate to the article. Then have students complete the middle column of the predictions chart on *Student Journal* page 147. They will finish the chart later.

## Preview the Selection

Have students survey the four pages of the article. Ask: *What do you think the article will be about? How is the information organized?*

## Make Predictions/ Set Purpose

Students should use the information they gathered in previewing the selection to make some predictions about the article. If students have trouble generating a purpose for reading, suggest that they read to learn how ants and bees are truly social insects.

## Comprehension
INFERENTIAL THINKING

To help students think inferentially, ask these questions.

- What do you already know about ants and bees?

- How are ants and bees similar to one another? How are they different?

- What new understandings do you have about ants and bees that are not directly stated in the article?

**Student Journal page 147**

Name _____ Date _____

**Building Vocabulary: Predictions**

How do you predict these words will be used in "Insect Cities"? Write your answers in the second column. Next, read the article. Then, clarify your answers in the third column.

| Word | My prediction for how the word will be used | How the word was actually used |
|------|------|------|
| social | | |
| colony | | |
| castes | | |
| chambers | | |
| cells | | |
| pollen | | |
| nectar | | |

Cities • Insect Cities                                                   147

## Places for Nests

Ants build nests in many places. Most ant nests are underground. The nest has many small rooms, or <u>chambers</u>. The ants crawl through tunnels to get from one room to the next. Sometimes you can see an ant nest because worker ants pile a large mound of dirt and twigs on the ground over the nest.

Other ants make a nest in the trunk or branch of a tree. Sometimes they choose an old log as their home. They chew tunnels in the wood to reach places where they stay.

## Inside an Ant Nest

An ant's nest may be big or small. A tiny nest has only one chamber. It's as little as your finger. Only about a dozen ants live in it. Other nests are much bigger. A giant nest can be forty feet deep in the ground. It has lots of tunnels and chambers. The nest might be as big as a tennis court. More than ten million ants can live in such a nest.

Each chamber in a nest is special. One chamber is home to the queen and her eggs. Many other chambers are "nurseries," where baby ants are raised. Still other chambers are resting places for workers. Other chambers are for growing and storing food.

As more ants are born, the workers add more rooms and tunnels to the nest. The ants move to the deepest rooms in the winter, where the nest is warmest. However, they move back "upstairs" in the spring.

This nest of slender ants is in a hollow thorn. In the nest are ant cocoons and scale insects.

Fire ants build mounded nests. They live in the southern United States. Fire ants can give a very painful sting.

52

# During Reading

## Comprehension
INFERENTIAL THINKING

Use these questions to model how to make inferences from "Classes of Honeybees." Then have students make inferences from another section.

- What does the text tell me about classes of honeybees?

- What do I know about bees?

- Using the text and what I already know, what can I infer?

(See Differentiated Instruction.)

### Teacher Think Aloud
*The text says that different honeybees have different roles, or belong to different classes. What I already know about bees is that they live in colonies, which are like little cities. With these pieces of information, I can infer that a colony of bees won't function very well if the different jobs within it aren't being done.*

## Comprehension
UNDERSTANDING TEXT STRUCTURE

Use these questions to model how to identify the classification text structure of the article. Then have students tell how the text structure helps them understand the information.

- How is the text structured?

- What details support my beliefs?

- Why did the author choose this text structure?

## A Bee Colony

Honeybees, like ants, are social insects. They live in a colony, either big or small. A small honeybee colony may have as few as ten members. A large colony may have up to eighty thousand bees in it.

### Classes of Honeybees

Like ants, honeybees belong to one of three classes. They are the queen, the drones, and the workers. The queen bee, like the queen ant, lays the eggs. The drones mate with the queen. The workers do all the work. Worker bees, like worker ants, are all females. They build the hive, or nest. They also care for the young and guard the hive. They collect and store honey in the hive.

### Building the Hive

Honeybees build their hive with beeswax. The wax forms on their bodies after they eat a lot of honey. Bees shape the wax into a group of six-sided cells called a *honeycomb*. Once a few cells are made, the queen lays an egg in each one. Workers build more cells, and the queen lays more eggs.

The cells with eggs are in the center of the hive. The area is called the *brood nest*. Workers store pollen and nectar in cells that surround the brood nest. Later, the nectar changes into honey.

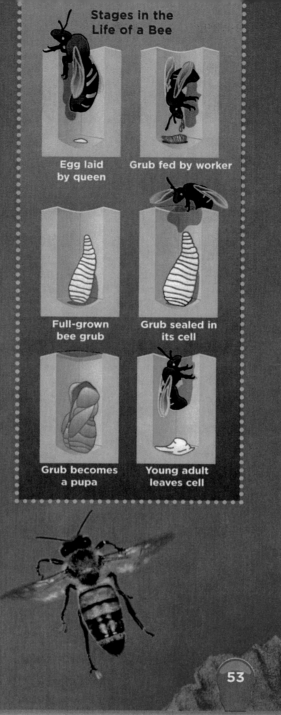

**Stages in the Life of a Bee**

Egg laid by queen

Grub fed by worker

Full-grown bee grub

Grub sealed in its cell

Grub becomes a pupa

Young adult leaves cell

53

---

# Teacher Think Aloud

*The headings show me that the information on ants and on bees is broken down in a similar way. This makes it easy for me to read about classes of ants, for example, and see how they compare to bee classes. The headings show how the text is classified. I like the classification structure because it keeps me focused on one aspect at a time.*

## Fix-Up Strategies

Offer these strategies to help students read independently.

**If you don't understand what you're reading:**

- Reread the difficult section to look for clues to help you comprehend.
- Read ahead to find clues to help you comprehend.
- Retell, or say in your own words, what you've read.
- Visualize, or form mental pictures of, what you've read.

**If you don't understand a word:**

- Reread the sentence. Look for ideas and words that provide meaning clues.
- Find clues by reading a few sentences before and after the confusing word.
- Look for the base or root word and think about its meaning.
- Think about the topic or plot at this point to see if either offers meaning clues.

## Vocabulary

### Multiple Meanings

If students need help with this activity, try the following steps:

1. Explain that *multiple* means "more than one." So a word with multiple meanings has more than one meaning. For example, the word *light* has two meanings: Turn on the *light*! This box is *light* as a feather.

2. Once students understand the concept of multiple meanings, ask them to work in pairs to fill in the chart.

### Student Journal page 148

Name _____ Date _____

**Writing: Draw and Label an Ant City**
Draw a detailed diagram of an ant city. Include the labels of the various workers and locations.

Be sure to include:

1. nursery
2. queen's chamber
3. storage chamber
4. workers' rest chamber
5. queen
6. males
7. workers

148      Cities • Insect Cities

## Life in the Hive

Worker bees stay very busy in their hive. They have many jobs to do. The youngest workers build the honeycomb and clean the cells. They also care for the young and store the nectar.

At two weeks old, workers fly out to the field. There they collect nectar and pollen from flowers. They gather food and water to feed the baby bees. Back at the hive, the workers then fly in a circle. Their "dance" tells other bees where food can be found in the flowers.

Some workers guard the hive by staying near the entrance. Sometimes bees from other hives try to get in. Guards can spot a stranger by its smell. Workers fight strangers and try to kill them.

In hot weather, some workers stay by the entrance of the hive. They flap their wings to fan in fresh air and force out stale air. In cold weather, all the bees crowd together in the hive to stay warm. ◆

**Drones**

The only job of a drone is to mate with the queen. After that, the drone is no longer needed. In the fall, worker bees let the drones starve to death, because they're afraid that the drones would eat too much stored honey.

54

# After Reading

Use one or more activities.

## Check Purpose

Have students decide if their purpose was met. Do they understand why ants and bees are social insects?

## Discussion Questions

Continue the group discussion with the following questions.

1. How are bees and ants both similar and different? (Compare-Contrast)

2. How would the world be different without bees? (Inferential Thinking)

3. What do you find most interesting about bees or ants? (Making Connections.)

## Revisit: K-W-L Chart

Have students revisit the chart that was started in Before Reading. What new information can students add? What questions do they still have? How can answers be found?

## Revisit: Predictions Chart

Have students return to *Student Journal* page 147 to complete the chart. How were the words actually used? Students can clarify their predictions in the right-hand column of the chart.

# Hidden Neighbors

Late at night, on city streets
hidden neighbors roam.
Coyote, fox, raccoon, and owl
call the city home.

While you sleep all safe inside,
a coyote or fox may stalk
mice and rats and insects, too,
on its <u>nocturnal</u> walk.

The raccoon lives in a hollow log
and hunts alone at night.
Raccoons eat almost anything
found within their sight.

An owl living in a tree
hears a mouse disturb the quiet.
Owl swoops on mouse and makes
it part of owl's diet.

Now you know the city's secret:
At night, a hunting place
for creatures who run wild and free,
and with whom we share our space.

55

## Poem: Hidden Neighbors

Have students read the poem on page 55. Then ask:

- What do you notice about the poem?
- What patterns do you see and hear?
- Are you familiar with any of the animals mentioned in the poem?
- Have you seen other "hidden neighbors" at night?

Possible answers to **Student Journal page 149** include *care*: source of worry, to be interested; *trunk*: the snout of an elephant, a suitcase; *spring*: a season, to dart forward.

Name _____ Date _____

**Building Vocabulary: Words with Multiple Meanings**

Write two definitions for each word below.

| Word | First Definition | Second Definition |
|------|-----------------|-------------------|
| cells | small compartments | rooms in a prison or jail |
| care | | |
| trunk | | |
| spring | | |

Cities • Insect Cities

149

## Writing Detailed Diagram

Have students draw a detailed diagram of an ant city on *Student Journal* page 148. Students should label the various workers and locations. Students can refer to the article for help.

## Vocabulary Multiple Meanings

Display the word *cell*. Ask students:

- What do you already know about the word *cell*?
- How is the word *cell* used in the article? (cells of honeycomb)
- What is another meaning of the word *cell*? (prison cell)

Now, have students complete the multiple meanings chart on *Student Journal* page 149. (See Differentiated Instruction.)

## Phonics/Word Study

### Ambiguous Vowel Sounds

Display this sentence and read it aloud: *The cool cook read a good book at noon.* Ask students which words have a long *u* sound. (*cool, noon*) Have students sort the *oo* words in the sentence into words with the long *u* sound and words with the more ambiguous vowel sound *oo* (as in *cook*). Now, work with students to complete the in-depth ambiguous vowel activity on TE page 354.

# Phonics/Word Study

## Ambiguous Vowel Sounds

▶ Write the following words on the board: *cool* and *good*. Tell students that the vowel sounds in these words are ambiguous, or undecided, and explain what that means. Students should notice that both words have the *oo* pattern but they sound different.

▶ Examine the *oo* in *cool*. Ask: *Does the* oo *in* cool *sound like any other long vowel we have learned?* Students should recognize the long *u* sound.

▶ Direct students to go through their Word Study notebooks and look at Long *u*: Sort Three. Have them find words with the *oo* pattern (such as *scoop* and *smooth*). The following sort is designed to have students compare the two *oo* patterns: one is long *u* and the other is ambiguous.

▶ Using the Ambiguous Vowels: Sort Three sheet, model the sorting process for the students. (See *Word Study Manual* page 79.) Write the headings *oo* = Long *u*, *oo*, and Oddball and the first few words in the appropriate columns. Complete the sort as a class.

▶ Discuss the sort and what students learned. There are two kinds of *oo* words: long *u*, and an ambiguous pattern.

▶ Hand out the Ambiguous Vowels: Sort Three sheet and ask the students to cut up the words and do the sort on their own or in groups.

▶ Check the final sorts for accuracy.

### Ambiguous Vowels: Sort Three

| oo = Long *u* | oo | Oddball |
|---|---|---|
| cool | good | could |
| proof | foot | would |
| noon | crook | should |
| stoop | wool | |
| zoom | book | |
| food | shook | |
| | brook | |
| | stood | |
| | look | |

For more information on word sorts and spelling stages, see pages 5–31 in the *Word Study Manual*.

# Focus on . . .

Use one or more activities in this section to focus on a particular area of need in your students.

## Comprehension [STRATEGY SUPPORT] INDEPENDENT

To help those students who need more practice using the strategies covered in this lesson, work one-on-one or in small groups to apply the strategy prompts below. Apply the prompts to a *Reading Advantage* paperback, a classroom library book, or a new or familiar selection in the magazine. Always model your own thinking first.

### Inferential Thinking

- What are the causes or effects of this event?
- What do I learn from the character or person's thoughts, words, or actions?
- What do I know (or infer) from the text that the author hasn't stated directly?
- What conclusions can I draw?

### Understanding Text Structure

- What kind of text is this? (book, story, article, guidebook, play, manual)
- How does the author organize the text? (cause-effect, problem-solution, chronological order, description, question-answer, comparison-contrast)
- What details support my thoughts about the text structure?
- What is the cause (effect, problem, solution, order, question, answer)?
- If fiction, who are the characters? What is the setting, plot, conflict, and resolution?

## Writing Compare and Contrast INDEPENDENT

Have students make a Venn diagram about ants and bees. Ask students to write two brief paragraphs explaining how bees and ants are similar and different. Students can write an introductory sentence that states that they are going to compare and contrast bees and ants, a first paragraph about how ants differ from bees, a second paragraph about how ants and bees are alike, and a wrap-up sentence.

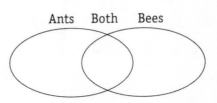

Ants   Both   Bees

For additional instruction on writing an introduction, see *Writing Advantage*, pages 13–29.

## CITY UNDER THE SEA

The story begins thousands of years ago. It takes place in the middle of an ocean. . . .

There was once an island nation. Gods and <u>mortals</u> created it. The people who lived there were <u>noble</u> and powerful. They had great wealth. This was the island of Atlantis.

The people of Atlantis were great builders. They built palaces and temples. They built harbors and docks. There were fountains with hot and cold water. There were stone walls covered with gold and silver.

The capital city was built on a hill. Rings of water surrounded it. Ships sailed from ring to ring through tunnels. On top of the hill was a temple. The people went there to honor Poseidon. He was the Greek god of the sea. A giant gold statue was built to honor him.

Outside the city were rich farmlands. Giant canals—long passages—collected water from rivers and streams. The climate was warm and good for growing things. The people enjoyed two <u>harvests</u> each year.

Beyond the farmlands were high mountains. There were villages, lakes, and meadows. Many fruits, nuts, and herbs grew on the island. Many animals roamed the land, too.

The people of Atlantis lived simple, good lives. But they began to change. They became greedy. They wanted more money and power.

Zeus was the king of the Greek gods. He was angry with the people of Atlantis. He decided they must be punished.

It happened quickly. A huge volcano erupted. An earthquake split the city. Atlantis was broken and in flames. Then a giant wave swelled in the sea. It crashed over the island. Beautiful Atlantis was gone!

Evidence, including a satellite photo and some volcanic rocks, convinced Jim Allen that he had found Atlantis in South America.

57

## DIFFERENTIATED INSTRUCTION
### MAKE A CONCEPT WEB

If students have trouble with this activity, you might want to provide more background.

1. Ask: *What do you think* gold fever *is?* Make sure students understand that a fever from illness can make you delirious. The illness may spread to other people. Likewise, the desire for gold, or wealth, can make people irrational and can affect many people at the same time.

2. You might want to direct the students to this website to learn more about gold fever in American history: http://www.pbs.org/wgbh/amex/gold/

## Preview the Selection

Have students look through the six pages of the article, pages 56–61 in the magazine. Ask:

- What do you notice first about the article?

- What do you think the article will be about? What makes you think that?

- What do the pictures and captions tell you?

- Do you think this is fiction or non-fiction? Why?

## Teacher Think Aloud

*When I flip through this article, I see that there are two subheads, and the background color is different for each subhead: blue for "City Under the Sea," and gold tones for "City of Gold." The subheads and color scheme show me that the article will tell about these two different cities.*

## Make Predictions/ Set Purpose

Students should use the information they gathered in previewing the selection to make some predictions about the article. If students have trouble generating a purpose for reading, suggest that they read to learn why people are so fascinated by Atlantis and El Dorado.

## Comprehension
MAKING CONNECTIONS

To help students make connections with the text, ask these questions.

1. What movies or books do you know about a fantastic city or place?

2. Why do you think the writers made up these places?

3. Why do you think people risked so much to find Atlantis and El Dorado?

The story of Atlantis comes from Plato. Plato was a great thinker from ancient Greece. He had heard about Atlantis from Solon. Solon was a Greek ruler and a relative of Plato's. Solon had heard of Atlantis from an Egyptian priest. Plato wrote about what he had heard.

Plato's writing fascinated many people. Some thought Atlantis was real. Others believed it was just a story.

Many people are interested in Atlantis. They want to know the truth. Is it a mysterious lost city? Or is it a myth?

Some people think Atlantis was part of the Greek islands. They believe it was destroyed by a volcanic blast. Other people think Atlantis was in the Atlantic Ocean. Still other people claim it was in Africa or in Central America or in South America.

There are many different theories. No one really knows the truth.

### Plato
Plato liked to write dialogues, or conversations. He wrote about Atlantis around 360 B.C. Plato's writing is the only known account of Atlantis.

## CITY OF GOLD

Explorers came to the northern part of South America from Spain. They came in the sixteenth century in search of a city of gold. They were looking for El Dorado. The explorers were looking for a "Golden Man," covered with gold dust. Some said he was the chief of the people who lived there. Others said he owned the "Golden Land." El Dorado was supposed to be a land of golden gardens and golden, life-sized statues.

The explorers weren't sure where to look. Mostly, they searched the area of the Orinoco and Amazon rivers. The people who lived there were not happy to see the explorers. "You can look for a city of gold, but it's not here," the people would say. "Keep on going. It's straight ahead."

### El Dorado
The term *El Dorado* is Spanish, meaning "The Gilded One." This refers to the chief of a Native American tribe said to live in the northern part of South America. Native American stories told of the chief having great wealth. Each year at festivals, he would cover his whole body with gold dust. The term later came to be used to refer to his kingdom. It was believed to be rich in gold and precious stones.

58

# During Reading

## Comprehension
MAKING CONNECTIONS

Use these questions to model for students how to make connections to the text. Then have students make their own connections.

- Does any of this sound familiar to me?

- What other fantasy places do I know about?

(See Differentiated Instruction.)

## Teacher Think Aloud
*I once read a fantasy novel about the discovery of a lost city under the ocean. I wonder if the author of the book I read knew about Atlantis. As I read this article, I'll look for similarities to my book.*

## Comprehension
DETERMINING IMPORTANCE

Use these questions to model how to determine the importance of ideas in "City Under the Sea." Then have students determine the importance of ideas as they read "City of Gold."

- What are the most important ideas in this section?

- How can I support my beliefs?

Sir Walter Raleigh was one of the explorers. He was determined to find El Dorado, but he never did. He never found any treasure at all. But he wrote a book about his trips. The book was very popular in England. Sir Walter Raleigh made many people aware of the legend of El Dorado.

## Sir Walter Raleigh

Sir Walter Raleigh was born around 1552 in England. He was a soldier, an explorer, a businessman, and a writer. He was a favorite of Queen Elizabeth I.

There is a legend that Raleigh laid his coat across a mud puddle so that the queen's feet would stay dry. While that story is probably not true, it is true that he spent a lot of time and money exploring the Americas. He tried to establish a colony in Roanoke, an island off the coast of North Carolina.

The first time settlers came to Roanoke, they stayed only a year. Sickness and fear drove them away. Raleigh tried again a year later, but when he returned after a trip to England for supplies, the colony had disappeared.

Later in his life, Raleigh led two searches for El Dorado. They both failed. In 1618, he was executed for disobeying King James I.

These are some of the ruins of Kuaua Pueblo at Coronado State Monument. The area was first visited by Spanish explorer Francisco Vasquez de Coronado in 1540.

59

## Fix-Up Strategies

Offer these strategies to help students read independently.

### If you don't understand what you're reading:

- Reread the difficult section to look for clues to help you comprehend.

- Read ahead to find clues to help you comprehend.

- Retell, or say in your own words, what you've read.

- Visualize, or form mental pictures of, what you've read.

### If you don't understand a word:

- Reread the sentence. Look for ideas and words that provide meaning clues.

- Find clues by reading a few sentences before and after the confusing word.

- Look for the base or root word and think about its meaning.

- Think about the topic or plot at this point to see if either offers meaning clues.

## Main Idea Chart

If students need help with this activity, use these steps to review different types of details.

1. The main idea is what the selection is mostly about and is supported by details that describe, tell, or explain. Not all details in a selection support the main idea; some give background or add interest.

2. Explain that supporting details give examples or information about the topic. The examples of people's theories about Atlantis on page 58 support the main idea that Atlantis is a fascinating mystery for many people.

### Student Journal page 151

Name _____ Date _____

**Writing: Main Idea Chart**

First, choose whether you are going to write about the section on Atlantis or El Dorado. Next, in the chart below, write three details about the section you chose. Then, figure out the main idea and write it in the top section. Finally, use the information in the chart to come up with a logical conclusion. Write it in the bottom part of the chart.

Main Idea:

Detail:        Detail:        Detail:

Conclusion:

Now retell the section you wrote about to a partner. Does your partner have any questions?

Cities • Atlantis & El Dorado: Fact or Fiction?                    151

Explorers searched for hundreds of years. They made many trips, but no one ever found the Golden Land.

Some explorers headed north to what is now Arizona and New Mexico. Francisco Coronado was one of the leaders. In 1549, he set out from Mexico to look for the Seven Golden Cities of Cibola. The cities had been the subject of many stories. The cities were supposed to be filled with gold and silver.

Coronado's expedition was large. It involved three hundred men. They brought hundreds of horses. They also brought herds of sheep, pigs, and cattle.

Coronado and his men explored the Grand Canyon and the mouth of the Colorado River. However, they found no gold in either place. They found no treasures at all, in fact. But they left behind something of great value. Many of their horses had escaped during their travels. The Plains Indians caught them and became great riders. The horses changed the lives of the Plains Indians.

Cheyenne Indians made use of horses descended from the Spanish horses left behind in the 1500s.

60

# After Reading  WHOLE CLASS  Use one or more activities.

## Check Purpose

Have students decide whether their purpose was met. Do they understand why Atlantis and El Dorado continue to fascinate people?

## Discussion Questions

Continue the group discussion with the following questions.

1. Why do you think people still want to uncover the truth about Atlantis and El Dorado? (Main Idea)

2. Would you like to live in a city like Atlantis or El Dorado? Why? (Making Connections)

3. How did "gold fever" affect the development of the United States? (Cause-Effect)

## Revisit: Concept Web

Return to the "gold fever" concept web started in Before Reading. Can students add any more information? What questions do students have? Record new ideas and questions on the web.

Many English, French, and Dutch explorers also caught "gold fever." They crossed the Atlantic Ocean to North America in search of treasure, but they did not find it.

Some of the gold seekers moved away. Most stayed to become permanent settlers. They raised crops to support themselves. They grew tobacco, indigo (plants from which blue dye can be made), and rice. These people had come looking for a city of riches, following a golden dream. They found no gold, but they helped build our country.

**Fact or Fiction?** It might help if we ask ourselves some questions. Why would people create such stories? Why would people risk their lives to discover if the stories were true?

The stories of places like Atlantis and El Dorado are fascinating. They <u>spark</u> our imaginations. We may never know the truth about these places.

But scientists, geologists, and deep-sea divers still search for Atlantis. People also have not given up their hope of discovering a city of gold. They live with their hopes and dreams.

Painting of Francisco Vasquez de Coronado by Newell Convers Wyeth (c. 1940–1945)

The Grand Canyon

61

Possible answers to **Student Journal page 152** include *covered*: topped with something, included; *capital*: a city that is the center of important activity, an upper case letter; *legend*: a mythical story, a list of symbols on a map; *subject*: an area of study, someone under the rule of another.

Name _____ Date _____

**Building Vocabulary: Words with Multiple Meanings**
Write two definitions for each word below.

| Word | First Definition | Second Definition |
|------|------------------|-------------------|
| spark | hot, glowing matter | to set in motion |
| covered | | |
| capital | | |
| legend | | |
| subject | | |

152      Cities • Atlantis & El Dorado: Fact or Fiction?

---

## Writing Main Idea Chart

First, have students choose whether they'd like to write about Atlantis or El Dorado. Then walk them through the main idea chart on *Student Journal* page 151. Suggest that students write the three details first. It's sometimes easier to figure out the main idea from the details. (See Differentiated Instruction.)

## Vocabulary Multiple Meanings

Display the word *spark*. Then ask:

- What do you know about the word *spark*?
- How is *spark* used on page 61?
- What are all the different meanings for *spark* that you know? (bit of burning material, to get something going)

Then have students work in pairs to complete the multiple meanings chart on *Student Journal* page 152.

## Phonics/Word Study
### Complex Consonant Clusters

Display and read these words aloud: *scream, stream, shrill, squire.* Ask: *How many consonant sounds do you hear at the beginning of each of these words?* (three) Explain that studying complex consonant clusters such as these will help students improve their spelling. Now, work with students to complete the in-depth consonant cluster activity on TE page 362.

## Phonics/Word Study

### Complex Consonant Clusters

▶ Write the following words on the board: *screech*, *stream*, *shrink*, and *square*. Direct students' attention to the beginning consonant sounds of the words. Students should notice that all four examples begin with a series of three consonant sounds.

▶ Using the Complex Consonants: Sort One sheet, model the sorting process for students. (See *Word Study Manual* page 80.) Write the headings *scr-*, *str-*, *shr-*, *squ-*, and the first few words under the appropriate columns. Complete the sort as a group.

▶ Discuss the sort and what students learned. Complex consonant clusters contain three consonant sounds, and they have certain patterns. You will find words beginning with *scr-* but not *skr-*, as in *scram*; you will find words with *shr-* as in *shrank*, but it will never be *schr-*; and, finally, words that sound like they begin with *skwa* are always spelled *squ-*.

▶ Once the sort is complete, hand out the Complex Consonants: Sort One sheet. Ask students to cut up the words and do the sort on their own or in groups.

▶ Check the final sorts for accuracy.

| Complex Consonants: Sort One | | | |
|---|---|---|---|
| *scr-* | *str-* | *shr-* | *squ-* |
| scramble | strange | shrink | square |
| scratch | straight | shrill | squelch |
| scribble | street | shriek | squall |
| scrod | strangle | shrimp | squid |
| scream | | | squirm |

For more information on word sorts and spelling stages, see pages 5–31 in the *Word Study Manual*.

## Focus on . . .

Use one or more activities in this section to focus on a particular area of need in your students.

### Comprehension    STRATEGY SUPPORT

To help those students who need more practice using the strategies covered in this lesson, work one-on-one or in small groups to apply the strategy prompts below. Apply the prompts to a *Reading Advantage* paperback, a classroom library book, or a new or familiar selection in the magazine. Always model your own thinking first.

#### Making Connections

- What does this story (article, passage) remind me of?
- What do I already know about this topic?
- Where have I heard about this topic before?
- What do I have in common with the characters, people, or situations in the text?
- What other books, stories, articles, movies, or TV shows does this text make me think about?

#### Determining Importance

- What is the most important idea in the paragraph? How can I prove it?
- Which details are unimportant? Why?
- What does the author want me to understand?
- Why is this information important (or not important) to me?

### Writing Paragraph

Discuss with students the appeal of gold for the explorers looking for El Dorado. Then lead students in a brainstorming session to collect ideas about the kinds of things that people search for now. When the list is finished, have students write a brief paragraph about why people search for one of the items on the list.

| What Do People Search for Now? |
|---|
| Gold |
| Money |
| Easy lives |
| Cures for diseases |
| Youth |
| Family members |
| Clues |

To help students strengthen their writing, see the lessons on writing techniques in *Writing Advantage*, pages 30–55.

## Fluency: Punctuation

After students have read the selection at least once silently, have partners take turns reading aloud the sections about Atlantis and El Dorado. Point out to students that if they read too fast, too slowly, or in a halting manner, their listeners will not be able to make sense of the words. Model the difference between natural-sounding reading and unnatural-sounding reading. Encourage partners to listen for (and comment on) appropriate pauses at commas and periods.

When students read aloud, do they—

✓ demonstrate appropriate meaning and usage of punctuation marks?

✓ incorporate appropriate timing, stress, and intonation?

✓ exhibit well-timed pauses between words and phrases?

## English Language Learners

To support students as they develop oral fluency, have them share thoughts and questions about Atlantis or El Dorado.

1. Have students complete the main idea chart on *Student Journal* page 151.

2. Pair students who wrote about different cities.

3. Have pairs share their thoughts and questions about the cities they wrote about.

## Independent Activity Options

While you work with individuals or small groups, others can work independently on one or more of the following options.

▶ Level A paperback books, see TE pages 371–376

▶ Level A *eZines*

▶ Repeat word sorts from this lesson

▶ *Student Journal* pages for this lesson

▶ *Writing Advantage* independent lessons

# Assessment

## Strategy Assessment

To help you and your students assess their use of comprehension strategies, ask the following questions. Students can complete a written response or provide verbal answers in a one-on-one reading conference.

1. **Making Connections** What connections did you make to this text? (Answers will vary. Students should specify one or more things from their prior knowledge or experience and how they helped them relate to the text, such as a movie that helped them picture El Dorado.)

2. **Determining Importance** What details do you think were most important in this article? Why do you think so? (Answers will vary. Students should cite one or more details from the article and explain why they were most important.)

For ongoing informal assessment, use the checklists on pages 61–64 of *Level A Assessment*.

## Word Study Assessment

Use these steps to help you and your students assess their understanding of complex consonant clusters.

1. Create a chart like the one shown, including only the words in the first column.

2. Have students read the words.

3. Then have students sort the words into the column with the correct spelling pattern. The answers are shown.

| Words | scr- | str- | shr- | squ- |
|-------|------|------|------|------|
| shrimp | scratch | strut | shrimp | square |
| strut | scram | strap | shred | squirrel |
| square | | | | |
| strap | | | | |
| squirrel | | | | |
| scratch | | | | |
| shred | | | | |
| scram | | | | |

### Level A Assessment

# Urban Transportation and Phone Call

*Cities*, pages 62–65

## SUMMARY

While the first **article** considers urban transportation, the second **article** focuses on time zones around the world.

## COMPREHENSION STRATEGIES

Making Connections

## WRITING

Compare and Contrast

## VOCABULARY

Words Within a Word

## PHONICS/WORD STUDY

Complex Consonant Clusters

### Lesson Vocabulary

public transportation
advantages
toxic fumes

## MATERIALS

*Cities*, pp. 62–end
*Student Journal*, pp. 153–155
*Word Study Manual*, p. 81
*Writing Advantage*, pp. 56–92

# URBAN TRA

**PEOPLE** who live in big cities need to get around the city. City dwellers depend on cars, subways, buses, and taxis. Some cities have great public transportation systems. Other cities do not. When a city does not have a good bus or subway system, people use their cars. Traffic and pollution are big problems when people drive their cars.

## Los Angeles

People who live in L.A. spend a lot of time in their cars. They are often stuck in heavy traffic. Traffic jams are no fun. They cause people to be late for work. They also cause air pollution. Smog is the dirty, brown air that hangs over parts of the city. Smog causes health problems. Scientists have linked smog to cancer and heart disease. Many new cars pollute less than older models. Still, there are a lot of cars in L.A. This means there is a lot of smog.

L.A. is working on a train system. Building problems and budget cuts have slowed down the project. City buses travel on major freeways. They run about every fifteen minutes almost all day long. (There is no bus service from 2 A.M. until 5 A.M.)

## San Francisco

Farther north in California, BART (Bay Area Rapid Transit) is a success story. This subway system started in 1972. It now covers 104 miles. There are forty-three stations. BART serves about four million people. By using BART, the people of San Francisco cut down on the traffic in the city.

62

# Before Reading

*WHOLE CLASS* Use one or more activities.

## Make a Transportation Web

Start a web with the phrase "city transportation" in the center oval. Ask: *What are some different forms of city transportation?* Revisit the web after students have completed the article to add any new information.

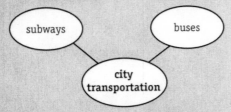

## Vocabulary Preview

Review the vocabulary list with students. Ask what associations students make to the words. There is no *Student Journal* page for this lesson.

## Preview the Selection

Have students look through the four pages of the two selections. Discuss what students notice and what they think they will learn.

## Make Predictions/ Set Purpose

Students should use the information they gathered in previewing the selections to make some predictions about them. If students have trouble generating a purpose for reading, suggest that they read to learn about issues of urban transportation.

# SPORTATION

DIFFERENTIATED INSTRUCTION · SMALL GROUP

## Comprehension
MAKING CONNECTIONS

To help students make connections with the text, use these questions.

1. What do you know about public transportation—from experience, books, TV, or movies?

2. How can you relate your knowledge to the descriptions of public transportation systems in L.A., San Francisco, and New York City?

## New York City

New York has a well-known subway system. New York City is very crowded. There is a great need for people not to use cars. The mayor is trying to set a good example. He has promised to take a bus or the subway at least once a day. Many New Yorkers are following the mayor's lead.

More than six million New Yorkers take a bus or subway every day. The buses and subways run twenty-four hours a day. Most of New York's schoolchildren take buses to and from school. Most New Yorkers don't drive a car to work. Many New Yorkers take taxis. There are more than twelve thousand taxis in the Big Apple. The bright yellow cars fill the city streets. Taxis fill the air with their honking. Taxis make it hard for walkers to get around.

Public transportation is a major issue. Even cities with good systems still have traffic jams and pollution. City planners need to think of ways to solve these problems. ◆

## A Different Kind of Taxi

Water taxis offer a solution to transportation problems. New York and Boston are using small boats to get people around. Water taxis have several <u>advantages</u> over cars, buses, and taxis. The boats don't create <u>toxic fumes</u>. They don't add to street traffic and noise. And they give workers a more relaxed way to get to and from work. Think about it. Would you like to be stuck in traffic on the highway every day for an hour? Or would you like to read the newspaper or listen to music while enjoying a beautiful view? The choice is easy. That's why cities near water are using water taxis as a clean, quick form of transportation.

63

# During Reading

Use these questions to model how to make connections to the text. Then have students make their own connections.

- Does any of this sound familiar to me?

- How do these connections help me understand the text?

(See Differentiated Instruction.)

## Teacher Think Aloud

*I grew up in a big city, so I used to ride on subways and buses a lot. The buses and subways were always packed—and there was still plenty of car traffic. I think transportation is a problem in many places.*

## Fix-Up Strategies

Offer these strategies to help students read independently.

**If you don't understand what you're reading:**

- Reread the difficult section to look for clues to help you comprehend.

- Read ahead to find clues to help you comprehend.

- Retell, or say in your own words, what you've read.

- Visualize, or form mental pictures of, what you've read.

## DIFFERENTIATED INSTRUCTION
### Writing

**Compare and Contrast**

To help students complete this activity, try the following steps:

1. Review discussion questions 2 and 3. What were some of the main points of these discussions? Write ideas on the board.

2. Tell students to use what they have discussed and to review the article to complete the compare and contrast chart.

3. When they have finished the chart, ask: *What conclusions can you draw about public transportation in these cities? What did you learn from this activity?*

### Student Journal pages 153–154

Name _____ Date _____

**Writing: Compare and Contrast Chart**

Fill in the chart below with details that compare and contrast each of the three cities mentioned in "Urban Transportation." Add your city or town to the end of the chart, and add details about your local transportation system.

| City | Transportation Details |
|------|----------------------|
| Los Angeles | |
| San Francisco | |
| New York | |
| | |

Cities • Urban Transportation   Phone Call   153

# Phone Call

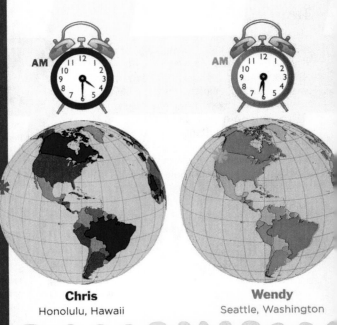

"**Jamie**, it's your turn," Mom said as she handed me the cell phone. This happens every Saturday morning about 9:30. We get free long distance calls on the weekend. My folks let me call anyone, anywhere I want. The calling plan is unlimited, but not in my house. I can have 30 minutes of free long distance calls. I can call one friend and talk for half an hour, or I can call ten friends and talk for three minutes each. Whom should I call? Maybe I should make a list first.

AM

AM

**Chris**
Honolulu, Hawaii

**Wendy**
Seattle, Washington

# After Reading
Use one or more activities.

## Check Purpose

Have students decide whether their purpose was met. What did they learn about urban transportation?

## Discussion Questions

Continue the group discussion with the following questions.

1. How does public transportation ease pollution? (Cause-Effect)

2. How would you describe the transportation issues in the three cities? (Compare-Contrast)

3. Now that you have read this selection, how do you feel about public transportation? (Making Connections)

## Revisit: Transportation Web

Return to the transportation web that was started in Before Reading. What new information can students add? Record new information on the web.

"Don't forget to check the time," Dad said as he walked by my room.

I looked at the clock on my desk. It's 9:30 A.M. here in Boston. I could call Nana in Miami, but her yoga class is at 9:30 A.M. What time is it for Chris in Honolulu, Hawaii? I checked my map. Hawaii is five hours earlier, so it's 4:30 A.M. for Chris. That's the middle of the night! I am most definitely not calling Chris. It's way too early to call her! Wait, I know whom to call. This is one friend who is always up with the birds!

## Time Zones of the World

Look at the globes. Each clock shows what time it is around the world when it's 9:30 A.M. Eastern Standard Time.

✱ Which friend might be setting the table for dinner? Where does this friend live?

✱ Who is playing an afternoon tennis game? Where does this friend live?

✱ Which friend is probably fast asleep?

### Daylight Saving Time

When Daylight Saving Time (DST) begins, clocks are moved ahead one hour so that there is more daylight at the end of the day. DST begins on the first weekend of April and lasts until the fourth weekend of October, when the clocks are turned back. You can remember which way to move the clock with this saying: Spring ahead, fall back.

Not all areas of the United States observe DST. Arizona does not observe DST, although the Navajo reservations in Arizona do. Parts of Indiana observe DST, but parts of the state do not. This causes a lot of confusion!

**AM**

**Jamie**

**PM**

**PM**

**Nana**
Miami, Florida

**Whitney**
London, England

**Gleb**
Moscow, Russia

## Short Feature: Phone Call

Have students read "Phone Call" to themselves. Then discuss the article by asking questions such as:

- What is a "long distance" call?
- Why is it important to know about different time zones when making a long distance call?
- How is Daylight Saving Time helpful?

### Student Journal page 155

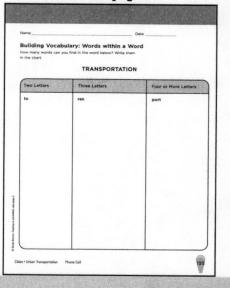

## Writing Compare and Contrast

Have students use the chart on *Student Journal* page 153 to fill in details that compare and contrast each city's transportation system. Students should add their own city or town to the end of the chart. Then have students use their chart to write a compare and contrast paragraph on *Student Journal* page 154. (See Differentiated Instruction.)

## Vocabulary

### Words Within a Word

Have students use *Student Journal* page 155 to complete a word challenge with the word *transportation*. Have students list all the words they can find within the word *transportation*. Look together as a group to find the first few.

## Phonics/Word Study

### Complex Consonant Clusters

Display these words and read them aloud: *reach, stretch, bench*. Also write these patterns on the board: *-ch, -tch, –Cch*. Ask: *Which word goes with which spelling pattern?* (reach, -ch; stretch, -tch; bench, -Cch) Now, work with students to complete the in-depth consonant cluster activity on TE page 368.

## Phonics/Word Study

### Complex Consonant Clusters

▶ Write the following words on the board: *catch, reach, lunch.* Direct students' attention to the ending sounds of the words. Students should notice that all three end with a series of consonants that create the *ch* sound.

▶ Using the Complex Consonants: Sort Two sheet, model the sorting process for students. (See *Word Study Manual* page 81.) Write the headings *-tch*, *-ch*, *-Cch*, Oddball and the first few words under the appropriate columns. Complete the sort as a group.

▶ Discuss the sort and what students learned. Complex consonant clusters at the ends of words generally make an *affricate* sound (like the *-tch* in *scratch*) and can have different patterns. You will find short vowel words generally end in *-tch* while long vowel words generally end in *-ch*. Also point out that in *-tch*, the *t* blends with the /ch/ sound.

▶ Students may initially put the Oddball words in different columns. If so, encourage them to resort the words, while keeping long vowel words in the *-ch* column and short vowel words in the *-Cch* column.

▶ Hand out the Complex Consonants: Sort Two sheet. Ask students to cut up the words and do the sort on their own or in groups.

▶ Check the final sorts for accuracy.

| Complex Consonants: Sort Two | | | |
|---|---|---|---|
| *-tch* | *-ch* | *-Cch* | Oddball |
| catch | reach | lunch | rich |
| pitch | screech | starch | such |
| stretch | peach | bench | much |
| hitch | | crunch | lurch |
| retch | | munch | church |

For more information on word sorts and spelling stages, see pages 5–31 in the *Word Study Manual.*

# Focus on . . .

Use one or more activities in this section to focus on a particular area of need in your students.

## Comprehension  STRATEGY SUPPORT  *INDEPENDENT*

To help those students who need more practice using the strategy covered in this lesson, work one-on-one or in small groups to apply the strategy prompts below. Apply the prompts to a *Reading Advantage* paperback, a classroom library book, or a new or familiar selection in the magazine. Always model your own thinking first.

### Making Connections

- What does this story (article, passage) remind me of?
- What do I already know about this topic?
- Where have I heard about this topic before?
- What do I have in common with the characters, people, or situations in the text?
- What other books, stories, articles, movies, or TV shows does this text make me think about?

## Writing Time Zones  *INDEPENDENT*

Have students divide a piece of paper into four sections—one for each mainland United States time zone. Students should write the time with the correct abbreviation at the top of each section. Then have them illustrate and write about what someone in each location might be doing at that time. When students finish writing, have them reread and edit their work.

To provide editing instruction, see the lessons in *Writing Advantage*, pages 56–92.

## Fluency: Phrasing

After students have read the two selections at least once silently, have them work in pairs to read them aloud. Students can practice reading aloud to their partner, who should give feedback to encourage naturally paced reading. Have partners help each other understand when to pause for commas, stop for periods, and raise their voices for questions.

When students read aloud, do they—

✓ demonstrate quick recognition of words and phrases?

✓ exhibit an understanding of phrasal construction?

✓ incorporate appropriate timing, stress, and intonation?

## English Language Learners

To support students as they prepare to read "Urban Transportation," build background knowledge.

1. Write the word *urban* on chart paper.
2. Discuss the meaning of the word *urban* ("relating to a city").
3. Have students cut out pictures from magazines that show urban areas. Tape them to the chart paper and discuss as a group.

## Independent Activity Options

While you work with individuals or small groups, others can work independently on one or more of the following options.

▶ Level A paperback books, see TE pages 371–376
▶ Level A *eZines*
▶ Repeat word sorts from this lesson
▶ *Student Journal* pages for this lesson
▶ *Writing Advantage* independent lessons

# Assessment

## Strategy Assessment

To help you and your students assess their use of comprehension strategies, ask the following question. Students can complete a written response or provide verbal answers in a one-on-one reading conference.

- **Making Connections** What connections did you make to the article? (Answers will vary. Students should specify one or more things from their prior knowledge or experience and how they helped them relate to the text, such as knowing that the public transportation system in Chicago is called the "el" or "L" for "elevated.")

See *Level A Assessment* page 50 for formal assessment to go with *Cities*.

## Word Study Assessment

Use these steps to help you and your students assess their understanding of complex consonant clusters.

1. Create a chart like the one shown, including only the words in the first column.
2. Have students read the words.
3. Then have students sort the words into the column with the correct spelling pattern. The answers are shown.

| Words | -*ch* | -*tch* | -C*ch* |
|-------|-------|--------|--------|
| batch | teach | batch | lunch |
| lunch | speech | witch | pinch |
| pinch | | | |
| teach | | | |
| speech | | | |
| witch | | | |

Great Source
Reading Advantage

**Level A Assessment**

# Great Source Reading Advantage
# Appendix

## Lessons for READING ADVANTAGE Paperbacks

The purpose of the paperbacks is to encourage independent reading. Minimal guidance is offered here and is optional. Additional sets of books can be ordered from Great Source.

## Graphic Organizers (Blackline Masters)

Make photocopies or transparencies of the graphic organizers to use in your classroom instruction.

## Leaping Lizards

**Synopsis** Lizards are reptiles, which means they are cold-blooded. Their body temperatures adjust to the temperatures around them. Lizards come in all shapes, sizes, and colors, and have particular features suited to their habitats. *Leaping Lizards* offers a look at a few of the most fascinating lizards— Gila monsters, Komodo dragons, chameleons, iguanas, geckos, and skinks. *32 pages, Lexile measure 530L*

**Strategy** Monitor Understanding (ask questions)

**Procedure** Have students use three sticky notes or fold a sheet of paper in thirds to provide places for them to respond to their reading. (Students may need some extra sticky notes. See the notations below.)

- If students use sticky notes, ask them to write their name, date, and book title on each of the sticky notes. Tell students to place one sticky note at the end of the first chapter, one halfway through the book (after Chapter 3), and a third at the end of the next-to-last chapter (Chapter 5).

- If students use a sheet of paper, have them write their name, date, and book title at the top of the paper. Students can then put the following headings on each third of the paper: After Chapter 1, After Chapter 3, After Chapter 5.

- At the first stopping point, ask students to write two or three questions about what they have read so far. If, in reading on, students discover answers to these questions, they can place extra sticky notes on appropriate pages and jot down the answers. Have students repeat this process at the next two stopping points. For questions that the book doesn't answer, discuss with students how to find the answers. Students might locate answers in books or on the Internet and discuss them with classmates.

**Activity (Optional)** Invite students to create a poster or TV commercial to advertise the book.

## No Ice? No Problem!
## The Story of the Jamaican Bobsled Team

**Synopsis** *No Ice? No Problem!* is the incredible story of the Jamaican bobsledding team that first captured world attention at the 1988 Winter Olympics. George Fitch, an American, saw a similarity between Jamaican "pushcart races" and the sport of bobsledding. In 1987, he selected a team of Jamaican athletes and gave them six months to train. The team's popularity with fans and its unusual story inspired the 1993 movie *Cool Runnings*. Having competed in every Winter Olympics since 1988, the Jamaican team now ranks among the world's top fifteen bobsled teams. *32 pages, Lexile measure 550L*

**Strategy** Monitor Understanding (visualize)

**Procedure** Have students use three sticky notes or fold a sheet of paper in thirds to provide places for them to respond to their reading.

- If students use sticky notes, ask them to write their name, date, and book title on each of the sticky notes. Tell students to place one sticky note at the end of the first chapter, one halfway through the book (after Chapter 3), and a third at the end of the next-to-last chapter (Chapter 5).

- If students use a sheet of paper, have them write their name, date, and book title at the top of the paper. Students can then put the following headings on each third of the paper: After Chapter 1, After Chapter 3, After Chapter 5.

- For this strategy, ask students to draw a picture at each stopping point based on a description of a setting, a situation, or an event that "grabbed" them during their reading. Or students might choose to list some words and phrases from the book that help them to see, hear, and feel something being described in the book. After students have read the book, encourage them to share and compare their pictures or word descriptions.

**Activity (Optional)** Invite students to give a book talk to convince other students to read the book.

## Big Rigs

**Synopsis** There are more than three million truckers in the United States. They carry goods thousands of miles across the country. *Big Rigs* gives readers a behind-the-wheel feel for the truckers' life—where they eat and sleep, how they communicate with one another, and what a typical run is like. Trucker "lingo" and the variety of big rigs that travel the highways are also presented. *32 pages, Lexile measure 480L*

**Strategy** Monitor Understanding (visualize)

**Procedure** Have students use three sticky notes or fold a sheet of paper in thirds to provide places for them to respond to their reading.

• If students use sticky notes, ask them to write their name, date, and book title on each of the sticky notes. Tell students to place one sticky note at the end of the first chapter, one halfway through the book (after Chapter 3), and a third at the end of the next-to-last chapter (Chapter 5).

• If students use a sheet of paper, have them write their name, date, and book title at the top of the paper. Students can then put the following headings on each third of the paper: After Chapter 1, After Chapter 3, After Chapter 5.

• For this strategy, ask students to draw a picture at each stopping point based on a description of a setting, a situation, or an event that "grabbed" them during their reading. Or students might choose to list some words and phrases from the book that help them to see, hear, and feel something being described in the book. After students have read the book, encourage them to share and compare their pictures or word descriptions.

**Activity (Optional)** Suggest that students choose a scene or event from the book and write a script to dramatize. Students might work up a conversation between two truckers using CB language as they talk on the radio.

## Shaq the Giant

**Synopsis** This is an inspirational biography of Shaquille O'Neal, one of basketball's greatest players. Starting out poor and feeling out of place due to his height and size, Shaquille's dream took root when his father gave him a basketball. Shaq credits his mother, stepfather (who really became a "father"), and high school and college coaches for being strict and setting limits for him. They helped him to keep out of trouble and be focused on doing his best on the court, in class, and in life. *32 pages, Lexile measure 540L*

**Strategy** Making Connections

**Procedure** Have students use three sticky notes or fold a sheet of paper in thirds to provide places for them to respond to their reading.

• If students use sticky notes, ask them to write their name, date, and book title on each of the sticky notes. Tell students to place one sticky note at the end of the first chapter, one halfway through the book (after Chapter 3), and a third at the end of the next-to-last chapter (Chapter 4).

• If students use a sheet of paper, have them write their name, date, and book title at the top of the paper. Students can then put the following headings on each third of the paper: After Chapter 1, After Chapter 3, After Chapter 4.

• For this strategy, ask students to make notes at each stopping point to connect the information they are learning about Shaquille O'Neal to experiences in their own lives or to other sources of similar information (e.g., newspaper, TV, books). After students have read the book, encourage them to share their thoughts with classmates.

**Activity (Optional)** Invite students to create a storyboard of the book, highlighting the main events, for a TV special documentary about Shaq. Students might find the story string graphic organizer useful in planning out their ideas. (See page 389.)

# PAPERBACKS

## Avalanche!

**Synopsis** *Avalanche!* focuses on the most common type of avalanche, the deadly snowslide, that often moves at 50 to 100 mph and buries everything in its path. The book explores reasons that avalanches occur and recounts some of history's most deadly slides. In addition, the book describes the work of scientists who start avalanches and study them in an effort to save lives in the future. The rescue efforts of St. Bernards, the breed of dog that has become famous for rescuing avalanche victims, are also highlighted. *32 pages, Lexile measure 530L*

**Strategy** Monitor Understanding

**Procedure** Have students use three sticky notes or fold a sheet of paper in thirds to provide places for them to respond to their reading. (For this strategy, students should have some extra sticky notes. See the notations below.)

- If students use sticky notes, ask them to write their name, date, and book title on each of the sticky notes. Tell students to place one sticky note at the end of the first chapter, one halfway through the book (after Chapter 3), and a third at the end of the next-to-last chapter (Chapter 4).

- If students use a sheet of paper, have them write their name, date, and book title at the top of the paper. Students can then put the following headings on each third of the paper: After Chapter 1, After Chapter 3, After Chapter 4.

- At the first stopping point, ask students to write two or three questions about what they have read so far. If, in reading on, students discover answers to these questions, they can place extra sticky notes on appropriate pages and jot down the answers. Have students repeat this process at the next two stopping points. For questions that the book doesn't answer, suggest to students that they do research to find the answers. Students might locate answers in books or on the Internet and discuss them with classmates.

**Activity (Optional)** Invite students to give a book talk to convince classmates to read this book.

## Training Wild Animals

**Synopsis** It's one thing to teach a pet a new trick; it's quite another to prepare a lion to do a movie scene. The people who train wild animals are quite a rare breed. *Training Wild Animals* profiles real people who talk about their jobs and the techniques they use in working with wild wolves, sharks, falcons, and mustangs. *32 pages, Lexile measure 470L*

**Strategy** Monitor Understanding

**Procedure** Have students use three sticky notes or fold a sheet of paper in thirds to provide places for them to respond to their reading. (For this strategy, students should have some extra sticky notes. See the notations below.)

- If students use sticky notes, ask them to write their name, date, and book title on each of the sticky notes. Tell students to place one sticky note at the end of the first chapter, one halfway through the book (after Chapter 3), and a third at the end of the next-to-last chapter (Chapter 5).

- If students use a sheet of paper, have them write their name, date, and book title at the top of the paper. Students can then put the following headings on each third of the paper: After Chapter 1, After Chapter 3, After Chapter 5.

- At the first stopping point, ask students to write two or three questions about what they have read so far. If, in reading on, students discover answers to these questions, they can place extra sticky notes on appropriate pages and jot down the answers. Have students repeat this process at the next two stopping points. For questions that the book doesn't answer, suggest to students that they do research to find the answers. Students might locate answers in books or on the Internet and discuss them with classmates.

**Activity (Optional)** Invite students to create a poster advertisement for the book.

## The Santini Puzzle

**Synopsis** *The Santini Puzzle* is the story of an eccentric benefactor who challenges the members of the Kidz Club with monthly puzzle contests. When Santini dies suddenly, he leaves the kids with a most challenging puzzle. Applying what they know about Mr. Santini (his fascination with Sherlock Holmes), the kids are able to solve all the clues. This leads them to Mr. Santini's final will, which ensures the survival of the Kidz Center. *48 pages, Lexile measure 350L*

**Strategy** Making Connections

**Procedure** Have students use three sticky notes or fold a sheet of paper in thirds to provide places for them to respond to their reading.

- If students use sticky notes, ask them to write their name, date, and book title on each of the sticky notes. Under this information, students should write the heading Predict. After leaving some space under Predict, students should write the heading Support. Tell students to place one sticky note at the end of the first chapter, one halfway through the book (after Chapter 5), and a third at the end of the next-to-last chapter (Chapter 8).

- If students use a sheet of paper, have them write their name, date, and book title at the top of the paper. Students can then put the following headings on each third of the paper: After Chapter 1, After Chapter 5, After Chapter 8. Under each of these headings, students should write the heading Predict, leave some space, and then write the heading Support.

- For this strategy, students write a prediction at each stopping point. They also write the information (the support) that led them to make this prediction. The second and third predictions may or may not be a confirmation or adjustment of the first one. When students finish the book, they can reread and discuss their predictions to review their thinking.

**Activity (Optional)** Invite students to give a book talk to convince classmates to read this book.

## Storm Chasers

**Synopsis** *Storm Chasers* focuses on two of the most dangerous weather conditions: tornadoes and hurricanes. The book points out that, while most people steer clear of bad weather, storm chasers move right into a storm's center. These are no average thrill-seekers. These men and women are serious scientists and meteorologists who study weather and climate with the hope of making more accurate predictions in the future.

Storm chasers use radar, maps, computers, video cameras, planes, and other tools to hunt hurricanes and track twisters. Some professional storm chasers conduct tours for tourists who are looking for an adventurous vacation of tracking twisters. *48 pages, Lexile measure 600L*

**Strategy** Making Connections

**Procedure** Have students use three sticky notes or fold a sheet of paper in thirds to provide places for them to respond to their reading.

- If students use sticky notes, ask them to write their name, date, and book title on each of the sticky notes. Tell students to place one sticky note at the end of the first chapter, one halfway through the book (after Chapter 3), and a third at the end of the next-to-last chapter (Chapter 5).

- If students use a sheet of paper, have them write their name, date, and book title at the top of the paper. Students can then put the following headings on each third of the paper: After Chapter 1, After Chapter 3, After Chapter 5.

- For this strategy, ask students to make notes at each stopping point to connect the information they are learning about storm chasers to experiences in their own lives or to other sources of similar information (e.g., movies, TV, books). After students have read the book, encourage them to share their thoughts with classmates.

**Activity (Optional)** Suggest that students write a book review of the book that might appear in a newspaper or magazine. Tell students to think of catchy, exciting phrases about storm chasers that will grab readers' attention.

## The Leading Edge

**Synopsis** *The Leading Edge* features biographical profiles of five extraordinary women who are leaders in their chosen fields. They are Lisa Ling, TV reporter/journalist; Lynne Cox, athlete who swam to Antarctica; Nydia Velázquez, member of the United States Congress; Katherine Dunham, creator of Afro-Caribbean dance; and Wilma Mankiller, Principal Chief of the Cherokee. Though different from one another in background and lifestyle, they all share a passion for what they do. *48 pages, Lexile measure 580L*

**Strategy** Making Connections

**Procedure** Have students use three sticky notes or fold a sheet of paper in thirds to provide places for them to respond to their reading. (For this strategy, students should have some extra sticky notes. See the notations below.)

• If students use sticky notes, ask them to write their name, date, and book title on each of the sticky notes. Tell students to place one sticky note at the end of the first chapter, one halfway through the book (after Chapter 3), and a third at the end of the next-to-last chapter (Chapter 4).

• If students use a sheet of paper, have them write their name, date, and book title at the top of the paper. Students can then put the following headings on each third of the paper: After Chapter 1, After Chapter 3, After Chapter 4.

• For this strategy, ask students to make notes at each stopping point to connect the information they are learning about storm chasers to experiences in their own lives or sources of similar information (e.g., books, TV, movies). After students have read the book, encourage them to share their thoughts with classmates.

**Activity (Optional)** Encourage students to make a collage, portrait, sculpture, or other visual representation of one of the women in the book.

## Projected into the Past: Book One

**Synopsis** Mrs. Drewin's history class comes alive (literally!) when she turns on an old film projector and Vendek, a caveman, talks to her and answers questions. Cleats and his two friends, Jinx and Mo, are immediately intrigued. They're not sure how Mrs. Drewin has made this happen, but they decide to find out. When no one is supposed to be around late one afternoon, the boys sneak into the classroom and turn on the projector. A menacing figure comes onto the screen just as Cleats notices someone peeking into the classroom. The story continues in *Projected into the Past, Book Two*. *48 pages, Lexile measure 480L*

**Strategy** Making Connections

**Procedure** Have students use three sticky notes or fold a sheet of paper in thirds to provide places for them to respond to their reading. (For this strategy, students should have some extra sticky notes. See the notations below.)

• If students use sticky notes, ask them to write their name, date, and book title on each of the sticky notes. Under this information, students should write the heading Predict. After leaving some space under Predict, students should write the heading Support. Tell students to place one sticky note at the end of the first chapter, one halfway through the book (after Chapter 4), and a third at the end of the next-to-last chapter (after Chapter 7).

• If students use a sheet of paper, have them write their name, date, and book title at the top of the paper. Students can then put the following headings on each third of the paper: After Chapter 1, After Chapter 4, After Chapter 7. Under each of these headings, students should write the heading Predict, leave some space, and then write the heading Support.

• For this strategy, students write a prediction at each stopping point. They also write the information (the support) that led them to make this prediction. The second and third predictions may or may not be a confirmation or adjustment of the first one. When students finish the book, they can reread and discuss their predictions to review their thinking.

**Activity (Optional)** Have students create a collage or drawing of a scene from the story or perhaps a sculpture of one or more of the main characters.

# Projected into the Past: Book Two

**Synopsis** Book Two begins at the point at which Cleats, Mo, and Jinx are secretly in Mrs. Drewin's classroom, trying out the film projector. A classmate, Meredith Blanchert, bursts in on the boys, steps in front of the film screen, and suddenly vanishes. After Cleats and Jinx tell Mo to get help, they jump into the film screen after Meredith and find themselves back in prehistoric time. They find Vendek (the caveman who had earlier appeared in Mrs. Drewin's classroom) and his clan. Mrs. Drewin and Mo eventually travel back in time to rescue the two boys and Meredith from a stampeding antelope herd. Everyone returns safely to the classroom, and the history of the strange projector is revealed. *64 pages, Lexile measure 480L*

**Strategy** Monitor Understanding (visualize)

**Procedure** Have students use three sticky notes or fold a sheet of paper in thirds to provide places for them to respond to their reading.

- If students use sticky notes, ask them to write their name, date, and book title on each of the sticky notes. Tell students to place one sticky note at the end of the first chapter, one halfway through the book (after Chapter 5), and a third at the end of the next-to-last chapter (Chapter 9).

- If students use a sheet of paper, have them write their name, date, and book title at the top of the paper. Students can then put the following headings on each third of the paper: After Chapter 1, After Chapter 5, After Chapter 9.

- For this strategy, ask students to draw a picture at each stopping point based on a description of a setting, a situation, or an event that "grabbed" them during their reading. Or students might choose to list some words and phrases from the book that help them see, hear, and feel something being described in the book. After students have read the book, encourage them to share and compare their pictures or word descriptions.

**Activity (Optional)** Invite students to give a book talk to convince classmates to read the book.

# In Search of a Giant Squid

**Synopsis** Fifteen-year-old J. D. Amber joins his father, a marine biologist, and his grandfather, a retired marine biologist, on a scientific expedition to New Zealand in search of a giant squid. A few dead specimens have been found, but this creature has never been seen alive in its natural habitat. J. D. learns much from the adults as well as from his first-hand experiences aboard the *Explorer*. The experiences include combat with a huge squid that attacks the boat. *64 pages, Lexile measure 550L*

**Strategy** Making Connections

**Procedure** Have students use three sticky notes or fold a sheet of paper in thirds to provide places for them to respond to their reading.

- If students use sticky notes, ask them to write their name, date, and book title on each of the sticky notes. Under this information, students should write the heading Predict. After leaving some space under Predict, students should write the heading Support. Tell students to place one sticky note at the end of the first chapter, one halfway through the book (after Chapter 6), and a third at the end of the next-to-last chapter (Chapter 11).

- If students use a sheet of paper, have them write their name, date, and book title at the top of the paper. Students can then put the following headings on each third of the paper: After Chapter 1, After Chapter 6, After Chapter 11. Under each of these headings, students should write the heading Predict, leave some space, and then write the heading Support.

- For this strategy, students write a prediction at each stopping point. They also write the information (the support) that led them to make this prediction. The second and third predictions may or may not be a confirmation or adjustment of the first one. When students finish the book, they can reread and discuss their predictions to review their thinking.

**Activity (Optional)** Create a storyboard of the book, highlighting the main events for a movie version. Students might find the story string graphic organizer useful in planning out their ideas. (See page 389.)

# Knowledge Rating Chart

Show your knowledge of each word by adding information to the boxes.

| Word | Define or Use in a Sentence | Where Have I Seen or Heard It? | How Is It Used in the Selection? | Looks Like (Words or Sketch) |
|---|---|---|---|---|
| | | | | |
| | | | | |
| | | | | |
| | | | | |
| | | | | |

# Predictions

How do you predict these words will be used in the selection? Write your answers in the second column. Next, read the selection. Then, clarify your answers in the third column.

| Word | My prediction for how the word will be used | How the word was actually used |
|------|----------------------------------------------|--------------------------------|
|      |                                              |                                |
|      |                                              |                                |
|      |                                              |                                |
|      |                                              |                                |
|      |                                              |                                |
|      |                                              |                                |
|      |                                              |                                |

Reading Advantage © Great Source. Copying is permitted; see page ii.

# Making Associations

Answer the questions for each word you write.

**Word** _____

What do you think about when you read this word? _____

_____

Who might use this word?_____

_____

What do you already know about this word? _____

_____

_____

**Word** _____

What do you think about when you read this word? _____

_____

Who might use this word? _____

_____

What do you already know about this word? _____

_____

_____

**Word** _____

What do you think about when you read this word? _____

_____

Who might use this word? _____

_____

What do you already know about this word? _____

_____

_____

# Word Map

**My Definition**

**Word**

**What does the word remind you of?**

1.

2.

**How might the word be used?**

1.

2.

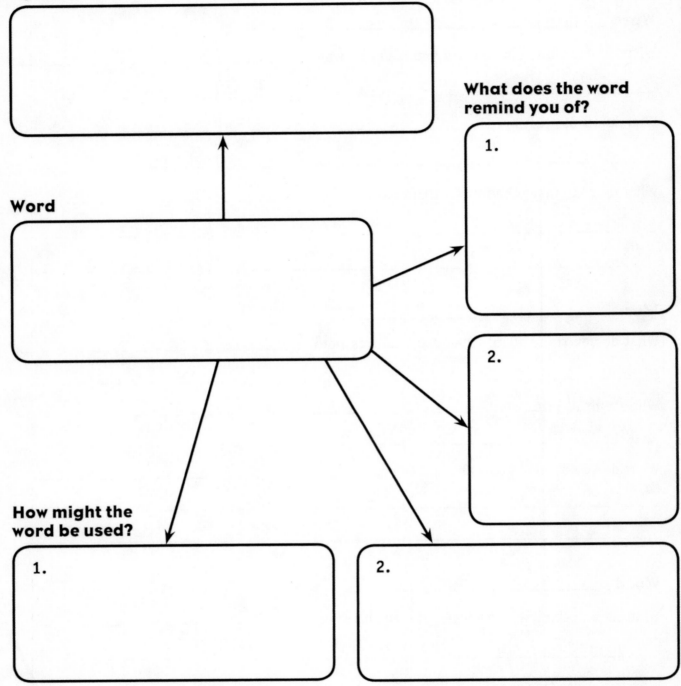

# Synonym and Antonym Chart

Think of two or three other words that are synonyms (similar in meaning) for each word. Then think of two or three words that are antonyms (opposite in meaning) for each word. Use a thesaurus to help you in your work.

| Word | Synonyms | Antonyms |
|------|----------|----------|
|  | 1.<br><br>2.<br><br>3. | 1.<br><br>2.<br><br>3. |
|  | 1.<br><br>2.<br><br>3. | 1.<br><br>2.<br><br>3. |
|  | 1.<br><br>2.<br><br>3. | 1.<br><br>2.<br><br>3. |
|  | 1.<br><br>2.<br><br>3. | 1.<br><br>2.<br><br>3. |

# Word Web

Write a word in the center oval. Add details around the oval that help to define the word. Then write the complete definition in the box at the bottom of the page.

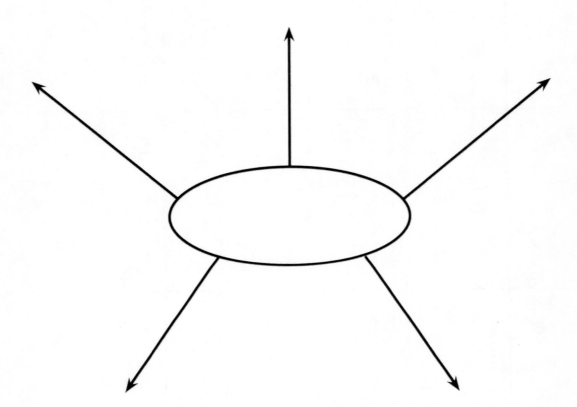

**Write the complete definition here:**

# Concept Ladder

| | Concept |
|---|---|
| | also called? |
| | kind of? |
| | replaces or replaced by? |
| | made of? |
| | parts are? |
| | made (used) for? |
| | looks like? |

# Double-entry Journal

| Quote | My Thoughts |
|---|---|
|  |  |
|  |  |
|  |  |
|  |  |
|  |  |

# Word Relationships

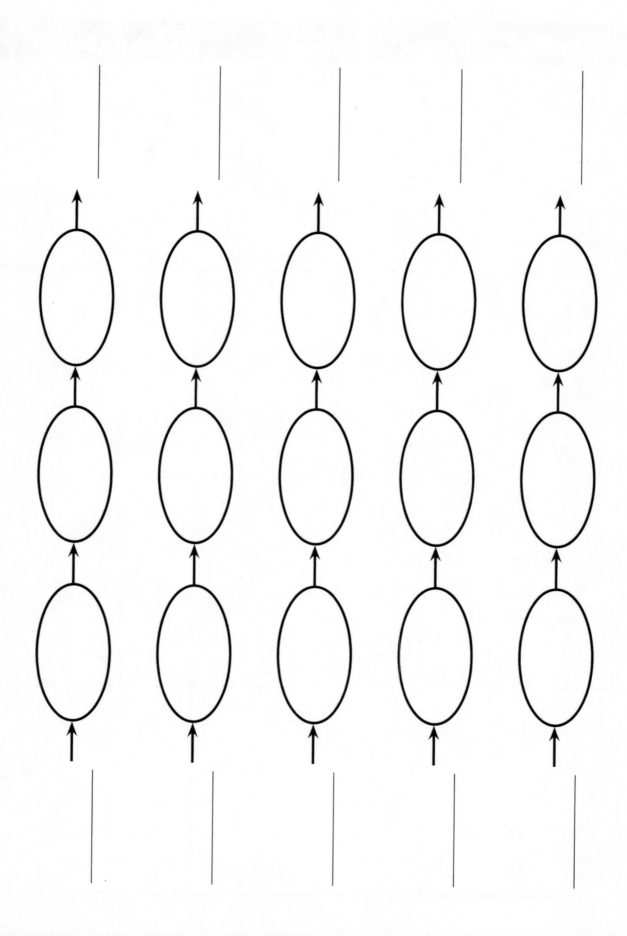

# Words with Multiple Meanings

| Word | First Definition | Second Definition |
|------|------------------|-------------------|
|      |                  |                   |
|      |                  |                   |
|      |                  |                   |
|      |                  |                   |

# Somebody Wanted But So

Use this chart to help you organize your thoughts for a summary.

| | My Notes |
|---|---|
| **Somebody** (an important character) | |
| **Wanted** (a key problem with details) | |
| **But** (conflict for the character) | |
| **So** (an outcome) | |

**Now write your summary.**

_____

_____

_____

_____

_____

_____

_____

_____

_____

# 5Ws Chart

The 5Ws—*who, what, where, when,* and *why*—give readers the basic
information about what happens in a news story or informational article.

| 5Ws | Details from the Selection |
|---|---|
| **Who** is the article about? | |
| **What** happens in the article? | |
| **Where** does the major event of the article take place? | |
| **When** does the major event of the article take place? | |
| **Why** is this event important? | |

# Main Idea Organizer for _____

First, write the details. They will help you figure out the main idea and conclusion.

**Main idea:**

| **Detail:** | **Detail:** | **Detail:** |
| --- | --- | --- |

**Conclusion:**

# Story String

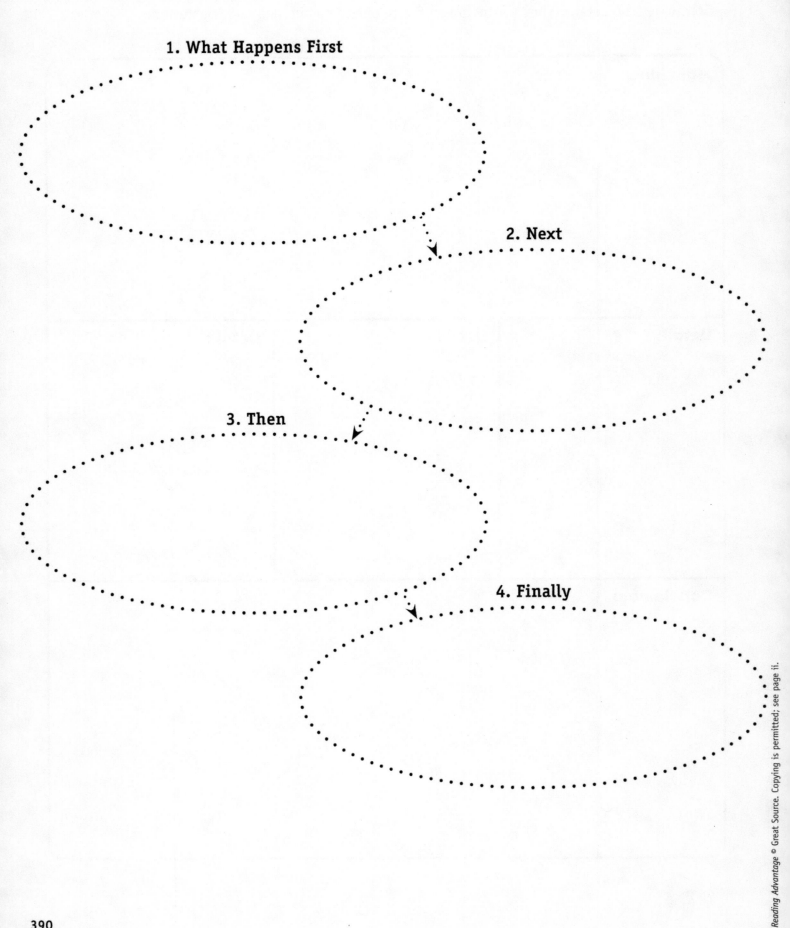

1. What Happens First

2. Next

3. Then

4. Finally

# Plot Organizer

A plot diagram helps you to see the main plot stages of a folktale, story, novel, or play. It highlights the five main parts of a fictional plot—exposition, rising action, climax, falling action, and resolution.

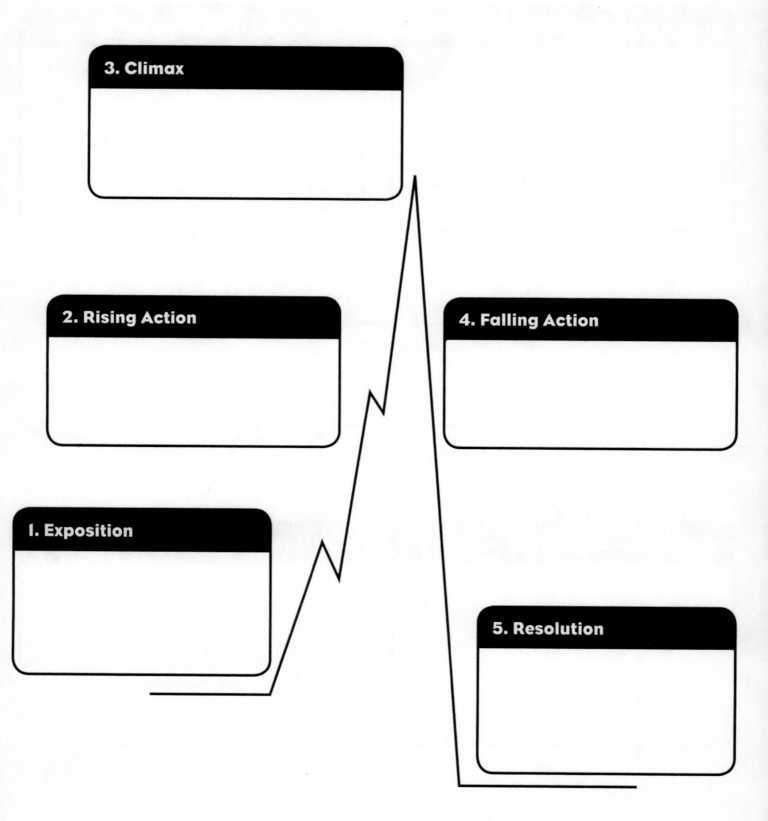

3. Climax

2. Rising Action

4. Falling Action

1. Exposition

5. Resolution

# Character Map

A character map helps you understand and analyze a character in a story, play, or novel. This tool helps you see how you—and other characters—feel about the character.

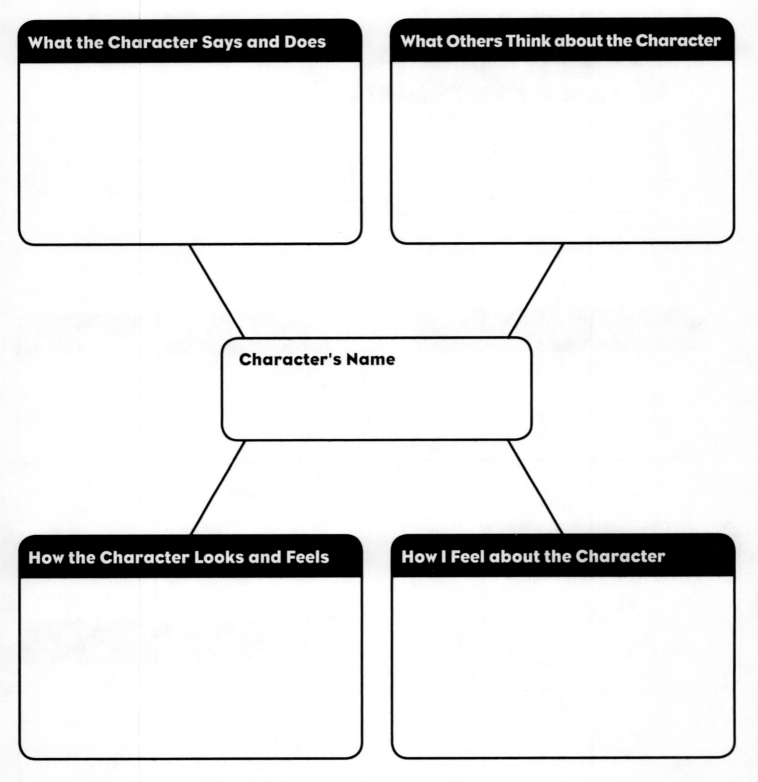

**What the Character Says and Does**

**What Others Think about the Character**

**Character's Name**

**How the Character Looks and Feels**

**How I Feel about the Character**

# Anticipation Guide

Do you agree or disagree with each statement? Check the appropriate box. Revisit your answers after you read the selection. Do you still feel the same way?

**Title** _____

| Agree | Disagree | |
|---|---|---|
| | | 1. |
| | | 2. |
| | | 3. |
| | | 4. |